Encyclopedia of Organizational Knowledge, Administration, and Technology

Mehdi Khosrow-Pour D.B.A.
Information Resources Management Association, USA

Volume V

Section 13: Marketing and Customer Relationship Management

Section 14: Operations and Service Management

Section 15: Organizational Management and Communications

A volume in the Advances in Logistics,
Operations, and Management Science (ALOMS)
Book Series

Published in the United States of America by
    IGI Global
    Business Science Reference (an imprint of IGI Global)
    701 E. Chocolate Avenue
    Hershey PA, USA 17033
    Tel: 717-533-8845
    Fax: 717-533-8661
    E-mail: cust@igi-global.com
    Web site: http://www.igi-global.com

Library of Congress Cataloging-in-Publication Data

Names: Khosrow-Pour, Mehdi, 1951- editor.
Title: Encyclopedia of organizational knowledge, administration, and
 technology / Mehdi Khosrow-Pour, D.B.A., editor.
Description: Hershey : Business Science Reference, 2020. | Includes
 bibliographical references and index. | Contents: v. 5. | Summary: "This
 book explores the latest concepts, issues, challenges, innovations, and
 opportunities covering all aspects of modern organizations. Moreover, it
 is comprised of content that highlights major breakthroughs,
 discoveries, and authoritative research results as they pertain to all
 aspects of organizational growth and development including methodologies
 that can help companies thrive and analytical tools that assess an
 organization's internal health and performance"-- Provided by publisher.

Identifiers: LCCN 2020000230 (print) | LCCN 2020000231 (ebook) | ISBN
 9781799834731 (v. 5 ; hardcover) | ISBN 9781799834748 (v. 5 ; ebook)
Subjects: LCSH: Knowledge management. | Technological
 innovations--Management. | Organizational effectiveness. |
 Organizational change.
Classification: LCC HD30.2 .E533 2020 (print) | LCC HD30.2 (ebook) | DDC
 658--dc23
LC record available at https://lccn.loc.gov/2020000230
LC ebook record available at https://lccn.loc.gov/2020000231

This book is published in the IGI Global book series Advances in Logistics, Operations, and Management Science (ALOMS) (ISSN: 2327-350X; eISSN: 2327-3518)

British Cataloguing in Publication Data
A Cataloguing in Publication record for this book is available from the British Library.

For electronic access to this publication, please contact: eresources@igi-global.com.

Advances in Logistics, Operations, and Management Science (ALOMS) Book Series

John Wang
Montclair State University, USA

ISSN:2327-350X
EISSN:2327-3518

MISSION

Operations research and management science continue to influence business processes, administration, and management information systems, particularly in covering the application methods for decision-making processes. New case studies and applications on management science, operations management, social sciences, and other behavioral sciences have been incorporated into business and organizations real-world objectives.

The **Advances in Logistics, Operations, and Management Science** (ALOMS) Book Series provides a collection of reference publications on the current trends, applications, theories, and practices in the management science field. Providing relevant and current research, this series and its individual publications would be useful for academics, researchers, scholars, and practitioners interested in improving decision making models and business functions.

COVERAGE

- Finance
- Information Management
- Computing and information technologies
- Decision analysis and decision support
- Marketing engineering
- Operations Management
- Risk Management
- Political Science
- Organizational Behavior
- Networks

IGI Global is currently accepting manuscripts for publication within this series. To submit a proposal for a volume in this series, please contact our Acquisition Editors at Acquisitions@igi-global.com or visit: http://www.igi-global.com/publish/.

The Advances in Logistics, Operations, and Management Science (ALOMS) Book Series (ISSN 2327-350X) is published by IGI Global, 701 E. Chocolate Avenue, Hershey, PA 17033-1240, USA, www.igi-global.com. This series is composed of titles available for purchase individually; each title is edited to be contextually exclusive from any other title within the series. For pricing and ordering information please visit http://www.igi-global.com/book-series/advances-logistics-operations-management-science/37170. Postmaster: Send all address changes to above address. Copyright © 2021 IGI Global. All rights, including translation in other languages reserved by the publisher. No part of this series may be reproduced or used in any form or by any means – graphics, electronic, or mechanical, including photocopying, recording, taping, or information and retrieval systems – without written permission from the publisher, except for non commercial, educational use, including classroom teaching purposes. The views expressed in this series are those of the authors, but not necessarily of IGI Global.

Titles in this Series

For a list of additional titles in this series, please visit: www.igi-global.com/book-series

AI and Future Management Tools for Business Transformation Emerging Research and Opportunities
Rami Shaheen (IAIDL, United Arab Emirates)
Business Science Reference • ©2021 • 220pp • H/C (ISBN: 9781799844174) • US $185.00

Handbook of Research on Sustainable Supply Chain Management for the Global Economy
Ulas Akkucuk (Boğaziçi University, Turkey)
Business Science Reference • ©2020 • 409pp • H/C (ISBN: 9781799846017) • US $265.00

Leadership Strategies for Global Supply Chain Management in Emerging Markets
Ashish Dwivedi (The University of Hull, UK) and Mohammed Saad Alshamrani (King Fahd Naval College, Saudi Arabia)
Business Science Reference • ©2020 • 333pp • H/C (ISBN: 9781799828679) • US $215.00

Managerial Issues in Digital Transformation of Global Modern Corporations
Thangasamy Esakki (Poompuhar College (Autonomous), India)
Business Science Reference • ©2020 • 270pp • H/C (ISBN: 9781799824022) • US $195.00

Contemporary Approaches to Military Operations Research
Mumtaz Karatas (National Defense University, Turkey) and Hakan Tozan (Istanbul Medipol University, Turkey)
Information Science Reference • ©2020 • 300pp • H/C (ISBN: 9781799844051) • US $195.00

Legal, Safety, and Environmental Challenges for Event Management Emerging Research and Opportunities
Vipin Nadda (University of Sunderland, London, UK) Ian Arnott (University of Westminster, London, UK) and Wendy Sealy (University of Chichester, UK)
Business Science Reference • ©2020 • 158pp • H/C (ISBN: 9781799832300) • US $195.00

Multi-Criteria Decision Analysis in Management
Abhishek Behl (Indian Institute of Technology, Bombay, India)
Business Science Reference • ©2020 • 422pp • H/C (ISBN: 9781799822165) • US $245.00

Handbook of Research on Project Management Strategies and Tools for Organizational Success
Nelson Antonio Moreno-Monsalve (Universidad EAN, Colombia) H. Mauricio Diez-Silva (Universidad EAN, Colombia) Flor Nancy Diaz-Piraquive (Universidad Catolica de Colombia, Colombia) and Rafael Ignacio Perez-Uribe (Universidad EAN, Colombia)
Business Science Reference • ©2020 • 537pp • H/C (ISBN: 9781799819349) • US $285.00

701 East Chocolate Avenue, Hershey, PA 17033, USA
Tel: 717-533-8845 x100 • Fax: 717-533-8661
E-Mail: cust@igi-global.com • www.igi-global.com

This book is dedicated to the memory of my late father for the love and care that he always displayed for his family, and for teaching me the importance of humanitarianism. Also, to my beautiful wife, Olga, and our handsome sons, Darius and Cyrus, for filling my life with so much love, joy, and happiness.

Editorial Advisory Board

List of Contributors

Alphabetical Table of Contents

Table of Contents by Volume

Volume I

Section 1: Accounting, Finance, and Economics

Section 2: Business and Organizational Development and Research

Section 3: Business Digital Economy and Knowledge

Volume II

Section 4: Business Information Systems

Section 6: Business Technological Innovations

Volume III

Section 7: Cyber and Network Security

Section 8: E-Business

Section 9: Entrepreneurship and SMEs

Section 10: Hospitality, Travel, and Tourism Management

Volume IV

Section 11: Knowledge Management

Section 12: Management Science

Section 13: Marketing and Customer Relationship Management

Section 14: Operations and Service Management

Section 15: Organizational Management and Communications

Preface

Technological innovations of the past few decades have had significant impacts on modern organizations worldwide forcing many of them to reevaluate their current infrastructures in terms of both efficiency and effectiveness. As the opportunity for further innovation progresses the goal of any organization is to identify more advanced and streamlined methods for managing organizational resources, human resources, as well as structural aspects. Successful organizations have been able to design and implement technology-driven infrastructures allowing them to use the most updated information in managing their resources to the level of accuracy and efficiency that until a few years ago was not imaginable!

The ushering in of the Fourth Industrial Revolution has been a catalyst to those companies that have not been able to reap the benefits of integrating modern technological innovation in support of managing their organizations more effectively. In modern times, many firms have begun looking into Artificial Intelligence (AI) in managing vast organizational knowledge to identify the most effective solutions, techniques, and management practices. The application and utilization of AI can now be found in most industries such as healthcare, education, engineering, tourism, government, transportation, retail, finance, etc. and offers many innovative and cost-effective solutions which are ultimately making organizations in these industries much more efficient and competitive.

Becoming a technology-driven organization does not just happen simply by acquiring technology resources and equipment, but rather begins through visionary leadership. Specifically, leadership that provides clear direction for the creation of a very innovative technology-centered infrastructure where technological evolution can be turned into a driving force in managing the organization. To ensure that an organization stays technology-driven, all administrative and management practices within the organization need to be continually assessed and redesigned in support of ongoing progress and sustainability of the organization. Regrettably, many organizations fail to understand that to properly utilize and benefit from technological innovations, they must have a modern administrative and management infrastructure in place, otherwise a lack thereof is a recipe for disaster.

Over the years, there have been many failures of technology experts – including a failure to understand that technological resources are not just hardware and software, but also humanware which includes all human elements from those in management to the end users who plan, implement, and manage technology applications and utilization. Also, a failure to understand how important it is to organizational leadership to develop state-of-the-art management practices where all human needs for utilizing the technology are carefully planned and managed. Technology-driven organizations cannot become successful unless there are strong modern management practices in place to support technological deployments. Therefore, modern successful organizations need to revolutionize their administrative and management practices first to pave the way for technology to become the driving force within their organization.

During the past few decades, there has been much research conducted by experts all over the world in determining what the critical factors are for developing successful technology-driven organizations. Much of the research has been centered around the human elements, organizational structures, management leadership and vision, as well as the impacts of external forces such as the economy and government policies, continuously expanding the body of literature in their important research areas. To provide access to some of the most valuable research findings relevant to organizational knowledge, administration, and technologies, the need to create a single publication where all this research can be found is of paramount importance. As such, this comprehensive five-volume *Encyclopedia of Organizational Knowledge, Administration, and Technology (First Edition),* was created and is designed to act as a single all-encompassing reference source on conceptual, methodological, and technical aspects of organizational knowledge and management and will provide insight into emerging topics including, but not limited to: organizational structure, strategic leadership, information technology management, business analytics, corporate social responsibility, supply chain management, and social networking. The chapters within this publication are aimed to provide researchers with contemporary research findings and results that are sure to pave the way for future research and discoveries pertaining to the creation of technology-driven organizations all over the globe.

The five-volume *Encyclopedia of Organizational Knowledge, Administration, and Technology (First Edition)* is organized into fifteen sections that provide comprehensive coverage of important topics. These sections are: 1) **Accounting, Finance, and Economics**, 2) **Business and Organizational Development and Research**, 3) **Business Digital Economy and Knowledge**, 4) **Business Information Systems**, 5) **Business Policy, Ethics, and Law**, 6) **Business Technological Innovations**, 7) **Cyber and Network Security**, 8) **E-Business**, 9) **Entrepreneurship and SMEs**, 10) **Hospitality, Travel, and Tourism Management**, 11) **Knowledge Management**, 12) **Management Science**, 13) **Marketing and Custom Relationship Management**, 14) **Operations and Service Management**, 15) **Organizational Management and Communications**.

Each of the focused sections include diverse chapters centered around a common theme, with each of the chapters then arranged by relevance to the theme and to each other. Two different tables of contents support the reader with navigating the contents by volume and alphabetically. Also, technical and managerial terms and their definitions are offered in addition to thorough reference sections.

SECTION 1: ACCOUNTING, FINANCE, AND ECONOMICS

This section opens this extensive reference source by highlighting the latest trends in the financial sector, from accounting practices to corporate finance and neuroeconomics. One of the initial chapters in the section, **"The Potential Role of Intellectual Capital in the Process of Accounting Convergence,"** authored by Prof. Ionica Oncioiu from Titu Maiorescu University, Romania, explores the importance of reviewing the fiscal policy of intangible assets in order to reestablish profit growth and promote business development. A following chapter, **"Technical Efficiency Through Innovative Methods and Estimations in Financial Markets"**, authored by Dr. Aikaterini Kokkinou from the Higher Military Academy, Greece, investigates technical efficiency estimation in financial markets, using both parametric and non-parametric techniques: parametric Stochastic Frontier Analysis (SFA) approach or non-parametric Data Envelopment Analysis (DEA). It focuses on reviewing the stochastic frontier analysis literature regarding estimating inefficiency in financial markets level, as well as explaining producer heterogeneity along with the relationships with productive efficiency level. Another chapter featured in this section, **"Financing Digital Innovation for Sustainable Development,"** authored by Dr. Danilo Piaggesi and Mrs. Helena Landazuri from K4D (Evidence and Knowledge for Development), United States, discusses establishing technical and financial support for the promotion of digital innovation and economic sustainability through the use of market development and efficient business models. The chapter that follows this, **"Auction-Based Pricing in Cloud Environment,"** authored by Ms. Branka Mikavica and Prof. Aleksandra Kostic-Ljubisavljevic from the University of Belgrade, Serbia, analyzes the benefits of allocation mechanisms using cloud resources, as well as the effects of improved bidding strategies within auction-based pricing methods. One of the closing chapters in this section, **"Neuroeconomic Perspectives for Economics"**, authored by Prof. Torben Larsen from the University of Southern Denmark, Denmark, outlines three macroeconomic focus points: 1) Equality by Universal Basic Income, 2) Environmental Protection by Carbon Emission Tax, and 3) Individualized Stress-Management.

SECTION 2: BUSINESS AND ORGANIZATIONAL DEVELOPMENT AND RESEARCH

This section includes chapters that investigate various business models and strategies that promote business development and a positive organizational culture. The first chapter in the section, **"Organizational Policy Learning and Evaluation using Monte Carlo Methods,"** authored by Prof. Clement Leung from the Chinese University of Hong Kong, China, Ms. Nikki Lijing Kuang of the University of California, San Diego, United States, and Prof. Vienne Sung from Hong Kong Baptist University, Hong Kong, explains the deployment of learning strategies in given organizational environments for reinforcing policy evaluation and review and promoting effective operation. Another noteworthy chapter found in this section, **"The Diversity Paradox,"** authored by Prof. J. Jacob Jenkins from California State University Channel Islands, United States, studies the false attainment of organizational diversity by emphasizing a singular form of individualism while neglecting alternative expressions. The chapter that follows this, **"Fab Labs, A Place for Innovation, Collaboration and Creation?"** authored by Prof. Diane-Gabrielle Tremblay from the University of Quebec, Canada and Prof. Arnaud Scaillerez from the University of Moncton, Canada, evaluates the implementation of digital workshops for developing organizational innovation and improving creativity among employees. The subsequent chapter, **"The Role of Networks in Local Governance,"** authored by Prof. Eugenio Salvati from the University of Pavia, Italy, identifies the characteristics of governmental networks in local communities and their connection to innovation in public administration. The final chapter in this section, **"A Model for Success in Agribusiness in the Portuguese Context,"** authored by Prof. Carla Negrão from the University of Coimbra, Portugal, supports developing a theoretical framework of achievement for agribusiness in today's digital economy through the application of novel factors including e-commerce, internationalization, and strategic alignment.

SECTION 3: BUSINESS DIGITAL ECONOMY AND KNOWLEDGE

This section presents coverage on the novel transformation of business practices with the implementation of digital systems. One of the opening chapters, **"Continuous Assurance as Digital Transformation Enabler of Audit, Risk Management, and Business Compliance,"** authored by Prof. Rui Pedro

Marques from the University of Aveiro, Portugal, provides an overview of continuous assurance services and its role in the evaluation and design of information systems, as well as the overall effectiveness of organizations. Another noteworthy chapter found in this section, **"Artificial Intelligence as an Enabler for Developing Business Systems,"** authored by Dr. N. Raghavendra Rao from FINAIT Consultancy Services, India, reviews the creation and improvement of modern business models using artificial intelligence. One of the chapters that succeeds this, **"Augmenting Organizational Knowledge Management Using Geographic Information Systems,"** authored by Prof. Colbert Jackson from the University of the Witwatersrand, South Africa and Prof. Dickson Kibetu from Chuka University, Kenya, examines the role of GIS technology in developing effective and efficient knowledge management systems within an organization. Another chapter featured within this section, **"Big Data, Data Management, and Business Intelligence,"** authored by Prof. Richard Herschel from Saint Joseph's University, United States, studies the application of big data in facilitating sound business intelligence, as well as key issues and effectiveness of data management in organizations. One of the last chapters presented, **"Data Discovery Systems for Not-for-Profit Organizations,"** authored by Prof. Joanna Palonka from the University of Economics in Katowice, Poland, discusses the integration of information and communication technologies, specifically data discovery systems, in nonprofit organizations to promote effective resource management methods and enhanced quality of services.

SECTION 4: BUSINESS INFORMATION SYSTEMS

This section discusses coverage and research perspectives on analytical approaches for integrating computing tools into corporate operations. The earliest chapter featured in this section, **"Research Trends in Information Systems from the Management Discipline Based on Co-Occurrence Analysis,"** authored by Prof. Beatriz Forés, Prof. Rafael Lapiedra, and Mr. José-María Fernández-Yáñez from Jaume I University, Spain, studies the impact of information systems in business practices and organizational performance based on the analysis of concurrences of key words used in publications of the specific topic. The next chapter, **"Organizations Operating in Real Time (Real-Time Enterprise) and the Role of IT as a Tool Supporting their Management Systems,"** authored by Prof. Jerzy Kisielnicki and Mr. Marek Markowski from the University of Warsaw, Poland, examines the benefits of implementing real-time information processing into an organization and its impact on the production of IT systems. Also included within this section is the chapter, **"An Approach for Estimating the Opportunity Cost Using Temporal Association Rule Mining and Clustering,"** authored by Prof. Reshu Agarwal from the G.L. Bajaj Institute of Technology and Management, India, which breaks down the application of data mining on evaluating penalty cost and determining opportunity cost for ensuring optimal inventory management and control. Following this chapter is, **"Systems, Services, Solutions of the Public Cloud,"** authored by Prof. Eduardo Correia from the Ara Institute of Canterbury, New Zealand. This chapter dissects the various models and platforms of the public cloud that are available for organizations, as well as highlights security risks and challenges that might arise. One of the final chapters found in this section, **"Automatic Detection of Semantic Clusters in Glossaries,"** authored by Ms. Marcela Ridao from the Universidad Nacional del Centro de la Provincia de Buenos Aires, Argentina and Prof. Jorge Doorn of Universidad Nacional del Oeste, Argentina, improves upon traditional visualization techniques in natural language models by applying a cluster detection method.

SECTION 5: BUSINESS POLICY, ETHICS, AND LAW

This section provides trending research on the latest best practices involving strategic planning and policy and examines corporate social responsibility initiatives. One of the opening chapters presented in this section, **"The Influence of Technology on the Strategic Planning Process,"** authored by Prof. Martin Mayer from the University of North Carolina at Pembroke, United States and Deputy Fire Chief Michael Martin of the Town of Cary (NC) Fire Department, United States, deliberates the transformation of public-sector strategic planning and organizational dynamics with the application of digital technology, as well as future opportunities and challenges. A proceeding chapter, **"Corporate Social Responsibility, Irresponsibility, and Citizenship,"** authored by Prof. Duane Windsor from Rice University, United States, addresses key issues in the field of corporate social responsibility, as well as analyzes its economic, ethical, and strategic influences. One of the concluding chapters presented in this section, **"What Can Organizations Do to Combat Human Trafficking?"** authored by Prof. Laura Dryjanska from Biola University, United States, converses effective organizational management techniques for fighting forms of modern slavery, including supply chain management and corporate social responsibility. Another closing chapter, **"A Guide to Cracking Down Cyber-Ethical Dilemmas,"** authored by Dr. Wanbil Lee from The Computer Ethics Society and Wanbil & Associates, Hong Kong, provides extensive research on cyber ethics and how to solve related issues using modern theories and technologies. A finishing chapter that follows this, **"Algorithms and Bias,"** authored by Ms. Julie Smith from the University of North Texas, United States, investigates the issue of discriminatory bias in algorithms as well as optimal solutions in the minimization of this problem.

SECTION 6: BUSINESS TECHNOLOGICAL INNOVATIONS

This section features the latest technological innovations including business intelligence, data mining, and decision support system applications that are being implemented in organizational practices. The first chapter featured in this section, **"ICT, Smart Systems, and Standardization,"** authored by Prof. Kai Jakobs from RWTH Aachen University, Germany, provides trending research on the relationship between standardization management strategies and the innovative sectors of smart systems and information and communication technologies. Another chapter that can be found within this section, **"Impact of Management Automation on the Processing of Business Information,"** authored by Prof. Alicia Martín-Navarro, Prof. María Paula Lechuga Sancho, and Mrs. Paula Algaba Berro from the University of Cádiz, Spain, analyzes the application of information systems into business management and its correlation to organizational development. Another noteworthy chapter, **"Quantification of Semantic Intelligence,"** authored by Prof. Maria Koleva from the Bulgarian Academy of Sciences, Bulgaria, discusses the various characteristics of semantic intelligence and speculates if there is a universal method for accurately measuring it. A closing chapter in this section, **"Data Mining for Fraud Detection,"** authored by Prof. Roberto Marmo from the University of Pavia, Italy, reviews the rising concerns of fraud as well as methods within data mining that provide viable solutions. The concluding chapter, **"Art Innovative Systems for Value Tagging,"** authored by Ms. Laurel Powell, Prof. Anna Gelich, and Prof. Zbigniew Ras from the University of North Carolina at Charlotte, United States, examines the use of big data analytics and recommender systems for accurately appraising specific artworks.

SECTION 7: CYBER AND NETWORK SECURITY

This section features in-depth analyses on contemporary findings in digital security methods. One of the initial chapters featured, **"Auditor Evaluation and Reporting on Cybersecurity Risks,"** authored by Prof. Jeffrey Zanzig from Jacksonville State University, United States and Prof. Guillermo Francia, III from the University of West Florida, United States, explores the implementation of guidance programs within audit agencies in order to understand modern cybersecurity risks and develop capable identification and defense techniques. The ensuing chapter, **"Threat and Risk Assessment Using Continuous Logic,"** authored by Profs. Aristides Dasso and Ana Funes from the National University of San Luis, Argentina, researches the use of logistical methods for assessing the threats and risks associated with computer systems in an organization. Another chapter included within this section, **"Phishing Attacks in Mobile Platforms,"** authored by Prof. Thangavel M., Miss Yaamine A.M., and Miss Nandhini J.T. from the Thiagarajar College of Engineering, India, studies the prominent hacking method of phishing and its modern assault on mobile operating systems. One of the concluding chapters, **"Blockchain Technology and Its Applications,"** authored by Mr. Ting Wang and Prof. Liguo Yu from Indiana University South Bend, United States and Prof. Yingmei Li from Harbin Normal University, China, dissects the fundamentals of blockchain technology as well as analyzes its impact on various industrial fields. Another closing chapter, **"Cyber Crime Threats, Strategies to Overcome, and Future Trends in the Banking Industry,"** authored by Prof. Atul Bamrara from the Indira Gandhi National Open University, India, examines the countless security risks that accompany electronic banking and enhanced protection and defense methods the financial industry can use against white collar crime.

SECTION 8: E-BUSINESS

This section presents informative chapters on electronic business models and the management of company websites. One of the opening chapters in this section, **"Digital Technologies in Wholesaling and Retailing,"** authored by Mr. Felix Weber from the University of Duisburg-Essen, Germany, investigates the effect of technological trends and their underlying elements in empowering the transformation of wholesaling and the retail industry. The following chapter, **"eLancing the Future Work Model: Opportunities and Challenges,"** authored by Prof. A. Mohammed Abubakar from Antalya Bilim University, Turkey, contemplates the idea of altering traditional work perceptions and regulations through the implementation of online freelance labor, or "eLancing". Another chapter that can be found within this section, **"Crowdsourcing Maturity and Its Application in Public Organization Management,"** authored by Prof. Regina Lenart-Gansiniec from Jagiellonian University, Poland, proposes an original and modern method for measuring crowdsourcing maturity within public administration bodies. The chapter that succeeds this, **"Theory and Practice of Search Engine Optimization,"** authored by Mr. Dimitrios Giomelakis and Prof. Andreas Veglis from the Aristotle University of Thessaloniki, Greece, provides an overview of the evolution of search engines, as well as trending practices and techniques in optimizing Internet search programs. One of the last chapters, **"Techniques for Developing Mobile-Friendly Web Sites,"** authored by Prof. J. Sandvig from Western Washington University, United States, discusses the current state of accessing webpages via mobile devices, as well as current attributes, popular design methods, and remaining limitations of mobile-friendly web sites.

SECTION 9: ENTREPRENEURSHIP AND SMEs

This section includes trending material and real-world studies on strategic approaches in the development of entrepreneurship, start-ups, and small and medium enterprises. An initial chapter identified in this section, **"Avatar-Based Intellectual Managing for Innovation Technologies Transfer in Nationals Entrepreneurships of Armenia,"** authored by Prof. Vardan Mkrttchian from HHH University, Australia, Prof. Serge Chernyshenko from Open University for the Humanities and Economics, Russian Federation, Prof. Mikhail Ivanov, Financial University under the Government of the Russian Federation, Russian Federation, and Prof. Leyla Gamidullaeva, Penza State University, Russian Federation, explains the promotion of sustainable economic growth, industrial competitiveness, and business attractiveness by facilitating the transfer of intellectual and innovative Internet technologies in the Republic of Armenia. Another recognized chapter, **"The ISO/IEC 29110 Software Lifecycle Standard for Very Small Companies,"** authored by Prof. Rory O'Connor from Dublin City University, Ireland, offers viable software development and improvement strategies for small organizations and start-up companies. The subsequent chapter, **"Design of a Strategic Knowledge Management Model to Evaluate Sales Growth in SMEs,"** authored by Prof. Leonardo Bermon-Angarita and Mrs. Lyda Rueda-Caicedo from the National University of Colombia, Colombia, proposes a knowledge management model for small and medium enterprises that analyzes marketing trends, promotes organizational learning in competitiveness, and evaluates the potential growth in sales. A chapter that follows this, **"A Theoretical Approach to Exploring Knowledge Transmission Across Generations in Family SMEs,"** authored by Prof. Filippo Ferrari from the University of Bologna, Italy, explores how knowledge is shared between the generations involved in business succession, along with cognitive and cultural insights on how this process can be improved. One of the final chapters presented, **"Role of Technology Startups in Africa's Digital Ecosystem,"** authored by Mr. Benjamin Assay from Delta State Polytechnic Ogwashi-Uku, Nigeria, examines the overarching role that technology startup companies have in the progression and growth of digital systems and mobile Internet adoption in Africa.

SECTION 10: HOSPITALITY, TRAVEL, AND TOURISM MANAGEMENT

This section highlights the latest findings on marketing and branding strategies, as well as technological applications within the travel and tourism sector. The first chapter of this section, **"Internationalization in the Hotel Industry and Modes of Entry,"** authored by Profs. Anna Moskalenko, Inês Silva, Juliana Gonçalves, Mafalda Brito, and Antonio Carrizo Moreira from the University of Aveiro, Portugal, analyzes globalization methods of hotel chains in relation to principal theories of international business. Another featured chapter, **"The Integrated Tourism Analysis Platform (ITAP) for Tourism Destination Management,"** authored by Dr. Francisco Gutierres from the Eurecat, Centre Tecnologic de Catalunya, Big Data & Data Science Unit, Spain and Mr. Pedro Gomes, Secretary General for Environment and Energy Transition, EEA Grants Unit, Portugal, demonstrates specific aspects of integrated geographical data within tourism planning for the promotion of interactive and innovative visitation experiences for travelers. Another chapter found within this section, **"Rapid Changes in Approaching First-Time Destination Historical Cities,"** authored by Profs. Annamaria de Rosa and Elena Bocci from Sapienza University of Rome, Italy and Prof. Laura Dryjanska from Biola University, United States, measures the social prominence of European cities by comparatively looking at a compilation of web-based media information about these targeted areas from first-time visitors. The following chapter, **"An Exploratory Study of In-Flight Safety Videos and Airline Marketing Strategy,"** authored by Prof. Norita Ahmad and Mrs. Nawal AlAnsaari from the American University of Sharjah, United Arab Emirates, investigates the effectiveness of in-flight safety videos and analyzes them through a marketing approach in order to gauge passenger attentiveness. The concluding chapter presented in this section, **"Model/Anti-Model Advocacy Responses to Hospitality Industry Sexual Harassment,"** authored by Profs. Jeffrey Brand and Gayle Pohl from the University of Northern Iowa, United States, studies how organizations and industries can address accusations against members (anti-model) and also propose and advocate for changes (model) to improve symbolic and material conditions for their industry, their employees, and their stakeholder communities.

SECTION 11: KNOWLEDGE MANAGEMENT

This section provides extensive chapters on knowledge harvesting, sharing and transfer. A preliminary chapter in this section, **"State of the Art in Semantic Organizational Knowledge,"** authored by Prof. Mamadou Kone from the International University of Grand-Bassam, Ivory Coast, studies the use of semantic web and linked data technologies in supporting the creation and distribution of knowledge within organizations. The subsequent chapter, **"Influential Factors on Reverse Knowledge Transfers in Multinational Organizations,"** authored by Ms. Rita Castro, Miss Sara Neves, and Prof. António Moreira from the University of Aveiro, Portugal, provides extensive research on the transfer of knowledge within multinational organizations from subsidiary companies to the headquarters which can lead to the promotion of productivity, performance, and global strategy formulation. Another prominent chapter found in this section, **"Knowledge Harvesting Concept Paves Way for Open Innovation Initiatives,"** authored by Dr. N. Raghavendra Rao from FINAIT Consultancy Services, India, investigates the relationship between collaborative knowledge sharing within organizational networks and the development of open innovation initiatives. Following this chapter is **"Information Overload"** authored by Prof. Tibor Koltay from Eszterhazy Karoly University, Hungary, which reviews the nature and types of information overload, as well as provides measures for prevention and mitigating symptoms using information management and literacy capabilities. A closing chapter, **"Big Data Analytics and Mining for Knowledge Discovery,"** authored by Prof. Carson Leung from the University of Manitoba, Canada, focuses on the discovery of organizational knowledge by mining through large collections of data, as well as discussing various methods that would assist in achieving this task.

SECTION 12: MANAGEMENT SCIENCE

This section provides global perspectives on current advancements within managerial methods in enterprises. One of the first chapters in this section, **"The Use of Design Thinking to Develop Corporate Skills and Competencies,"** authored by Miss Lucia Cuque from Pontifícia Universidade Católica de São Paulo, Brazil and Prof. Joao Mattar from Pontifícia Universidade Católica de São Paulo (PUC-SP) and Centro Universitário Internacional Uninter, Brazil, discusses the promotion and development of 21st century skills for in the corporate environment using design thinking methodologies along with information and communication technologies. One of the ensuing chapters, **"Global Project Manage-**

ment: Achieving Sustainability in Diverse Multinational Organizational Development Initiatives," authored by Profs. Emad Rahim and Terrence Duncan from Bellevue University, United States, examines the benefits of project management initiatives within an international context in order to improve organizational development. Following this chapter is **"Managing Workplace Conflicts Through Self-Mediation"** authored by Prof. Ndifon Obi from the University of Calabar, Nigeria, which researches how to effectively control conflict within the workplace by implementing self-mediation principles. Another highlighted chapter, **"Modern Downsizing,"** authored by Prof. Grzegorz Wojtkowiak from the Poznan University of Economics and Business, Poland, provides an in-depth review on the concept of downsizing which includes the evolution of the term, various directions of development, and future research trends of its use within the management field. The finishing chapter of this section, **"Women at Leadership Positions in Bangladesh Civil Service,"** authored by Prof. Fardaus Ara from Rajshahi University, Bangladesh, investigates the consistent lack of power and influence women have within the government of Bangladesh, despite their increasing presence in leadership roles.

SECTION 13: MARKETING AND CUSTOMER RELATIONSHIP MANAGEMENT

This section discusses explorative approaches and research perspectives on current innovations in promotional strategies and advertising. The opening chapter of this section, **"Green Marketing,"** authored by Prof. Teresa Paiva from Guarda Polytechnic Institute, Portugal, explores the evolution of marketing practices in order to achieve environmental sustainability while maintaining organizational success and customer satisfaction. A proceeding chapter that is featured, **"Intelligent Assistants and the Internet of Things as the Next Marketing Landscape,"** authored by Profs. Edward Forrest, Christina McDowell-Marinchak, and Bogdan Hoanca from the University of Alaska Anchorage, United States, examines the current adoption of smart technologies and the Internet of things within the business and marketing industry through the analysis of prominent applications of digital assistants in the field. Also found in this section is the chapter, **"The New Technological Trends in Customer Relationship Management (CRM) to Unveil Opportunities for Developing Countries,"** authored by Prof. Cagla Seneler and Miss Rana Kadioglu from Yeditepe University, Turkey, which discusses how the use of technological concepts including artificial intelligence, cloud computing, and the Internet of things are transforming the way organizations manage their relationship with customers, specifically in developing regions of the world. Following this, is the chapter, **"The Ubiquitous Role of Mobile Phones in Value Co-Creation Through Social Media Marketing,"** authored by Mr. Syed Hossain, Ms. Xu Shan, and Mr. Abdul Qadeer from Xi'an Jiaotong University, China. This chapter evaluates the contemporary function of mobile phones and social media in developing value co-creation and customer engagement strategies by surveying various universities in China and compiling primary data. A concluding chapter, **"Emotional Intelligence and Customers Satisfaction of Online Health Information,"** authored by Dr. Ionica Holban from the European Academy of the Regions, Belgium, Profs. Ioana Duca and Diana Andreea Mândricel from Titu Maiorescu University, Romania, Prof. Rodica Gherghina of The Bucharest University of Economic Studies, Romania, and Prof. Elena Nicolescu from Valahia University, Romania, researches online health service qualities that influence consumers' behavioral intentions toward using health information systems in Romania and analyzes the congruence of digitalization in healthcare and the improvement of customer satisfaction.

SECTION 14: OPERATIONS AND SERVICE MANAGEMENT

This section presents extensive research and reportage on systematic advancements in operational tasks, supply chain management, and the service industry, as well as initiatives to reduce a company's carbon footprint. A primary chapter found in this section, **"Artificial Neural Network in Operation Management Regarding Communication Issue,"** authored by Mr. Ayan Chatterjee from S.P. Jain Institute of Management and Research, India, Miss Susmita Sarkar and Prof. Mahendra Rong from Bangabasi Evening College, India, and Prof. Debmallya Chatterjee of S P Jain Institute of Management & Research (SPJIMR), India, explores the different models of artificial neural networks and their ability to solve key communication issues in the operation management area. Another featured chapter, **"Decision Support for Smart Manufacturing,"** authored by Prof. Marzieh Khakifirooz from Tecnológico de Monterrey, Mexico, Prof. Mahdi Fathi from the University of North Texas, United States, Prof. Panos M. Pardalos from the University of Florida, United States, and Prof. Daniel J. Power from the University of Northern Iowa, United States, reviews the implementation of decision-making templates based on operations research modeling and optimization techniques in smart manufacturing environments. It aims to provide insights into the system engineering design, emphasizing system requirements analysis and specification, the use of alternative analytical methods and how systems can be evaluated. The next chapter, **"Green Supply Chains and Enabling RFID Technology,"** authored by Prof. Alan Smith from Robert Morris University, United States, studies the promotion of environmentally conscious business practices by incorporating radio-frequency identification tactics. Another chapter contained within this section, **"A Review of Future Energy Efficiency Measures and CO2 Emission Reduction in Maritime Supply Chain,"** authored by Profs. Muhamad Fairuz Ahmad Jasmi and Yudi Fernando from Universiti Malaysia Pahang, Malaysia, evaluates the adoption of low carbon technologies and other energy efficient practices within the shipping industry in order to reduce harmful emissions and preserve marine ecosystems. One of the concluding chapters, **"Big Data Analytics in Supply Chain Management,"** authored by Prof. Nenad Stefanovic from the University of Kragujevac, Serbia, discusses applications, challenges and new trends in supply chain big data analytics and background research of big data initiatives related to supply chain management is provided.

SECTION 15: ORGANIZATIONAL MANAGEMENT AND COMMUNICATIONS

This section contains integral research on novel communicative practices within professional firms and trending management perspectives. This section starts with the chapter, **"Types and Challenges of Expatriation,"** authored by Miss Carla Morence, Miss Marta Esteves, Miss Núria Silva, and Prof. António Moreira from the University of Aveiro, Portugal, which covers research on the contemporary perspectives of corporate migration and relocation within multinational enterprises. Another chapter found within this section, **"Strategic HRM and Organizational Agility Enable Firms to Respond Rapidly and Flexibly to the Changing Environment,"** authored by Prof. Nibedita Saha from Tomas Bata University in Zlín, Czech Republic, demonstrates how companies use agile capabilities including knowledge development and strategic human resource management to react and adapt to modern challenges within the business industry. Following this chapter is **"Social Media and Organizational Communication"** authored by Profs. Victor Briciu and Arabela Briciu from Transilvania University of Brasov, Romania, which studies the transfer of professional activity and organizational interaction into online environments through the use of social networking. Also presented in this section is the chapter, **"Examination of Quality of Life in Workplace Environments,"** authored by Prof. Lesley Clack from the University of Georgia, United States, which breaks down the numerous factors that impact the quality of life of workers in healthcare, and provides effective management solutions to improve the overall well-being of medical professionals. One of the final chapters of this section, **"Leader Ambidexterity in Research Teams",** authored by Prof. Montserrat Boronat-Navarro and Ms. María P. Mora-Crespo from Jaume I University, Spain, builds on organizational ambidexterity literature to determine the antecedents at the individual level of the main researcher to successfully achieve both research and commercialization activities. The authors review the ambidexterity literature to identify these antecedents and illustrate their framework with two research teams at different Spanish universities that have achieved scientific- and commercial-oriented results.

In summary, the authoritative contents included in this comprehensive reference publication is intended to provide a much better understanding of the issues, challenges, trends, solutions, and opportunities surrounding the themes of its fifteen sections; delivering thorough coverage of the most recent research conducted by various experts all over the world. Collectively, the authors of the chapters in this encyclopedia bring about the most current thoughtful and comprehensive overviews of many important topics related to organizational development and advancement in light of modern emerging technological innovations, providing a much better understanding of this particular area of research. We hope that their diverse and comprehensive coverage offered within their chapters will contribute to a broader awareness of all topics, research, discoveries, opportunities, and solutions in developing dynamic and progressive organizations that can survive and thrive in our modern competitive global economy with all its recent challenges. We are also hopeful that the contents of this publication will inspire other researchers to further explore the expansion of existing research to discover new ways of stretching beyond the current boundaries and identify new opportunities in the field that can be further developed to better serve the inhabitants of our planet and organizations worldwide.

Mehdi Khosrow-Pour
Editor-in-Chief
Encyclopedia of Organizational Knowledge, Administration, and Technology

User's Guide

The *Encyclopedia of Organizational Knowledge, Administration, and Technology (First Edition)* is a five-volume set comprised of 188 chapters. All chapters are divided into categories relevant to their topical coverage. There are fifteen different category sections, with each volume containing multiple categories. All category sections are arranged alphabetically across the five volumes. Within each category section, the chapters are arranged by their relevance to the theme and to each other. As each new category section is introduced, section dividers represent the transition from one category section to the next. Tabs on the right-hand side of each of the pages have numbers representing each corresponding category section number.

To assist with easy navigation, there are two different tables of contents compiled at the beginning of each volume. The first represents the "Contents by Volume," which displays the arrangement of the content in its respective category sections, and the second represents the "Contents in Alphabetical Order," which displays the arrangement of content from A to Z by the chapters' titles.

EACH VOLUME CONTAINS

- A **preface and user's guide.**
- The **Editor-in-Chief's biography and acknowledgment.**
- **Two different tables of content** are compiled at the beginning of each volume: "Contents by Volume" and "Contents in Alphabetical Order."
- **Several authoritative, research-based chapters** contributed by researchers and experts from all over the world.
- A **comprehensive index** supporting the extensive system of cross-references.

EACH CHAPTER INCLUDES

- A brief **introduction to the topic area** describing the general perspective and objectives of the chapter.
- A **background** providing the broad definitions and discussions of the topic and incorporating the views of others (i.e., a literature review) into the discussion to support, refute, or demonstrate the author's position on the topic.

- Various perspectives examining the **issues, controversies, and problems** as they relate to the theme. Also provided are arguments supporting the position as well as a comparison and contrast with regards to what has been and/or is currently being done as it relates to the chapter's specific topic and the overall theme of the encyclopedia.
- A discussion of **solutions and recommendations** in dealing with the issues, controversies, or problems presented in the preceding section.
- **Charts, graphs, tables, and formulae** are included as illustrative examples whenever appropriate.
- A discussion of **future research directions.**
- A **conclusion** to discuss the overall coverage of the chapter and present concluding remarks.
- An extensive **list of references** so that readers can benefit from the sources cited within the text.
- An **additional reading section** consisting of sources that complement the topical coverage within the chapter.
- A **key terms and definitions section** providing 7-10 terms related to the topic of the chapter with a clear and concise definition for each term.

Acknowledgment

Editing and completing an authoritative and comprehensive scholarly research publication such as the five-volume *Encyclopedia of Organizational Knowledge, Administration, and Technologies (First Edition)* requires tremendous contributions and a great deal of assistance from large groups of scholars, researchers, and professional staff. The primary objective of this encyclopedia is to provide the most up-to-date scholarly coverage of all topics related to the conceptual, methodological, and technical aspects of organizational knowledge, management, and technologies.

The contributed chapters from expert researchers from all over the world provide an in-depth look into topics such as organizational structure, strategic leadership, information technology management, business analytics, corporate social responsibility, supply chain management, social networking, and much more. I am indebted to all the authors for their excellent contributions to this publication.

All submitted chapter manuscripts to this publication underwent a double-blind peer review process in order to achieve the highest level of validity, reliability, accuracy, and quality of the submitted research. I am thankful to all the reviewers of this encyclopedia for providing their expertise and their rigorous, unbiased assessment of the chapter manuscripts assigned to them on a double-blind basis, as well as the members of the Editorial Advisory Board for their wisdom, guidance, and assistance with various decisions throughout the editorial process.

I would also like to convey my deepest appreciation and gratitude to all those individuals who assisted me in editing this publication, which include Lindsay Wertman, Managing Director of IGI Global, Jan Travers, Director of Intellectual Property and Contracts at IGI Global, Melissa Wagner, Managing Editor of Acquisitions at IGI Global, Maria Rohde, Assistant Development Editor at IGI Global, Crystal Moyer, Assistant Development Editor at IGI Global, Eric Whalen, Assistant Development Editor at IGI Global, Josh Christ, Assistant Development Editor at IGI Global, Chris Shearer, Copy Editing Manager at IGI Global, Michael Brehm, Managing Editor of Book and Journal Production at IGI Global, and Deanna Zombro, Production Assistant at IGI Global. Additionally, I would like to thank the IGI Global Sales and Marketing Department, especially Nick Newcomer, Senior Director of Marketing and Sales at IGI Global, Caroline Campbell, Marketing Manager at IGI Global, Brittany Haynes, Marketing Editorial Assistant at IGI Global, and Tori Parks, Graphic Design Coordinator at IGI Global, for their endless support in promoting this invaluable reference source.

Thanks to everyone who has provided me immeasurable amounts of knowledge, wisdom, and support over the last 30 years.

Mehdi Khosrow-Pour
Editor-in-Chief
Encyclopedia of Organizational Knowledge, Administration, and Technologies

About the Editor

Mehdi Khosrow-Pour, D.B.A., received his Doctorate in Business Administration from the Nova Southeastern University (Florida, USA). Dr. Khosrow-Pour taught undergraduate and graduate information system courses at the Pennsylvania State University – Harrisburg for almost 20 years. He is currently Executive Editor at IGI Global (www.igi-global.com). He also serves as Executive Director of the Information Resources Management Association (IRMA) (www.irma-international.org) and Executive Director of the World Forgotten Children Foundation (www.worldforgottenchildren.org). He is the author/editor of more than 100 books in information technology management. He is also currently the Editor-in-Chief of the *International Journal of E-Politics (IJEP)* and the *International Journal of Semiotics and Visual Rhetoric (IJSVR),* and is also the founding Editor-in-Chief of the *Information Resources Management Journal (IRMJ), Journal of Electronic Commerce in Organizations (JECO), Journal of Cases on Information Technology (JCIT),* and the *Journal of Information Technology Research (JITR),* and has authored more than 50 articles published in various conference proceedings and scholarly journals.

Crisis Communication in the Age of Social Media and the Case of Dairy Khoury

Nisrine Zammar

Faculty of Information, Lebanese University, Lebanon

INTRODUCTION

The rise of social media was a game changer for consumers and companies alike. It gave the consumers clear and direct voice in many aspects related to the products they consume. On the other hand, it provided the organizations with a new tool to communicate with their audiences everywhere, especially in response to an occurring crisis.

At times, crisis strike due to factors beyond the company's management control (natural disasters, war, stock market drop, boycotts, competition's malevolence etc…), and sometimes due to the management's misconduct, deception or lack of values. For a reason or another, "crises are considered to be common parts of the social, psychological, political, economic and organizational landscape of modern life" (Matthew et al. 2003).Consequently, a predetermined crisis-management plan and an adaptable communication strategy will always play a pivotal role in defining the survival of an organization or an industrial sector as a whole.

According to Willmer (2016), organizations should invest in preparing crisis-management plans on different scales, supported by comprehensive analysis of the organization's environment, activity and potential risks. Risks are known to be all the potential activities or events that could harm the organization's finances, revenues, reputation, market position and capacity to deliver services.

Whereas, crises are known to be unforeseen events that may occur at a specific point in time and they tend to:

- Place the organization in serious financial jeopardy
- Cause damage to the employees and the public
- Cause image and reputation damages:
  - Threaten the viability of the organization
  - Alter the reputation of the company and its leadership
  - Weaken or destroy the confidence of stakeholders and consumers in the company.

Furthermore, the SCCT (Situational Crisis Communication Theory) developed by Coombs (2011) classifies different types of crises as follows:

The rise of social media made it very difficult for any company to survive a failure in responding to a crisis through social networks, such as Facebook and Twitter. "Crises affect more people than ever before, are more widely reported in the media, and have a wider impact on increasingly interconnected, dynamic and complex social-technical systems" (Matthew et al. 2003).

For instance, 2017 witnessed on huge failures of some organizations that didn't have the experience, nor the right knowledge to sail with the company on social media during the crisis. Therefore, we will present three cases:

DOI: 10.4018/978-1-7998-3473-1.ch151

Table 1. SCCT (Situational Crisis Communication Theory) CRISIS TYPES*

Crisis cluster	Crisis type	Description
Victim	Natural disaster	Earthquake, flood, etc would damage an organization
	Rumor	A rumor is disseminated about an organization
	Hacking	Attackers perform computer hacking
	Workplace violence	An employee attacks other employees
Accidental	Challenges	Stakeholders claiming that the organization is operating inappropriately
	Technical-error product harm	A technology failure resulting in a faulty product
	Technical-error accident	A technology failure causing an accident
Preventable	Human-error accident	A human error causes an accident
	Human-error product harm	A human error results in a faulty product
	Organizational-misdeed	Management taking actions that it knows may place stakeholders at risk

* (Adapted from Coombs, 2011).

The first is when Pepsi launched a new advertising campaign featuring the basketball star Kendall Jenner while joining a street protest, then, she hands a can of Pepsi to a police officer who takes a sip and smiles at his partners. The company was accused of taking advantage of serious social issues and the crisis began. Pepsi pulled the video and apologized, but the social media audience was not merciful and blamed Pepsi for trivializing the demonstrations.

The second is when the Environmental Protection Agency accused Volkswagen of selling vehicles that didn't meet environmental requirements. The company recalled millions of vehicles and promised to reimburse some of the customers. On social media, the customers expressed their suspicion that the company was handling the crisis in an inconsistent and dishonest way by publishing contradictory statements as to whether they knew or didn't know about the cheating.

The third is when the United Airlines told a passenger to give up his seat for airline staff due to flight overbooking. When the passenger (69-year-old doctor) refused to leave the plane, he was forcefully dragged from his seat and was struck in the process. The crisis started when a cell phone video recording of the incident was published on social media. The CEO Oscar Munoz apologized for "having to re-accommodate" the customer. This statement triggered a huge amount of criticism accusing the CEO for being disrespectful and lacking accountability. This case demonstrates how an apology on social media should be carefully put into words and communicated, taking into consideration the feelings of the victims.

In an era of growing consumption consciousness in the Lebanese market, the conventional media created frenzy about the Labneh (strained yogurt) production in Lebanon. The case gained pubic interest and triggered public health concerns when the media framed the Natamycin as a carcinogen.

Suddenly Dairy Khoury was at the center of a product harm/food safety crisis (Yehya& Coombs, 2014) and decided to counter campaign via conventional media. But the social media forced itself as a medium to be reckoned with, when the consumers started to voice their opinions on Facebook. What distinguishes the Dairy Khoury case is its being one of the earliest cases in Lebanon in which a dairy company, facing a crisis, used the social media to generate support for its cause. And yet, no apologies were addressed and there were no recalling for the product in question.

The main purpose of this paper is to provide a clear understanding of the crisis communication strategy adopted by Dairy Khoury on social media, at a time when the social media's full potential was yet to be recognized.

As a case study, the author will highlight the elements in dealing with Dairy Khoury's crisis via social media, and what are the efficient and inefficient elements of this communication strategy in today's standards. Hence, the author will highlight the necessity of a preset crisis communication strategy and a vigilant use of social media platforms while dealing with crisis.

This paper will be divided as follows: first the author will draw a theoretical background followed by a description of the research method, and then the author will present the findings. Finally, a few remarks and suggestions will be offered.

After determining the cause of crisis, a carefully-prepared communication plan should be able to minimize most of these negative impacts and, in some cases, ultimately stanch the damage.

BACKGROUND

Long before the rise of the Social Media, an impressive number of scholars have been studying crisis and many researchers have agreed that a crisis is an unpredictable event which results in uncertainty and is perceived as a threat to high priority values of the organization goals.

Table 2. What is crisis according to the scholars?

Scholar	Definition
Fearn-Banks (2010)	"A crisis is a major occurrence with a potentially negative outcome affecting an organization as well as its public, products, services, or good name".
Coombs (1999)	"Crisis is a risk manifested… an event that is an unpredictable, major threat that can have a negative effect on the organization, industry, or stakeholders if handled improperly".
Seeger et al. (2003)	"An organizational crisis is an unexpected, non-routine organizationally based event which results in uncertainty, threat, or perceived threat to an organization's high priority goals."
(Matthew et al. 2003).	"The term crisis evokes a sense of threat, urgency and destruction, often on a monumental scale. Crisis suggests an unusual event of overwhelmingly negative significance that carries a high level of risk, harm, and opportunity for further loss".
Hermann (1963)	"Crisis includes three main conditions: (1) threatens high priority values of the organization goals, (2) presents a restricted amount of time in which a decision can be made, and (3) is unexpected or unanticipated by the organization".

Managing a Crisis Through Communication

Richardson (1994), Coombs (2007), and Maisonneuve (2010), classify the crisis communication strategy into three main: pre-crisis, during crisis and post-crisis.

a. Pre-Crisis

Pre-planned emergency response is most effective for the immediate tackling of any unpredictable event. The author emphasized in the afore-introduction the importance of having a pre-crisis plan to deal efficiently with potential external and internal hazards. The author hereby names the EXXON Valdez oil spill as an example of the absence of pre-planning, which drastically affected the management of the crisis.

The Exxon Valdez tanker ran aground on Bligh Reef in Alaska on March 24, 1989, releasing nearly 11 million gallons of crude oil into Prince William Sound.

More than anything else, the running aground of the tanker Exxon Valdez underscores the fact that crises in business are inevitable and companies must have crisis-management plans in place well before disaster strikes (The New York Times – April 30, 1989).

b. Key Factors During and Post Crisis: Reputation, Image, and Public Response

Watrick (1992) states that "A reputation is an aggregate evaluation that the stakeholders make about how well an organization is meeting stakeholder expectations, based on its past behaviors"

Table 3. Benoit's Typology of Image Restoration Strategies

Strategy	Specific Tactic	Course(s) of Action
Denial		Denying the act or shifting the blame
Evading responsibility *With 4 tactics*	1- Provocation	the firm declares that its action was a response to another's offensive act
	2- Defeasibility	the firm alleges a lack of information or knowledge related to the situation
	3- Inadvertent	claiming that the act in question happened accidentally, unintentionally
	4- Good intentions	suggesting that the action was based on good intentions
Reducing offensiveness *With 6 tactics*	1- Bolstering	reminding the audience of previous positive acts
	2- Minimization	telling the audience that the act is less serious than it appears
	3- Differentiation	comparing the act with other more offensive acts
	4- Transcendence	putting the act in a broad context so it looks less offensive
	5- Attacking accuser	questioning the credibility of the source
	6- Compensation	suggesting offers (payments, reimbursement, …)
Corrective Action	Restoring the state of affairs existing	promising to correct the situation and prevent its reoccurrence
Mortification	Confessing	By admitting the responsibility of the occurrence and asking the audience's forgiveness

Source: https://www.ou.edu/deptcomm/dodjcc/groups/98A1/Benoit.htm

The Image Repair Discourse and Crisis Communication theory focuses on message options (Benoit, 1997) and consider that the communication strategy is a goal directed activity in order to maintain a favorable reputation for individual or organizations when their image is compromised. This theory outlines a typology for image restoration as follows:

Moreover, Sellnow et al. (1998) suggests "Corrective Action" as one of the successful strategies in image restoration. They recommend corrective action in order to ensure the priority of safety for stakeholders and thus reduce pressure.

Pushing the Image Restoration Theory ahead, The Situational Crisis Communication Theory (SCCT) designed by Coombs (2007) provides an evidence-based framework for understanding how to maximize the reputational protection through *post crisis* communication strategy. Coombs SCCT identifies how key facets of the crisis situation influence attributions about the crisis and the reputations held by stakeholders. In turn, understanding how stakeholders will respond to the crisis informs the post-crisis communication. In this empirical research, Coombs (2007) provides a set of guidelines for how crisis managers can use crisis response strategies to protect a reputation from the ravages of a crisis, as follows:

Furthermore, Szczepanik (2003) considers that the public support is especially important when facing a crisis. The public can both turn against an organization and harm its credibility and reputation, or it could provide support and assist in efforts to solve the crisis. In her study she stresses on the fact that a proper communication during a crisis is fundamental to gain public support. For her, organizations that face crises unprepared, such as Exxon, fail to address the importance of public perception and damage the company's reputation, maybe forever! And because a corporate reputation is a valuable asset (Fombrun and Van Riel, 2004) and a crisis is a threat to the corporate reputation, crisis communication can be an *integral part* of repairing that harm/protecting the reputational assets (Barton, 2001; Benoit, 1995). Therefore, reputational attacks can be defended through communicative effort called corporate apologia. In his qualitative research, Coombs (2010) found that corporate apologia is the key point upon which crisis communication should be developed. It is a communicative effort to defend the corporation against reputation attacks.

Table 4. SCCT crisis response strategy guidelines - (Coombs, 2007)

1	Informing and adjusting information can be enough when crises have minimal attributions of crisis responsibility (victim crises), with no history of similar crises and a neutral or positive prior relationship reputation.
2	Victimage can be used as part of the response for workplace violence, product tampering, natural disasters and rumors.
3	Diminish crisis response strategies should be used for minimal-attribution crisis responsibility (victim crises), coupled with a history of similar crises and/or negative prior relationship reputation.
4	Diminish crisis response strategies should be used for low-attribution crisis responsibility (accident crises), which have no history of similar crises, and a neutral or positive prior relationship reputation.
5	Rebuild crisis response strategies should be used for low-attribution crisis responsibility (accident crises), coupled with a history of similar crises and/or negative prior relationship reputation.
6	Rebuild crisis response strategies should be used for strong-attribution crisis responsibility (preventable crises), regardless of crisis history or prior relationship reputation.
7	The deny posture crisis response strategies should be used for rumor and challenge crises, when possible.
8	Maintain consistency in crisis response strategies. Because mixing the deny crisis response with either the diminished or the rebuild strategies will erode the effectiveness of the response as a whole.

Source: https://link.springer.com/article/10.1057/palgrave.crr.1550049

Corporate apologia is also a key factor for Chung (2011) who investigates how corporate apologies can relieve the level of public anger under a crisis situation. In his study, he proved that an apology statement with active responsibility is more likely to relieve public anger than that with passive responsibility.

All the above studies were made prior to the advent of the social media as a key player when handling a crisis situation. Nowadays, with social media tools, individuals and organizations have new ways to engage interactively by means of creative and collaborative platforms. Thus, social media can be seen as the means for gathering a variety of information, in order to enhance the understanding of a crisis.

c. The Role of Social Media in Crisis Communication

Social media has been recognized as an increasingly important source of information that supports decision making processes during crisis situations.

By definition, social media is "an umbrella term that is used to refer to a new era of Web-enabled applications that are built around user-generated or user-manipulated content, such as wikis, blogs, podcasts, and social networking sites" (Pew Internet & American Life Project, 2010). Because social media possesses characteristics of participation, openness, conversation, community, and connectedness (Mayfield, 2006), it allows private individuals to become sources of information and 'sharing opinions, insights, experiences and perspectives with others' online (Marken, 2007).Therefore, the news of a crisis can be shared and reach millions of people without the "traditional" control of the "news room". While there can be a considerable lag between the occurrence of a crisis situation and news reports about it, social media has been recognized for its potential to provide complementary and relevant information for crisis management in near real-time (Meier, 2013).

However, disseminating information about organization crisis on social media can be a double edged sword and a contestable opinion because they give a vast spectrum for users to voice their opinions, which can lead to new challenges facing crisis managers. On that behalf, Coombs (2011) advises that when meeting a crisis, a quick response is an active response because it tries to fill the vacuum with facts. A slow response allows others to fill the vacuum with speculation and misinformation.

MAIN FOCUS: THE DAIRY KHOURY CASE

Social networks can instigate rumours, amplify the damage of a crisis, bypass a crisis or even put out its flames. Therefore, the author decided to examine the case of "Dairy Khoury"- a dairy products company in Lebanon-through observation, and also through analysing its crisis management by means of social networks. It is important to mention that the author gave a particular attention to Dairy Khoury because it is considered to be the first Lebanese dairy company to face such a crisis, while the use of Social Media in Lebanon was growing exponentially and imposing new communication practices on the Lebanese scene.

By means of conducting a case study, the author has the chance to go beyond the limitations of quantitative and statistical limitations (Zainal, 2007). Case study allows the researcher to explore, describe and provide an in depth-explanation of the problems in question. It helps explain both the process and the outcome of a phenomenon through complete observation, reconstruction and analysis of the cases under investigation (Tellis, 1997).

For the purpose of this case study, the author decided to conduct an email in-depth interview with Mr. Ziad Akiki the *Project & Process Improvement Director at Dairy Khoury*, who was in charge of dealing with the crisis. An email in-depth interview provides necessary information from people who prefer to be interviewed online rather than face-to-face. It also overcomes many boundaries such as time constrains and geographical difficulties.

E-mail in-depth interviews can be employed quickly, conveniently, and inexpensively and can generate high-quality data when handled carefully (Lockman, 2006). Aware of the method's challenges, the author found that an in-depth e-mail interview can be viable and efficient for the qualitative approach adopted in this study.

Further, and in order to shed the light on the context in which Dairy Khoury was trying to encounter the damage of the crisis, the author found it interesting to examine the comments made by the audience on the Dairy Khoury's Facebook page during and post crisis. The time frame of this study covers the following years of the crisis which allows us to make a critical examination of the efficiency or inefficiency of Dairy Khoury's communication strategy.

1. Data Collection

A. The Interview

Mr. ZiadAkiki, the *Project & Process Improvement Director at Dairy Khoury*, confirmed that the Dairy Khoury's crisis broke up on the 18th of March 2014, because of the usage of a natural mold inhibitor called Natamycin in Labneh. First, the traditional media spread the news and treated the Natamycin as a chemical dangerous ingredient to be aware of. At that time, Dairy Khoury didn't anticipate such a claim, because for them, Natamycin is a natural mold inhibitor with no harm on human beings health's.

According to Mr. Akiki, their first response, when the crisis stroke and became widely spread, was to hold a press conference and to explain the truth about what happened. Dairy Khoury's strategy was to recognize the fact of using the Natamycin. Mr.Akiki stated "…recognition, because we believed that we were rather advanced in our production method". In the press conference, it was clear that the board took full responsibility of using the Natamycin. Board members held speeches to share responsibility in dealing with the crisis.

Part of their strategy to respond through media, Mr. Akiki said that they used both traditional and social media. They held press conferences and invited TV stations to produce TV documentaries on the subject, all for transparency reasons.

The author asked Mr. Akiki whether they used the social media during or after the crisis and why? He answered: "We only used the social media after the crisis, because back in 2014, social media were not active as much as they are nowadays".

Nevertheless, during the crisis, Dairy Khoury's crisis manager focused on communicating with the partners. He communicated with them via Facebook, also addressing their social media audiences with the same message. Dairy Khoury made a clever move by resorting to opinion leaders and active partners on social media, particularly Facebook, in order to ease the tension of the crisis.

As a post-crisis response, always according to Mr. Akiki, Dairy Khoury followed-up on the information that was circulating on social media. He confirmed that the impact of social media on the crisis was "positive, because social media users made researches about for Natamycin and found out that it is not a harmful substance". Nevertheless, for Mr. Akiki, it is not possible to overcome a certain crisis solely by conducting a communication campaign on social media. Because when facing the crisis "we also had to target older people who did not use the social media".

The damages due to the crisis (material, reputation, market share…) were estimated to have reached 12 million US dollars. Surprisingly, Dairy Khoury didn't conduct a post-crisis assessment in order to measure the effectiveness of its adopted communication plan!

Figure 1. Candia (One Competitor)'s reaction to the crisis
Source: https://blogbaladi.com/the-lebanese-labneh-scandal/

Mr. Akiki revealed that, in the aftermath of the crisis Dairy Khoury developed a communication plan in order to face any potential crisis, based on the experience gained from dealing with the Natamycin crisis. Mr. Akiki confirmed to the author, that eight months after the crisis, Dairy Khoury started to recover gradually until it totally did.

B. Dairy Khoury's Facebook Activity

Examining the Facebook's page, the author found that Dairy Khoury's usage of Facebook was not limited during the crises period, contrast to what M. Akiki had told us about social media's limited impact during the time of crises.

- We can see on the 23rd of March, the announcement of TV press conference will take place, the date and the TV channel (LBC, Lebanese Broadcasting Channel at 5:00 PM,).
- There are also photos of M. Khoury, owner of Dairy Khoury, in a dinner with the Health minister and other important Lebanese personality
- Photos of Dairy Khoury's team receiving the CPC (Colder Products Company) certificates from the Lebanese Health Minister
- The speech of Mr.GirgiKhoury during the CPC's awarding ceremony on the Facebook page
- The video made on TV in a program called "Tahkik" (Investigation), as the photo below
- An announcement that the crises will be the subject matter of a TV program called "Lilnacher" (to be spread)

Figure 2. Announcement of "Tahkik" on Dairy Khoury Facebook's Page
Source: Dairy Khoury's Facebook Page

- Articles taken from local newspapers
- Photos from the factory and for the products
- Photos of the cows Milking and being showered
- Photos of the team during HORECA's (HOtel, REstaurant, CAfé) exhibition in Lebanon and photos of the Health Minister eating Dairy Khoury's products in the exhibition.
- We can read also a message from Dairy Khoury Dairy thanking the Facebook users for their "kind and gentle support" and asking them to invite their friends to like Dairy Khoury's Facebook page and to "share the press conference videos so the truth can spread as much as we can to beat all these rumors" (March 23, 2014).

C. Crisis Type, Reputation, and Crisis History

Firstly, it is important to mention that according to the crisis typology determined by Coombs (2007), and presented in Table 1, the Dairy Khoury's case fall into the "Preventable" type; because the crisis was provoked when the "Natamycin" was intentionally added to a dairy product, in this case the Labneh. Secondly, based on the SCCT crisis response strategy guidelines elaborated by Coombs (2007), Dairy Khoury has no history of similar crises and the company has a positive prior relationship reputation. No prior crises information was found in the conventional media nor on the Internet platforms. Finally, none of the unit of analysis (comments) referred to prior dishonesty.

D. The Dairy Khoury's Facebook comments

In order to corroborate the information deducted from the in-depth interview, and in order to give a better understanding of the use of social media by Dairy Khoury for crisis communication, the author found it interesting to examine the comments written on Dairy Khoury's Facebook page. From March 20 till May 24 2014 (Date where Dairy Khoury resumed to a normal activity), 193 of Dairy Khoury's Facebook comments during the crises were collected and analyzed qualitatively. These comments were made accessible to the public and provided invaluable opportunities for studying the crises.

The guidelines that the author followed for messages classification are suggested by Helsoot & Groenendaal's (2013). They are comprised of (1) questions (2) giving information (3) suggestions and

(4) messages intended to be funny. Roshan et al. (2016) enlarged this cluster and added three clusters comprising (5)objections (6) appreciations and (7) comparison of the organization with others. This study identified one additional cluster which is (8) support

Table 5. Audience's Comments on Dairy Khoury's Facebook Page

Qualification	Category	Comments
Positive	**Suggestions**	Comments suggested that the competitors and the media of being the responsible of this coup and how they could help
	Appreciation	Especially mothers, claiming that they and their families are consuming the Dairy Khoury's products every day, appreciating and testifying that these products are the safest and the best in the Lebanese market.
	Support	Many users supported Dairy Khoury and said that they are the best, trustworthy and professional, ideal, being the leader in the market, having delicious products, respecting hygiene standards... also, we read encouragement statements such as: *" God be with you"; "go forward"; "go gogo"; "wish you the best"; "Best of luck"*... As well as congratulating comments, for example, those who are congratulating the Dairy Khoury's owner and team after receiving the CPC certificate.
	Messages intended to be funny	Using cheering phrases such as "خوري الأساس وعلم كل الناس" Meaning "Khoury is the basis and it taught everyone else"
	Comparison of the organization with others	Comments compared Dairy Khoury's product with all the others dairy products companies in Lebanon: "If you see what other companies are producing, you would stop eating Labneh and cheese".
Negative	**Accusations/Condemnation**	People also accused the Health Minster for celebrating the CPC award ceremony with the owner of Dairy Khoury and said that "it is a condemnation that the minister is celebrating with you. The minister also wants to fill (his pocket with money), like the others". In addition, users accused Dairy Khoury for not respecting the ISO's certificates they hold, and for using.
	Objections	Objections on the fact that Dairy Khoury for using harmful additives and some call for boycotting Dairy Khoury's products
Inquiry	**Question**	Inquiries about Natamycin, about the media and about Dairy Khoury's production
	Giving information	One of the Facebook users gave explanation about the Natamycin based on the demanded of another Facebook user. As aforementioned, Dairy Khoury invited those who commented positively on Facebook to circulate the true facts and to help fighting the rumors.

Source: https://www.facebook.com/DairyKhoury/

Accordingly, the author tried to classify and categorize the audience's comments on Dairy Khoury's Facebook Page. The author adopted a qualitative approach in order to analyze and classify into categories this unstructured data. Therefore, the author:

- Read every unit (Facebook's comment)
- Identified the different categories
- Put the unit of analysis into the corresponding category
- Highlighted the recurring patterns
- Defined the different categories of the recurring patterns.
- Qualified the categories: positive, negative, inquiry

It is important to note that when the collected data didn't match the above prefigured categories, new category was developed

2. Discussion

In Lebanon, few studies on social media content are being conducted. This study may contribute to a better understanding of the use of social media platforms during certain crises. The findings suggest several gaps in the response of Dairy Khoury firm according to what the crisis communication literature implies.

Firstly, through the analysis of Dairy Khoury's Facebook users comments, and based on the findings of Helsoot & Groenendaal's (2013) and Roshan et al. (2016), the author were able to identify a new category cluster which was the "support" category that comprised messages defending the company, encouraging its team and congratulating the company on new achievements.

Secondly, the author states that no response to stakeholders on Dairy Khoury's Facebook Page could be identified, at a time when a "Corrective Action", such as recalling the Labneh from the market and promising to replace the Natamycin by a safer component, would have reduced stakeholder's pressure. Scholars stresses that if an organization fail to communicate with stakeholders in a timely manner, negative content and rumors will start circulating via social media affecting organizational reputation and stakeholders' behavioral intention (Roshan et al., 2016)).

Thirdly, the organization didn't address any apology neither to the public nor to the stakeholders, while Chung (2011) considers that those corporate apologies are crucial to decrease public anger when facing a crisis. Surprisingly, none of the Facebook users and none of the consumers of Dairy Khoury's Labneh did ask for an apology. And the reason maybe that the concept of demanding an apology from the company's management was not mature enough among the Lebanese consumers.

Fourthly, the author didn't find full status updates about the crisis as studies suggest (Freberg, 2012; Veil et al., 2011). Therefore, due to the increase use of social media in crisis communication, Lebanese organizations are invited to fully understand how to take advantages of these interactive platforms in times of crisis. Since, a lack of understanding can result in mishandling a crisis and endangering the organizational competitive position (Roshan et al., 2016).

Fifthly, in terms of organizational response to stakeholders and public's messages in a social media context as classified by Helsloot & Groendaal's (2013), this study found that Dairy Khoury didn't use Facebook to address messages to stakeholders, but only replied to specific comments of some of the users, although the public had been using Facebook platform to express their feelings and support towards the firm, as already mentioned. The reason that kept Dairy Khoury from using Facebook to address stakeholders maybe because, as M. Akiki stated, back at the time of the crisis, social media platforms where not considered to be an essential part of a crisis communication strategy.

Sixthly, this case meets the "Rumor" type in the SCCT elaborated by Coombs (2002), which is the circulation of information designed to harm an organization. This fact is solidified by the claims of Mr. Akiki, and supported by some of the comments on Dairy Khoury's Facebook page. "Weird is that the TV program addressed a totally legal additive when there is 127 unlicensed dairy factory" (Jack Al Kallasi – President of Lebanese Dairy Board)

These rumors created a domino effect and shook the whole sector of dairy production in Lebanon "The expose had a negative impact on the dairy's sales, dropping by 60 or 70 percent". Executive Magazine – issue of December 22, 2014

Seventhly, the study showed the predominance of "one-way communication" on Dairy Khoury Facebook Page, although some "two-way communication" or selective responses exist. For instance, we can recall the message posted from Dairy Khoury on their Facebook page thanking the Facebook users for their "kind and gentle support" and asking them to invite their friends to like Dairy Khoury's Facebook page and to "share the press conference videos so the truth can spread as much as we can to beat all these rumors" (2014).According to Stenger (2014), such behavior might be due to the lack of persons trained and prepared to face such situations or fear of aggravating the crisis.

Eighthly, the study highlighted that the organization didn't have a pre-crisis plan as suggested by several scholars such as Richardson (1994), Coombs (2007) and Maisonneuve (2010). The organization didn't anticipate such a pre-plan crisis, as Mr. Akiki confirmed, and as per the findings of a study conducted by Steven Fink (2000) who found that 89 percent of the chief executive officers of Fortune 500 companies reported that a business crisis was almost inevitable, and yet, 50 percent admitted that they did not have a prepared crisis management plan!

Ninthly, Dairy Khoury, appears to have violated multiple crisis response guidelines due its lack in preparedness of a potential crisis, yet, according to Mr. Akiki the company succeeded to sail through the crisis and recover by 90 percent. As suggested by Yehya and Coombs (2014), this was possible due to a large and long-term crisis response strategy that is still ongoing until today.

At the end, this study highlighted some key differences between the findings and some of the literature's suggestions. It is important to mention that, according to the SCCT for example, a few theories on crisis communication were developed in the social media context. Therefore, we suggest a reassessment of these theories, in order to verify their applicability in a social media context.

FUTURE RESEARCH DIRECTIONS

Crisis communication is an expanding field where numerous theory-based approaches and practices aim at dealing with hazardous and sudden situations. However, crisis communication has been an increasingly complicated type of management, due to the ongoing and fast progress of social media. Therefore, the communication strategies of crisis management should be developing towards:

- Tailored messages for multiple audiences that use a variety of media outlets
- Envisaged plans for a two-way communication process.
- Understanding how the crisis is perceived by the audience
- Researchers must shed the light on the possibility of having a proactive discourse aiming to help an organization to defend itself toward critics. Future researches should verify to what extend this type of proactive discourse can help the organization during a crisis to minimize the audience's tension and neutralize critics.

- Moreover, researchers should be more sensitive to the new trends in corporate communications (considering reputation as a currency, keep feeding fresh stories, the death of press releases… etc.). They should aim at providing the elements that'd help the crisis management to situate its corrective messages in a Corporate Social Responsibility context. And that requires working towards an after-crisis communication strategy, within the margins of local and global norms and values, which can contribute to furthering social good.

CONCLUSION

This paper explored the use of social media by Dairy Khoury during the crisis that stroke in 2014. The study used an in-depth email interview conducted with Mr. Akiki combined to a qualitative content analysis of Facebook messages posted during the crisis. The author provided important understanding of how the organization used Facebook during the crisis, suggesting the establishment of a well-tailored communication plan to resolve a crisis.

The author was able to identify that the organization didn't fully benefit from the added value of social media platform such as Facebook in the Dairy Khoury's crisis communication. However, this study highlighted modest use of Facebook due to an underestimation of the usefulness of such platforms back at the time of the crisis. Moreover, the study shed the light on a total absence of apology supported by Chung (2011).

The author was able to provide insights from the study, suggesting that organizations exhibited little understanding of the effectiveness of social media in a crisis situation. Given that in Lebanon, social media usage especially Facebook, developed exponentially since Dairy Khoury's crisis, the author suggests more research to be done in this area.

Thus, when an organization recovers from a crisis, it can benefit from the experience and improve its communication strategies, in order to avoid such impromptu incidents and increase preparedness for any unexpected crisis. Whether an organization is on high or low risk activity, crisis should always be considered and efficient crisis plan should always be maintained.

Researchers note that an individual's need to obtain information increases in times of conflict and ambiguity in order to provide comfort, mitigate tension and cope with uncertainty (Hong and Cameron, 2018). And as underlined by Kim and Rhee (2005), people tend to read others 'online comments in order to explore the climate of opinion before they establish their own perspectives.

Therefore, the author suggests more reliance on social media as part of crisis communication strategy, for the benefits of communicating the information on time with transparency and expertise. And this can't but have a positive impact, improve the organization's recovery and minimize the loss.

REFERENCES

Barton, L. (2001). *Crisis in organizations II* (2nd ed.). College Divisions South Western.

Benoit, W. (2007). Image repair discourse and crisis communication. *Public Relations Review, 23*(2), 177–186. doi:10.1016/S0363-8111(97)90023-0

Benoit, W. L. (1995). *Accounts, Excuses, and Apologies: A Theory of Image Restoration*. State University of New York Press.

Chung, S. (2011). Corporate apology and crisis communication: The effect of responsibility and sympathetic expression on public anger relief. Graduate Theses and Dissertations, Iowa State University

Coombs, T., & Holladay, S. H. (2002). *Helping crisis managers protect reputational assets. Initial Tests of the Situational Crisis Communication Theory.* Eastern Illinois University.

Coombs, W. T. (2007). Protecting organization reputations during a crisis: The development and application of situational crisis communication theory. *Corporate Reputation Review*, *10*(3), 163–176. doi:10.1057/palgrave.crr.1550049

Coombs, W. T., Frandsen, F., Holladay, S. H., Johansen, W., & Denmark, A. (2010). Why a concern for apologiaand crisis communication? *Corporate Communications*, *15*(4), 337–349. doi:10.1108/13563281011085466

Coombs, W. T., & Holladay, S. H. (2010). *The handbook of crisis.* Wiley Blackwell Publishing Ltd. doi:10.1002/9781444314885

Fearn-Banks, K. (2010). Crisis Communications: A casebook approach (4th ed.). Mahwah, NJ: Lawrence Erlbaum.

Fombrun, C. J., & van Riel, C. B. M. (2004). *Fame & Fortune: How successful companies build.* Pearson Education.

Freberg, K. (2012). Intention to comply with crisis messages communicated via social media. *Public Relations Review*, *38*(3), 416-421. doi:10.1016/j.pubrev.2012.01.008

Helsloot, I.&Groenendaal, J. (2013). Twitter: an underutilized potential during sudden crises? *Journal of Contingencies and Crisis Management*, *21*(3), 178-183. Retrieved from doi:10.1111/1468-5973.12023

Hermann, C. F. (1963). Some Consequences of Crisis Which Limit the Viability of Organizations. *Administrative Science Quarterly*, *8*(1), 61–82. doi:10.2307/2390887

Hong, S., & Cameron, G. T. (2018). Will comments change your opinion? The persuasion effects of online comments and heuristic cues in crisis communication. *Journal of Contingencies and Crisis Management*. Retrieved 1st of June 2017 from http://www.instituteforpr.org/crisis-management-communications

Kim, E., & Rhee, J. (2005). Rethinking "reading" online: The effects of online communication. *The Korean Journal of Journalism & Communication Studies*, *50*(4), 65–94.

Lokman, I. M. (2006). E-mail interviewing in qualitative research: A methodological discussion. *Journal of the American Society for Information Science and Technology*, *57*(10), 1284–1295. doi:10.1002/asi.20416

Roshan, M., Warren, M., & Carr, R. (2016). Understanding the use of social media by organizations for crisis communication. Computers in Human Behavior, 63, 350-361.

Seeger, M. W., Sellnow, T. L., & Ulmer, R. R. (2003). Communication, organization and crisis. Westport, CT: Quorum.

Sellnow, T. L., Ulmer, R. R., & Snider, M. (1998). The compatibility of corrective action in organizational crisis communication. *Communication Quarterly*, *46*(1), 60–74. doi:10.1080/01463379809370084

Staffaroni, S. (2012). *Crisis communication &natural disasters:communication plan for Rome, Italy in the case of an earthquake*. Thesis presented to the USC Graduate School University of Southern California.

Stenger, T. (2014). Social media and online reputation management as practice: First steps towards social CRM? *International Journal of Technology and Human*, *10*(4).

Szczepanik, A. (2003).The importance of crisis Communication: What lessons did we learn fromTylenol and Exxon? Oxford, Ohio

Tellis, W. (1997, July). Introduction to case study. *Qualitative Report*, *3*(2). http://www.nova.edu/ssss/QR/QR3-2/tellis1.html

Veil, S. R., Buehner, T., &Palenchar, M. J. (2011). A work in process literature review: Incorporating social media in risk and crisis communication. *Journal of Contingencies and Crisis Management*, *19*(2), 110-122. doi:10.1111/j.1468-5973.2011.00639.x

Wartick, S. (1992). The relationship between intense media exposure and change in corporate reputation. *Business & Society*, *31*(1), 33–49. doi:10.1177/000765039203100104

Wilcox, D., Cameron, G., & Reber, B. (2015). *Public Relations: Strategies and Tactics* (11th ed.). Prentice-Hall/Financial Times.

Willmer, J. (2016). *Crisis Management Versus Risk Management: Do You Know the Difference?* Retrieved from https://probonoaustralia.com.au/news/2016/09/crisis-management-versus-risk-management-know-difference/

Yehya, N. & Coombs, T. (2014). Catalytic defiance as a crisis communication strategy: the risk of pursuing long-term objectives. *Business Horizons, 60*(4), 463-472.

Zainal, Z. (2007). Case study as a research method. *Journal Kemanusiaan bil.9*.

ADDITIONAL READING

Austin, L., & Jin, Y. (2017). *Social media and crisis communication*. Routledge. doi:10.4324/9781315749068

Brataas, K. (2018). *Crisis Communication: Case Studies and Lessons Learned from International Disasters*. Routledge. doi:10.4324/9781315368245

Clark, R. (2018). Crisis Management: Is Social Media its new best friend or its worst nightmare? Manchester, UK

Ndlela, M. (2018). *Crisis Communication: A Stakeholder Approach*. Palgrave Macmillan.

Phelps, R. (2018). *Crisis Management: How to develop a powerful program*. Chandi Media.

Telang, A., & Deshpande, A. (2016). Keep calm and carry on: A crisis communication study of Cadbury and McDonalds. *Management & Marketing: Challenges for the Knowledge Society*, *11*(1), 371–379. doi:10.1515/mmcks-2016-0003

Zhang, D. (2013, October). Communication Strategies of the Chinese Dairy Industry Manufacturers to Rebuild Reputation and Maintain a Quality Relationship. *Journal of Media and Communication*, 5(1), 118–130.

KEY TERMS AND DEFINITIONS

Communication Strategy: A set of communication activities to reach an organizational objective(s). It targets a well-defined audience with strategic messaging, using a choice of communication tools that would best reach that audience. A communication strategy aims to achieve a high level of performance, create values for its shareholders and satisfaction for the target audience in a competitive market

Corporation: The legal entity of a group of companies or a large company owned by shareholders. The Corporation is liable by law to conduct the actions and finances of the business, while the shareholders are not.

Crisis Management: The actions taken to deal with unpredictable and sudden events often based on pre-designed strategies, in order to limit – and eventually halt- the occurring damages as quickly as possible.

Image: Is the public perception of an organization/corporation, and the way it presents itself to the public. As it is a perception, it might not be a real reflection of the actual state of the organization/corporation nor of its brand (s). The main challenge is to match reality with the desired image.

Organization: It is the process of organizing a group of people in a given structure and being managed to pursue and meet particular purposes. Organizations have an authority that structures and determines activities, roles, tasks, and responsibilities that members should carry out. Organizations are shaped by their member's relationships. Organizations are dynamic structures that affect and are affected by their environment. Organizations are units, in which offices, or positions, have distinct but interdependent duties, working to achieve financial or on-financial goals. An organization can be part of a corporation.

Reputation: Is the trust and confidence (or the lack of) of consumers and shareholders in an organization. It is what people hear and say about an organization and how its good or bad standing is reported in the media. It affects the number of customers, operations, and profit margins. Good reputation takes a lot of efforts to build and requires excellent crisis management to maintain in times of adversities.

Social Media: Are computer-based platforms that enable people to connect with each other's, to share and generate content (opinions, ides, photos, videos…), to establish and maintain relationships. These platforms allow organizations to reach, to engage with and persuade their target audiences. Social media includes forums, blogs, social networking sites and other forms of online discussions.

Social Advertisements and Recall

Anish Yousaf

🔘 https://orcid.org/0000-0002-5234-7474

ICFAI Business School (IBS), Hyderabad, India

Roktim Sarmah

Mittal School of Business, Lovely Professional University, India

INTRODUCTION

Kotler (1971) proposed the concept of social advertising as "the design, implementation and control of programs calculated to influence the acceptability of social ideas and involving considerations of product planning, pricing, communication and marketing research'. Social advertising approach is used for informing, educating and persuading the society on basic issues (Cismaru, Lavack, and Markewich, 2009). Social advertising identifies social problems and it informs about them, but it does not try to offer immediate solutions (Choi, Eldomiaty, and Kim, 2007; Elliott, 1999). Social advertising do not promote any product, firm or service; its main goal is to evoke a sense of responsibility or to make people do a change in their behavior and attitudes. Social advertising is also an important part of Indian public policy where that policy relates to communications, Family Welfare, Education, Health, and Environment and National Integration (Chauhan, 1995).

Research in the area of social advertising is very narrow as majority of the studies are done in European Nations with few exceptions in India (Biener, Keeler, and Nyman, 2000; Hawkings et al., 2011). Causes that have been studied in the area of social advertisements include tobacco television advertisements (Biener, Keeler, and Nyman, 2000), ethical challenges (Brenkert, 2000), sexual social marketing (Reichert, Heckler, and Jackson, 2001), attitude of college students towards economic, social and ethical consequences (Beard, 2003), AIDS prevention messages and condom usage (Pfeiffer, 2004), cigarette advertising (Gibson et al., 2010; Bansal, John, and Ling, 2005), gambling issues among Youths (Messerlian and Derevensky, 2007), effectiveness of obesity programmes and health behaviour (Suarez-Almazor, 2011; Cismaru and Lavack, 2007), consumer trust and ethics of welfare exchange (Choi, Eldomiaty, and Kim, 2007), and drunk driving (Cismaru, Lavack, and Markewisc, 2009).

There are many social causes existing in a highly diverse country like India. Central as well as State Governments are running many social advertisement campaigns related to these social causes so as to spread awareness to target audiences. For policy makers, evaluation and measuring the effectiveness of these social advertisements is an important part that needs to be evaluated. Cornwell, Weeks and Roy (2005) studied the outcomes of one form of communications, sponsorship, and argued that recall or top-of-mind awareness is an important test to judge its effectiveness. Similar views were presented by other researchers in similar domain (Wakefield and Bennett, 2010; Wakefield, Becker-Olsen, and Cornwell, 2007, Lardinoit and Derbaix, 2001, Boshoff and Gerber, 2008). Same could be applied to social advertisements also where one can judge the effectiveness of various social advertisements by measuring their recall among target audience.

DOI: 10.4018/978-1-7998-3473-1.ch152

BACKGROUND

Social advertising tries to bring change in the perception of individuals, which at large would bring change in the society. Generally, individuals want them to be the cause of a good cause. It is highly welcomed by all ages than action, humor and sexual appeal in commercial. Research in the area of social advertising is not new though initial researches were carried out in the area of advertising related to tobacco marketing, HIV and similar diseases (Sharma, 2012; Cismaru, Lavack, and Markewisc, 2009). Doing an ethnographic study, Ritson and Elliott (1999) explored the social uses of advertising, within an adolescent audience, arguing that social implications of advertising changes consumer behaviour positively. Advertising text can provide an independent source for rituals that are enacted in a variety of social contexts in order to confer meaning onto their participants and audience. Advertising can form the basis for a wide variety of social interactions that can potentially influence both the qualitative nature and quantitative magnitude of the effect of a particular execution on members of the target audience.

Sharma (2012) conceptually explored the impact of creativity on advertising and discusses campaigns that have left strong impressions on consumers. The presented review study tries to come up with some evidence of creativity by reviewing expert views, past literature in advertising, advertising campaign and marketing activities. Cismaru, Lavack and Markewisc (2009) examined social marketing programs using protection motivation theory (PMT) for preventing drunk driving, and explored how protection motivation theory (PMT) can be used to create effective anti drunk driving communications using qualitative analysis of anti-drunk driving communication materials posted on Internet. The campaigns described are designed to motivate the public to undertake a variety of behaviors, including drinking in moderation or abstaining from alcohol use, choosing a designated driver, or choosing a safe ride home such as a taxi or public transit. The researcher found that social marketing campaigns aimed at preventing drunk driving in English-speaking countries were very successful, and the research showed that PMT can be successfully used in this type of campaigns.

Tangari and Netemeyer (2007) also worked on similar lines and studied the impact of anti-tobacco campaigns and smoking status of user beliefs and intentions. They found that social anti-smoking campaigns and efforts are successful in preventing of trial behavior of adolescents potentially offer a room for considerable profits. Also, young adult smokers had stronger beliefs about secondhand smoke and were also likely to consider quitting. Such young smokers give receptive market for future considerations of antismoking campaigns. Biener, Keeler and Nyman (2000) assessed adults' receptivity to the Massachusetts television anti-tobacco campaign as a function of respondents' demographics, baseline tobacco control attitudes, and changes in smoking status during the campaign, and advertisements' affective qualities. Findings of the study revealed anti-tobacco media campaign achieving high levels of penetration into the adult population and a favorable reaction to the television campaigns. The results suggest that social advertisements depicting suffering as a result of tobacco use may be instrumental in promoting cessation or reinforcing the decision to quit.

Gibson et al. (2010) studied the impact of social advertisements on HIV prevention among injecting drug users (IDUS) and social advertisements were found as a cost effective strategy to prevent HIV among IDUs. This study also represented the involvement of social marketing in applying marketing principles to promote social goods. The research is all about success of social marketing campaign in reaching majority of the estimated 7000 heroin users in Sacramento, California. It was found that exposure to HIV prevention messages with small posters and a newsletter significantly reduced the community-wide prevalence of HIV-related injection risk behavior. On similar lines, Yaminidevi (2014) studied the relationship between peer education and change in behaviour of people towards HIV and other similar issues using social advertisement campaigns and also shows personal interaction with volunteer as an effective way to convey the social message and information of the cause to educate people. It summarized the impact of different tools like peer to peer education, brochure, documentary movies etc through the in depth interview with different NGO of the Tamil Nadu area.

Maheshwari and Suresh (2013) studied the preference of social advertisement among youths and conceptually examined the adoption of social advertisements by gathering views from respondents who are mostly influencing the success of social advertising. They found that social advertisements are mainly attracting youths and argued that present youth is expecting changes in advertisements without compromising the India's value system. The internet (email, videos, research articles, and Social media) is a big platform to do this thought provoking exercise. Singh et.al (2013) also assessed the awareness, perception and myths regarding Swine Flu among educated common public in Patiala District of Punjab. They found that around 88% of the study population had heard of Swine flu out of which only 36.5% respondents know that hand washing as a mode of prevention and around 40% of the population has myths regarding mode of spread. Authors were of the view that social advertisement campaigns play an important role in spreading awareness for such kind of issues in rural areas and government should focus more on providing scientific and effective information through the prime media. There are plenty of researches focusing on social advertisements and measurement of their effectiveness. Majority of these researches are done in European context and very few studies have focused the measurement of effectiveness of social advertisement campaigns in Indian context. The present study, thus, aimed at empirically measuring the effectiveness of popular social advertisement campaigns that are running in India.

FOCUS OF THE ARTICLE

This study is an attempt towards exploring the popularity of various social advertisement campaigns of India among youths via measuring their recall. One of the main objectives of the current study is to measure the recall of these social advertisements and exploring the most recalled (popular) social advertisements in India. Another objective of the current stud is to explore the reasons for the high recall of these social advertisements by doing exploratory study with target audience. The scope of the study is limited to the rural areas of Jalandhar, Kapurthala and Hoshiarpur districts of Punjab. The measurement of social advertisement effectiveness was divided into two phases. Initially, an exploratory study was done to explore popular social advertisement for the study followed by measuring their recall and the reasons thereof. The detailed procedure is discussed in the research methodology section followed by discussion of results and conclusion.

RESEARCH METHODOLOGY

Sampling Procedure and Participants

The sample of this study consists of students enrolled in a large Private Indian University (Lovely Professional University, Punjab). Convenience sampling technique was used for data collection from the respondents. Data was collected from 350 students intercepted at different locations within the university using a structured questionnaire. After omitting outliers and half-filled forms, 300 were kept for further analysis with a response rate of 86%. The participation of the respondents was entirely voluntary.

Instrumentation and Measurement

A structured questionnaire was designed in order to achieve the objectives. The questionnaire was divided into two sections. Section A consists of demographic related information of respondents whereas Section B consists of measurement of respondent's awareness of the select social advertisement campaigns. Section A of the questionnaire consists of questions about the demographic and psychographic characteristics of the participants related to participant's gender, age, nationality, education. Filler question was also asked in this section. Section B was designed to measure the awareness towards different social causes by asking respondents to rank these social causes in order of their preference in a way similar to Maheshwari and Suresh (2013). Open ended questions were also asked in this section to know about the reason for the recall of these campaigns individually.

Demographic Profiling of Respondents

Data analysis revealed that 52.33% (47.67%) of the respondents were male (female) showing an equal (approximately) gender distribution. Majority of the respondents were in the age group of 20-25 years (50%). In terms of the place of residence, it was found that 35.33% respondents were from Kapurthala district, 30% were from Hoshiarpur district and 34.67% were from Jalandhar district. The district wise regional break includes Kapurthala district including Mahehru, Chaheru and Domeli village where as Hoshiarpur includes Sangowal and Badowal village and Jalandhar includes Randhawa Masandan and Nakodar. Data analysis revealed that the respondents for the current study have a good educational background with 41.67% graduate respondents and 35% post-graduates.

A filler question was asked initially regarding respondents awareness of the concept of social advertisements. It was found that 98% respondents were aware about social advertisements and only 2% were not aware of the various social advertisements. In terms of the importance of social advertisements, 96% respondents reported that social advertisements are important for the society whereas only 4% think that social advertisements are not important. Also, 91.33% of the respondents find social advertisements being telecasted attractive while 8.67% find the social advertisements unattractive.

Selecting Social Advertisements

Pilot Study 1

In the first phase of the research a focus group was conducted and data was collected from 37 respondents aged between 18 to 35 years having awareness about various social advertisements being aired by government (NGO) agencies, both state and central. The main purpose of this focus group was to generate a pool of social causes that could be used for further use. The respondents were asked to recall three social advertisements/causes that come to their mind first. The pool of social advertisements / causes that were generated after the first focus group were the social advertisements related to Aids, Cancer, Polio, Drug Abuse, Female Foeticide, Tuberculosis, Malnutrition, Child Labor, Female Illiteracy, Swachh Bharat Abhiyaan, Human Trafficking, Sanitation, Dowry, Gambling, Domestic Violence. It is important to mention that all these are prominent social causes existing in India and social advertisements are being aired by the state as well as central government via different media.

DISCUSSION OF RESULTS

13

Measuring Effectiveness of Social Advertisements

Few questions were asked to respondents in Section A related to social advertisements. Analysis of these questions generates interesting findings. 53.67% of the respondents feel that social advertisements telecasted on television are the most attractive whereas 26.67% of the respondents find social advertisements on social media like Facebook, twitter etc. the most attractive. 11.67% of the respondents feel print media social advertisements are the most attractive. 4% respondents feel outdoor media like bill boards and hoardings etc. are the most attractive medium for social advertisements followed by 4% respondents being attracted through radio advertisements.

When asked about what purpose social advertisements solves, respondents were divisive in their opinions. 24% of the respondents believe that the social advertisements create reasonable social impact 19% respondents thinks it forces to think about the social issue. 13% of the respondents say that social advertisements gives information. 11.67% of the population says that social advertisements generates curiosity, 11% respondents thinks that it increase the level of knowledge, 10% of the respondents thinks social advertisements transfers beliefs and values to the society, 9.67% of the respondents thinks that social advertisements creats awareness about prevention and cure of the epidemics. 39.67% respondents believe social advertisements to have a positive impression on their minds. 25.67% respondents think that social advertisements have the desire to explore their minds. 24% respondents are interested in the social advetisments. 8.67% of the respondents have the impression to recall the social advertisements. 2% of the respondents are not interested in the social advertisements. 31.33% respondents believes that picture depicting a scene /story advertisements are more attractive, 28.67% respondents thinks that a moving action oriented advertisments are attractive. 20% respondents reported in favor of words with the visuals make the social advertisements attractive. 10.33% respondents say words with sound social advertisments are attractive. 8.33% respondents think celebrity endorsements social advertisements are attractive. 1.33% respondents think just the printed words in the social advertisements makes it attractive.

Another important dimension was the duration of impact of social advertisements on the respondent's memory. 38.33% respondents say social advertisements have the impression on their minds for one week. 16.67% respondents says social advertisements have the impression on their minds for one month. 15.67% respondents have the impression of social advertisements on their minds for only one day. 15% respondents say the impression of the social advertisements on their minds lasts for more than a month. 9.33% respondents say social advertisements have the impression on their minds only for few hours. 4.67% respondents are least bothered about the impression of the social advertisements. 0.33% respondents have the impression of social advertisements for one week. 34.33% respondents think that the message is the important aspect in the social advertisements. 23.67% respondents think punch line of the social advertisements is the important aspect of the advertisements. 14% respondents says the captions in the social advertisements are important aspects of the ad. 13.33% respondents thinks theme of the social advertisements are important.13.33% respondents thinks that models in the social advertisements are important aspects.1.33% respondents thinks the background of the social advertisements is the important aspect of the advertisements. 69% respondents think that the celebrity endorsing the social advertisements is more influential. 31% respondents think that the non-celebrity social advertisements are more influential.

Table 1. Evaluating Social Advertisements on Various Parameters*

PARAMETER	Mean	Std. Dev
Creative	3.71	1.07
Informative	**3.98**	**1.00**
Memorable	3.42	1.03
Strong Social Message	**4.02**	**1.10**
Entertaining	3.31	1.01
Effective	**3.80**	**1.02**
Presence of celebrity is influential	**4.11**	**1.04**
*mean measured on a 5-poiint Likert scale		

Evaluation of Social Advertisements on Select Parameters

In terms of reasons for recalling social advertisement campaigns, it was found that social campaigns that have the presence of celebrity (mean = 4.11, s.d = 1.04), strong social message (mean = 4.02, s.d = 1.10) and are informative (mean = 3.98, s.d = 1.00) and effective (mean = 3.80, s.d = 1.02) are the best determinant of enhancing people to recall them. Please see Table 1. Analysis of data revealed that respondents agree that the social advertisements that are telecasted are creative. The ad elements used to convey the story to the target group involves a good amount of creativity, informative and add to the information and awareness of the audience. Respondents also agree that the social advertisements having celebrities as social cause ambassadors are influential and change target audiences behaviour. Respondents also agree a celebrity endorsing a social cause give a positive image and creates a lasting impression regarding the social advertisement campaign. Regarding the message content of the social advertisements, respondents agree that the social advertisements leave a strong social message for the audience and have a neutral opinion on the entertainment aspect of social advertisements. Respondents also agree that the social advertisements telecasted are effective in delivering the social value they are meant to deliver and that the social advertisements with celebrity endorsements create more awareness due to the presence of celebrities agreeing to the fact that presence of a celebrity in a social advertisement campaigns is influential in bringing attention towards social causes.

Top Recalled Social Advertisements

Out of the social awareness campaigns mentioned in the questionnaire "Clean India (Swachh Bharat)" was recalled by 87.66% of the surveyed respondents which was followed by Polio advertisements (recalled by 82.33%). Please see Table 2. Results of exploratory study revealed that heavy participation of top political leaders and celebrities in these causes have led to their high recall. Also, Celebrity endorsements and catchy slogans also play a very important role in social advertisement, which cannot be denied. For example, the campaign slogan of Polio advertisements "Do boond zindagi ki" and the presence of Mr. Amitabh Bachchan lead to this campaign among the top recalled social advertisement campaign. The awareness advertisement that runs before the movie starts in a cinema hall depicting a cancer patient struggling for his life left a great impression on the population which was recalled by 69.66%. This was followed by the social advertisement of female foeticide which was recalled by 67.33% respondents.

Table 2. Recall Of Select Social Advertisement Campaigns

S. No	SOCIAL ADVERTISEMENTS	PERCENTAGE RECALL	RANK
1	Swachh Bharat Abhiyaan (Clean India)	87.66	1
2	Polio	82.33	2
3	Cancer	69.66	3
4	Female Foeticide	67.33	4
5	Female illiteracy	64	5
6	Child labor	62.33	6
7	Aids	59.33	7
8	Domestic violence	53	8
9	Drug abuse	49	9
10	Sanitation	47	10
11	Dowry	44.33	11
12	Malnutrition	37.66	12
13	Tuberculosis	36.33	13
14	Human trafficking	33.33	14
15	Gambling	30	15

Reason for the same can be attributed to the "Beti Bachao, Beti Padhao" campaign recently launched by Central Government of India. Beti Bachao activities include large rallies, campaigns, wall paintings, billboards, and television commercials and short animations and video films. Also people were able to recall the advertisement because celebrities such as Priyanka Chopra are involved in "Save the girl child" initiatives. Moreover, Bollywood actor Aamir Khan devoted the first episode "Daughters Are Precious" of his show "Satyamev Jayate" to increase the awareness about this issue, focusing primarily on Western Rajasthan. In addition to it, 64% of the respondents were able to recall the awareness campaigns aimed on female illiteracy. Sarva Shiksha Abhiyan aimed at providing free education to children also have a good recall followed by "National Programme for Education of Girls at Elementary Level (NPEGEL)". Child labor was also one of the social campaign that was recalled in good numbers by respondents (62.33%) because of the Indian TV drama show "Udaan - Sapno ki" which telecast a girl child being practiced upon child labor by the master who owns her.

FUTURE RESEARCH DISCUSSIONS

Social advertisements are quite popular and governments of different countries have laid emphasis on their awareness from time to time. Our study provides various insights into the awareness of social advertisement campaigns run in India and highlight the most popular campaigns. Despite the efforts made, like other studies, this study too has few limitations which needs to be taken care of by future researchers. We have made a descriptive attempt to explore the popularity of social campaigns in India but failed to explore why these campaigns are more popular relative to other campaigns which were given the same resources. Future researchers can do an analytical or qualitative research into this issue to explore why few campaigns are more popular over other campaigns and completely dominate consumer recall. Also, the detailed impact of celebrities endorsing social cause needs to be studied by future researchers.

Government needs to prepare more advertisement campaigns and need to create more awareness among rural population. Also, future researchers also need to study the role of collaboration between non-govt agencies and government agencies to market a social cause. Government agencies, NGOs, other regional bodies and advertising agencies need to focus on the issues like human trafficking, gambling, sanitation, dowry and need to come up with some creative and interesting campaigns so that it can leave an impression on the minds of the viewers and they can recall it easily even after a long time.

CONCLUSION

Previous studies have focused on social advertisements in different contexts but to our knowledge no study has made an attempt to study their relative effectiveness and reasons for the same. Results revealed that social advertisements having a strong and informative message as content are rated high by target audience. Selection of print media also plays a very important role in achieving its objectives. Social advertisements telecasted on television and social media sites are believed to have a strong impact and are believed to create impact and generate awareness about the social issue and gives information to the target audience. It was also explored that social advertisements are believed to have a positive impression on the minds of target audience generating curiosity to know more about the cause. While measuring the recall of different social advertisements it was found that out of all select social advertisements "Swatch Bharat Abhiyaan" was having the highest recall followed by social advertisements of Polio and Cancer campaign. Results of open ended questions revealed that social causes having celebrity (ies) and politicians as ambassadors have high recall and acceptability among target audience. The findings of the study can be used in public-policy making. In direction with the findings of the study, policy makers can make effective use of various communication tools and media to achieve their objectives. For example, the social issues related to youths need to use television and social networking sites as communication media. Also, policy makers need to identify celebrities having a high fit with the social cause who can convey the message to target audience to spread maximum awareness of social advertisements.

REFERENCES

Bansal, R., John, S., & Ling, P. M. (2005). Cigarette advertising in mumbai, india: Targeting different socio economic groups,women & youth. *British Medical Journal, 14*(3), 201–206. PMID:15923471

Beard, F. K. (2003). College student attitudes toward's advertising's ethical economic & social consequences. *Journal of Business Ethics, 48*(3), 217–228. doi:10.1023/B:BUSI.0000005782.44337.c2

Biener, L., Keeler, M. G., & Nyman, A. L. (2000). Adults' response to massachusetts anti-tobacco television advertisements: Impact of viewer & advertisement characteristics. *British Medical Journal, 9*(4), 401–407. PMID:11106710

Boshoff, C., & Gerber, C. (2008). Sponsorship recall & recognition. The case of the 2007 Cricket World Cup. *South African Journal of Business Management, 39*(2), 1–8. doi:10.4102ajbm.v39i2.556

Brenkert, G. G. (2002). Ethical challenges of social marketing. *Journal of Public Policy & Marketing, 21*(1), 14–25. doi:10.1509/jppm.21.1.14.17601

Chauhan, M. R. (1995). *Advertising: The Social AD Challenge*. Anmol Publications Pvt. Ltd.

Choi, C. J., Eldomiaty, T. I., & Kim, S. W. (2007). Consumer trust, social marketing & ethics of welfare exchange. *Journal of Business Ethics*, *74*(1), 17–23. doi:10.100710551-006-9128-z

Cismaru, M., & Lavack, A. M. (2007). Social marketing campaigns aimed at preventing & controlling obesity: A review & recommendations. *International Review on Public and Nonprofit Marketing*, *4*(2), 9–30. doi:10.1007/BF02893617

Cismaru, M., Lavack, A. M., & Markewich, E. (2009). Social Marketing Campaigns Aimed at Preventing Drunk Driving:A Review & Recommendations. *International Marketing Review*, *26*(3), 292–311. doi:10.1108/02651330910960799

Cornwell, T. B., Weeks, C., & Roy, D. (2005). Sponsorship-Linked Marketing: Opening the Black Box. *Journal of Advertising*, *34*(2), 21–42. doi:10.1080/00913367.2005.10639194

Elliott, M. R. (1999). The Social Uses of Advertising: An Ethnographic Study on Adolescent Advertising Audiences. *The Journal of Consumer Research*, *26*(3), 260–277. doi:10.1086/209562

Gibson, D. R., Zhang, Z., Cassady, D., Pappas, L., Mitchell, J., & Kegeles, S. M. (2010). Effectiveness of HIV prevention social marketing with injecting drug users. *American Journal of Public Health*, *10*(10), 1828–1830. doi:10.2105/AJPH.2009.181982 PMID:20724686

Hawkins, J., Bulmer, S., & Eagle, L. (2011). Evidence of IMC in Social Marketing. *Journal of Social Marketing*, *1*(3), 228–239. doi:10.1108/20426761111170722

Kotler, P., & Gerald, Z. (1971). Social Advertising: An Approach to Planned Social Charge. *Journal of Advertising*, *35*(July), 3–12. PMID:12276120

Lardinoit, T., & Derbaix, C. (2001). Sponsorship & recall of sponsors. *Psychology and Marketing*, *18*(2), 167–190. doi:10.1002/1520-6793(200102)18:2<167::AID-MAR1004>3.0.CO;2-I

Maheshwari, R., & Suresh, D. G. (2013). A study on the preference of social advertisements among the adults in Erode. *Asia Pacific Journal of Marketing & Management Review*, *2*(2), 112–119.

Messerlian, C., & Derevensky, J. (2007). Evaluating the Role of Social Marketing Campaigns to Prevent Youth Gambling Problems: A Qualitative study. *Canadian Journal of Public Health*, *98*(2), 101–104. doi:10.1007/BF03404318 PMID:17441531

Pfeiffer, J. (2004). Condom social marketing, pentecostalism, & structural adjustment in mozambique: A clash of aids prevention message. *Medical Anthropology Quarterly*, *18*(1), 77–103. doi:10.1525/maq.2004.18.1.77 PMID:15098428

Reichert, T., Heckler, S. E., & Jackson, S. (2001). The effects of sexual social marketing appeals on cognitive processing & persuasion. *Journal of Advertising*, *30*(1), 13–27. doi:10.1080/00913367.2001.10673628

Ritson, M., & Elliot, E. (1999). The social uses of advertising: An ethnographic study of adolescent advertising audiences. *The Journal of Consumer Research*, *26*(2), 260–267. doi:10.1086/209562

Sharma, P. (2012). Advertising effectiveness: Underst&ing the value of creativity in advertising. A review study in India. *Online Journal of Communication and Media Technologies*, *2*(3), 1–10. doi:10.29333/ojcmt/2386

Singh, S., Kaur, P., & Singh, G. (2013). Study to assess the awareness, perception & myths regarding swine flu. *International Journal of Research & Development of Health*, 6(2), 54–60.

Suarez-Almazor, M. E. (2011). Changing health behaviors with social marketing. *Osteoporos International Review*, 22(3), 461–464. doi:10.100700198-011-1699-6 PMID:21847766

Tangari, A. H., & Netemeyer, S. B. (2007). How do antitobacco campaign & smoking status affect beliefs & intentions? Some similarities & differences between adults & adolescents. *American Marketing Journal*, 26(1), 60–74.

Wakefield, K. L., Becker-Olsen, K., & Cornwell, T. B. (2007). I spy a sponsor. The effects of sponsorship level, prominence, relatedness, & cueing on recall accuracy. *Journal of Advertising*, 36(4), 61–74. doi:10.2753/JOA0091-3367360405

Wakefield, K. L., & Bennett, G. (2010). Affective intensity & sponsor identification. *Journal of Advertising*, 39(3), 99–111. doi:10.2753/JOA0091-3367390307

Yaaminidevi. (2014). A study on the behavior change communication in the soical marketing of condoms. *International Review on Public & Nonprofit Marketing, 11*(2), 181-193.

ADDITIONAL READING

Aral, S., & Walker, D. (2012). Identifying influential and susceptible members of social networks. *Science, 337*(6092), 337–341. doi:10.1126cience.1215842 PMID:22722253

Bakshy, E., Eckles, D., Yan, R., & Rosenn, I. (2012). Social influence in social advertising: Evidence from field experiments. In: *Proceedings of the ACM Conference on Electronic* Commerce. ACM. 10.1145/2229012.2229027

Furlow, N. E. (2011). Find us on Facebook: How Cause Marketing has Embraced Social Media. *Journal of Marketing Development and Competitiveness, 5*(6), 61–64.

Lina, D. (2015). 40 Of The Most Powerful Social Issue Ads That'll Make You Stop And Think. Retrieved from https://www.boredpanda.com/powerful-social-advertisements/

McPherson, M., Lovin, L. S., & Cook, J. M. (2001). Birds of a feather: Homophily in social networks. *Annual Review of Sociology, 27*(1), 415–444. doi:10.1146/annurev.soc.27.1.415

Veloutsou, C., Saren, M., & Tzokas, N. (2002). Relationship Marketing: What If...? *European Journal of Marketing, 36*(4), 433–449. doi:10.1108/03090560210417255

Zubcsek, P. P., & Sarvary, M. (2011). Advertising to a social network. *Quantitative Marketing and Economics, 9*(1), 71–107. doi:10.100711129-010-9093-9

KEY TERMS AND DEFINITIONS

Advertising: Is a means of communication with the users of a product or service. Advertisements are messages paid for by those who send them and are intended to inform or influence people who receive them.

Advertising Recall: Is a measure of advertising effectiveness in which a sample of respondents is exposed to an ad and then at a later point in time is asked if they remember the ad.

Celebrity Endorsements: Are forms of advertising that uses famous personalities or celebrities who command a high degree of recognition, trust, respect, or awareness amongst the people. Such people advertise for a product lending their names or images to promote a product or service.

Social Advertising: Advertisements that promote a community's health and well-being, such as programs that educate people about drugs, diseases, and other social issues.

Social Advertising Effectiveness: Is a measure of effectiveness of the social advertising in a way similar to measuring the effectiveness of the campaign.

Social Marketing: Is an approach used to develop activities aimed at changing or maintaining people's behaviour for the benefit of individuals and society as a whole. Social marketing aims to develop and integrate marketing concepts with other approaches to, in turn, influence behaviors that benefit individuals and communities for the greater social good.

Social Marketing Campaigns: In public health, many social marketing campaigns include a specific behavior change component.

Impact of Advertisements on Demand for Fairness Products Among University Students in Pakistan

Tansif Ur Rehman
University of Karachi, Pakistan

Sajida Parveen
University of Karachi, Pakistan

Kiran Jawaid
Institute of Business and Technology, Karachi, Pakistan

Muhammad Ajmal Khan
Karachi Institute of Economics and Technology, Pakistan

INTRODUCTION

Pakistani cosmetics industry is flourishing at a rapid pace; which is evidenced by its presence in different markets at a global level. It has more comprehensively been enlightened that the local cosmetic industry of Pakistan makes its mark not only at the domestic level, but also at the global level. Kalsoom (2011) elaborated that the demand for fairness creams exist and is rising in female as well as male consumers. This rise in demand leads to an increase in its supply in different South Asian regions.

The dilemma in Pakistan is standardization. Individuals have a propensity to link beauty with a lighter skin tone. This has driven females to take excessive measures to apply dangerous chemicals to their skin, because they promise mesmerizing fairness. Consequently, there has been an immense demand of skin brightening items in Pakistan.

There are in addition social as well as monetary implications with respect to beauty. It takes a lot of endeavor to embellish as well as modify one's appearance in order to look stylish. The inspiration to be forever young as well as appealing exists in every society. Society imposes the rules of beauty. Today, what is considered as beautiful, might be mocked in the future. The perception regarding beauty changes with the evolution of society (Sunaina, 2016).

Society plays a significant function regarding the concept of attractiveness. For example, youthfulness is the aim of attractiveness in USA, whilst in Europe unblemished skin is considered as being ideal. In most Asian countries, fairness is desirable. As the globalization progressed, individuals started associating beauty by means of contentment as well as affluence. Thus, females from Asia started to crave the Western idyllic of attractiveness, i.e. being fair, slim, and tall (Sunaina, 2016).

In the contemporary era, despite women are more powerful and have a professional success. A new type of social control exists in the form of beauty myth. It is an obsession with physical perfection that traps women in an endless spiral of self-consciousness, hope, and self-hatred as they try to accomplish society's impossible explanation of being a flawless beauty (Wolf, 2013). This chapter focuses on the impact of television advertising on the demand for fairness products among university students in Pakistan.

DOI: 10.4018/978-1-7998-3473-1.ch153

BACKGROUND

Beauty lies in the eye of the beholder. The sensitivity regarding attractiveness is led by social influences as well as a notion of aesthetics decided by elites. Females and sometimes males go as far as possible to achieve that 'ideal' look. The quest for perfect looks has been as old as time itself. (Sunaina, 2016).

Moral beauty was considered to be the *telos* (purpose) of human virtues by Aristotle. Displays of moral beauty have been shown to inspire the moral sentiment of elevation and can cause an aspiration to become a better individual. Researches propose that by encouraging individuals to connect with moral beauty can amplify their wish to become more humane. As, moral emotions stimulate ethical behavior (Diessner, Iyer, Smith, & Haidt, 2013).

Different methods are employed to accomplish fairness in Pakistan. One of the most prominent is 'formula cream'. It is usually made at home and often sold at beauty parlors across Pakistan. Bleaching agents are its main ingredients. Fairness products mostly contain steroids according to dermatologists, and often lead to pigmentation, telangectasias, acne, scarring, early aging, as well as massive facial hair growth. Females use these products and later wax their facial hair, which leads to loss of skin elasticity, thus leaving it old as well as saggy ("Attitude: Obsession with fairness," 2012).

In the process of lightening the skin tone, layers of melanin are depleted from skin. It is actually a pigment which determines skin color. Darker skin means higher content of melanin. Melanin absorbs the ultraviolet solar radiation, and thus it is transformed into nontoxic heat. Its basic purpose is to protect the skin from DNA damage. Thus, it is a human's natural defence against the UV. Fighting with nature could have detrimental effects. When the melanin layer is depleted for fairness, it also depletes healthy skin. Skin whitening creams makes the skin thin and deprive the skin of melanin. Because, skin color is strictly genetic and to some extent is influenced by environmental factors ("Attitude: Obsession with fairness," 2012).

Kapoor (2012) highlights that time and the concept of beauty are related to fair skin complexion. Carreiro (2009) has discussed regarding current fairness trends developed in India and Pakistan revealing that with Indians, Pakistanis are also getting crazy to get fairer complexion. Venkataswamy (2016) stated that the biggest consumer market of skin whitening products fall under the age bracket of 20 to 29 years.

From the review of literature, it is apparent that neither any previous research covers the impact of product claims and frequency of fairness TV advertisements on demand for fairness products in Pakistani context, nor any one of them studied the relationship between them. This was the very inspiration behind this study. Hence, to some extent, this research gap was visible, which was also evidenced by the review of detailed literature.

This research intended to study the impact of two factors, namely, product claim and frequency of fairness TV ads. It also aimed to find out the factors which had a stronger influence regarding the demand for fairness products in Pakistan. On the basis of detailed review of above literature, respective hypotheses and conceptual framework were formulated.

FOCUS OF THE ARTICLE

This study asses and analyze the impact of advertisements on demand for fairness products among university students in Pakistan. The purpose of this research is to assist legislators, marketing executives, academicians, students, as well as other professionals.

PAKISTANI COSMETIC INDUSTRY AND DEMAND FOR FAIRNESS PRODUCTS

Components of success with regards to beauty business include particular kinds of creativity, fashion sense, and cultural affinity that are not easily quantified or readily susceptible to analysis. Moreover, the industry has always lacked a cohesive identity as the business enterprise, encompassing significantly different sectors in fragrances, color cosmetics, hair care, skin care, and toiletries that often have little in common (Jones, 2010).

According to Memon (2000), when Pakistan came into being, i.e., 1947, the Pakistani cosmetic industry was also nascent. Now, there exists many local as well as foreign brands of fairness products that sell hopes worldwide and particularly in Pakistan (Andrew, 2011). For instance, Fair & Lovely, Fair & Lovely Menz Active, Fair & Lovely Max Fairness for Men, Emami Fair & Handsome, Emami Naturally Fair Pearls Intensive Herbal Fairness Cream, Stillman's Skin Bleaching Cream, Olivia Bleach Creams, Skin White Goat Milk Whitening Cream, Soap & Face Wash, etc.

Business Recorder (2010) discussed about the establishment of Pakistani cosmetic industry. It claimed that the Pakistani cosmetic industry is flourishing tremendously. Local brands of Pakistan are also now getting much more popular along with global brands introduced in Pakistan. According to Ashaduzzaman and Rahman (2011), TV advertisements have a great impact on consumers' buying attitude and product selection usually leads to an increasing demand for respective products.

In South Asian countries, the trend of consumption of fairness products began specially during the last decade. Fairness TV ads through their dramatic stories greatly influence the young population of Pakistan, who often buy these fairness products (Kamran, 2010).

Venkataswamy (2016) discussed about the new emerging market of fairness products. Females are the target market for beauty products for many years. Many fairness brands are now stepping into the new emerging market, which comprises of the male along with female consumers. It can be evidenced from the survey of KuicK Research (2012) conducted in India that currently there is a significant increase in the male consumer market for personal care products, like fairness creams. For this reason, in this research study, males are also included.

TELEVISION ADVERTISEMENTS

Advertising can be understood in terms of a non-personal way to communicate with an audience about ideas, goods or services by means of a recognized sponsor (Kotler & Keller, 2005). The main purpose of advertising is to provide satisfactory information about product's attributes, to persuade consumers to buy those products and repeatedly reminding them regarding the product's existence within the market. This can only be possible when the content of the advertisement is sound enough to obtain audiences' reaction as it is anticipated (Soliha & Dharmmesta, 2012). Advertising helps to retain potential buyers that can lead the companies to improve their income (Eze & Lee, 2012).

It is believed by most of the consumers that television advertising also has a strong impact on their buying behavior (Priya, Baisya, & Sharma, 2010). According to Shabbir, Kirmani, and Hassan (2008), television advertisements play an essential part in the propagation of messages around the world. According to Daud, Farooq, and Anwar (2011), advertisements have a major impact on human thoughts, beliefs, and attitude. Because, they use different techniques and appeals like, slice of life, humor, romance, adventure, etc., in order to stimulate human mood.

A number of TV advertisements in Pakistan portray that a dark complexioned girl is undesirable and utterly unhappy and after discovering and using a magical skin whitening cream all her dreams come true — not only does she get married, but also gains self-confidence. These advertisements project the notion that girls who are of a darker skin tone are worth nothing — they don't deserve success in any aspect of their lives, let alone marriage. In Pakistani society, while prioritizing people, after nepotism skin color surely takes the lead ("Attitude: Obsession with fairness," 2012).

FACTORS IN TV ADS AFFECTING DEMAND OF FAIRNESS PRODUCTS

Different early researches have discussed about various factors in TV advertisements that are accountable for influencing the demand of product. The claims in fairness TV ads have a significant impact on viewers. Such ads exaggerate the product promise and often lack credibility. Sometimes, they are even considered unacceptable by the viewers (Kamran, 2010). Female consumers are more influenced by the promises made in TV advertisements. One of the main aspects of advertisements is to raise sales rate by making big product claims and promises (Ashaduzzaman & Rahman (2011).

According to Vikkraman and Kumaravel (2012), the viewers are often influenced by deceptive claims in advertisements promising hope for their better future. Today, the majority of fairness TV ads are involved in exploiting product benefits, which often results in raising an inappropriate demand within the market. As, these ads portray that their products can change dark complexion to fair. Unfortunately, the overstatements stated in fairness TV ads are not true at all in reality (Kamran, 2010).

According to Ashaduzzaman and Rahman (2011), the repeated exposure of TV ads can persuade viewers towards buying behavior. The repeated exposure (frequency) of advertisement helps to boost the demand for products, because a direct relationship exists between TV advertisements and increased demand (All-share & Salaimeh, 2010). The high rate of repeated exposure of viewers towards ads consequently upsurge the demand in the market. The young population as well as housewives are more inclined in buying items which are repeatedly advertised on TV (Ashaduzzaman & Rahman, 2011). Vikkraman and Kumaravel (2012) are of the view that, the buyers tend to purchase more advertised goods and services.

OBJECTIVES OF STUDY

1. To find out the relationship between product claims in fairness TV ads and demand for fairness products in Pakistan.
2. To find out the relationship between the frequency of fairness TV ads and demand for fairness products in Pakistan.

RESEARCH QUESTION

Do factors in fairness TV ads cast a negative or positive impact on demand for fairness products in Pakistan?

RESEARCH LIMITATIONS

1. The sample size was small because of the limitation of resources.
2. The financial constraints did not warrant taking samples from other big cities of Pakistan besides Karachi.

RESEARCH METHODOLOGY

This research is descriptive in terms of research design, while the approach adopted was deductive. It is a quantitative research by nature. One of the non-probability sampling techniques employed in this research study was convenience sampling. The size of sample units comprised 200 students from the University of Karachi, Federal Urdu University of Arts, Science and Technology, Allama Iqbal Open University, i.e., three government operating universities in Karachi, Pakistan. A self-administered questionnaire was designed as an instrument for conducting research. The Five-Point Likert scale was used to generate the questionnaire for this research. It consisted of 12 questions that were closed-ended. The responses received from the questionnaires were evaluated by using SPSS.

Hypothesis #1

H_1 = There is a relationship between product claims in fairness TV ads and demand for fairness products in Pakistan.

H_0 = There is no relationship between product claims in fairness TV ads and demand for fairness products in Pakistan.

Hypothesis #2

H_2 = There is a relationship between the frequency of fairness TV ads and demand for fairness products in Pakistan.

H_0 = There is no relationship between the frequency of fairness TV ads and demand for fairness products in Pakistan.

CONCEPTUAL FRAMEWORK

In this research, different factors in TV ads were discussed under review of literature in order to calculate the impact of TV advertisements on demand for fairness products. The conceptual framework used in this research study can be illustrated in the following figure.

Figure 1. Factors Affecting Demand for Fairness Products

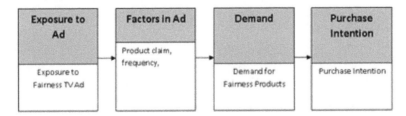

DATA ANALYSIS

13

Demand for Fairness Products

When respondents were asked whether there exists a demand for fairness products within their friends/ peer group? 44% of respondents strongly agreed, 29% were somewhat agreeing, 19% were neutral about it, 5% somewhat disagreed and only 3% of respondents strongly disagreed.

Figure 2.

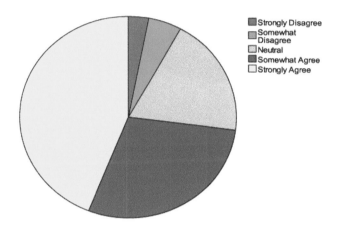

When respondents were asked, whether their friends/peer group often made use of fairness products? 45% of respondents strongly agreed, 37% were somewhat agreeing, 13% were neutral about it, 3% somewhat disagreed and only 2% of respondents strongly disagreed.

Figure 3.

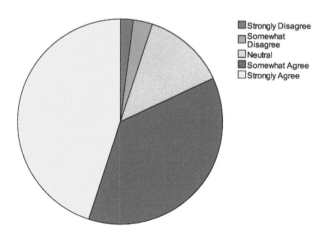

When respondents were asked whether their friends/peer group give priority to fairness products over other skin care products? 34% of respondents strongly agreed, 31% were somewhat agreeing, 25% were neutral about it, 6% somewhat disagreed and only 4% of respondents strongly disagreed.

Figure 4.

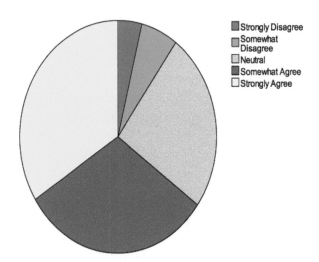

When respondents were asked, whether fairness products are now in demand due to increasing desire to get fairer skin complexion? 55% of respondents strongly agreed, 21% were somewhat agreeing, 9% were neutral about it, 7% somewhat disagreed and only 8% of respondents strongly disagreed.

Figure 5.

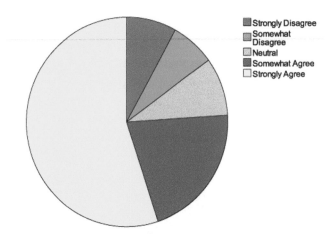

Product Claims in Fairness TV Ads

When respondents were asked whether product claims/promise was an important element to create demand within the market? 32% of respondents somewhat agreed, 27% of respondents strongly agreed, 21% of respondents somewhat disagreed, 14% of respondents were strongly disagreed and only 6% of respondents were neutral about it.

When respondents were asked whether the product claims/promise in fairness TV ads diverts their attention? 41% of respondents somewhat agreed, 39% were strongly agreeing, 10% somewhat disagreed, 5% were neutral about it and only 5% of respondents strongly disagreed.

Figure 6.

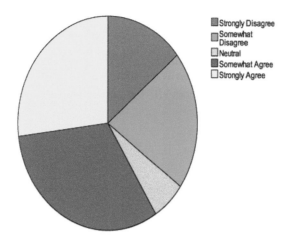

Figure 7.

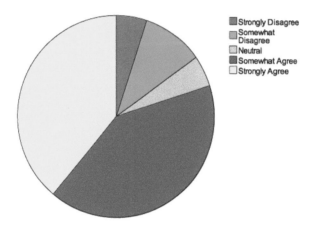

Figure 8.

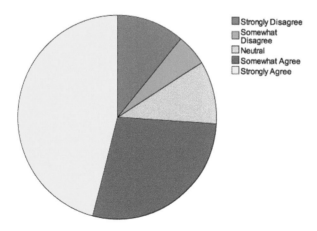

When respondents were asked if almost every fairness TV commercials involve claim/promise of achieving idealized skin? 46% of respondents strongly agreed, 28% were somewhat agreeing, 11% strongly disagreed, 10% were neutral about it and only 5% of respondents somewhat disagreed.

When respondents were asked whether the product claims/promise demonstrated in fairness TV commercials sometime compels people to buy fairness products? 51% of respondents strongly agreed, 36% were somewhat agreeing, 7% were neutral about it, 4% somewhat disagreed and only 2% of respondents strongly disagreed.

Figure 9.

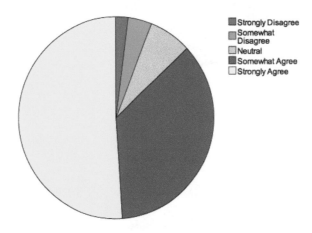

Frequency of Fairness TV Ads

When respondents were asked if repeated exposure of fairness TV ads is an important element to create demand within the market? 42% of respondents strongly agreed, 32% of respondents somewhat agreed, 12% of respondents were neutral about it, 11% of respondents were somewhat disagreeing and only 3% of respondents strongly disagrees about it.

Figure 10.

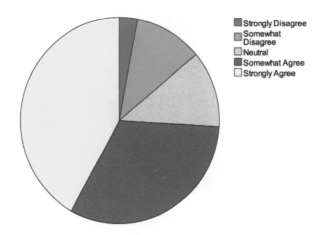

Figure 11.

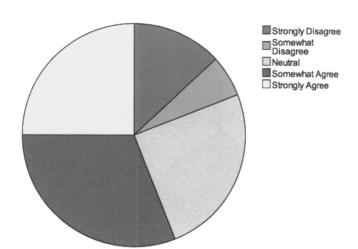

When respondents were asked if repeated exposure of fairness TV ads diverts their attention? 31% of respondents somewhat agreed, 25% were strongly agreeing, 25% were neutral about it, 13% somewhat disagreed, and only 6% of respondents strongly disagreed.

Figure 12.

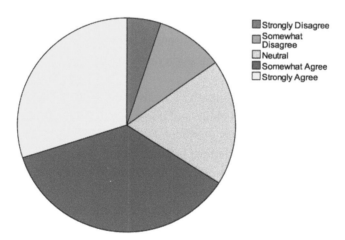

When respondents were asked whether almost every TV channel relays fairness TV commercials many times a day? 36% of respondents somewhat agreed, 30% were strongly agreeing, 19% were neutral about it, 10% were somewhat disagreed and only 5% of respondents strongly disagreed.

When respondents were asked if the repeated exposure of fairness TV ads increases their curiosity towards a particular brand? 37% of respondents strongly agreed, 28% were somewhat agreeing, 14% somewhat disagreed, 11% of respondents strongly disagreed and only 10% were neutral.

Figure 13.

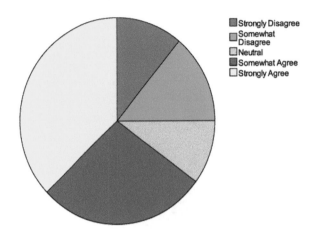

DISCUSSION

According to All-share and Salaimeh (2010), one of the most important functions of TV advertisements is to create demand for products. TV advertisements influence youth towards buying behavior (All-share & Salaimeh, 2010; Ashaduzzaman & Rahman, 2011). In this way, most of the youth population (nearly 73%) believed that they did find a demand for fairness products within their friends/peer group. Nearly 82% of the young population agreed that their friends/peer group often made use of fairness products. Simultaneously, the findings also revealed that the majority of university students (nearly 65%) believed that their friends/peer group gives priority to fairness products over other skin care products. Mostly respondents (approx. 76%) believed that fairness products are now in demand due to increasing desire to get fair skin complexion.

In this research, different aspects of fairness TV ads were analyzed in relation to the demand for fairness products which includes product claim and frequency. It can be analyzed that these aspects are meant to increase the demand for fairness products. Nearly 59% of the young population agreed that product claims/promise is an important element to create demand within the market. About 80% of respondents agreed that the product claims/promise in fairness TV ads diverts their attention. Nearly 74% of respondents agreed that almost every fairness TV commercial involves claims/promises of achieving an idealized skin. About 87% of university students agreed that the product claims/promise demonstrated in fairness TV commercials sometime compels people to buy fairness products.

The young population strongly believes that fairness claims made by advertisers about their products are true, so it is possible to achieve those ideal features (Javid, Namin, & Noorai, 2012; Saadeghvaziri & Hosseini, 2011). It has a strong impact on their buying behavior (Kamran, 2010) and thus leads to an increased demand for fairness products.

By the correlation analysis, we have come to know that a strong relationship exists between product claims in fairness TV ads and demand for fairness products with a significance level of .000. The value of R-square of 0.308, which indicates that 30% of the variation in demand for fairness products can be explained by variations in the product claims in fairness TV ads. The P-Value 0.000 is less than 0.05, therefore, the alternative hypothesis is accepted. The value of regression coefficients 0.529 and the constant 1.987, which is the expected value of the dependent variable (demand for fairness products) when the values of the independent variables (product claims in fairness TV ads) is equal to zero. The best-fitting regression equation for this data, as under;

Demand for fairness products = 1.987 + (0.529 x Product claims in fairness TV ads)

The Alternate hypothesis is proved.

H1= There is a relationship between product claims in fairness TV ads and demand for fairness products in Pakistan.

The findings also specified that the more TV ad flashes on a TV screen, the deeper it will strike the mind of the audience (Ashaduzzaman & Rahman, 2011). In this way, most of the youth (nearly 74%) believed that the repeated exposure of fairness TV ads is an important element to create demand within the market. Nearly 56% of the young population agreed that the repeated exposure of fairness TV ads diverts their attention.

Simultaneously, the findings also revealed that majority university students (nearly 66%) believe that almost every TV channel relay fairness TV commercials many times a day. Mostly respondents (approx. 65%) believe that the repeated exposure of fairness TV ads increases their curiosity towards a particular brand.

By the correlation analysis, we have come to know that a strong relationship exists between the frequency of fairness TV ads and demand for fairness products with a significance level of 0.000. The value of R-square of 0.352, which indicates that 35% of the variation in demand for fairness products can be explained by the variability in the frequency of fairness TV ads. The P-Value 0.000 is less than 0.05, therefore, the alternative hypothesis is accepted. The value of regression coefficients is 0.652 and the constant is 1.621, which is the expected value of the dependent variable (demand for fairness products) when the values of the independent variables (frequency of fairness TV ads) is equal to zero. The best-fitting regression equation for this data:

Demand for fairness products = 1.621 + (0.652 x frequency of fairness TV ads)

Alternate hypothesis is proved.

H2= There is a relationship between the frequency of fairness TV ads and demand for fairness products in Pakistan.

SOLUTIONS AND RECOMMENDATIONS

1. It is better not to exaggerate product claims in fairness TV ads. As, it often leads to create an inappropriate demand within the market. People are often compelled to buy products which they actually do not need.

2. Advertisers must keep in mind that too much repetition of TV ads leads to irritation within viewers, often resulted in clutter within their mind and instead of noticing TV ads they start ignoring them by switching channels.

3. The TV advertisements of fairness products need to improve its ad contents (concepts of storyline), as well as the way they execute its contents. Because, instead of creating prejudice regarding skin tone, they must convey a positive and constructive message to their consumers.

4. Fair skin models cast in fairness TV ads often leads to an objectionable comparison among skin tones, which results in the humiliation of dark skin people within society.

5. Pakistan Electronic Media Regulatory Authority (PEMRA) must regulate the objectionable content regarding fairness TV ads in order to induce improvement.

6. General public awareness programs should be initiated with regards to the health issues associated with skin whitening products in Pakistan.

7.   During the process of legislation regarding cosmetics in Pakistan, expert opinion should be included, like dermatologists, psychologists, health and physical professionals, etc.
8.   Pakistan should maintain proper data with regards to the cases associated with skin damage.
9.   In Pakistan, victims of skin damage are large in number, there should be easy access for the victims where they can lodge their complaint.
10. Private companies should develop a strong liaison with the Government of Pakistan regarding their product development.
11. The Pakistani legal department should be equipped with the latest investigating technologies encompassing the damage from using inferior quality skin whitening products.
12. Pakistani scholars should discuss the issue of color on different forums, specially in print as well as electronic media.

FUTURE RESEARCH DIRECTIONS

Further researches can be conducted on the following encompassing themes:

1.   The declining demand of local fairness brands in Pakistan.
2.   To study the impact of skin tone partiality on self-esteem of consumers in Pakistan.
3.   How can local fairness brands in Pakistan achieve competitive advantage over global brands.

CONCLUSION

Pakistani cosmetics industry is flourishing at a rapid pace. The demand for fairness creams exist and is rising in female as well as male consumers. The dilemma in Pakistan is standardization, individuals have a propensity to link beauty with a lighter skin tone. There are in addition social as well as monetary implications with respect to beauty. It takes a lot of endeavor to embellish as well as modify one's appearance in order to look stylish.

Society plays a significant function regarding the concept of attractiveness. Pakistani females crave to the Western idyllic of attractiveness, i.e. being fair, slim, and tall. A new type of social control exists in the form of beauty myth. It is an obsession with physical perfection that traps women in an endless spiral of self-consciousness, hope, and self-hatred as they try to accomplish society's impossible explanation of being a flawless beauty.

Different methods are employed to accomplish fairness in Pakistan. One of the most prominent is 'formula cream', and bleaching agents are its main ingredients. Fairness products mostly contain steroids according to dermatologists, and often lead to pigmentation, telangectasias, acne, scarring, early aging, as well as massive facial hair growth. In the process of lightening the skin tone, layers of melanin are depleted from skin. When the melanin layer is depleted for fairness, it also depletes healthy skin.

A number of TV advertisements in Pakistan portray that a dark complexioned girl is undesirable and utterly unhappy and after discovering and using a magical skin whitening cream all her dreams come true — not only does she get married, but also gains self-confidence. These advertisements project the notion that girls who are of a darker skin tone are worth nothing — they don't deserve success in any aspect of their lives, let alone marriage. In Pakistani society, while prioritizing people, after nepotism skin color surely takes the lead.

There is a strong impact of fairness products TV advertisements on demand among university students in Karachi, Pakistan. In this research, one of the factors, namely, product claim and another factor that is the frequency of fairness TV ads help to find the impact of fairness TV ads on demand for fairness products. These variables are correlated with each other that can be evidenced by the help of Pearson correlation. By the correlation analysis of these two variables we come to know that a strong relationship exists between product claims and frequency of fairness TV ads and demand for fairness products.

Finally, the findings also revealed that TV ads of fairness products holds a lasting impact on the minds of consumers and consequently leads to stimulate its demand due to its product claim. While, the frequency of fairness TV ads also leads to a positive relationship between these two factors.

REFERENCES

All-share, F., & Salaimeh, M. A. (2010). The effects of television advertisement on the behavior of canned food consumer in small industries. *European Journal of Soil Science, 16*(3), 332–341.

Andrew, M. (2011). *Aspirations of beauty*. Retrieved from http://auroramagazine.blogspot.com/2011/11/aspirations-of-beauty.html

Ashaduzzaman, M., & Rahman, S. M. A. U. (2011). Impact of television advertisements on buying pattern of women in Dhaka city. *European Journal of Business and Management, 3*(3), 16–27.

Attitude: Obsession with fairness. (2012, June 6). *Dawn*. Retrieved from https://www.dawn.com/news/727085

Business Recorder. (2010, July 26). *Pakistan cosmetics market takes big strides*. Retrieved from http://www.brecorder.com/br-research/44:miscellaneous/1059:pakistan- cosmetics-market-takes-big-strides/?date=2010-07-26

Carreiro, H. (2009). *Perception of race and skin color in Pakistan*. Retrieved from http://voices.yahoo.com/perception-race-skin-color-2552023.html?cat=16

Daud, U., Farooq, U., & Anwar, F. (2011). Impact of advertisement on the life style of Pakistani youth. *Interdisciplinary Journal of Research in Business, 1*(7), 39–44.

Diessner, R., Iyer, R., Smith, M. M., & Haidt, J. (2013). Who engages with moral beauty? *Journal of Moral Education, 42*(2), 139–163. doi:10.1080/03057240.2013.785941

Eze, U. C., & Lee, C. H. (2012). Consumers' attitude towards advertising. *International Journal of Business and Management, 7*(13), 94–108. doi:10.5539/ijbm.v7n13p94

Javid, M. H., Namin, A. T., & Noorai, M. (2012). Prioritization of factors affecting consumers' attitudes toward mobile advertising. *Journal of Basic and Applied Scientific Research, 2*(9), 9293–9300.

Jones, G. (2010). *Beauty imagined: A history of the global beauty industry*. Oxford University Press.

Kalsoom. (2011, June 30). *The white standard of beauty*. Retrieved from https://changinguppakistan.wordpress.com/2011/06/30/the-white-standard-of-beauty/

Kamran, S. (2010). Potential issues of skin fairness creams TV advertisements in Pakistan. *Electronic Journal of Business Ethics and Organization Studies, 15*(1), 15–20.

Kapoor, A. (2012). *The nuances of fairness ads*. Retrieved from http://www.asianage.com/health-fitness/nuances-fairness-ads-146

Kotler, P., & Keller, K. L. (2005). *Marketing management*. Prentice Hall.

Kuic K. Research. (2012). Retrieved from http://www.kuickresearch.com/company-buy- report.php?reporttitle=IndiaMaleCosmetics Market-ConsumerInsight2012

Priya, P., Baisya, R. K., & Sharma, S. (2010). Television advertisements and children's buying behaviour. *Emerald Group Publishing Limited, 28*(2), 151–169.

Saadeghvaziri, F., & Hosseini, H. K. (2011). Mobile advertising: An investigation of factors creating positive attitude in Iranian customers. *African Journal of Business Management, 5*(2), 394–404.

Shabbir, M. S., Kirmani, S., & Hassan, F. (2008). Children attitude towards TV advertisements in Pakistan. *European Journal of Scientific Research, 21*(4), 693–699.

Soliha, E., & Dharmmesta, B. S. (2012). The effect of source credibility and message framing on consumer risk perceptions with consumer product knowledge as a moderating variable: A literature review. *International Research Journals, 3*, 108–117.

Sunaina. (2016, April 6). *How Culture Influences Beauty*. Retrieved from http://www.drsunaina.com/blog/how-culture-influences-beauty/

Venkataswamy, S. (2016). Transcending Gender: Advertising fairness cream for Indian Men. *Media Asia, 40*(2), 128–138. doi:10.1080/01296612.2013.11689961

Vikkraman, P., & Kumaravel, K. (2012). A study on impact of T.V. advertisements on buying pattern of adult girls at Erode city. *European Journal of Economics. Finance and Administrative Sciences, 48*(48), 36–41.

Wolf, N. (2013). *The beauty myth: How images of beauty are used against women*. Random House.

ADDITIONAL READING

Burger, P. (2016). Skin whitening cosmetics: Feedback and challenges in the development of natural skin lighteners. *Cosmetics, 3*(30). www.mdpi.com/journal/cosmetics

Das, S. (2013). Consumer's perception on fairness cream in India. *Journal of Research, Extension and Development, 1*(11) 64-66. Retrieved from https://papers.ssrn.com/sol3/papers.cfm?abstract_id=2592358

Jha, B. (2016). Representation of fair-skin beauty and the female consumer. *IOSR Journal of Humanities And Social Science, 21*(2), 1–12.

Karnani, A. (2007). *Case Study: Fair & Lovely whitening cream*. The University of Michigan.

Raja, A. S., & Kumar, M. (2014). A study on mens preference towards fairness cream and factors influencing the purchase behaviour. *Indian Journal of Applied Research, 4*(11).

Watson, S., Thornton, C. G., & Engelland, B. T. (2010). Skin color shades in advertising to ethnic audiences: The case of African Americans. *Journal of Marketing Communications*, *16*(4), 185–201. doi:10.1080/13527260802707585

Williamson, J. (1978). Decoding advertisements: Ideology and meaning in advertising. Retrieved from http://bookzz.org/

KEY TERMS AND DEFINITIONS

Advertisement: Paid, non-personal, public communication about causes, goods and services, ideas, organizations, people, and places, through means such as direct mail, telephone, print, radio, television, and internet.

Cosmetics: Products used to enhance the appearance of the face or texture of the body.

Demand: The quantity of a good that consumers are willing and able to purchase at various prices during a given period of time.

Fairness Products: Skin lightening products.

Government Universities: Public sector universities.

Repeated Exposure: People tend to develop a preference for things because they are familiar with them.

Target Market: A particular group of consumers at which a product or service is aimed.

Youth: The time between childhood and adulthood (maturity).

Examining the Value, Satisfaction, and Loyalty Relationship Under Online Framework Using PLS–ANN

Himanshu Sharma
University of Delhi, India

Anu G. Aggarwal
 https://orcid.org/0000-0001-5448-9540
University of Delhi, India

Abhishek Tandon
University of Delhi, India

INTRODUCTION

The digital era has revolutionized the way of conducting businesses by converting brick-and-mortar firms into brick-and-click or pure-click firms. This has forced the firms to restructure their corporate strategies, which now consider customer-retailer interaction in online framework. With abundant options available for online shoppers in each domain, the e-tailers are facing a fierce market competition to gain a major market share in the economy. The dynamicity of markets resulting from these technological advancements poses a question on the loyalty of customers towards these e-commerce websites. Online retailers have shown interest in studying the variables influencing the e-loyalty among browsers. This has motivated extant researches to focus on exploring greater insights into the website loyalty frameworks. According to a report, customers who express continuance intention to shop from a website spend 67% more than new customers, and 60% will recommend the website to his family and friends in return of their loyalty (Statista, 2018). Thus, even though the topic of loyalty in online framework is less explored, recent researchers are finding this field of study attractive.

Loyalty may be defined as "the preferential, attitudinal and behavioral response toward one or more object category expressed over a period of time by a consumer" (Hirschman, 1970). Researchers have explained loyalty in both attitudinal and behavioral measures (Hill & Alexander, 2017). The attitudinal loyalty is represented by a preference desire towards an object, whereas the behavioral measures concentrate on the proportion of time the customer purchase same object in the present of other objects in same category. The advent of internet technologies has shifted the loyalty concept towards online framework. Website loyalty may be defined as the attitude of a consumer towards a website and his willingness to make a revisit as well as recommend that website to his family and friends (Kabadayi & Gupta, 2005). The success of an e-business can be judged on the basis of its stable customer base, which in this digital world can be attained with the help of a user friendly and well-built website, that makes the shopping experience of customers smooth and enjoyable. The advancements in the information and communication technology (ICT) has showered the online customers with many blessings such as in-depth knowledge regarding the retailer and his offerings, information about the suppliers, comparing prices from various sites, availing discounts and various incentives available for membership holders, and many more ad-

DOI: 10.4018/978-1-7998-3473-1.ch154

vantages. All these benefits inculcate uncertainty in shopper behavior and pose a challenge for marketers to create a loyal group of customers (Veloutsou & McAlonan, 2012).

Previous studies have evaluated loyalty in terms of the level of satisfaction achieved by the shopper while using the website (Anderson & Srinivasan, 2003; Anderson & Swaminathan, 2011). A desirable customer experience while using the website leads to its success, which eventually results in formation of a favorable attitude towards that platform in the presence of other alternatives (Ayo, Oni, Adewoye, & Eweoya, 2016). However, a delighted customer may show intent to make a revisit as well as suggest the site to his family or friends or peers, which leads to a loyalty intention. Moreover, a purchaser will stick to a site only if he perceives it to be beneficial in return of his investments, and is thought to create value for customers, which may be either monetary or non-monetary (Kumar Roy, M. Lassar, & T. Butaney, 2014). Thus, this study considers two antecedents of website loyalty namely customer satisfaction and customer value.

Customer value is defined as "the ratio of the customer's outcome/input to that of the service provider's outcome/input" (Patterson & Spreng, 1997). The concept is based on equity theory which considers that the customers should be offered fair and right product/service in return to his cost inputs. Customer value mainly focuses on the importance of an object (here website) and the extra benefits provided by it. The literature mentions two types of value i.e. transactional value and emotional value (Sweeney & Soutar, 2001). The transactional value concentrates on the price related issues. For example in the online framework, e-firms strategize many incentive appraisal programs so as to attract customers and generate traffic towards their site. On the other hand, emotional value takes care of the cognitive issues such as time or stress or feelings of the customers. Online firms achieve this task by practicing good business ethics and indulging corporate social responsibility (CSR) programs (Loureiro, Sardinha, & Reijnders, 2012).

Customer satisfaction is a vital concept in consumer related studies and has been vastly covered by previous researches (Quester et al., 2007; Söderlund, 1998). Satisfaction may be defined in two terms namely transaction related and overall satisfaction. The transaction related customer satisfaction is defined as "an emotional response by the customers to the most recent transactional experience with an organization" (Cardozo, 1965). On the other hand, overall satisfaction is defined as "a cumulative sum of the satisfaction associated with the specific products and various facets of the firm" (Cardozo, 1965). In online context, it may be defined as the optimistic feelings aroused in reaction to the aggregate experience during his browsing sessions. Many researchers have noticed that a satisfied customer embraces the success of an e-commerce website, which in turn leads to the popularity of the owner (Brown & Jayakody, 2008; Tandon, Sharma, & Aggarwal, 2019). Delighted customers convey positive messages regarding the website, however, negative messages by unhappy customers tend to diffuse faster and hamper the sales of the firm (Arbore & Busacca, 2009). Thus, it is important to incorporate customer satisfaction in the website loyalty framework.

Website service quality (WSQ) is asserted to be a combination of technical and customer-oriented dimensions of key features of an e-commerce website. The technical concept takes care of the system quality and content quality measures of the retailers, whereas customer-oriented concept involves the service quality measures (Wang & Tang, 2003). The web page of the company acts as the first contact point of the customers with the vendors. This page plays a key role in attracting the customers and its design motivates its usage by a large population. The concept of website quality is well known among researchers and included the variables such as trust, interactivity, ease of understanding, visual appeal, and consistency. The WSQ variable considered here makes use of the information system (IS) success factors which were defined to find the variables that improve the effectiveness of the systems (DeLone & McLean, 1992). Along with these factors, the construct also incorporates the items that customers look out for while requesting a service using the website. Various measures have been introduced by previous studies in each category (Sá, Rocha, & Cota, 2016; Sharma & Lijuan, 2015; J. D. Xu, Benbasat, & Cenfetelli, 2013), but we consider the most comprehensive and distinct list of dimensions such as trust, tangibility, navigation, ease-of-use, ease-of-ordering, responsiveness, and customization. These dimensions help the customers to evaluate the utility of the website, an indicator of value generation for them.

With the emergence of digital mediums, people all over the world are knit closely in a social web. This has led to the introduction of various social media sites that allow its members to generate content and network with other users, over the internet (A. J. Kim & Ko, 2012). Social media reviews (SMR) is the phenomena of providing review related to a product/service over social media platforms, which can only be accessed by near and dear ones like family and friends (Y. Chen, Fay, & Wang, 2011). The role of these customer generated text is continuously trending upwards and is found to be highly influential for the purchasing decision making (Chu & Kim, 2011). This practice is being supported by the online retailers, as they have enabled the shoppers to post their comments related to the products/services in the form of text or ratings over their platforms, which helps in improving their services (Mishra, Maheswarappa, Maity, & Samu, 2018). Customers generally show a strong tie with the people in his list under a social media platform. Also, companies have starting developing their profile over these social platforms, where the customers can comment, complain, or request service, which is visible to mass population, other than his friends and family members. Therefore, SMR may be considered as an extension of electronic word-of-mouth (EWOM) concept over public network sites, with a rapid diffusion rate (Chu & Kim, 2011). Thus, is plays a non-monetary value generation approach for the customers.

In aggregation, this chapter focuses on the following research questions:

a) Is there a significant relationship of WSQ and SMR over CV; CV over CS; and CV and CS over LOY?
b) Does switching cost play a moderating role between CS and LOY relationship?
c) Which is the most influential predictor in each causal relationship considered?

Partial least squares (PLS) is an extension of the covariance based SEM (CBSEM) approach, with few major improvements (Hulland, 1999). Structural equation modeling (SEM) is an improvement made by researchers over first generation techniques such as ANOVA and multiple regression, which can predict the causal relationship between the independent and dependent variables with hierarchical or non-hierarchical structural equations (Hox & Bechger, 1998). The covariance based SEM laid emphasis on the overall fit of the covariance matrix constructed under the hypothesized model. The tools usually preferred for it are LISREL, AMOS, EQS, and MPlus, whereas smartPLS is usually preferred for component based SEM (PLS-SEM). SEM performs estimation of the model parameters in such a way so as to minimize the error between the estimated and original sample covariance matrices (Ali, Rasoolimanesh, Sarstedt, Ringle, & Ryu, 2018). On the other hand, PLS emphasizes on utilizing the explained variance of the endogenous latent constructs by estimating the parameters of the model using ordinary least squares (OLS) method. Another advantage of PLS over its predecessor is that it is a soft modeling technique without any distributional assumption on the data. A major assumption in path modeling models using PLS is that the latent variables (LV) are made up of linear combinations of manifest variables (MV) and that the latent variables themselves are also associated linearly (Puig & Ming, 2017). This poses a relationship degree between these latent variables. This drawback can be rectified by using Artificial Neural Network (ANN). ANN has the ability to predict the non-linearity association among the variables and also evaluate the most important predictor in a causal model (Chong & Bai, 2014). But, ANN is not capable of testing the hypotheses and measuring the path loadings. Therefore, this chapter uses PLS followed by ANN to measure the path loadings and to check the type of relation between the variables.

13

Previous studies considering website loyalty as endogenous variable have been performed (Bilgihan, 2016; X. Chen, Huang, & Davison, 2017; Hsieh & Tsao, 2014; O'Cass & Carlson, 2012). Most of these studies used path modeling such as SEM or PLS-SEM. Also, the independent variables considered in these studies are information quality, system quality, customer satisfaction, utilitarian and hedonic factors, and many more. To the best of our knowledge, this is the first chapter that utilizes the combination of PLS and ANN to determine key determinants of website loyalty. The PLS determine the path loadings for the conceptual framework while ANN helps in determining the most determining variable in each cause-effect relationship. Moreover, the distinguishing part of the chapter is validating the moderating role of switching cost between customer satisfaction and website loyalty. The rest of the paper is sequentially organized into sections that discuss the literature and formulate the hypotheses relevant to the study; describe the methodology employed to check the significance of the proposed model; then the results on the data analysis are provided in detail; afterwards, the discussions and implications for practitioners are provided; lastly, conclusion and limitation faced during the study are aggregated.

BACKGROUND

Website Service Quality (WSQ)

Last two decades have noticed a remarkable increase in the studies emphasizing success of online businesses, which rely mainly on their platforms. Literature supports the fact that online service is basically an interaction between the customers and information systems (DeLone & McLean, 1992, 2003; Molla & Licker, 2001). Therefore, today's website service quality literature is a mix of service quality studies and information system or website design quality studies (Zhou, Lu, & Wang, 2009). The service quality measures mainly focus on the traditional SERVQUAL model whereas the website quality studies concentrates on computer and networking based impersonal interactions. The pioneer study in the area of service quality defined it to be "the degree of discrepancy between the customer's normative expectations for the service and their perceptions of the service performance" (Parasuraman, Zeithaml, & Berry, 1988). They proposed five dimensions of SQ namely assurance, responsiveness, empathy, tangibility, and reliability, which were aggregated to be known as SERVQUAL. However, researchers observed that this traditional service quality was incapable of handling quality under online framework, as the former concentrated over customer-firm interaction. Later, this problem was rectified by the introduction of the concept of e-SERVQUAL (Zeithaml, Parasuraman, & Malhotra, 2002). On the other hand, the pioneer study under website design quality monitored the impact of system and content quality over the success of an information system (DeLone & McLean, 1992). This study has played a key reference point for many extensions based on customer's perspective or industrial ones. The development of WebQual concept aligned system quality, content quality, and service quality in online framework under one roof, termed as website service quality (Loiacono, Watson, & Goodhue, 2002).

Social Media Reviews

Recently social media has emerged as a communication platform for consumers and firms. Social media is defined as "a group of internet-based applications that build on the ideological and technological foundations of Web 2.0 and allow the creation and exchange of user-generated content (UGC)" (Abirami, Askarunisa, Gayathri, & Jeyalakshmi, 2015). Various types of social media applications have been observed such as internet forums, message boards, product review websites, weblogs, wikis, and picture/video-sharing websites. They provide an incomparable platform for past purchasers to post their product experiences and opinions through electronic word-of-mouth (EWOM) or customer reviews (Schultz & Peltier, 2013). In the presence of such platforms, these messages are generated in abundant volume, diffuse at an unmatched speed, and consequently creates a high impact on firm strategies and customer's purchase behavior. Previous researchers have emphasized the importance of reviews and their impact on the purchase decision of the shoppers (Schindler & Bickart, 2012; Ye, Law, & Gu, 2009). It is believed that most of the potential purchasers make use of these online customer reviews (OCRs) or blogs or other UGC present on these social platforms in addition to the ones available on the e-commerce sites, before turning into actual purchasers. These reviews result in reducing the level of risk perceived by shoppers and participate in an enjoying shopping experience (Chu & Kim, 2011). Thus, with the unprecedented growth in internet technology and incorporation of socially connecting links, the role of social media reviews (SMR) is over-clouding the effect of online customer reviews considered under e-commerce systems.

Customer Value

The customer value is defined as "the proportion of the net output/input of the customer with respect to the net output/inputs of the service provider" (Woodruff, 1997). It was developed under the theoretical fundamentals of equity value, which emphasized that the equity of a customer can be evaluated on the basis of his expected returns in relation to the cost incurred by him (Carpenter & Fairhurst, 2005). This cost may be monetary or non-monetary such as time invested or energy and stress experienced. Thus, customer value may be measured as a trade-off between the reward-sacrifice relationships. An equitable situation is achieved when the desired outcome in relation to inputs invested is almost equivalent to the outcome/input ratio of the organization. Recent studies have shown interest in value related studies as it is considered to be a predictor of purchasing behaviour of the customers and also that it is a multidimensional construct which depends on the circumstances and other situations of the customer (C. M. Chiu, Wang, Fang, & Huang, 2014). The topic of customer value in the online context is less explored by the researchers. Availability of numerous website options and low browsing cost has transformed the purchasing behaviour of the customer to be more hedonic and unplanned. The emotional or attitudinal state of the customers has a major impact on their online pre-purchasing behaviour. Moreover, the product characteristics too influence the proactive buying behaviour. These characteristics may be external such as price, brand which are not part of the physical product or they may be internal such as size, design which are part of the physical product and can be manipulated (Eggert & Ulaga, 2002). Since in online shopping the customers cannot feel the product, the extrinsic attributes dominate the intrinsic ones. A detrimental factor for value is the amount of risk perceived by the consumers while shopping (Featherman & Pavlou, 2003). Customers assume themselves risk averse from lack of trust on website's security facilities and prone to personal information breaching by hackers. Another factor that affects value inversely is the price of the product. Latest technological advancements allow online customers to compare products and their prices through multiple websites, and also provide a low transaction fee. Thus, above mentioned monetary and non-monetary aspects influence customer value.

Customer Satisfaction

Customer satisfaction is the level of pleasure experienced by the customer during the purchasing process and its consequences on the future perceptions. It is the net evaluation of the products/services post purchase (Hallowell, 1996). Satisfaction in online context asserts the holistic, complex, and subjective shopping experience encountered by the customers between him and the online platforms such as shopping websites and social media (Bai, Law, & Wen, 2008). The behavioural consequences of a purchaser are highly influenced by the relative measure of satisfaction and dissatisfaction experienced on using the product/service provided by the e-firm. A satisfied shopper conveys positive words related to the product/service and is willing to recommend it to others. On the other hand, dissatisfied customers may prove to be a detrimental factor in terms of spreading bad word-of-mouth, switching to competitor website, and complaining to external and internal agencies (Caruana, 2003). It has been shown by researchers that the negative impact overtakes the positive one with respect to satisfaction (Ye et al., 2009). Thus, with the dynamicity in customer purchasing behaviour, generating satisfaction is a very tough task for these online vendors.

Website Loyalty

Loyalty may be defined as the consequence of a relationship between the customer and a brand or a product or a store or a website. Loyalty is a multidimensional construct with both behavioural and attitudinal constructs (Ariff, Yun, Zakuan, & Ismail, 2013). Website loyalty reflects the relative attitude of the customer towards a website in the presence of other competitor's websites. This preference should be maintained in the presence of decrease in price sensitivity, lower selling costs, increase in positive WOM, and competitive messages (Reichheld & Schefter, 2000). Loyalty leads to the phenomena of repeat purchase from the same online vendor, leading to customer retention, which in turn contributes to the profitability of the firm, apart from the increasing market share (Casaló, Flavián, & Guinalíu, 2008). A number of factors such as availability of alternative websites, low cost of surfing, facility of comparing prices from various sites, incentives to premium members, and low switching cost have resulted in fierce competition among these online platforms to retain their customer base, which is a determinant of online loyalty (Aydin, Özer, & Arasil, 2005). Moreover, loyalty measures are assumed to be market or situation specific, where for stable markets the marketers consider the behavioural measures for loyalty evaluation and make use of attitudinal measures in the presence of uncertainty in markets. In the online context, some retailers believe that the site image, price of product, quality of the product/service provided, and the payment options contribute to loyalty generation (Lin & Sun, 2009). Others highlight the importance of design and relevant content of the website, a healthy dialogue with the browser, and availability of rewards or incentives (for example loyalty points) lead to customer retention (Qian, Peiji, & Quanfu, 2011). Although it may be considered true that compared with the vast body of literature focusing on loyalty in general, website loyalty is a relatively under-investigated concept, with few studies investigating the concept and the antecedents of website loyalty. A comprehensive list of loyalty studies for online markets is provided in Table 1.

Table 1. Previous Research on Website Loyalty

Variables	Author(s)	Analysis Technique
trust, satisfaction, and flow	(Kabadayi & Gupta, 2005)	Second order confirmatory factor analysis (CFA)
perceived usability, satisfaction, and trust	(Flavián, Guinalíu, & Gurrea, 2006)	Structural equation modelling (SEM)
Perceived ease of use, perceived social presence, perceived usability, trust, and enjoyment	(Cyr, Hassanein, Head, & Ivanov, 2007)	Partial least square (PLS) - SEM
perceived usability, reputation, satisfaction, and consumer familiarity	(Casaló et al., 2008)	SEM
technology acceptance factor, website service quality, specific holdup cost, and satisfaction	(Lin & Sun, 2009)	SEM
perceived service quality, satisfaction, and trust	(Kassim & Asiah Abdullah, 2010)	SEM + Analysis of variance (ANOVA)
website quality and satisfaction	(Hur, Ko, & Valacich, 2011)	SEM
Website quality, trust, and word-of-mouth	(O'Cass & Carlson, 2012)	PLS-SEM
service quality and satisfaction	(Ariff et al., 2013)	Hierarchical regression analysis
System quality, information quality, e-service quality, and perceived risk	(Hsieh & Tsao, 2014)	SEM
information quality, system quality, service quality, trust, and customer satisfaction	(J. V. Chen, Yen, Pornpriphet, & Widjaja, 2015)	SEM
hedonic features, utilitarian features, brand equity, flow, and trust	(Bilgihan, 2016)	SEM
social capital and website quality	(X. Chen et al., 2017)	PLS-SEM
Website service quality, social media reviews, customer value, and customer satisfaction	Proposed model	PLS-SEM-ANN

HYPOTHESES DEVELOPMENT

Website Service Quality and Customer Value

A number of combinations of dimensions have been studied up by researchers focusing on the concept of WSQ. The aggregate list of these dimensions consist of usability, design, trust, empathy, information, security, privacy, functionality, responsiveness, reliability, enjoyment, usefulness, ease-of-use, and content (Ariff et al., 2013; J. D. Xu et al., 2013). This study provides a unique combination consisting of trust, tangibility, customization, responsiveness, ease of ordering, navigation, and ease of use. An amalgamation of these attributes puts a major impact on customer value. Since the online platforms enable the potential buyers to check prices of the products, make comparisons among alternative offerings, and find unusual products (Andam, 2003). Thus, quick access to low cost, relevant information has a beneficiary effect over the online purchasers. Moreover, website design that encourages more of cognitive efforts and is less user-friendly deems to assert a negative impact on value generation (Kumar & Desai, 2016). Thus, we posit that

H1: there is a significant positive association between WSQ and CV

Social Media Reviews and Customer Value

Social media reviews (SMR) enables a previous purchaser to express his attitude and experience regarding a website or a particular product/service of that website with their family members, peers, friends, or the people with whom he is connected online (Zhang, Li, & Chen, 2012). Online firms have started noticing the impact of SMR on their sales as well as on the buyers, in terms of impression management, emotion regulation, information acquisition, social bonding, and persuasion (Abirami et al., 2015). Purchasing decisions are highly influenced by the cognition cost involved during shopping (Andreou et al., 2005). It basically supports the cost-benefit tradeoff considered by online buyers before making a purchase. According to this theory, the customer keeps looking forward for additional information regarding a product/service until the benefits obtained from that information exceeds the cognitive cost incurred during the search process (Kwahk & Ge, 2012). The above discussions interpret the impact of social reviews over various aspects of customer value. Hence, we posit that

H2: there is a significant positive association between SMR and CV

Customer Value and Customer Satisfaction

Customer value is measured in terms of the net benefits obtained in return for the net cost invested i.e. it is an indicator of net utility generated by an online firm. Customer satisfaction is the amount of positive or negative feeling created in relation to the product/service provided by the e-tailers. Therefore, customer value evaluates the level of customer cognition whereas satisfaction mirrors the feeling portrayed by values (C. Xu, Peak, & Prybutok, 2015). In literature, value is considered to be a cognition dependent variable which reflects the benefit-discrepancy relationship, whereas satisfaction is basically affective and evaluative variable (Puig & Ming, 2017). It is believed that while shopping if the buyer asserts his benefits to outnumber his discrepancies, there is a relevant amount of satisfaction engendered (Gallarza, Arteaga-Moreno, Del Chiappa, & Gil-Saura, 2016). Keeping in mind the social theories which state that the cognitive process leads to affective responses, we posit the following.

H3: there is a significant positive association between CV and customer satisfaction

Customer Value and Website Loyalty

A customer is loyal to an object only if that object meets his expected value. The customer value may be defined as the ratio of the output generated by a firm in comparison to the level of inputs incurred by the customer. Because loyalty is a behavioral intention, it is considered to be a subordinate goal whereas customer value is deemed to be a super-ordinate goal (Gallarza et al., 2016). As per the goal-action relationship, it has been argued that super-ordinate goals are very likely to influence the subordinate goals (Abelson, 1983). In the online environment, value driven loyalty is generated if the website provides an attractive interface, low cost products, and risk free transactions so as to make online payments (C. M. Chiu et al., 2014). It is not just price that influence the value of a customer (Veloutsou & McAlonan, 2012). An e-tailer may charge a high price for an offering, but if they attach few additional fringe benefits to it, the customer may not feel hesitant in accepting that commodity. Thus, customer value acts as a determinant for website loyalty till the proportional measurements indicate utility for the customer (Puig & Ming, 2017), and this leads us to posit that.

H4: there is a significant positive relationship between CV and website loyalty

Customer Satisfaction and Website Loyalty

Previous studies indicate that customer satisfaction and loyalty assume to have some intuitive association as some marketing analysts believe that satisfaction precedes loyalty whereas some believe that satisfaction positively affects loyalty (Chadha & Kapoor, 2009). Satisfaction is believed to be the key determinant factor for customer loyalty (M.-J. Kim, Chung, & Lee, 2011). Satisfied customers are expected to have a healthy and longer bond with the product provider, be it in offline mode or online (Anderson & Srinivasan, 2003). This may be due to the fact that the customers perceive that since the organization fulfilled his expectation, they will continue to do so in the future too (Limbu, Wolf, & Lunsford, 2011). Thus, this self-actualization of the expectations will increase the buying intention from that website for the future needs, resulting in more frequent visits to the website, which eventually may result in more purchases more even at premium prices (T. S. H. Pham & Ahammad, 2017). Here, we posit as follows.

H5: there is a significant positive relationship between CS and website loyalty

Moderating Effect of Switching Cost

Switching cost consists of the economic, psychological, and emotional dimensions of the consumers. This cost may vary with the type of product, businesses, or customers (H.-C. Chiu, Hsieh, Li, & Lee, 2005). The technological incompatibility within brands for technology products increases the switching costs. In business sector, switching costs can be classified as hard and soft assets. The monetary, behavioral, search and learning related issues contribute to the switching cost with respect to customers. Few studies have considered the role of switching cost in the satisfaction-loyalty relationship (Huang & Hsieh, 2012; Minarti & Segoro, 2014). However, these studies emphasize on the fact that this role is dependent on situational variables such as businesses, products and consumers, and this relationship may not always be significant. However, the significance of the moderator is supported in the mobile phone sector (Aydin et al., 2005; Oyeniyi & Abiodun, 2010). In this digital era, the firms now own their websites and help shoppers reduce searching costs for price and quality information, as well as allow comparisons across e-stores by eliminating physical travel. Since the competitors are just a click away, the shoppers face minimum barriers for switching e-commerce platforms (Chuah, Marimuthu, Kandampully, & Bilgihan, 2017). Therefore, the role of switching cost as a moderator warrants further investigation. Thus, we posit that

H6: the relationship between CS and website loyalty is moderated by switching cost

METHODOLOGY

Data Collection

A questionnaire was prepared to perform a web based survey sent over some popular social media platforms. This type of survey is useful as the respondents come from a population which is socially connected over the internet and can make meaningful responses on statements related to impact of the social reviews, as well as those who do shopping online. 250 responses were registered, out of which 174 were considered for study, after removing the incomplete and wrongly filled up questionnaires. A simple random probability sampling technique was adopted as each respondent had an equal chance of being selected in the sample; however the overall population was limited to the number of connections over that platform. The survey was conducted from 1 May, 2018 to 31 July, 2018. To get accurate response and reduce ambiguity, pilot study was conducted on 30 respondents which mainly consisted of academician and management experts dealing with e-commerce websites. The pilot group correctly filled the questionnaire and suggested few changes in the questionnaire language. The final questionnaire with closed ended questions on 5-point likert scale was prepared after incorporating the suggested corrections. Moreover, the sample seems apt as it consists of respondents that are active on social media, perform online shopping, and make frequent transactions online. The demographic profiles of the respondents are presented in Table 2.

Measures

This chapter aims to study the relationship between website service quality (WSQ), social media reviews (SMR), perceived value (PV), customer satisfaction (CS), and website loyalty (LOY); and also check the moderating effect of switching cost in the association between customer satisfaction and website loyalty. A conceptual model is constructed here on the basis of hypotheses developed in this study, as shown in Figure 1. A self-administered questionnaire with 19 constructs was used to check the support for the hypotheses. The respondents were asked about their shopping experience with respect to a particular website in the past three months. This provided us with meaningful responses rather than the ones which we would have received on asking about their most visited website. The respondents were questioned about website service quality measures (seven items, 5-point likert scale), the influence of reviews available on their social media accounts (three items, 5-point likert scale), the value generated by the website towards its customers (two items, 5-point likert scale), level of satisfaction achieved while using the e-commerce website (two items, 5-point likert scale), loyalty generated (three items, 5-point likert scale), their perspective on switching website (two items, 5-point likert scale), amount of time spent on online shopping, and general demographic characteristics. Scaling was done using agreement-type of 5-point likert scale, where 1 = strongly disagree and 5 = strongly agree. The statements of the constructs used in the questionnaire are provided in the appendix. All the variables considered here are multi-item measures. Though it has been proved by researchers that single-item measures best represent an overall evaluation, but when it is not possible to define a construct in terms of single item, researchers must make use of multi-item measures (Hoeppner, Kelly, Urbanoski, & Slaymaker, 2011).

Figure 1. Hypothesized Model

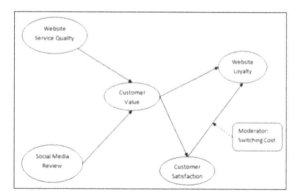

DATA ANALYSIS

Validity and Reliability of Measures

To rectify the scales of the considered measures, exploratory factor analysis (EFA) was performed. For EFA, principal component analysis with varimax rotation and eigenvalue greater than 1 was considered and attributes with factor loadings above .5 were retained for further analysis. Kaiser-Mayer-Olkin (KMO) value of .836 and valid Bartlett's Sphericity Test suggest the usefulness of factor analysis. All the constructs had Cronbach alpha value above .7 and composite reliability (CR) value above .7, which substantiated construct reliability. Confirmations of discriminant validity of the constructs were observed with AVE (average variance extracted) values above .5 and that the square roots of AVE for each latent variable more than absolute correlations between these variables. Above mentioned results are given in Table 3 and 4.

Table 2. Demographic Profile

Respondent's Demographic Profile	Variables	Usable responses	Percentage
Gender	Male	103	59.20
	Female	71	40.80
Age (in years)	Below 18	7	04.02
	18 – 30	114	65.52
	31 – 45	33	18.97
	Above 45	20	11.49
Education Qualification	Undergraduate	5	02.87
	Graduate	46	26.44
	Postgraduate	67	38.51
	Other	56	32.18
Occupation	Student	82	47.13
	Self employed	43	24.71
	Service	49	28.16
Annual Household Income (in lacs of Rupees)	Below 4 (Low)	45	25.86
	4 – 8 (Lower Middle)	60	34.48
	8 – 12 (Upper Middle)	32	18.39
	Above 12 (High)	37	21.27
Hours spent on online shopping (in a month)	Below 6	36	20.69
	6 – 12	48	27.59
	Above 12	90	51.72
Hours spent on social media (in a month)	Below 6	40	22.99
	6 – 12	55	31.61
	Above 12	79	45.40

Table 3. Dimensionality and Reliability Results

Variable	Items	Loadings	Cronbach Alpha	CR
Website Service Quality (WSQ)	WSQ1	.730	0.756	0.87
	WSQ2	.656	0.768	
	WSQ3	.592	0.764	
	WSQ4	.863	0.751	
	WSQ5	.746	0.759	
	WSQ6	.850	0.749	
	WSQ7	.900	0.753	
Social Media Reviews (SMR)	SMR1	.891	0.766	0.96
	SMR2	.631	0.768	
	SMR3	.873	0.768	
Customer Value (CV)	CV1	.671	0.762	0.82
	CV2	.611	0.756	
Customer Satisfaction (CS)	CS1	.887	0.774	0.93
	CS2	.620	0.772	
Website Loyalty (LOY)	L1	.681	0.768	0.92
	L2	.830	0.761	
	L3	.806	0.768	
Switching Cost (SC)	SC1	.878	0.778	0.94
	SC2	.859	0.792	

Table 4. Discriminant Validity Results

	AVE	WSQ	SMR	CV	CS	LOY	
WSQ	.67	**0.82**					
SMR	.79	0.64	**0.89**				
CV	.58	0.61	0.63	**0.76**			
CS	.74	0.62	0.70	0.67	**0.86**		
LOY	.72	0.76	0.74	0.77	0.72	**0.85**	
SC	.76	0.68	0.70	0.72	0.65	0.79	**0.87**

Common Method Bias (CMB)

A common instrument used for surveying both independent and dependent entities may result in the problem of CMB. The most efficient method to detect this issue, as suggested by many researchers is the Harman's Single Factor Analysis. From the results of the present study, we may infer that there is no CMB error as a single factor is able to explain less than 50% of total variance explained (Anderson & Swaminathan, 2011).

PLS-SEM Results

The hypothesised relationships among the considered latent variables were examined through PLS-SEM. For this, smartPLS (2.0) software was used to determine the path loadings between each pair of variables, coefficient of determination value for the endogenous latent variables, and lastly the t-value to test the significance of the assumptions. The coefficient of determination value for CV, CS, and LOY were found to be .602, .430, and .460, respectively, and bootstrapping technique was used to obtain the t-test values, which were greater than the threshold value of 1.96 for acceptance. The results of the hypothesis testing are shown in Table 5.

Table 5. Hypotheses Results

Path	Loading	T - value	Status
WSQ → CV (H1)	0.476	2.363	Accept
SMR → CV (H2)	0.358	2.610	Accept
CV → CS (H3)	0.641	4.685	Accept
CV → LOY (H4)	0.402	3.361	Accept
CS → LOY (H5)	0.354	2.996	Accept

Moderating Effect of Switching Cost

In addition to the above analysis, we wish to study the significance of switching cost as a moderator over the relationship between customer satisfaction and website loyalty. The moderation test was performed by generating the interaction effect between SC and CS, by setting the LOY as the endogenous variable. The PLS test was again run and the bootstrapping results were obtained. The path loading obtained after the analysis was .224 with t-value equal to 2.860. This supports the significance of hypothesis H6 at 5% level of significance. The results are provided in Table 6.

Table 6. Moderating Effect Results

Path	Loading	t-value	Status
CS → LOY	0.387	3.308	
SC → LOY	0.204	2.335	Accept
CS*SC → LOY	0.224	2.860	

After performing the hypotheses testing and obtaining the respective path loadings using PLS-SEM, we next proceed to find the best determinant variable in each causal relationship considered in the developed hypothesized model by making use of ANN.

Artificial Neural Network (ANN) Analysis

The literature supports various multivariate assumptions such as normality in data, linearity of relationships, absence of outliers and multi-collinearity, homoscedasticity, and sufficient data elements, which need to be fulfilled by the analytical techniques (Sarstedt, Ringle, Henseler, & Hair, 2014). For covariance based SEM, all these assumptions are vital for its application to exist. PLS takes care of outliers, small sample size, and non-normality, during its application, however it is unable to detect the linearity or non-linearity among the relationships. ANN is the most robust technique towards all these assumptions and is capable of handling both linear and non-linear associations (Hsu, Chen, & Hsieh, 2006). Based on the above discussion, we first check the feasibility of using ANN. The foremost objective is to examine the normality, which was tested using one sample Kolmogorov-Smirnov (KS) normality test.

Table 7. One Sample KS Test Results

Items	N	Normal Parameters		Most Extreme Differences			Kolmogorov-Smirnov Z	Asymp. Sig. (2-tailed)
		Mean	Std. Deviation	Absolute	Positive	Negative		
WSQ1	174	3.6552	1.11041	.214	.130	-.214	2.821	.000
WSQ2	174	2.7816	1.43793	.181	.172	-.181	2.386	.000
WSQ3	174	2.0172	1.26525	.301	.301	-.211	3.968	.000
WSQ4	174	2.9425	1.29344	.184	.163	-.184	2.427	.000
WSQ5	174	1.5747	.99283	.385	.385	-.281	5.083	.000
WSQ6	174	3.5805	1.19337	.183	.141	-.183	2.419	.000
WSQ7	174	3.4368	1.25575	.196	.113	-.196	2.587	.000
SMR1	174	2.4310	1.36147	.228	.228	-.147	3.003	.000
SMR2	174	3.1092	1.19953	.176	.157	-.176	2.327	.000
SMR3	174	2.0920	1.32676	.301	.301	-.205	3.964	.000
CV1	174	2.6494	1.26220	.197	.197	-.151	2.593	.000
CV2	174	2.8046	1.39644	.172	.172	-.155	2.266	.000
L1	174	3.1034	1.14331	.192	.132	-.192	2.527	.000
L2	174	1.9253	1.21653	.305	.305	-.223	4.027	.000
L3	174	2.9943	1.32777	.166	.135	-.166	2.195	.000
CS1	174	1.8678	1.18751	.325	.325	-.232	4.287	.000
CS2	174	3.2011	1.26756	.161	.161	-.138	2.120	.000

Table 8. ANOVA Result

Path	F - value	Sig
WSQ → CV	2.548	.012
SMR → CV	2.806	.000
CV → CS	5.944	.000
CV → LOY	5.605	.000
CS → LOY	5.763	.000

The results presented in Table 7 show that all the p-value are less than 5% level of significance, which cancels the normality in distribution. Moreover, we look for linearity assumption, which is taken care of by Analysis of Variance (ANOVA) approach. For all the causal relationships considered here, we noticed the p-value to be less than 5% level of significance, which confirms non-linearity among the latent variables, as provided in Table 8.

ANN is an interconnected network consisting of neurons connected through synaptic weights. The structure consists of three layers of neurons namely input, hidden, and output layer, known as multilayer perceptrons (Holcomb & Morari, 1992). During the training process, the neurons in the input layer are processed through the hidden layers to finally reach the output layer. This is generally termed as feed-forward back-propagation algorithm. In case of supervised learning, these hidden layers act as knowledge bank for predicting the future and the synaptic weights acts plays the role of catalyst during this process. The error terms are produced at the output layer, which are propagated back to the input with the help of hidden layer (Chong & Bai, 2014). This cycle is repeated till the error becomes minimal and prediction capacity becomes efficient. Though, ANN has few advantages over other similar techniques such as SEM, MRA, logistic or discriminant regression (Hsu et al., 2006). (1) The learning ability of the approach makes it superior than these traditional techniques. (2) It can identify both compensatory as well as non-compensatory associations, in comparison to conventional ones which could involve only compensatory ones. (3) It does not depend on p-value, the value which nullifies as the sample size increases, and is thus capable of identifying complicated linear and non-linear relationships. (4) Non-parametric ANN makes it possible to study the cause-effect relationships without testing the hypotheses.

This study applies ANN to determine the most influential predictor in each causal relationship. To minimize over-fitting of the model, we perform ten-fold cross validation. The data ratio in training to testing is set to 9:1. The numbers of hidden layers were automatically generated, whereas sigmoid activation function was used for hidden and output layer. To evaluate the prediction accuracy we make use of RMSE (root mean square error). Finally, sensitivity analysis was used to measure the normalized importance of each predictor on the basis of relative importance. In this analysis, we consider three models. Model 1 consists of WSQ and SMR as the input neurons and CV as the output layer. Model 2

Table 9. RMSE Results

Neural Networks	Model 1		Model 2		Model 3	
	Training	Testing	Training	Testing	Training	Testing
NN1	.0932	.0868	.1214	.0976	.1464	.1488
NN2	.0949	.0637	.1169	.1334	.1405	.1559
NN3	.0933	.0855	.1329	.1294	.1418	.1438
NN4	.0999	.0924	.1316	.1492	.1367	.1218
NN5	.0946	.0748	.1262	.1225	.1498	.1247
NN6	.0944	.0729	.1212	.1074	.1410	.1492
NN7	.0985	.1008	.1201	.1144	.1410	.1549
NN8	.0986	.1080	.1221	.0922	.1397	.1598
NN9	.0937	.0827	.1374	.0981	.1421	.1049
NN10	.0933	.0847	.1232	.0685	.1479	.1427
Mean	0.0954	0.0852	.1253	.1113	0.1427	0.1407
S.D.	0.0026	0.0131	.0066	.0235	0.0041	0.0178

Table 10. Sensitivity Analysis Results

Neural Networks	Model 1		Model 2	Model 3	
	WSQ	SMR	CV	CV	CS
NN1	.497	.503	.100	.195	.805
NN2	.504	.496	.100	.294	.706
NN3	.356	.644	.100	.196	.804
NN4	.427	.573	.100	.459	.541
NN5	.723	.277	.100	.546	.454
NN6	.306	.694	.100	.650	.350
NN7	.375	.625	.100	.697	.303
NN8	.445	.555	.100	.217	.783
NN9	.821	.179	.100	.397	.603
NN10	.620	.380	.100	.618	.382
Mean	0.5074	0.4926	.100	0.4269	0.5731
Normalized	100.00	97.08	100.00	74.49	100.00

considers CV as input whereas CS acts as output neuron. Model 3 takes CS and CV as inputs and LOY as output. The RMSE results are provided in Table 9. Moreover, the sensitivity analysis results are given in Table 10. The RMSE results for the ten-fold analysis shows that for all the three models there is less variation between the training and testing outcomes with the values .0105, .0169, and .0137, respectively. Moreover, the sensitivity results show the most important predictors in each model i.e. WSQ, CV, and CS, respectively.

DISCUSSIONS AND IMPLICATIONS

The acceptance of hypothesis H1 validates the direct association between website service quality and customer value. This is consistent with the results provided in previous studies (Ariff et al., 2013; Kumar & Desai, 2016; J. D. Xu et al., 2013). The first thing that the shopper comes in contact with is the firm's webpage. It is necessary for a company to own its website so as to reach wider audience not only within country but also across borders. Previous studies have laid emphasis on system quality, content quality, and service quality dimensions for the success of an e-commerce website. The chapter covers these dimensions under one umbrella, namely the website service quality. The online shoppers expect these items while purchasing through a website and so marketers must concentrate on these concepts so as to increase their website traffic. These dimensions are trust, tangibility, customization, responsiveness, ease of ordering, navigation, and ease of use. Moreover, equity theory embarks the importance of customer value during their purchasing process. The theory suggests that customers prefer those products/services that provide them with equal benefits in return for their inputs. These inputs may be in form of price (monetary) or in terms of time or sentiments (non-monetary). The acceptance of the hypothesis registers the relationship between WSQ and CV. Therefore, the online marketers must have a website which is compatible to the shopper's need and wants such as a safe and secure transaction medium, a platform which is easily accessible, makes it possible to order products/services with ease and at affordable prices, availability of customer support system which is very affordable. In addition to these, customers also expect a platform that is available 24X7, displays correct and precise information regarding their offerings, and most importantly allowing shopper to compose his shopping cart as per his requirements. Moreover, the strategy of providing cash-backs, discounts, free shipping, and other incentives seems a beneficial decision for customers, and helps in generating value in them.

The direct association between social media reviews and customer value is validated by the support of hypothesis H2. This is similar to the analysis results obtained by the previous studies (Abirami et al., 2015; Andreou et al., 2005; Kwahk & Ge, 2012). As discussed earlier, customer value is an aggregation of price and cognitive activities. The SMR is the form of electronic word-of-mouth, where the messages related to an object are spread by near and dear ones as well as acquaintances over social platforms. Extant researchers have noticed the influence of these social stimuli in the purchase decision making of a customer. Therefore, these online customer reviews plays the emotional role in customer value generation. The online vendors must keep a track of the feedbacks provided by previous purchasers, and try to solve their issues related to its offering, if any. This will help in retaining present customer base and also adding potential purchase in their database. Thus, e-firms must be active on social platforms in order to maintain a continuous dialogue with their potential and actual customers, which in turn lead to enhancement in value generation.

The support for hypothesis H3 verifies the positive direct association between customer value and customer satisfaction towards a website. Similar validation has been provided in previous studies (Gallarza et al., 2016; Puig & Ming, 2017; C. Xu et al., 2015). CV is the basically an evaluation of net benefit generation. If this net benefit valuation turns out be a positive number, and then it will lead to a feeling of satisfaction among the customers. They will be happy with their returns and a feeling of contentment will be showcased by them. Also, customer satisfaction towards an e-commerce system is judged to be an indicator of e-business success. Therefore, it validates the sociological theories of cognitive processes resulting into affective responses.

The direct relationship between customer value and website loyalty is validated by the acceptance of hypothesis H4. The theoretical implications can be verified through the past studies (Gallarza et al., 2016; Puig & Ming, 2017; Veloutsou & McAlonan, 2012). If a customer perceives that he is getting good return for his investments, which may be monetary or non-monetary, he will try to stick to that organization. But, this process is supported until his marginal utility is maximized. Therefore, marketers must track the shopping patterns of buyers so as to provide them enjoyable and hedonic shopping experience. This will increase the loyalty intent towards that website and resistant to switching barriers, however small they may be. Thus, if the shoppers find a website good worth for their inputs, they will be ready to recommend it to his family and peers.

The acceptance of hypothesis H5 signifies the positive direct relationship between customer satisfaction and website loyalty. This relationship has well been justified by previous studies, and suggests marketers to focus on their previous purchasers so that they are inclined to make a revisit to their website and make contribution towards market value generation for the firm (M.-J. Kim et al., 2011; Limbu et al., 2011; T. S. H. Pham & Ahammad, 2017). Therefore, only when the buyers are satisfied with their shopping experience as well as with the purchased product/service, they will consider that website superior to other similar alternatives and will be willing to suggest it to others.

Next, the question arises whether there is a catalyst that can intensify or de-intensify the direct relationship between customer satisfaction and website loyalty. Few researchers have considered the role of switching cost under this association but have stated its significance as per situation. This motivated us to take it as a moderator in this chapter. The hypothesis testing results provided in Table 6 gives a glimpse of a parallel relationship between the between the combined effect of CS and switching cost

Figure 2. Interaction Effect

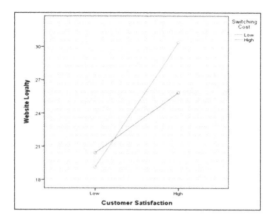

over website loyalty. The significant positive path loading along with acceptable t-value validates our hypothesis H6 that customer satisfaction acts as a moderator in this relationship. Also, to gain deeper insight, we studied the interaction effects among these variables. The graphical representation is provided in Figure 2. The curves show that website loyalty increases with increase in customer satisfaction; however switching cost facilitates this impact.

Lastly, after hypotheses testing, artificial neural network was used to find the best predictor of the endogenous variable. For this, we divided our conceptual framework into three models. The first model considered SMR and WSQ as independent variables whereas the dependent variable was CV. The second model considered CV as independent and CS as dependent constructs. The third model considered CS and CV are explanatory variables whereas LOY played the role of explained variable. The RMSE results provided in Table 9 show that the variation between the training and testing results for each model considered is very less, which validated the three models. Moreover, sensitivity analysis was provided to investigate the best predictor of each causal relationship (Table 10). For Model 1, WSQ is more important predictor of CV in comparison to SMR. This may be due to the fact that many customers feel that the user generated contents are skeptical as they may be fake or posted by the firm itself. For Model 2, since the relationship involves only one predictor, CV is itself the best determinant of CS. For Model 3, CS is more important predictor of website loyalty in comparison to CV. This may be attributed to the fact that a customer who wins the price-return tradeoff may not be eventually happy with the quality of offering provided or that the customers do not feel content with the website.

CONCLUSION

Thus, this chapter attempts to examine the relationship between website service quality (WSQ), social media reviews (SMR), customer value (CV), customer satisfaction (CS), and website loyalty (LOY); with the moderating effect of switching cost between CS and LOY. Also, the most influential predictor in each cause-effect relationship is determined. The hypothesized conceptual framework is validated using a two-stage approach. In the first stage, the hypotheses are tested and path loadings are generated using PLS-SEM approach. Also, the moderating effect is studied. Second stage utilizes the advantages of artificial neural network (ANN) to obtain the best explanatory variable in each independent-dependent association. The two approaches were applied on 174 meaningful responses obtained through a web-based questionnaire to get to the conclusion of the study. PLS-SEM results show that all the hypotheses considered in the study s well as the moderating effect of switching cost are significant. ANN results proved that WSQ, CV, and CS are the best predictors of CV, CS, and LOY, respectively.

FUTURE RESEARCH DIRECTIONS

Though the study has the limitation of geographic location, and so the results may not be generalized for sample in other developing or developed economies. Future studies may consider involving the moderating role of various demographic characterises in the conceptual framework.

REFERENCES

Abelson, R. P. (1983). Whatever became of consistency theory? *Personality and Social Psychology Bulletin, 9*(1), 37–54. doi:10.1177/0146167283091006

Abirami, A., Askarunisa, A., Gayathri, K., & Jeyalakshmi, M. G. (2015). Social Media Analysis for TamilNadu Tourism Places using VIKOR Approach. *Artificial Intelligent Systems and Machine Learning, 7*(5), 133–138.

Ali, F., Rasoolimanesh, S. M., Sarstedt, M., Ringle, C. M., & Ryu, K. (2018). An assessment of the use of partial least squares structural equation modeling (PLS-SEM) in hospitality research. *International Journal of Contemporary Hospitality Management, 30*(1), 514–538. doi:10.1108/IJCHM-10-2016-0568

Andam, Z. R. (2003). *E-commerce and e-business, e-primer for the information economy*. Society and Polity Series, UNDP-APDIP and e-ASEAN Task Force.

Anderson, R. E., & Srinivasan, S. S. (2003). E-satisfaction and e-loyalty: A contingency framework. *Psychology and Marketing, 20*(2), 123–138. doi:10.1002/mar.10063

Anderson, R. E., & Swaminathan, S. (2011). Customer satisfaction and loyalty in e-markets: A PLS path modeling approach. *Journal of Marketing Theory and Practice, 19*(2), 221–234. doi:10.2753/MTP1069-6679190207

Andreou, A. S., Leonidou, C., Chrysostomou, C., Pitsillides, A., Samaras, G., Schizas, C., & Mavromous, S. M. (2005). Key issues for the design and development of mobile commerce services and applications. *International Journal of Mobile Communications, 3*(3), 303–323. doi:10.1504/IJMC.2005.006586

Arbore, A., & Busacca, B. (2009). Customer satisfaction and dissatisfaction in retail banking: Exploring the asymmetric impact of attribute performances. *Journal of Retailing and Consumer Services, 16*(4), 271–280. doi:10.1016/j.jretconser.2009.02.002

Ariff, M. S. M., Yun, L. O., Zakuan, N., & Ismail, K. (2013). The impacts of service quality and customer satisfaction on customer loyalty in internet banking. *Procedia: Social and Behavioral Sciences, 81*, 469–473. doi:10.1016/j.sbspro.2013.06.462

Aydin, S., Özer, G., & Arasil, Ö. (2005). Customer loyalty and the effect of switching costs as a moderator variable: A case in the Turkish mobile phone market. *Marketing Intelligence & Planning, 23*(1), 89–103. doi:10.1108/02634500510577492

Ayo, C. K., Oni, A. A., Adewoye, O. J., & Eweoya, I. O. (2016). E-banking users' behaviour: E-service quality, attitude, and customer satisfaction. *International Journal of Bank Marketing, 34*(3), 347–367. doi:10.1108/IJBM-12-2014-0175

Bai, B., Law, R., & Wen, I. (2008). The impact of website quality on customer satisfaction and purchase intentions: Evidence from Chinese online visitors. *International Journal of Hospitality Management, 27*(3), 391–402. doi:10.1016/j.ijhm.2007.10.008

Bilgihan, A. (2016). Gen Y customer loyalty in online shopping: An integrated model of trust, user experience and branding. *Computers in Human Behavior, 61*, 103–113. doi:10.1016/j.chb.2016.03.014

Brown, I., & Jayakody, R. (2008). B2C e-commerce success: A test and validation of a revised conceptual model. *The Electronic Journal Information Systems Evaluation, 11*(3), 167–184.

Cardozo, R. N. (1965). An experimental study of customer effort, expectation, and satisfaction. *JMR, Journal of Marketing Research, 2*(3), 244–249. doi:10.1177/002224376500200303

Carpenter, J. M., & Fairhurst, A. (2005). Consumer shopping value, satisfaction, and loyalty for retail apparel brands. *Journal of Fashion Marketing and Management: An International Journal, 9*(3), 256–269. doi:10.1108/13612020510610408

Caruana, A. (2003). The impact of switching costs on customer loyalty: A study among corporate customers of mobile telephony. *Journal of Targeting, Measurement and Analysis for Marketing, 12*(3), 256-268.

Casaló, L., Flavián, C., & Guinalíu, M. (2008). The role of perceived usability, reputation, satisfaction and consumer familiarity on the website loyalty formation process. *Computers in Human Behavior, 24*(2), 325–345. doi:10.1016/j.chb.2007.01.017

Chadha, S., & Kapoor, D. (2009). Effect of switching cost, service quality and customer satisfaction on customer loyalty of cellular service providers in Indian market. *IUP Journal of Marketing Management, 8*(1), 23.

Chen, J. V., Yen, D. C., Pornpriphet, W., & Widjaja, A. E. (2015). E-commerce web site loyalty: A cross cultural comparison. *Information Systems Frontiers, 17*(6), 1283–1299. doi:10.100710796-014-9499-0

Chen, X., Huang, Q., & Davison, R. M. (2017). The role of website quality and social capital in building buyers' loyalty. *International Journal of Information Management, 37*(1), 1563–1574. doi:10.1016/j.ijinfomgt.2016.07.005

Chen, Y., Fay, S., & Wang, Q. (2011). The role of marketing in social media: How online consumer reviews evolve. *Journal of Interactive Marketing, 25*(2), 85–94. doi:10.1016/j.intmar.2011.01.003

Chiu, C. M., Wang, E. T., Fang, Y. H., & Huang, H. Y. (2014). Understanding customers' repeat purchase intentions in B2C e-commerce: The roles of utilitarian value, hedonic value and perceived risk. *Information Systems Journal, 24*(1), 85–114. doi:10.1111/j.1365-2575.2012.00407.x

Chiu, H.-C., Hsieh, Y.-C., Li, Y.-C., & Lee, M. (2005). Relationship marketing and consumer switching behavior. *Journal of Business Research, 58*(12), 1681–1689. doi:10.1016/j.jbusres.2004.11.005

Chong, A. Y.-L., & Bai, R. (2014). Predicting open IOS adoption in SMEs: An integrated SEM-neural network approach. *Expert Systems with Applications, 41*(1), 221–229. doi:10.1016/j.eswa.2013.07.023

Chu, S.-C., & Kim, Y. (2011). Determinants of consumer engagement in electronic word-of-mouth (eWOM) in social networking sites. *International Journal of Advertising, 30*(1), 47–75. doi:10.2501/IJA-30-1-047-075

Chuah, S. H.-W., Marimuthu, M., Kandampully, J., & Bilgihan, A. (2017). What drives Gen Y loyalty? Understanding the mediated moderating roles of switching costs and alternative attractiveness in the value-satisfaction-loyalty chain. *Journal of Retailing and Consumer Services, 36*, 124–136. doi:10.1016/j.jretconser.2017.01.010

Cyr, D., Hassanein, K., Head, M., & Ivanov, A. (2007). The role of social presence in establishing loyalty in e-service environments. *Interacting with Computers, 19*(1), 43–56. doi:10.1016/j.intcom.2006.07.010

DeLone, W. H., & McLean, E. R. (1992). Information systems success: The quest for the dependent variable. *Information Systems Research, 3*(1), 60–95. doi:10.1287/isre.3.1.60

Delone, W. H., & McLean, E. R. (2003). The DeLone and McLean model of information systems success: A ten-year update. *Journal of Management Information Systems, 19*(4), 9–30. doi:10.1080/07421222.2003.11045748

Eggert, A., & Ulaga, W. (2002). Customer perceived value: A substitute for satisfaction in business markets? *Journal of Business and Industrial Marketing, 17*(2/3), 107–118. doi:10.1108/08858620210419754

Erkan, I., & Evans, C. (2018). Social media or shopping websites? The influence of eWOM on consumers' online purchase intentions. *Journal of Marketing Communications, 24*(6), 617–632. doi:10.1080/13527266.2016.1184706

Featherman, M. S., & Pavlou, P. A. (2003). Predicting e-services adoption: A perceived risk facets perspective. *International Journal of Human-Computer Studies, 59*(4), 451–474. doi:10.1016/S1071-5819(03)00111-3

Flavián, C., Guinalíu, M., & Gurrea, R. (2006). The role played by perceived usability, satisfaction and consumer trust on website loyalty. *Information & Management, 43*(1), 1–14. doi:10.1016/j.im.2005.01.002

Gallarza, M. G., Arteaga-Moreno, F., Del Chiappa, G., & Gil-Saura, I. (2016). Intrinsic value dimensions and the value-satisfaction-loyalty chain: A causal model for services. *Journal of Services Marketing, 30*(2), 165–185. doi:10.1108/JSM-07-2014-0241

Goutam, D., & Gopalakrishna, B. (2018). Customer loyalty development in online shopping: An integration of e-service quality model and commitment-trust theory. *Management Science Letters, 8*(11), 1149–1158. doi:10.5267/j.msl.2018.8.009

Hallowell, R. (1996). The relationships of customer satisfaction, customer loyalty, and profitability: An empirical study. *International Journal of Service Industry Management, 7*(4), 27–42. doi:10.1108/09564239610129931

Hill, N., & Alexander, J. (2017). *The handbook of customer satisfaction and loyalty measurement.* Routledge. doi:10.4324/9781315239279

Hirschman, A. O. (1970). *Exit, voice, and loyalty: Responses to decline in firms, organizations, and states* (Vol. 25). Harvard University Press.

Hoeppner, B. B., Kelly, J. F., Urbanoski, K. A., & Slaymaker, V. (2011). Comparative utility of a single-item versus multiple-item measure of self-efficacy in predicting relapse among young adults. *Journal of Substance Abuse Treatment*, *41*(3), 305–312. doi:10.1016/j.jsat.2011.04.005 PMID:21700411

Holcomb, T., & Morari, M. (1992). PLS/neural networks. *Computers & Chemical Engineering*, *16*(4), 393–411. doi:10.1016/0098-1354(92)80056-F

Hox, J. J., & Bechger, T. M. (1998). *An introduction to structural equation modeling*. Academic Press.

Hsieh, M.-T., & Tsao, W.-C. (2014). Reducing perceived online shopping risk to enhance loyalty: A website quality perspective. *Journal of Risk Research*, *17*(2), 241–261. doi:10.1080/13669877.2013.794152

Hsu, S.-H., Chen, W., & Hsieh, M. (2006). Robustness testing of PLS, LISREL, EQS and ANN-based SEM for measuring customer satisfaction. *Total Quality Management & Business Excellence*, *17*(3), 355–372. doi:10.1080/14783360500451465

Huang, L.-Y., & Hsieh, Y.-J. (2012). Consumer electronics acceptance based on innovation attributes and switching costs: The case of e-book readers. *Electronic Commerce Research and Applications*, *11*(3), 218–228. doi:10.1016/j.elerap.2011.12.005

Hulland, J. (1999). Use of partial least squares (PLS) in strategic management research: A review of four recent studies. *Strategic Management Journal*, *20*(2), 195–204. doi:10.1002/(SICI)1097-0266(199902)20:2<195::AID-SMJ13>3.0.CO;2-7

Hur, Y., Ko, Y. J., & Valacich, J. (2011). A structural model of the relationships between sport website quality, e-satisfaction, and e-loyalty. *Journal of Sport Management*, *25*(5), 458–473. doi:10.1123/jsm.25.5.458

Iqbal, S., Bhatti, Z. A., & Khan, M. N. (2018). Assessing e-service quality of B2C sites: a proposed framework. *International Journal of Information Technology*, 1-12.

Kabadayi, S., & Gupta, R. (2005). Website loyalty: An empirical investigation of its antecedents. *International Journal of Internet Marketing and Advertising*, *2*(4), 321–345. doi:10.1504/IJIMA.2005.008105

Kassim, N., & Asiah Abdullah, N. (2010). The effect of perceived service quality dimensions on customer satisfaction, trust, and loyalty in e-commerce settings: A cross cultural analysis. *Asia Pacific Journal of Marketing and Logistics*, *22*(3), 351–371. doi:10.1108/13555851011062269

Kim, A. J., & Ko, E. (2012). Do social media marketing activities enhance customer equity? An empirical study of luxury fashion brand. *Journal of Business Research*, *65*(10), 1480–1486. doi:10.1016/j.jbusres.2011.10.014

Kim, M.-J., Chung, N., & Lee, C.-K. (2011). The effect of perceived trust on electronic commerce: Shopping online for tourism products and services in South Korea. *Tourism Management*, *32*(2), 256–265. doi:10.1016/j.tourman.2010.01.011

Kumar, S., & Desai, D. (2016). Web Personalization: A Perspective of Design and Implementation Strategies in Websites. *KHOJ: Journal of Indian Management Research and Practices,* 109-119.

Kumar Roy, S., & Lassar, M., W., & Butaney, G. (2014). The mediating impact of stickiness and loyalty on word-of-mouth promotion of retail websites: A consumer perspective. *European Journal of Marketing*, *48*(9/10), 1828–1849. doi:10.1108/EJM-04-2013-0193

Kwahk, K.-Y., & Ge, X. (2012). *The effects of social media on e-commerce: A perspective of social impact theory.* Paper presented at the System Science (HICSS), 2012 45th Hawaii International Conference on. 10.1109/HICSS.2012.564

Limbu, Y. B., Wolf, M., & Lunsford, D. L. (2011). Consumers' perceptions of online ethics and its effects on satisfaction and loyalty. *Journal of Research in Interactive Marketing, 5*(1), 71–89. doi:10.1108/17505931111121534

Lin, G. T., & Sun, C.-C. (2009). Factors influencing satisfaction and loyalty in online shopping: An integrated model. *Online Information Review, 33*(3), 458–475. doi:10.1108/14684520910969907

Loiacono, E. T., Watson, R. T., & Goodhue, D. L. (2002). WebQual: A measure of website quality. *Marketing Theory and Applications, 13*(3), 432-438.

Loureiro, S. M., Sardinha, I. M. D., & Reijnders, L. (2012). The effect of corporate social responsibility on consumer satisfaction and perceived value: The case of the automobile industry sector in Portugal. *Journal of Cleaner Production, 37*, 172–178. doi:10.1016/j.jclepro.2012.07.003

Minarti, S. N., & Segoro, W. (2014). The influence of customer satisfaction, switching cost and trusts in a brand on customer loyalty–The survey on student as IM3 users in Depok, Indonesia. *Procedia: Social and Behavioral Sciences, 143*, 1015–1019. doi:10.1016/j.sbspro.2014.07.546

Mishra, A., Maheswarappa, S. S., Maity, M., & Samu, S. (2018). Adolescent's eWOM intentions: An investigation into the roles of peers, the Internet and gender. *Journal of Business Research, 86*, 394–405. doi:10.1016/j.jbusres.2017.04.005

Molla, A., & Licker, P. S. (2001). E-commerce systems success: An attempt to extend and respecify the Delone and MacLean model of IS success. *Journal of Electronic Commerce Research, 2*(4), 131–141.

O'Cass, A., & Carlson, J. (2012). An e-retailing assessment of perceived website-service innovativeness: Implications for website quality evaluations, trust, loyalty and word of mouth. *Australasian Marketing Journal, 20*(1), 28–36. doi:10.1016/j.ausmj.2011.10.012

Oyeniyi, O., & Abiodun, A. (2010). Switching cost and customers loyalty in the mobile phone market: The Nigerian experience. *Business Intelligence Journal, 3*(1), 111–121.

Parasuraman, A., Zeithaml, V. A., & Berry, L. L. (1988). Servqual: A multiple-item scale for measuring consumer perc. *Journal of Retailing, 64*(1), 12.

Patterson, P. G., & Spreng, R. A. (1997). Modelling the relationship between perceived value, satisfaction and repurchase intentions in a business-to-business, services context: An empirical examination. *International Journal of Service Industry Management, 8*(5), 414–434. doi:10.1108/09564239710189835

Pham, L., Williamson, S., & Berry, R. (2018). Student perceptions of e-learning service quality, e-satisfaction, and e-loyalty. *International Journal of Enterprise Information Systems, 14*(3), 19–40. doi:10.4018/IJEIS.2018070102

Pham, T. S. H., & Ahammad, M. F. (2017). Antecedents and consequences of online customer satisfaction: A holistic process perspective. *Technological Forecasting and Social Change, 124*, 332–342. doi:10.1016/j.techfore.2017.04.003

Phuong, N. N. D., & Dai Trang, T. T. (2018). Repurchase Intention: The Effect of Service Quality, System Quality, Information Quality, and Customer Satisfaction as Mediating Role: A PLS Approach of M-Commerce Ride Hailing Service in Vietnam. *Marketing and Branding Research*, *5*(2), 78–91. doi:10.33844/mbr.2018.60463

Puig, L. C. M., & Ming, X. (2017). Experience Value, Satisfaction and Loyalty of International Tourists in Shanghai: A PLS-SEM Analysis. *International Business Research*, *10*(8), 114. doi:10.5539/ibr.v10n8p114

Qian, S., Peiji, S., & Quanfu, Y. (2011). An integrated analysis framework for customer value, customer satisfactory, switching barriers, repurchase intention and attitudinal loyalty: Evidences from China mobile data services. *Management Science and Engineering*, *5*(3), 135–142.

Quester, P., Neal, C., Pettigrew, S., Grimmer, M., Davis, T., & Hawkins, D. (2007). *Consumer behaviour: Implications for marketing strategy*. McGraw-Hill.

Reichheld, F. F., & Schefter, P. (2000). E-loyalty: Your secret weapon on the web. *Harvard Business Review*, *78*(4), 105–113.

Sá, F., Rocha, Á., & Cota, M. P. (2016). From the quality of traditional services to the quality of local e-Government online services: A literature review. *Government Information Quarterly*, *33*(1), 149–160. doi:10.1016/j.giq.2015.07.004

Sarstedt, M., Ringle, C. M., Henseler, J., & Hair, J. F. (2014). On the emancipation of PLS-SEM: A commentary on Rigdon (2012). *Long Range Planning*, *47*(3), 154–160. doi:10.1016/j.lrp.2014.02.007

Schindler, R. M., & Bickart, B. (2012). Perceived helpfulness of online consumer reviews: The role of message content and style. *Journal of Consumer Behaviour*, *11*(3), 234–243. doi:10.1002/cb.1372

Schultz, D. E., & Peltier, J. (2013). Social media's slippery slope: Challenges, opportunities and future research directions. *Journal of Research in Interactive Marketing*, *7*(2), 86–99. doi:10.1108/JRIM-12-2012-0054

Sharma, G., & Lijuan, W. (2015). The effects of online service quality of e-commerce Websites on user satisfaction. *The Electronic Library*, *33*(3), 468–485. doi:10.1108/EL-10-2013-0193

Söderlund, M. (1998). Customer satisfaction and its consequences on customer behaviour revisited: The impact of different levels of satisfaction on word-of-mouth, feedback to the supplier and loyalty. *International Journal of Service Industry Management*, *9*(2), 169–188. doi:10.1108/09564239810210532

Statista. (2018). Retrieved September, 2018, from https://www.statista.com/study/42335/ecommerce-report/

Sweeney, J. C., & Soutar, G. N. (2001). Consumer perceived value: The development of a multiple item scale. *Journal of Retailing*, *77*(2), 203–220. doi:10.1016/S0022-4359(01)00041-0

Tandon, A., Sharma, H., & Aggarwal, A. G. (2019). Assessing Travel Websites Based on Service Quality Attributes Under Intuitionistic Environment. *International Journal of Knowledge-Based Organizations*, *9*(1), 66–75. doi:10.4018/IJKBO.2019010106

Veloutsou, C., & McAlonan, A. (2012). Loyalty and or disloyalty to a search engine: The case of young Millennials. *Journal of Consumer Marketing*, *29*(2), 125–135. doi:10.1108/07363761211206375

Wang, Y.-S., & Tang, T.-I. (2003). Assessing customer perceptions of website service quality in digital marketing environments. *Journal of Organizational and End User Computing, 15*(3), 14–31. doi:10.4018/joeuc.2003070102

Woodruff, R. B. (1997). Customer value: The next source for competitive advantage. *Journal of the Academy of Marketing Science, 25*(2), 139–153. doi:10.1007/BF02894350

Xu, C., Peak, D., & Prybutok, V. (2015). A customer value, satisfaction, and loyalty perspective of mobile application recommendations. *Decision Support Systems, 79*, 171–183. doi:10.1016/j.dss.2015.08.008

Xu, J. D., Benbasat, I., & Cenfetelli, R. T. (2013). Integrating service quality with system and information quality: An empirical test in the e-service context. *Management Information Systems Quarterly, 37*(3), 777–794. doi:10.25300/MISQ/2013/37.3.05

Ye, Q., Law, R., & Gu, B. (2009). The impact of online user reviews on hotel room sales. *International Journal of Hospitality Management, 28*(1), 180–182. doi:10.1016/j.ijhm.2008.06.011

Zeithaml, V. A., Parasuraman, A., & Malhotra, A. (2002). Service quality delivery through web sites: A critical review of extant knowledge. *Journal of the Academy of Marketing Science, 30*(4), 362–375. doi:10.1177/009207002236911

Zhang, Z., Li, X., & Chen, Y. (2012). Deciphering word-of-mouth in social media: Text-based metrics of consumer reviews. *ACM Transactions on Management Information Systems, 3*(1), 5. doi:10.1145/2151163.2151168

Zhou, T., Lu, Y., & Wang, B. (2009). The relative importance of website design quality and service quality in determining consumers' online repurchase behavior. *Information Systems Management, 26*(4), 327–337. doi:10.1080/10580530903245663

ADDITIONAL READING

Ali, F., Rasoolimanesh, S. M., Sarstedt, M., Ringle, C. M., & Ryu, K. (2018). An assessment of the use of partial least squares structural equation modeling (PLS-SEM) in hospitality research. *International Journal of Contemporary Hospitality Management, 30*(1), 514–538. doi:10.1108/IJCHM-10-2016-0568

Cao, Y., Ajjan, H., & Hong, P. (2018). Post-purchase shipping and customer service experiences in online shopping and their impact on customer satisfaction: An empirical study with comparison. *Asia Pacific Journal of Marketing and Logistics, 30*(2), 400–416.

Erkan, I., & Evans, C. (2018). Social media or shopping websites? The influence of eWOM on consumers' online purchase intentions. *Journal of Marketing Communications, 24*(6), 617–632. doi:10.1080/13527266.2016.1184706

Goutam, D., & Gopalakrishna, B. (2018). Customer loyalty development in online shopping: An integration of e-service quality model and commitment-trust theory. *Management Science Letters, 8*(11), 1149–1158. doi:10.5267/j.msl.2018.8.009

Iqbal, S., Bhatti, Z. A., & Khan, M. N. (2018). Assessing e-service quality of B2C sites: a proposed framework. *International Journal of Information Technology*, 1-12.

Lin, M.-J., & Wang, W.-T. (2018). Explaining Online Customer Repurchase Intentions from a Relationship-Marketing Perspective: An Integration of the 4Rs Marketing Strategy and Customer Trust Mobile Commerce: Concepts, Methodologies, Tools, and Applications (pp. 1230-1259): IGI Global.

Pee, L. G., Jiang, J., & Klein, G. (2019). E-store loyalty: Longitudinal comparison of website usefulness and satisfaction. *International Journal of Market Research*, *61*(2), 178–194. doi:10.1177/1470785317752045

Sharma, H., & Aggarwal, A. G. (2019). Finding determinants of e-commerce success: A PLS-SEM approach. *Journal of Advances in Management Research*, *16*(4), 453–471. doi:10.1108/JAMR-08-2018-0074

Tandon, A., Sharma, H., & Aggarwal, A. G. (2019). Assessing Travel Websites Based on Service Quality Attributes Under Intuitionistic Environment. *International Journal of Knowledge-Based Organizations*, *9*(1), 66–75. doi:10.4018/IJKBO.2019010106

Wu, G. (2005). The mediating role of perceived interactivity in the effect of actual interactivity on attitude toward the website. *Journal of Interactive Advertising*, *5*(2), 29–39. doi:10.1080/15252019.2005.10722099

KEY TERMS AND DEFINITIONS

Customer Satisfaction: The deviation between the expectation and actual outcome for a customer.

Customer Value: In context of online platform: a potential customer will make a purchase only if the item is consistent with his monetary and non-monetary requirements; and also provides some incentives.

Social Media Reviews: The reviews regarding a product/service provided by experienced customers over social media platforms.

Switching Cost: Monetary and non-monetary factors that compel a customer to shift his website preference.

Website Loyalty: It means a customer willing to make online purchase through same platform while buying.

Website Service Quality: The variable consisting of information and system quality related to a website.

APPENDIX

Website Service Quality

WSQ1: E-commerce website makes me feel safe while making a transaction
WSQ2: E-commerce website offers multiple ways of searching product/service online
WSQ3: E-commerce website correctly answers my queries
WSQ4: E-commerce website provides correct information about the product/service
WSQ5: E-commerce website provides a smooth interface for requesting and obtaining information
WSQ6: E-commerce website provides a smooth interface for ordering goods/services online
WSQ7: E-commerce website provides a smooth interface to opt the product/service according to my preferences

Social Media Reviews

SMR1: E-commerce website is introduced by peers/family
SMR2: E-commerce website is introduced by media
SMR3: E-commerce website is introduced by customer reviews

Customer Satisfaction

CS1: I am overall satisfied with the website
CS2: Website is ideal to my expectations

Customer Value

CV1: Compared to alternative websites, the website charges me fairly for similar products
CV2: Comparing what I pay to what I get, the company provided me with good value

Website Loyalty

LOY1: I will recommend the website to my friends and relatives
LOY2: I will again make a purchase from the e-commerce website
LOY3: I will make a purchase from this website in the presence of other competitors

Switching Cost

SC1: It takes me a great deal of time and effort to switch to another website
SC2: It costs me too much to switch to another website

Emotional Intelligence and Customer Satisfaction of Online Health Information

Ionica Holban
European Academy of the Regions, Belgium

Ioana Duca
Titu Maiorescu University, Romania

Rodica Gherghina
The Bucharest University of Economic Studies, Romania

Diana Andreea Mândricel
Titu Maiorescu University, Romania

Elena Denisa Nicolescu
Valahia University, Romania

INTRODUCTION

The healthcare sector is probably one of the most dynamic sectors of the economy and society contiguously changing in response to a whole range of forces: patient expectations, changing social patterns, public policies and new technology (Agarwal & Labrique, 2014). As a consequence, the consumer of online health information is now viewed in a new perspective as a combination between the traditional patient and the contemporary consumer, having much more knowledge about the health system, open to innovations and with an active role in the process of diagnosis, treatment and maintaining health (Feng & Xie, 2015).

Romania has been and continues to undertake a variety of activities related to the implementation and adoption of technology in its health care system. These efforts have been particularly successful in the primary care sector in all regions of Romania but development of health IT projects must encourage successful adoption and implementation efforts. Withal, Romanian patients may also make use of health IT products, especially those designed to encourage healthier living habits and to enable patients to make appointments with providers.

The importance of various service qualities for customer satisfaction and subsequent adoption of online health services has been evidenced in numerous studies, but there is a paucity of research that explores the linkage between online health service quality satisfactions and customer adoption intentions in the context of Romania (Powell et al., 2011; Thackeray, Crookston & West, 2013; Grande & Taylor, 2010; Bansil et al., 2006).

Emotional intelligence directly influences the performance of an entity in both positive and negative ways because it determines the performance of the entity, the credibility of managers by promoting their values, beliefs, attitudes and behaviors (Ashkanasy & Humphrey, 2011). These approaches point to the fact that the core of emotional intelligence is the managers' value system, which influences their

DOI: 10.4018/978-1-7998-3473-1.ch155

satisfactions, decisions and behaviors with a major impact on the entity's activities. Organizational effectiveness and efficiency, productivity, open, creative and stimulating work environment, entity role in the community, social responsibility are just some of the values shown by top managers (Gevers & Peeters, 2009). It is also why the employees agree to be evaluated and motivated, as do all the actors involved, in relation to established standards. Where the environment is a mobilizer, they can they work together to maximum effectiveness.

There is a direct link between the need for an entity of change, having as its rationale its evolution, development, the gaining of new markets, or sometimes the staying in the competitive market and the influence of a strong emotional intelligence (Petrides et al., 2016). The latter may be either the key element in the transfer of the entity to another economic level, or the element that salvages the entity from a situation that might have led to its exit from the market. Under the pressure of the external and internal influences, emotional intelligence comes with a substantial contribution that guides the processes of change of entities through decisions and actions of managers (Campo et al., 2016).

The present chapter intends to identify the construct a set of factors that influence customers' behavioral intentions towards using online health information in Romania. The research questions have been formulated as following: Are health care institutions today making efficient use of the online health information they have available? How to use emotional intelligence in health IT?

This chapter is structured in the following way: in the first section, the authors will introduce a radiography of current situation regarding assessment of the potential for online health service; in the second section, research methodology will be discussed; in the third section, the results of the study and statistics analysis will be discussed; finally, the authors will argue the conclusions and will presented this paper's limitation.

BACKGROUND

Controversies about health IT implementation have been, and are still, generated by the difficulty of accurately determining demand, unequal access to participants' information, regulated pricing and pricing mechanisms and intervention of the third paying party, as well as ethical and moral aspects related to the patient-doctor relationship, the limit between research and treatment, the perception of health and illness, etc. (Beig et al., 2007; Hallyburton & Evarts, 2014; Kontos et al., 2014).

On the one hand, online healthcare consumers differ from those of other goods and services, due to certain peculiarities that arise from the specifics of the market, the supplier-client relations, and the way of organizing the health system (Rezai-Rad, Vaezi & Nattagh, 2012). Unlike other areas where, as a rule, the number of consumers is limited in traditional health services, in online health anyone can become theoretically the consumer at some point, so the potential market is very high.

In response to the necessity of online health information, consumer behavior is structured on two basic components, with important implications for online health services, namely purchasing behavior and consumption behavior (Li et al., 2010; Kelly, Jenkinson & Ziebland, 2013). Therefore, studying the behavior of the online healthcare consumer should not be limited to the individual as the end user, but should also focus on studying the relationship between the provider and the consumer, and in particular on set of factors may influence this behavior. In online healthcare, purchasing decisions require the most presence of multiple participants, who fulfil different roles: the influence, the decision-maker, the buyer, or the user (Carpenter et al., 2011; Khoja et al., 2007; Galdas, Cheater & Marshall, 2005).

On the other hand, emotional intelligence equips individuals with the attitude needed for a customer service position. Consumer behavior is the object of the permanent concerns of modern firms (Sillence et al., 2007; Jaiswaland & Gupta, 2015; Grosso, Castaldo & Grewal, 2018). In the face of increasingly strong competition on the market, it is necessary to know the behavior of the consumer in order to pre-serve market position, but also to expand, to increase the market share (Kim et al., 2012; Mittal, 2017). Understanding consumer behavior and knowing customers is never a simple job because consumer behavior is dynamic, constantly changing and evolving (Campo et al., 2016). This means that many statements about consumer behavior will probably become inappropriate, similar to fashion, with the change in concepts and social conditions. It is necessary to know what consumers think (perception), what they feel (impressions) and what they do (conduct); which are the things and places that influence or are influenced by what they think, feel and do (the environment). Not only can thoughts and emotions give the value of behavior, but behavior itself leads to related behavior (Biswas et al., 2014). Indeed, emotional intelligence equips the employee with the attitude needed for a customer service position.

RESEARCH METHODOLOGY

The primary data of this research were gathered from a questionnaire distributed online for the multi-functional platform designed to optimize diagnostic and decision making methods in medical services in Romania. - PROMED. The questionnaire was pre-tested and revised to ensure reliability. Apart from respondents' personal information that are measured by a categorical scale, the main questionnaire contains 9 items that are measured by a 5-point Likert-type scale ranging from 1 (strongly disagree) to 5 (strongly agree). It is by design to minimize the total number of items for encouraging the willingness of responses.

The experiment was conducted from April 2017 until December 2017. A total of 850 valid returns were obtained from the 1,000 distributions, representing 85% response rate. From 850 valid returns, Table 1 illustrates the sample's demographics. Majority of the respondents are female, at 68.47% (n = 582). By age, 52.35% (n = 445) of the respondents are between 31 and 40 years old. By marital status, 68.82% (n = 585) of the respondents are married. Females tend to be more willing to participate in the survey and mailing questionnaires back.

Then, collected data were analyzed using SPSS 20.0 statistical software for Windows. After perform-ing factor analysis to identify the attitude of Romanian consumers towards online health service quality, demographic differences were examined through one-way analysis of variance (ANOVA). In the next stage, in order to confirm questionnaire reliability, its internal consistency was measured by Cronbach alpha. The alpha coefficient of each item indicates appropriate reliability of the instrument. Thus, it was revealed that the questions are internally homogenous, that is, they measure one common construct.

According to the results obtained Mean ratings of the 9-item scale are presented in Table 2. Among them, Q_6: "Using online health service suits my living environment" received the highest mean, at $M = 5.66$ and Q_8: "It is more beneficial for patients make use of online health information" ($M = 5.46$). On the other end of the spectrum, the lowest mean was found in Q_2: "Help is available if I have problems in using online health service" ($M = 3.24$), followed by Q_1: "I consciously try to choose online health service because they are easy to access" ($M = 3.31$), and Q_3: "I believe online health service provides me complete health information" ($M = 3.70$). It is interesting to note that the standard deviation (SD) is higher among items with the lower mean (i.e. Q_1: $M = 3.31$, SD = 1.513; Q_2: $M = 3.24$, SD = 1.616; Q_3: $M = 3.70$, SD = 1.534). Conversely, items receiving higher mean tend to have lower standard deviation

Table 1. Demographic characteristics of the respondents

Demographics	Number	Percentage
Gender		
Male	268	31.53
Female	582	68.47
Age		
18 to 30	92	10.82
31 to 40	445	52.35
41 to 50	297	34.94
Over 50	16	1.89
Marital status		
Single	233	27.41
Married	585	68.82
Divorced/Widowed	32	3.77
Education		
High school or less	32	3.76
Junior college	81	9.53
College	298	35.06
Post graduate	439	51.65

(i.e. Q_6: $M = 5.66$, SD = 1.233). The phenomenon implies that the respondents tend to agree in unison on items that receive higher mean.

The nine attributes of "online health service" analysed are presented in Table 3. The first identified attribute can be attributed to "Social Influence", which is explained by 20.317% of the total variance with an eigenvalue of 2.862. The second online health service attribute, "Behavioural Intention", accounts 20.415% of the total variance with an eigenvalue of 2.814. The last attribute, "Facilitating Conditions", explains 18.417% of the total variance with an eigenvalue of 2.578. The Cronbach's alpha (α) across

Table 2. Measurement of online health service attributes

Items of measurement	Mean	SD
Q_1. I consciously try to choose online health service because they are easy to access	3.31	1.513
Q_2 Help is available if I have problems in using online health service	3.24	1.616
Q_3. I believe online health service provides me complete health information	3.70	1.534
Q_4. People who are important to me think that I should use online health service	5.19	1.479
Q_5. I prefer use the Internet to look for health information	5.17	1.274
Q_6. Using online health service suits my living environment	5.66	1.233
Q_7. I believe it is worthwhile for me to solve my health problem using health IT	4.98	1.445
Q_8. It is more beneficial for patients make use of online health information	5.46	1.357
Q_9. I systematically choose the online health service to protect my privacy	5.12	1.393

Table 3. The key Statistics

Online health service attributes	Factor loadings		
	1	2	3
Factor 1: Social Influence ($M = 5.172$)			
Q_4. People who are important to me think that I should use online health service	.849		
Q_5. I prefer use the Internet to look for health information	.836		
Q_8. It is more beneficial for patients make use of online health information	.705		
Factor 2: Behavioural Intention ($M = 5.272$)			
Q_7. I believe it is worthwhile for me to solve my health problem using health IT		.808	
Q_3. I believe online health service provides me complete health information		.742	
Q_9. I systematically choose the online health service to protect my privacy		.740	
Factor 3: Facilitating Conditions ($M = 3.442$)			
Q_6. Using online health service suits my living environment			.851
Q_1. I consciously try to choose online health service because they are easy to access			.759
Q_2 Help is available if I have problems in using online health service			.741
Eigenvalues	2.862	2.814	2.578
Cronbach's alpha	.872	.881	.874
Variance (%)	20.317	20.145	18.417
Cumulative variance (%)	20.317	40.462	58.575

these three attributes ranged from .872 to .881, indicating adequate consistency. The factor loadings (λ) ranged from .705 to .851 across all items.

According to the findings of the present study, owners of online health information must understand the importance of designing a website which inspires pleasant emotions of online health service users, directs their occasional feelings, and satisfies them with interaction with the website.

DISCUSSION

In health services, due to their characteristics, demand has to be seen from two points of view, namely the consumer / patient and the provider. The client / patient's point of view regarding the demand for health services may differ from that of the physician because: a) the consumer / patient has a less "scientific" perception of the disease, its causality, its evolution and its treatment ; b) the consumer / patient only partially knows the characteristics of a particular disease because the diseases are scientifically defined; c) for the consumer / patient, the period is limited in time because it emphasizes the current manifestations of the disease rather than its subsequent consequences; d) the consumer / patient is more concerned about the impact of the illness in terms of discomfort and interference with the activities of a normal lifestyle as defined by its place in society. However, knowledge of consumers' needs and their image regarding health services are not sufficient unless accompanied by a number of specific strategies at the level of the organizations in the field.

For businesses, this study has implications that go beyond the simple fact of making consumers choose a health service. Once involved with emotional intelligence, managers can gamble from sensing customer preferences and motivations to engaging enough to communicate clients / patients to a positive state. As it can be seen from the results of this study, there is no miraculous recipe for the success of the interaction, but if certain empathy manifests, there will be an economic and emotional gain. And if emotions are so contagious, any organization that provides online health services needs to remember that it can improve its performance.

SOLUTIONS AND RECOMMENDATIONS

This study systematically examines whether the online health service quality of the health system can influence the behavioral intention of customers by providing them the satisfaction expected from such alternate reliably service. As such, the takeaway for the health care institutions will be to adopt or improve these qualities of their online health services in order to achieve customer satisfaction and thereby, result in an increased growth rate in the use of health IT services in Romania. Also, the health care institutions should actively inform their customers about the processes and time needed for certain services under the online health system in order to ensure quality information.

Furthermore, the results of this study claims that respondents who expect less effort input in the service consuming process are more likely to show positive attitude in embracing the concept of online health services. Along the same line, facilitating conditions is found to be yet another determinant that can influence respondents' behavioral intention and use of online health services. Facilitating conditions generally tend to be the wide availability of computers, strong mobile networks and fast internet services in the context of Romania. The findings from this research generally supports the results of various recent studies in the field of health IT service quality like Rains (2007) and Shahab et al. (2014).

Implementation of health IT system might be a long-term project, but the fairly positive perception and an equally positive attitude of customers towards such services clearly paves the way of a higher rate of adoption of online health services in Romania.

FUTURE RESEARCH DIRECTIONS

Through the goals set, this chapter has touched its target. The presented and analyzed issues are a synthesized part of the vast amount of information that has been developed by the authors to create the framework for understanding Romanian customers' satisfaction of online health information. Therefore, there are new directions of future research such as:

§ Use technology to generate statistics and management indicators to better measure and plan care;
§ Incorporating safety screening into patient portal-based surveys that are keyed to emergency department visits, hospital discharge, or office encounters;
§ Analyzing and interpreting the dilemma situations faced by online health services from the former socialist countries that have not been analyzed in this chapter.

CONCLUSION

In order to explain the behavior of the online health consumer, it is not enough just to study the behavior of the healthcare consumer, but also the relationship between medical staff - especially the doctor - and the consumer as the main determinant of his behavior and consumption. The significance of this relationship is extremely important for online health services because the creation and delivery of services and their quality depend to a large extent on the relationship between the two. Medical staff can help improve this relationship by constantly informing the consumer through a realistic picture of the illness and the judicious use of the possibilities and resources available to the consumer.

The nature of the relationship between the doctor and the patient does not fall within certain limits, it is always problematic and can be affected by conflicting views and attitudes and a number of communication difficulties. Thus, in the physician-patient relationship, two types of behaviors appeared: the social or social behavior developed within the community and the personal behavior, which manifests according to the nature of each of the two participants in the process of performance. For all that, despite a significant number of initiatives in Romania related to online health information, lack of interoperability remains one of the major challenges in implementing successful health IT systems.

At the same time, the emotional intelligence exerts a major role in organizational culture when managers are willing to affect an appreciable share of their time for employee communication and training as regards managerial philosophy and the set of core values of the firm and consequently are aware of their role on which they have in their firm, not only at formal but also informal level.

In this regard, suppliers of online health information are making efforts to change the optics of approaching business, moving to consumer orientation. Beside on the results of this study we can say that the Romanian health IT is a growing business.

Like most empirical research, this study has several limitations. First, the conclusions drawn from this study are based solely on the users of the PROMED platform. Second, the study can be more constructs characterizing online health services or moderator effects like that of age, gender, recognition of benefits, engagement readiness of doctor, etc. that can be added in the research model to enhance the understanding of service qualities that customers expect from online health information.

REFERENCES

Agarwal, S., & Labrique, A. (2014). Newborn health on the line: The potential mHealth applications. *Journal of the American Medical Association, 312*(3), 229–230. doi:10.1001/jama.2014.6371 PMID:24953141

Ashkanasy, N. M., & Humphrey, R. H. (2011). Current emotion research in organizational behavior. *Emotion Review, 3*(2), 214–224. doi:10.1177/1754073910391684

Bansil, P., Keenan, N. L., Zlot, A. I., & Gilliland, J. C. (2006). Health-related information on the web: Results from the Health Styles Survey, 2002-2003. *Preventing Chronic Disease, 3*(2), A36. PMID:16539777

Beig, L., Montazer, G., & Ghavamifar, A. (2007). Adoption a proper tool for e-readiness assessment in developing countries (case studies: Iran, Turkey and Malaysia). *Journal of Knowledge Economy & Knowledge Management, 2,* 54–69.

Biswas, D., Labrecque, L., Lehmann, D., & Markos, E. (2014). Making choices while smelling, tasting, and listening: The role of sensory (dis)similarity when sequentially sampling products. *Journal of Marketing, 78*(1), 112–126. doi:10.1509/jm.12.0325

Campo, C., Pauser, S., Steiner, E., & Vetschera, R. (2016). Decision making styles and the use of heuristics in decision making. *Journal of Business Economics, 86*(4), 389–412. doi:10.100711573-016-0811-y

Carpenter, D. M., DeVellis, R. F., Hogan, S. L., Fisher, E. B., DeVellis, B. M., & Jordan, J. M. (2011). Use and perceived credibility of medication information sources for patients with a rare illness: Differences by gender. *Journal of Health Communication, 16*(6), 629–642. doi:10.1080/10810730.2011.551 995 PMID:21476166

Feng, Y., & Xie, W. (2015). Digital divide 2.0: The role of social networking sites in seeking health information online from a longitudinal perspective. *Journal of Health Communication, 20*(1), 60–68. doi:10.1080/10810730.2014.906522 PMID:25119019

Galdas, P. M., Cheater, F., & Marshall, P. (2005). Men and health help-seeking behaviour: Literature review. *Journal of Advanced Nursing, 49*(6), 616–623. doi:10.1111/j.1365-2648.2004.03331.x PMID:15737222

Gevers, J. M. P., & Peeters, M. A. G. (2009). A pleasure working together? The effects of dissimilarity in team member conscientiousness on team temporal processes and individual satisfaction. *Journal of Organizational Behavior, 30*, 379–400. doi:10.1002/job.544

Grande, E., & Taylor, A. (2010). Sampling and coverage issues of telephone surveys used for collecting health information in Australia: Results from a face-to-face survey from 1999 to 2008. *BMC Medical Research Methodology, 10*(1), 77. doi:10.1186/1471-2288-10-77 PMID:20738884

Grosso, M., Castaldo, S., & Grewal, A. (2018). How store attributes impact shoppers' loyalty in emerging countries: An investigation in the Indian retail sector. *Journal of Retailing and Consumer Services, 40*, 117–124. doi:10.1016/j.jretconser.2017.08.024

Hallyburton, A., & Evarts, L. A. (2014). Gender and online health information seeking: A five survey meta-analysis. *Journal of Consumer Health on the Internet, 18*(2), 128–142. doi:10.1080/15398285.2 014.902268

Jaiswal, A. K., & Gupta, S. (2015). The influence of marketing on consumption behavior at the bottom of the pyramid. *Journal of Consumer Marketing, 32*(2), 113–124. doi:10.1108/JCM-05-2014-0996

Kelly, L., Jenkinson, C., & Ziebland, S. (2013). Measuring the effects of online health information for patients: Item generation for an e-health impact questionnaire. *Patient Education and Counseling, 93*(3), 433–438. doi:10.1016/j.pec.2013.03.012 PMID:23598293

Khoja, S., Scott, R. E., Casebeer, A. L., Mohsin, M., Ishaq, A., & Gilani, S. (2007). E-health readiness assessment tools for healthcare institutions in developing countries. *Telemedicine Journal and e-Health, 13*(4), 425–432. doi:10.1089/tmj.2006.0064 PMID:17848110

Kim, N. E., Han, S. S., Yoo, K. H., & Yun, E. K. (2012). The impact of user's perceived ability on online health information acceptance. *Telemedicine Journal and e-Health, 18*(9), 703–708. doi:10.1089/tmj.2011.0277 PMID:23072632

Kontos, E., Blake, K. D., Chou, W. Y., & Prestin, A. (2014). Predictors of eHealth usage: Insights on the digital divide from the Health Information National Trends Survey 2012. *Journal of Medical Internet Research, 16*(7), e172. doi:10.2196/jmir.3117 PMID:25048379

Li, J. H., Land, L. P. W., Ray, P., & Chattopadhyaya, S. (2010). E-Health readiness framework from Electronic Health Records perspective. *International Journal of Internet and Enterprise Management, 6*(4), 326–348. doi:10.1504/IJIEM.2010.035626

Mittal, B. (2017). Facing the Shelf: Four Consumer Decision-making Styles. *Journal of International Consumer Marketing, 29*(5), 303–318. doi:10.1080/08961530.2017.1318732

Petrides, K. V., Mikolajczak, M., Mavroveli, S., Sanchez-Ruiz, M. J., Furnham, A., & Perez-Gonzales, J. C. (2016). Developments in trait emotional intelligence research. *Emotion Review, 8*(4), 335–341. doi:10.1177/1754073916650493

Powell, J., Inglis, N., Ronnie, J., & Large, S. (2011). The characteristics and motivations of online health information seekers: Cross-sectional survey and qualitative interview study. *Journal of Medical Internet Research, 13*(1), e20. doi:10.2196/jmir.1600 PMID:21345783

Rains, S. A. (2007). Perceptions of traditional information sources and use of the World Wide Web to seek health information: Findings from the health information national trends survey. *Journal of Health Communication, 12*(7), 667–680. doi:10.1080/10810730701619992 PMID:17934943

Rezai-Rad, M., Vaezi, R., & Nattagh, F. (2012). E-Health Readiness Assessment Framework in Iran. *Iranian Journal of Public Health, 41*(10), 43–51. PMID:23304661

Shahab, L., Brown, J., Gardner, B., & Smith, S. G. (2014). Seeking health information and support online: Does it differ as a function of engagement in risky health behaviors? Evidence from the health information national trends survey. *Journal of Medical Internet Research, 16*(11), e253. doi:10.2196/jmir.3368 PMID:25380308

Sillence, E., Briggs, P., Harris, P. R., & Fishwick, L. (2007). How do patients evaluate and make use of online health information? *Social Science & Medicine, 64*(9), 1853–1862. doi:10.1016/j.socscimed.2007.01.012 PMID:17328998

Thackeray, R., Crookston, B. T., & West, J. H. (2013). Correlates of health-related social media use among adults. *Journal of Medical Internet Research, 15*(1), e21. doi:10.2196/jmir.2297 PMID:23367505

ADDITIONAL READING

Ahmed, A., Arshad, M. A., Mahmood, A., & Akhtar, S. (2016). Holistic human resource development: Balancing the equation through the inclusion of spiritual quotient. *Journal of Human Values, 22*(3), 165–179. doi:10.1177/0971685816650573

Darvishmotevali, M., Altinay, L., & De Vita, G. (2018). Emotional intelligence and creative performance: Looking through the lens of environmental uncertainty and cultural intelligence. *International Journal of Hospitality Management, 73*, 44–54. doi:10.1016/j.ijhm.2018.01.014

Dubois, C. L., & Dubois, D. A. (2012). Strategic HRM as social design for environmental sustainability in organization. *Human Resource Management, 51*(6), 799–826. doi:10.1002/hrm.21504

El-Chaarani, H. (2016). Exploring the impact of emotional intelligence on portfolio performance: An international exploratory study. *Humanomics, 32*(4), 474–497. doi:10.1108/H-02-2016-0012

Freshman, B., & Rubino, L. (2002). Emotional intelligence: A core competency for health care administrators. *The Health Care Manager, 20*(4), 1–9. doi:10.1097/00126450-200206000-00002 PMID:12083173

Hanefar, S. B., Siraj, S., & Sa'ari, C. Z. (2015). The application of content analysis toward the development of Spiritual Intelligence Model for Human Excellence (SIMHE). *Procedia: Social and Behavioral Sciences, 172*, 603–610. doi:10.1016/j.sbspro.2015.01.409

Khalid, J., Khaleel, M., Janee Ali, A., & Islam, M. (2018). Multiple dimensions of emotional intelligence and their impacts on organizational commitment and job performance. *International Journal of Ethics and Systems, 34*(2), 221–232. doi:10.1108/IJOES-07-2017-0096

Mikolajczak, M., & Van Bellegem, S. (2017). Increasing emotional intelligence to decrease healthcare expenditures: How profitable would it be? *Personality and Individual Differences, 116*, 343–347. doi:10.1016/j.paid.2017.05.014

KEY TERMS AND DEFINITIONS

Benchmarking: A technique for determining competitive advantages and learning about products, services, own operations, by comparing with the best.

Emotional Intelligence: The ability to understand and manage emotions of the client and can make the difference in whether the customer decides to come back to the online health services.

Motivation: Is a problem of temperament: on one hand, we will always meet individuals that are more passionate than others, who are more dedicated to their work, and on the other hand, there are methods likely to contribute to changes in attitude towards work, decisive, both for the success of the individuals in organizations, and for the organization's success on the market..

Online Health Service: The utility obtained by the consumer as a result of interdependent activities based on the client-client relationship and which materialize in a physical, mental and social welfare.

Organization: A system, which includes employers and employees aiming at achieving common objectives.

Organizational Culture: Values and behaviors that contribute to creating a social and psychological environment of an organization.

Performance: The ability of an organization to exploit its environment to access scarce resources.

When Do Working Consumers Become Prosumers?
Exploring Prosumer Characteristics for Organizational Value Creation Strategies

13

Sabina Alina Potra
Politehnica University Timisoara, Romania

Adrian Pugna
Politehnica University Timisoara, Romania

INTRODUCTION

Recent debates have outlined a substantial movement from an organizational dyad to a triad (Gabriel, Korczynski, & Rieder, 2015). The dominant organizational characters, namely the manager and the worker, behold a newcomer, the consumer. Thus, the sphere of consumption is modified and new terms emerge (Fontenelle, 2015). Concepts like the 'working consumer' (Cova, Dalli & Zwick, 2011), 'consum-actor', 'post-consumer' (Firat & Dholakia, 2006) or even 'prosumer'(Cova & Cova 2012; Ritzer & Jurgenson, 2010; Toffler 1980) are blurring the producer and consumer spheres (Cochoy, 2014), without significant delimitation between them.

Working consumers are consumers reconsidered as workers (Cova, Pace, & Skålén (2015), or even 'partial employees' (Mills & Morris, 1986), enrolled for their competencies, either intellectually or physically, with the final scope of consumer exploitation (Arvidsson, 2005). Even if Cochoy (2014) argues that the work of the consumer is not necessarily seen as a chore and depending on the context, it does not automatically transform him/her into a worker; the term 'working consumers' is often associated with self-service activities, where consumers work is needed at the end of the production chain.

Prosumers on the other hand, are seen not only as participants in the co-creation of value (providing work in the last stages of production) but active designers of product and service experiences (Chandler & Chen, 2015). Giannopoulou, Gryszkiewicz and Barlatier (2014) even argue that prosumer participation in the co-creation of value can change the structure and boundaries of service configuration and design. Pitt, Watson, Berthon, Wynn and Zinkhan (2006) and Xie, Bagozzi and Troye (2008) state the fact that prosumption is different than mere customer participation in firm service, delimiting working consumers from prosumers.

BACKGROUND

In the last decade there has been a growing academic interest in different forms of prosumer collaboration (Cova, Kozinets & Shankar, 2007). In practice, prosumers have been associated with value added activities in corporate environments or governmental spheres. Prosumers have the power to create value for themselves and for their peers, but especially for businesses in an open innovation approach

DOI: 10.4018/978-1-7998-3473-1.ch156

(Chesbrough, 2003). Thus, they are becoming an extremely important external partner in delivering added value in a competitive environment. Kotler (1986) argues that managers together with marketing specialists should look for opportunities to facilitate prosumption activities. Companies are motivated to involve prosumers in product or service design at any stage due to several benefits: reduced risk and customer satisfaction (Cova et al., 2011), development of products that match and satisfy customers' needs (Enkel, Perez-Freije & Gassmann, 2005), the design, improvement and marketing promotion of new services (Sigala, 2012).

But we merely have some definitions and guidance for prosumer behavior. How can organizations increase their participation? Knowing prosumers' relevant characteristics will help managers engage them effectively in pursuit of the benefits listed above. In this line of reasoning, the present paper aims to provide a thorough conceptualization of prosumer characteristics in the co-creation context of organizational studies.

The present study seeks to understand how prosumers behave and what makes them co-create alongside companies. Denegri-Knott (2006) suggested that an increased control, information availability, aggregation and participation are triggering consumer power on the web. Gamble and Gilmore (2013) consider that co-creational marketing depends on the degree of consumer control and involvement. But studies of prosumer behaviour and triggering factors are scarce. Thus, our purpose is to uncover the characteristics which make consumers become prosumers and co-create valuable outcomes. With this purpose in mind we have developed the following research questions:

- What is the motivation for prosumption?
- What enables people to prosume?
- Which are the dominant prosumer characteristics companies must take into consideration when designing new co-creative strategies?

The research questions are designed to extend current theoretical frameworks using a theory building qualitative research approach with a high importance for management theory and practice. Because grounded theory (GT) is best used in the absence of hypotheses (Thornberg, 2012), the authors have chosen to use this approach to investigate the characteristics of prosumption.

The objective of this study is to advance the prosumer concept and the co-creational strategies as to enable managers to develop a prosumer-oriented relationship with their customers (Izvercian & Seran, 2013) in a natural pursuit of market position and marketing management advantages.

FOCUS OF THE ARTICLE

Grounded Theory Methodology – Prosumer Characteristics Analysis

Grounded theory (GT), originally developed by the sociologists Glaser and Strauss (1967) and defined as the discovery of theory from data, offers systematic and at the same time flexible guidelines for data collection and analysis to construct theories that consist of abstract conceptualizations of substantive problems that people experience. Accordingly, the present research proposes to identify and analyse prosumer abilities, scope and generic behaviour patterns to better understand the "why" and "how" prosumption takes place.

As the theory-building process occurs via recursive cycling among the case data, emerging theory, and later extant literature (Eisenhardt & Graebner, 2007), GT is built upon two key concepts (Suddaby, 2006): constant comparison (no separation between data collection and analysis) and theoretical sampling (envisages decisions about which data to collect by on-going interpretation of data and emerging conceptual categories). Bryman and Bell (2007) consider the constant comparison and theoretical sampling together with coding (whereby data is broken down into component parts which are given names) and theoretical saturation, the most important tools of GT. These stages of continuous data sampling and data analysis are detailed in Figure 1 which represents the theoretical process of grounded theory development regarding prosumer characteristics.

Figure 1.

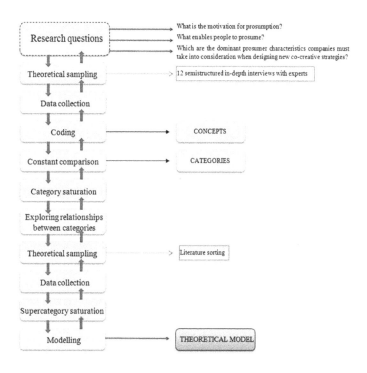

Because theory-building research using cases typically answers research questions that address "how" and "why" in unexplored research areas particularly well (Edmondson & McManus, 2007), we have chosen multiple cases for the likelihood that they will offer theoretical insight and better ground the theory (Eisenhardt & Graebner, 2007).

Due to the fact that the prosumer concept is not yet debated by the public, remaining a topic in the research area of experts, we need to find highly knowledgeable informants who share critical similarities related to our research questions. Thus, for the first theoretical sampling step, a representative homogenous sample of experts from Delft University of Technology were chosen with ages ranging from 28 till 62, both male and female, with 3 to 20 years of experience in research, who view the focal phenomenon from diverse perspectives because they use the prosumer concept in different areas of research (energy, large scale distributed systems, educational games and simulation gaming, system engineering of infrastructures, crisis management, learning organizations, computer science). They research the subject and use the prosumer concept in their projects.

Saturation of the categories has been reached after 12 interviews with 20 hours of observation.

Research based on qualitative interviews contributes to conceptual and theoretical knowledge advancement. From Bryman and Bell (2007)'s major types of interviews, we have chosen the semi-structured interview because it offers the possibility of an a priori organization of the proposed subjects for discussion and the liberty to detect topics and in-depth details based on the respondent's ideas and observations.

The interview guide was built upon 14 open questions, starting with introductory questions about professional area of expertise, projects and interests (for contextualizing their next answers) followed by specific, direct and projective questions regarding the prosumer concept.

The interviews have been placed over a period of three months, in which the interviewees were contacted by e-mail and asked if they are interested to schedule a meeting inside their university, at their workplace (main office or discussion room). The specific location has been chosen because the experts needed to remain in the physical context of their organizational role and therefore focused on their research and professional opinion. The discussions have been tape recorded with the permission of each interviewee to assure a thorough examination of the data in the analysis phase. Each interview recording was fully transcribed for data analysis.

The data coding process for the in-depth interviews with experts was a constant comparison between the theory under construction and theoretically sampling cases. Data from interview notes and transcriptions has been conceptualized line by line, segment by segment, while the particular iterative phenomena in the text has been temporary labeled.

The process of coding has been accomplished by a sequence of coding steps (Strauss & Corbin, 1990): open coding (labels and categorizes phenomena, grouping concepts at an abstract level), axial coding (develops main categories and their sub-categories) and selective coding (integrates the categories to form the initial theoretical framework).

The analysis started with the chronologic order of the interview data and the retrieved codes have been numbered sequentially, adding new codes with each interview data analysis. Because the codes are always changing to fit the right data, the constant comparison of data has been used to find similarities and differences between them. Clusters of initial codes have been formed till basic categories emerged.

In this analysis stage for each case study (transcribed interview) a memo has been established. Memos are concisely written reports of the case study analysis. They work like a set of ideas written in a bank of concepts and relations between concepts, which will furthermore lead towards a written theory.

The open coding phase comprises a total number of 12 memos which contain 417 concepts. It continues with an axial coding stage where initial codes have been explored to reveal which of them best cover the ideas drawn from collected data. Therefore, the complex codes are raised at a conceptual preliminary category level. For the formation of categories two main criteria have been taken into consideration (Van Staalduinen, 2012): clarity (the main theme of a category must be clearly stated even from the title and must emerge from its associated key-words) and distinction (categories must be different from one another to avoid confusion). Each category has specific notes for the ease in its further analysis.

The constant comparison process continued until all possible categories have been concluded.

The category notes have been completed with properties and dimensions for each category. Properties have been established according to associated key-words, unlike dimensions in which attached concepts have been used to ascertain the qualitative extent of properties. In conclusion, the axial coding phase comprises 31 categories based on 401 of the concepts retrieved from the open coding phase, 16 concepts have been abandoned due to lack of relevance for the present study.

The selective coding represents the last step towards a first sketch of the theoretical model of prosumer characteristics. It explores the relations between categories in the search of the core category to which all the codes will furthermore relate to. For this reason, the open access SocNetV tool (Kalamaras, 2010) has been used. It enables a visual understanding of the strong relations between the 31 already chosen categories (Figure 2).

Figure 2.

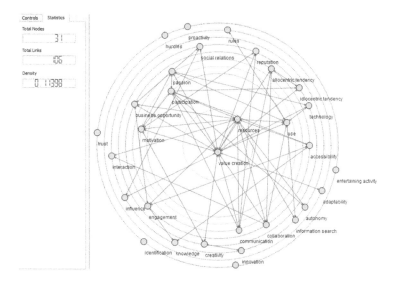

Findings

From Figure 2 we can easily see the core variable "value creation" which has the strongest links with the majority of other categories. The next strong category is represented by "resources". Therefore, the main prosumer characteristics are envisaged by these two key-words which can be translated into production of value (value creation) through the consumption of resources. Based on the 31 categories, the relations between them and the analysis observations, a hierarchy of the most important categories has been realized together with their distribution in six specific groups called 'super categories' (Table 1).

Table 1. Super categories formed based on initial categories

Super categories Initial categories	Creative potential	Motivation	Social interaction	Engagement	Used resources	Objective
1	adaptability	entertaining activities	collaboration	accessibility	search for information	business opportunity
2	awareness	motivation	communication	autonomy	rules	allocentric tendency
3	value creation	passion	influence	trust	resources	idiocentric tendency
4	creativity	reputation	social relations	identification	technology	
5	knowledge		interaction	participation	use	
6	innovation			hurdles		
7				proactivity		

The value creation category represents the core category and it is included in the most representative super category of the research, which encapsulates the most relevant prosumer feature, his or her *creative potential*. Without this feature, prosumption would not be possible. This creative potential is typical for a flexible person, aware of his or her potential and creativity level, capable of using accumulated knowledge for value creation. Innovation is a final feature, the result of the creative potential, which offers the most important competitive advantage in the market. But without *motivation*, prosumers would not act. It comprises entertaining activities, passion and reputation.

Prosumers are compelled to interact in the majority of their activities, and *social interaction* is one of their distinctive traits. Proactive prosumers are living for the purpose of influencing others being also affected by the social relations they develop through collaboration and communication. Their *engagement* takes place only if the respective activity allows access, the desired autonomy and develops trust. The feature known as *proactive* facilitates engagement due to personal initiative. Prosumer participation can suffer from hurdles if there is a need for anonymity or a lack of some of the features listed before.

We cannot talk about engagement if there are no *resources* for the prosumer to use. If the creative potential means production, the use of resources designates consumption. These two concepts are complementing each other. Prosumers are engaged through their search for information and use of technology. Rules are also important, even if they refer to system rules of security or the rules which define responsibilities in consumption.

The objective through which the prosumer realizes different activities can be oriented towards the commercial sphere becoming a business opportunity, towards satisfying personal wishes and needs (idiocentric tendency) or towards helping others (allocentric tendency).

Table 2. Literature findings regarding the prosumer concept

Authors	Findings
Toffler (1980)	- a prosumer is a person that *creates* goods, services or experiences for his *own use or satisfaction*, rather than for sale or exchange - the prosumer is a person who *produces* and *consumes* his own output
Kotler (1986)	- the prosumer is an individual that *produces* many of his *own* goods - prosumers are *another market segment* for which specialists will need to develop new opportunities and research tools
Tapscott and Williams (2008)	- true prosumption entails deeper and earlier *engagement* in design processes and products that facilitate customer hacking and remixing - prosumers are able to *create value for everyone*, not just for their *own use* and they are *sharing* it globally - prosumers *co-innovate* and co-produce the products they *consume*
Humphreys and Grayson (2008)	- prosumers appear when consumers are *producing exchange value* for companies, producing a fundamental change in economic organization
Ritzer (2010); Ritzer and Jurgenson (2010)	- prosumers are seen as individuals who *take on tasks* from corporations and *produce* value in the process
Hellman (2010)	- prosumption is when we *make a contribution* in the *usage value* of a product or service for *own use*, without which the product process remains incomplete, regardless if there is or not a *payment* for his activity - the prosumer is seen as a consumer that *makes a contribution* in the usefulness of a product or service that he furthermore *consumes* therefore *adding* both work and *value* for the market

Literature Sorting and Discussions

The study of the grounded theory approach is continued with a second theoretical sampling stage named literature sorting. Thornberg (2012) defines bibliographic analysis as a constructive method of grounded theory, which gives liberty to the researcher without forcing data. Literature sorting is left until this moment for not jeopardizing data from the start with preconceived ideas (Glaser, 1998). By comparing the emergent theory of super categories to the existing literature, the internal validity of the theory is reached. The literature review has taken into consideration the most significant scientific contributions to the prosumer concept definition (Table2).

From this literature review it can be concluded, that prosumers start as consumers who act/contribute/create (value production) due to engagement (involvement in an activity), through usage (resource consumption) for a purpose/objective (own use, others' use).

Engagement is an essential feature for prosumption because it envisages a consumer role expansion that changes consumption behaviour. If usual consumers are defined by passivity, prosumers are known as active actors in co-production. But an active role (participation/engagement) in production activities does not automatically make someone a prosumer. Engagement alone does not transform a consumer into a prosumer. In this line of reasoning, Tapscott and Williams (2008) argue that prosumption is more than customization because customization entails mixing and matching pre specified components, which limits flexibility and innovation, considering that flexibility of thought is important for innovative results.

Ritzer and Jurgenson (2010), on the other hand, associate the prosumer concept with the self-service domain. They argue that prosumers are involved consumers 'put at work' by smart companies in the end phases of the production process through self-service technologies (SSTs) or Do It Yourself (DIY) techniques, like unpaid employees. These tasks do not comprise flexibility of thought, originality or a real added value (contribution). Therefore, customization and self-service/DIY techniques are not able to offer flexibility and autonomy for prosumption to occur.

Based on the present analysis and literature sorting, the main trait that differentiates prosumers from other market segments is represented by their latent qualities and abilities that may be developed and lead to creative contribution. Without a certain amount of creativity or originality, they do not have the power to make a contribution (to add value), and the provided work is solely self-service (they remain in the consumer segment). The creativity dimension refers to the productive thinking, which is necessary for today's urge for innovation (Seran, Kolfshoten & Izvercian, 2013).

If an engaged person cannot become a prosumer without creativity, both creativity and engagement are the consequences of adequate *motivation*.

Social interaction is also seen as an important prosumer characteristic because social environment is claimed to influence both the level and the frequency of creative behaviour (Amabile, Conti, Coon, Lazenby & Herron, 1996). Tapscott and Williams (2008) argue that even the participation in an online community makes a contribution to the new digital commons, due to the fact that community members engage and support each other in solving problems and generating ideas.

The use of resources, as seen from the interview analysis, is the second must connected feature, enabling a creative output. Without the consumption of resources we cannot produce value. Therefore, the fifth major prosumer characteristic is considered to be the *use of resources*.

Prosumers engage due to an adequate motivational drive, create by using resources and collaborating with peers or being influenced by their social environment, but the ultimate *objective* of prosumption can differ. If the motivation for prosumption represents in the majority of cases an unconscious impulse for engagement, a specific objective becomes a target wilful planned, an ambition toward which effort is directed.

The Prosumer Characteristics Theoretical Model

After the conceptualization of the super categories, the 31 categories have been merged and reinterpreted based on literature sorting, brainstorming and discussions. From the undertaken research, a honeycomb structure of prosumer characteristics (Figure 3) is built based on six main prosumer characteristics: creative potential, motivation, social interaction, engagement, resources used and objective, each with specific concepts.

Figure 3.

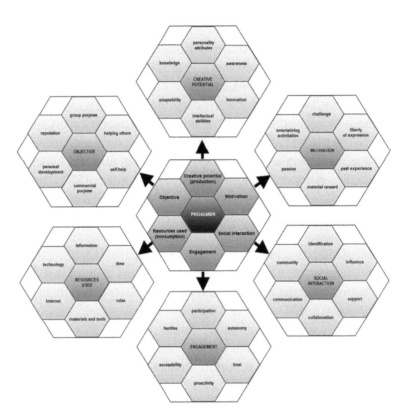

The prosumer is inserted in the middle as the starting point of the proposed model. For each main prosumer characteristic, specific honeycombs are formed. In each specific honeycomb the main prosumer characteristic is inserted in the middle to envisage that the elements it comprises organize around it. In the following, each main concept will be presented in a sub-heading with an adequate definition based on literature, a link to the prosumer concept and citations from the in-depth interviews undertaken in the qualitative research to give an example of how it was recognized as an aspect of prosumption.

The Creative Potential

13

Creative potential, according to Kristensson, Gustafsson and Archer (2004), is the ability to generate creative ideas defined as original (new), valuable (solve a perceived problem) and realizable (can be transformed into a commercial product). They also agree that customers should be thought of as a valuable source to initiate exploitable ideas. Izvercian and Seran (2013b) claim that if a customer is adequately empowered, he or she is likely to become a creator of value, namely to transform into a prosumer. Therefore, creative potential, as noted in the literature sorting and discussion section of the present article, represents a main prosumer characteristic. It was also recognized as such by the expert in education and technology who stated that "I consider creativity and involvement as the essential factors for prosumption."

Creative potential is composed by: adaptability, intellectual abilities, knowledge, specific creative personal attributes, awareness of self-competence and value creation/innovation.

Adaptability to different situations determined by flexibility of mind is considered by Dundon (2002) as a trait of a creative thinker; flexibility of thought makes the difference between a personal touch and a standard setting, an adaptive characteristic of the prosumer. In this line of reasoning, the expert in crisis management defined prosumers as "creative in handling a situation and also in using technology completely different from what it was designed for."

The *intellectual abilities* refer to the confluence of synthetic, analytic and practical contextual abilities (Sternberg, 1999). To make a creative contribution a person needs to see problems in new ways, surpassing conventional thinking.

Knowledge is necessary to make a contribution to a field (Sternberg, 1999). It requires preliminary understanding of the field for an entrenched perspective for the purpose of moving it forward. Too much knowledge can hinder creativity due to preconceptions but also a low amount of knowledge can limit creativity due to domain gaps. The lesson learned expert explained that "this is why programming communities stay relatively small, because if you want to prosume, you have to possess extensive knowledge of programming languages."

Creativity is also characterized by specific *personality attributes* as perseverance, self-efficacy, and willingness to overcome obstacles, to take risks and tolerate ambiguity (Sternberg, 1999), together with openness to new experiences, stand up to conventions and act in creative ways. Individuals engage into an activity when they perceive themselves as capable of doing a specific task, becoming *aware* of their competences. Ryan and Deci (2000) argue that to adopt a goal, it requires that one feels efficacious with respect to it, supporting the importance of competence awareness. The interviewed experts also argued that: "when teenagers become prosumers, they are aware of their creativity", "the prosumer seems the perfect entrepreneur, taking risks and creatively handling difficult situations."

Innovation represents the successful implementation of creative ideas within an organization (Amabile et al., 1996). The crisis management expert claimed that "prosumers are very creative and innovative to me, designing and using technology different than the rest."

Motivation

Motivation involves an individual's reasons for engaging in a task (Amabile et al., 1996). Motivation concerns the "why" of actions (Ryan & Deci, 2000), becoming critical for prosumption. Regarding the incentives for prosumption, the opinions of the interviewed experts differ. Some claimed that "financial incentives are most important", others considered "a fun activity triggers prosumption", all concluding that "there is no motivation to match the needs of all prosumers". Therefore, motivation can be represented by: passion, entertaining activities, challenging activities, liberty of expression, past experience and material rewards.

We can make a distinction between intrinsic and extrinsic motivation. Intrinsic motivation reflects the natural human propensity to learn and assimilate (Ryan & Deci, 2000) and also refers to doing an activity because it is inherently interesting or enjoyable.

Passion refers to an interest in some kind of work (Amabile et al., 1996). Ritzer and Jurgenson (2010) confirm the fact that prosumers enjoy, even love what they are doing and are willing to devote long hours to it for no pay. The expert in educational games argues that "there are a lot of people that find technology interesting and start to produce, you have a lot of people that find a game interesting and then learn themselves how to program in order to mod it. So I think it depends on where your interest lies, based on that you are eager to act."

Entertaining activities (e.g. online games which trigger addiction) can mobilize masses of consumers to transform them into prosumers. Geo-cashing is an example of an entertaining activity provided by the expert in systems engineering of infrastructure due to the fact that "it is entertaining, like the joy to solve a puzzle."

The *challenge* of a task has the potential to trigger creativity (Amabile et al., 1996). The crowdsourcing phenomenon materializes in all kind of contests, where companies promote a competition and launch a challenge for prosumers to improve something or to find a solution for a problem they are confronted with. The majority of the interview experts argued that "the main incentive for clients to become prosumers is the product or service which is not there", namely the need for a new one. The challenge to create the product or service you need is extremely motivating.

Liberty of expression is also known as self-expression. Multiple experts agree that prosumers want to stand out of the crowd, to share information and experience, to express their thoughts, ultimately to "make their voice heard". The expert in education and technology argued "As a prosumer, I want to influence people and express my opinion, therefore I blog."

Past experience determines habits or product familiarity and prior knowledge. It also refers to others' experiences or creative results that are setting goals or aspirations that direct action (Price, Arnould, & Zinkhan, 2004). Creativity in prosumption, as the education and technology expert opinions, has a lot to do with past experience. "Once I have taken part in an activity which I did not know and everything went bad. But the second time, I could be more creative because I had experience with the tools."

Extrinsic motivation refers to doing something because it leads to a separable outcome, an instrumental value (Ryan & Deci, 2000). *Material rewards* (coupons, money, tickets, products or free services) used alone tend to have a negative influence on creativity, but used together with intrinsic motivation, they increase creativity. The game expert argues in this direction "if I get paid to play a game, then, depending on the amount of money, I will play it. But as soon as they stop paying me and the game has not an addictive quality that engages me to play, I would probably stop."

Social Interaction

Sigala (2012) opinions that in order to fully exploit customer creative potential we must enable customers to perceive themselves as members of a group or community and create a platform and a community environment that will be mentally stimulating, enjoyable, entertaining and a source of fun for active customers. Therefore, social interaction is composed by the following sub-elements: community, communication, collaboration, support, influence and identification.

A prosumer is not able to create without the help of others. Csikszentmihalyi (1997) estimates that creativity results from the interaction of: a culture with symbolic rules, a person who brings novelty into the symbolic domain and a field of experts who recognize and validate the innovation. The experts (*communities*) are extremely important due to the fact that, by social interactions, the creative idea is presented and validated as valuable and worth pursuing. The expert in lessons learned argues that "I used discussion forums to give and receive feedback in problematic areas or programming, I helped my community and they helped me."

In groups, prosumers are able to *communicate*. *Collaboration* refers to working together for a purpose (Seran & Izvercian, 2014). Prosumers form communities online, share information, collaborate and swap tips, tools and product hacks (Tapscott & Williams, 2008), therefore, working together for everyone's gain. The educational games expert has noticed that recent games are designed as a social environment, "so you can both work with other people or you can share your own achievements and experience with others. If you share your experience apparently the enjoyment of the experience becomes slightly larger or more intense."

Support through prosumption has been widely seen on forums and the health domain is researching this particular feature for peer support in psychological and physical recovery. The *influence* element of social interaction can be understood as prosumers influence others or are being influenced by the community they belong to. The expert in simulation gaming concluded that "people have different visions and they inspire one another by collaborating." Also, the more consumers *identify* themselves with the group, the more involved they become in the co-creation process and put greater effort into the collaborative contribution.

Engagement

As discussed earlier, engagement is a very important prosumer characteristic, a differentiating factor for prosumption in general (Izvercian & Seran, 2013b). Engagement comprises: participation, autonomy, trust, proactive behaviour, accessibility and hurdles.

Tapscott and Williams (2008) envisage the new model of prosumption formed by customers who *participate* in the creation of products in an active and on-going way. Thus, prosumption starts with participation. We use the term engagement for both participation (observable behaviour) and involvement (psychological state). Involvement becomes activated when personal needs, values or self-concept are stimulated within a given situation (Price, Arnould and Zinkhan, 2004).

Engagement is maintained by a facilitating environment. *Autonomy* refers especially to having a choice in how to play, accomplish tasks, and contribute in some form. The expert in learning organizations shared a personal engagement model in education: "the elements important in this approach are trust and autonomy which belong to the idea of participation". *Trust* in a brand for example can be understood as the consumer tendency to believe that the specific brand can keep its promises regarding performance (Chaudhuri & Holbrook, 2001).

Proactive behaviour determines the ease in future engagement. But trust, autonomy and a proactive behaviour appear when users are given *accessibility* to an activity, product, service, tool, community or experience. The large scales distribution systems expert estimated that "by providing information to people you allow them to take decisions." Also another expert emphasized the fact that "prosumption appeared in some domains when the technology became accessible." Therefore, the main *hurdle* for engagement can be understood by the absence of the elements which trigger and sustain it.

Resources Used

Resource allocation to projects is directly related to the projects' creativity levels. This prosumer characteristic is formed by the following elements: materials and tools, time, technology, Internet, rules and information.

The consumption of (material or immaterial) resources in prosumption is mandatory. In the physical world we use mainly *materials and tools* to engage in an activity.

Time is also a valuable resource. Time pressure is generally associated with high creativity when it regards challenging work and not workload pressure (Amabile et al., 1996). Like one of our experts emphasized, "social networking, blogs, user reviews, I just don't have time for them. I sometimes think what I would say but I don't ever come to write about it. Prosumption is a time issue."

Technology was an important element for the interviewed experts, because it enables prosumers to actively participate in the experience, to appropriate the goods to new uses, to combine and alter the goods to create entirely new experiences.

With the rise of the *Internet* and Web 2.0, considered means of presumption byRitzer and Jurgenson (2010), consumers are now able to produce their own content and interact with one another. As the expert in educational gaming emphasized, "the Internet provides a platform for prosumption." Ultimately, the main resource we are handling and by which we are empowered is *information*.

Objective

We become prosumers due to adequate motivation, but we continue to prosume due to the objective we are trying to achieve. Price, Arnould and Zinkhan (2004) argue that by pursuing goals, motivated people may feel interest, excitement, anxiety, passion, engagement and flow. Prosumer objectives are consistent with their subjective culture. As Triandis (1995) identified, people have two opposed tendencies for different contexts: the idiocentric (when focusing on personal goals, needs and rights) and the allocentric tendency (when prioritizing communal goals). Thus, the six objectives we have proposed can be classified into allocentric tendencies (helping others, group purpose) and idiocentric tendencies (self-help, commercial purpose, personal development and reputation).

People can gain social value from joy of group activities with persons of similar interests. We call this objective *group purpose*. But in the same time people contribute also because they desire the experience of having social ties with others. This objective is oriented towards *helping others*, and it is mostly seen in discussion forums where as the lessons learned expert argues, "people discuss programming language and help one another." But, as the educational games expert emphasized, "it depends on the person, some people actually want to *help others* and others just want to gain social status." Therefore, prosumers can have different objectives, some want to share, to contribute for the sake of others; some are oriented towards their own goals.

Self-realization or personal development is the main reason people blog, act as DJs without being paid for that, take leadership roles in online communities and engage in practices of 'prosumerism' (Tapscott & Williams, 2008). This objective motivates prosumers on the long run to learn continuously from all experiences as considered by the interviewed experts and to engage in activities which enhance a positive sense of self (Csikszentmihalyi, 1997).

The *self-help* element has a distinct purpose. It refers mainly at engaging in an activity for the final purpose to achieve the desire consumption experience or a better quality for the product/service (Kotler, 1986). As several experts argued, "when you modify a game in your own spare time, you do it for yourself" and "some people participate just because they like to create things."

The concept of *reputation* appears for a validity assessment of self. The questioned experts concluded that "ultimately everyone wants to be recognized by their contribution to a certain community or society", and "especially in the programming world, users create, modify and contribute open source for status."

The last possible objective of a prosumer can be oriented towards the commercial aspect of his or her work. A *commercial purpose* is typical for a category of prosumers who create not entirely for self or others to share, but also for sale (Izvercian & Seran, 2013b), because, as the computer science expert claimed, "they are as capable or even more capable as companies to design and produce useful new products."

SOLUTIONS AND RECOMMENDATIONS

The limitations of the study emerge from the principle of contextualization of Klein and Myers (1999) due to the fact that the separate messages of the experts interviewed may be dependent on the global context of the organization they belong to. Therefore, further extended research in other research institutions focused on the prosumer concept can provide a wider generalization and strengthening of prosumer characteristics. The conclusions of the study are also limited by external validity; we cannot generalize the prosumer characteristics model for all situations, people or stimuli. But the present research is a step closer to a more thorough understanding of the prosumer trend in today's knowledge society. Other studies on this topic envisage the construction of practical strategic steps for prosumer inclusion in corporate product or service development based on the model of prosumer characteristics.

FUTURE RESEARCH DIRECTIONS

Scholars and practitioners alike feel the need to better understand the prosumer concept and its characteristics in the broad organizational culture for an adequate management of the new active consumer generation. Based on the findings of the present article, new business trends and strategies can emerge. By addressing prosumer characteristics, organizations can design engaging information technology architecture, build marketing 4.0 strategies and collective intelligence networks, improve customer relationship management, outsource intellectual capital and promote its offer in new ways. Governmental organizations may develop open innovation platforms and scholars can use prosumer characteristics for delineating prosumer-oriented management alternatives to current management practices.

CONCLUSION

Based on observations and literature considerations, three research questions have been proposed, which, adequately answered can advance theory and practice towards the development of specific targeted strategies for co-creation. With the help of the grounded theory methodology, the main motivational drives for prosumption have been analysed. The incentives for prosumption have been classified in intrinsic and extrinsic motivational elements, each examined and explored both by a literature review and expert data. Second, it has been revealed what enables prosumers to act and contribute.

The most important prosumer characteristics have been scrutinized for an accurate model construction, with the final purpose of answering the third research question for a further development of an effective design for new prosumer-oriented co-creative strategies. The advancement of the prosumer concept through theory will ultimately lead towards prosumer management for innovative organizational and social results. The findings can be applied to a wide sphere of domains. The gaming industry needs an engaging design and a continuous communication and collaboration with users for game improvement. In this situation, the prosumer characteristics may determine new strategies and partnership ideas. The tendency for open government also needs to address prosumer characteristics for innovative projects and engaging citizen contributions. Marketing specialists use crowd sourcing contests for loyalty building and customer attraction. Social media platforms are based on prosumer co-creation. In so many contexts and industries, prosumers are key for continuous and innovative development. Therefore, by taking into consideration prosumer features, specialists can better design platforms, projects or campaigns for prosumer engagement and creative outsourcing.

REFERENCES

Amabile, T. M., Conti, R., Coon, H., Lazenby, J., & Herron, M. (1996). Assessing the Work Environment for Creativity. *Academy of Management Journal*, *39*, 1154–1184.

Arvidsson, A. (2005). Brands: A Critical Perspective. *Journal of Consumer Culture*, *5*(2), 235–258. doi:10.1177/1469540505053093

Bryman, A., & Bell, E. (2007). *Business Research Methods*. Oxford University Press.

Chandler, J., & Chen, S. (2015). Prosumer motivations in service experiences. *Journal of Service Theory and Practice*, *25*(2), 220–239. doi:10.1108/JSTP-09-2013-0195

Chaudhuri, A., & Holbrook, M. B. (2001). The Chain of Effects from Brand Trust and Brand Affect to Brand Performance: The Role of Brand Loyalty. *Journal of Marketing*, *65*(2), 81–93. doi:10.1509/jmkg.65.2.81.18255

Chesbrough, H. (2003). *Open Innovation: The New Imperative for Creating and Profiting from Technology*. Harvard Business School Press.

Cochoy, F. (2014). Consumers at work, or curiosity at play? Revisiting the prosumption/value cocreation debate with smartphones and two-dimensional bar codes. *Marketing Theory*, *15*(2), 1–21.

Cova, B., & Cova, V. (2012). On the Road to Prosumption: Marketing Discourse and the Development of Consumer Competencies. *Consumption Markets & Culture*, *15*(2), 149–168. doi:10.1080/10253866.2012.654956

Cova, B., Dalli, D., & Zwick, D. (2011). Critical Perspectives on Consumers' Role as 'Producers': Broadening the Debate on Value Co-creation in Marketing Processes. *Marketing Theory*, *11*(3), 231–241. doi:10.1177/1470593111408171

Cova, B., Kozinets, R. V., & Shankar, A. (2007). *Consumer Tribes*. Butterworth.

Cova, B., Pace, S., & Shålén, P. (2015). Marketing with working consumers: The case of a carmaker and its brand community. *Organization*, *22*(5), 882–701. doi:10.1177/1350508414566805

13

Csikszentmihalyi, M. (1997). *Creativity. Flow and the psychology of discovery and invention.* Harper Perennial.

Denegri-Knott, J. (2006). Consumers behaving badly: Deviation or innovation? Power struggles on the web. *Journal of Consumer Behaviour, 5*(1), 82–94. doi:10.1002/cb.45

Dundon, E. (2002). *The Seeds of Innovation. Cultivating the Synergy that Fosters New Ideas.* AMACOM.

Edmondson, A. C., & McManus, S. E. (2007). Methodological fit in organizational field research. *Academy of Management Review, 32*(4), 1155–1179. doi:10.5465/amr.2007.26586086

Eisenhardt, K. M., & Graebner, M. E. (2007). Theory building from cases: Opportunities and challenges. *Academy of Management Journal, 50*(1), 25–32. doi:10.5465/amj.2007.24160888

Enkel, E., Perez-Freije, J., & Gassmann, O. (2005). Minimizing market risk through customer integration in new product development: Learning from bad practice. *Creativity and Innovation Management, 14*(4), 425–437. doi:10.1111/j.1467-8691.2005.00362.x

Firat, A. F., & Dholakia, N. (2006). Theoretical and Philosophical Implications of Postmodern Debates: Some Challenges to Modern Marketing. *Marketing Theory, 6*(2), 123–162. doi:10.1177/1470593106063981

Fontenelle, I. A. (2015). Organizations as producers of consumers. *Organization, 22*(5), 644–660. doi:10.1177/1350508415585029

Gabriel, Y., Korczynski, M., & Rieder, K. (2015). Organizations and their consumers: Bridging work and consumption. *Organization, 22*(5), 629–643. doi:10.1177/1350508415586040

Gamble, J., & Gilmore, A. (2013). A new era of consumer marketing? An application of co-creational marketing in the music industry. *European Journal of Marketing, 47*(11/12), 1859–1888. doi:10.1108/EJM-10-2011-0584

Giannopoulou, E., Gryszkiewicz, L., & Barlatier, P.-J. (2014). Creativity for service innovation: A practice-based perspective. *Managing Service Quality, 24*(1), 23–44. doi:10.1108/MSQ-03-2013-0044

Glaser, B. G. (1998). *Doing grounded theory: Issues and discussions.* Sociology Press.

Glaser, B. G., & Strauss, A. L. (1967). *The discovery of grounded theory: Strategies for qualitative research.* Transactions.

Hellmann, K. U. (2010). Eine inführung, Prosumer Revisited: Zur Aktualität einer Debatte. Wiesbaden: VS, Verlag für Sozialwissenschaften 36.

Humphreys, A., & Grayson, K. (2008). The Intersecting Roles of Consumer and Producer: A Critical Perspective on Co-production, Co-creation and Prosumption. *Sociology Compass, 2*(3), 2. doi:10.1111/j.1751-9020.2008.00112.x

Izvercian, M., & Seran, S. (2013a). An Extended CRM model: Prosumer-oriented Relationship Management Tools and Their Functionalities. *Applied Mechanics and Materials, 411-414*, 2391–2394. doi:10.4028/www.scientific.net/AMM.411-414.2391

Izvercian, M., & Seran, S. (2013b). The Web 2.0 and the globalization impact on new consumer emergence and classification. *Advances in Intelligent Systems Research, 44*, 158–161. doi:10.2991/icemss.2013.42

Klein, H. H., & Myers, M. D. (1999). A Set of Principles for Conducting and Evaluating Interpretive Field Studies in Information Systems. *Management Information Systems Quarterly*, *23*(1), 67–93. doi:10.2307/249410

Kotler, P. (1986). The Prosumer Movement, a New Challenge for Marketers' NA. *Advances in Consumer Research. Association for Consumer Research (U. S.)*, *13*, 510–513.

Kristensson, P., Gustafsson, A., & Archer, T. (2004). Harnessing the Creative Potential among Users. *Journal of Product Innovation Management*, *21*(1), 4–14. doi:10.1111/j.0737-6782.2004.00050.x

Mills, P. K., & Morris, J. H. (1986). Clients as 'Partial' Employees of Service Organizations: Role Development in Client Participation. *Academy of Management Review*, *11*(4), 726–735.

Pitt, L. F., Watson, R. T., Berthon, P., Wynn, D., & Zinkhan, G. (2006). The penguin's window: Corporate brands from an open-source perspective. *Journal of the Academy of Marketing Science*, *34*(2), 115–127. doi:10.1177/0092070305284972

Price, L. L., Arnould, E. J., & Zinkhan, G. M. (2004). *Consumers* (2nd ed.). McGraw-Hill Irwin.

Ritzer, G. (2010). Focusing on the Prosumer: On Correcting an Error in the History of Social Theory. *Prosumer Revisited, 1*, 61-79.

Ritzer, G., & Jurgenson, N. (2010). Production, Consumption, Prosumption. The nature of capitalism in the age of the digital 'prosumer'. *Journal of Consumer Culture*, *10*(1), 13–36. doi:10.1177/1469540509354673

Ryan, R. M., & Deci, E. L. (2000). Intrinsic and Extrinsic Motivations: Classic Definitions and New Directions. *Contemporary Educational Psychology*, *25*(1), 54–67. doi:10.1006/ceps.1999.1020 PMID:10620381

Seran, S. A., Kolfshoten, G., & Izvercian, M. (2013). Consumer Behaviour Elements for Innovative Co-Production of Value. *Lecture Notes in Management Science*, *15*, 70–75.

Seran (Potra), S. & Izvercian, M. (2014). Prosumer Engagement in Innovation Strategies – The Prosumer Creativity and Focus Model. *Management Decision*, *52*(10), 1968–1980. doi:10.1108/MD-06-2013-0347

Sigala, M. (2012). *Web 2.0 and Customer Involvement in New Service Development: A Framework, Cases and Implications. In The Handbook of creativity.* Cambridge University Press.

Strauss, A., & Corbin, J. M. (1990). *Basics of qualitative research: Grounded theory procedures and techniques.* Sage Publications, Inc.

Suddaby, R. (2006). From the editors: What GT is not. Academy of Management Journal, 49, 633-642.

Tapscott, D., & Williams, A. D. (2008). *Wikinomics. How Mass Collaboration Changes Everything.* Penguin Group.

Thornberg, R. (2012). Informed Grounded Theory. *Scandinavian Journal of Educational Research*, *56*(3), 243–259. doi:10.1080/00313831.2011.581686

Toffler, A. (1980). *The Third Wave.* Bantam Books.

Tourism. (n.d.). *Social Media in Travel, Tourism and Hospitality: Theory, Practice and Cases*, Ashgate Publishing Limited 25-37.

Triandis, H. C. (1995). *Individualism and Collectivism.* Westview Press.

Van Staalduinen, J. P. (2012). *Gamers on Games and Gaming: Implications for Educational Game Design* (Thesis Disertation). Technishe Universiteit Delft, The Netherlands.

Xie, C., Bagozzi, R. P., & Troye, S. V. (2008). Trying to prosume: Toward a theory of consumers as co-creators of value. *Journal of the Academy of Marketing Science, 36*(1), 109–122. doi:10.100711747-007-0060-2

ADDITIONAL READING

Potra, S. (2017). What Defines a Prosumer? An Insight in Participative Consumer Behaviour, *Proceedings of the 5th International Conference on Management, Leadership and Governance*, 380-385.

Potra, S., Branea, A., & Izvercian, M. (2015). How to Foster Prosumption for Value Co-creation? The Open Government development Plan, *Proceedings of the 15th European Conference on eGovernment*, 239-245.

Potra, S., Izvercian, M., & Ivascu, L. (2015). Prosumer-Oriented Relationship Management Architecture for the Innovative Enterprise. *Applied Mechanics and Materials, 701-702*, 1294–1297. doi:10.4028/www.scientific.net/AMM.701-702.1294

Potra, S., Izvercian, M., & Miclea, S. (2016). Changes in CRM Approach: Refined Functional Blocks for Customer Creative Engagement in Services. *International Journal of Information Systems in the Service Sector, 8*(1), 45–57. doi:10.4018/IJISSS.2016010104

Ritzer, G. (2018). *The McDonaldization of Society: Into the Digital Age.* SAGE Publications Inc.

Surowiecki, J. (2005). *The Wisdom of Crowds.* Anchor.

Tapscott, D. (2008). *Grown Up Digital: How the Net Generation is Changing Your World.* McGraw-Hill Education.

Wuebben, J. (2017). *Future marketing: Winning in the prosumer age.* Content Launch Press.

KEY TERMS AND DEFINITIONS

Co-Creation: The result of a joint creative collaboration between an organization and its customer, with benefits for both parties.

Consumer Engagement: The participation and psychological involvement of the consumer in the creation of products, experiences, or services with an organization.

Creativity: The production of something novel which is perceived as original and valuable by significant others.

Grounded Theory: A qualitative research method that builds theories from various forms of data (case studies, interviews, observations) through theoretical sampling and constant data comparison.

In-Depth Interview: A semi-structured interview based on an adaptable interview guide for information exploration.

Prosumer: A consumer who exceeds his/her role by creatively engaging and co-producing value alongside an organization or platform.

Technology: The principles and processes needed for the development of useful tools.

Eye Tracker Technology in Sports Sponsorship Research

Ho Keat Leng

(iD) https://orcid.org/0000-0002-7349-6540

Nanyang Technological University, Singapore

Philip Phua

Nanyang Technological University, Singapore

INTRODUCTION

Sports sponsorship is a common marketing strategy for many commercial organisations. While the objective for sponsoring a sports event can vary across companies, many companies see sponsorship as a means to raise awareness and increase profit (Fullerton, 2010; Mullin, Hardy, & Sutton, 2007; Walliser, 2003). Coupled with the large financial cost in sponsoring sports events, there has been much interest in examining the effectiveness of sports sponsorship particularly in terms of the recall rate of sponsored brands (Walliser, 2003). While it has been established that sports sponsorship is generally effective, there are still many unanswered questions in this area.

In recent years, eye trackers have been employed to provide deeper insights in sports sponsorship research. While the use of eye trackers is established in other research areas, its use in sports sponsorship research is still relatively new. The aim of this paper is to provide an overview of the potential contributions and methodological challenges in the use of eye trackers in sports sponsorship research. The paper will conclude with a discussion on the future directions of sports sponsorship research using other technologies.

BACKGROUND

Many research studies in sports sponsorship have focused on whether spectators are able to recall the sponsors after watching an event (Chadwick & Thwaites, 2005; Cornwell & Humphreys, 2013; Meenaghan & O'Sullivan, 2013; Walliser, 2003). As spectators of sports events are exposed to sponsors at the sporting venues for a prolonged period of time, it is not unexpected that spectators will be able to recall sponsors (Bennett, 1999; Walliser, 2003). Research across many sports including American football (Moore, Pickett, & Grove, 1999; Newell, Henderson, & Wu, 2001), basketball (Maxwell & Lough, 2009; Turley & Shannon, 2000), car racing (Kinney, McDaniel, & DeGaris, 2008), cricket (Boshoff & Gerber, 2008), soccer (Bennett, 1999; Biscaia, Correia, Ross, & Rosado, 2014; Dekhil, 2010; J. H. Lee & Bang, 2005), swimming (Leng, 2017) and tennis (Herrmann, Corneille, Derbaix, Kacha, & Walliser, 2014) have largely established that sports sponsorship is effective. The proportion of respondents who correctly identifies at least one sponsor ranged from 60% of respondents (J. H. Lee & Bang, 2005; Stotlar & Johnson, 1989) to more than 85% of respondents (Biscaia et al., 2014; Moore et al., 1999; Turley & Shannon, 2000). Other studies using the mean number of correctly recalled sponsors as an alternative

DOI: 10.4018/978-1-7998-3473-1.ch157

measure of sponsorship effectiveness have also found that sports sponsorship can be effective (Dekhil, 2010; Kinney et al., 2008).

Such measures of sponsor recall are based on explicit memory. Explicit memory refers to the intentional and conscious effort to recollect a specific past event (Balasubramanian, Karrh, & Patwardhan, 2006; Herrmann, Walliser, & Kacha, 2011; Holden & Vanhuele, 1999; Yang, Roskos-Ewoldsen, Dinu, & Arpan, 2006). As such, spectators will need to devote cognitive resources in order to recall a sponsor as a substantial degree of mental construction is required (Johar & Pham, 1999; Walliser, 2003). It is thus not surprising that some studies have found that spectators are unable to recall sponsors (Maxwell & Lough, 2009). Mere exposure within the sports venue does not necessarily lead spectators to process the message extensively and encode it for retrieval at a later stage (Lardinoit & Derbaix, 2001). According to the Limited Capacity Model of Mediated Message Processing, spectators have limited cognitive capacity for processing information and will need to allocate cognitive resources between watching a game and processing other peripheral information (Lang, 2000). When spectators are attracted to the game, they will be less likely to attend to peripheral messages from sponsors and as a result less likely to recall sponsors.

It becomes apparent that there is a need to examine the relationship between exposure and brand recall further. Eye trackers have been used in research studies in other fields including advertising and marketing communications. In such studies, the physiological responses of eye movements to advertising stimulus is examined to determine what the respondents is attracted to and how the visual stimuli becomes memory (J. Lee & Ahn, 2012; Taylor & Herbert, 2013). It is only recently that eye trackers are used in sports sponsorship studies (Breuer & Rumpf, 2012). Eye movements are typically characterised by 2 distinct components; fixations and saccades. Fixations are defined as a state where the eye is relatively still for a minimum amount of time typically for a duration of 200 to 500 milliseconds. Saccades, on the other hand, refer to quick and sharp movements, or 'jumps' of the eyes lasting around 20 to 40 milliseconds (Wedel & Pieters, 2008).

EYE TRACKER IN SPORTS SPONSORSHIP RESEARCH

The following describes a sports sponsorship study using an eye tracker to examine the relationship between glance duration and sponsor. This will serve to illustrate the potential contributions of the usage of eye trackers in this field of research.

60 respondents were recruited from a tertiary educational institution in an Asian country for the study. They were asked to watch a five-minute video clip of the FINA World Championship Shanghai 2011 50 meters men's Freestyle finals swimming event. The video clip was played on a computer desktop equipped with a 19-inch monitor, a headset and the SensoMotoric Instrument Remote Eye-tracking Device 250mobile (SMI RED250m). The SMI RED250m can track eye movement at a rate of 250 Hz with a gaze position accuracy of 0.4 degrees. By projecting an infrared light to the surface of the eye, the mini camera in the eye tracker detects the resulting corneal reflection to measure and record the position of the pupil as well as gaze direction. A nine-point calibration and four-point validation process for the participant's eye movements was carried out prior to watching the video clip. This was consistent with other studies using eye tracker (Breuer & Rumpf, 2012; Taylor & Herbert, 2013). The participants were not informed of the actual purpose of the study. This was essential so as to ensure that the participants were not primed to pay attention to the perimeter boards while watching the swimming event (Leng, 2011; Schneider & Cornwell, 2005). At the end of the video, respondents completed a survey instru-

Figure 1. Visual Depiction of Glance Duration. Adapted from Eye Tracking Definitions: Basic Definition of Terms by Fattahi, P (2011)

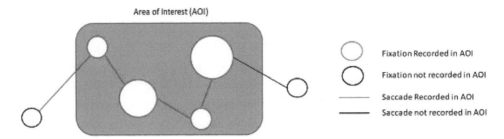

ment which collected data on the sponsor recall rate. Subsequently, participants were given a token of appreciation for their time and informed of the actual objective of the study.

The eye-movement data collected was analyzed using the BeGaze 3.5 program. To demarcate the areas for analysis, areas of interest (AOI) for each sponsor's banner were marked out using the computer software. For this study, the extent of attention of participants toward the event sponsors was measured by their glance duration toward the respective advertising boards. Glance duration is defined as the sum of all fixations and saccades between and within the AOI, including the duration of the initial saccade entering the AOI (Figure 1). This was then compared to the sponsor recall data from the questionnaire to determine the relationship between exposure and memory (Breuer & Rumpf, 2012).

The six official sponsors for the event were Nikon, Yakult, Myrtha Pools, Omega, Midea and Speedo. Each sponsor appeared on two equal sized perimeter banners along the competition pool. The mean recall rate was 2.53 (SD = .19) sponsors. Logistic regression was performed to assess the impact of glance duration on the likelihood that respondents are able to recall each sponsor. The full model was statistically significant for four of the brands: Midea (χ^2 (2, N = 60) = 6.37, $p < .05$); Omega (χ^2 (2, N = 60) = 7.23, $p < .05$); Speedo (χ^2 (2, N = 60) = 21.67, $p < .01$); Yakult (χ^2 (2, N = 60) = 26.32, $p < .01$). The models explained variance between 10.1% and 19.6% for Midea; 11.4% and 15.3% for Omega; 30.3% to 41.0% for Speedo; and 35.5% to 49.8% for Yakult. The odds ratio for glance duration across the four brands were 2.19 for Midea, 2.20 for Omega, 20.66 for Speedo and 7.76 for Yakult. This indicated that for every second increase in glance duration, the probability of sponsor recall increases between 2 to 21 times for these 4 brands.

This study shows that an eye tracker can provide additional data in understanding the effectiveness of sports sponsorship. The results show a clear relationship between exposure and memory. While this concurs with earlier research, the data from the eye tracker is able to quantify that for each second increase in glance duration, the probability of sponsor recall can increase between 2 to more than 20 times.

Table 1. Logistic regression of sport involvement and glance duration on recall of sponsor (n=60)

Brand	χ^2	p	Explained Variance	Odds Ratio
Midea	6.37	<.05	10.1-19.6%	2.19
Omega	7.23	<.05	11.4-15.3%	2.20
Speedo	21.67	<.01	30.3-41.0%	20.66
Yakult	26.32	<.01	35.5-49.8%	7.76

More importantly, the data also shows that exposure is not the only factor affecting recall. In this study, it was found that glance duration for two of the sponsors, Nikon and Myrtha Pools, did not significantly affect the likelihood that respondents are able to recall the sponsor. The variability in the explained variance and odds ratio across the four sponsors further suggests that the relationship between glance duration and sponsor recall is complex and requires further study. Rate of sponsor recall is likely to be affected by other variables besides glance duration. This was supported by earlier studies in the literature (Walliser, 2003).

METHODOLOGICAL CHALLENGES

Given that the use of an eye tracker can potentially provide more data for understanding sports sponsorship, it seems surprising that it was only recently that there is an interest in employing them for research in this area. There may be several reasons for this.

It is necessary to remember that the eye tracker can only track eye movement. As such, the researcher will need to understand if the data is relevant to the needs of the study and how to make sense of this data. In this light, it is a widely accepted belief that attention is only a precondition to other psychological and cognitive factors that take place in the brain (Wedel & Pieters, 2008). This, combined with the assumption that obtaining attention is a simple task for marketers, plays a large role in the lack of eye-tracking centered research thus far. It is possible that previous researchers in the field of sport marketing perceive a diminished role of visual attention, and thus opt to concentrate on other aspects of consumer behavior.

Another possible methodological challenge are cost-associated issues. For the study outlined in the previous section, the total cost of the equipment, which include the eye-tracking device and the associated software to run the analysis amounted to approximately $50,000. The nature of stimuli being studied i.e. frame by frame video analysis, also requires powerful computer hardware, which makes such studies less economically viable. Without research grants or other forms of funding, it will be difficult to embark on such studies.

The third challenge is related to the time required to code and analyze eye tracking data. This issue is especially prevalent in the field of studying sports events as they are often of long duration and consist of dynamic images. As such, coding these videos, which involve the drawing of AOIs and shifting them across different frames, is extremely time consuming. For example, in the study outlined in the previous section, it took approximately one month to code a video clip of five minutes that featured six sponsors. Clearly, as the event gets longer and the number of sponsors increase, it will take more time and resources to code the AOIs.

Finally, such eye tracking studies are conducted in a laboratory setting, where there are specific conditions that participants have to adhere to when viewing the visual stimuli. This may prime the participant's attention towards certain aspects of the visual stimuli that he or she would otherwise not have paid attention to if viewing the same stimuli outside of the study. In addition, the eye tracking software used in the study described in the previous section requires participants to minimize head movement throughout the study. This may be unnatural to the participant and may cause the participant to exhibit different viewing behaviors when viewing the sport event, as compared to a more natural setting i.e. watching the event on the television at home.

SOLUTIONS AND RECOMMENDATIONS

Technological advancements in both eye tracking hardware and software have improved the practicality and ease of execution of studies in this field. Eye tracking studies in the past involved the researcher physically observing and recording an individual's eye tracking movement. This is very different from the equipment that researchers have at their disposal today. As eye-tracking technologies continue to improve, accessibility and cost will reach a point where it becomes more readily available to researchers.

Likewise, the current limitations with regard to participant constraints i.e. unnaturally still head positions and having the conduct of experiment only in a laboratory setting could also be resolved with improvements to technology. Already, there is some promising research using mobile eye trackers.

FUTURE RESEARCH DIRECTIONS

Recent studies have employed physiological instruments to measure arousal and attention as they allow for a more valid measure of the effectiveness of advertisements compared to cognitive and affective measures (Gangadharbatla, Bradley, & Wise, 2013). Future studies in sports sponsorship studies should also include physiological measures such as heart rate and skin conductance to provide additional information on the attention and arousal generated by the images of sponsors.

Eye movement data alone may only indicate exposure. The process of how exposure becomes memory suggests that more work needs to be done to examine factors such as brand familiarity, prominence of sponsors including size, colors and placement, etc and their effect on brand recall.

Sponsorship effectiveness is not only about recall. At the end of the day, sponsors require a return from their investment in sponsorship. As such, future work should also examine attitudes and purchase intention of sponsors' products and their relationship with exposure. According to Mere Exposure Theory, prolonged exposure leads to favorable attitudes towards a brand. It will be interesting to examine whether this can be generalized to the field of sports sponsorship.

CONCLUSION

The use of eye tracker can potentially shed new light in the field of sports sponsorship. Technological advancements have made eye trackers easier to use and more accessible. However, there are still several methodological challenges, mainly related to cost and time related factors. These can potentially inhibit the viability of such studies, especially in projects that involve a large number of respondents. As technologies continue to improve, it is expected that eye trackers will become less expensive and easier to use. This may allow more research studies using eye trackers to be conducted and improve the analysis of eye movement data in future.

REFERENCES

Balasubramanian, S. K., Karrh, J. A., & Patwardhan, H. (2006). Audience response to product placements: An integrative framework and future research agenda. *Journal of Advertising*, *35*(3), 115–141. doi:10.2753/JOA0091-3367350308

Bennett, R. (1999). Sports sponsorship, spectator recall and false consensus. *European Journal of Marketing, 33*(3/4), 291–313. doi:10.1108/03090569910253071

Biscaia, R., Correia, A., Ross, S., & Rosado, A. (2014). Sponsorship effectiveness in professional sport: An examination of recall and recognition among football fans. *International Journal of Sports Marketing & Sponsorship, 16*(1), 7–23. doi:10.1108/IJSMS-16-01-2014-B002

Boshoff, C., & Gerber, C. (2008). Sponsorship recall and recognition: The case of the 2007 Cricket World Cup. *South African Journal of Business Management, 39*(2), 1–8. doi:10.4102ajbm.v39i2.556

Breuer, C., & Rumpf, C. (2012). The Viewer's Reception and Processing of Sponsorship Information in Sport Telecasts. *Journal of Sport Management, 26*(6), 521–531. doi:10.1123/jsm.26.6.521

Chadwick, S., & Thwaites, D. (2005). Managing sport sponsorship programs: Lessons from a critical assessment of English soccer. *Journal of Advertising Research, 45*(3), 328–338. doi:10.1017/S0021849905050312

Cornwell, T. B., & Humphreys, M. S. (2013). Memory for sponsorship relationships: A critical juncture in thinking. *Psychology and Marketing, 30*(5), 394–407. doi:10.1002/mar.20614

Dekhil, F. (2010). The effects of the type of audience, involvement, interest and socio-demographic variables on sponsor recall: The soccer African Nations Cup. *International Journal of Sports Marketing & Sponsorship, 11*(2), 158. doi:10.1108/IJSMS-11-02-2010-B005

Fullerton, S. (2010). *Sports marketing* (2nd ed.). Irwin Professional Pub.

Gangadharbatla, H., Bradley, S., & Wise, W. (2013). Psychophysiological responses to background brand placements in video games. *Journal of Advertising, 42*(2-3), 251–263. doi:10.1080/00913367.2013.775800

Herrmann, J. L., Corneille, O., Derbaix, C., Kacha, M., & Walliser, B. (2014). Implicit sponsorship effects for a prominent brand. *European Journal of Marketing, 48*(3/4), 785–804. doi:10.1108/EJM-11-2011-0624

Herrmann, J. L., Walliser, B., & Kacha, M. (2011). Consumer consideration of sponsor brands they do not remember: Taking a wider look at the memorisation effects of sponsorship. *International Journal of Advertising, 30*(2), 259–281. doi:10.2501/IJA-30-2-259-281

Holden, S. J., & Vanhuele, M. (1999). Know the name, forget the exposure: Brand familiarity versus memory of exposure context. *Psychology and Marketing, 16*(6), 479–496. doi:10.1002/(SICI)1520-6793(199909)16:6<479::AID-MAR3>3.0.CO;2-Y

Johar, G. V., & Pham, M. T. (1999). Relatedness, prominence, and constructive sponsor identification. *JMR, Journal of Marketing Research, 36*(3), 299–312. doi:10.1177/002224379903600301

Kinney, L., McDaniel, S. R., & DeGaris, L. (2008). Demographic and psychographic variables predicting NASCAR sponsor brand recall. *International Journal of Sports Marketing & Sponsorship, 9*(3), 169. doi:10.1108/IJSMS-09-03-2008-B005

Lang, A. (2000). The limited capacity model of mediated message processing. *Journal of Communication, 50*(1), 46–70. doi:10.1111/j.1460-2466.2000.tb02833.x

Lardinoit, T., & Derbaix, C. (2001). Sponsorship and recall of sponsors. *Psychology and Marketing*, *18*(2), 167–190. doi:10.1002/1520-6793(200102)18:2<167::AID-MAR1004>3.0.CO;2-I

Lee, J., & Ahn, J. H. (2012). Attention to banner ads and their effectiveness: An eye-tracking approach. *International Journal of Electronic Commerce*, *17*(1), 119–137. doi:10.2753/JEC1086-4415170105

Lee, J. H., & Bang, J. S. (2005). An analysis of brand recall of 2002 FIFA Korea/Japan World Cup on official sponsor corporation. *International Journal of Applied Sports Sciences*, *17*(1), 30–41.

Leng, H. K. (2011). A Study on the Effectiveness of In-Game Advertisements. *International Journal of Sport Management, Recreation and Tourism*, *8*, 65–80. doi:10.5199/ijsmart-1791-874X-8d

Leng, H. K. (2017). Sponsor recall in sports events of short duration: Empirical evidence from swimming competitions. *International Journal of Sports Marketing & Sponsorship*, *18*(2), 138–148. doi:10.1108/IJSMS-05-2017-091

Maxwell, H., & Lough, N. (2009). Signage vs. no signage: An analysis of sponsorship recognition in women's college basketball. *Sport Marketing Quarterly*, *18*(4), 188–198.

Meenaghan, T., & O'Sullivan, P. (2013). Metrics in Sponsorship Research—Is Credibility an Issue? *Psychology and Marketing*, *30*(5), 408–416. doi:10.1002/mar.20615

Moore, J. N., Pickett, G. M., & Grove, S. J. (1999). The impact of a video screen and rotational-signage systems on satisfaction and advertising recognition. *Journal of Services Marketing*, *13*(6), 453–468. doi:10.1108/08876049910298739

Mullin, B. J., Hardy, S., & Sutton, W. A. (2007). *Sport marketing* (Vol. 13). Human Kinetics Publishers.

Newell, S. J., Henderson, K. V., & Wu, B. T. (2001). The effects of pleasure and arousal on recall of advertisements during the Super Bowl. *Psychology and Marketing*, *18*(11), 1135–1153. doi:10.1002/mar.1047

Schneider, L. P., & Cornwell, T. B. (2005). Cashing in on crashes via brand placement in computer games: The effects of experience and flow on memory. *International Journal of Advertising*, *24*(3), 321–343. doi:10.1080/02650487.2005.11072928

Stotlar, D. K., & Johnson, D. A. (1989). Assessing the impact and effectiveness of stadium advertising on sport spectators at Division 1 institutions. *Journal of Sport Management*, *3*(2), 90–102. doi:10.1123/jsm.3.2.90

Taylor, G., & Herbert, J. S. (2013). Eye tracking infants: Investigating the role of attention during learning on recognition memory. *Scandinavian Journal of Psychology*, *54*(1), 14–19. doi:10.1111jop.12002 PMID:23198776

Turley, L. W., & Shannon, J. R. (2000). The impact and effectiveness of advertisements in a sports arena. *Journal of Services Marketing*, *14*(4), 323–336. doi:10.1108/08876040010334547

Walliser, B. (2003). An international review of sponsorship research: Extension and update. *International Journal of Advertising*, *22*(1), 5–40. doi:10.1080/02650487.2003.11072838

Wedel, M., & Pieters, R. (2008). *A review of eye-tracking research in marketing. Review of Marketing Research*. Emerald Group Publishing Limited.

Yang, M., Roskos-Ewoldsen, D. R., Dinu, L., & Arpan, L. M. (2006). The effectiveness of "in-game" advertising: Comparing college students' explicit and implicit memory for brand names. *Journal of Advertising*, *35*(4), 143–152. doi:10.2753/JOA0091-3367350410

ADDITIONAL READING

d'Ydewalle, G., & Tamsin, F. (1993). On the visual processing and memory of incidental information: Advertising panels in soccer games. In *Visual search 2: Proceedings of the 2nd international conference on visual search* (pp. 401-408). London: Taylor & Francis.

Holmqvist, K., Nyström, M., Andersson, R., Dewhurst, R., Jarodzka, H., & Van de Weijer, J. (2011). *Eye tracking: A comprehensive guide to methods and measures*. OUP Oxford.

Shapiro, S., & Krishnan, H. S. (2001). Memory-based measures for assessing advertising effects: A comparison of explicit and implicit memory effects. *Journal of Advertising*, *30*(3), 1–13. doi:10.1080/00913367.2001.10673641

Venkatraman, V., Dimoka, A., Pavlou, P. A., Vo, K., Hampton, W., Bollinger, B., Hershfield, H. E., Ishihara, M., & Winer, R. S. (2015). Predicting advertising success beyond traditional measures: New insights from neurophysiological methods and market response modeling. *JMR, Journal of Marketing Research*, *52*(4), 436–452. doi:10.1509/jmr.13.0593

Wedel, M., & Pieters, R. (2000). Eye fixations on advertisements and memory for brands: A model and findings. *Marketing Science*, *19*(4), 297–312. doi:10.1287/mksc.19.4.297.11794

KEY TERMS AND DEFINITIONS

Area of Interest (AOI): The area marked out in eye tracking software that is of interest to researchers.

Eye Tracking: The measuring and recording of the eye movements of an individual.

Fixation: The state where an individual's eye is not moving for a set amount of time.

Glance Duration: The sum of all fixations and saccades between and within the AOI, including the duration of the initial saccade entering the AOI.

Saccade: The fast and rapid movement of the eye.

Sports Event: An organized event of physical activity that is governed by rules and regulations.

Sports Sponsorship: A relationship where a sporting entity obtains financial or non-financial benefits from a commercial organization, in exchange for imaging rights to the sporting entity's name, logo and other aspects of branding.

Section 14

Operations and Service Management

Business Process Management

Matthias Lederer

International School of Management (ISM), Munich, Germany

Peter Schott

REHAU AG+Co, Germany

INTRODUCTION

The historical development of the business organization as well as the management theory took place in three fundamental phases. Until the 30s, the focus of the company organization was on technical problems in production and administration. At the beginning of the 80s, companies were structured into a hierarchies and processes. In this dualistic viewpoint, the focus of process was on the execution of tasks and the focus of organizational structure was on departments and positions (Krallmann et al., 2002). In the last and current phase, companies are increasingly focusing on value chains and workflows (vom Brocke & Schmiedel, 2015). Modern companies understand corporate structures as continuous procedures and value chains (Jeston & Nelis, 2010), which may also connect companies across organizational boundaries (Manuel, 2011). Instead of focusing on individual functions and optimizing individual business units, productivity and quality in seen in the overall business context and especially business processes influence the value of companies (Franz & Kirchmer, 2012).

Processes can be found in almost every company and every organization. They describe patterns (e.g., processing information) of how a company responds to events (e.g., a customer request). It has been confirmed in studies that with the optimization of processes the classical business goals like time, cost and quality can be improved (Weske, 2012).

There are many definitions of business processes. All have in common (Weske, 2012; Allweyer, 2014; Lehmann, 2012; Gadatsch, 2012) that a process consists of a sequence of activities (e.g., delivery of material, processing steps in the factory, outbound logistics). It typically has a defined start (input, trigger, e.g., a customer order) and completes with a defined end (output, e.g., automobile was provided to the customer). The result is of value to an internal or external customer (e.g., price of an automobile) and the procedure uses specific information (e.g., order data).

Some textbooks and standard works make a distinction between processes and **business processes**. The latter is characterized by two further properties (Weske 2012; Allweyer, 2014; Lehmann 2012; Gadatsch 2012). First, a business process is usually carried out with division of labor by several organizations or organizational units (for example, sales, production, logistics). Business processes are thus cross-functional. Second, the business process describes the creation of services according to the given objectives cascaded from an enterprise strategy (e.g., focus on quality leadership leads to more quality assurance steps in the process).

Business processes are understood as the set of goal-oriented operations that are carried out in several functional areas of a company and whose results are of value to a customer (Hammer & Champy, 2003). While processes generally transform a given input into an output (Schmelzer & Sesselmann, 2008), business processes always deliver a performance that is oriented towards the respective customer and generates significant added value for him/her (Allweyer, 2014).

DOI: 10.4018/978-1-7998-3473-1.ch158

Business process management (BPM) is understood as an integrative concept of leadership, organization and controlling that enables control of these operations. It is also about meeting the needs of customers and other interest groups (Schmelzer & Sesselmann, 2008; vom Brocke & Schmiedel, 2015; Franz & Kirchmer, 2012).

In contrast to projects that take place only once, processes usually have multiple **instances**. This term is defined as a concrete execution of the business process. For example, the ordering from one customer of a specific car of a particular type carries individual information (e.g., color, equipment, etc.) as an instance, but follows the general model of manufacturing processes in production. The number of instances varies from process to process. Development processes can sometimes have only one process instance per year, while for example complaints or payroll processes may have thousands of instances per year (Weske, 2012).

It usually makes a difference in the definition whether a process is purely manual (e.g., hairdressing service) or at least partially automated (e.g., assignment of calls in a service center, robots in a manufacturing line). A **workflow** is defined as formally described business process that is fully or partially automated. Through a specified model, the workflow includes temporal, functional and resource-related specifications, so that an automatic control of the workflow at the operational level gets possible (Draheim, 2010).

PROCESS ORIENTATION

Process orientation describes the structuring of organizations/company design on the basis of coherent processes (Weske, 2012). This orientation in modern management can overcome challenges such as shorter product life cycles, increasing customer demands, globalization, increasing cost pressure, and information technology developments (Allweyer, 2005). It is thus becoming increasingly important in modern and digital companies.

The process orientation origins from **Business Process Reengineerings** as a findings from various consulting firms from the 90s. This concept by Hammer and Champy (2003) describes that companies need to radically rethink their procedures (processes) and should not remain thinking in the existing functions (Hammer & Champy, 2003).

Traditionally, companies differentiate between the organizational structure and the process organization. In internal and external communication, the focus is usually on so-called "work in the line", that is the structure of departments and positions. However, since the daily work processes go beyond the functional and departmental boundaries, the orientation towards processes has central advantages (McCormack & Johnson, 2016; Becker, Kugeler & Rosemann, 2013; vom Brocke & Rosemann, 2010): The interfaces between teams and departments are well defined. Cross-functional work gets more effectively and efficiently. Through a holistic process responsibility, the roles do not only ensure the fulfillment of internal goals (e.g. the department strategy), but rather focus on the achievement of holistic specifications in the customer's sense. Optimizing processes means focusing on value-adding activities rather than examining internal procedures of teams or departments. Through defined steps and ongoing optimization of processes, resources can be reduced and time can be saved.

Typically, there are three types of business processes (Lehmann, 2012; vom Brocke & Rosemann, 2010). **Management processes** include planning, control and controlling activities. All processes of this level serve the continuous improvement and strategic alignment. The **core processes** realize the essential business of a company. These should not be outsourced. For classic companies (e.g. from manufacturing industry), these processes typically include Supply Chain Management (SCM), Product Lifecycle Management (PLM), and Customer Relationship Management (CRM). **Support processes** are often not directly visible to customers, but they make significant contributions to enable core processes (e.g., human resources, financial accounting).

In order to ensure a professional execution of processes on all levels in all domains, there are usually five roles of responsibility (Lederer, Butz & Bodendorf, 2015):

- The **Chief Process Officer** (CPO) is responsible for the entirety of all business processes of a company and establishes the holistic process orientation in the company.
- The same applies to the **process owner** who is in contrast responsible for one or more concrete processes.
- **Process managers** are usually located at a lower organizational level. They are responsible for the performance of all instances of a specific process.
- The **process team** executes the process (e.g., clerks).
- Depending on the process, **supportive roles** (e.g., modelers and auditors) can be provided.

Process Lifecycle

The different tasks of BPM can be described along the typical process lifecycle (see Figure 1) (vom Brocke & Rosemann, 2010; Weske 2012; von Rosing, van Scheel & Scheer, 2014):

- **Strategy**: A process should achieve goals that are cascaded from corporate strategy. Key figures are defined to measure process performance.
- **Modeling**: To understand how the process works, an actual and a target model are usually created. This can be based on employee statements, observations, document analyzes or digital traces (such as timestamps and actions within an IT system). Steps, tasks, documents, responsibilities and interfaces are typical entities of process models.
- **Optimization**: There are many different methods to identify optimization potentials. To increase internal efficiency, for example, it is questioned which process steps are particularly disruptive and which interfaces are not defined. To increase efficiency, tools, control flows and documents can be changed.
- **Implementation**: Good ideas for process optimization are implemented. This implementation may involve tools (e.g., other attributes, data or interfaces), teams (e.g., new departments, roles or forms of collaboration) and artefacts/documents (e.g., templates).
- **Execution**: If optimizations are implemented, the process instances can follow the new process.
- **Monitoring**: Have the goals of optimization been achieved? This is checked in the context of monitoring in various dimensions.

Strategy

Numerous indications and evidences show that business processes and also IT support (for example Enterprise Resource Planning Systems [ERP]) are only efficiently applied, when a corporate strategy was determined before (Schmelzer & Sesselmann, 2008; Allweyer, 2005) Explicitly stated strategic objectives should serve as the basis for selection of required resources, such as personnel and information systems in BPM.

Figure 1. BPM lifecycle (vom Brocke & Rosemann, 2010; von Rosing, van Scheel & Scheer, 2014)

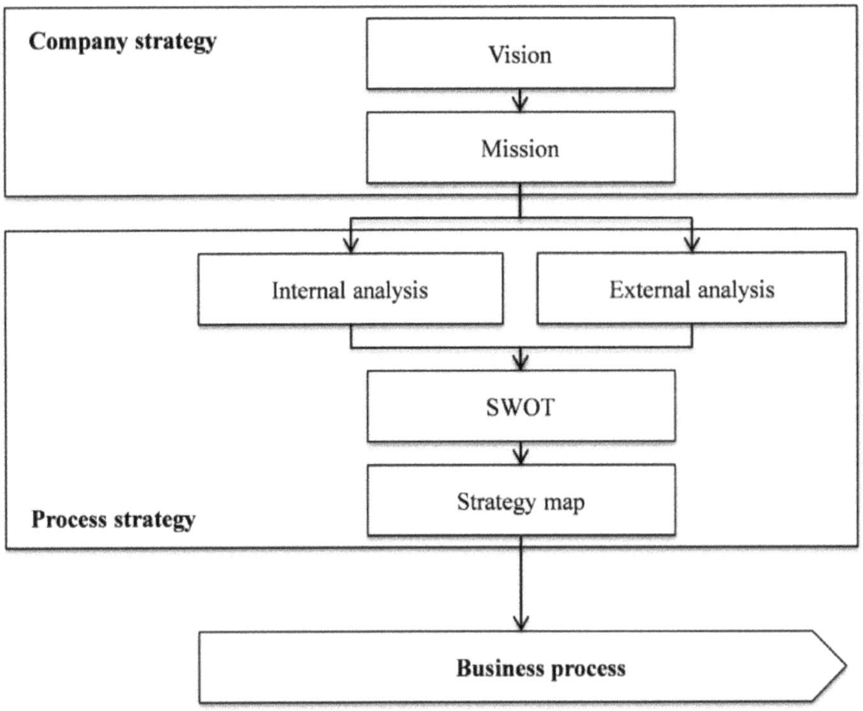

Company strategy

Vision

Mission

Internal analysis

External analysis

SWOT

Process strategy

Strategy map

Business process

Figure 2. BPM strategy (Lederer, 2016)

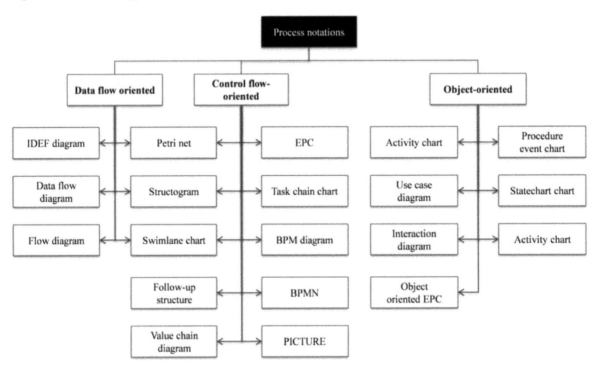

There is a variety of different methods and tools available for defining a strategy in the company. As Figure 2 shows as a general summary of many existing approaches, it is relevant for process management that individual strategic or tactical objectives are named (e.g., "High quality of service", "Efficient handling of customer inquiries" or "High repurchase rate " for a CRM process). This process strategy is described, for example, as a strategy map or balanced scorecard. It results from the cascaded business strategy and can be generated by combining an internal (e.g., resource analysis) and external analysis (e.g., PEST analysis) (Lederer, 2016).

Modeling

Modeling generally refers to the representation of perceptions that an individual makes of procedures in the environment (Wittges, 2005; Schmelzer & Sesselmann, 2008). Models consist of individual building blocks interacting with each other, with syntax rules and model types ensuring that the formal or semi-formal models can be used by IT systems in subsequent lifecycle phases (Wittges, 2005; vom Brocke & Schmiedel, 2015). In terms of companies and IT-based modeling of business processes, this means that the process components, such as activities, organizational units, data and events, are usually linked as symbols in terms of time and collaboration (Hansmann, 2006; Franz & Kirchmer, 2012). Depending on the desired focus (for example, detail specification for automation of a workflow vs. rough schemata of a top management discussion), different notations are used for the modeling. Gadatsch (2012) classifies available process notations according to their focus on data, control flow (i.e., activities), and objects (e.g., object-oriented programming) as a recognized division. His well-known and accepted classification is shown in Figure 3.

Figure 3. BPM modeling notations (Gadatsch 2012)

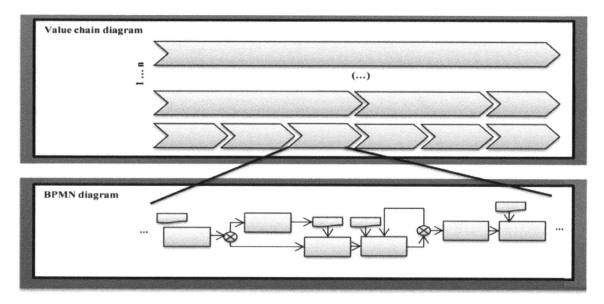

Since there are probably several hundred different notations (Lederer, Avci &Schmidt, 2017), studies come to different estimates of which notation has the widest distribution. However, it is generally accepted that in research and practice two notations are quite common.

Value chains are an extension of Porter's classic process chains. Functions (i.e., process steps) are described at a very high level of abstraction and in a purely sequential order. This representation is very intuitive and dispenses with the description of details (e.g., roles, IT systems, documents). This notation is used in particular for process maps, which serve as entry points for discussion or detailing.

Business Process Modeling and Notation (BPMN) is a graphical notation with a variety of symbols. The current standard BPMN 2.0 defines four basic types of elements: *Flow objects* are the nodes (Activity, Gateway and Event) in the diagrams and represent the actual contents like handling or checking steps. *Connecting objects* are edges in the form of sequence flows) as well as message flows. *Pools and Swimlanes* represent areas of responsibility of the roles and systems involved. *Artifacts* summarize all explanatory and supplementary elements such as groups and annotations. The main advantages of this notation are its power to visualize different procedure and flexibility as well as the possibility of digital translation. For example, diagrams can be automatically converted into machine-readable form (e.g. for workflow management systems, see later).

Figure 4. BPMN as detailed process modelling of value chain steps
(Lederer, Schott & Keppler, 2015)

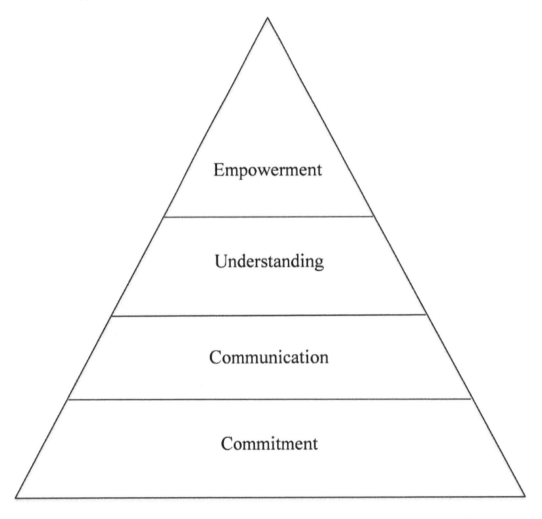

The two notations described model processes at different levels of detail. Figure 4 shows in this context the possibility of detailing a PLM process chain in sub-processes with more details in BPMN.

Optimization

As part of the process analysis, business processes are assessed from the inside view of a company in order to identify room for improvement (Schmelzer & Sesselmann 2008). This is to be done before the process is implemented in the structure, teams and IT systems of a company. For example, a validation answers the question whether the established process model actually reflects reality (Richter von Hagen & Stucky 2004).

In general, processes can be analyzed to optimize according to the following criteria (Lederer et al., 2012):

- **Process costs** (C1): Process analysis methods of this category make processes more transparent in terms of their cost structure. The methods establish possible cost saving potentials in processes and identify cost drivers.
- **Process time** (C2): Methods of this category analyze processes with respect to the time dimensions in the process execution. They outline processing time, deadlines, critical paths/points and show their impact on value-adding processes and interfaces.
- **Process quality** (C3): This category describes the focus on quality of the process output, of process throughput and of the process structure.
- **Process outcomes** (C4): As one main goal a business process creates benefits to meet customer needs. Benefit represents the achievement of customer satisfaction and is analyzed in this category.
- **Process structure** (C5): This focus evaluates the process landscape of a company from an organizational and operational point of view. Analysis methods of this category show interdependencies, redundancies, and networks of processes. Moreover, these methods describe the general process orientation of the corporate structure.
- **Process information** (C6): Methods in this category analyze the supply of information, the availability of information and information transparency in the process. Moreover, the quality of information within processes can be analyzed.
- **Process communication** (C7): This focus category summarizes analysis methods outlining the efficiency and effectiveness of information exchange. Furthermore, the transmission of information within a process and across processes is examined. However, not the information itself, but the quality of the information transport is the main objective of analysis.
- **Process risks** (C8): This focus category groups risk analysis methods to identify possible process-relevant events which can have negative impacts. The most relevant aspects are the probability of these events as well as the level of impact of their consequences.
- **Process resources** (C9): Methods of this focus category look at process resources, meaning the supply and demand situation of all goods and resources necessary to execute a certain process.
- **Process flexibility** (C10): The flexibility of processes includes their temporal, spatial and functional adaptability to changing conditions.

The process analysis includes methods of performance evaluation (Richter von Hagen & Stucky, 2004). For this purpose, modern tools generally offer the possibility to compare alternative process models. At the end of the performance assessment, statements are drawn up about process models that show to what extent a model fulfills the qualitative and quantitative process objectives compared to alternative processes or workflows (Gadatsch, 2012).

Simple and general hints for an intuitive optimization of processes are (Bleicher, 1991; Gadatsch, 2012):

- **Leaving out**: If activities are not necessary or are not rewarded by customers, they can be removed. The process becomes less prone to errors and faster.
- **Eliminating media breaks**: Media breaks (such as printing and rescanning) slow processes and unnecessarily bind resources.
- **Outsourcing**: Activities that are not core processes can be meaningfully outsourced.
- **Summarizing**: Pooling activities can create synergies and accelerate processes.
- **Parallelization**: If activities are performed in parallel rather than sequentially, the division of labor increases.
- **Relocating**: Occasionally, it makes sense to provide activities further up the workflow or even later in the process.
- **Accelerating**: By providing more resources, task completion can be optimized and waiting times can be avoided.
- **Avoiding loops**: If, for example, data is checked directly for plausibility when typing in, queries can be avoided.
- **Adding**: Adding process steps, sub-processes, e.g. for quality and result assurance, may lead to optimizations as well.

Lederer et al. (2012) show in their compilation a comprehensive picture of which concrete methods can be used to achieve which specific goals (marked with "X" in Table 1). Depending on the company's strategy, specific methods may be applicable.

Implementation

To implement a business process and also to introduce the underlying IT tools, a roll-out strategies should be chosen, which plans the timing of new processes or process changes (Hansmann et al., 2008). The opposing implementation approaches are the "Big Bang Approach", in which new processes or IT systems are introduced at a specific point in time throughout the entire company, and the "step-by-step approach", in which the implementation in successive steps (Upton & Staats 2008).

In general, the implementation can relate to adjustments to teams/roles (humans) or to IT systems. Basic information on both approaches will be presented briefly (see the following sections).

Humans

Employee coordination focuses on new or changed process steps that are not automated but executed by a process team. In many cases, employees are involved in process activities and operationalize process objectives in their daily work. Employee coordination describes that process teams accept and follow the processes. Whether concepts such as open communication and individual incentives are possible and meaningful depends on many internal factors of a company (Lederer, Raake & Kurz 2014).

Figure 5 shows a maturity approach to how new processes should be introduces to process teams, as described as result of a meta-study by Lederer, Raake, & Kurz (2014).

Table 1. BPM analysis methods classified according to analysis focus categories

Analysis method \ Analysis focus	C_1	C_2	C_3	C_4	C_5	C_6	C_7	C_8	C_9	C_{10}
Critical path analysis	X	X								
Core process / core competence analysis					X					X
ABC analysis					X					
Information requirements analysis			X			X				
Communication Analysis		X				X	X			
Networking analysis					X		X			
Vulnerability analysis	X		X					X		
Cause and effect analysis			X					X		
FMEA		X	X					X		
Value analysis		X		X						
Force field analysis			X							X
Fragmentation / concentration analysis		X							X	
Runtime analysis		X								
Dependency Analysis		X	X							
Fault analysis			X					X		
Process cost analysis	X		X							
"Moments of truth" analysis				X						
"Voice of the customer" analysis				X	X					
Interface analysis		X	X							X
IT resource analysis						X	X	X		
Analysis the operational structure					X					X
Organizational structure analysis			X						X	X
Knowledge-centered process analysis			X			X	X			
Quality cost analysis	X		X							
Portfolio analysis				X	X					
Process potential analysis			X	X	X				X	
Process environment analysis					X			X		
Process-oriented SWOT Analysis				X				X		
Cost Benchmarking	X									

(Lederer et al., 2012)

Commitment means that the process manager is committed to the goals and new processes. This self-commitment is important at an early stage and an essential foundation for further steps in employee motivation (Harber, 1998). Lacking this foundation often results in disrespect or misunderstanding of the strategic objectives (Kaplan and Norton 2001, Blackall 2007).

In recent years, **communication** and knowledge has become a core resource of organizations and can have a significant impact on the overall success of process management. Process teams, for example, need knowledge about new process flows, documents, interfaces, functions, and roles after optimizing processes. The transfer of knowledge by the process manager thus follows the commitment. Functional knowledge describes specific knowledge that employees have to handle a function (such as activity in

Figure 5. Human-centric implementation steps of BPM

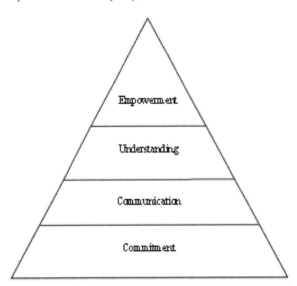

BPMN diagrams). They are aware of these abilities (e.g., knowledge of masks to be filled in) or implicitly carry them (e.g., presentation skills). Knowledge that is relevant for working in processes from an individual's point of view is called knowledge in processes. They include both internally described information (e.g., manuals, checklists for testing activities, etc.) and external knowledge (e.g., methodology, best practices, etc.). Knowledge about processes describes knowledge about the organization of a process (e.g., process steps and resources).

Building **understanding** of new processes in the process team follows the commitment and communication of concrete content. Understanding means that the process team is motivated for processes, has relevant information, and now gathers experience in dealing with it. The understanding of the objectives and the processes are important for the overall success.

Empowerment stands for the highest level of motivation and support of process teams. It describes the ability and will of process teams, objectives, and theirs

Operationalization. Empowerment characterizes a shift in power away from the managers to the employees (Hammer, Champy & Künzel, 1994), because without an overview of the entire process and its environment, employees entrusted with executive activities cannot shape their business processes (Kurz & Hartmann, 2011). This aspect is reiterated in the last section of the post with Social BPM.

IT-Systems

This article is not intended to depict specific manufacturers or tools. Rather, different classes of IT systems will be explained using the integration pyramid (see Figure 6). All of these typically support automated or semi-automated process management. In the modern IT landscape, data, functions and methods are integrated along the value chain (horizontally) and across the various management levels (vertical). Depending on whether operational or strategic views on processes are necessary, different IT system classes are used.

In addition to many modeling and visualization tools (from simple as Powerpoint to complex CASE tools), there are six key IT classes, shown in Figure 6. Depending on the hierarchical level and degree of vertical or horizontal integration the following classes can be distinguished:

Figure 6. IT tools supporting BPM classified in the integration pyramid of an organization

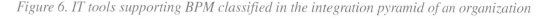

14

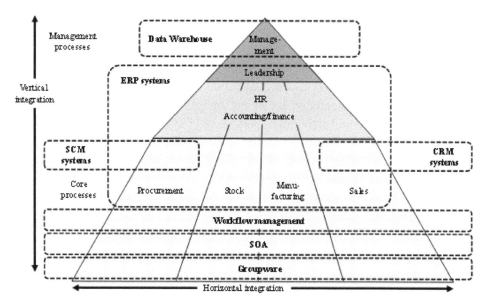

- **Data warehouse**: Systems of this class manage data and allow rough as well as detailed data analysis. For example, a dashboard is used to interactively show a divisional manager whether the process meets key performance indicators. Various visualizations (for example as diagrams or cubes) are available, depending on the intended use.

- **ERP systems**: These systems provide the highest level of integration because they consistently manage all corporate data and operations of all processes. These powerful systems claim to define all the process-relevant information and steps in one central database. Even though many success stories of ERP systems are well known, they sometimes overwhelm companies with their holistic approach.

- **SCM/CRM systems**: These specific systems support e.g. sales, marketing, logistics or customer management. Much of these solutions are now offered as cloud software. For example, depending on the focus, these systems offer predefined sales funnel (steps from an interested party to the loyal customer) and provide very specific support for managing each step (for example, campaign monitoring, cross-channel action planning, etc.).

- **Workflow management**: If all process model contents can be modeled in standard procedures (for example, payroll processes), they can be automated in this system class. A rule engine manages the norms of the process (e.g., when to send a request to whom) and ensures all the constraints from the process model. Unlike the previous class, these IT systems can be customized to the specific enterprise, regardless of a specific domain.

- **Service-oriented architectures**: The idea of this system class is to encapsulate all the steps (services) of a process. The overall process flow can thus be flexibly realized from a compilation of services available.

- **Groupware**: In addition to standard processes, there are also weak or unstructured processes (for example, creative phases in product development). This class of systems supports knowledge work (e.g., through authoring systems or coordination mechanisms), which follows a process model but has high degrees of freedom.

Execution

The business process execution includes all the activities of starting and controlling instances, which contains concrete data of a specific application case (Scheer 1999). In principle, the instantiation of a process model can be done either manually (e.g. by the action of a person) or automatically (e.g. within the framework of a formulated rule) (Dustdar et al., 2003).

After a business process is instantiated, it can in principle be executed manually or with IT support. In the execution, the work steps and activities of persons or IT systems designed in the process model are processed (Fischer et al., 2006). Coordination is done by the responsible manager and/or an IT system. In corporate practice, in particular process exceptions, that is, events not provided for in the process model, lead to intensive coordination.

Monitoring

In addition to the operational monitoring of concrete process instances, this phase also includes strategic controlling. It includes the activities of the process documentation, the determination of key performance indicators (KPI) and their collection, as well as the implementation and control of improvement plans in response to the actual measured values. The main objective of this lifecycle phase is to increase the efficiency and effectiveness of the processes and thus of the company (Schmelzer & Sesselmann, 2008).

Starting point of almost all known monitoring approaches of BPM, such as process benchmarking, the Balanced Scorecard or cause-and-effect, is the collection of performance and key figures from processes. In contrast to the pure recording of process performance, process indicators represent the repeated and recurring measurement of certain points of interest (Köster, 2008). Geich (2001) summarizes in his review general tasks of process monitoring:

- Modern performance measures include both financial and non-financial metrics (Geich, 2001) as it often turns out in practice that not only the costs of a business process should be the focus of attention (Fischer et al., 2006).
- Since monitoring strives for well-balanced KPIs as well as a perfect match between defined operational and strategic plans, a monitoring tool must offer comparative and analyzing controlling possibilities. In this context, four essential analyzes are used in practice: (i) target/actual comparisons (e.g. information from the execution), (ii) actual comparisons (e.g. time comparisons), (iii) Analysis of deviations (e.g. weak point analysis) and (iv) procedural/ behavioral control (e.g. reconciliation of decisions).
- Although many companies currently design only a small degree of detail of their processes (Fink, 2003), the importance of increasingly stronger power level differentiation and target reconciliation at all levels of performance measurement performance will increase. As a logical consequence, the monitoring on an aggregated level (e.g. for overall processes) is needed as well as detailed evaluations (e.g. of a single activity or groups of activities within the process).
- Due to increasing stakeholder influence the preparation and presentation of key performance indicators and performance parameters is getting more important. This is due to the fact that stakeholders often have different specialist know-how and thus also often place very different interests in terms of process indicators.

Figure 7. Upcoming BPM trends (Lederer, Schott & Knapp, 2017)

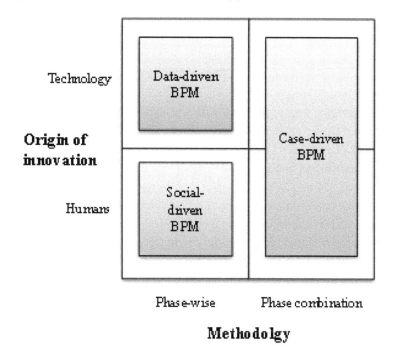

Trends

The experiences with the phases of the classical lifecycle as well as the availability of new technologies result in new approaches for BPM. A compilation of modern trends should serve as closing of this contribution (Lederer, Schott & Knapp, 2017).

Based on a study by (Lederer, Schott & Knapp, 2017), it was shown that three major trends continue to enrich the BPM in the future.

Trends of the first trend (subsumed under *Social-driven BPM*) use the ideas, initiatives and experiences of the process team in procedures to gain important impulses for the BPM life cycle. Employees or customers who are active or even involved in the process execution get the power to independently identify improvement potentials. Proposals are prepared and made available by teams. Depending on the actual approach, employees/customers can only report improvements or make them directly in the process model. IT supports this further development (e.g. by virtual post-its in process models) that humans play a more important role for BPM. An explicit approach of this trend is known under the term BPM 2.0, which introduces specific approaches (e.g. tool support, role models) how unstructured or semi-structures ideas from front-line workers can be translated into process optimizations. This trend explicitly addresses the fact that process teams know best about customer needs and expectations. Their valuable input in the BPM lifecycle is used to enable process innovations. Frameworks and especially modeling notations from the trend of Subject-oriented BPM (S-BPM) have been developed to support this general development. S-BPM is no longer driven from a top-down view on processes, but to offer solutions for modeling and optimizing processes from the point of view of individual employees.

Due to the increasing automation of business processes, the presence of intelligent algorithms as well as many available sensors, data can also be used for the optimization of the processes (subsumed under *Data-driven BPM*). In this category, data consist for example of events, functions, resources and time, relevant to analyze a process. Processes are for example increasingly supported and controlled by information systems that store events such as messages and transactions. Information systems in companies generate and collect data, which can be used, for example, by using process mining to identify, monitor and improve processes. Aspects of prediction based on data lead to the idea of Intelligent BPM. It leverages the connection of digital processes with physical objects in order to optimize business processes on a data-driven basis.

In principle, the individual approaches subsumed under the trend *Case-driven BPM* use the same sources for optimization. However, they deviate from the classic BPM lifecycle by operating business following cases instead of routine process instances. Methods of this trend use the inputs of people involved in processes as well as available data. However, in order to enable a general flexibility of procedures, certain processes instances are performed in the way of cases (Case-driven BPM). Case management is about supporting knowledge workers who require a higher degree of flexibility than it can be provided by the traditional process management. The processing of cases is originally from the medical field where procedures include both highly structured (e.g., performing an x-ray) but also very poorly structured (e.g., finding a complicated diagnosis).

CONCLUSION

Business process management already has a long tradition in organizations, because it focuses in the core on the continuous management of workflows across functional boundaries. The increasing digitalization results in numerous new starting points for optimization along the BPM life cycle, for example through simulation and automation.

REFERENCES

Allweyer, T. (2014). *BPMS: Einführung in Business Process Management-Systeme*. Norderstedt: BoD.

Becker, J., Kugeler, M., & Rosemann, M. (2013). *Process Management: A Guide for the Design of Business Processes*. Springer.

Bleicher, K. (1991). *Organisation*. Gabler. doi:10.1007/978-3-322-82918-4

Draheim, D. (2010). *Business Process Technology: A Unified View on Business Processes, Workflows and Enterprise Applications*. Springer. doi:10.1007/978-3-642-01588-5

Dustdar, S. (2005). Architecture and design of an internet-enabled integrated workflow and groupware system. *Business Process Management Journal*, *11*(3), 275–290. doi:10.1108/14637150510600452

Fink, C. A. (2003). *Prozessorientierte Unternehmensplanung*. DUV. doi:10.1007/978-3-663-11194-8

Fischer, H., Fleischmann, A., & Obermeier, S. (2006). *Geschäftsprozesse realisieren*. Vieweg.

Franz, P., & Kirchmer, M. (2012). *Value-Driven Business Process Management: The Value-Switch for Lasting Competitiv*. McGraw.

Gadatsch. (2012). *Grundkurs Geschäftsprozess-Management*. Wiesbaden: Springer.

Gleich, R. (2001). *Das System des Performance Measurement*. Vahlen.

Hammer, M., & Champy, J. (1994). *Business Reengineering Work.* Campus.

Hammer, M., & Champy, J. (2003). *Reengineering the Corporation.* Campus.

Hansmann, K. W. (2006). *Industrielles Management.* Oldenbourg. doi:10.1524/9783486840827

Jeston, J., & Nelis, J. (2010). *Business Process Management.* Routledge. doi:10.4324/9780080557366

Köster, D. (2008). *Marketing und Prozessgestaltung am Baumarkt.* DUV.

Krallmann, H., Frank, H., & Gronau, N. (2002). *Systemanalyse im Unternehmen.* Oldenbourg.

Kurz, M., & Herrmann, C. (2011). *Adaptive Case Management.* University of Bamberg Press.

Laguna, M. (2011). *Business Process Modeling, Simulation and Design. Dorling.* Pearson.

Lederer, M. (2016). *Business Process Transparency Management.* University Erlangen-Nürnberg.

Lederer, M., Avci, R., & Schmidt, W. (2017). Should Process Management Add its Two Cents? A Classification Approach for the Selection of Process Management Build-Time Techniques for Software Development Purposes. In *Proceedings of the 43nd Euromicro Conference on Software Engineering and Advanced Applications.* Vienna: IEEE. 10.1109/SEAA.2017.40

Lederer, M., Butz, F., & Bodendorf, F. (2015). *Der mittlere Prozessmanager: Aufgaben der Transfer-funktion.* University Erlangen-Nürnberg.

Lederer, M., Raake, D., & Kurz, M. (2014). The BSC Cookbook: Vol. 1 - Ingredients for a Successful Balanced Scorecard. Ingolstadt: I2P.

Lederer, M., Schott, P., Huber, S., & Kurz, M. (2013). Strategic Business Process Analysis: A Procedure Model to Align Business Strategy with Business Process Analysis Methods. In *5th International Conference S-BPM ONE 2013 Proceedings.* Berlin: Springer. 10.1007/978-3-642-36754-0_16

Lederer, M., Schott, P., & Keppler, A. (2015). Using a Strategy-oriented Business Process Modeling Notation for a Transparent Company-wide Business Control System. *International Journal of Decision Support Systems, 1*(3), 325–347. doi:10.1504/IJDSS.2015.070152

Lederer, M., Schott, P., & Knapp, J. (2017): The Digital Future has Many Names - How Business Process Management drives the Digital Transformation. In *Proceedings of the 6th International Conference on Industrial Technology and Management.* Cambridge: IEEE. 10.1109/ICITM.2017.7917889

Lehmann, C. F. (2012). *Strategy and Business Process Management: Techniques for Improving Execution, Adaptability, and Consistency.* CRC.

Mc Cormack, K. P., & Johnson, W. C. (2016). *Supply Chain Networks and Business Process Orientation: Advanced Strategies and Best Practices.* Boca Raton: CRC.

Richter von Hagen, C., & Stucky, W. (2004). *Business-Process- und Workflow-Management.* Teubner. doi:10.1007/978-3-322-84807-9

Scheer, A. W. (1999). *ARIS.* Springer.

Schmelzer, H. J., & Sesselmann, W. (2013). *Geschäftsprozessmanagement in der Praxis.* Munich: Carl Hanser.

Schütte, R., & Vering, O. (2004). *Erfolgreiche Geschäftsprozesse durch standardisierte Warenwirtschafts-systeme*. Springer.

vom Brocke, J., & Rosemann, M. (2010). *Handbook on Business Process Management 2: Strategic Alignment, Governance, People and Culture*. Springer. doi:10.1007/978-3-642-01982-1

vom Brocke, J., & Schmiedel, T. (2015). *BPM - Driving Innovation in a Digital World*. Springer. doi:10.1007/978-3-319-14430-6

von Rosing, M., von Scheel, H., & Scheer, A. W. (2014). *The Complete Business Process Handbook*. Morgan Kaufmann.

Weske, M. (2012). *Business Process Management: Concepts, Languages, Architecturese Advantage*. McGraw. doi:10.1007/978-3-642-28616-2

Wittges, H. (2005). *Verbindung von Geschäftsprozessmodellierung und Workflow-Implementierung*. DUV. doi:10.1007/978-3-322-81937-6

KEY TERMS AND DEFINITIONS

Business Process: Set of several activities that transform a given input in several stages into a valuable output.

Enterprise Resource Planning: IT system aiming to integrate all processes and data of a company.

Process Modelling: The mapping of procedure in a diagram.

Process Re-Engineering: Complete redesign of procedures without considering existing structures/workflows.

Social BPM: Approach to use the ideas, initiatives, and experiences of the process team in procedures to gain important impulses for the process life cycle.

Workflow: A business process that is completely or partially automated.

Artificial Neural Network in Operation Management Regarding Communication Issue

14

Ayan Chatterjee
S. P. Jain Institute of Management and Research (SPJIMR), India

Susmita Sarkar
Bangabasi Evening College, India

Mahendra Rong
Bangabasi Evening College, India

Debmallya Chatterjee
ⓘD https://orcid.org/0000-0002-3395-691X
S. P. Jain Institute of Management and Research (SPJIMR), India

INTRODUCTION

Communication through a proper and optimal network by meeting demand in satisfactory level is an important part of decision-making in operation management. Proper and optimal network can be defined in a significant way. The term 'optimal' refers to optimization of cost, use of resources, like fuel, manpower etc. 'Proper' signifies congestion handling. More specifically, the term 'proper' follows the research question "How is congestion reduced in a specific network?" Considering these facts with different motivations and contexts, various decision-making models were developed in this area. Among all these models, ANN based models play a significant role for decision-making. In this chapter, a set of ANN based models are taken into account for analysing the efficacy of ANN as a tool. All the developed ANN based models are not taken as consideration. The specific models are selected based on three following criterion:

- Revolutionary change in goal over earlier models
- Revolutionary change in technical outcome
- Introducing a real scenario in modelling

Before going to the detail of the modelling analysis, a small outline of three major wings- Travelling Sales Problem (TSP), Vehicle Routing Problem (VRP) and Transportation Problem (TP) is given in the following:

Travelling Salesman Problem (TSP)

Travelling Salesman Problem is a combinatorial optimization problem as well as it is NP hard in nature. It is equally important in the area of operation research and operation management. The basic objective

DOI: 10.4018/978-1-7998-3473-1.ch159

of this problem is to identify an optimal path for a traveller among a set of cities/nodes. Optimality of network can be described in terms of cost, time, distance etc. But in generally, optimization of cost is taken into account. The crucial assumption of this problem is that each city should be covered once only. Mathematical structure of TSP model is,

$$\text{Minimize } Z = \sum_i \sum_j c_{ij} X_{ij} \tag{1}$$

Subject to

$$\sum_i X_{ij} = 1 \forall j \tag{2}$$

$$\sum_j X_{ij} = 1 \forall i \tag{3}$$

$$X_{ij} \in \{0,1\} \tag{4}$$

The list notations and corresponding significance is given below:

c_{ij} : Cost of travelling through the edge (i, j)

$$X_{ij} = \begin{cases} 1, \text{if the edge}(i, j) \text{ is considered in optimal network} \\ 0, Otherwise \end{cases}$$

Equation (1) denotes the objective function of TSP and that is minimization of total cost. Equations (2) and (3) ensure that each city is visited exactly once. Equation (4) represents that the only decision variable X_{ij} is binary in nature.

Transportation Problem (TP)

Transportation Problem (TP) is an optimization based problem. It is very much useful to connect the phases of supply chain. Also, it is useful to each phase of supply chain, i.e. in the cases of multiple production units, multiple retailing units, multiple warehouses etc. It is equally important to the critical issues of operation research. The objective of the problem is to minimize the transportation costs to ship goods from 'm' number of origins to 'n' number of destinations. Here, the transportation costs of goods from origins to destinations are given through a cost matrix. But there should be a balance between demand and supply of products. The LP structure of Transportation Problem is,

$$\text{Minimize } Z = \sum_i \sum_j d_{ij} X_{ij} \tag{5}$$

Subject to

$$\sum_j X_{ij} \leq S_i \qquad \forall i \tag{6}$$

$$\sum_i X_{ij} = d_j \qquad \forall j \tag{7}$$

$$X_{ij} \geq 0 \tag{8}$$

Here, d_{ij} represents cost of transportation of goods from $i-th$ origin to $j-th$ destination. Only decision variable X_{ij} is amount of goods to be transferred from $i-th$ source to $j-th$ destination. Objective (5) represents the minimization of cost. Constraints (6) and (7) represent the fulfillment of supply and demand of products respectively. Constraint (8) maintains feasibility condition of decision variable(s).

Vehicle Routing Problem (VRP)

Vehicle routing is also combinatorial optimization problem. It is very much realistic as well as it has wild range applications in present decade with different conditions and criterions. The objective of this problem is finding optimal set of ways for a finite set of vehicles to deliver a set of products to the customers properly. This is basically an extension of TSP. More particularly, objective function and constraints of TSP are same in VRP. Other assumptions of VRP are (i) balance between number of incoming and outgoing vehicles and (ii) capacities of vehicles must be greater than demand on each route. The particular NP hard problem is critical to handle in reality. The LP formulation of VRP is,

$$\text{Minimize } Z = \sum_i \sum_j d_{ij} X_{ij} \tag{9}$$

Subject to

$$\sum_i X_{ij} = 1 \forall j \tag{10}$$

$$\sum_j X_{ij} = 1 \forall i \tag{11}$$

$$\sum_i X_{i0} = K \tag{12}$$

$$\sum_j X_{0j} = K \tag{13}$$

$$\sum_i \sum_j X_{ij} \geq r(P) \tag{14}$$

$$X_{ij} \in \{0,1\} \tag{15}$$

Here, d_{ij} is cost of travelling by a single vehicle from $i-th$ node to $j-th$ node and the decision variable. X_{ij} determines that a particular edge is selected or not. Objective (9) represents minimization of vehicle traveling cost. Constraints (10) and (11) maintain the condition that each node is visited exactly once. Constraints (12) and (13) ensure that number of incoming and outgoing vehicles is same. Constraint (14) handles the condition that vehicle capacity on a particular path must be greater or equal to the demand of that route.

Artificial Neural Network (ANN) is a popular optimization tool in now a day. Actually different structures of Neural Network enhance the convergence of optimality in different ways. Also, in the area of operation management, decision makers can use the ANN based models for configuring the communication network corresponding to a particular firm. Among the techniques of ANN; Hopfield Network, co-adaptive network, Kohonen's network and Boltzman machines are popular most. The objective of the chapter is to develop a comprehensive analysis about the utilities of these specific neural network approaches with respect to the mentioned three fields.

Remaining parts of the chapter are maintained as follows: In the next section, a literature survey is developed on previous review articles of this field. After that different models are described with proper classification and analysis. At the end of the chapter, a conclusion is drawn with future direction of research in the field of communication management.

BACKGROUND

In the review article of artificial neural network based TSP models (Potvin, 1993), a comparative study is developed depending on three major architectures of neural network. These are elastic net, Hopfield Tank network and self-organizing map. TSP models are divided into two categories according to their implementation and performance. These are exact algorithms and heuristic algorithms. The major concern of this paper is to analyse the application of ANN in heuristic based themes. A thorough analysis of this paper says that Hopfield Tank network is not very much suitable to develop TSP models. But elastic net and self-organizing maps are better than that to find shortest way for a large number of cities.

Another important review (Daniel Graupe, 2001) is developed on TSP models using continuous Hopfield network. The objective of this paper is to develop a comparative study between Hopfield network and Kohonen self-organizing map in view of TSP models. In this development, it is shown that Hopfield network is better than Kohonen self-organizing map. This conclusion is drawn based on number of iterations to solve TSP models.

But these two previously mentioned reviews were developed in 1993 and 2001 respectively. After that some highly efficient TSP models are built up using ANN till today. In the proposed chapter, all such type of models are considered to analyse efficacy of ANN in TSP. But previously reviewed models are not excluded.

Another important field of communication management is Vehicle Routing Problem (VRP). A taxonomic review (Burak Eksioglu, 2009) was developed in the field of vehicle routing irrespective of tools and solution approaches. The main concern of this paper is how different solution approaches improve VRP. According to different application areas of VRP, the models are classified into some categories. The main attraction of the specific contribution is the synthesis of gradually improvement of VRP models using several approaches. But efficacy of neural network in this particular field was not analysed properly in this specific review article.

An excellent survey (M. Monica Subashini, 2014) was developed in the field neural network structure. In this particular contribution, different models of ANN are considered in comparative nature. These techniques are tested in the field Image processing. This particular paper is taken into account for choosing the required ANN models.

In the next section, the proposed discussion on communication management models is developed with suitable categorization.

Decision Making Models

In this section, different ANN based TSP, VRP and TP models are discussed with their corresponding unique efficiencies. For this purpose, 45 decision making models are collected from 29 different journals including conference proceedings. These models are selected based on technical efficiencies and consideration of significant realistic conditions. Among these, 8 are TSP models, 32 are VRP models, 1 is TP model and 4 are hybrid models. This categorization of models is listed in Table 1.

TSP Models Using Artificial Neural Network

An important approach (Beasley, 2003) of TSP was developed considering the Euclidean distance among the pair of nodes. This particular model takes Co-Adaptive Net architecture of ANN. The speciality of this dignified approach is less time complexity with a huge number of nodes considerations. Actually, to find the shortest path by maintain all the principles of TSP with a huge number of cities, this particular model is developed. Experimentally, it is observed that this specific model is well suited up to consideration of 85,900 cities with less time and space requirement. Ultimately, this efficacy is much better in view of large data set handling in computation.

Another technique (Hassan Ghaziri, 2003) of TSP was developed by considering a backhaul condition. More specifically, all the visited customers are partitioned into two categories using Kohonen mapping network. Beginning side of the neurons represents line haul customers and the end side of neuron represents back haul customers. Uniqueness of this approach is development of two separate chains of neurons based new network architecture. In this particular case, four type interactions are considered. These are interaction of line haul customers in the first chain, interaction of backhaul customers in the second chain, interaction of the two chains together at the tails and interaction with the depot with the heads of two chains. As a result, it can be easily decided that the number of revisited customers in the next iteration. This chaining system enhances the procedure of finding two clusters easily iteration wise. Experimental analysis shows that it provides very good result up to 1000 customers' problem. This

Table 1. Categorization of the communication management models wings wise

Models	TSP	VRP	TP
(Beasley, 2003)	✓		
(Hassan Ghaziri, 2003)	✓		
(Hui-Dong Jin, 2004)	✓		
(Junying Zhang, 2012)	✓		
(F. Jolai, 2010)	✓		
(Bert F. J. La Maire, 2012)	✓		
(Emile H.L. AARTS, 1989)	✓		
(Ricardo Insa Franco, 2016)		✓	
(Pedro M. Talavan, 2002)	✓		
(JEAN-YVES POTVIN, 1992)		✓	
(Jean-Yves Potvin, 1995)		✓	
(Linsen Chong, 2013)		✓	
(Xiaolei Ma, 2015)		✓	
(Weiliang Zeng, 2016)			✓
(Sina Dabiri, 2018)		✓	
(Jian Zheng, 2014)		✓	
(Peng, 2015)		✓	
(Abdolhamid Torki, 1997)		✓	
(Fabio Rafael Segundo, 2016)		✓	
(Koichi Maekawa, 2018)		✓	
(Georgios P. Mazarakis, 2007)		✓	
(Jae-Gon Kim, 2018)		✓	
(Nur E. Ozdemirel, 2000)		✓	
(Ke Song, 2018)		✓	
(Subramanya P. Nageshrao, 2017)		✓	
(Zhang Yi, 2016)	✓	✓	
(Jiaqiu Wang, 2016)	✓	✓	✓
(Irena Ištoka Otkovic, 2013)		✓	
(Aleksandar D. Jovanovic, 2014)		✓	
(Dragan Pamucar, 2014)		✓	
(Juan de Oña, 2014)		✓	
(Yajie Zou, 2018)		✓	
(Jian Zhang, 2018)		✓	
(Nuno Coutinho, 2015)		✓	
(Zhang Lei, 2014)		✓	
(Douglas K.Swift, 2018)		✓	
(Hong Qu, 2012)		✓	✓
(LORENZO Mussone, 2013)		✓	✓
(Xiaogang Ruan, 2012)		✓	
(Zhongyi Zuo, 2014)		✓	
(Jittima Varagul, 2016)		✓	
(José S. C. Martini, 2017)		✓	
(Van-Suong Nguyen, 2018)		✓	
(Yang Zhao, 2016)		✓	
(Carl Goves, 2015)		✓	

particular approach is developed based on SOFM (Self Organizing Feature Maps) 2 opt strategy. The limitation of this particular approach is failure of addressing non-Euclidean instances.

To reduce this problem, a TSP technique (Hui-Dong Jin, 2004) is developed using extended SOFM. This extension is dependent on two important properties of Operation Research (OR): neighbourhood preserving and the convex-hull properties. Specification of this approach is the closing property of excited neurons to input city and pushing these towards cooperative convex hull of the cities iteration wise. Efficiency of the scheme is analysed through both of theoretical and experimental ways. Experimentation is developed using standard data sets with various number of cities, ranging from 50 to 2400. This typical approach ensures that it is more efficient than some popular approaches, like- Budinich approach, KNIES algorithms and convex elastic net techniques. The complexity of this approach is very much less as well as it is sophisticated heuristic approach to handle a large amount of data set easily. Actually implicit property of convex hull with ESOM is implemented here to acquire topological neighbourhood among the preserved and inspected nodes of cities. As a result, it is tried to assure the necessary and sufficient conditions of optimal routes. So, it is observed that the particular approach is efficient logically; but it is not compared with some popular complicated heuristics approaches.

A particular methodology (Junying Zhang, 2012) of solving TSP is developed for symmetric Euclidean matrices. This novel approach is designed by combining two selective rules- overall and regional competition. These two competition methods are used to separate less competitive and more competitive neurons. More specifically, overall competition method is used to locate less competitive neurons and regional method is implemented to find more competitive neurons. After preparing the neurons priority wise, three important properties of operation research- preservation, convex hull and infiltration are used to find the optimal tour. The utility of infiltration is easily handling of complex TSP (both of symmetric and asymmetric cost matrices). Computational complexity of this approach is $O\left(N^3\right)$; N is the number of cities in a particular network.

Another efficient TSP technique (F. Jolai, 2010) is developed merging Hopfield network and data transformation. More specifically, logarithmic and z-score approaches are used as data transformations to enhance the efficacy of TSP over only using the Hopfield Network. Actually in Hopfield Network, only local optimum value is obtained. But inclusion of data transformation enhances the result to global optimum. This particular technique is tested with 10 cities and comparative analysis with other approaches shows the effectiveness of this particular scheme.

An innovative concept (Emile H.L. AARTS, 1989) is developed in the field of TSP with Boltzman machines. The idea of binary variable is introduced here to develop the decision making model. This is very much suitable to select a particular edge easily. The speciality of Boltzman structure is handling of the discrete models easily. Also, in the case of continuous problems, both of linear and quadratic forms are handled easily. The particular TSP model is developed on the basis of two consecutive approaches-(1) A Boltzman structure is selected in such a way that a particular TSP instance is directly mapped to the combinatorial structure and (2) the strength of connections are chosen in a specific manner such that cost function is represented with consensus function.

An important TSP model (Pedro M. Talavan, 2002) is developed by new types of parameter settings in Hopfield continuous network. Normally the drawback of Hopfield continuous network is occurrence of non-feasible solutions. More specifically, the trial-and-error approach brings a lot of non-feasible solutions in the optimal scenario. Here, some new parameters are introduced to ensure that an equilibrium point distinguishes an optimal feasible path. The particular enhancement is analysed through a set of 'n' cities, in both of using only CHN (Continuous Hopfield Network) and this extended model.

An important analytical review (Bert F. J. La Maire, 2012) is developed regarding Neural Network based TSP models. This particular analysis develops a comparative analysis of efficacy among Genetic Algorithm (GA), Hopfield Network and Kohonen Self Organizing Map. These three are basically taken into account due to soft computing efficiencies. Also, TSP is considered as NP complete in now a day. So, it is a good problem for analysing the efficacy of these three approaches. Ultimately, through various experiments it is observed that Self Organizing Map is efficient more among these three approaches.

VRP Models Using Artificial Neural Network

The vehicle routing problem (or demand responsive dial-a-ride problem) is concerned with the allocation of vehicles to service the customers properly. Decision making regarding dispatching of vehicles and corresponding crews is still dependent on manually expertise. From experience, it seems very difficult to develop model explicitly that expertise via a symbolic approach.

An alternative neural network model (JEAN-YVES POTVIN, 1992) is proposed as a sub-symbolic and empirical alternative for modelling the decision process of expert dispatchers. Preliminary results about the ability of the network to reproduce various decision rules are reported. This paper focuses on the problem: the dynamic dispatching of vehicles and crews. Utility of the neural network approach in this particular case is solved of dial-a-ride problems dynamically and feasibility of the dispatcher system. The flexibility of the neural network approach is very attractive in this context, because it can be trained in several dispatching platforms, and adapts them dynamically at the time of training phase.

A competitive neural network model (Jean-Yves Potvin, 1995) is developed to enhance the VRP with time windows. Basically, seed customers are identified over the whole distributed network properly. Here, ANN converges towards the centroid of clusters if such clusters are present. Here, the use of a competitive neural network during the initialization phase of an insertion heuristic for the Vehicle Routing Problem with Time Windows (VRPTW) is described. First, the neural network initialization is based on spatial considerations only. Better results are achieved by considering both spatial and temporal issues during the initialization phase. In this case, a third input unit relating to the time window at each customer would be added to the neural network. This specific approach of neural network is considered as ART network. Solomon's standard set is used for testing purpose.

A rule-based neural network model (Linsen Chong, 2013) is proposed to simulate driver behaviour in terms of lateral and longitudinal actions in two situations, car-following and safety critical events. The main attraction of this contribution is consideration of fuzzy for developing the rule based network. An approach of machine learning is introduced to mimic behaviour of individual driver. This particular method is equally applicable in both of homogeneous and heterogeneous data sets. Here, the importance of fuzzy logic is to divide reinforcement learning method and traffic state variables. The major extensions in this approach are inclusion of driver merging and lane changing behaviour.

Another model (Xiaolei Ma, 2015) on speed prediction is developed using a special type of neural network. This particular long short-term network is used to confine traffic dynamically in non-linear structure. The novelty of this model is automatic determination of optimal time lags with removing the error of back propagation.

In now a day, green vehicle routing is one of the most important research topics worldwide. A model (Sina Dabiri, 2018) is developed regarding this using convolution neural network. Here, this particular architecture is prepared with GPS trajectories. A channel is developed with four attributes (speed, acceleration, bearing and jerk). Then the large population segment is divided into small terms and it is prepared according to the model requirement of CNN. These small segments are handled individually and merging these solutions, ultimate path is obtained. The speciality of this methodology is obtaining more optimal result due to use of multiple layers iteration wise. The result is near about 84.8% accurate to the actual position. Another specification of this approach is removing the exposure to traffic and consideration of environmental conditions.

A great contribution (Jian Zheng, 2014) is developed for prediction of track changing decision of drivers using neural network architecture. The importance of this development are behavioural analysis of changing left and right track of the path. Also, path changing decision is considered in quantitative nature. This particular model is developed as multinomial model and the utility of this are estimation of model and validation checking. This is an initial enhancement in this particular field. So, the outcome of the model is not very well. Different experiments show that only 13.25% left track and 3.33% right track can be extracted correctly using this model.

To improve the accuracy of the particular model, another model (Peng, 2015) is developed with various criterions and different parameters. One of the most important parameter in this particular is time window and that is introduced here. Other considered parameters are visual search nature of drivers, vehicle operation, speed and condition of driving. The concept of back propagation together with neural network is used for predicting track changing behavior.

A self-organization Neural Network based VRP model (Abdolhamid Torki, 1997) is introduced in this paper for handling a group of Vehicle Routing Problems. Motivated by the outstanding performance of adaptive Neural Network approach in the Traveling Salesman Problem, an algorithm is devised to extend the domain of applicability of this approach to more complex problems. In this research, a new algorithm is designed based on SOFM for solving a class of routing problems. The simulation results demonstrate the capability of the algorithm to yield favourable solutions. Speciality of this particular model is that it is equally applicable to other type routing problems by a self-effacing modification.

A multi-copy routing strategy (Fabio Rafael Segundo, 2016) for a DTN built on the top of an Urban Bus Transportation System (UBTS) is presented with high efficiency. Using the buses as nodes, the contact history of nodes is used to improve the DTN communication. Depending on a journey predictor, a multi graph is built up in this formulation. The uniqueness of this approach is introducing minimal delay factor. Implementation of copy control algorithm enhances the concert of the system. In the UBTS context, the proposed multi-copy routing strategy outperforms the Max Prop strategy in terms of delivered messages, delivery rate, delivery delay, network load and cost of network messages per delivered message. The results indicate potential advantages of the ANN strategy over other ones in a real scenario.

A multi-scale simulation model with the pseudo-cracking method (Koichi Maekawa, 2018) is developed to estimate fatigue life of real RC bridge decks with a wide variety. An artificial neural network model is used for quick diagnosis for the remaining fatigue life at the site. The particular ANN model aims at quick but sound judgment equivalent to the pseudo-cracking method at the site.

In the model (Georgios P. Mazarakis, 2007) of signal processing work, the use of a time-domain encoding and feature extraction method is investigated to produce simple, fixed size matrices from complex acoustic and seismic signatures of vehicles for classification purposes. Classification is accomplished using an artificial Neural Network and a basic, L1 distance, archetype classifier and 8 bit microcontroller based sensor node. The TESPAR/FANN method provided high recognition rates between two types of vehicles using their acoustic and seismic signature. Different encoding alphabets have been tested and the effect on performance has been discussed. Classification performance is comparable with existing methods while computational cost is greatly reduced. A hardware implementation on a prototype wireless sensor node showed the effectiveness of that method to the vehicle classification task.

Another study (Jae-Gon Kim, 2018) proposes a neural network based predictive control (NNPC) approach that finds suitable weights for multiple factors dynamically so that the best performance of the intelligent parking guidance system can be achieved. This model enhances the efficiency of parking guidance system through dynamic control by selecting the parking lot in the best manner. Considering the fact that finding the best performance under public policy requires extensive processing time, the relatively low processing burden makes the proposed NNPC more applicable to real-time environments. Moreover, NNPC can adjust weight configurations in response to diverse parking environments.

A unique model (Nur E. Ozdemirel, 2000) of Automated Guided Vehicle routing is developed using the concept of artificial neural network. The main objective of this development is to find the shortest path for a single and free-ranging AGV that carry out more than one pick and deliver requests. This is NP hard in nature. Kohonen's self-organizing feature maps is developed to solve the problem. The developed algorithm outperforms the nearest neighbour rule for all request patterns and problem sizes in terms of the solution quality. But the nearest neighbour rule is always superior in computation time. A general result of these comparisons is that the algorithm provides good solutions within reasonable computation time for certain request patterns. The solution qualities for other patterns are acceptable but not as good. The main reason for this, is the unstable behaviour and that is considered as a major drawback also.

A learning vector quantization (LVQ) based neural network model (Ke Song, 2018) is developed for designing the driving patterns depending on the driving information of a vehicle. This multi-mode strategy shows the efficacy and it can automatically switch to the genetic algorithm under particular driving conditions depending on recognition results. The results show that the multi-mode energy management strategy can satisfy the needs of vehicle dynamic performance. And the energy management strategy can transform into a more suitable one based on driving conditions and produce a more economic performance than the thermostat strategy under the same dynamic conditions. In addition, a complex driving cycle is designed to verify the actual effect of this strategy MM_LVQ under complex driving conditions. The results show the efficacy under specific driving conditions. At the same time, the condition recognition effect helped the multi-mode strategy to adapt to real driving conditions.

An offline optimal charging strategic model (M. Gholami, 2013) is developed by taking the objective with minimizing the energy cost. This is done by exploiting the periodicity and predictable operation of the city buses. In this particular case, the actual demand of the energy of electric bus should be known and it has an important priority. A predictor is designed for addressing and the neural network model is capable to indicate the estimation of the energy demand of the next day. Three different optimal charging strategies are implemented using this. This shows considerable cost minimization i.e., capacity of charging the full battery at each available opportunity. A cost optimization between 32%− 54% is obtained at the time of comparing with the non-optimal strategy.

Another ANN based architecture (Douglas K.Swift, 2018) is developed to model and predict the traffic network. Application on the Connexion by Boeings (CBB) global broadband network was evaluated to establish feasibility. Exact classification and prediction regarding traffic network is very much essential for sizing network resource and for real-time network management. The purpose of this study was to examine whether or not network traffic on a large-scale broadband network could be modelled by adaptive, artificial intelligence, and computing techniques. The experimental results demonstrated that ANNs could indeed be used for network traffic modelling and have the potential for significant increases in accuracy and increased capability for adaptation.

A micro simulation based traffic model (Irena Ištoka Otkovic, 2013) represents the results of research on the applicability of neural networks in the process of computer calibration. VISSIM micro simulation model is used for calibration done at roundabouts in an urban area. It is developed on prediction of neural network for the traveling time between measuring points. Besides this, the process involves a comparison between the modelled and measured queue parameters at the initial level. The process of validation includes an analysis of traveling time and queue parameters on new sets of data gathered both at the modelled and at a new round about.

A neuro fuzzy approach (Aleksandar D. Jovanovic, 2014) is developed for authorities of local city with a serious effort to expand the number of low-greenhouse gas vehicles (green vehicles) at home. A system has been developed to optimize the green capacity in urban green vehicle routing. The objective of this paper is to propose a green vehicle distribution model in a public transportation network. The problem has been defined as a problem of non-linear optimization with dispersed input parameters, requiring neuro-fuzzy logic. An adaptive neural network was developed, taking into account the costs to be borne by operators and users, and the environmental parameters along the observed vehicle route. One of the advantages of this model is consideration of uncertainties in predicting the operator/passenger costs and environmental parameters. Besides, the model allows for planning the vehicle routes with the maximum of positive environmental effects, including reduced greenhouse gas emissions, and a better air quality in most densely populated areas.

Another model (Dragan Pamucar, 2014) of neuro fuzzy is built up for the routing of light delivery vehicles by logistics operators. The model takes into account the fact that logistics operators have a limited number of environmental friendly vehicles (EFV) available to them. At the time of defining a route, EFV vehicles and environmental unfriendly vehicles (EUV) are considered separately. For routing the particular model, an adaptive neural network is used to train by a simulated annealing algorithm. In this model, the input parameters are logistics operating costs, exhaust emissions and noise for the given vehicle route. This model has been developed to minimize air pollution, noise level and logistics operating costs. Although the benefits of using EFV are well-known, their introduction is gradual, and their optimal allocation on routes is very important, which gives the model presented here great practical significance. The practical value of this algorithm lies in the fact that the collected experience of a number of experts is incorporated into the model, thus avoiding a situation in which the routing of EFV is limited to the knowledge of individuals who find themselves in a position where they have to solve these problems alone.

A model (Juan de Oña, 2014) on service quality of public transportation is carried out using ANN. Here the service quality perceived by the passengers is analysed. The ANN is proposed in this research because of its numerous advantages over more traditional parametric models (such as regression models, structural equation models or logit/probit models), and other non-parametric models, such as decision trees. ANN allows to mitigate the inherent instability of ANN models, which is an important improvement in the field of ''black-boxes'' techniques, to which ANN belong, since until now there is no consensus about what method of relative importance must be used for determining the variables relative importance.

A lane changing predictor based on Adaptive Fuzzy Neural Network (AFNN) model (Yajie Zou, 2018) is proposed to predict steering angles. The prediction model includes two parts: fuzzy neural network based on Takagi–Sugeno fuzzy inference, in which an improved Least Squares Estimator (LSE) is adopted to optimize parameters; and adaptive learning algorithm to update membership functions and rule base. The prediction results indicate effectiveness and stability of this model.

A neural network model (Jian Zhang, 2018) is employed with carefully selected traffic trajectory data. The virtual vehicle production is organized by a unique structure. The mobility model comes from the observed real-world traffic data, and is learnt by using a neural network. Differs from prediction in macro-level, detailed behaviours of vehicles is considered. Since the traffic flow is complicated and sensible may be faced in some unknown traffic situations, the mobility model is more reliable and produces more realistic traffic data than using a conventional car-following mode. A way is proposed on managing and organizing the vehicles that makes the proposed model to be executed efficiently. Finally, the presentation is implemented by employing the SUMO simulator.

An autonomous Quality of Experience management approach (Nuno Coutinho, 2015) is proposed for multiservice wireless mesh networks, where individual mesh nodes apply reinforcement learning methods to dynamically adjust their routing strategies. Within the forwarding nodes, a novel packet dropping strategy is developed that takes into account the impact on QoE. A novel source rate adaptation mechanism is considered here with the available network capacity. The introduction of source rate control improves further the QoE of each service types and for different WMN topologies. In addition, this approach exhibits a significantly smaller control traffic overhead.

A residual capacity estimation model (Zhang Lei, 2014) is built up based on an ANN. Both of charging and discharging current together with temperature are taken into account. This model comprises of three inputs (temperature, current and voltage) and one output (residual charge). The result shows that the proposed model can provide an accurate prediction of residual charge while maintaining good generalization capability. The established model can be used to precisely monitor the state of charge of the ultra-capacitors in ESS, and lays a reliable foundation for control strategy implementation and operation safety.

A method (Xiaogang Ruan, 2012) of realizing vehicle's photo taxis and negative photo taxis through a neural network is developed. A randomly generated network is used for computation purpose. During training only weights of the output units are changed during training.

An approach (Zhongyi Zuo, 2014) combining historical data and real-time situation information is developed to forecast the bus arrival time. This includes two phases: Radial Basis Function Neural Networks (RBFNN) model and an online oriented method. RBFNN is used to learn and to approximate the nonlinear relationship in historical data and online oriented method is introduced to adjust the actual situation. Ultimately, the system designing outline is given to summarize the structure and components of the system.

An algorithm (Jittima Varagul, 2016) is simulated for detecting object for Automated Guide Vehicle (AGV) guidance problem to avoid obstacle. This system is designed in security of internal transportation system to prevent collision. Depending on classification of obstacles, the system is designed. The obstacles recognition system using ANN with back-propagation learning algorithm by learning HOG features, 100% accuracy is achieved.

An adaptive biologically-inspired neural network model (José S. C. Martini, 2017) is made to receive the system state and is able to change the behaviour of the control scheme and order of semaphore phases. This particular adaptive control is evaluated on a single intersection scenario. The performance evaluation ensures that the model has higher adaptability and capacity than the previous traffic responsive control method, which is mainly attributed to its flexible and constant system monitoring and acting possibility.

A novel ANN controller (Van-Suong Nguyen, 2018) by using the head-up coordinate system is proposed to control automatically the ship into the berth in different ports without retraining the ANN structure. Numerical simulations are performed for two ports which verified the effectiveness of the proposed model.

A novel descriptor (Yang Zhao, 2016) is developed with road occupancy rate, for measuring campus traffic congestion level and it is statistically proved to be the most effective descriptor among other descriptors. Markov model and back propagation neural network (BPNN), are combined with the proposed descriptors. Experimental results show that the proposed methods can achieve desirable performance for detecting traffic congestion in campus, while the BPNN based method obtains more stable performance.

The results also point towards the importance of the proposed method for traffic congestion detection in campus.

By using Artificial Neural Networks (ANN), an excellent model (Carl Goves, 2015) is developed that 90% of the time predicts future traffic density 15 minutes into the future within 2.6 veh/km/lane of accuracy.

An energy consumption based ANN model (Ricardo Insa Franco, 2016) is developed to calculate the energy consumption of electric trains. It shows a good agreement with the target data. Output is compared with another subset of measured data and it provided a good estimation of the energy consumption with slight underestimation of negative energy peaks.

Transportation Model Using Artificial Neural Network

An ANN based transportation model (Weiliang Zeng, 2016) depending on theory of vehicle dynamics is developed to predict the vehicle CO_2 emission per kilometer and determine an eco-friendly path that results in minimum CO_2 emissions while satisfying travel time budget. The importance of this approach are-

(1)   The relative importance analysis indicates that the average speed and average acceleration occupy 85.6% relative importance to the CO_2 emission model.

(2)   Eco-friendly path offers significantly reduced CO_2 emissions at little cost in terms of increased travel time and the tours. On average, an eco-friendly path can reduce CO_2 emissions by 6.98%, 5.15%, and 10.17% relative to the observed path, the shortest distance path, and the least travel time path respectively.

(3)   Compared to the observed path as selected empirically by the driver,the eco - friendly path offers significant advantage in terms of travel time(reducedby16.95%) and CO_2 emissions (reduced by 6.98%) though the travel distance is slightly longer (by 0.3 km).

(4)   In an eco-routing experiment using all the observed OD pairs, it is found that the percentage of trips in which CO_2 emissions are reduced increases as the travel time buffer increases. Interestingly, when the travel time buffer reaches 10%, a certain degree of CO_2 emissions reduction is achieved for almost all trips.

(5)   The average reduction in CO_2 emissions achieved by the eco-friendly path reaches a maximum of around 11% for trip OD distances between 6 km and 9 km and when the travel time buffer is around 10%. This indicates that setting a travel time buffer of 10% is appropriate for this eco-routing model, because this results in the greatest reduction in CO_2 emissions for the least cost in terms of travel time.

Hybrid Models Using Artificial Neural Network

A pulse coupled neural network model (Zhang Yi, 2016) is developed to find a single pair shortest path. A unique structure (on-forward/off-backward) is introduced to reduce the search space. In this mechanism, neighbourhood forward region is excited and backward region is inhibited at the time of firing a neuron. As a result, shortest path can be obtained quickly with less time complexity. Also, shortest path is involved in both of TSP and VRP. Therefore, it is considered in both these fields.

A space time delay network model (Jiaqiu Wang, 2016) is developed for merging temporal and spatial auto correlation of a network through both of local and dynamic approach. The concept of dynamic approach enhances the prediction of travel time efficiently.

Another modified continued pulse coupled network model (Hong Qu, 2012) was developed for large scale nonlinear shortest path computation. The idea of tree structure is used to handle the nonlinear structure. The specialty of the model is lateral connection among neurons through wave propagation. An approach (LORENZO Mussone, 2013) of multilayer forward network is developed to estimate Origin Destination (O-D) matrix of traffic. Here, the speciality is dynamic computation and due to that reason efficiency of the scheme is enhanced. Ultimately, missing data can be taken into account in this model for decision making.

CONCLUSION

In this critical review and discussion, three important categories (TSP, VRP and TP) of communication management are described shortly. Trends of research of these three particulars in last few years are realized properly. Moreover new policy enhancement, like- environment issue, zero carbon emission issue etc. are taken into consideration. From another view, the utility of artificial neural network can be comprehended properly in this particular research and development area. In the analysis of Potvin (Potvin, 1993), it was shown that ANN is not a sufficient approach in the area of communication management. But huge improvement ANN methodologies in last few years improve the decision making models with new policies efficiently.

FUTURE DIRECTION

Artificial Neural Network (ANN) is an important tool in the area of pattern recognition. In now a day, quantitative management research is using machine learning as a tool in different interdisciplinary fields, like- marketing, finance, human resource etc. Artificial Neural Network is also a part of machine learning. So, future researchers will be benefited by knowing about the different approaches of artificial neural network from this chapter. In view of optimization, researchers will be benefited from two sides- methods and applications. First, different methods of ANN that are discussed in this paper will give an overview about ANN regarding optimization. Second, the different application areas of optimization, like- VRP, TP and TSP can be enhanced in future by considering a lot of other real factors with other optimization models. That will also help to the researchers in the area of operation research and operation management.

REFERENCES

Abdolhamid Torki, S. S. (1997). A Competitive Neural Network Algorithm for Solving vehicle. *Computers & Industrial Engineering, 33*(3-4), 473–476. doi:10.1016/S0360-8352(97)00171-X

Beasley, E. C. (2003). The co-adaptive neural network approach to the Euclidean Travelling Salesman Problem. *Neural Networks*, 1499–1525. PMID:14622879

Bert, F. J., & La Maire, V. M. (2012). Comparison of Neural Networks for Solving the. *11th Symposium on Neural Network Applications in Electrical Engineering* (pp. 21-24). Belgrade, Serbia: IEEE.

Coutinho, N., Matos, R., Marques, C., Reis, A., Sargento, S., Chakareski, J., & Kassler, A. (2015). Dynamic dual -reinforcement-learning routing strategies for quality of experience-aware wireless mesh networking. *Computer Networks*, *88*, 269–285. doi:10.1016/j.comnet.2015.06.016

Daniel Graupe, R. G. (2001). Implementation of traveling salesman's problem using neural network. *ECE 559 Neural Networks*.

de Oña, J. (2014). Neural networks for analyzing service quality in public transportation. *Expert Systems with Applications*, *41*(15), 6830–6838. doi:10.1016/j.eswa.2014.04.045

Eksioglu, B., Vural, A. V., & Reisman, A. (2009). The vehicle routing problem: A taxonomic review. *Computers & Industrial Engineering*, *57*(4), 1472–1483. doi:10.1016/j.cie.2009.05.009

Emile,, H. L., & Aarts, J. H. (1989). Boltzmann machines for travelling salesman problems. *European Journal of Operational Research*, 79–95.

Franco. (2016). Modelling electric trains energy consumption using Neural Networks. In *XII Conference on Transport Engineering, CIT, 7-9 June* (pp. 59 – 65). Valencia, Spain: Elsevier.

Gholami, M., Cai, N., & Brennan, R. W. (2013). An artificial neural network approach to the problem of wireless sensors. *Robotics and Computer-integrated Manufacturing*, *29*(1), 96–109. doi:10.1016/j.rcim.2012.07.006

Goves, C. (2015). Short term traffic prediction on the UK motorway network using neural networks. *European Transport Conference– from Sept-28 to Sept-30*, 184 – 195.

Hassan Ghaziri, I. H. (2003). A neural network algorithm for the traveling salesman problem with backhauls. *Computers & Industrial Engineering*, *44*(2), 267–281. doi:10.1016/S0360-8352(02)00179-1

Hui-Dong Jin, K.-S. L.-B. (2004). An expanding self-organizing neural network for the traveling salesman problem. *Neurocomputing*, 267–292.

Jean-Yves Potvin, C. R. (1995). Clustering for vehicle routing with a competitive neural network. *Neurocomputing*, *8*(2), 125–139. doi:10.1016/0925-2312(94)00012-H

Jian Zheng, K. S. (2014). Predicting driver's lane-changing decisions using a neural. *Simulation Modelling Practice and Theory*, *42*, 73–83. doi:10.1016/j.simpat.2013.12.007

Jolai, F., & Ghanbari, A. (2010). Integrating data transformation techniques with Hopfield neural networks for solving travelling salesman problem. *Expert Systems with Applications*, *37*(7), 5331–5335. doi:10.1016/j.eswa.2010.01.002

Jovanovic, A. D., Pamučar, D. S., & Pejčić-Tarle, S. (2014). Green vehicle routing in urban zones – A neuro-fuzzy approach. *Expert Systems with Applications*, *41*(7), 3189–3203. doi:10.1016/j.eswa.2013.11.015

Junying Zhang, X. B. (2012). An overall-regiona lcompetitive self-organizing map neural network for the Euclidean traveling salesman problem. *Neurocomputing*, *89*, 1–11. doi:10.1016/j.neucom.2011.11.024

Kim, J.-G. (2018). Dynamic control of intelligent parking guidance using neural network. *Computers & Industrial Engineering*, *120*, 15–30. doi:10.1016/j.cie.2018.04.023

Lei, Z., W. Z. (2014). Residual Capacity Estimation for Ultracapacitors in Electric Vehicles Using Artificial Neural Network. *Proceedings of the 19th World Congress* (3899-3904). Cape Town, South Africa: The International Federation of Automatic Control. 10.3182/20140824-6-ZA-1003.00657

Linsen Chong, M. M. (2013). A rule-based neural network approach to model driver. *Transportation Research Part C, Emerging Technologies*, *32*, 207–223. doi:10.1016/j.trc.2012.09.011

Maekawa, K. (2018). Remaining fatigue life assessment of in-service road bridge decks based. *Engineering Structures*, 602–616.

Martini. (2017). Adaptive traffic signal control based on bio-neural network. In *International Workshop on Adaptive Technology* (pp. 1182-1187). Elsevier.

Mazarakis, G. P., & Avaritsiotis, J. N. (2007). Vehicle classification in Sensor Networks using time-domain. *Microprocessors and Microsystems*, *31*(6), 381–392. doi:10.1016/j.micpro.2007.02.005

Monica Subashini, M., & Sahoo, S. K. (2014). Pulse coupled neural networks and its applications. *Expert Systems with Applications*, *41*(8), 3965–3974. doi:10.1016/j.eswa.2013.12.027

Mussone, L. (2013). OD Matrices Network Estimation from Link Counts by Neural Networks. *Journal of Transportation Systems Engineering and Information Technology*, *13*(4), 84–93. doi:10.1016/S1570-6672(13)60117-8

Nguyen, V.-S. (2018). Artificial neural network controller for automatic ship berthing using head-up coordinate system. *International Journal of Naval Architecture and Ocean Engineering*, *10*(3), 235–249. doi:10.1016/j.ijnaoe.2017.08.003

Otkovic, I. I. (2013). Calibration of microsimulation traffic model using neural network. *Expert Systems with Applications*, *40*(15), 5965–5974. doi:10.1016/j.eswa.2013.05.003

Ozdemirel, N. E. (2000). A self-organizing neural network approach for the single AGV. *European Journal of Operational Research*, *121*(1), 124–137. doi:10.1016/S0377-2217(99)00032-6

Pamucar, D. (2014). Green logistic vehicle routing problem: Routing light delivery vehicles in urban areas using a neuro-fuzzy model. *Expert Systems with Applications*, *41*(9), 4245–4258. doi:10.1016/j.eswa.2014.01.005

Pedro, M., & Talavan, J. Y. (2002). Parameter setting of the Hopfield Network applied to TSP. *Neural Networks*, 363–373. PMID:12125891

Peng, J., Guo, Y., Fu, R., Yuan, W., & Wang, C. (2015). Multi-parameter prediction of drivers' lane-changing behaviour with. *Applied Ergonomics*, *50*, 207–217. doi:10.1016/j.apergo.2015.03.017 PMID:25959336

Potvin, Y. S.-M. (1992). Neural networks for automated vehicle dispatching. *Computers Ops Res.*, 267-276.

Potvin, J.-Y. (1993). The Traveling Salesman Problem:A Neural Network Perspective. *ORSA Journal on Computing*, 1–60.

Qu, H., Yang, S. X., Yi, Z., & Wang, X. (2012). A novel neural network method for shortest path tree computation. *Applied Soft Computing*, *12*(10), 3246–3259. doi:10.1016/j.asoc.2012.05.007

Ruan, X. L. D. (2012). Vehicle Study with Neural Networks. Physics Procedia, 25, 814 – 821.

Segundo, F. R. (2016). A DTN routing strategy based on neura lnetworks fo rurban bus. *Journal of Network and Computer Applications*, 216–228. doi:10.1016/j.jnca.2016.02.002

Sina Dabiri, K. H. (2018). Inferring transportation modes from GPS trajectories using a. *Transportation Research Part C, Emerging Technologies*, *86*, 360–371. doi:10.1016/j.trc.2017.11.021

Song, K., Li, F., Hu, X., He, L., Niu, W., Lu, S., & Zhang, T. (2018). Multi-mode energy management strategy for fuel cell electric vehicles based. *Journal of Power Sources*, *389*, 230–239. doi:10.1016/j.jpowsour.2018.04.024

Subramanya, P., & Nageshrao, J. J. (2017). *Charging cost optimization for EV buses. In International Federation of Automatic Control*. Elsevier.

Swift, D. K., & Dagli, C. H. (2018). A study on the network traffic of Connexion by Boeing:Modeling with artificial neural networks. *Engineering Applications of Artificial Intelligence*, *21*(8), 1113–1129. doi:10.1016/j.engappai.2008.04.019

Varagul, J. (2016). Simulation of Detecting Function object for AGV using Computer Vision with Neural Network. In *20th International Conference on Knowledge Based and Intelligent Information and Engineering Systems* (pp. 159 – 168). Elsevier. 10.1016/j.procs.2016.08.122

Wang, J., Tsapakis, I., & Zhong, C. (2016). A space–time delay neural network model for travel time prediction. *Engineering Applications of Artificial Intelligence*, *52*, 145–160. doi:10.1016/j.engappai.2016.02.012

Weiliang Zeng, T. M. (2016). Prediction of vehicle CO2 emission and its application. *Transportation Research Part C, Emerging Technologies*, *68*, 194–214. doi:10.1016/j.trc.2016.04.007

Xiaolei Ma, Z. T. (2015). Long short-term memory neural network for traffic speed. *Transportation Research Part C, Emerging Technologies*, 187–197.

Yi, Z. (2016). Shortest path computation using pulse-coupled neural networks with restricted autowave. *Knowledge-Based Systems*, 1–11.

Zhang, J., & El Kamel, A. (2018). Virtual traffic simulation with neural network learned mobility model. *Advances in Engineering Software*, *115*, 103–111. doi:10.1016/j.advengsoft.2017.09.002

Zhao. (2016). Research on campus traffic congestion detection using BP neural network and Markov model. *Journal of Information Security and Applications, 31*, 54-60.

Zou, Y. (2018). Lane-changes prediction based on adaptive fuzzy neural network. *Expert Systems with Applications*, *91*, 452–463. doi:10.1016/j.eswa.2017.09.025

Zuo, Z. (2014). Bus Arrival Time Prediction Using RBF Neural Networks Adjusted by Online Data. In *The 9th International Conference on Traffic & Transportation Studies (ICTTS'2014)* (pp. 67 – 75). Elsevier.

KEY TERMS AND DEFINITIONS

Artificial Neural Network: A framework for handling machine learning procedures critically. More specifically, it is one of the best ways to realize a certain pattern automatically.

Communication Management: Organization of communication through vehicles properly with meeting the demand in an optimal way.

Transportation Problem: TP is management of production unit to retailing market in an optimal way such that cost is minimized and maximum amount of resources can be utilized.

Travelling Salesman Problem: TSP is a NP hard problem to find the shortest path in a particular network with covering all the nodes.

Vehicle Routing Problem: VRP is an extension of TSP. It is basically routing/scheduling of a set of different type vehicles in a specific network.

Enablers of Servitization Roles and Action Mechanism

14

Flair Karaki

Al Quds Open University, Palestine

INTRODUCTION

To build a long-term competitive advantage, the manufacturing industry has begun a movement to transform itself from simply offering products to offering customer-based services and solutions in addition to their products. This new business model is known as "servitization." There are several business service models that manufacturers can use according to their level of service integration.

In order to transform into a service-driven organization effectively, various types of servitization enablers have been presented and examined in this study. This paper is organized to investigate servitization enablers thoroughly and to analyze their interrelations. Perona et al. (2017) pointed out that enablers have not been discussed comprehensively by servitization literature. Moreover, the enablers for servitization have been, in general, investigated individually without analyzing their interactions, which are important to facilitate the desired transition.

The first section of this paper addresses the most influential enablers by focusing on:

1. Type of organizational cultural in servitized manufacturing.
2. Leadership behavior and personnel management during the process of servitization.
3. The role of digital technologies in supporting servitization.
4. Organizational structure and operations that facilitate servitization.

The second section emphasizes the interrelations between servitization enablers. In order to make appropriate decisions, it is essential to understand how enablers can be redesigned to achieve servitization as a new business strategy, and to analyze the nature of interactions between enablers, as lacking a holistic view of their collaboration may lead to servitization failure.

BACKGROUND

The term "servitization" was firstly introduced by researchers Vandermerwe and Rada (1988). Since then, researchers have studied it from different perspectives. Baines et al. (2009) defined servitization as "The innovation of an organizations' capabilities and processes to create mutual value by shifting from selling products to selling integrated solutions." The early literature introduces servitization as adding services to supplement the existing product (Vandermerwe & Rada, 1988). The more recent literature introduces service offering and customization as a dynamic and central activity (Ng et al., 2011). Servitization enablers have gained the attention of researchers, and they have classified them into multiple categories. Matthyssens and Vandenbempt (1998) identified organizational culture, organizational structure, and human resources as the key enablers, whereas Mathieu (2001) and Galbraith (2002) believed that

DOI: 10.4018/978-1-7998-3473-1.ch160

strategy, people, structure, rewards, and processes were the key enablers. Gebauer and Fleisch (2007) also presented the latter key enablers and extended them to include market-oriented service processes, relationship marketing, customer-oriented services, and creating a separate service organization.

The impact of servitization enablers is important to organizational stakeholders, and therefore this paper offers a great opportunity to add new knowledge regarding the understanding of servitization.

FOCUS OF THE ARTICLE

Organizational Culture (OC)

Management literature defines OC in different ways based on their related variables. Ravasi and Schultz (2006) gave a simple definition of OC as "A set of shared assumptions that guide what happens in organizations by defining appropriate behavior for various situations," and "it forms the basis to solve company's problems" (Dubruc el al., 2014).

Servitization is all about innovation of business offers, which consequently demands a service orientation OC (Dubruc et al., 2014). Zeithaml and Bitner (2003) defined service culture as "Culture where an appreciation for good service exists, and where giving good service to internal as well as ultimate, external customers is considered a natural way of life and one of the most important norms by everyone." Shifting from product-oriented OC to service-oriented OC means shifting the focus from achieving efficiency, economics of scales (Bowen et al., 1989) to innovation, flexibility, variety, and customization.

Schein (2004) determined three levels of culture:

1. The artifacts such as physical infrastructure, processes, structures, technology, and published values that can be seen and felt.
2. Espoused values such as norms, values, and beliefs that employees use to represent themselves within the OC.
3. Basic assumptions that are unconscious and taken for granted by employees.

Kinnunen (2011) suggested that changing OC would be in artifacts and espoused values only, because since the last level is not easy to recognize. Kinnunen (2011) argued that within the service transition, the artifacts will be concentrated on the role of the customer, type of customer relationship, and tools to measure performance, while espoused values will relate to the observation of the organization's basic mission, its philosophy, and its competitiveness. Nuutinen and Lappalainen (2012) revealed that in a product-oriented organization, the product history was positioned in the firms' mentality, existed in the structure and in management practices, therefore, the existing OC obscured new ways of thinking and the ability to develop a real service business.

Gebauer et al. (2012) emphasized modifying the company's values and employee behaviors in order to have a service organization and people-oriented OC. However, service OC is not rooted at the early stage of a transition, but is promoted when the service offering becomes recognizable and profitable (Geabuer et al., 2010).

In terms of OC change during the servitization process, there are several issues to examine:

1. The change of managers and employees' roles, and their service awareness are necessary (Nuutinen & Lappalaineen, 2012). Service awareness at the managers' level means changing their thinking

from services as "add-on" to services as "value added" activities (Gebauer et al., 2012), and doing business in new ways (Gebauer & Fleisch, 2007). At the employee level, it means changing employee roles from selling products to providing services (Gebauer et al., 2012).

2. Servitization requires OC characterized by flexibility, personality of services, and co-development with customers (Kinnunen, 2011).
3. Organizations are obligated to specify the amount and the type of required change of OC (Cameron, 2008).
4. It is not easy to change core beliefs about work and its purposes. When a more radical change is required, then changing deep-rooted beliefs regarding an organization's purposes and its key success factors is needed (Nuutinen & Lappalaineen, 2012).
5. It is essential that a service orientation be accepted in all business units (Gebauer & Fleisch, 2007), which depends on the required service awareness level (Gebauer et al., 2012).
6. The essential characteristics of service OCs are emphasizing service as a core task, developing integrative and cross-functional work practices, managing practices on the bases of flexibility and end results, and shifting customer relationships from short-term, transaction-based relations to long-term, development-based relations (Nuutinen & Lappalainen, 2012; Oliva & Kallenberg, 2003).

Cameron (2008) explored the steps necessary to establish a service OC by defining a type of OC to integrate and communicate values about the future OC, determining activities (to start with, to enhance, or to stop performing), beginning with easy tasks or concerns to change, setting milestones to measure and monitor change, enhancing communication channels, and training leaders for the job.

Leadership Behavior and Personnel Management

Within servitization, employees are encouraged to allow more interaction with customers, since customers are recognized as partners in creating value. From that perspective, practicing leadership in service-oriented organizations will not be the same as in product-oriented organizations. Consequently, leaders are expected to change their leadership style to direct and motivate their workforce effectively through the service transition process.

Leaders of service-driven organizations face challenges to direct employees due to the intangibility of their duties as they are related to communicating with customers. Therefore, the improvement of employees' self-motivation and the encouragement of more creative behavioral attitudes are essential (Yong et al., 2013).

Nie et al. (2013) stated that in servitized businesses, the areas of leadership that need change are:

1. **Fellowship:** Changing the focus from discipline and obedience to the effectiveness of followers.
2. **Value Source:** Deriving value from employees' thoughts rather than from blind procedures.
3. **Communication:** Solving problems through conversations with staff members regardless of their positions.
4. **Goal Setting**: Shifting from path goal leader to a leader who directs by setting an inspirational goal for the employees and letting them proceed, especially in a process to create a new brand, e.g. innovative services.
5. **Influential Power:** Using personality power instead of position power.
6. **Corporate Climate:** Replacing a hierarchy climate with a cooperative climate.

7. **Decision-Making Tools**: Shifting from a dependence on rigid databases or software to a societal-oriented software to share knowledge through joint communications and dialogs.

In the context of servitization, there are two comprehensive and well-adopted leadership styles that have been recognized: the transactional style and the transformational style. The transformational leadership style is centered on motivating staff to achieve superior results. It is about enhancing trust and confidence in the organizational environment and encouraging personal excellence. This is achieved by creating vision (Popli & Rizvi, 2015), enhancing communication, inspiring employees, and fulfilling employees' intrinsic needs (Yong & Kosak, 2014). Conversely, the transactional leadership style focuses on using authority, power, position, and policy to maintain control, and gets the job done through adopting transactions of reward and punishment (Popli & Rizvi, 2015).

Popli and Rizvi's (2015) work showed that the transformational leadership style is suitable for integrating service orientation into an organization, because it has direct and strong capabilities to create an environment for higher employee engagement.

Management studies have addressed human capital challenges with servitization, such as developing the abilities to build long-term relationships with customers and identifying employees' tasks to design and to deliver services (Rese & Maiwald, 2013). In that context, Gebauer et al. (2010) described a leader as a mentor, problem solver, and customer performance developer, and believed that employees should be hired for their behavioral capabilities and technical skills. According to Rese and Maiwald (2013), the number of employees who have direct contact with customers should be increased.

Gotsch (2014) identified the following individual capabilities required for service transition:

1. **Professional Expertise:** Refers to the technical competence and knowledge of conditions and corporate, which are essential for task-oriented services.
2. **Social Skills:** Refer to employees' behaviors and interactions with others, especially customers, which are essential for relationship-oriented tasks.
3. **Personal Skills:** Skills such as openness, resilience, self-confidence, good judgment, and readiness to learn.

However, Gebauer et al. (2010) also suggested that at the introduction level of services to an organization, technical competencies are required, and when service offerings become complex and dominant, then technical, social, and personal competencies become essential for job purposes. Gotsch (2014) suggested that employees who are involved in core service tasks would need new capabilities more than other employees in order to meet servitization challenges. Baines and Lightfoot (2013) agreed with Gotsch (2014), and suggested that enhanced capabilities were required for front office employees for service-related duties. They suggested five sets of skills that front office members were expected to hold, namely: 1). Flexibility to respond to customer needs; 2). Relation development, primarily with customers; 3). A service-centricity attitude; 4). Authenticity and; 5). Technical expertise in using systems and subsystems. Effective leaders have an obligation to build a cooperative OC amongst the employees, especially among the front office staff and, at the same time, maintain a comparable power balance between the front and back offices (Baines & Lightfoot, 2013).

Rese and Maiwald (2013) stated that managers might face two possible behavioral responses during a transition process, as employees could be either promoters or opponents to change. They viewed management's duty as being to reward the promoters, in order to gain more support from them, affect the behavior of others, and overcome opponents' resistance. Furthermore, they believed that management could also consider the opponents' arguments as valuable feedback.

Rese & Maiwald (2013) explained that resistance to change evolves as employees' attitudes and beliefs are influenced by the transition process. Gabouer et al. (2010) emphasized that convincing employees about change must be related to their appreciation of the added services based on their recognition of the opportunities accompanying change. However, this could lead to creating multiple values and beliefs within the organization, which could result in internal organizational conflict (Rese & Maiwald, 2013). Rese & Maiwald (2013) also argued that communication is effective to managing employees' resistance. They stated that at the early stage of applying the change, a downward communication channel is essential to inform employees about the upcoming change. During the actual change phase, the communication channel delivers how tasks are altered; face-to-face communication is a recommended at this phase. At later stages, communication content focuses on publicizing the success of the change process (Rese & Maiwald, 2013).

Digital Technologies

It has been stated that the service revolution and the information revolution are two sides of the same coin (Ardolino et al., 2016). Moving an organization towards a service-oriented business model demands an adoption of digital technologies (Oliva & Kallenberg, 2003). Ardolino et al. (2016) assured that making an investment in information and communication technologies (ICT), such as customer-relationship management (CRM) and enterprise resource planning (ERP) will contribute to applying services successfully and automating key internal processes related to manufacturing, accounting, and customer engagement (Bevan, 2015).

The works of Ardolino et al. (2016) presented the following key digital capabilities as being possible through the use of high-level technologies:

1. User Identification, such as a customer's personal ID to access to the service.
2. Product identification, such as product serial numbers and database to identify service.
3. Geo Localization, such as using GPS for allocating customer location.
4. Timing assessment, such as determining the time for billing services for customers.
5. The amount of product usage, such as connecting printers to a remote data platform in order to determine the paying invoice per user.
6. Condition monitoring, such as monitoring of equipment for incident faults by connecting it to a remote database.
7. Usage monitoring, such as sending notifications to customers whenever they use the remotely monitored machine inappropriately.
8. Prediction, such as using predictive models to estimate the reliability of critical components of a product.
9. Remote control to solve product parameters, such as sending a notification to a car driver to stop a car for safety issues.
10. Maintenance Optimization, such as making adjustments on a product from a remote surveillance center to increase efficiency.
11. Autonomy, by allowing a product to make certain actions by using data and system connections, such as allowing an air conditioner to automatically adjust the temperature as the weather changes.

The concepts of smart manufacturing and digitalization have been used intensively to illustrate technology as a servitization enabler to create smart products, services, equipment, and processes (Kang et al, 2016). The following are classifications of the most accepted, well-known technologies that enable servitization in product-oriented organizations:

1. Predictive analytics to forecast product failure (Paschou et al., 2017, Danges et al., 2015; Cimini, 2018).
2. Remote communications to fix or bend products remotely (Danges et al., 2015).
3. Observation of customer-related aspects by using advanced customer relationship management tools in coordination with consumption monitoring (Danges et al., 2015; Cimini, 2018).
4. Publication of information to employees or customers (Danges et al., 2015).
5. Mobile platforms to communicate with customers and to obtain data access for enterprise resources planning purposes (Danges et al., 2015).
6. Internet of things (IoT) for purposes of data exchanging and interaction (Paschou et al., 2017; Cimini, 2018).
7. Cloud computing that opens access to a shared pool of resources by different stakeholders (Paschou et al., 2017; Cimini, 2018).
8. Additive manufacturing (technologies that build 3-D objects) to produce customized goods with minimum waste of resources (Paschou et al., 2017; Cimini, 2018).
9. Big data, to gather and store a large amount of data for further analysis (Paschou et al., 2017).
10. Cyber security to develop protection of Internet-connected systems, including hardware, software, and data, against cyber attack (Paschou et al., 2017).

Cimini et al. (2018) stated that at the early introduction of service orientation to the organization, cyber-physical systems (CPS) are utilized to make products smarter, traceable, identifiable, and to give updated information on the system's status. As business progresses in the journey of servitization, digitalization becomes more critical and complex in supporting service offerings and enhancing supplier-customer relations (Cimini et al., 2018). Baines et al. (2009) stated that the main aim of technologies utilized in service driven organizations was to deliver value through facilitation and mediation, and that this was achieved by using intensive mediating technology.

Organizational Structure (OS) and Operations

The literature on servitized organizations neither presents empirical evidence about successful or unsuccessful organizational design (Kreye & Jensen, 2014), nor identifies the relationship between servitization strategy and the OS (Lobert, 2016). Servitized organizations face the challenges of integrating different levels of customer services into their operations, as well as adapting to market changes and customer requirements (Kreye & Jensen, 2014).

OS shows how activities, coordination, and supervision are managed in order to achieve organizational goals, and where the decision-making power and authority is located within an organization (Galbraith, 2002). According to Galbraith (2002), OS is identified by four areas: specialization, shape, distribution of power, and departmentalization. Generally, developing the appropriate OS by an organization depends on how the OS will fit and serve the organization's status (Mintzberg, 1979).

There are key differences between the OS of product-oriented businesses and service-oriented businesses. Product-oriented organizations are structured according to their product business. The involved functions of an organization are defined by the product kind and category, with hierarchical control (Galbraith, 2002; Shah et al., 2006). In general, sales are performed through intermediaries (Baines & Lightfoot, 2013), and the responsibility of service sales falls under the product sales units (Gebauer & Kowalkowski, 2012). Conversely, the service-oriented organization is described as an organization focusing on analyzing customer needs and creating values by obtaining the necessary knowledge of its clients (Lobert, 2016). Moreover, products and services are recognized as tools to solve customer problems. Customer or market segments are created to replace products, with several business units to offer products and services (Gebauer & Kowalkowski, 2012). In such organizations, front office functions and customer teams that supervise customer relationships are established (Galbraith, 2002).

A well-known service-oriented OS model is the front-back hybrid organizational model, or "interdependent system of profit centers" (Galbraith, 2002). It consists of two types of functions; front-end functions related to customer or market segments responsible for developing and delivering solutions, and back-end functions related to technologies and product lines responsible for developing and manufacturing products and services (Galbraith, 2002). These offices do not work separately, as the linkage between product, service, and customer-focused units is necessary (Galbraith, 2002), and is utilized through liaison devices to coordinate activities across the organizational units, e.g. informal processes, e-coordination, integrators, and formal groups (Galbraith, 2002). Kobashi and Konomi (2015) explained that front offices focus on a region or a country, and back offices focus on products. Thus, all or parts of products are developed in back offices in a standardized way, and then each product is customized in the front offices to meet the needs of the customers or the market (Kobashi & Konomi, 2015).

There are contrasting views about how service functions are designed and coordinated, and whether these functions should be integrated into the existing OS or separated (Lobert, 2016). Many scholars set different service typologies in order to design the proper service-oriented OS. Baines and Lightfoot (2013) focused on three broad service levels based on the customer integration into the organization's operations: 1). Base level (product, equipment, and spare part provision); 2). Intermediate level (training, maintenance, repair, overhaul and; 3). Help desk and advanced level (customer support agreement, outcome-oriented contracts, e.g. advanced rental and leasing solutions).

Gebauer et al. (2010) suggested the following classifications for service transition:

1. Customer service provider (supplementary services such as delivery, information, and billing services)
2. After-sales provider (spare parts, maintenance, inspection, and basic training)
3. Customer support provider (preventive maintenance, consulting, and advanced operating training)
4. Development partner and outsourcing partner (providing of customer solutions)

Schmenner (1986) built a service matrix of four types following the degree of labor intensity and the degree of customization. They are: 1). Mass service (high labor intensity and low customization); 2). Service factories (low labor intensity and low customization); 3). Service shops (low labor intensity and high customization) and; 4). Professional services (high labor intensity and high customization). Examining the literature related to product service systems (PSS), another significant platform of service appears (Tukker, 2004) as:

1. Product-oriented services (selling products with some extra services)
2. User-oriented services (selling functions of the product as leasing).
3. Result-oriented services (selling results or utility as an outcome)

Auguste et al. (2006), Gebauer and Kowalkowski (2012), and Raddats and Burton (2011) discussed types of OS related to service-oriented organizations, which are combined product and service business units, separate service business units, and customer focused business units.

The decision regarding the appropriate OS to adopt is made according to an organization's service-led growth strategies. As organizations find profitable opportunities from offering service, the transition begins in stages, starting with a few product-related services and ending up with a broad set of services or solutions offered. During the early phase, base level (Baines & Lightfoot, 2013) or customer service provider (Gebaure et al., 2010), the organization decides to offer services to support a product. The combined product and service business units will be a proper OS for this level (Gebauer et al, 2010, Oliva & Kallenberg, 2003; Raddats & Burton, 2011). This OS will include product-related units and service management functions (Lobert, 2016).

As organizations increase their service offerings, they will enter the next stage, the intermediate level (Baines and Lightfoot, 2013) or after-sales service provider and customer support provider (Gebaure et al., 2010). In this stage, the expansion of services is recognizable and profitable. Service offerings are created to support product differentiation (Raddats & Burton, 2011). At this stage, the use of separated product and service business units is appropriate (Bustinza et al., 2015; Oliva Kallenberg, 2003; Raddats & Burton, 2011). Gebauer et al. (2008) suggested that at the after-sales stage, offers should include only basic services and could be integrated into the existing OS, whereas, at the customer support provider stage, separate service units would be more suitable. Oliva & Kallenberg (2003) pointed out that if offers are related to building a relationship or process-oriented services, creating independent business units for services is essential. At this level, the growth of service offers leads to increasing service orientation in OC (Raddats & Burton, 2011).

The last stage is the advanced level (Baines & Lightfoot, 2013), or development partner and outsourcing partner level (Gebauer et al., 2010). During this stage, designing customer solutions is targeted, which means shifting from selling products to many customers to selling a broader set (products and services) to a limited number of customers (Raddats & Burton, 2011). At this phase, organizations started to re-locate their OS around customer groups (Gebauer et al., 2005; Raddats & Burton, 2011) and, therefore, the separation of product and business units is no longer a suitable OS, as the organization is expected to satisfy customers by integrating the efforts of all functions. Core teams in sales units, or designing customer-focused business units, are appropriate for this stage (Gebauer et al., 2008; Raddats & Burton, 2011). Consequently, a hybrid OS or matrix OS are formulated with two dimensions, customer units at the front end, and product and service units at the back end, and decision-making then shifts from product units to customer units (Galbraith, 2002). Gebauer et al. (2010) pointed out that R&D teams were necessary to work with customers and find solutions to their needs, and outsourcing partners are developed to overcome operational risks and to focus on customer operating requirements (Gebauer et al., 2010).

In summary, combined product and service units are appropriate for companies that sell products as a core business (Auguste et al., 2006). Independent service units are suitable for organizations that invest in service-driven growth (Raddats & Burton, 2011). Finally, customer focused units are appropriate if service is dominant, sales growth is decreasing, and separate product and service units are inappropriate (Raddats & Burton, 2011).

From an operations perspective, managing a service operation depends on the changes in OS, operation processes, and the identified type and number of tasks and people in the organization (Buzacott, 2000). Smith and Maull (2014) suggested that the challenges of servitization were not only associated with developing effective services, but also the actual integration between service (front offices) and production operation (back offices). Furthermore, they stated that the degree of customer orientation was the critical element for operational change. Thus, the concept of "lean service" has been used recently in the service operation literature as a proposition to concentrate on the value creation, and to eliminate non-value activities from processes (Resta et al., 2015).

In summary, Table 1 illustrates the differences between production and service operations.

Table 1. Differences between production and service operations

Items	Production Operation	Service Operation
Role of Goods	Goods are end products	Goods are either intermediate product or offer package of products and services with service dominance
Value Characteristics	Creating value through a transformation of raw materials, (transactional activities).	Creating value through activities focused on building a customer relationship along with transactional activities related to product sales
Design of Work	Work is divided into units; people are assigned to execute their specified duties.	Preferable to work as staff teams from different departments and from outside the organization.
Main Concern	Product innovation	Quality of services and solving customer problems in addition to offering products
Processes and Technologies	1-Physical transformation of materials into tangible goods 2- Automation of processes in order to achieve quality conformity and decrease employees' involvement.	1. Delivering value through facilitation and mediation 2. The use of intensive, mediating technologies. 3. Processes and technologies must facilitate service delivery.
Capacity	Meeting market demand aiming to maximize the uses of resources.	1. Lower capacity is accepted in order to respond to customer needs 2. Increasing capacity is allowed without changes in the service process 3. Capacity can be measured through a number of customers served by the service unit per day
Facilities (Baines, 2009)	1. Large factories; assemble closer to production location. 2. Vertical integration is preferable to minimize costs, to control over quality and supply chain.	Smaller, multiple friendly facilities close to the market, or centralized manufacturing area, and service points located close to customer operations.
Customer Data and Knowledge	Used for Controlling	Used as a Valuable Asset
Quality Control	Techniques focus on achieving product conformity and utilization of resources.	Delivering service is measured through the subjective judgment of individuals and customer surveys.
Product and Service Range	Producing a higher volume of limited product range	Producing a limited product range with bundles of supporting services.
Introduction of New Products and Services	New product is designed and tested before releasing into the market.	New service is designed in cooperation with the customer.
Work Structure	Hierarchal, vertical structure is preferable	Network flatter structure is preferable
Performance Measurements	1. Parameters: cost, specification, and delivery time. 2. Measurements: profitability, market share, productivity, low operation cost	1. Parameters: customer expectation of service, co-location, and response speed 2. Measurements: customer satisfaction, customer lifetime value, collaboration between employees and management. 3. Difficult to measure satisfaction as every customer has his/her own mindset to recognize the acceptable service.

Source: Baines, 2009; Buzacott, 2000; Martin & Horne, 1992; Neil et al., 2013; Nuutinen & Lappalainen, 2010; Shah et al., 2006

DISCUSSION

This paper investigates the enablers of servitization and four elements are examined, reviewed, and the interaction between the enablers is analyzed. Generally speaking, it is not easy to study servitization enablers and their interrelations due to their complexity and the abundance of their aspects.

The Interrelation Between OC and Leadership Behavior

OC is among the major concerns in research work and business practices, which represents a crucial dimension to all aspects of organizational behavior. Developing service OC on the basis of customization and close relations with customers is vital. Based on Scien's OC model (2004), changing OC requires changes to the espoused values (social context) and the artifacts (operating systems). Transformational leadership has been suggested to drive organizational change (Popli & Rizvi, 2015). Leaders can utilize their knowledge of OC to change an organization's climate towards innovation and customization (Brooks, 1996).

However, Pawar and Eastman (1997) pointed out that organizational context will impact transformational leadership functions. Porras and Hoffer (1986) stated that cultural context shapes leadership style. Furthermore, the extent of leadership impact on organizational performance is mediated by OC (Ogbonna & Harris, 2000). However, servitization is perceived as business model innovation, and transformational leadership style is essential in shaping and monitoring a desired OC (Sharma & Sharma, 2010). Dubruc et al. (2014) clarified that changing OC within service-centric businesses depends on managerial behavior and structure transformation.

Recently, many scholars have concentrated on the proposition of the bilateral relationship between leadership and OC (Kargas & Varoutas, 2015). Through servitization, the transformation leader will act as a visionary, a strategic change authorizer, and a facilitator of organizational context change.

However, personal resistance may appear against a leader's actions within the service transition process, and this can disturb the leader's attention. Therefore, a comprehensive assessment of existing cultural values, assumptions, and interactions, is necessary to form an operational framework used to perform gap analysis between the current situation and the desired outcome.

The Interrelation Between OC and Digital Technologies

The interaction between the introduction of new technologies and OC is a two-way relationship. Creating a service OC demands the integration of advanced technologies to facilitate service creation and value delivery. However, when new information technology is introduced, different employee reactions are expected and, at the same time, OC context will assist the employees to acclimate themselves to the technological development (Xie, et al., 2013). Employees' acclimation to the use of new IT depends on the employees' interactions with one another, such as expressing their reactions, sharing stories and tales, and the effectiveness of the embedded knowledge communication channels within the organization (Xie, et al., 2013). Technology, as an OC artifact, acts to reshape the existing OC values, as long as these technologies meet employees' expectations (Xie, et al., 2013). However, engaging in OC rituals can serve as a kind of social protection against employee anxieties about new technology developments in the workplace (Perona et al., 2017).

The Interrelation Between OC, OS, and Operations

Janicijevic (2013) stated that the relationship between OS and OC is reciprocal, thus new cultures legitimizes new structures, and new structures serve to shape new cultures in a condition of employees' acceptance of a new structure proposition. For the servitized organization, it is conclusive that a model of the organic OS is more likely applicable in a service OC, as it is more flexible, innovative, and has the ability to adapt to changes (Garg & Krishnan, 2003). Galbraith (2002) proposed a well-known model for service-oriented business called the "front back hybrid model," which emphasizes the assumptions of an organic model, with distinctive features of establishing front and back offices or divisions.

The Interrelation Between Leadership Behavior and OS and Operations

Leaders can change their roles from directing internal production processes to developing outside relations with customers (Nie et al, 2013). Moreover, they can change their focus from "operand resources" management, e.g. materials and equipment, to "operant resources" management, such as skills and knowledge, which primarily depend upon employees' intellect (Nie et al., 2013).

Burns (1978) stated that transformational leader is an independent power in changing OS. Pawar and Eastman (1997) argued that transformational leader suits the "adaptation organization," which is described as a dynamic environment that introduces change in response to the demands of environmental conditions. Further, the transformational leader will adopt a revolutionary act as long as he or she faces an organizational context with a bureaucratic-based OS; otherwise, the leader will act as a reformer and exploiter of organizational context (Pawar & Eastman, 1997).

The Interrelation Between Leadership Behavior and Digital Technologies

In general, leaders have the power and authority to influence, support, and execute, the needed service transition in technological systems. In the competitive and complex business environment that is facing servitized organizations, it is necessary that leaders create an OC that facilitates innovation and IT integration. The philosophy of management and the OC plays a primary role in determining the consequences that will result from the introduction of technology (Peyman et al., 2011).

The Interrelation Between Digital Technologies, OS, and Operations

Digital technology clearly impacts OS (Peyman et al., 2011). It determines the complexity of the OS, as the more the technology in use advances, the greater the complexity of the built OS must be in order to ensure additional coordination, control, and communication mechanisms (Peyman et al., 2011).

Peyman et al. (2011) stated that applying IT would facilitate organizational restructuring from the traditional hierarchal OS into a flexible matrix design, with minimum organizational borders. All tasks are integrated using information technology networks, the tasks' pattern changes from one task performed by an individual to group of tasks performed individually, and employee roles change from routine, simple tasks to designing customized solutions (Peyman et al., 2011). IT is also used within organizational operations to fulfill many different purposes. For a product-oriented organization, it is used to automate processes. For service companies, it is used to facilitate service offering and relationships with customers (Baines et al, 2009).

Figure 1. The interaction between servitization enablers

CONCLUSION

Presently, servitization as a new business model is recognized by many manufactures. However, the service transition is accepted when the transition is consistent with the different elements of the organizational culture. The more the direct attempts and efforts to change an organization's culture, the more the employees show resistance, therefore, the OC change attempts will end up in improving only the visible parts of the organizational culture. Thus, the transformational leadership style is recommended for integrating service orientation into an organization as it has strong capabilities to create an environment for higher employees engagement. Moreover, implementing servitization requires employees with more social, personal, and technical skills. It is also suggested that successful businesses incorporate the latest digital technologies into their business models to accelerate the organization's transition to services, develop new service offerings and ways of delivery. It should be noted that as the organization shifts its core business from selling products to selling services and building long- term customer relations, independent service units are required with redesigning of its internal operations. Finally, servitization enablers are interrelated deeply within servitization processes. The paper examined these relations at a macro level. However, the extent of change or transition of these enablers depends primarily on the required level of service integration.

FUTURE RESEARCH DIRECTIONS

This paper, being of an investigative nature, suggests a number of opportunities for future research in terms of theoretical improvement and concept validation. Further work is essential in:

1. Examining these enablers and their interactions within empirical research.
2. Examining the impact of these enablers on the different levels of servitization design.

REFERENCES

Ardolino, M., Saccani, N., Gaiardelli, P., & Rapaccini, M. (2016). Exploring the key enabling role of digital technologies for PSS offerings. *Procedia CIRP*, *47*, 561–566. doi:10.1016/j.procir.2016.03.238

Auguste, B. G., Harmon, E. P., & Pandit, V. (2006). The right service strategies for product companies. *The McKinsey Quarterly*, *1*(1), 41–51.

Baines, T., & Lightfoot, H. (2013). *Made to serve*. John Wiley & Sons Ltd.

Baines, T. S., Lightfoot, H. W., Benedettini, O., & Kay, J. M. (2009). The servitization of manufacturing. *Journal of Manufacturing Technology Management*, *20*(5), 547–567. doi:10.1108/17410380910960984

Bevan, D. (2015). Conceptual Model for the Use of ICT Systems to Facilitate Manufacturing SME Servitization. *The Journal of Innovation Impact*, *8*(2), 107–120.

Bowen, D. E., Siehl, C., & Schneider, B. (1989). A framework for analyzing customer service orientation in manufacturing. *Academy of Management Review*, *1*(14), 75–95. doi:10.5465/amr.1989.4279005

Brooks, I. (1996). Leadership of a cultural change process. *Leadership and Organization Development Journal*, *17*(5), 31–37. doi:10.1108/01437739610127496

Burns, J. M. (1978). *Leadership*. Harper & Row.

Bustinza, O., Bigdeli, A., Baines, S., & Elliot, C. (2015). Servitization and Competitive Advantage: The importance of organizational structure and value chain position. *Research Technology Management*, *58*(5), 53–60. doi:10.5437/08956308X5805354

Buzacott, J. A. (2000). Service system structure. *International Journal of Production Economics*, *68*(1), 15–27. doi:10.1016/S0925-5273(99)00133-4

Cameron, K. S. (2008). A process for changing organizational culture. In T. G. Cummings (Ed.), *Handbook of Organizational Development* (pp. 429–445). Sage.

Cimini, C., Rondini, A., Pezzotta, G., & Pinto, R. (2018). Smart manufacturing as an enabler of servitization: a framework for the business transformation towards a smart service ecosystem. Presented at XXIII Summer School "Francesco Turco" – Industrial Systems Engineering, Palermo.

Dinges, V., Urmetzer, F., Martinez, V., Zaki, M., & Neely, A. (2015). *The future of servitization: Technologies that will make a difference*. Working Paper, Cambridge University. Available at http://cambridgeservicealliance.eng.cam.ac.uk/resources/ Downloads/MonthlyPapers/150623FutureTechnologiesinServitization.pdf

Dubruc, N., Peillon, S., & Farah, A. (2014). The Impact of Servitization on Corporate Culture. *Procedia CIRP*, *16*, 289–294. doi:10.1016/j.procir.2014.01.028

Galbraith, J. R. (2002). *Designing organizations*. John Wiley & Sons Inc.

Garg, G., & Krishnan, V. R. (2003). Transformational leadership and organizational structure: The role of value-based leadership. In S. Bhargava (Ed.), Transformational leadership: Value-based management for Indian organization (pp. 82-100). New Delhi: Response Books (Sage Publications).

Gebauer, H., Bravo-Sanchez, C., & Fleisch, E. (2008). Service strategies in product manufacturing companies. *Business Strategy Series*, 9(1), 12–20. doi:10.1108/17515630810850073

Gebauer, H., Edvardsson, B., & Bjurko, M. (2010). The impact of service orientation in corporate culture on business performance in manufacturing companies. *Journal of Service Management*, 21(2), 1–43. doi:10.1108/09564231011039303

Gebauer, H., & Fleisch, E. (2007). An investigation of the relationship between behavioral processes, motivation, investments in the service business and service revenue. *Industrial Marketing Management*, 36(3), 337–348. doi:10.1016/j.indmarman.2005.09.005

Gebauer, H., & Kowalkowski, C. (2012). Customer-focused and service-focused orientation in organizational structures. *Journal of Business and Industrial Marketing*, 27(7), 527–537. doi:10.1108/08858621211257293

Gebauer, H., Paiola, M., & Edvardsson, B. (2012). A Capability Perspective on Service Business Development in Small and Medium-Sized Suppliers. *Scandinavian Journal of Management*, 28(4), 321–339. doi:10.1016/j.scaman.2012.07.001

Gotsch, M., Hipp, C., Erceg, P. J., & Weidner, N. (2014). The impact of servitization on key competences and qualification profiles in the machine building industry. In *Servitization in Industry* (pp. 315–330). Springer International Publishing. doi:10.1007/978-3-319-06935-7_19

Janicijevic, N. (2013). The mutual impact of organizational culture and structure. *Economic Annals*, 58(198), 35–60. doi:10.2298/EKA1398035J

Kang, H. S., Lee, J. Y., Choi, S., Kim, H., Park, J. H., Son, J. Y., & Do Noh, S. (2016). Smart manufacturing: Past research, present findings, and future directions. *International Journal of Precision Engineering and Manufacturing-Green Technology*, 3(1), 111–128. doi:10.100740684-016-0015-5

Kargas, A. D., & Varoutas, D. (2015). On the relation between organizational culture and leadership: An empirical analysis. *Cogent Business & Management*, 2(1), 1–18. doi:10.1080/23311975.2015.1055953

Kinnunen, R. E. (2011). *Servitisation of manufacturing companies – framework for analyzing servitisation capabilities* (Master thesis). Aalto University, School of Economics, Department of Business Technology, Espoo, Finland.

Kobashi, T., & Konomi, N. (2015). Idiosyncrasies of the front-back organization. *Aichi Institute of Technology, 50*. Retrieved from http://repository.aitech.ac.jp/dspace/bitstream/11133/2882/1/%E7%B4%80%E8%A6%8150%E5%8F%B7%28p200-p203%29.pdf

Kreye, M., & Jensen, P. L. (2014). *Key variables of organization design in servitization*. Paper presented at 21st International EurOMA Conference European Operations Management Association, Palermo, Italy.

Lobert, L. (2016). *Organizing for Servitization: Developing a framework to guide the transition for manufacturing firms* (Master Thesis). Retrieved from https://repository.tudelft.nl/islandora/object/uuid:bc079a36-45f6-4b84-934a-786bf03e4a08?collection=education

Martin, C. R., & Horne, D. A. (1992). Restructuring towards a Service Orientation: The Strategic Challenges. *International Journal of Service Industry Management*, 3(1), 25–38. doi:10.1108/EUM0000000002809

Mathieu, V. (2001). Service strategies within the manufacturing sector benefits costs and partnership. *International Journal of Service Industry Management*, 5(5), 451–475. doi:10.1108/EUM0000000006093

Matthyssens, P., & Vandenbempt, K. (1998). Creating competitive advantage in industrial services. *Journal of Business and Industrial Marketing, 13*(4/5), 339–355. doi:10.1108/08858629810226654

Mintzberg, H. (1979). *The structuring of organizations*. Prentice Hall.

Ng, I., Parry, G., Wild, P., McFarlane, D., & Tasker, P. (2011). *Complex engineering service systems: Concepts and Research*. Springer. doi:10.1007/978-0-85729-189-9

Nie, Y., & Kosaka, M. (2014). A new perception on leadership for achieving servitization of business. *Journal of Management Research, 6*(4), 50–62. doi:10.5296/jmr.v6i4.6088

Nie, Y., Shirahada, K., & Kosaka, M. (2013). Value co-creation oriented leadership for promoting service-centric Business. *Intercultural Communication Studies, 22*, 1, 216–228.

Nuutinen, M., & Lappalainen, I. (2012). Towards service-oriented organizational culture in manufacturing companies. *International Journal of Quality and Service Sciences, 4*(2), 137–155. doi:10.1108/17566691211232882

Ogbonna, E., & Harris, L. C. (2000). Leadership style, organizational culture and performance: Empirical evidence from UK companies. *International Journal of Human Resource Management, 11*(4), 766–788. doi:10.1080/09585190050075114

Oliva, R., & Kallenberg, R. (2003). Managing the transition from products to services. *International Journal of Service Industry Management, 14*(2), 160–172. doi:10.1108/09564230310474138

Paschou, T., Adrodegari, F., Perona, M., & Saccani, N. (2017). *The digital servitization of manufacturing: a literature review and research agenda*. Paper presented at 27th RESER Conference, Bilbao, Spain.

Pawar, B. S., & Eastman, K. K. (1997). The nature and implications of contextual influences on transformational leadership: A conceptual examination. *Academy of Management Review, 22*(1), 80–109. doi:10.5465/amr.1997.9707180260

Perona, M., Saccani, N., & Bacchetti, A. (2017). Research vs. Practice on manufacturing firms' servitization strategies: a gap analysis & research. *System, 5*(1), 19. . doi:10.3390ystems5010019

Peyman, Y., Mohsen, A. S., Hassan, G., Aboulghassim, F., & Zaman, A. (2011). The Analysis of the relationship between organizational structure and information technology (IT): And the barriers to its establishment at the university of isfahan from the faculty member's viewpoints. *Higher Education Studies, 1*(1), 98–104. doi:10.5539/hes.v1n1p98

Popli, S., & Rizvi, I. A. (2015). Exploring the relationship between service orientation, employee engagement and perceived leadership style: A study of managers in the private service sector organizations in India. *Journal of Services Marketing, 29*(1), 5–70. doi:10.1108/JSM-06-2013-0151

Porras, J. I., & Hoffer, S. J. (1986). Common behavior changes in successful organization development efforts. *The Journal of Applied Behavioral Science, 22*(4), 477–494. doi:10.1177/002188638602200409

Raddats, C., & Burton, J. (2011). Strategy and structure configurations for services within product-centric businesses. *Journal of Service Management, 22*(4), 522–539. doi:10.1108/09564231111155105

Ravasi, D., & Schultz, M. (2006). Responding to organizational identity threats: Exploring the role of organizational culture. *Academy of Management Journal, 49*(3), 433–458. doi:10.5465/amj.2006.21794663

Rese, M., & Maiwald, K. (2013). *The individual level of servitization: creating Employees service orientation*. Paper presented at 7th IFAC Conference on Manufacturing Modeling, Management, and Control, Saint Petersburg, Russia. 10.3182/20130619-3-RU-3018.00429

Resta, B., Powell, D., Gaiardelli, P., & Dotti, S. (2015). Towards a frame-work for lean operations in product-oriented product service systems. *CIRP Journal of Manufacturing Science and Technology, 9,* 12–22. doi:10.1016/j.cirpj.2015.01.008

Schein, E. H. (2004). *Organizational Culture and Leadership*. Jossey-Bass.

Schmenner, R. W. (1986). How can services businesses survive and prosper? *Sloan Management Review, 27*(3), 21–32. PMID:10300742

Shah, D., Rust, R. T., Parasuraman, A., Staelin, R., & Day, G. S. (2006). The Path to customer centricity. *Journal of Service Research, 9*(2), 113–124. doi:10.1177/1094670506294666

Sharma, S., & Sharma, A. (2010). Examining the relationship between organizational culture and leadership styles. *Journal of the Indian Academy of Applied Psychology, 36*(1), 97–105.

Smith, L., Maull, R., & Ng, I. C. L. (2014). Servitization and operations management: A service dominant-logic approach. *International Journal of Operations & Production Management, 34*(2), 242–269. doi:10.1108/IJOPM-02-2011-0053

Tukker, A. (2004). Eight types of product-service system: Eight ways to sustainability? Experiences from sus- Pronet. *Business Strategy and the Environment, 13*(4), 246–260. doi:10.1002/bse.414

Vandermerwe, S., & Rada, J. (1988). Servitization of business: Adding value by adding services. *European Management Journal, 6*(4), 314–324. doi:10.1016/0263-2373(88)90033-3

Xie, S., Helfert, M., Lugmayr, A., Heimgärtner, R., & Holzinger, A. (2013). Influence of organizational culture and communication on the successful implementation of information technology in hospitals. In P. L. P. Rau (Ed.), Lecture Notes in Computer Science: Vol. 8024. *cross-cultural design. Cultural differences in everyday Life. CCD 2013*. Springer. doi:10.1007/978-3-642-39137-8_19

Yong, N., Shirahada, K., & Kosaka, M. (2013). Value co-creation oriented leadership for promoting service-centric business. *Journal of Intercultural Communication Studies, 22*(1), 216–228.

Zeithaml, V., & Bitner, M. (2003). *Service Marketing: integrating customer focus across the firm*. McGraw-Hill.

ADDITIONAL READING

Akaka, M. A., & Vargo, S. L. (2014). Technology as an operant resource in service (eco)systems. *Information Systems and e-Business Management, 12*(3), 367–384. doi:10.100710257-013-0220-5

Brady, T., Davies, A., & Gann, D. M. (2005). Creating value by delivering integrated solutions. *International Journal of Project Management, 23*(5), 360–365. doi:10.1016/j.ijproman.2005.01.001

Gong, Y., Huang, J. C., & Farh, J. L. (2009). Employee learning orientation, transformational leadership, and employee creativity: The mediating role of employee creative self-efficacy. *Academy of Management Journal*, *52*(4), 765–778. doi:10.5465/amj.2009.43670890

Kobashi, T. (2004). Front-Back Organization: A structure in the age of globalization. *Journal of Business and Management*, *11*, 28–38.

Payne, A. F., Storbacka, K., & Frow, P. (2008). Managing the co-creation of value. *Journal of the Academy of Marketing Science*, *36*(1), 83–96. doi:10.100711747-007-0070-0

Porter, E. M., & Heppelmann, E. J. (2014). How smart, connected products are transforming competition. *Harvard Business Review*, *92*, 65–88.

Sebastiani, R., & Paiola, M. (2010). Rethinking service innovation: Four pathways to evolution. *International Journal of Quality and Service Sciences*, *2*(1), 70–94. doi:10.1108/17566691011026612

KEY TERMS AND DEFINITIONS

Digital Technology: Device or application to record, process, receive, transmit, or display information in a numerical form.

Service Culture: Culture where employees have a desire and ability to serve customers and solve their problems.

Service Structure: Set of people, technologies, and shared information designed to perform services.

Servitization: A shift of firms, mainly manufacturers, from selling products to selling customer solutions coupled with their existing products.

Transformational Leadership: Leadership style that motivates change of individuals and social systems.

Ambient–Intelligent Decision Support System (Am–IDSS) for Smart Manufacturing

Marzieh Khakifirooz

 https://orcid.org/0000-0002-1721-2646

Tecnológico de Monterrey, Mexico

Mahdi Fathi

 https://orcid.org/0000-0001-6863-4761

University of North Texas, USA

Yiannis Ampatzidis

University of Florida, USA

Panos M. Pardalos

University of Florida, USA

INTRODUCTION

Competitiveness among companies and nations is forcing decision makers in companies to strategically re-creating manufacturing processes and supply chains toward smart production. The goals of smart manufacturing include: 1) optimizing production and increasing profitability and innovation, 2) responding to market changes faster and with agility, 3) better-informed decisions, and 4) more flexibility in physical processes, cf., Clemons, 2018. Smart manufacturing can create dynamic, competitive operations, and global supply chains by using intelligent computerized control, advanced information technologies, the Internet of Things (IoT) technologies, and flexible manufacturing systems.

Research in the broad area of smart manufacturing and its challenges for encompassing IDSS into the production process appeared in a wide range of topics and methodologies. For instance, Simeone et al. (2019) investigated the requirements for cloud manufacturing platform for making a sharing platform in the smart manufacturing network. Weber (2018) introduced effective stakeholders in measuring key performance indicators (KPIs) for the smart production process in the high-tech industry. Meng et al. (2018) considered the smart recovery decision-making process for sustainable manufacturing purposes. Latorre-Biel et al. (2018) designed a Petri net model of a smart factory regarding the Industry 4.0 paradigm as virtualization for decision making support. Avventuroso et al. (2017) introduced a networked production system to implement virtual enterprise and product lifecycle information loops. Preuveneers et al. (2017) reviewed the emerging trends on the smartness of manufacturing, including the relevant research challenges and opportunities to shape an IDSS. Brodsky et al. (2014) investigated the decision support system for reusable components, including knowledge, data, control variables, and decisions, for leading the environment to the smartness. However, there is a lack of a good snapshot of quantitative modeling approaches and trends based on system engineering design, emphasizing system requirements analysis and specification, the use of alternative analytical methods and systems' evaluation.

DOI: 10.4018/978-1-7998-3473-1.ch161

The purpose of this article is to introduce an IDSS based on AmI technology for smart manufacturing landscape, emphasizing on design and structure of AmI technology and covers the technological foundations of smart manufacturing. To build essential knowledge around AI technology and its role in influencing Am-IDSS platform, we are focusing almost exclusively on issues relevant to understanding, constructing, and analyzing the different challenges of smart manufacturing from the system engineering point of views based on human-centric computer (HCC) interaction design.

Our approach is to explain the basic principles of Am-IDSS structure in the area of smart manufacturing. First, we address the new and rapidly growing role of the internet and high-tech computing in manufacturing. Other topics include the definition of smart manufacturing, smart DSS, AI potentials for smart manufacturing, and the necessity for advance Am-IDSS in smart manufacturing. Thereafter, problems of coordinating the advanced robotics, Cyber-Physical systems (CPS), IoT and admitting the big-data, machine learning, and cloud and cognitive computing in industrial development will discuss. Following these topics, the structure of Am-IDSS including component of collaborations, services and logical issues in Am-IDSS, infrastructural layers of Am-IDSS such as physical, functional, integrated, and human-computer layers, architecture of human-centered DSS, components of database module, information collection components, components of knowledge management (KM) module, decision making process components, and user-interface components will be reviewed. The system engineering design of each model implements the role of AI in different segments of Am-IDSS. Models and applications of Am-IDSS for smart manufacturing will be explored, including (not limited) the advanced manufacturing processes, rapid prototyping, collaborative virtual factory (VF) platforms, advanced human-machine interaction (HMI), machine-to-machine (M2M) communication, and open manufacturing. The development and future trend of IDSS for smart manufacturing such as HCC and Information architect (IA) will discuss.

The study will be concluded by providing recommendations for further research and align our mindset for the next step. From the gap in the literature, we propose some areas for further investigation, for those who are interested in walking into the field of IDSS for smart manufacturing.

BACKGROUND

AmI is becoming an interesting emerging topic after the birth of the fourth industrial revolution and smart manufacturing. In a manufacturing environment with AmI setting, human's senses and their actions, machine and materials, temperature, etc. are becoming feasible; therefore, creating a platform or software to interpret and act on data from sensors in real-time is a significant problem. In this sphere of influence, several studies have been done to show how AmI can bring impact for decision makers in different fields, such as transportation (Ocalir-Akunal, 2016), healthcare (Tawfik & Anya, 2015), and disaster management (Fersini et al., 2017). However, only limited works consummated in this sphere for smart manufacturing.

A unified structure of an integrated expert system and DSS for designing an IDSS for the first time was discussed in the late 80s by Teng et al. (1988). Later, after the birth of AmI in the late 1990s and increase of interest in user-experience and user-evaluation, during the revolution from mass production to mass customization, Kim et al. (2004) were among of the first researchers who integrated the human-centered knowledge into the IDSS. Following them, Filip (2008) designed the IDSS for large-scale complex systems with the perspective of advanced IDSS, including the AI-based techniques, the concept of the AmI, and mixed-knowledge IDSS approach. Marreiros et al. (2009) invented the augmented DSS based on intelligent sensors which can simulate the behavior of human users. Vrana and Aly (2009) enter to this area from reverse engineering solution, where they design the infrastructure of AmI into DSS after the implementation of smart decision making into the managerial level, and analyzing the system requirements, quality, and performance from human performance.

Although, almost all researches investigated on the benefits and bright future of consolidation of AmI and decision making and production process, Gandy (2010) surveyed on challenges, difficulties and disadvantage of using AmI in DSS including, ethical concerns, data quality, human emotionalism, and economical concerns due to technological assessments and discriminations. Some studies considered knowledge management, and re-usability of knowledge from the machine for human users or human users for machines into the IDSS (Brodsky et al., 2017; Kim et al. 2008; Urosevic et al. 2006). In the work of Chen & Chen (2010) ubiquitous computing environment is combined into decision-making process and presented the context-aware DSS.

More recently, after the genesis of the fourth industrial revolution, literature involved with the concept and application of smart and intelligent manufacturing multiplied. Kaklauskas (2015) deliberated the ideas of AmI and IoT and their link into the IDSS; however, the article mainly discussed on concepts rather than the design of the systems. Robinson et al. (2015) investigated the application of AmI in manufacturing for energy saving and efficiency. In their study, in addition to presenting a comprehensive survey on the use of AmI, they suggested general information regards to the system implementation and requirements of AmI adhered processes. Tyrychtr et al. (2016) merged the concept of online analytical processing (OLAP) into the AmI for constructing a smarter DSS. Martinho et al. (2017) introduced a ubiquitous group decision support system for facilitating human-human interaction in IDSS. Gomes et al. (2016) had an in-depth look at the architecture of production and control planning of a system merged with AmI technology. Similarly, Menascé et al. (2015) designed a structure for automated smart manufacturing upon the IDSS for production and control planning.

Our approach in this study is the general framework of the used case analysis presented in Gomes et al. (2016) for Am-IDSS. In this study, we flashback to the past, when Kim et al. (2004) brought the human-centered knowledge into the decision-making system. Regards to their modeling and design, we update it with the AmI and smart manufacturing perspective.

SYSTEM DESIGN OF IDSS: CHALLENGES AND COMPONENTS

The collaborative component is the first and most constructive component of an Am-IDSS. It can provide different aspects of design for an Am-IDSS. It also helps the nature of organizations or businesses to become more distributed and dynamic. The distributed concepts could be any properties or entities of an organization such as knowledge, humans, specialization, tasks, and contexts when there is no limitation regarding roles, time, geography, and structure. A collaborative component can describe through the 1) application of collaboration, 2) collaborators (human users), 3) fundamental, process, and issues of collaboration, and 4) collaboration enable technology and environment.

Knowledge is the next and the most vital component for Am-IDSS. It can be originated from data, expert system, collaboration, documents, and intelligent models (Power et al., 2018). It can increase the level of understanding of problem-solving and decision making. Knowledge should be shareable (knowledge sharing, KS), producible (knowledge production, KP), integrative (knowledge integration, KI), and acquisitional (Knowledge acquisition, KA). Within the decision-making process, firstly, knowledge is captured (KA) either manually or automatically. Knowledge is represented in different

14

formats and is required to be stored and fusion (KI) for further analysis. Later knowledge needs to be shared (KS) among different parts of an organization for human brainstorming or system enhancement and preventive maintenance. KS causes the creation of new knowledge or innovation (KP). At the end of each loop, KP should be validated to become KA for the next loop.

Interaction among the participants in a collaborative Am-IDSS to use the knowledge can take place in a distributed environment. A distributed environment for intelligent processing required actuators, sensors, and mobile devices to make collaboration and communication possible, depending on how wide the environment is expanded. Besides, the interaction and processing should proceed in a real-time but virtual system. Additional technologies, such as word sense disambiguation (Ruas et al., 2019), are enforced to interpret the knowledge of different languages (such as image, signal) and formats to a unique and singular terminology. AI, as a comprehensive and intelligent tool, can deal with different parts of the knowledge processing from KA to KP.

In a collaborative environment, the participants' interaction is not entirely accepted and respected by all users. Decision makers may have arguments for supporting or ignoring alternative solutions. The level of acceptance or rejection is highly depended on the level of interaction and understanding the shared knowledge. Therefore, communication in any scale from M2M, human-to-machine (H2M) or human-to-human (H2H) depends on the point of interaction called interface. The better the interface is, the higher the level of interaction will be.

Interfaced interaction should be independent of time, location, and the number of users (group or individual). Consider the independence characteristic of interfaced interactions, semantic web could be as one of the best environments for sharing and interaction. Semantic web increases the accessibility and interface-ability, and a consequently higher number of users, which leads to more innovative and accurate decisions.

An increase in the number of users brings diversity. Therefore, considering the independence characteristics of interfaced interaction, an interactive user interface system is required for better communication and interaction among users (human or machine). HCC can manage the interaction between users through human-computer interaction. Note that HCC can manage the H2H interaction, since, in a distributed environment and semantic web, humans communicate through the machine with each other, either in hierarchy or anarchy level. However, regardless of the levels of interfaces, in any level of interaction, either in H2H, M2M, or H2M communication and interaction may not be understandable for all users. Additional technologies (such as word sense disambiguation) are required to determine the sense of ambiguous interactions according to its context and prepare it for the needs of all levels of users.

Consider the aforementioned components of an Am-IDSS; Figure 1 illustrates a collaborative Am-IDSS module, and Figure 2 performs the class diagram for AmI based design.

Figure 1. A collaborative module of an intelligent decision support system based on AmI

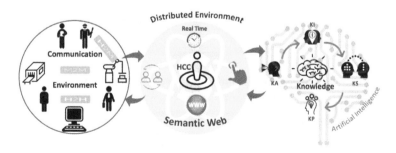

Figure 2. Class diagram for AmI based design

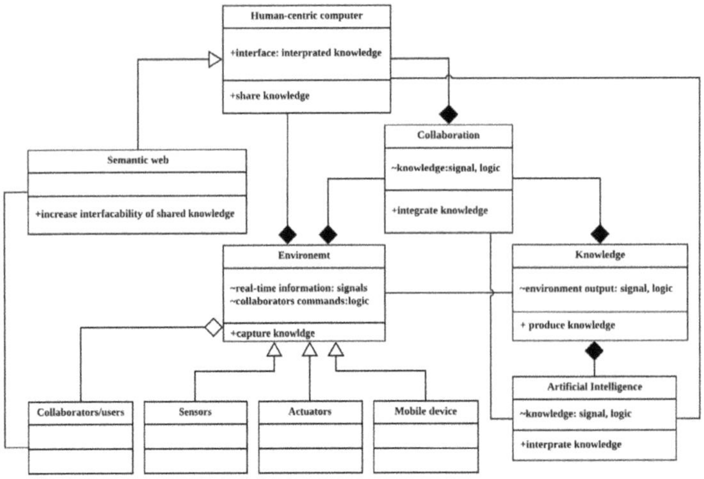

MODEL AND APPLICATION OF AMBIENT INTELLIGENCE FOR IDSS

A. AmI's components

According to the Aarts & Marzano (2003), the main components of AmI are classified into two classes of intelligent aspects including "personalization," "adaptability" and "anticipatory," and ambient aspects including "context-aware" and "embedded." Following we describe the meaning of each concept.

Am-IDSS is embedded (Agana et al., 2019; Bonci et al., 2019). In an embedded system, many networked devices are integrated into the environment and environment intelligently processes in a real-time setting. The core part of the embedded system is microcontrollers or microprocessors, which are available in a wide range of devices such as the smartwatch, intelligent traffic light, hybrid vehicle, and medical devices.

Am-IDSS is context-aware (Mahfooz Ul Haque et al., 2019; Triboan et al., 2019; Belkadi et al., 2019). In a context-aware system, a mobile device in a network is integrated into the environment to identify the situation (mainly location) of the user. The essential requirement of a context-aware system is connecting devices into the pervasive or ubiquitous computing system to deal with the network linking and environmental ambiguous.

Am-IDSS is personalized (Park et al., 2019; Bag et al., 2019). In a personalized system, environment and information are customized for users' preference. Personalization is included the behavior, context, historical data, technology, and collaborators. The goal of personalization is user/customer satisfaction. Therefore, AmI is tightly engaged with mass customization or mass personalization.

Am-IDSS is adaptive (Murphy et al., 2019). In an adaptive system, the setting of the environment is changeable based on the need and preference of the user; in fact, the user can change the setting. The intelligent adaptation is from the machine, algorithm, or decision for humans, but the diverse form of adaptation from human to machine is not in the context of the Am-IDSS. In other words, humans will not adapt themselves to machines.

Am-IDSS is anticipatory (Lughofer, 2019; Panetto et al., 2019). In an anticipated system, the environment can make a decision and act based on that decision in an appropriate way. The Am-IDSS takes

Figure 3. The use case diagram to identify the action and relation among users and components of Am-IDSS

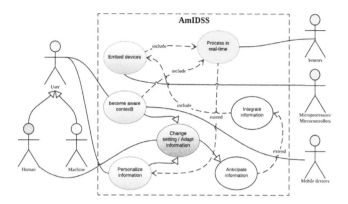

future events into account and builds, predicts, and evaluates a model for the future. Anticipation has employed the concepts of the AI, such as case-based reasoning (CBR) to anticipate the user's desire.

The use case diagram in Figure 3, illustrates the relationship, performance, and actions among the users and the components of the Am-IDSS system.

B. AmI's Features

AmI is applied for smart manufacturing for supporting industrial communication among components involved in the production process, manufacturing data flow, and advanced machinery. The shareable information should be understandable between users and ambiance. Following features identify how AmI can merge and help to the IDSS.

In the manufacturing process, a part of the information is explicated from human operators.

- The information could be in the form of natural input such as spoken language and handwriting through the touch screen panel and gesture. Technologies which can help in capturing information in this step could be digital pen or handwriting and speech recognition.
- The information could be in the form of observations and experiences about the statue and problems in the process and from the environment. Wireless handheld devices, tablet, mobile phones, wearable devices such as keyboards, in-cloth, data gloves, smart glasses or augmented reality (AR) can be used for recording the information during the observation or experience. Biometric authentication and authorization can help the operator to be identified and record the observed or experienced information.
- The information could be in the form of a request from the operator. Consider operator has the lowest knowledge about the information (no name of information, no information about the location or format), mobile communication and interoperability technologies such as Bluetooth, wireless local area network (WLAN), general packet radio service (GPRS), and universal mobile telecommunications system (UMTS) can aid operator to access to get an update the information. The collaborative working environment is the core for providing these services to the operator.
- Information could be unstructured, about any needs, or forwarding materials from a single operator, or during the collaborative work. For the unstructured information, the interoperability network and ubiquitous communication system could handle the information sharing procedure task.

In the manufacturing process, a part of the information is the output of devices in AmI system.

- The output information could be in the form of personalized information about the operator, or context-dependent. Wireless handheld devices or wearable output devices, such as the headset, head-mounted display, AR or other display attached devices could record this information from the operator.
- The output information could be assistance or answer from active users in return of operator's question. The active assistance or answer could deliver to the operator through visual infrastructure equipment or optical/acoustic output devices such as light, pointer, and horn.
- Any other communication in the form of visual and voice user interfaces for communication with a collaborative partner or ambiance can be done in network interoperability and ubiquitous communication system.
- Information which is impossible and inaccessible to be captured or recorded can be simulated from haptic or kinesthetic computing for remote control.

In the manufacturing process, a part of the information is the environmental input.

- The information could be from sensors of the underlying environmental conditions such as temperature, humidity, and vibration. Basic ambient sensors could capture this information.
- The information could be in the form of the spatial situation. The camera system or spatial surveillance and change detectors could identify the location and identification of things.
- The information could be about the hazardous changes in the environment. The sensitive sensors could alert about these critical changes.

In a manufacturing process, a part of the information is the knowledge about the ambiance, process, and interactions.

- The information could be about the status of the process, machine, products, and material, such as spatial structure, location, and movement. The radio frequency identification (RFID) tags, camera system, and geographical positioning system (GPS) could capture the location and movement information, and service-oriented architecture (SOA) in collaboration with the data acquisition system could handle the device communication targeting on the internet or web-based system.
- The knowledge could be about the current or historical status of manufacturing components, devices, and products. The manufacturing status could show environmental characteristics, date/time information, or human activities. For KM, the multi-agent technology can be employed in a distributed information and communication technology (ICT) environment and executive information systems (EIS) such as CBR and rule-based reasoning (RBR) for managing knowledge sharing and interpretation.
- The knowledge could be about the business process or semantic relationship of user activities and production process. This form of knowledge can be restored, shared, and analyzed through the SOA, semantic web, ontologies, network interoperability, and ubiquitous communication system.

The features of AmI are described through the elicitation, documentation, and managerial aspects of a system in Figure 4.

Figure 4. Analysis methodology for features of Am-IDSS

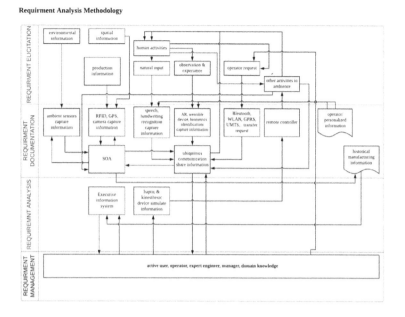

C. AmI's Implementation into IDSS

Analytical techniques for decision making continue to advance in efficacy, as well as complexity. However, it is sometimes unrealistic to employ complex analyses during time-constrained. Embedded analytics tools provided by AmI can offer an effective and practical means for real-time decision making and emergencies. For this purpose, embedded devices can be implemented in the manufacturing tools and machinery to collect and record all the necessary information, on the other side, decision-makers can be equipped with *embedded* intelligent devices to capture online data and analyzed the system configuration.

To deal with different working situations, users and decision makers have to be aware of essential elements in the situation and to interpret it correctly. Being constantly aware of all these elements is a difficult task for human users and may lead to cognitive overload. Based on contextual knowledge re-use, high-speed simulation, and advanced visualization techniques, context-aware products can provide proactive support for different manufacturing tasks. The context-aware roadmap can support decision makers to be aware of sudden changes in the manufacturing environment when they are facing a massive pool of decision information.

In a smart manufacturing environment, decentralized DSS can be used and managed by decentralized decision makers. In such cases, local decision-makers require a customized DSS system based on their knowledge, working environment, and decision tasks. AmI can support IDSS to be personalized for different levels of users and decision makers.

Smart manufacturing is a dynamic manufacturing environment which is flexible with any change from customer orders to scheduling, inventory, supply chains, and retails. Therefore, all components of the production process are adaptable with any changes, including an IDSS. Also, decision making for smart manufacturing is a group decision-making process (centralized) where each in the group has their authority to make and implement a regional decision (decentralized). Therefore, a decentralized IDSS in the inner layer and a centralized IDSS in the outer layer are adaptable with all types of assessments, theory, and pleasant thoughts.

Preventive maintenance, cost prediction, customer order forecasting, response-based supply chain, remanufacturing program, time-dependent sustainability, open manufacturing, and many other phenomena in this era of digital transformation are all possible under the umbrella of anticipated IDSS. Anticipation is required to prepare the current setting to face future trends. Future trends can be based on national strategy roadmaps, potential co-manufacturing (i.e., the case of fabless companies or open manufacturing), and customer expectation and evaluation.

FUTURE RESEARCH DIRECTIONS

Developing IDSS for AmI environments such as homes, hospitals, industrial factories, touristy spots, cultural-heritage sites, and work-places is required for advanced technological research and development. For implementing AmI, three questions should be asked about products or services, including: How this product is intelligence? Where is the location of the intelligent device? Is it a single item or aggregation of different items?

For proposing future research directions, we attempt to offer a broader vision of the requirements for designing a smart DSS associated with ambient intelligence. These requirements are barely addressed in the literature with regards to analytic context and thus are known as being the new obligations for the next step towards smart decision making. In the following, we discuss some of the highlighted topics in this chain.

Game and Am-IDSS: Applying game theory and learning algorithm for Am-IDSS and behavioral modeling in the IoT-based system would be novel future research. Players decide to leave or stay in their node by receiving the information from the neighbor nodes. The utilities of players' actions in the game will be changed by the rewards and penalties of interaction with the environment, which can be considered as a bargaining game model.

Am-IDSS Applications in Agriculture: Am-IDSS is very critical in precision agriculture, including farm processes, farm management, data chain, network management organization, and network management technology. The cloud-based cyber-physical management cycle of smart agriculture has three aspects of smart sensing & monitoring, smart control, and smart analysis & planning. More researches are needed on AmI based farm management, which is based on sensing and monitoring the farm performance, analysis, and decision making to reach the vision performance, and intervention to revise the farm processes. Moreover, in Am-IDSS agriculture environment, there are many challenges in data ownership associated with security and privacy, data quality, farm intelligent processing and analytics, sustainable integration of farm big data sources, stockholders' business models, and openness of farm solution platforms. A fruitful future research direction would be Am-IDSS for agricultural environment considering the big data challenges.

Combining AI and Operations Research in the planning of Am-IDSS Systems: Planning can be divided into deliberative (plan and execute without dealing with unexpected events), reactive (reacting to stimulus in a much more fundamental way) or hybrid (combining the best of deliberative and reactive policies). The environment of ambient systems should support planning and guide users intelligently. Planning should be intelligent either offline or online, and most of the time is related to some optimization task. Intelligent-computational and nature-inspired algorithms such as Taboo Search, Genetic Algorithm, Particle Swarm Optimization, Simulated Annealing, and Ant Colony could play the role of optimization engine. For example, in intelligent transportation DSS, the driver should get feedback both from inside the vehicle and outside such as pickup and delivery route planning under time windows, three-dimensional loading, and network congestion. Developing more integrated optimization and AI techniques (such as hidden Markov models, logical programming, fuzzy systems, case-based programming, multi-agent programming, and ontologies) for the planning of Am-IDSS would be another challenging topic.

Am-IDSS in healthcare: Our final suggestion as a future research possibility is to integrate interconnected Am-IDSS, service innovation, and open innovation in Health 4.0 and smart hospitals. In a smart hospital, the IDSS can be used by different layers of users, including, patients, staff, and patients' accompaniers. Ambiance can be classified in various departments and sections, such as pharmacy, patient room, operation room, nursing station, waiting room, emergency department, laboratory, etc.

Digital Twins and Am-IDSS: Personalized production and distributed manufacturing are in the center of attention during this revolutionary period in industrial technology. On the other hand, mass customization and production required additional investigation on the cost and time for design and production. Digital twins, as a digital representation of products, can be utilized for configuration of manufacturing elements, synchronized information, and functional units. In the Am-IDSS real-time monitoring of the present production, tracking information from the past, and operational decision-making support for the future is feasible for implementation of digital twins.

Blockchain and Am-IDSS: In an open and distributed decision-making system, trust, efficiency, and accuracy are the key important factors for decision makers. A platform that can guarantee the quality of data and identify trustee users is necessary for an Am-IDSS. Blockchain is a platform that can be used to express and enforce inter-organizational agreements, control all H2H interactions, and provide an immense interfaced interaction environment for human users.

CONCLUSION

IDSS is critical for intelligent decision making in smart manufacturing. In this study, we have reviewed the roles of human factors in IDSS to design an AmI structure for smart manufacturing systems and engineering applications. Integrating HCC modeling, human factors, SOA, semantic web, and AI propose novel ideas for making smart decisions with complex objectives in smart manufacturing. In smart manufacturing and Industry 4.0, communication among machine users and human users play a critical role in automating strategic, knowledge sharing, and tactical decision making. Therefore, the implementation of an IDSS in manufacturing ecosystem will lead managers towards smarter decision making for the efficiency and effectiveness uses of human resources. In conclusion, there are many large scale optimization problems in IDSS based on AmI in smart manufacturing that we encourage readers for further investigation refer to Fathi et al., (2019) and Velasquez et al., (2019).

REFERENCES

Aarts, E., & Marzano, S. (2003). *The new everyday: Views on ambient intelligence.* 010 Publishers.

Agana, M. A., Ofem, O. A., & Ele, B. I. (2019, March). A Framework for a Fuzzy Smart Home IoT e-Health Support System. In *Future of Information and Communication Conference* (pp. 432-447). Springer.

Avventuroso, G., Silvestri, M., & Pedrazzoli, P. (2017). A networked production system to implement virtual enterprise and product lifecycle information loops. *IFAC-PapersOnLine, 50*(1), 7964–7969. doi:10.1016/j.ifacol.2017.08.902

Bag, S., Ghadge, A., & Tiwari, M. K. (2019). An integrated recommender system for improved accuracy and aggregate diversity. *Computers & Industrial Engineering*, *130*, 187–197. doi:10.1016/j.cie.2019.02.028

Belkadi, F., Dhuieb, M. A., Aguado, J. V., Laroche, F., Bernard, A., & Chinesta, F. (2019). (in press). Intelligent Assistant System as a context-aware decision-making support for the workers of the future. *Computers & Industrial Engineering*.

Bonci, A., Carbonari, A., Cucchiarelli, A., Messi, L., Pirani, M., & Vaccarini, M. (2019). A cyber-physical system approach for building efficiency monitoring. *Automation in Construction*, *102*, 68–85. doi:10.1016/j.autcon.2019.02.010

Brodsky, A., Krishnamoorthy, M., Menascé, D. A., Shao, G., & Rachuri, S. (2014, October). Toward smart manufacturing using decision analytics. In *Big Data (Big Data), 2014 IEEE International Conference on* (pp. 967-977). IEEE. 10.1109/BigData.2014.7004330

Brodsky, A., Shao, G., Krishnamoorthy, M., Narayanan, A., Menascé, D., & Ak, R. (2017). Analysis and optimization based on reusable knowledge base of process performance models. *International Journal of Advanced Manufacturing Technology*, *88*(1-4), 337–357. doi:10.100700170-016-8761-7 PMID:31274946

Chen, N., & Chen, A. (2010, March). Integrating context-aware computing in decision support system. In *Proc. The international Multiconference of Engineers and Computer Scientists (Vol. 1)*. Academic Press.

Clemons, J. (2018, March 19). The Anatomy Of Smart Manufacturing. *Forbes*. Retrieved from https://www.forbes.com/sites/forbestechcouncil/2018/03/19/the-anatomy-of-smart-manufacturing

Fathi, M., Khakifirooz, M., & Pardalos, P. M. (2019). Optimization in Large Scale Problems: Industry 4.0 and Society 5.0 Applications. Springer Optimization and Its Applications. (in press)

Fersini, E., Messina, E., & Pozzi, F. A. (2017). Earthquake management: A decision support system based on natural language processing. *Journal of Ambient Intelligence and Humanized Computing*, *8*(1), 37–45. doi:10.100712652-016-0373-4

Filip, F. G. (2008). Decision support and control for large-scale complex systems. *Annual Reviews in Control*, *32*(1), 61–70. doi:10.1016/j.arcontrol.2008.03.002

Gandy, O. H. Jr. (2010). Engaging rational discrimination: Exploring reasons for placing regulatory constraints on decision support systems. *Ethics and Information Technology*, *12*(1), 29–42. doi:10.100710676-009-9198-6

Gomes, M., Silva, F., Ferraz, F., Silva, A., Analide, C., & Novais, P. (2016, December). Developing an Ambient Intelligent-Based Decision Support System for Production and Control Planning. In *International Conference on Intelligent Systems Design and Applications* (pp. 984-994). Springer.

Kaklauskas, A. (2015). Intelligent decision support systems. In *Biometric and Intelligent Decision Making Support* (pp. 31–85). Springer.

Kim, D. H., Song, J. Y., & Cha, S. K. (2008, April). Knowledge-Evolution based Intelligent Machine Tools based on M2M. In *2008 International Conference on Smart Manufacturing Application* (pp. 214-218). IEEE. 10.1109/ICSMA.2008.4505644

Kim, S. Y., Godbole, A., Huang, R., Panchadhar, R., & Smari, W. W. (2004, November). Toward an integrated human-centered knowledge-based collaborative decision making system. In *Information Reuse and Integration, 2004. IRI 2004. Proceedings of the 2004 IEEE International Conference on* (pp. 394-401). IEEE.

Latorre-Biel, J. I., Faulín, J., Juan, A. A., & Jiménez-Macías, E. (2018). Petri Net Model of a Smart Factory in the Frame of Industry 4.0. *IFAC-PapersOnLine, 51*(2), 266–271. doi:10.1016/j.ifacol.2018.03.046

Lughofer, E. (2019). *Predictive Maintenance in Dynamic Systems: Advanced Methods, Decision Support Tools and Real-World Applications.* Springer. doi:10.1007/978-3-030-05645-2

Mahfooz Ul Haque, H., Zulfiqar, H., Ahmed, A., & Ali, Y. (2019). (in press). A context-aware framework for modelling and verification of smart parking systems in urban cities. *Concurrency and Computation.* Advance online publication. doi:10.1002/cpe.5401

Marreiros, G., Ramos, C., Machado, J., & Neves, J. (2009). Argument-based decision making in ambient intelligence environments. *IJRIS, 1*(3/4), 182–190. doi:10.1504/IJRIS.2009.028017

Martinho, D., Carneiro, J., Marreiros, G., & Novais, P. (2017, June). Defining an Architecture for a Ubiquitous Group Decision Support System. In *International Symposium on Ambient Intelligence* (pp. 246-253). Springer. 10.1007/978-3-319-61118-1_30

Menascé, D. A., Krishnamoorthy, M., & Brodsky, A. (2015). Autonomic smart manufacturing. *Journal of Decision Systems, 24*(2), 206–224. doi:10.1080/12460125.2015.1046714

Meng, K., Qian, X., Lou, P., & Zhang, J. (2018). Smart recovery decision-making of used industrial equipment for sustainable manufacturing: Belt lifter case study. *Journal of Intelligent Manufacturing*, 1–15.

Murphy, R., Gill, D., & Brown, L. (2019). The Importance of Adaptive Technology on Data Mining. *Computer Science and Information Technology Journal, 2*(1).

Ocalir-Akunal, E. V. (2016). A Web Based Decision Support System (DSS) for Individuals' Urban Travel Alternatives. In Using Decision Support Systems for Transportation Planning Efficiency (pp. 145-167). IGI Global.

Panetto, H., Iung, B., Ivanov, D., Weichhart, G., & Wang, X. (2019). Challenges for the cyber-physical manufacturing enterprises of the future. *Annual Reviews in Control, 47*, 200–213. doi:10.1016/j.arcontrol.2019.02.002

Park, K. T., Nam, Y. W., Lee, H. S., Im, S. J., Noh, S. D., Son, J. Y., & Kim, H. (2019). Design and implementation of a digital twin application for a connected micro smart factory. *International Journal of Computer Integrated Manufacturing, 32*(6), 1–19. doi:10.1080/0951192X.2019.1599439

Power, D. J., Khakifirooz, M., Fathi, M., & Pardalos, P. M. (2018, April 8). *How can decision support aid smart manufacturing initiatives?* Retrieved from http://dssresources.com/faq/index.php?action=artikel&id=416

Preuveneers, D., & Ilie-Zudor, E. (2017). The intelligent industry of the future: A survey on emerging trends, research challenges and opportunities in Industry 4.0. *Journal of Ambient Intelligence and Smart Environments, 9*(3), 287–298. doi:10.3233/AIS-170432

Robinson, D. C., Sanders, D. A., & Mazharsolook, E. (2015). Ambient intelligence for optimal manufacturing and energy efficiency. *Assembly Automation*, *35*(3), 234–248. doi:10.1108/AA-11-2014-087

Ruas, T., Grosky, W., & Aizawa, A. (2019). Multi-Sense embeddings through a word sense disambiguation process. *Expert Systems with Applications*, *136*, 288–303. doi:10.1016/j.eswa.2019.06.026

Simeone, A., Caggiano, A., Boun, L., & Deng, B. (2019). Intelligent cloud manufacturing platform for efficient resource sharing in smart manufacturing networks. *Procedia CIRP*, *79*, 233–238. doi:10.1016/j.procir.2019.02.056

Tawfik, H., & Anya, O. (2015). Evaluating practice-centered awareness in cross-boundary telehealth decision support systems. *Telematics and Informatics*, *32*(3), 486–503. doi:10.1016/j.tele.2014.11.002

Teng, J. T., Mirani, R., & Sinha, A. (1988, January). A unified architecture for intelligent DSS. In *System Sciences, 1988.* Vol. III. *Decision Support and Knowledge Based Systems Track, Proceedings of the Twenty-First Annual Hawaii International Conference on* (Vol. 3, pp. 286-294). IEEE.

Triboan, D., Chen, L., Chen, F., & Wang, Z. (2019). A semantics-based approach to sensor data segmentation in real-time Activity Recognition. *Future Generation Computer Systems*, *93*, 224–236. doi:10.1016/j.future.2018.09.055

Tyrychtr, J., Pelikán, M., Štiková, H., & Vrana, I. (2016, April). Multidimensional design of OLAP system for context-aware analysis in the ambient intelligence environment. In *Computer Science On-line Conference* (pp. 283-292). Springer. 10.1007/978-3-319-33622-0_26

Urosevic, L., Kopacsi, S., Stokic, D., Campos, A. R., & Bognar, G. (2006, February). Knowledge Representation and Case-based Reasoning in a Knowledge Management System for Ambient Intelligence Products. In Artificial Intelligence and Applications (pp. 329-334). Academic Press.

Velasquez, J., Khakifirooz, M., & Fathi, M. (2019). Large Scale Optimization in Supply Chains and Smart Manufacturing- Theory and Applications. *Springer Optimization and Its Applications*. https://books.google.com/books?id=D7Q8xQEACAAJ

Vrana, I., & Aly, S. (2009). Conceptual Models for Managerial Ambient Intelligence. In AMIF (pp. 53-63). Academic Press.

Weber, A. (2018, September). Smart Manufacturing Stakeholders and Their Requirements. In *2018 e-Manufacturing & Design Collaboration Symposium* (pp. 1-3). IEEE.

ADDITIONAL READING

Bibri, S. E. (2015). *The Human Face of Ambient Intelligence: Cognitive, Emotional, Affective, Behavioral and Conversational Aspects*. Atlantis Press. doi:10.2991/978-94-6239-130-7

Doumpos, M., & Grigoroudis, E. (2013). *Multicriteria Decision Aid and Artificial Intelligence: Links, Theory and Applications*. John Wiley & Sons. doi:10.1002/9781118522516

Krumm, J. (Ed.). (2016). *Ubiquitous Computing Fundamentals*. CRC Press.

Power, D. J. (2009). *Decision support basics*. Business Expert Press. doi:10.4128/9781606490839

Power, D. J. (Ed.). (2013). *Engineering Effective Decision Support Technologies: New Models and Applications*. IGI Global. doi:10.4018/978-1-4666-4002-3

Power, D. J., Khakifirooz, M., Fathi, M., & Pardalos, P. M. (2018, April 8). How can decision support aid smart manufacturing initiatives? Retrieved from http://dssresources.com/faq/index.php?action=artikel&id=416

Power, D. J., Sharda, R., & Burstein, F. (2015). *Decision Support Systems*. John Wiley & Sons.

Zopounidis, C., & Pardalos, P. M. (Eds.). (2010). *Handbook of Multicriteria Analysis* (Vol. 103). Springer Science & Business Media. doi:10.1007/978-3-540-92828-7

Zopounidis, C., & Pardalos, P. M. (2013). *Managing in Uncertainty: Theory and Practice* (Vol. 19). Springer Science & Business Media.

KEY TERMS AND DEFINITIONS

Ambient Intelligence (AmI): Refers to a data-intensive environment that senses changes in state and responds appropriately to correct, act and alert. The goal of this sensor-rich AmI environment is stability and homeostasis.

Case-Based Reasoning: The process of learning to solve new problems based on the solutions of similar past problems.

Context Awareness: The property of mobile devices which define the location awareness. The location is used to identify how a particular process is operating around a contributed device, such as a smartphone.

Executive Information Systems (EIS): A branch of management information system which facilitates the decision-making system's needs. EIS merges with user-experience knowledge. In recent years, by entering advance technologies such as augmented reality, and turning to a smarter environment, EIS lost its popularity.

Haptic/Kinesthetic Computing: A mechanical simulation for creating the sense of touch by applying vibrations, forces, or motions to users for controlling the virtual devices or remote-control machines or robots.

Human-Centric Computer (HCC): The design, development, and analysis of a mixed-initiative human-computer system. It emerges two concepts of human-computer interaction and information science together to increase the usability of information and system by human and machine.

Pervasive/Ubiquitous Computing: Accessibility of computing in any place at any device and with any format, through the aid of mobile computing, sensors, internet, AI, context awareness and human-computer interaction.

Rule-Based Reasoning: The process of learning to solve new problems based on the research and the application of AI.

Semantic Web: An integrator which provides a framework for sharing and reusing data for every application, enterprise, and community. It is an extension or the World Wide Web.

Service-Oriented Architecture (SOA): The software-based design of services for application components over a network and communication protocol. One individual SOA system can contain other sub-SOA, it is self-contained and acts and updates independently from its vendor.

Decision Support for Smart Manufacturing

Marzieh Khakifirooz

https://orcid.org/0000-0002-1721-2646

Tecnológico de Monterrey, Mexico

Mahdi Fathi

https://orcid.org/0000-0001-6863-4761

University of North Texas, USA

Panos M. Pardalos

University of Florida, USA

Daniel J. Power

University of Northern Iowa, USA

INTRODUCTION

A post-industrial revolution is encouraging the deployment of novel concepts both for designing smart factories and for creating a new generation of monitoring, control and man-machine collaboration systems. In general, companies are embracing an era of smart manufacturing built upon Cyber Physical Systems (CPS), the Internet of Things (IoT), and Cloud and Cognitive computing. Using digital technologies with advanced manufacturing tools can provide opportunities for building smart decision support systems (DSS) to improve manufacturing analysis, monitoring, output, and performance. Despite the potential of improved Decision Support Systems (DSS), the major challenge is successfully adapting smart manufacturing processes to use new digital technologies that can enable the implementation of Intelligent systems and improved DSS.

Additionally, to move towards smart manufacturing, better means are required for technology deployments. The speed of technology implementation should be significantly faster, and machines should have greater accuracy of calibration in comparison to traditional manufacturing. One approach to enhancing deployment is incorporating optimization models into manufacturing systems. This change should provide a design that provides ease of use for operators and decision makers in real-time during the manufacturing process.

This chapter defines requirements for various types of DSS (see Power, 2002 and 2004, for details on the typology of DSS) in a smart manufacturing environment based upon increased use of optimization. It focuses on identifying key barriers which prevent the development and use of enhanced or "smart" DSS in manufacturing and then provides the requirement and architecture for a system engineering design for using optimization and other techniques with advanced computing and manufacturing technologies.

This review aims to promote a standard design or framework that is useful for both the manufacturing and academic communities that can facilitate needed efforts and innovation while stimulating adoption and use of smart manufacturing technologies.

DOI: 10.4018/978-1-7998-3473-1.ch162

BACKGROUND

Mathematical models and optimization techniques are the driver for model-driven DSS. With regards to the structure of data and a problem's objective and constraints, many programming tools and mathematical algorithms are available to aid decision-makers in building a DSS with optimal recommendations. The critical step is to know the type of optimization algorithm needed to solve the problem. For more details on a taxonomy of optimization problems, one can refer to a comprehensive collection of optimization resources at https://neos-guide.org/.

Mathematical algorithms support convergence towards optimal solutions. This review classifies optimization problems in terms of traditional and intelligent approaches. The most commonly used intelligent optimization models are search-based (i.e., metaheuristic models), learning-based (i.e., machine learning models), uncertainty-based (i.e., robust optimization; stochastic optimization), simulation-based (i.e., Markov Chain Monte Carlo) and Markov Decision Process (MDP) (see Tao et al., 2016, for a comprehensive review on intelligent optimization).

Although using an intelligent optimization algorithm can gradually adapt a specific model-driven DSS for smart manufacturing, such a DSS requires several other criteria be met to be adequately intelligent. More intelligent DSS are created with a learning algorithm, a knowledge sharing system, and with cognitive computing capabilities. Nevertheless, in a smart manufacturing system, with connectivity among all manufacturing processes, an intelligent, integrated DSS is required to manage a manufacturing system. Features of an integrated, intelligent DSS include expert knowledge, risk management, production control, quality monitoring, marketing and sales management, project management, and supply chain (SC) support. Guo (2016) provides an extensive collection of DSS capabilities and features needed for managerial tasks of smart manufacturing integrated with intelligent optimization algorithms.

There is a gap in the literature on the applications of optimization techniques in DSS for smart manufacturing. Moreover, there is a lack of a comprehensive system design which can cover all types of DSS and managerial decision making (DM). This analysis identifies the requirements of parameter alignment, and conceptual design of an integrated, intelligent DSS for smart manufacturing by considering the core of an optimization procedure.

DECISION SUPPORT CAN AID SMART MANUFACTURING INITIATIVES

Manufacturing in developed nations must incorporate more data capture and decision support to control costs and maintain product quality. Digital transformation of manufacturing means production must be transformed using technologies like robotics, IoT, Intelligent systems, and real-time analytics. Smart manufacturing means all aspects of production are transformed so they are data, computing, and decision support intensive. Smart manufacturing has been defined by i-SCOOP.eu as the "fully-integrated, collaborative manufacturing systems that respond in real time to meet changing demands and conditions in the factory, in the supply network, and in customer needs." Various decision support and data-driven capabilities must be incorporated in smart manufacturing systems, including:

Knowledge-Driven DSS

In a smart manufacturing environment, sharing expert domain knowledge at the manager-operator and operator-machine interface level is very important. Recommender systems and opinion mining can support real-time, data-based decision making. Machine/user relationship mining and clustering can increase the self-awareness, self-learning, and self-maintenance of production systems. Finally, Reciprocal Learning-Based DSS (RL-DSS) can make repetitive decisions and reduce the human decision making load. Routine decision tasks can be programmed and learning algorithms can enhance performance. Then decision makers can update their knowledge and the improved system helps create better decisions than previously possible for semi-structured decisions. Research challenges include:

- **Providing Man-Machine Knowledge-Sharing**
- **Knowledge-Mining**
- **Creating Reciprocal Learning-Based DSS**

Data-Driven DSS / Document-Driven DSS

Big Data Management in the Cloud can improve data management and distribution for both "machine-generated data" and "human-generated data." Real-time automated fault detection, classification and root-cause detection should be optimized using data from sensors. Finally, data-driven DSS should integrate real-time and special study data analytics. New and expanded data sources can enhance predictive analytics and output can be quickly shared using visualization tools.

Model-Driven DSS

Factories of the Future (http://www.effra.eu/factories-future) require integrated supply chain management, improved demand forecasting, and technology integration throughout the supply chain management process. Sensors combined with quantitative models can reduce costs and identify faults in the supply network itself, such as sensor failure and degradation. Ideally models will optimize the frequency and timing of sensor measurement and will eliminate or reduce supply chain network delays.

Creation of an Intelligent Feedback Control System can improve product quality and can provide feedback for system management, which can be used to improve production scheduling, to maintain machinery, and improve proactive maintenance.

Communication-Driven DSS

More machine to machine and person to machine decision support can facilitate the sharing of machines across different tasks or under different conditions. Developing simulation tools can help train operators and decision makers, prevent impending problems, and help in taking corrective action in a timely manner. If Artificially Intelligent machines communicate, then security challenges will increase, but shared decision making will increase in the capabilities of the production network.

Challenges to Improving DSS

Smart manufacturing requires intelligent systems and decision support for human participants. Improving DSS capabilities is necessitated by the development and deployment of smart manufacturing systems. The main sources of challenge are:

14

- **Innovation:** The fast growth of start-up firms has lead to accelerating change in manufacturing environments. The production function has become a source of innovation. On the other hand, innovation in an organization often leads to increased personalization. However, the sustainability in innovation due to rapid change in technology is often temporary. Invest in decision support may be delayed.

- **Changes in Social Behavior:** Customers are becoming more knowledgeable; and their demand for quality, customer service, and rapid product adaptation to new technologies is increasing. Therefore, manufacturing servitization, developing capabilities needed to provide services and solutions that supplement traditional product offerings, is required. New service capabilities often necessitate creating more integrated products, increased customer focus, more automated services, support, and more knowledge integration in an effort to produce value-added products. Additionally, rapid changes in leadership and culture must occur to respond to rapid market, business, and technological change.

- **Changes in Technology:** Changes in technology set new standards for evaluating the performance of manufacturing firms, such that from a quality management perspective, since 1987 (ISO 9000 series) society has moved to environmental management in 1992 (ISO 14000 series) and, recently, to an energy management perspective (ISO 50000 series). Other indices, such as the Key

Table 1. Optimization-based solutions for overcoming DSS challenges in smart manufacturing

Quick Solutions	Detailed Solutions
Digitalize knowledge-based DSS	• Incorporating the behavior of human decision makers with proposed solutions. • Automating decisions previously made by humans. • Improving the interface of Information Systems for humans.
Incorporate dynamics into the solutions	• Developing stochastic and dynamic versions of solutions and deterministic models. • Anticipating stochasticity in the models based on dynamic programming, robust optimization, and stochastic programming.
Design software-based solutions with a user-friendly interface	• Considering the role of high-tech computing techniques, including cloud computing techniques in DM and parallel computing on Graphics Processing Units (GPU). • Knowing the restrictions of management software for smart manufacturing management, process, and production. • Proposing alternative software solutions, including service-oriented computing and software agents for planning and scheduling applications.
Create a hybrid configuration of optimization models	• Facilitating planning problems and a DM-based optimization and data analysis perspective. • Implementing "Manufacturing Execution System" (MES), "Enterprise Resource Planning" (ERP), and "Advanced Planning and Scheduling" (APS) for developing integrated production planning and scheduling solutions. • Decreasing measurement uncertainty by merging the hybrid metrology with state-of-the-art statistical analyses.
Enable Simulation and Data-driven solutions	• Simulating the physical environment to comprehend the connections amid real-world circumstances; and planning to find solution-based approaches in a risk-free environment before applying those solutions. • Visualizing production planning processes by use of event-driven process. • Modeling and analyzing manufacturing challenges by utilization of various simulation paradigms. • Supporting the different aspects of DM in smart manufacturing by embedding the actual simulation methods in existing and forthcoming information systems.
Encourage Process integration	• Integrating decisions made by the different elements of the system to avoid *ad hoc* situations. • Integrating high-tech computing procedures to derive computationally tractable models, and to engage in discourse regarding the diverse uncertainties encounterable in the industry. • Incorporating sustainability aspects into proposed solutions and deterministic models. • Taking the product's lifetime into account and integrating with demand planning.

Performance Indicators (KPI), must radically change in both definition and metrics due to cross-factory integration.

- **Changes in Market Behavior:** Merging of small, medium, and large enterprises changes the nature of competition in many markets. Lowering the general cost of IT infrastructure like server and networks and market forces that are increasing the cost of innovative technologies are increasing the dynamism and volatility in many industries. Robots and machines participate in smart manufacturing systems by means of Artificial Intelligence (AI). Therefore, the concept of a supply chain is not limited to moving services and products from the supplier to customers; rather, supply chains must describe all transactions among different parts of production systems and of the network both inside and outside of a manufacturing environment.

Despite the challenges mentioned above, Table 1 summarizes some specific suggestions for developing DSS and smart manufacturing solutions that can overcome them.

KEY COMPONENTS OF INTELLIGENT, INTEGRATED DSS

This section defines a framework and a reference architecture to support the requirements for more intelligent, "smarter" DSS. Three components are explored: 1) the environment, 2) the architecture, and 3) the requirements. The discussion is based upon common principles, assumptions, and terminology for better integration and interoperability.

A. Environment

Cyber-Physical Systems (CPS) integrate computation, networking, and physical processes. A CPS links cyberspace with the physical world through a network of interrelated elements such as sensors and actuators, robotics, and computational engines. These systems are highly automated, intelligent, and collaborative. A CPS is sufficient when only standalone model-driven, data-driven, and document-driven DSS are implemented. However, when knowledge-driven and communication-driven DSS are integrated with other types of DSS, the CPS itself cannot adequately cover interactions among the system components. In this case, only a Cyber-Physical-Social System (CPSS) can support all aspects of decision support needed in the system. Semantic integration transfers information between the physical world and CPSS, and delivers knowledge between a CPSS and communities of practice. In smart manufacturing, communities include expert engineers/managers and/or machines/manufacturing tools. Communication can be defined in terms of its occurrence either on a vertical level (between members at different expertise and application levels) or on a horizontal level. Machines in the same group and similar application can form a community if they are carrying out knowledge activities and if they can either learn from or teach other members of the group. A schematic of the CPSS is illustrated in Figure 1.

Ideally, the CPSS environment will be an autonomous, sustainable, and intelligent system that can gather and organize resources into semantically rich forms that both machines and decision makers can efficiently use. Additionally, each space is required to be capable of self-evaluation.

The evolution of socialnomics, especially social network peer reviews, related to products/services in manufacturing organizations and more integrated operational structures defines a new concept of social manufacturing systems, see Jiang et al. (2016). Information technology and decision support must process these new data sources, especially for consumer facing goods.

Figure 1. Schematic of a Cyber-Physical-Social System

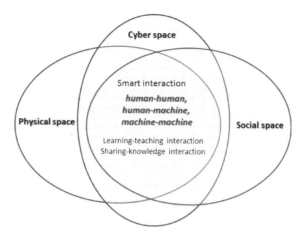

B. Architecture

DSS can create a sophisticated management system. In general, DSS can integrate multidisciplinary data sources and related tools to generate value-added information to support DM. This section outlines a functional description of components required for realizing a system based on CPSS. The architecture comprises inherent layers that are typically considered in requirements specifications for production systems and associated analytics, and decision processes. The ten proposed architecture layers are as follows:

1. **Data Layer:** Contains distributed spatial, constraint, and relational databases—and their metadata information. This layer provides transparent access to data without concern for their original formats. Since the data layer is the most frequently accessed layer, a data warehouse system usually exists to help improve performance. The data layer also provides the base for building data-driven and document-driven DSS.
2. **Information Layer:** Contains a collection of domain-specific mathematic or analytic tools or simulation models that help aggregate data into information. The analytic tools can be distributed over a network of computers in each of the other layers in the architecture. The analytic tools include domain-specific statistics, optimization, and simulation models. These domain-specific tools can provide value-added information based on raw data from the data layer.
3. **Knowledge Layer:** Knowledge is created or discovered by combining information when it transfers from an expert/intelligent engineer/machine to other parties in the system. Tools or applications that provide or recognize domain-specific knowledge include data mining, knowledge discovery algorithms, or traditional statistical inference approaches. The tools in the knowledge layer do not make decisions. Instead, they contribute and organize knowledge that is used in the decision making process. This layer also provides the knowledge base needed to build a knowledge-driven DSS.
4. **Integration Layer:** In a smart manufacturing context, additional adapters for sensor and IoT object integration are required. Due to the extensive variety in the use of various sensors, an initial classification into an ontology-based enterprise data model is needed. The integration layer can provide access for all types of DSS. In the integration layer, data from multidisciplinary sources is combined into information that can be used as domain knowledge either by non-experts or by machines. Those multidisciplinary data sources and related tools can be organized under a hier-

archical architecture structure to clarify their relationship. The system in this layer cannot express the information context inside a domain-specific application for decision making.

5. **Physical Configuration Layer:** This layer deals with the practical deployment of essential hardware for implementing CPSS such as sensors, actuators, machines, and personnel. Information about the task, process plans, quality requirements, and real-time data can be stored in the physical devices, which can repeatedly be read and written for production management usage. The physical devices flow via wireless communications in the manufacturing environment, and the information network and databases extracted from physical devices are configured and connected with each other for information sharing.

6. **Social Interaction Layer:** The social interaction layer plays the role of a mediator to assist the communication and collaboration among manufacturing components as described in the social space of the CPSS. This layer also provides the base to build more comprehensive communication-driven DSS.

7. **In-Memory Data Management and Connectivity Layer:** Due to the high volume of data and the velocity by which it is generated by physical devices, an in-memory data management platform is utilized, allowing for distributed in-memory data management with predictable latency and fast data access for real-time data handling. An in-memory data store will act as a central point of coordination, aggregation, and distribution. Besides data management, events such as alerts or system messages communicate with users in this layer.

8. **Predictive Learning Layer:** Real-time data access via the in-memory data management platform can be preprocessed, and the results are fed back to the in-memory data store. The aggregated data are used for in-situ analysis. Historical data can be analyzed for pattern detection and correlated with respective manufacturing process behaviors. Based on these patterns, manufacturing abnormalities can be detected, learned, optimized, and applied to monitor real-time data streams. Furthermore, modern Markov Decision Process (MDP) approaches could be combined with historical data to optimize the learning procedure.

9. **Presentation Layer:** To enable decision makers to make quality real-time decisions, all relevant data needs to be aggregated and visualized appropriately. Additionally, process engineers must be notified proactively if a decision is required or when a deviation in the current state of a process is detected. Moreover, a recommendation should be generated based on historical process analysis, and drill-down functionality should allow for navigation to Bayesian information and enable decision makers to make high quality decisions. Also, the presentation layer creates a user interface platform for displaying decision rules to decision makers. It manages the multidisciplinary meta-information from the layers beyond it. Based on the meta-information, it can reflect and provide internal data and services to users by means of a user interface diagram. The user interface can take many forms, such as a Web portal.

10. **Intelligent Action Layer:** DM happens in this layer based upon presented information. Manufacturing processes can be adapted by adjusting the current decision. However, adaptations in one process can lead to necessary changes in other interlinked processes. A consistent transition of changes must be fed back into the process execution system(s) when adaptations have taken place.

Figure 2 illustrates the relationship among the different layers.

Figure 2. The schematic of the relationship among different layers of architecture

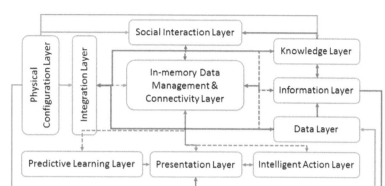

C. Requirements

To create the architecture needed required reasoning about a CPSS. A generalized framework of methods, tools and concepts can describe the needed components required for all types of DSS in a smart enterprise manufacturing environment. We define the following requirements:

- **Engineering Methodologies:** The combining of different engineering tools to build different models of a smart plant; this may be expressed in the form of process models using different process modeling languages. Methodologies decide which model to produce and which modeling languages to use to describe the model.
- **Modeling Languages:** Used for shaping the different aspects of the system and its entities—aspects including human roles, operational processes, functions, information, the workplace, and production technologies.
- **Engineering Tools:** Used for implementing modeling languages, which are supported by engineering methodologies, and model concepts to create, use, manage, analyze, evaluate, and enact models for simulation and to provide a shared design repository or database.
- **Model Concepts:** Define and formalize the most generic concepts of models in the form of ontological models, meta-models, or reference models.
- **Modules:** Used to implement the operating systems supported by models.
- **Functional Components:** For connecting to DSS in the operation phase. The functional components of DSS are included in all defined phases of software development and support the rapid adaptability and reconfigurability of manufacturing within the smart environment.
- **Information Analysis:** Consists of the analytical process modeling, statistical data and information modeling and analysis, quality management, and optimization.
- **System Management:** Involves the definition of requirements and parametric constraints. The reference structure of system management is open, which permits the possibility of expansion and improvement of the system. It can also specify hardware, processes, personnel, and facilities.
- **Mathematical Models:** Adequate models of the processes for achieving the control tasks of the system modules and equipment are required. The mathematical models allow for the optimization of the process parameters, function, and behavior of the system, information maintenance, operations and data management, and organizational structure.

- **Database:** Methods, tools, and models are arranged in a database. The methods and tools have to be characterized by their attributes for a database. Attributes determine their applicability from the system requirements. The database contains a case library and a set of solutions related to these cases. The attributes represent the objects in the database.

- **Attributes:** Defined within the ontology model as relating to properties for each concept. The attributes which are only used by the corresponding methods in each group, form the basis for choice of a suitable method or tool for the given task. Attributes characterize the prepared cases in detail and are stored in the database to be utilized in case-based reasoning.

- **Ontology:** Describes the meaning and relationships among modeling concepts (definitions) available in modeling languages, to improve the analytic capability of engineering tools and the usefulness of the models. Different components have different ontologies that coincide only partially or even mismatch. However, ontologies can merge and create a single coherent ontology; or they can align and reuse information from one another.

- **Monitoring Agents:** These follow system behavior after applying the recommended method for design and control. The "data collection and acquisition" subsystem is available and connected with monitoring agents.

- **Control Agents (Actuators):** These execute control algorithms. During the real-time control, the actuators interfere with an equipment control block initiated by some industrial controller devices or which may occur following operator manipulation. State feedback regulators can be implemented after receiving signals from measuring devices.

- **Equipment Control:** Usually designed by equipment producers. It includes sources of the actual measurement of data for the state of the physical or cyberspace equipment by sensors or other measuring devices.

- **Object-Based Architectures:** The most promising approach in modeling interactive systems. These model the interface software as a composition of co-operating objects. These models are highly modular and support concurrency, distribution of applications, and multithread dialogues.

- **Interference Monitoring of a User's Requirements:** Defines outputs and inputs for the identification of control work for making connection of external applications via the internet or a local network for distributed computing. It is required to start as an independent component and to connect to a server for computing. The resources could be physically accessible in cyberspace.

- **Readability of Knowledge:** Knowledge has to be represented in a form which can be read by a human or by a machine/computer.

- **Reusability of Data:** All data about the specific domains have to be stored, archived, and organized for future reuse.

- **Reproducibility:** New knowledge has to be reproducible (based on historical information), and it should be organized as a structured database.

- **Contestability:** Monitoring agents update the database with newly achieved results for subsequent usage and application if all of the requirements are satisfied – or else the monitoring and control agents have to repeat their operations.

- **Connectivity:** The data collection and acquisition, the information system, and system management have to connect to DSS to provide decision makers, operators, and managers with key information that enables them to make efficient and consistent decisions.

- **Knowledge Sharing:** Representation is the application of logic, computation, and ontology for the task of constructing models for an application domain. Knowledge can integrate with conjoint use of ontology and software patterns inside each component.

Figure 3. Block diagram of requirements for intelligent, integrated DSS

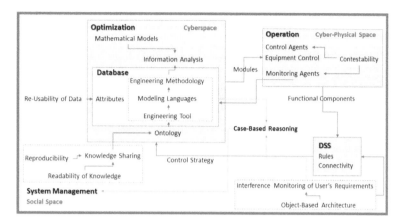

- **Rules:** Defined within an interference engine; serve to find solutions for the user according to the user's requirements.
- **Control Strategies:** Defined for searching solutions by predefined rules in both forward chaining and backward chaining.
- **Case-Based Reasoning:** Used within the system to find a solution that matches best with the user's requirements, using data stored in a database.

With regards to the environment and the architecture mentioned previously relative to intelligent, integrated DSS, Figure 3 is a block diagram of requirements for improved DSS to support the essential characteristics of smart manufacturing.

FUTURE RESEARCH DIRECTIONS

In proposing future research directions, we attempt to provide a broad vision of a design for "smart" DSS for "smart" manufacturing. These design requirements are not discussed in the literature with regards to an analytic and decision support context and thus are new directions for the next step towards smart manufacturing. In the following bullet points, we discuss some of the highlighted topics in this technology chain.

- **Area 1: *Bi-level optimization*** is an approach where the outer optimization problem is embedded (nested) within an inner optimization problem (including lower-level variables). Many multi-level DMs exist—DMs such as strategic planning of marketing and sales channels; global SC simulation models based on a marketing-operations perspective; and positioning order penetration points (OPP) in global SCs in smart manufacturing, which can be modeled by Bi-level optimization approach. As an example, in a Bi-level DM, both the leader and the follower may have multiple objectives with uncertain values and constraints which can be modeled as a *fuzzy multi-objective* **Bi-level** *programming* DSS.
- **Area 2:** Developments in electronic communication, computing, and DM – coupled with new interest on the part of organizations to improve meeting effectiveness – are spurring research in the area of ***group DSS*** (GDSS). GDSS combines communication, computing, and DM to facili-

tate the formulation and solution of unstructured problems by a group of people. Another area of future research would be developing mathematical models of group DM in DSS of the smart manufacturing environment.

- **Area 3:** Optimizing the product design process in smart manufacturing has a significant impact on the global SC. The role of having a smart DSS for optimal product design in smart manufacturing is crucial. ***Multi-level DM programming*** can be applied for capturing different features in design stages and for evaluating design alternatives based on correlated criteria such as functionality, reliability, and manufacturability to perform automated DSS for product design criteria. Consequently, multi-level optimization – as a useful and practical tool – provides the what-if analysis for product design (i.e., "What would happen if a particular decision is taken?).

- **Area 4:** Smart manufacturing employs computer control and high levels of adaptability. There are an increasing number of computer systems in smart manufacturing which can be considered as autonomous agents. Another area of future research would be developing Game Theory models for making rational choices—***DSS in a negotiation and bargaining game***.

- **Area 5:** Applying ***cooperative and noncooperative multi-level programming*** is a generalized future research direction in control and optimization of cooperative systems in the smart manufacturing environment.

- **Area 6:** Other topics in SC and operation management in smart manufacturing: 1) Integrated DSS for operation and maintenance optimization; 2) Integrated and coordinated DSS for SC optimization; and 3) Integrated DSS for maintenance, spare parts, inventory, and logistics.

CONCLUSION

More sophisticated decision support is critical for intelligent decision making in smart manufacturing environments. In this analysis, we have reviewed briefly the role of optimization and other mathematical and machine learning models in DSS to solve complex decision making tasks in smart manufacturing systems. We have proposed a systematic structure for engineering decision support applications. Integrating operations research modeling, optimization, big data analytics, and AI provide a means for making better decisions with complex objectives in a smart manufacturing setting. In smart manufacturing and in an Industry or Manufacturing 4.0 context, optimization techniques can play a critical role in automating strategic, operational, and tactical decision making and can provide more precise error analysis. Smarter decision support should lead managers to make better decisions to improve the efficiency and effectiveness of smart manufacturing systems.

We are early in the journey toward smarter manufacturing and personalization of goods. We are moving towards automation and using and integrating data capture is facilitating process improvements.

REFERENCES

Guo, Z. (2016). *Intelligent Decision-Making Models for Production and Retail Operations*. Springer. doi:10.1007/978-3-662-52681-1

Jiang, P., Leng, J., & Ding, K. (2016, July). Social manufacturing: A survey of the state-of-the-art and future challenges. In *2016 IEEE International Conference on Service Operations and Logistics, and Informatics (SOLI)* (pp. 12-17). New York, NY: IEEE. 10.1109/SOLI.2016.7551654

Power, D. J. (2002). *Categorizing decision support systems: A multidimensional approach. In Decision Making Support Systems: Achievements and Challenges for the New Decade*. Idea Group.

Power, D. J. (2004). Specifying an Expanded Framework for Classifying and Describing Decision Support Systems. *Communications of the Association for Information Systems, 13*(1), 52.

Tao, F., Zhang, L., & Laili, Y. (2016). Configurable intelligent optimization algorithm. In *Configurable Intelligent Optimization Algorithm. Springer Series in Advanced Manufacturing*. Springer.

ADDITIONAL READING

Floudas, C. A., & Pardalos, P. M. (Eds.). (2008). *Encyclopedia of Optimization*. Springer Science & Business Media.

Kearfott, R. B., & Kreinovich, V. (Eds.). (2013). *Applications of Interval Computations* (Vol. 3). Springer Science & Business Media.

Pardalos, P. M., Kallrath, J., Rebennack, S., & Scheidt, M. (Eds.). (2009). *Optimization in the Energy Industry* (p. 533). Springer.

Pardalos, P. M., & Yatsenko, V. A. (2010). *Optimization and Control of Bilinear Systems: Theory, Algorithms, and Applications* (Vol. 11). Springer Science & Business Media.

Power, D. J. (2009). *Decision support basics*. Business Expert Press. doi:10.4128/9781606490839

Power, D. J. (Ed.). (2013). *Engineering Effective Decision Support Technologies: New Models and Applications*. IGI Global. doi:10.4018/978-1-4666-4002-3

Power, D. J., Sharda, R., & Burstein, F. (2015). *Decision Support Systems*. John Wiley & Sons.

Sakawa, M., & Nishizaki, I. (2009). *Cooperative and Noncooperative Multi-Level Programming* (Vol. 48). Springer Science & Business Media.

Zopounidis, C., & Pardalos, P. M. (Eds.). (2010). *Handbook of Multicriteria Analysis* (Vol. 103). Springer Science & Business Media. doi:10.1007/978-3-540-92828-7

Zopounidis, C., & Pardalos, P. M. (2013). *Managing in Uncertainty: Theory and Practice* (Vol. 19). Springer Science & Business Media.

KEY TERMS AND DEFINITIONS

Advanced Planning and Scheduling: Refers to a manufacturing management process by which raw materials and production capacity are optimally allocated to meet demand.

Case-Based Reasoning: The process of learning to solve new problems based on the solutions of similar past problems.

Enterprise Resource Planning: The real-time integrated management of core business processes, mediated by software and technology.

Manufacturing Execution System: Computerized systems used in manufacturing to track and document the transformation of raw materials to finished goods.

Markov Decision Process: Describes the environment for solving the optimization problem by reinforcement learning or dynamic programming. Provides a mathematical framework for modeling DM in situations where outcomes are fully or partially observable.

Order Penetration Point (OPP): Defines the stage in the manufacturing value chain, where a particular product is linked to a specific customer order.

Semantic Integration: The process of integrating information from diverse sources. In this regard, semantics focuses on the organization of, and action upon, information by acting as an intermediary between heterogeneous data sources which may conflict not only in structure but also in context or value.

Modelling Quality and Pricing in Next Generation Telecom Networks

Vesna Radonjic Djogatovic

Faculty of Transport and Traffic Engineering, University of Belgrade, Serbia

Marko Djogatovic

Faculty of Transport and Traffic Engineering, University of Belgrade, Serbia

INTRODUCTION

Business processes in telecommunication sector have evolved from rigid structures to a highly competitive environment due to the dynamics of the open market. Future telecommunications infrastructure are expected to be built upon the concept of next generation network (NGN) referring to an architecture of telecommunication core and access networks, which assumes transport of all information and services over a common network, typically built around the Internet Protocol (IP).

Many service providers (SPs) are looking to NGN services as a means to attract and/or retain the most gainful users. In NGN users are expected to choose the SP offering the best price and quality of service (QoS) combination. As a result, SPs operating in the same telecommunication market will end up competing for users by adjusting QoS they offer and the price they charge for their services.

Quality of NGN services can be estimated based on the three aspects: QoS, quality of experience (QoE) and quality of business (QoBiz). The main goal for SP is to maximize his revenue while providing users the required QoS at the acceptable price. QoS can be defined as a set of characteristics of a telecommunications service that bear on its ability to satisfy users' requirements (ITU-T E.800, 2008). While QoS is related to the service performances that can be measured and controlled, QoE relates to the experience realized by a user when using the service and it depends upon users' actions and subjective opinions. In addition to SPs' aspirations to ensure the required QoS to their users, profitability is of the most importance to them. QoBiz in particular covers service providers' profitability. It deals with the financial aspects of service provisioning and refers to all those parameters that are expressed in monetary units. QoS, QoE and QoBiz are integral parts of a service level agreement (SLA) which can be contracted between two SPs or a SP and a user.

This chapter aims to provide new possibilities for SPs to enhance their revenues using the appropriate pricing scheme. Features and applicability of responsive pricing scheme and hybrid pricing for charging end users in NGN are discussed. Game theory is used as an underlying concept for the implementation of pricing. In addition, transparent mapping of QoS parameters to QoBiz are considered, encompassing service price dependence on QoS violation, which is consequently reflected on SP's revenue.

BACKGROUND

Pricing with QoS guarantees has gained a strong momentum in telecommunication networks in past decade. It has led to a new interdisciplinary research area of "Telecommunication Economics", which

DOI: 10.4018/978-1-7998-3473-1.ch163

investigates telecommunication networks from an economical rather than from a technical perspective and allows innovative solutions in network management, control and pricing (Courcoubetis & Weber, 2003).

QoS describes the ability of a network to provide a service with an assured service level but it appears that in NGN QoS differentiation will not provide a suitable economic framework for the trade-off between quality delivered by SPs and willingness to pay from users' side. QoE is an alternative framework for pricing service quality according to the user perception (ITU-T G.1011, 2013). It is affected not only by technical (i.e. QoS) aspects, but on non-technical aspects of service too, such as service set-up, content, price and customer support, which are essential for both QoE and QoBiz evaluation.

The distinction between QoS, QoE and QoBiz metrics in case of Internet services are first emphasized by Moorsel (2001). In Wolter and Moorsel (2001) possible relationships between QoS and QoBiz metrics are pointed out, particularly the effects of QoS degradations on the profitability of e-services. This research considers dynamic relationship between QoS and QoBiz metrics with pricing as an important tool for balancing users' behaviour. Further, for the purpose of evaluating the impact of service composition and utility computing on QoBiz aspects of SPs, a distributed architecture of control systems that manages SLAs is proposed in Machiraju et al. (2002). Yu and Bouguettaya (2007) proposed the model for supporting optimized access of web services through service-oriented queries. Besides QoBiz parameters, this model captures functionality and users' behaviour, as the key features of web services. Bjekovic and Kubicki (2011) address the need for an integration of non-functional aspects of service from the business perspective with aim of improving cooperation among business enterprises. Rivera et al. (2016) presented a framework for evaluating QoE of a web-based over the top (OTT) service from QoS, QoE, and QoBiz perspective. In focus of QoBiz consideration was revenue maximization. In Radonjic Djogatovic, Djogatovic and Stanojevic (2018) the model performing transparent mapping from QoS to QoBiz parameters is proposed. This model is based on several QoS parameters that significantly affect both users' demand and a SP's requirements from the business perspective.

Telecom provider's QoBiz is tightly related to the selection of the appropriate network pricing method. Price based bandwidth allocation has been the focus of many research efforts that aimed to guarantee an appropriate QoS to users. Some methods allow congestion which results in blocking of the lower-priced traffic classes and the acceptance of the higher-priced traffic classes in case of congestion (Marbach, 2004). The concept of responsive pricing was proposed with the aim to incorporate a feedback generated by the network. When the network announces a price based on the cost of using network resources price-sensitive users adjust their traffic in accordance of their own network service valuation (MacKie-Mason, Murphy, L. & Murphy, J., 1997). Chod and Rudi (2005) considered responsive pricing with resource flexibility as well as effects of demands variability and correlation, assuming normally distributed demand curve. In Ninan and Devetsikiotis (2005) a model for incorporating pricing in NGNs with users sharing bandwidth under a fixed charge per bandwidth amount was presented. Optimal resource allocation of NGN services under a flat pricing scheme and QoS policies were considered by Kallitsis et al. (2007). Congestion pricing with various user demands over time was analyzed by Hande et al. (2010). With the goal of maximization SPs' revenue the same authors applied the optimal combination of flat-rate and usage-based access price components. The importance of selection of the appropriate pricing method for a business model framework in case of providing assured quality services is emphasized in Ghezzi et al. (2014). An overview of usage-based pricing schemes and accounting protocols that can be used in NGN are given in Radonjic Djogatovic and Kostic-Ljubisavljevic (2015). The significance of quality and pricing as major causes of customer churn is highlighted in Floris (2017). In the same publication QoE-aware collaboration approach between OTT and Internet SP has been proposed, which is driven by revenue maximization based on pricing, quality, user churn, and marketing actions. Jin et al. (2019)

proposed a location-dependent pricing strategy, taking into consideration the congestion level of different sites within the framework that integrates the advantages of information-centric forwarding and content delivery networks.

PRICING AND QUALITY ISSUES IN NGN

The evolution of networks to NGNs must allow the continuity of, and interoperability with, existing networks while enabling the implementation of new capabilities (ITU-T Y.2012, 2010). Suitable pricing and business models need to be designed which is expected to provide the appropriate incentives for both SPs and users.

Generally, the concept of pricing implies the process of determining prices which should be based on the appropriate pricing model and controlled by a pricing policy. It is expected that competition will force SPs to rapidly create and deploy different pricing concepts with aim of fulfilment a trade-off between providing satisfying user's utility and provider's profit, still preserving implementation efficiency and feasibility. User's utility can be expressed as a function of available network resource offered to a user which indicates a user's sensitivity to changes in QoS. A wide range of different pricing schemes is likely to be applied in NGN (Ninan & Devetsikiotis, 2005; Pandey, Ghosal & Mukherjee, 2007; Radonjic & Acimovic-Raspopovic, 2010). Pricing schemes that should be implemented in NGN have to be defined and evaluated with respect to the heterogeneous technical, economic and social aspects. The main evaluation criteria encompass efficiency in the context of maximizing utilities of users and providers, fairness and feasibility.

In NGN there is a need for shifting from static pricing schemes, in which users are charged independently of the resource consumption and QoS delivered, towards dynamic pricing schemes. In dynamic pricing, price is determined as a cost per unit of consumption and according to the level of QoS guarantees provided for the observed service class. The main problem with dynamic pricing refers to the need of intensive monitoring of network resources in order to dynamically adjust per-class prices to resources usage and the QoS provided for each service class. Any NGN architecture must guarantee fair access to the shared resources in the access network and control load distribution with aim of avoiding focused overload in the core. Also, NGN should support hard guarantees to users and pricing different QoS classes.

Due to the rapidly increasing deployment of interactive and multimedia applications in telecommunication services, QoS becomes an integral part of various protocols and mechanisms for enabling computing and telecommunication systems. QoS is defined by SLA which consists of two parts: the technical part and the administrative part. The technical part encompasses a set of descriptors and associated attributes that describe the particular service class and the traffic profile. The administrative part covers financial and legal aspects: information about pricing, charging, billing and payment, penalties for both user and service provider in the case of contract violation, etc. (Stojanovic, Kostic-Ljubisavljevic & Radonjic Djogatovic, 2013). As users' needs are constantly increasing, as well as competition between service providers, SLA becomes more complex.

Although QoS is usually represented by delay, loss and jitter, which are difficult to measure precisely, frequently used QoS parameters for determination whether a required service level is being achieved, are network availability and bandwidth. Network availability includes the availability of many items the network consists of, e.g. multiple physical connections, networking device redundancy. It is also important to distinguish available and guaranteed bandwidth. In many dynamic pricing schemes users are allowed to compete for the available bandwidth and their obtained bandwidth depends upon amount of traffic from other users in the network at any observed time (Chod & Rudi, 2005). The term guaranteed bandwidth implies a guaranteed minimum bandwidth SP provides or burst bandwidth in SLA. The service with guaranteed bandwidth has higher priority and is priced higher compared to the available bandwidth service.

By introducing QoS differentiation users are encouraged to choose the service that meets their needs in the most adequate manner, which can be achieved through pricing. Providing service with strong QoS guarantees keeps users satisfied and thereby maintains the confidence in the SP. However, it is necessary to take into account user experience and business indicators too. Therefore, quality of NGN services can be estimated based on three aspects: QoS, QoE and QoBiz.

Obviously, QoS is related to the service performances that can be measured and controlled, while QoE relates to the experience realized by a user when using the service. QoE depends upon users' actions and subjective opinions. It takes into consideration users' satisfaction with the service, subjective evaluation, the degree of their expectations fulfilment and in what context they use it or intend to (Barakovic, S., Barakovic, J. & Bajric, 2010).

In addition to SPs' aspirations to ensure the required QoS to their users, QoBiz is an important aspect in providing quality of NGN services that is being increasingly used in the pursuit of better business. It deals with the financial aspect of service provisioning and refers specifically to measures such as service price, service provisioning costs, revenue from the service provisioning, revenue per transaction, lost transactions etc. In general, QoBiz parameters are all those parameters that are expressed in monetary units. According to the more precise interpretation, it is a monetary value that matches the quality of delivered service, expressed through connection of QoS parameters with monetary value within the SLA (Radonjic Djogatovic et al., 2018).

SOLUTIONS AND RECOMMENDATIONS

A model for QoBiz improvement of next generation telecom network should include business aspects that are specific and important for telecom sector. It should reflect involved parties' preferences which allow discovering, negotiating and contracting a service between a user and a provider. In this chapter we propose two models for pricing and quality improvement. The first model is designed for eliminating or at least alleviating congestion along with service price optimization regarding QoS and QoE and revenue maximization, which is reflected on QoBiz. Since it relies on responsive pricing, we will denote it as the responsive model. The second model assumes that SP offers tariff packages based on users' requirements and transparent mapping of QoS parameters to QoBiz including direct reflection of QoS violation on service prices and consequently on SP's revenue. Therefore, the second model is denoted as the mapping model.

In the responsive model, congestion and pricing management have been done via proper bandwidth assignment considering the capacity constraint, i.e. adapting the network price to optimize network performances. It is achieved by a usage-based scheme with users getting charged for the amount of traffic they consume. For maintaining social optimality these charges would have to be set equal to the marginal cost of usage. Since bandwidth scarcity occurs only during congestion, this marginal cost is essentially the same as the congestion cost. In order to achieve satisfying network and economic efficiency the responsive pricing scheme is used (Chod & Rudi, 2005). Price is emphasized as an alternative means for congestion control to ensure proper network operation and in particular to guarantee different service levels. In this pricing scheme, in the case of high network utilization, provider increases the prices for the resources and adaptive users then reduce traffic offered to the network. Similarly, in the case of low network utilization, by decreasing the price adaptive users are encouraged to increase their offered traffic.

Bandwidth management server (BMS) is introduced in order to enhance scalability and to allow connection control functions independently of the underlying network, which makes it suitable for NGN. BMS acts as an interface between the connection control functions and the network specific bearer functions. The interface between BMS and the underlying network elements is provided to allow BMS to set up and tear down aggregate bandwidth reservations across the network. The most important features of BMS are the ability to release bandwidth when it is no longer needed and to reserve bandwidth to the particular destination of the particular QoS class. The underlying network elements must be able to inform BMS of any changes affecting current reservations. The interface should allow this information to be passed upwards to BMS immediately such an event takes place and the information should reach BMS with the shortest possible delay.

During SLA negotiation, the SP estimates resource usage according to the required traffic profile. Although it is common that the agreement between the SP and a user for a service consumption has to be settled for a long time period, in this model allocations are performed in short time scales. In practice, it would be impossible for each user to update his bandwidth in a short time scale. Instead of that, with the aim of maximizing SP's revenue, updates are performed by BMS considering network congestion and network capacity utilization. Updates are based on users' parameters of desired bandwidth, maximal price they are willing to pay and their individual utility functions. During the service provisioning interval, the usage-based traffic monitoring should be applied only with respect to deviations from the contracted traffic profile. Such approach is called hybrid pricing scheme. It needs less storage of monitoring data in comparison with monitoring per unit of consumption (i.e. dynamic pricing) and should be implemented only at the edge routers, in which traffic conditioning is performed. The solution of the problem encompasses the optimal bandwidth allocation and the optimal price for that allocation. The actual price is calculated at the end of service provisioning interval according to SP's specific policy, which should aim to force users to wisely select the most appropriate traffic profiles and to properly adjust to them. Each user has to pay the price that is equal to the sum of products of each optimal price and his bandwidth consumption during all his sessions in the agreed time period.

In the responsive model, problem of determining service prices is divided into optimization with respect to users' utility and the optimization of the provider's revenue. In this fashion, the model incorporates not only QoS but QoE and QoBiz too. Users' preferences may be modelled with utility functions that describe users' sensitivity to changes of QoS. Since it is not easy to predict actual QoS parameters, such as delay or packet losses in most real networks, utility is often expressed as a function of the amount of available network resources (i.e. bandwidth) offered to each user (Ninan & Devetsikiotis, 2005). Thus, the utility indirectly indicates user's sensitivity to changes in QoS.

The optimization procedure is performed for different categories of users, which can be alternatively done for different service classes. According to the elasticity criteria, users are classified into three categories: inelastic, partially elastic and elastic users (Radonjic Djogatovic & Kostic-Ljubisavljevic, 2015). Inelastic users are users who have strict requirements in terms of delay but can tolerate losses to some extent and their utility has been most commonly described by the sigmoid function. A utility function which best models elastic and partially elastic users' behaviour is a generalization of the logarithmic function. Elastic users do not tolerate losses but can accept a delay to some extent. Partially elastic users are also not tolerant of losses but they have stronger requirements in respect to delay. Users' utility functions vary in accordance to the elasticity criterion of a user. For all users' types, QoS is defined by bandwidth, θ obtained from the SP. Users are assumed to be non-cooperative, meaning that they refuse to reveal their utility functions to one another in the fear of being misused.

The SP employs a usage-based pricing policy by charging M per unit bandwidth consumed. Depending upon the QoS requested, i.e. the class of service he chose, each user would require a minimum bandwidth γ. Fewer bandwidth than γ on average is of no utility to the user (Ninan & Devetsikiotis, 2005). The law of diminishing marginal utility ensures that the user derives the same amount of satisfaction from any bandwidth more than the maximum π. It is considered that the user is willing to pay a maximum price m per unit of bandwidth. When the price M equals the maximal price m, the user will desire only the minimum acceptable bandwidth, γ. For all types of users, any price beyond the maximal price reduces a user's desired bandwidth to zero. Each user will try to choose his bandwidth θ so as to maximize his net benefit (i.e., utility minus cost). Ideally any resource allocation between users should ensure that the total user utility is maximized. On the other hand, the SP's utility T depends on the total revenue generated and hence is a function of the market price and the bandwidth allocated to the various users. In order to maximize his revenue, the SP settles the price per bandwidth unit according to the concept of responsive pricing reflecting the state of resource utilization.

The interaction of the SP and users is defined as a Stackelberg leader-follower game within responsive pricing scheme driving the system towards optimality. Generally, in Stackelberg model at least one player is defined as the leader who can make the decision and commit the strategy before other players who are defined as followers (Briest, Hoefer & Krysta, 2008). In the proposed model, players are the SP, acting as the leader and users, acting as followers. They act in a definite sequence and interaction between them is dynamic rather than static. The strategy chosen by the SP can be observed by users, so they can adapt their decisions in accordance to their preferences. The SP can choose such a strategy which allows him to maximize revenues, assuming that users will choose their best responses. With backward induction, the best responses of users are obtained first. The best responses of both SP and users in this leader-follower competition can be obtained in the following way. Given the price offered by the SP, based on a demand function, the amount of bandwidth users requested can be determined. For example, if the price is high, the amount of bandwidth requested by users will be small and vice versa. Then, this best response is used to compute the revenue of the SP, and he chooses a strategy that leads to his revenue maximization.

In the proposed usage-based pricing algorithm within the responsive model (Figure 1), prices optimization is performed for a single critical resource link in a SP's network. Such a link usually does not behave badly all the time, but only under certain worst-case conditions. On the observed link, the total number of users is N. For each user, bandwidth and price parameters, representing QoS and QoE respectively, are parts of the SLA. Each user gives his parameters of desired bandwidth and maximal price that can't be changed during the agreement period. The bandwidth allotment to user i is denoted as θ_i^* and that is his best response to the price SP determined. The algorithm can be performed for scenarios with different number of service classes in order to optimize bandwidth usage, price per bandwidth unit and a total capacity of the critical link in the network.

There are S rounds in total and in each round s, l_s iterations are performed, where $s = 1, 2, \ldots S$. Each round s consists of several iterative steps. The algorithm, shown in Figure 1, converges quickly after few tens of rounds. Optimization is performed for each service class j. The algorithm begins when the provider assigns an initial price, M^0 for each service class j. The initial price can be set either randomly or based on historical data. BMS simulates users' behavior in a manner that for each user requiring a certain service class, calculates the desired bandwidth and forwards the data to the provider. The provider then checks whether all user requirements can be met with the existing capacity and if the answer

Figure 1. Pricing algorithm (Radonjic & Acimovic-Raspopovic, 2010)

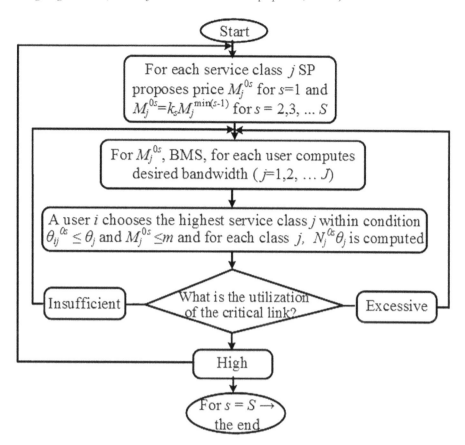

is yes and if the facilities are not used enough, it proceeds to a new iteration with lower prices. In case that requests exceed the network capacity, next iteration is performed with higher prices. In this fashion, users' responses are adapted to the state of network capacity utilization. A round ends when satisfactory utilization of the network capacity is achieved (over 90%). In each round different values of the network capacity are adopted as well as different values of the initial price for each service class. The price offered by the SP, which maximizes his revenue along with the best response bandwidth of each user constitutes the Stackelberg equilibrium (Radonjic & Acimovic-Raspopovic, 2010). In this manner, revenue, as a significant aspect of QoBiz can be improved.

Further, we propose the mapping model, considering that SP strives to maximize its revenue while providing users the required QoS at the acceptable price. We focus on mapping QoS to QoBiz parameters (Radonjic Djogatovic et al., 2018). In the mapping model we take into account only requirements regarding QoS that are significant and transparent enough to users and thereby relevant for SP's QoBiz. Before the development of the model it is necessary to select QoS parameters that significantly affect QoBiz requirements, and identify key QoBiz parameters. Next step include finding the most appropriate solution for mapping QoS to QoBiz. We choose available bit rate, i.e. download and upload speed, as well as security as key QoS parameters for mapping to QoBiz. Considering price is one of the most significant parameters for users while the main goal for SP is to maximize its revenue, we focus on a service price and SP's revenue, as key QoBiz parameters.

We propose the spiral solution for mapping QoS to QoBiz with different settings for each QoS parameter (Figure 2):

- download speed (s_{d1}, s_{d2}, s_{d3}, s_{d4}, s_{d5}), where $s_{d1} > s_{d2} > s_{d3} > s_{d4} > s_{d5}$,
- upload speed (s_{u1}, s_{u2}, s_{u3}, s_{u4}, s_{u5}), where $s_{u1} > s_{u2} > s_{u3} > s_{u4} > s_{u5}$ and
- security (s_1, s_2, s_3, s_4, s_5), where s_1 indicates the highest level of security while each subsequent level indicates a bit lower security, so s_5 point out to the lowest level of security.

Each of these values corresponds to a specific price, as it is illustrated in Figure 2. Service with the best performances (s_{d1}, s_{u1}, s_1) is charged with maximum price, denoted as p_0. It is assumed that a price equally depends on each QoS parameter, i.e. it decreases for 5% with any QoS degradation, which implies that a service with the worst performances by all QoS parameters (s_{d5}, s_{u5}, s_5) is charged with 60% lower price compared to a service with the best performances.

Figure 2. Spiral QoS to QoBiz mapping (Radonjic Djogatovic et al., 2018)

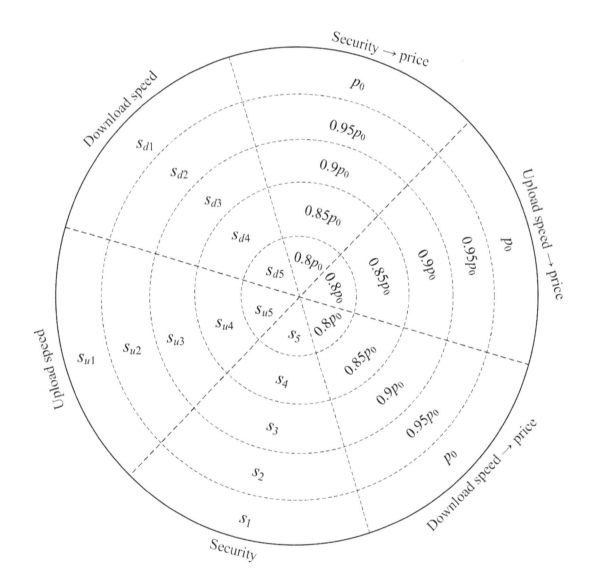

Users are classified in eight different types according to their preferences regarding to QoS and price:

1. Users who prefer high speed Internet access with maximum download speed,
2. Users who prefer high speed Internet access with maximum upload speed,
3. Users who prefer maximum security protection,
4. Users who can tolerate slightly lower download speed
5. Users who can tolerate slightly lower upload speed
6. Users who can tolerate slightly lower level of security
7. Users who are willing to pay no more than p_1 ($p_1 > 0.4\,p_0$) for monthly Internet usage and
8. Users who are willing to pay no more than p_2 ($p_2 \geq .0.4\,p_0$) for monthly Internet usage (the assumption is that $p_2 < p_1$).

Users can belong to more than one type but some types are mutually exclusive. We assume type 7 and 8 don't have any QoS preferences specified for previous types, so they will be assigned lower QoS values than previous types and consequently they will be charged with lower prices. Based on QoS parameters combinations and users' requirements, SP defines tariff packages (TPs), shown in Table 1.

Table 1. Tariff packages (Radonjic Djogatovic et al., 2018)

QoS/ QoBiz	Download speed	Upload speed	Security	Price
TP1	s_{d1}	s_{u1}	s_1	p_{TP1}
TP2	s_{d1}	s_{u1}	s_2	p_{TP2}
TP3	s_{d1}	s_{u2}	s_1	p_{TP3}
TP4	s_{d2}	s_{u1}	s_1	p_{TP4}
TP5	s_{d1}	s_{u1}	s_3	p_{TP5}
TP6	s_{d1}	s_{u3}	s_1	p_{TP6}
TP7	s_{d3}	s_{u1}	s_1	p_{TP7}
TP8	s_{d1}	s_{u3}	s_3	p_{TP8}
TP9	s_{d3}	s_{u1}	s_3	p_{TP9}
TP10	s_{d3}	s_{u3}	s_1	p_{TP10}
TP11	s_{d4}	s_{u4}	s_4	p_{TP11}
TP12	s_{d5}	s_{u5}	s_5	p_{TP12}

Acordingly, SP's revenue can be determined as:, where is monthly price per tariff package *TPi*, is number of users per tariff package *TPi* and k is the number of TPs (in this case $k=12$). Monthly prices are determined according to spiral QoS to QoBiz mapping. Thus, $p_{TP1} = p_0$, $p_{TP2} = p_{TP3} = p_{TP4} = 0.95p_0$, $p_{TP5} = p_{TP6} = p_{TP7} = 0.9p_0$, $p_{TP8} = p_{TP9} = p_{TP10} = 0.8p_0$, $p_{TP11} = 0.55p_0$, $p_{TP12} = 0.4p_0$.

Finally, we assume SP applies hybrid pricing scheme, which is implemented in a fashion that the monthly price is reduced by a certain percentage if users, due to excessive network load, experience significantly lower speed than declared during period longer than defined time interval (typically several minutes). Based on simulation model and the results for an example of the mapping model, given in Radonjic Djogatovic et al. (2018), it is shown that prices decrease for most tariff packages. Applying hybrid pricing scheme, SP is likely to attract new users, but in order to maximize his revenue, his aspiration should be directed towards improving QoS parameters, which can be performed by additional investments in the network.

FUTURE RESEARCH DIRECTIONS

In order to provide the appropriate incentives for providers, suitable business and pricing models need to be designed. QoBiz stands out as a significant concept which deals with the financial aspects of service provisioning. For QoBiz evaluation, it is essential to consider service demand, price structures and revenue trends. The need for new pricing solutions that coordinate the competing requirements of providers and users in NGN environment is evident.

In future research, new possibilities for solving similar problems of pricing and interconnection between multiple providers in NGN should be considered. A general research direction should comprise market modelling, cost and risk consideration as well as network design. The proposed models can be extended to cover cost optimization for SP in order to optimize trade-off between cost investments and expected revenue from new users. Moreover, the proposed models may include contemporary real market situation in which several service providers compete for users. Different types of providers should be considered along with quantifying their impact on the price setting and overall QoBiz. More specific research direction could include applying different game models (e.g. repeated/cooperative games, Cournot and Bertrand games) under dynamic and hybrid pricing schemes. Furthermore, future research should be directed towards more precise mapping between QoE and QoBiz parameters.

CONCLUSION

The adoption of an appropriate pricing scheme can significantly affect business operation of a NGN provider. NGNs must be flexible enough to enable the use of different pricing and business models. Growth in demand due to the popularity of NGN applications requires significant investment in infrastructure but brings a negligible return.

Service providers, therefore, strive for a new network model giving priority to managed services whose usage is controlled by a particular pricing scheme. They are searching for ways to brand and bundle new services, achieve operational cost reductions and strategically position themselves in relation to their competition. Many SPs are looking to NGN services as a means to attract and/or retain the most gainful users. In NGN users are expected to choose the SP offering the best price and QoS combination. As a result, SPs operating in the same telecommunication market will end up competing for users by adjusting QoS they offer and the price they charge for their services.

With the aim of telecom provider's QoBiz improvement, in this chapter two models for the service price optimization are proposed. It has been shown that applying responsive pricing scheme along with Stackelberg game, leads to improvement of the SP's revenue, as a significant aspect of QoBiz. The target market for the application of the responsive model are business users, such as small and medium enterprises. The introduction of the responsive model should be done gradually to the coexistence with the current pricing models. The main advantage of the mapping model is transparent mapping QoS parameters to QoBiz with direct reflection of QoS violation on service prices and accordingly on SP's revenue. In addition, the mapping model implies that users are charged based not only to declared QoS but also with regards to achieved QoS, which results in lower prices.

REFERENCES

Barakovic, S., Barakovic, J., & Bajric, H. (2010). QoE Dimensions and QoE Measurement of NGN Services. In *Proceedings of 19th Telecommunications Forum* (pp. 15-18). Belgrade Telecommunications Society.

Bjekovic, M., & Kubicki, S. (2011). Service quality description – a business perspective. In *Proceedings of the Federated Conference on Computer Science and Information Systems*, (pp. 513-520). IEEE.

Briest, P., Hoefer, M., & Krysta, P. (2008). Stackelberg Network Pricing Games. In *Proceedings of 25th International Symposium on Theoretical Aspects of Computer Science*, (vol. 1, pp.133-142). Springer-Verlag.

Chod, J., & Rudi, N. (2005). Resource Flexibility with Responsive Pricing. *Operations Research, 53*(3), 532–548. doi:10.1287/opre.1040.0191

Courcoubetis, C., & Weber, R. (2003). *Pricing Communication Networks*. John Wiley & Sons Ltd. doi:10.1002/0470867175

Floris, A. (2017). Quality of Experience: modelling and application scenarios. PhD in Electronic and Computer Engineering, University of Cagliari.

Ghezzi, A., Dramitinos, M., Rangone, A., Agiatzidou, E., Johanses, F. T., Balocco, R., & Løsethagen, H. (2014). Internet Interconnection Techno-Economics: A Proposal for Assured Quality Services and Business Models. *Proceedings of 47th Hawaii International Conference on System Science*, Waikoloa, HI, USA. (pp. 708-717). IEEE. 10.1109/HICSS.2014.95

Hande, P., Chiang, M., Calderbank, R., & Zhang, J. (2010). Pricing under Constraints in Access Networks: Revenue Maximization and Congestion Management. In Proceedings of IEEE INFOCOM 2010, (pp. 1-9). IEEE.

ITU-T Recommendation E.800 (2008). Definitions of terms related to quality of service.

ITU-T Recommendation G.1011 (2013). Reference Guide to Quality of Experience Assessment Methodologies.

ITU-T Recommendation Y.2012 (2010). Functional requirements and architecture of next generation networks.

Jin, M., Luo, H., Gao, S., & Feng, B. (2019). Joint Location-Dependent Pricing and Request Mapping in ICN-Based Telco CDNs for 5G. *Future Internet, 11*(6), 125. doi:10.3390/fi11060125

Kallitsis, M., Michailidis, G., & Devetsikiotis, M. (2007). Pricing and Measurement-based Optimal Resource Allocation in Next Generation Network Services. In *Proceedings of the First IEEE Workshop on Enabling the Future Service-Oriented Internet*, (pp. 1-6). IEEE. 10.1109/GLOCOMW.2007.4437788

Machiraju, V., Rolia, J. & Moorsel, A. (2002). *Quality of Business Driven Service Composition and Utility Computing*. Software Technology Laboratory, HP Laboratories Palo Alto, HPL-2002-66.

MacKie-Mason, J., Murphy, L., & Murphy, J. (1997). Responsive Pricing in the Internet. In L. W. McKnight & J. P. Bailey (Eds.), *Internet Economics* (pp. 279–303). MIT Press.

Marbach, P. (2004). Analysis of a static pricing scheme for priority services. *IEEE/ACM Transactions on Networking, 12*(2), 312–325. doi:10.1109/TNET.2004.826275

Moorsel, A. (2001). Metrics for the Internet Age: Quality of Experience and Quality of Business. In *Proceedings of the Fifth International Workshop on Performability Modeling of Computer and Communication Systems*, (vol. 34, pp. 26-31). University of Erlangen.

Ninan, B. M., & Devetsikiotis, M. (2005). Game-Theoretic Resource Pricing For The Next Generation Internet. In A. Girard, B. Sanso, & F. Vazquez Abad (Eds.), *Performance Evaluation and Planning Methods for the Next Generation Internet* (pp. 141–163). Springer. doi:10.1007/0-387-25551-6_6

Pandey, V., Ghosal, D., & Mukherjee, B. (2007). Pricing-based approaches in the design of next-generation wireless networks: A review and a unified proposal. *IEEE Communications Surveys and Tutorials, 9*(2), 88–101. doi:10.1109/COMST.2007.382409

Radonjic, V., & Acimovic-Raspopovic, V. (2010). Responsive Pricing Modeled with Stackelberg Game for Next Generation Networks. *Annales des Télécommunications, 65*(7-8), 461–476. doi:10.100712243-010-0174-2

Radonjic Djogatovic, V., Djogatovic, M., & Stanojevic, M. (2018). Simulation Analysis of Quality of Business in IP Networks. In *Proceedings of the XIII Balkan Conference on Operational Research*, (pp. 373-380). Mathematical Institute – Serbian Academy of Sciences and Arts.

Radonjic Djogatovic, V., & Kostic-Ljubisavljevic, A. (2015). Telecommunications Pricing Fundamentals. Belgrade, Serbia: University of Belgrade – Faculty of Transport and Traffic Engineering.

Rivera, D., Cavalli, A. R., Kushik, N., & Mallouli, W. (2016). An Implementation of a QoE Evaluation Technique Including Business Model Parameters. In *Proceedings of the 11th International Joint Conference on Software Technologies*, (pp. 138-145). SciTePress. 10.5220/0006005001380145

Stojanovic, M., Kostic-Ljubisavljevic, A., & Radonjic Djogatovic, V. (2013). SLA-controlled Interconnection Charging in Next Generation Networks. *Computer Networks, 57*(11), 2374–2394. doi:10.1016/j.comnet.2013.04.013

Wolter, K. & Moorsel, A. (2001). *The Relationship between Quality of Service and Business Metrics: Monitoring, Notification and Optimization*. HP Labs Technical Report, HPL-2001-96.

Yu, Q., & Bouguettaya, A. (2007). Framework for Web Service Query Algebra and Optimization. *ACM Transactions on the Web*, 1–34.

ADDITIONAL READING

Collins, H. (2009). *Next Generation Networks Creating a Dedicated Cost Model*. InterConnect Communications Ltd.

ITU-T Recommendation Y.2233 (2010). Requirements and framework allowing accounting and charging capabilities in NGN.

Karamchati, S., Rawat, S., & Varma, V. (2017). A novel architecture to enhance Quality of Service in IP networks. *Proceedings of the 31st International Conference on Information Networking*, Da Nang, Vietnam (pp. 616-621). IEEE. 10.1109/ICOIN.2017.7899567

Krogstie, J. (2016). *Quality in Business Process Modeling*. Springer International Publishing Switzerland. doi:10.1007/978-3-319-42512-2

Sharif, S. M., & Ahmed, A. (2015). Next Generation Networks (NGN) Billing and Charging System. *International Journal of Engineering and Computer Science, 4*(1), 9825–9830.

Stankiewicz, R., Cholda, P., & Jajszczyk, A. (2011). QoX: What is It Really? *IEEE Communications Magazine, 49*(4), 148–158. doi:10.1109/MCOM.2011.5741159

Stojanovic, M., Vukasinovic, M., & Radonjic Djogatovic, V. (2015). Approaches to Quality of Experience Management in the Future Internet, *Proceedings of the 12th International Conference TELSIKS*, Nis, Serbia (pp. 281–288). IEEE. 10.1109/TELSKS.2015.7357788

Webb, J. N. (2007). *Game Theory - Decisions, Interaction and Evolution*. Springer.

KEY TERMS AND DEFINITIONS

Dynamic Pricing: The process of allocating the price as a cost per unit of resource consumption and according to level of QoS guarantees provided for the particular service class.

Hybrid Pricing: The process of applying the static price in regular network operation mode while during congestion the dynamic pricing is enforced allowing deviations from contracted traffic profile.

Next Generation Network (NGN): An architectural concept of future telecommunication core and access networks, which assumes transport of all information and services over a common network, typically built around the IP.

Quality of Business (QoBiz): A monetary value that matches the quality of delivered service, expressed through connection of QoS parameters with monetary value within the SLA.

Quality of Experience (QoE): The overall acceptability of an application or service, as perceived subjectively by the end-user.

Quality of Service (QoS): A set of service requirements that a network should meet when transferring traffic flows.

Responsive Pricing: A pricing scheme which incorporates feedback generated by a network assuming that users are adaptive to the service price changes.

Service Level Agreement (SLA): A contract between service providers or a service provider and a user, which defines responsibilities of all contracting parties, QoS guarantees, performance metrics, measurement methods and pricing principles.

Service Provider (SP): A general reference to an enterprise that provides telecommunication services to users.

Stackelberg Game: A strategic game in which at least one player is defined as the leader who can make a decision and commit a strategy before other players who are defined as followers.

Resources, Recycling, Regulations, and Reputation in the Comparison of Operations Sustainability Techniques

Alan D. Smith

Robert Morris University, USA

INTRODUCTION

Sustainability as a Strategy Sustainability is a growing concern and challenge for companies around the globe. Batra (2012), McDonagh and Clark (1995), Menon, Menon, Chowdhury, and Jankovich (1999), and Moisander (2007) attribute this challenge to the over-consumption of the Earth's resources, especially in developed countries, and the unexpected rapid increase in the world's population throughout the last century. Many corporate management have realize that in a world with decreasing resources and increasing population, that it is imperative to consider sustainability in their own operations (Simintiras, Schlegelmilch, & Diamantopoulos, 1994; Straughan & Roberts, 1999; Thogersen, 2006; Van Liere & Dunlap, 1981; Vesilind, Heine, & Hendry, 2006). When evaluating sustainability in production processes the four "R's" of sustainability is a useful tool. These are the resources used by the production process, the recycling of production materials and product components, the regulations that apply, and the firm's reputation (Hooley, Saunders, & Pierry, 1998; Iyer & Banerjee, 1993; Jain & Kaur, 2006). A company can assess their organization and use the four "R's" to determine where improvements can be made. Companies are often unaware of the advantages sustainability can bring. Searcy (2009) points out that there were few published examples of indicators being used either in Board-level and strategic decision-making, or in managing supply chains or even business units. The world would benefit if more corporations began implementing sustainability processes.

Resources are used primarily by the firm's operations segment. This suggests that there are many opportunities to use human, financial, and material resources in a sustainable manner (Kayas, McLean, Hines, & Wright, 2008; Kilbourne, 1995; Kroes & Ghosh, 2010; Laroche, Bergeron, & Barbaro-Forleo, 2001). Reducing resources is the most common way companies implement the four "R's". When a firm reduces the amount of resources used, costs will also be lowered. Low costs and resource use help increase the company's profit margins while also incorporating a sustainable approach. There are many different ways that a company can reduce their resource consumption. One common approach is to lower energy and water costs. Another example is reducing the amounts of materials used in a process. Advancing technology allows firms to become more efficient in their materials use.

DOI: 10.4018/978-1-7998-3473-1.ch164

BACKGROUND

Waste Management

Waste is another aspect of sustainability that every company must deal with. There are only 3 things that can be done with waste: burn it, bury it, or reuse it (Hooley, et al. 1998; Jain & Kaur, 2006). Burning waste is not a sustainable practice because it pollutes the atmosphere and increases greenhouse gasses. Burying creates even more problems; we have a limited amount of space that will eventually run out and it also pollutes ecosystems and can have dangerous consequences. Therefore, it is essential that management attempt to design products and services that utilize the cradle to cradle approach. In this process design, we can follow the product from creation to destruction while having no effect on the environment. There are numerous ways that a firm can recycle whether plastic; glass, or metals, and there are always opportunities for a firm to become more sustainable in the recycling arena.

Laws and regulations affecting transportation, waste, and noise are proliferating and can be as much of a challenge as reducing resource use (Kroes & Ghosh, 2010; Laroche, et al., 2001). Regulations may impact a company negatively but they are necessary in a world with finite resources. Governmental agencies are aware that we will not be able to take from the environment indefinitely and are attempting to correct the imbalance. Companies can face fines or taxes for not complying with regulations; therefore, it is in the best interest of the company as well as the environment for firms to attempt to curb pollution as much as possible. This is often referred to as a carbon footprint reduction and represents the firm's impact on the environment.

Another evaluation criterion of sustainability is the firm's reputation. Many companies today are realizing that sustainability can be an advantageous marketing technique. Consumers are becoming more aware of sustainability practices and will do business with companies that reflect these values (Granzin & Olsen, 1991; Haanpää, 2007; Hooley, Saunders, & Pierry, 1998; Iyer & Banerjee, 1993). Although firms are not required to commit to sustainable values, they often gain market share because they embrace the techniques. A comment made in a recent Harvard Business Review article stated, "Impressive as the cost efficiencies are, more intriguing is the growth that companies in emerging markets have gained by extending their sustainability efforts to the operation of their customers. Companies are building unique business models by boosting customers buying power and, in the process, creating interdependencies that are difficult for competition to copy" (Haanaes et al., 2013). Seeing that sustainability is unlikely to disappear, firms would be suited to use this marketing technique to their advantage.

Purpose of Study

This paper will use the case study approach to evaluate two different firms and the sustainability of their operations. The first company is the University of Pittsburgh Medical Center (UPMC), which is a global nonprofit health enterprise. They are considered one of the leading healthcare providers in the U.S. and one of the largest employers in the Pittsburgh region. The second company is Seneca Resources Corporation (SRC), which is a subsidiary of National Fuel Corporation. Seneca Resources handles the prospecting for, development of, and purchase of natural gas and oil reserves. Their primary focus is on the Marcellus Shale in Pennsylvania. The paper will analyze these companies in terms of general characteristics, operations sustainability and compare these two different companies.

CASE STUDIES

Company Profile: University of Pittsburgh Medical Center (UPMC)

UMPC is comprised of 4 major divisions: Hospital and Community Services, Physician Services, Insurance Services, and International and Commercial Services. UPMC's system wide revenue reached $10.19B for FY 2012, making it the largest non-profit healthcare system in the United States in terms of gross revenue (UPMC, 2012). It is also Pennsylvania's largest employer with over 58,000 employees (UPMC, 2012). UPMC has consistently gained national recognition for providing excellent patient care and was ranked 10 on U.S. News and World Report's 2012-2013 Honor Roll (Romoff, 2012). Shortly after establishing its Insurance Services division, UPMC launched the International and Commercial Services division. The goal of this division is to expand UPMC's reach and influence to different markets, both nationally and internationally. Hospitals specializing in transplants and cancer treatments have since been established in foreign nations such as Italy and Ireland. The division also seeks to share ideas and processes through consulting services and various international partnerships.

No single factor, however, will present a greater challenge than the recently passed Patient Protection and Affordable Care Act (PPACA). In summary, the act aims to increase health insurance coverage for all citizens while reducing the cost and increasing the quality of healthcare. While this act will eventually benefit individuals, it will put tremendous pressure on healthcare providers and hospitals to tighten operations and become leaner and more efficient than ever before. The provision of the act that could possibly have the greatest effect on operations deals with Medicare reimbursements to hospitals and healthcare providers. Currently, care providers are reimbursed by Medicare on a fee-for-service basis. This means that each medical service is billed and reimbursed separately. Under PPACA effective in 2014, Medicare will only be disbursing "bundled payments" in which one lump sum will be paid to cover all aspects and stages of treatment. For a hip replacement under the current system, for example, Medicare makes separate disbursements for aspect of treatment (e.g., surgery, surgeon fee, post-op care, rehab, etc.) based on what is billed by each department. Under the new system, however, Medicare will pay one standard lump-sum amount based on the type of episode. According to Cutler and Gosh (2012), an analysis of the costs associated with some of the more expensive episodes showed that bundled payments do have the potential to significantly reduce costs by forcing hospitals to increase efficiency in the provision of care. Another provision of the act that has begun to take effect is a penalty fee that is charged based on certain types of re-admittances. If a care provider reports a certain amount of unnecessary readmittances, they will in turn be docked a percentage (up to 3%) of their Medicare reimbursement.

A major challenge that has recently arisen is the city of Pittsburgh's decision to challenge the tax-exempt status of UPMC as a charitable organization. Mayor Luke Ravenstahl issued the following statement regarding the city's decision to challenge the status: "They haven't been operating as a charity and it's time that this community step up in that regard. The reality of the situation is the taxpayers ... are currently subsidizing UPMC's non-profit status." (Balingit, 2013). A ruling in favor of the city could result in UPMC absorbing over $30M in property taxes that it is currently except from as a charitable organization (Schooley, 2013).

Healthcare Sustainability Considerations

In order for UPMC to remain a major player in the healthcare provider industry and overcome these challenges, the company must rely on the key success factors and core competencies that allowed it to rise to its current position. UPMC's major key success factor is its broad and diverse network of healthcare facilities that range from physician's offices to hospitals to rehabilitation centers. It allows for a patient to be diagnosed, treated, and rehabilitated without having to go outside of UPMC. This contributes greatly to the improvement of operations management in a number of ways. First, it allows UPMC to better manage costs, especially in the era of PPACA. Controlling all aspects and stages of patient treatment allows for UPMC to control entire processes instead of individual stages as other hospitals might do. Quality of treatment is better maintained when UPMC is able to monitor a patient's progress throughout various stages of treatment. According to Donald Riefner, Vice President of Finance and Chief Revenue Officer, the number one detriment to quality is the handoff, which is when patients are transferred from one care division to another (Riefner, personal communication, 2013). By integrating and monitoring a diverse network of healthcare divisions, UPMC is better able to monitor patient handoff and a patient's overall experience at facilities. According to Mechanic and Tompkins (2012), UPMC will have additional opportunities to fine-tune operations as the bundled-payment initiative provides an opportunity for hospitals to gain experience with coordinating care across a continuum of services for discrete clinical conditions.

Sustaining Operations for the Future at UPMC

The healthcare that UPMC offers is award winning, recently receiving an excellence accreditation from the National Committee for Quality Assurance (UPMC Health Plan, 2013). Over the past few years UPMC has been working to take their excellence a step further beyond the area of healthcare and into the realm of operational sustainability coinciding with environmental concerns. UPMC recognizes that they not only have a responsibility to provide great healthcare, but also to be more socially accountable, which will not only positively affect their patients but also the western Pennsylvania region. According to Laura Kinney, the healthcare industry spends $8.3 billion on energy each year as well as being the largest water user in communities and producing two tons of waste per year (Kinney, L., 2010). Not only will social responsibility by UPMC improve the quality of life for the surrounding communities, but can significantly lower the costs that the company incurs. To show their commitment to green sustainability, UPMC has incorporated environmental sustainability in all aspects of the company. Sustainability measures in the areas of regulations, resources, recycling, and reputation are necessary for UPMC to continue its success and meet patient demands.

UPMC is continually working towards improved management and reduction in the use of resources as well as encouragement of recycling throughout the company. Their goal is to promote sustainability throughout their company, on all levels. A partnership with Duquesne Light has allowed UPMC to more actively handle its use of power and reduce it. Duquesne Light has established software within UPMC that puts computers into "sleep" mode at a suitable intermission of non-use. This small change alone has resulted in computer power usage being reduced by fifty percent ("A Network for Sustainable Business," 2013). UPMC also reduced its use of paper and the resulting paper waste by promoting paperless meetings, making medical records available electronically, switching to direct deposit for employee pay, and appropriately recycling paper that is used. As a result of these changes in paper usage, more than one million pounds of paper is recycled on an annual basis. UPMC also incorporates recycling and resource management into hospital services by not only changing to biodegradable products for use in food services, but they also use locally grown produce in healthy meals serviced throughout the hospital. UPMC purchases produce from local vendors, promoting local sustainability and community, as well as growing their own produce and herbs in gardens at Magee-Women's Hospital.

UPMC demonstrated their commitment to recycling and resource reduction when building the new Children's Hospital of Pittsburgh. UPMC used recycled building materials as well as local materials; a water reduction and air filtration system was put in place, green roofing and shading systems were installed to lower costs of cooling the hospital, among many other areas of environmental concern being addressed. This successful commitment to efficiency resulted in Children's Hospital of Pittsburgh of UPMC receiving Leadership in Energy and Environmental Design (LEED) certification. Renovations of the UPMC offices located in the U.S. Steel Tower also resulted in LEED certification. Green renovations in the U.S. Steel Tower consisted of low-flow water systems, rapidly renewable finishes, and low-emitting furniture, carpeting, and paint ("U.S. Steel Tower," 2012). UPMC is also in the process of expanding its presence in the western Pennsylvania region by building a campus in Monroeville, PA as well as expanding the existing campus in McCandless, PA. It can certainly be expected that UPMC will continue its success in green sustainability with these expansions and strives to earn additional LEED certifications.

The healthcare industry uses a significant amount of water, energy, and resources, resulting in considerable amounts of waste and pollution. There are a variety of agencies, both on the state and federal level, which are responsible for the regulation of functions in various healthcare facilities. The U.S. Environmental Protection Agency (EPA) focuses on protecting our planet, and primarily needs to regulate the healthcare industry due to the hazardous chemicals and drugs used. The Clean Water Act (CWA), Clean Air Act (CAA), and Resource Conservation and Recovery Act (RCRA) are all in place in an attempt to curtail contamination and make sure waste is properly disposed of within healthcare facilities. The Centers for Disease Control and Prevention (CDC) also has a noteworthy authority on healthcare facilities by focusing on disease control as well as cleanliness and sterilization. If CDC recommendations are followed, then the general public can be protected from outbreaks of infection as well as medical waste disposed of improperly. UPMC has in a way gone a step further and begun regulating itself through the creation of policy and programs focused on social and environmental responsibility. UPMC has focused on promoting environmentally preferred purchases within its supply chain management purchasing policy. As a part of this policy, contracts must include an option for green products or services, promotion conducting business with suppliers that are concerned with green sustainability, and working with the UPMC appointed team to identify new environmentally friend services and products as well as industry standards that can impact the environment (Sustainability, 2013). UPMC is also working directly with the U.S. Department of Energy to focus on creating a national healthcare industry program that will focus on cutting costs, minimizing pollution, and lowering energy use (Environmental Initiatives, 2013).

UPMC has successfully maintained a reputation of superior medical services and quality patient care. UPMC has succeeded at taking their positive standing a step further by improving their value of patient care through environmental and social responsibility. In 2007, UPMC banned smoking in all of their facilities, which is an effort made with the goal of improving quality of life for patients and reducing pollution. UPMC has also been a strong supporter of education for patients, staff, and the community. Free smoking-cessation classes offered for staff and patient classes such as childbirth for new mothers includes education on environmental-related health concerns as well as lectures on environmental-related topics being offered for the local community to attend (Environmental Initiatives, 2013). The positive results of UPMC taking the time to educate those within the facility and the local community is two-fold. Not only is UPMC helping to break the cycle of misinformation and illnesses that can easily be avoided, but according to EcoHealth there is significant evidence that human related environmental changes, such as urbanization, has resulted in a considerable amount of health challenges facing the world today (Patrick, R., Capetola, T., Townsend, M., & Hanna, L., 2011). Hopefully by UPMC educating the community on the impact of their carbon footprint and how to reduce it, the impact on our planet can be minimized. UPMC has also shown their concern for quality of life by making the majority of facilities mercury, DEHP, and PVC free, as these substances can cause a variety of illnesses. UPMC has also built a positive reputation by looking beyond the region where it is located and towards the international stage. In an effort to reduce waste and recycle, UPMC has partnered with Global Links to provide surplus medical supplies, previously meant for the landfills, to developing countries in need of these medical supplies (Recycling to Save Lives, 2008). The sustainability efforts made by UPMC have led to a leaner, more environmentally friendly, and higher quality operation.

Company Profile: Seneca Resources Corporation (SRC)

SRC is a subsidiary of National Fuel Gas Company, and is in the business of exploring, developing, and purchasing natural gas and oil reserves in California, in the Appalachian region of the U.S. and in Kansas. SRC (and its predecessor affiliates) has been in this business for over 100 years, and can be broken down into a West Division and an East Division. The West Division was established through the acquisition of several properties across the west coast of the U.S. West coast operations are focused on the development of current properties and future acquisitions of new properties that will have low to moderate risk. The East Division includes over 3,000 shallow wells and is known for its stable, long life natural gas reserves. This division is also known for its Marcellus Shale production which, in recent years, has become one of the most fruitful natural gas fields in the world. With control over 745,000 acres of Marcellus drillable land, this division offers a significant future cash flow opportunity for the company.

SRC has announced significant Marcellus shale well results over the past several months. In January 2013, they completed 15 new wells in Lycoming County, PA, with five of the wells representing the highest peak production rates of any wells previously or currently operated by Seneca. They expect to have 16 more wells completed in fiscal year 2013, and 25 more wells completed in fiscal year 2014. David F. Smith, CEO of Natural Fuel Gas Company, stated that "The success we are achieving in Lycoming County validates the prolific nature of the Marcellus in this area" (National Fuel Announces, 2013). SRC 2013 first quarter production of crude oil and natural gas increased by 34% over the prior year's first quarter. When considering production in only the Appalachian region (primarily Marcellus shale wells), production increased by 48% (National Fuel Reports, 2013).

SRC would not be able to maintain profitable operations without the presence of key success factors and core competencies in the natural gas field. Key success factors of SRC include sufficiency of financial resources, technological capabilities, and capacity of reserve. The oil and gas industry is an expensive one; profitability cannot be achieved without the financial means to purchase the expensive drilling equipment and the vast amount of land that is necessary for drilling. The company must possess highly skilled engineers who have the appropriate knowledge and the proper technology required to complete the job. Additionally, the company must have reserves that extend far enough into future years to ensure that the wells will not dry up before they have had the chance to develop new ones. All of these things are key success factors that SRC does well, although they are not enough on their own to ensure a competitive advantage in the industry.

To remain competitive, SRC must also have a core competency on which to focus. The concept of a core competency explores how competitive advantage is related to the unique resources of a firm that provide for a value added process (Hafeez, 2007). SRC remains competitive by having a core competency of innovation. They are able to quickly adapt new processes and ideas into profitable solutions for long term problems. For example, SRC was the first company in the state to successfully convert its drilling rigs to use natural gas (Boyer, 2012). The company wanted to set an example that natural gas is a safe, reliable, and efficient energy source in this country, and what better example is there than to use natural gas itself to power the drilling rigs that they use every day. Studies show that using natural gas reduces the emission of carbon dioxide and other harmful pollutants, thus allowing for a safer and cleaner environment for the future. Innovative ideas such as this one set SRC apart from their competition, and will allow them to remain profitable for many years to come.

The Marcellus Shale boom in the Appalachia region has provided great opportunities to the SRC. In recent years, SRC has spent the capital to position itself as a major player in the Marcellus Shale natural gas boom, and the demand for natural gas is expected to continue to increase. According to William Liss (2012), from the Gas Technology Institute, the United States is on a path toward the elimination of gas imports and the EIA has projected that the anticipated U.S. demand for natural gas in year 2020 will amount to 26 Tcf with U.S. production slightly below the demand. This implies that the amount of opportunity for SRC is high, but with this opportunity comes the need to increase awareness of how present actions will impact the future.

SRC: Sustaining Operations to Keep Pace with Demand

With this optimistic projection in demand for natural gas comes a great responsibility for SRC as the company has been faced with many business decisions concerning the sustainability of their operations for years to come. Sustainability provides incentive for SRC to perform well and protect the environment as the company develops and refines the production process of natural gas. Without implementing sustainability into a firm's operations management strategy, a firm risks misusing precious resources (Dey, 2011). SRC must also ensure that they are using their resources wisely, and must continuously seek out acquisition opportunities for new drilling sites to replenish resources as they are used. SRC employs "best practice" techniques in all of its operations, including regulatory requirements. They strive to conduct their business in a way that protects the environment and ensures safety. SRC has implemented policies and measures focused on abiding by industry regulations, effectively managing and procuring resources, promoting recycling, and building reputation.

A large part of sustainability for a company in the oil and gas industry involves the need to remain compliant with the various regulations of the industry. The oil and gas industry is a highly regulated primarily by the U.S. Environmental Protection Agency (EPA) with the use of the several statutes. These statues include the Resource Conservation and Recovery act (RCRA), the Clean Air Act (CAA), the Safe Drinking Water Act (SDWA) and the Clean Water Act (CWA), and the Toxic Substances Control Act (TSCA) (Ternes, 2012). These acts regulate the production and transportation of natural gas produced in Appalachia and provides increasing pressure on SRC to reduce by-products that yield greenhouse gasses and pollute the air and water. SRC has not only risen to the regulatory challenges of the natural gas industry, but also they have excelled in surpassing them. Recently, SRC converted their drilling rigs from diesel use to liquefied natural gas use (Boyer, 2012). The cost of the conversion is a huge capital expenditure, but it yields a very friendly impact to the environment. In fact, Rob Boulware, Public Relations Manager for SRC noted that the Liquefied Natural Gas (LNG) engine is the first drill rig engine in the country to be operated on LNG and is even certified by the EPA. The new engine is cleaner for the environment and even quieter than the traditional diesel engines (Boyer, 2012). Not only has SRC provided a more environmentally friendly engine, but SRC also anticipates a reduction in fuel costs to power the rigs which can result in 60% lower fuel costs and reduce overall combustion emissions up to 25% (Diesel & Gas Turbine Worldwide, 2012). The benefit of the LNG engine has also allowed SRC to start creating a new vehicle fleet to run off LNG engines, which can reduce fuel costs by more than 25%. Diesel to LNG conversions can be seen as a win-win for the SRC as there is a significant friendly emission impact while saving on fuel costs. The change to LNG engines clearly supports the conservation of the environment.

SRC realizes that sustainability cannot be achieved through meeting regulatory requirements alone. Recently, SRC has had two major projects that promote recycling and waste reduction of resources. First, SRC has developed a water project that withdrawals water from a creek when water levels are high to support their hydraulic fracturing operations. SRC's water project was a result of a recent Pennsylvania Department of Conservation and Natural Resources (DCNR) lease that presented a unique challenge as there were poor road conditions to the leased land. Hydraulic fracturing operations for SRC alone require over 70,000 truck trips in a highly populated area with a small road system that is also used by other operators with land rights in the area (Jacobs, 2012). These conditions lead to congestion, layout issues, and increased pollution due to the high number trucks. In order to alleviate these problems, SRC plans on making a pipeline available to other operators to help cover capital costs and to reduce the number of water trucks in the region which could have totaled more than 200,000 truckloads including the other operators (Jacobs, 2012). The new water pipeline would withdrawal water from the Johnson creek in Lycoming County under strict conditions which focused on when water can be withdrawn and how the water needs to be continuously monitored for contamination (Jacobs, 2012). In addition to the elimination of water truck traffic, SRC also picked a creek that has been contaminated by an abandoned coal mine and the creek currently has no life. Doug Keppler, a VP and Biologist of SRC, was the individual who presented the idea to SRC officials and determined that there are no ill effects produced from using the contaminated water (Phillips, 2013). Taking the water from the contaminated creek helps minimize the amount of pollution that flows into the Tioga River. The creation of a water pipeline was a tremendous capital expenditure to SRC; however, it has greatly improved environmental conditions by reducing truck traffic and emissions while using contaminated water withdrawn from the Johnson Creek.

The second project geared toward recycling and waste reduction is a mission to recycle and to treat all of their fracturing fluid used in operations so that it can be reused on future hydraulic fracturing operations. Hydraulic fracturing has many environmental concerns, and there have been great strides in the industry toward recycling water that is flowed-back to the surface after the hydraulic fracturing process. This "flowback" fluid poses great challenges for companies, and technology has been introduced that allows companies to recycle this byproduct. According to David Grottenthaler (2011), general manager of Kroff Well Services, Inc., the challenge to Marcellus Shale companies is that a recycling plan needs adopted to manage water so the shale will be a sustainable resource in the future. The challenge for recycling "flowback" water is that the solids in the water need removed before the water can be treated and reused in future hydraulic fracturing jobs. For "flowback" fluid to be reusable, the recycling process must involve removing iron deposition, suspended solids and microorganisms while addressing pH levels so that the right water attributes are obtained to achieve adequate friction reduction (Grottenthaler, 2011). According to National Fuel (2013), the parent company of SRC, SRC has a goal to recycle 100% of all hydraulic fracturing fluid (frac fluid) to use in other well operations. Frac fluid is the hazardous chemical that poses a risk to the environment and needs to be separated from the water and sand as part of the recycling process. The end result of this recycling process is a zero discharge of its operations, which means reuse of the "flowback" fluid while recycling the water, sand, and hydraulic fracturing fluid for use in other well operations (National Fuel, 2013).

SRC has been at the forefront of innovation in operations sustainability and has created a reputation that focuses on the sustainability of the shale boom. As mentioned earlier, SRC has done a variety of things to promote a clean environment that can potentially save the company money in the long run through large, up-front capital investments. SRC believes that a good reputation can lead to future business ventures, especially since the PA DCNR has historically made available large quantities of land for gas exploration and production. So far, SRC has leased four major tracts of land from the DCNR and has established a strong working relationship with the state agency. Currently, SRC and the DCNR are looking into contracts with other gas operators that would utilize the SRC built roads to minimize the impact in the state forests. In 2012, DCNR forest program specialist Dix (2019) identified a problem on state access roads, and SRC promptly obtained emergency permits from the DEP for streambank stabilization. The road was eroding and all work was done at SRC's expense. Cooperation between SRC, the DEP, the DCNR, and the Pennsylvania Fish and Boat Commission allowed for quick completion of the project before the collapse of the road into the parallel stream. An appealing retaining wall was built and Rich Glinksi, District Forester of Loyasock State Forest, stated that "If the DCNR were to have done the repair in the future, it would have taken funding away from other projects such as bridges and facilities" (Dix, 2019, p. 1). The response and sections of SRC in this case highlights their focus on reputation, commitment to environmental sustainability, and desire to build relationships with organizations who promote similar goals. Establishing relationships of this type can lead to cooperation and collaboration in future sustainability efforts.

In a separate matter, SRC also fully discloses the chemicals used in their hydraulic fracturing process voluntarily to "FracFocus," which is a nationally recognized non-profit organization that provides public transparency in the oil and gas industry by disclosing what ingredients are used during hydraulic fracturing. The website www.fracfocus.org allows anyone to search for the ingredients used in each well that has been registered with the organization. SRC believes that a strong reputation is a key to future operations and understands that the oil and gas industry is a free enterprise system that operates on a voluntary basis. If SRC is unable to obtain leases on land for drilling, then SRC will not be able to continue to utilize and share their sustainable operations techniques throughout the remainder of the Marcellus Shale boom.

Comparison of Sustainability Techniques

The policies, processes, and techniques implemented by UPMC and SRC presented in this research, provide evidence that shows how operations sustainability presents various incentives to firms, and also how it benefits people, the community, and the environment. Even though these companies operate in two vastly different industries, they share the feeling of responsibility to change in order to create a better future. "SRC employs best practices in all aspects of its operations, and continues to revise those practices in keeping with technological advances, regulatory requirements and the lessons learned through daily operations" ("Best Practices", 2013). They both exhibit this devotion and understanding of being sustainable in numerous ways. Both companies leveraged their core competencies into their sustainability practices: UPMC by running many unmatched specialty care facilities as compared to their competitors and SRC by exhibiting its core competency of being innovative. More specifically, UPMC and SRC both focus on utilizing resources and emphasize the importance of recycling. These operational techniques allow the companies to be recognized as reputable businesses in the Pittsburgh region, and both not only satisfied the regulatory requirements of their respective industries, but also set internal standards that exceeded those set by external agencies.

Both companies exhibited their dedication to being a sustainable business by responsibly using resources. UPMC uses locally grown produce as well as their own grown produce and herbs in meals served at the hospitals. They exhibited the insight of knowing how green is better than using biodegradable products in foods. They also practiced sustainability by making their facilities free of Mercury, DEHP and PVC, since they knew the harm these products can cause to the environment. Similarly, SRC strived to reduce the amount of truck traffic from water trucks travelling in and out of the fracking sites. To accomplish this, the company built a pipeline that SRC and other Operators can use to transport water to the drilling locations which would drastically reduce congestion. Not only does this initiative result in fewer truck trips that reduced diesel gas use and costs, but also allows SRC plans to create a new revenue stream that will offset their costs for establishing the new water pipe.

The importance of recycling by re-using waste products is a technique used by SRC and UPMC. SRC used the cradle-to-cradle practice by recycling 100% of all hydraulic fracturing fluid to use in other wells, which leads to extra cost saving. The need to recycle resources was not only formed based on the extra monetary incentives for SRC, but also based on creating a win-win situation through their reuse of the contaminated coal waste water, indirectly leading to replenishing the natural resources that had been improperly disposed of in the past. UPMC transformed many waste products into the UPMC Children's Hospital during construction of the facility. This not only promotes a great use of supposed waste, but also it highlights the importance of realizing that reuse opportunities are typically possible no matter the industry. Effective management of resources and recycling also leads to improvement in reputation. UPMC and SRC did not simply satisfy their social obligations, but instead went over and above them, which contributes to the positive image these firms try to maintain. "The strategic issues of environmental and socio-economic stewardship have already and will continue to be the focus of economic activities and innovations worldwide" (Lee, Pati, & Roh, 2011, p. 74). UPMC and SRC both illustrate this. Another similarity between both firms was the impact that laws, acts, and regulations played on each firm's willingness and quickness to adapt sustainable practices. This illustrates the significant role that the government plays in setting sustainability standards and how companies are adopting standards that exceed government requirements. What may have once been an inconvenience is now a routine function in the daily activities of both UPMC and SRC. Both external and internal regulations indirectly helped UPMC and SRC to control costs and improve performance. UPMC has gone beyond the environmental and health regulations set forth by the EPA and CRC and adopted practices to create and maintain a green supply chain. SRC has satisfied the requirements of the oil and natural gas industry through disclosure to third party firms such as "FracFocus," but also raised the industry standard through their water recycling and diesel to LNG conversion projects.

CONCLUSION

Sustainability Case Studies

The research conducted on the sustainability practices of UPMC and SRC has highlighted some major techniques and practices that other firms can adapt to ensure the sustainability of their own operations. Both companies in this study illustrated how reuse of resources can lower costs, improve performance, and help the environment. For these reasons alone, companies would surely benefit by investigating how resources in their particular industry could be used for other purposes internally and also externally. This study indicated that environmental stability and improvement of social welfare cannot be achieved by just abiding by predetermined standards and existing regulations. Firms must strive to set their own standards that surpass what exists and collaborate with the governing bodies of their industries to determine and improve best practices. In a society with growing concern over global warming, recycling has proved to be as important as ever. In some cases, however, significant capital investment is required in order to implement effective recycling practices such as with SRC's innovative solutions and UPMC's building construction projects. Lastly, this study has shown that there is a clear linkage between social responsibilities and reputation. Creating and maintaining a positive image is directly related to the amount of time and effort companies place on giving back to society and creating a safer and healthier world for the future.

FUTURE RESEARCH DIRECTIONS

Ultimately, the best actions to take in order to increase operational sustainability are those that fall within the core competencies of a firm and make the firm successful. UPMC is a healthcare provider, and the majority of examples provided in this study revolve around UPMC creating a healthier and safer environment for patients and safer work place for their employees. SRC has been characterized as an innovative firm. Throughout this study, we have shown that SRC's success in sustainability has come from their ability to implement new products, technologies, and processes in the natural gas industry. Both firms also face their share of challenges, which makes achieving sustainability difficult. UPMC has had to deal with new Medicare policies forcing them to adopt leaner operations, new competition within the Pittsburgh area, and the threat of losing tax-exempt status. SRC has also faced fierce competition during the Marcellus shale boom in Pennsylvania as well as the continuous battle to maintain a positive reputation. These challenges have not stopped either firm from taking initiative to protect the environment and fulfill their social responsibilities to create a more sustainable business and future for others. In fact, the sustainability measures discussed in this study have aided both firms in facing and in some cases overcoming the difficulties they face. This should provide a sense of hope and motivation for all firms to promote sustainability from within, especially by finding ways to use resources more effectively, recycling to protect the environment, satisfying and exceeding industry regulations, and improving the way they are perceived by their customers and the world.

REFERENCES

Balingit, M. (2013). *Ravenstahl pledges challenge to UPMC's tax-exempt status*. Retrieved from http://www.post-gazette.com/stories/local/region/ravenstahl-pledges-challenge-to-upmcs-tax-exempt-status-680094/

Batra, M. M. (2012). The Sustainability Challenge and its Business Solution. *Competition Forum, 10*(3), 182-190.

Boyer, B. (2012). *Seneca Resources converts drilling rigs to use natural gas*. Retrieved from http://www.wjactv.com/news/news/seneca-resources-converts-drilling-rigs-use-natura/nTGHL/

Cutler, D., & Ghosh, K. (2012). The potential for cost savings through bundled episode payments. *The New England Journal of Medicine, 366*(12), 1075–1077. doi:10.1056/NEJMp1113361 PMID:22435368

Dey, A., LaGuardia, P., & Srinivasan, M. (2011). Building sustainability in logistics operations: A research agenda. *Management Research Review, 34*(11), 1237–1259. doi:10.1108/01409171111178774

Dix, E. (2019). *Pennsylvania Department of Conservation and Natural Resources – Energy development contributes to maintaining state forest access.* Retrieved from http://www.apps.dcnr.state.pa.us/news/resource/res2012/12-0912-loyalsocksf.aspx

Granzin, K., & Olsen, J. (1991). Characterising participants in activities protecting the environment: A focus on donating, recycling and conservation behaviours. *Journal of Public Policy & Marketing, 10*(1), 1–27.

Grottenthaler, D. (2011). Recycling water for hydraulic fracturing. *Mechanical Engineering (New York, N.Y.), 133*(12), 21–22, 24.

Haanaes, K., Michael, D., Jurgens, J., & Rangan, S. (2013). Making sustainability profitable. *Harvard Business Review, 91*(3), 110–115.

Haanpää, L. (2007). Consumers' green commitment: Indication of a postmodern lifestyle? *International Journal of Consumer Studies, 31*(5), 478–486. doi:10.1111/j.1470-6431.2007.00598.x

Hafeez, K., & Essmail, E. A. (2007). Evaluating organization core competences and associated personal competencies using analytical hierarchy process. *Management Research News, 30*(8), 530–547. doi:10.1108/01409170710773689

Hooley, G., Saunders, V., & Pierry, N. (1998). *Marketing Strategy and Competitive Positioning* (2nd ed.). Prentice Hall Inc.

Iyer, E., & Banerjee, B. (1993). Anatomy of green advertising. *Advances in Consumer Research. Association for Consumer Research (U. S.), 20*, 494–501.

Jacobs, N. (2012). *Seneca Resources gets innovative to reduce impacts.* Retrieved from http://eidmarcellus.org/marcellus-shale/seneca-resources-gets-innovative-to-reduce-impacts/9745/

Jain, S., & Kaur, G. (2006). Role of socio-demographics in segmenting and profiling green consumers: An exploratory study of consumers in India. *Journal of International Consumer Marketing, 18*(3), 107–117. doi:10.1300/J046v18n03_06

Kayas, O. G., McLean, R., Hines, T., & Wright, G. H. (2008). The panoptic gaze: Analysing the interaction between enterprise resource planning technology and organisational culture. *International Journal of Information Management, 28*(6), 446–553. doi:10.1016/j.ijinfomgt.2008.08.005

Kilbourne, W. (1995). Green advertisement: Salvation or oxymoron? *Journal of Advertisement, 24*(2), 7–19. doi:10.1080/00913367.1995.10673472

Kinney, L. M. (2010). Environmental sustainability in healthcare. *Journal for Quality and Participation, 33*(2), 23–26.

Kroes, J. R., & Ghosh, S. (2010). Outsourcing congruence with competitive priorities: Impact on supply chain and firm performance. *Journal of Operations Management, 28*(2), 124–143. doi:10.1016/j.jom.2009.09.004

Laroche, M., Bergeron, J., & Barbaro-Forleo, G. (2001). Targeting consumers who are willing to pay more for environmentally friendly products. *Journal of Consumer Marketing, 18*(6), 503–520. doi:10.1108/EUM0000000006155

Lee, J., Pati, N., & Roh, J. J. (2011). *Relationship between Corporate Sustainability Performance and Tangible Business Performance: Evidence from Oil and Gas Industry*. Academic Press.

Liss, W. (2012). Demand outlook: A golden age of natural gas. *Chemical Engineering Progress*, *108*(1), 35–40.

McDonagh, P., & Clark, A. (1995). Corporate communications about sustainability: Turning clever companies into enlightened companies. *Greener Management International*, *11*(1), 49–62.

Mechanic, R., & Tompkins, C. (2012). Lessons learned preparing for Medicare bundled payments. *The New England Journal of Medicine*, *367*(20), 1873–1875. doi:10.1056/NEJMp1210823 PMID:23150955

Menon, A., Menon, A., Chowdhury, J., & Jankovich, J. (1999). Evolving paradigm for environmental sensitivity in marketing programs: A synthesis of theory and practice. *Journal of Marketing Theory and Practice*, *7*(1), 1–15. doi:10.1080/10696679.1999.11501825

Moisander, J. (2007). Motivational complexity of green consumerism. *International Journal of Consumer Studies*, *31*(4), 404–409. doi:10.1111/j.1470-6431.2007.00586.x

National Fuel Announces Significant Marcellus Shale Well Results. (2013). Retrieved April 26, 2013, from http://natfuel.com/news/1-22-13%20Tract%20100%20Pad%20M%20Results%20-%20WEB1222013-152528.pdf

National Fuel Reports First Quarter Earnings. (2013). Retrieved from http://natfuel.com/news/02-07-13%201st%20Quarter%20Earnings%20-%20FINAL%20-%20WEB272013-17535.pdf

National Fuel – The Marcellus Shale. (2019). Retrieved from http://natfuel.com/seneca/marcellus_shale.aspx

Patrick, R., Capetola, T., Townsend, M., & Hanna, L. (2011). Incorporating sustainability into community-based healthcare practice. *EcoHealth*, *8*(3), 277–289. doi:10.100710393-011-0711-0 PMID:22045434

Phillips, S. (2013). Using abandoned mine drainage to frack. *State Impact*. Retrieved from http://stateimpact.npr.org/pennsylvania/2013/03/12/using-abandoned-mine-drainage-to-frack/

Powering LNG-fueled drilling rigs. (2012). *Diesel and Gas Turbine Worldwide*. Retrieved from http://www.dieselgasturbine.com/November-2012/Powering-LNG-Fueled-Drilling-Rigs/#.UX8Kj8qCWSo

Recycling to save lives. (2008). *UPMC*. Retrieved from http://extra.upmc.com/103108/3-global-links.htm

Romoff, J. A. (2013). *Restructuring Healthcare: Daunting Challenges are Upon Us* [PowerPoint slides]. PowerPoint supplementation for presentation for advisory board CCM event on April 10, 2013.

Schooley, T. (2013). City to challenge UPMC's tax-exempt status. *Pittsburgh Business Times*. Retrieved from http://www.bizjournals.com/pittsburgh/news/2013/03/20/city-to-challenge-umpcs-tax-exempt.html?page=2

Searcy, C. (2009). *The Role of Sustainable Development Indicators in Corporate Decision-making*. IISD, Winnipeg, Manitoba, Canada. Retrieved from http://www.iisd.org/pdf/2009/role_of_sustainability_indicators.pdf

Shale Gas Boom. (2013). Retrieved from http://planningpa.org/wp-content/uploads/D3_Shale-Gas-Industrys-Role-in-Sustainable-Community-Development.pdf

Simintiras, A., Schlegelmilch, B., & Diamantopoulos, A. (1994). Greening the marketing mix: A review of the literature and an agenda for future research. In M. Baker (Ed.), *Perspectives on Marketing Management, 4* (pp. 1–25). John Wiley and Sons.

Straughan, R., & Roberts, J. (1999). Environmental segmentation alternatives: A look at green consumer behaviour in the new millennium. *Journal of Consumer Marketing, 16*(6), 558–575. doi:10.1108/07363769910297506

Sustainability. (2019). *UPMC: Life Changing Medicine*. Retrieved from http://www.upmc.com/about/partners/supply-chain/pages/sustainability.aspx

Ternes, M. E. (2012). Regulatory programs governing shale gas development. *Chemical Engineering Progress, 108*(2), 36–43.

The Regulatory Environment. (2019). *Sustainability Roadmap for Hospitals*. Retrieved from http://www.sustainabilityroadmap.org/drivers/regulatory.shtml#.UX3VSUq3qZg

Thogersen, J. (2006). Media attention and the market for 'green' consumer products. *Business Strategy and the Environment, 15*(3), 145–153. doi:10.1002/bse.521

UPMC facts & stats. (2013). Retrieved from http://www.upmc.com/about/facts/Pages/default.aspx

U.S. Steel Tower. Property Overview. (2012). *CBRE United States - Commercial Real Estate Services*. Retrieved from http://www.cbre.us/o/pittsburgh/properties/ussteeltower/Pages/overview.aspx

Van Liere, K., & Dunlap, R. (1981). Environmental concern: Does it make difference how it is measured? *Environment and Behavior, 13*(6), 651–676. doi:10.1177/0013916581136001

Vesilind, P., Heine, L., & Hendry, J. (2006). The moral challenge of green technology. *TRAMES. Journal of the Humanities and Social Sciences, 10*(1), 22–31.

Wan, H.-D., & Chen, F. F. (2008). A leanness measure of manufacturing systems for quantifying impacts of lean initiatives. *International Journal of Production Research, 46*(23), 6567–6584. doi:10.1080/00207540802230058

Wenner, D. (2013). Highmark reports strong finances, steady membership, even with UPMC fight. *PennLive*. Retrieved from http://www.pennlive.com/midstate/index.ssf/2013/04/highmark_upmc_health_insurance.html

Young, W., Hwang, K., McDonald, S., & Oates, C. (2010). Sustainable consumption: Green consumer behaviour when purchasing products. *Sustainable Development, 18*(1), 20–31.

Zimmer, M., Stafford, T., & Stafford, M. (1994). Green issues: Dimensions of environmental concern. *Journal of Business Research, 30*(1), 63–74. doi:10.1016/0148-2963(94)90069-8

KEY TERMS AND DEFINITIONS

LEED Certification: Leadership in Energy and Environmental Design is probably the world's most widely used green building rating system. It is noted for an eco-friendly framework for evaluation the energy conservation of most building, community, home projects that is both highly efficient and cost-savings.

Patient Protection and Affordable Care Act (PPACA): The PPACA is part of a healthcare reform or Obamacare and was a law enacted on March 23, 2010. It provided new rules and guidelines on healthcare coverage and administration in the U.S.

Sustainable Operations: Due to changes in the market conditions, operations and production management continue to innovate to remain competitive, management must adapt their SC strategies well. Currently, consumers, both internal and external, are more conscious about the change happening in the environment and what steps corporations are taking to prevent the pollution. International laws and local laws have come into the effect so that every company has to follow those rules and guidelines (hopefully).

RFID Technologies and Warehouse Applications:
Case Studies

14

Alan D. Smith

Robert Morris University, USA

INTRODUCTION

Chapter Overview of RFID Technologies and its Applications

Although radio frequency identification (RFID) technologies have been around for some time, the use of the technology in supply chain management (SCM) and its associated operations is still being explored and yet to be fully implemented/adopted by many companies. Basically, RFID uses electromagnetic fields to help with identifying and tracking objects. The number of ways that the technology can be used is almost endless as many examples can be found in preventing theft, expediting inspections, keeping track of surgical sponges, safeguarding pharmaceuticals, helping farmers with vital crop and social moisture information, to name a few (Hamidi, Farahmand, Sajjadi, & Nygard, 2012; Kumar, Shankar, & Yadav, 2011; Mathirajan, Manoj, & Ramachandran, 2011; More & Babu, 2012). RFID technology used in warehouses for receiving product, picking orders, packaging shipments, and tracking deliveries can save a company time and money and is part of an array of available Automatic identification and data capture technologies (AIDC), including the universally accepted barcodes. For growing companies such as the University of Pittsburgh Medical Center (UPMC) and Boeing, the introduction can help them remain efficient during these times of prosperity and growth.

BACKGROUND

Overview of RFID Technology

RFID is defined any method of identifying unique items using radio waves. This is usually done when a reader (or an interrogator) communicates with a transponder (Smith, 2017a, 2017b, 2017c). This transfer of information happens without the devices making any actual physical contact and is used in items we use every day like car keys, employee identification cards, medical history, highway toll tags, and security access cards. In essence, RFID is a modern and impactful technology that is changing the way a logistics operates. As this research paper has shared in earlier sections, the technology surrounding RFID technology has existed since the earlier 1900's and has more recently been implemented to support the transportation industry due to technology and cost improvements. Formally, according to the RFID journal is "any method of identifying unique items using radio waves such as through a reader which communicates with a transponder and holds digital information in a microchip. There are chipless forms of RFID tags that use material to reflect back a portion of the radio waves beamed at them (Radio

DOI: 10.4018/978-1-7998-3473-1.ch165

Frequency Identification)." RFID has been a way of continuing to evolve in many practices specifically as it relates to SCM. Historically, as this course has demonstrated, SCM productivity evolved from the human based way of tracking and transporting inventory for companies to more automated systems such as bar codes and RFID technology. RFID systems are important components in the Toyota Production System (TPS) in effective manufacturing and SCM.

Probably, the first venture began with bar code technology as a way of tracking and transmitting information. The optical nature of barcode requires labels to be within the proper line-of-sight between label and reader, which is often difficult, if not impractical, to achieve in industrial environments. A barcode reader must have typically clean, clear optics, the label must be clean and free of abrasion, and the reader and label must be properly oriented with respect to each other" ("Advantages of RFID," 2018, p. 1). RFID-enabled technology helps to solve many of the issues and challenges caused by direct line of sight technology by allowing information to be transmitted through a receiving device. Improvements in such technology have allowed tag reading from greater distances and in harsh environments. RFID technology is the next wave, arguably the current and sustainable wave in industrial applications, of being able to efficiently track and transmit information in order to provide greater efficiency improvements to logistics and SCM systems (Zelbst, Green, Sower, & Reyes, 2012).

Low-frequency systems were developed first then products moved up the radio spectrum to high frequency which means there is a greater range and data can be transferred at much higher rates (Roberti, 2005). High-frequency systems are used to track cargo containers, payment systems, and contactless smart cards. In the 1990s, IBM developed ultra-high frequency (UHF) RFID systems which offered even greater ranges and faster data transfers. They originally worked with Wal-Mart in their development and then in warehouses and farming. UHF RFID technology was taken to the next level in 1999 when the Uniform Code Council, EAN International, Procter & Gamble, and Gillette funded the establishment of the Auto-ID Center at MIT. They developed a low-cost RFID tag to put onto all products to track them through the supply chain and then linked this information to the Internet (Roberti, 2005). This was the first time that information contained in an RFID tag was available beyond the tag and reader themselves. The Auto-ID Center received support from over 100 large companies between 1999 and 2003 including the Department of Defense. It then opened up facilities in Australia, the United Kingdom, Switzerland, Japan, and China. Protocols, a numbering system called Electronic Product Code (EPC), and a network were developed and in 2003 the technology was licensed to the Uniform Code Council.

Currently, many companies are trying to develop smaller and smaller tags, some containing just 2 components (Landt, 2005). This means that RFID tags can now be found even in paper-like labels which can be affixed to almost anything. Advancements in RFID technology continues to grow at faster rates and the applications for use continue to grow as well.

Implications for Technology-based Supplier Integrations

A lack of universal application and its fully implementation of RFID-based technologies is very typically that in the absence of proactive management, the companies under consideration would find itself under this situation to not see the vision of implementation of such technologies to suppler integrations (Basu & Nair, 2012; Paksoy & Cavlak, 2011; Pettersson & Segerstedt, 2011; Pradhananga, Hanaoka, & Sattayaprasert, (2011; Von Haartman, 2012). With the current climate with top management in many companies regarding any change is "if it is not broken do not fix it" and "how much is it going to cost us?" no wonder they find themselves in this predicament. It is a wonder they even perceive that there is a problem. Perhaps, one of the first steps is to see if the firm's management really want to have a formal supplier development program or is it something they heard of as a good thing and do not want to be perceived as a traditional, backward company. Some more traditional, backward-looking companies that only wants to a superficial approach to a supplier development program, having a plan for change is difficult. Before proceeding, there needs to be formal recognition of top-management support, a written commitment to such a program, a detailed listing of its objectives and potential benefits, a budget that would allow such a program to be successfully implemented. After all, individual reputation is at risk as well and qualified people would not serve as a consultant in such a project unless there is a clear path to success. If not, such people would be part of the firm's deceptive program of "suppler development wash!"

In defining, what management hopes to gain from a supplier development program and assuming that management is serious about such a venture, there must be a series of metrics that all suppliers agree upon as having a common unifying thread that binds them together (Smith, 2019; Smith, Shock, & Beaves, 2019). An interesting study by Farris II and Hutchison (2002), the authors discuss what a cash-to-cash (C2C) metric in within the supply chain partners may be and how to calculate it. C2C is the average days required to turn a dollar invested in raw material into a dollar collected from a customer. Companies like Dell and Cisco have implemented this model to help their businesses become more cost efficient and profitable; thus rewarding its various suppliers with cash bonus and more orders. However, Farris II and Hutchison state that approximately two-thirds of companies are even aware of this concept. In order to use this metric effectively, a business must understand what comprises the metric. It explains the importance of measuring C2C as it relates to accounting and supply chain, and how it can be strategically leveraged in a supplier development program. As noted by Melnyk, Davis, Spekman, & Sandor, 2000; Trebilcock, 2015, if suppliers are willing to negotiate and meet costs targets, will they be forced to continually lower their costs and potential profit margins. There needs to be some level of both cost and profit sharing programs may be worthwhile. Suppliers must be able to understand the premise of such a proposed supplier development program, learn to trust each other, have informational transparency, and mutually agree on the long-term strategic benefit of such a program (Brito & Botter, 2012; Hamidi, Farahmand, Sajjadi, & Nygard, 2012; Kumar, Shankar, & Yadav, 2011). With such a disparity among supplier partners, building trust would be difficult and the suppliers with the larger share of the buyer's business has no interesting in sharing that business with the other suppliers (Bulcsu, 2011; Carvalho, Cruz-Machado, & Tavares, 2012).

The C2C concept to specific principles of supplier development and how valuable C2C is from a supply chain perspective would be helpfully to implement RFID-based technologies within a supply integration program. An efficient supply chain focuses on achieving the lowest total cost through interactional of all supply chain components instead of silos. The C2C metric is important because it bridges together many supply chain activities. Measuring C2C cycle time helps to determine how well a supply chain is performing and if there is room for improvement. Many companies who use C2C as a standard performance measure outperform their competitors by significant amounts. In such actions, it would to helpful to point out because we often hear and learn about the same types of performance metrics for a supply chain and yet there is no differentiation among supplier performance. Thus, everyone simply meets the minimum standards set by the parent company and there is essentially no competition among suppliers to performance better than their peers. Perhaps, introducing C2C and how it can relate to a supply chain can be useful for future business analysis and decisions to foster competition among suppliers.

Another useful aspect of the work by Farris II and Hutchison (2002) is that it gives specific ways a business can improve its C2C metric. These "leverage points" can be considered for any type of business and are a great starting point for evaluating a C2C metric. The authors state that the three advantage points for managing a C2C metric are to extend average accounts payable, to shorten production cycle to reduce inventory days of supply and to reduce average accounts receivable. These are a great starting point for someone in a firm who has never measured C2C before but wants to start. These things will help measure C2C and are goals a firm should strive for even if it was not measuring C2C because it would help profitability. The article also goes into the importance of collaboration among firms within the supply chain. This is important for many reasons, including cost reduction and efficiency, and can help improve the C2C metric. The authors recognize that C2C is a relatively new concept in the business world. While there is proof that it can help a firm become more profitable, there is still research to be completed. Questions such as what target for C2C is appropriate and if one target is right for different types of business will be helpful to explore and can benefit firms once more research is complete.

In the definitions of mutual benefits of supplier development goals, it would be important to emphasize a very clear description of this process. This may be obtained by applying an industry standard in information technologies and contractual procedures. This not only enhances one firms supply chain, but this makes supply chains in the entire industry much more efficient. This forces supply chain partners to have a collaborative relationship, which as we have seen in other articles we have read, makes supply chains more efficient and less expensive. The overall goal of supplier development is for the ultimate customer to realize the savings of the efficient supply chain.

CASE STUDIES

Overview of UPMC Central Distribution Center

The University of Pittsburgh Medical Center (UPMC) is a US$17-billion-dollar healthcare provider and insurer based in Pittsburgh, PA. UPMC currently operates over 30 hospitals, more than 600 doctors' offices and outpatient centers, has over 4,000 physicians employed, along with a variety of rehabilitation centers, retirement communities, and long-term care facilities. To operate and run all of these locations UPMC needs many supplies delivered JIT and to maintain their operating margins via inventory control principles; hence, they need the supplies in the most efficient means possible. The goal of UPMC's supply chain is simple: establish the most cost effective and efficient means of supporting UPMC facilities and their patients. Part of this goal includes the utilization of a Centralized Distribution Center. Having a centralized warehouse allows supply chain to purchase products at lower prices by eliminating traditional healthcare distributors such as Cardinal Health or Owens & Minor. With one warehouse supporting all hospital locations, savings are also found in consolidating products such as all facilities use the same brand of exam glove which again gives supply chain the ability to leverage contract prices.

The UPMC Central Distribution Center has over 60 employees, is 150,000 square feet and maintains over 4,000 SKUs. The distribution center operates 24 hours a day 5 days a week and picks, packs, and ships over 2.3 million lines per year. It also manages over 250,000 cross-docked non-stock parcels annually. There are 9 delivery vehicles which run over 490,000 miles per year. The distribution center also utilizes Voice Directed Picking technology, which helped them reduce their picking errors by 25%, leaves the pickers hands free for picking and labeling, and is environmentally friendly with the reduction of paper. All of these numbers are for UPMC at its current size but UPMC just bought an additional 18 hospitals from Jamestown, New York to Harrisburg, PA. The addition of these new facilities will mean an increased need to be even more efficient and effective. Part of this would be to explore the option of using RFID technology.

Overview of Boeing Factory in Everett, WA

14

The Boeing Company Factory based in Everett, WA is a highly coordinated logistics and manufacturing operation that helps produce commercial and military aircraft for the worldwide aviation market. The Boeing Company is the "world's largest aerospace company and leading manufacturer of commercial jetliners and defense, space and security systems. A top U.S. exporter, the company supports airlines and U.S. and allied government customers in 150 countries. Boeing products and tailored services include commercial and military aircraft, satellites, weapons, electronic and defense systems, launch systems, advanced information and communication systems, and performance-based logistics and training. Boeing is noted as having the largest manufacturing building in the world, producing the 747, 767, 777, and the 787 airplanes. Their manufacturing product facilities employ thousands in aircraft fabrication and production, product development, aviation safety and security and airplane certifications. This factory covers nearly 100 acres of land under one roof in order to assemble and coordinate the various components required to build aircraft with over 30,000 people supporting the daily construction of this aircraft.

There are numerous logistical and transportation needs to build the aircraft. The 747 and 767, the older and original aircraft of this factory, follow a traditional assembly process that combines components such as wings, elevators, rudders, and other parts at one of four stage of assembly. The parts of this aircraft are assembled in a nearby bay which arrives via rail and truck from various U.S. suppliers from across the world. However, through this assembly process which dates back to the mid-1960s, Boeing has been able to innovate their logistics and assembly practice with modern processes. The 777 and 787 process, mostly in part due to the aircraft being new and one of the first in the world to be designed completely using a computer rather than an actual model, implement just-in-time (JIT) practices for the delivery of the various components and assemble the aircraft on a slow moving assembly line.

This process is successful due to a very close and transparent partnership with suppliers from across the world which is engaged to ensure the parts - as large as an aircraft fuselage - arrive exactly when they are required. From this point, each task and step of assembly is precisely timed out for workers to complete in order to maximize productivity. The parts for the workers assembling the various aspects of the aircraft are delivered through mobile robotic carts in the factory which are delivered to the exact location of the workers as the aircraft assembly line ever so slowly moves. This orchestra of various parts and workers ensure the products are assembled on time as well as uses barcode and RFID technology to ensure products are able to be tracked and easily moved throughout the factory.

Managerial Implications

For companies such as UPMC and Boeing which have been reviewed in this chapter, these 2 companies operate in 2 separate industries though hold various applicability of how RFID technology can impact managerial decisions. RFID-based technologies, through its evolution since WWII technology, have found many ways to benefit managers in various types of industries who are looking to quickly, efficiently, and accurately track the inventory of their product. In particular, companies with large amounts of individual components to complete a service or products, such as UPMC and Boeing respectively, have numerous benefits for managers. First, the reduction of human errors and implementation of consistency that RFID technology can provide is impactful for managers. RFID allows the constant and consistent flow of information through an established system of transmitters and receivers that is not dependent on humans who may collect information differently. This also ensures that human errors, even by the best of employees, can be reduced and even eliminated.

Secondly, RFID technology allows for the delivery of information and components exactly when it is needed. At the Boeing factory, the right amount and type of components is delivered precisely when workers require the components which reduces errors and ensures maximum efficiency. For a company such as UPMC which is growing the number of hospitals in their network, RFID can provide the company a consistent source of data collection across a wide range of employees and staff. Overall implications of RFID technology to manager in SCM and to leaders in companies such as UPMC and Boeing is noticeable with the ability to be quantified in time, costs, and efficiency savings. The efficiency of RFID technology to collect this information with reduced errors translates into more accurate information for managers to make decisions at often a much lower potential cost.

Research has been done on the effectiveness and success of introducing RFID technology into the supply chain. A study by Wu and Ku (2013) investigated what happens in upstream and downstream firms when RFID technology is brought into the supply chain. The authors used the Adaptive Structuration Theory and Structural Equation Modeling to analyze upstream and downstream firms who had business in manufacturing, logistics, warehousing, retailing, and selling. Due to the benefits of RFID technology including reducing costs and reducing data entry errors, which have their own downstream effect, Wu and Ku wanted to see if there were any difficulties upstream and downstream that firms encountered when RFID technology is introduced. They researched 7 different ways RFID could prove difficult for firms including its effect on operation structure, group cooperation, and influence on issues derived from RFID technology. Although almost all of their findings confirmed that RFID technology has a positive influence on supply chains, there were a couple of negative outcomes. These were mostly around the changes that would take place with the introduction of RFID technology to a firm and the extent of this change is largely unknown.

RFID technology applicability can be applied to an even greater sense at both companies. UPMC for example has a large hospital system with multiple staff members covering a wide variety of shifts at the hospital. This dynamic in the healthcare industry is also more complex with all the various supplies and tools needed to treat patients in a hospital. While much of the supplies are tracked with bar codes today, RFID tags can help to collect data and perform an inventory in real time. This inventory can be more easily known as needed as well as tracked through its usage throughout a time period to better predict when supplies or tools may be needed for predictable procedures or treatments. UPMC as a result can better predict when a supply may be needed and can also reduce storage space in a hospital. In turn, Boeing Company is moving more towards RFID technology from the bar coded technology that was historically used at the factory. Boeing today uses the RFID chips to track and guide the movement of robots with the components for their aircraft. However, for Boeing their use can also be far greater by being able to integrate RFID technology not only in the logistical process to assemble the aircraft but also in the actual maintenance of an aircraft. For example, safety checks for inspections of aircraft can be more efficient and accurate if RFID technology could be implemented to monitoring the existing systems of their aircraft. Mechanics could then know precisely where to look onboard an aircraft with this more accurate information to better maintain their fleet. While RFID technology at Boeing cannot fully take the place of a human inspection, it can help to ensure the accuracy and speed at to which inspections could occur. For companies such as UPMC and Boeing, surveying the work force that interacts with these components and the management can be an important step to understand the potential impact and scope of RFID technology at both these companies.

CONCLUSIONS

General Conclusions and Implications

RFID technology has demonstrated its ability to evolve into a logistics solution since its inception in the 1900's. As technology has improved by becoming less expensive on a per chip basis and through a much smaller size, RFID technology is a competitive advantage for managers involved in SCM. Various aspects of the supply chain process are now able to be more accurately and easily tracked based upon their location and the data associated with the chip rather than through line of sight technology that exists through bar code technology. Managers can now be empowered with time and a constant flow of data that allows them to make fact based decisions and projections which have helped to save time and money through efficiency for their companies. Companies such as Boeing are demonstrating the existing potential of RFID technology while companies such as UPMC can take RFID technology the next level by tracking thousands of supplies that exist in a hospital.

DIRECTIONS FOR FUTURE RESEARCH

As with any technology, there is an initial and substantial investment that is required to implement RFID-based technologies. While this group recognizes the benefit of RFID technology, performing a case study on individual companies to understand the cost-benefit of this technology is important. Additionally, completing a detailed survey of UPMC and Boeing is a key aspect of future work that would allow for a strong understanding of RFID at each of the companies. Overall, the benefits of RFID technology are likely to improve as the technology for transmitting and receiving devices continues to be more cost efficient and widely implemented in the SCM system. As shown in the case studies, RFID solutions and its the approach is to assume that the outcome is acceptable to all (e.g., return of assets, from a financial perspective, elapsed lead time from an operational perspective) and that after it communicated to all stakeholders, and there must be agree of how to address it. Therefore, from a metric-intensive perspective, using predictive measures such as overtime dollars or reducing the number of steps would be a logical approach to properly management the desired outcomes. Technology coordination, which recognizes the presence of interdependency between processes, activities or functions, needs to be properly manage, as coordination can reduce potential conflicts that can occur when individuals want to use their own priorities. All priorities much match the organization's established goals. Future research could focus on how best to satisfy all those competing needs.

REFERENCES

Advantages of RFID. (2018). Retrieved March 02, 2018, from http://www.activewaveinc.com/technology_rfid_advantage.php

Basu, P., & Nair, S. K. (2012). Supply chain finance enabled early pay: Unlocking trapped value in B2B logistics. *International Journal of Logistics Systems and Management*, *12*(3), 334–353. doi:10.1504/IJLSM.2012.047605

Brito, T. B., & Botter, R. C. (2012). Feasibility analysis of a global logistics hub in Panama. *International Journal of Logistics Systems and Management*, *12*(3), 247–266. doi:10.1504/IJLSM.2012.047601

Bulcsu, S. (2011). The process of liberalising the rail freight transport markets in the EU: The case of Hungary. *International Journal of Logistics Systems and Management*, *9*(1), 89–107. doi:10.1504/IJLSM.2011.040061

Carvalho, H., Cruz-Machado, V., & Tavares, J. G. (2012). A mapping framework for assessing supply chain resilience. *International Journal of Logistics Systems and Management*, *12*(3), 354–373. doi:10.1504/IJLSM.2012.047606

Farris, M. T. II, & Hutchison, P. D. (2002). Cash-to-cash: The new supply chain management metric. *International Journal of Physical Distribution & Logistics Management*, *32*(4), 288–298. doi:10.1108/09600030210430651

Hamidi, M., Farahmand, K., Sajjadi, S. R., & Nygard, K. E. (2012). A hybrid GRASP-tabu search metaheuristic for a four-layer location-routing problem. *International Journal of Logistics Systems and Management*, *12*(3), 267–287. doi:10.1504/IJLSM.2012.047602

Kumar, P., Shankar, R., & Yadav, S. S. (2011). Global supplier selection and order allocation using FQFD and MOLP. *International Journal of Logistics Systems and Management*, *9*(1), 43–68. doi:10.1504/IJLSM.2011.040059

Landt, J. (2005). The history of RFID. *IEEE Potentials*, *24*(4), 8–11. doi:10.1109/MP.2005.1549751

Mathirajan, M., Manoj, K., & Ramachandran, V. (2011). A design of distribution network and development of efficient distribution policy. *International Journal of Logistics Systems and Supply Management*, *9*(1), 108–137. doi:10.1504/IJLSM.2011.040062

Melnyk, S. A., Davis, E. W., Spekman, R. E., & Sandor, J. (2000). Outcome-driven supply chains. *MIT Sloan Management Review*, *51*(2), 33–38.

More, D., & Babu, A. S. (2012). Benchmarking supply chain flexibility using data envelopment analysis. *International Journal of Logistics Systems and Management*, *12*(3), 288–317. doi:10.1504/IJLSM.2012.047603

Paksoy, T., & Cavlak, E. B. (2011). Development and optimisation of a new linear programming model for production/distribution network of an edible vegetable oils manufacturer. *International Journal of Logistics Systems and Management*, *9*(1), 1–21. doi:10.1504/IJLSM.2011.040057

Pettersson, A. I., & Segerstedt, A. (2011). Performance measurements in supply chains within Swedish industry. *International Journal of Logistics Systems and Management*, *9*(1), 69–88. doi:10.1504/IJLSM.2011.040060

Pradhananga, R., Hanaoka, S., & Sattayaprasert, W. (2011). Optimisation model for hazardous material transport routing in Thailand. *International Journal of Logistics Systems and Management*, *9*(1), 22–42. doi:10.1504/IJLSM.2011.040058

Radio Frequency Identification (RFID): What is it? (2017). U.S. Department of Homeland Security. Retrieved July 23, 2018 from https://www.dhs.gov/radio-frequency-identification-rfid-what-it

RFID for What? 101 Innovative Ways to Use RFID. (2011). *RFID Journal*, 11-14.

14

Roberti, M. (2005). The History of RFID Technology. *RFID Journal*. Retrieved July 23, 2018 from: http://www.rfidjournal.com/articles/view?1338

Smith, A. D. (2017a). Case Studies of RFID Practices for Competitive Inventory Management Systems. In J. Wang (Ed.), *Management Science, Logistics, and Operations Research* (pp. 1–25). IGI Global. doi:10.4018/978-1-4666-4506-6.ch001

Smith, A. D. (2017b). Operational Strategies Associated with RFID Applications in Healthcare Systems. In I. Lee (Ed.), *RFID Technology Integration for Business Performance Improvement* (pp. 199–217). IGI Global. doi:10.4018/978-1-4666-6308-4.ch010

Smith, A. D. (2017c). Inventory Management, Shrinkage Concerns, and Related Corrective RFID Strategies. In I. Lee (Ed.), *RFID Technology Integration for Business Performance Improvement* (pp. 218–246). IGI Global. doi:10.4018/978-1-4666-6308-4.ch011

Smith, A. D. (2019). JIT Inventory Management Strategy. In V. X. Wang & G. Torrisi-Steele (Eds.), *Handbook on Research in Transdisciplinary Knowledge Generation* (pp. 57–74). IGI Global. doi:10.4018/978-1-5225-9531-1.ch005

Smith, A. D., Shock, J. R., & Beaves, R. G. (2019). Customer relationship management and the impact of e-coupons on B2C retail markets. *International Journal of Business Information Systems*, *30*(2), 203–231. doi:10.1504/IJBIS.2019.097535

Trebilcock, B. (2015). How they did it: Supply relationship at Raytheon. *Supply Chain Management Review*, 18-23.

Von Haartman, R. (2012). Beyond Fisher's product-supply chain matrix: Illustrating the actual impact of technological maturity on supply chain design. *International Journal of Logistics Systems and Management*, *12*(3), 318–333. doi:10.1504/IJLSM.2012.047604

Wu, M. Y., & Ku, C. W. (2013). A study of key factors in the introduction of RFID into supply chains through the Adaptive Structuration Theory. *International Journal of Industrial Engineering*, *20*(5/6), 429–443.

Zelbst, P., Green, K. W., Sower, V. E., & Reyes, P. M. (2012). Impact of RFID on manufacturing effectiveness and efficiency. *International Journal of Operations & Production Management*, *32*(3), 329–350. doi:10.1108/01443571211212600

ADDITIONAL READING

Hu, G., Wang, L., Fetch, S., & Bidanda, B. (2008). A multi-objective model for project portfolio selection to implement lean and Six Sigma concepts. *International Journal of Production Research*, *46*(23), 6611–6648. doi:10.1080/00207540802230363

Jain, V., Benyoucef, L., & Deshmukh, S. G. (2008). What's the buzz about moving from 'lean' to 'agile' integrated supply chains? A fuzzy intelligent agent-based approach. *International Journal of Production Research*, *46*(23), 6649–6678. doi:10.1080/00207540802230462

Kamhawi, E. M. (2008). System characteristics, perceived benefits, individual differences and use intentions: A survey of decision support tools of ERP systems. *Information Resources Management Journal*, *21*(4), 66–83. doi:10.4018/irmj.2008100104

Okoniewska, B., Graham, A., Gavrilova, M., Wah, D., Gilgen, J., Coke, J., Burden, J., Nayyar, S., Kaunda, J., Yergens, D., Baylis, B., & Ghali, W. A. (2010). Multidimensional evaluation of a radio frequency identification Wi-Fi location tracking system in an acute-care hospital setting. *Journal of the American Medical Informatics Association*, *19*(4), 674–679. doi:10.1136/amiajnl-2011-000560 PMID:22298566

Ustundag, A. (2010). Evaluating RFID investment on a supply chain using tagging cost sharing factor. *International Journal of Production Research*, *48*(9), 2549–2562. doi:10.1080/00207540903564926

Visich, J. K., Li, S., Khumawala, B. M., & Reyes, P. M. (2009). Empirical evidence of RFID impacts on supply chain performance. *International Journal of Operations & Production Management*, *29*(12), 1290–1315. doi:10.1108/01443570911006009

KEY TERMS AND DEFINITIONS

Automatic Identification and Data Capture Technologies (AIDC): Types of AIDC-related technologies to leave the human element out of the data collection and storage functions of information derived from manufacturing, integrated through the manufacturing process, types of authentication concerns and/or e-security strategies, and relationship links to customer profiles. Typical types of AIDC include, bar-coding, RFID, magnetic strips, touch memory, and smart cards.

Inventory Control: Inventory control is the concept by which the negative aspects of maintaining inventories (i.e., less capital to invest elsewhere, costs associated with shrinkage and storage) are balanced with its positive aspects (i.e., having goods and services available in a JIT fashion). A number of traditional models are used to optimize levels of inventory (i.e., Minimum Stock, Economic Order Quantity (EOQ), and Safety Stock methods) that help determine minimum stock necessary to adequately maintain production levels.

JIT: JIT methodologies are intended to maximize the ability to respond to consumer preferences but simultaneously reduce levels of inventories via lean or cost-sensitive approaches. It is hoped by the eliminating any wasteful or non-value added activities, a firm can strategically level automation and its highly skilled.

Radio Frequency Identification (RFID): RFID technologies are types of automatic data capture techniques that use a combination of active and passive senders and receivers to collect and store codified information for further uses. The implementation of such technologies should lead to improved managerial and/or supply chain performance. On the surface, there appears to be few drawbacks to implementing such technology into a production process, assuming it enhances performance and improves output of the product. The main issues surrounding the RFID applications are whether the initial costs and labor required to utilize this technology are worth it, and will result in a positive outcome of revenues.

Toyota Production System (TPS): TPS is an optimum set of approaches to inventory production planning systems by creating economies of scale while producing in relatively small-batch volumes. The aim of the process is to apply scientific methods to obtain the best available quality, lowest costs, and shortest lead times via simultaneously reducing of waste or non-value added activities. TPS has two major considerations, JIT and jidoka.

Green Supply Chains and Enabling RFID Technology

Alan D. Smith

Robert Morris University, USA

INTRODUCTION

Green, Supply Chains, and RFID

There is considerable evidence the next frontier for achieving a competitive advantage in marketplace is taking up the idea of a green supply chain (GSC) by introducing corporate responsibility (CSR) and sustainability into your day-to-day operations. This chapter of applications of supply chain management (SCM) emphases the role of radio frequency identification (RFID) technology. RFID-embedded has been a major technological advance that appears to be on the verge of universal acceptance as an industrial standard that will enable companies with improved data gathering. Therefore, helping managers make more informed decisions, saving capital while improving their environmental friendliness. Since the beginning of RFID since the early 1980s, the technology has blossomed into many sectors and different purposes but there is no consensus on the actual popularity, familiarity, and overall likeability of RFID in any of this. Some of these business sectors include retail, finance, information technology (IT), healthcare, and aerospace industry. As consumers continue to educate themselves and become more environmentally conscious, they will begin looking at a company's green profile or their energy efficiency profile and begin making their purchasing decisions with that in mind. The speed at which companies peruse these indicatives will be directly related to the dollars spent on product by customers demanding green indicatives. Many firms are requiring their suppliers to be cognizant of these ideas and these customer demands, which will in turn drastically affect B2B commerce between the firm and its suppliers. With the wave of environmental friendliness emerging, these supply chains still have to deal with the challenges of keeping their strategy cost-conscious and effective; this is where RFID comes into play.

In a world that is bent on eliminating waste from its operations (i.e. eliminating redundancies, streamlining manual data collections, etc.), there is another form of west that occurs, physical waste. In other words, the waste that is created by transportation, outside warehousing, damaged inventory, wasted effort in managing these larger fleets, etc. RFID can increase the visibility for manufacturers, distributors, suppliers and retailers, and with real time information, firms can access much more accurate information regarding inventory movement and usage. This will not only reduce wasted costs but can have a large impact on the company's overall environmental standing by reducing the operational west in the supply chain.

Purpose

The purpose of this research study is to find out, using a wide birth questionnaire to real world, multi-sector participants, how people feel about the use of radio frequency identification (RFID) technology. RFID technology, which is not only a multi-billion-dollar industry but also the grandchild of Radar

DOI: 10.4018/978-1-7998-3473-1.ch166

technology, has only been recently becoming more popular across many business sectors, far more than run of the mill retail security tags. This diversification comes at the forefront of oftentimes, the problems of RFID persisting or even getting worse across a supply chain.

The expressed purpose of the propositions presented in this study is to aid in the discovery process of what is the best business practice concerning the usage of RFID technology in the manufacturing and service industries and see if the results corroborate with that much of the current literature says about the popularity of the technology. Across practitioner and scholarly research, have generated many different and often contrasting opinions on how well RFID works in the real world. As well, because the technology has changed so much, many of the articles about RFID scholarly articles and research models are simply obsolete. This study stands to make a more modern look at whom is using RFID technology, based on sector, business, size, longevity, and most of all, the feelings of the business/respondent on the matter.

DISCUSSION

Current Trends

According to Goldenhersh (2009), RFID technology assists firms with the three "R's" of sustainability.

1. Reducing the number of logistics assets needed to operate the supply chain
2. Reusing those assets as frequently as possible
3. Recycling whenever possible

RFID plays a key role as it can vastly improve the managerial use and visibility of their inventory. A company can track everything from returnable inventory to raw materials, therefore increasing their asset utilization and reducing the strain that maintaining and storing these additional assets has on the environment. Studies have shown that RFID-tracking performance in industrial sites by developing methods that integrate Multidimensional Support Vector Regression (MSVR) and a Kalman filter have been very successful (Zhong, 2015; Song, Xiao, Zhang, & Zipkin, 2017). Zhong (2015) demonstrated that RFID technology can be used in manufacturing industries to create an RFID-enabled ubiquitous environment to advanced real time production planning and scheduling. This can be achieved with the goal of collective intelligence. Song, et al. (2017) investigated SCM inventory policy problem for a dual source with equal success. Rogers (2017, p. 276) empirically determined the key advantages of Military Information System Technology (MIST) as an optimal viscosity RFID system that improves fault toler- ance, decreases entropy, decreases costs and decreases backorders. Hence, the technical and business literature have demonstrated that there are many benefits of RFID technology for reducing inventory shrinkage and optimization of SCM

For example, an empirical study case study was performed on several industries, including food and dairy industries, to assess the effectiveness of RFID technology has had on the sustainability goals of each industry (Smith, 2017; Smith & Smith, 2017). It was found that RFID had many practical uses in the food industry and has a major impact on reducing food wastage and perishability. In one company alone, a producer of about 60% of U.S. pistachio crop and exports uses RFID primarily to rationalize the processing of deliveries from its suppliers, which is a critical part of the firm's supply chain. Because Paramount's inventory, Pistachios, has a relatively short time horizon in which they can be harvested and processed, time spent picking, shipping and packaging are of great concern as perishability issues can arise. Paramount went on to say that, their keeping of accurate tracking of inventory delivered was key in maintaining a good working relationship with its suppliers.

RFID has enabled this relationship because Paramount can now weigh its trailers with the nuts to determine the exact amount of inventory that each truck contains. That truck is then RFID tagged as it enters the processing plant to help the manages at Paramount understand exactly how much inventory they have on hand and how much they still need to cover current demand forecast for its product. However, there are some issues Paramount has had with this new technology. First, the surface in which the tags are placed, the metal hulls of the trailers, poses a problem because the metal reflects back the signal, therefore causing some interference. To get around this they now place a "spacer" between the RFID tag and the truck, reducing the interference they were getting when applying it directly to the truck hull. Another issue they were having was the climate in which they were exposing the tags too. By exposing the trailers to extreme temperature swings, Paramount had to use extra durable tags to withstand to change in temperature they would be going through.

Even with these extra costs coming about by the challenges, Paramount reported a staggering success stemming from the utilization of RFID tagging. First, the relationship between them and their suppliers grew and improved considerably by eliminating bad information and disagreements over payment amount and delivery times. Second, the throughput of trucks significantly increased therefore saving the company from having to build a second scale house to handle the increased volume through the facility. Third, there have been better informed management decisions being made by the plant because delivery information is highly accurate, timely, and accessible. Fourth, the company has saved money and gained efficiencies in being able to track expensive assets, like trailers, whose usage was reported to be increasing by 30% since the RFID tagging began.

Another study that was done in the food industry was in Greengard (2007), where the author explored how RFID helps ensure the freshness of processed foods that went through multiple factory operations like the dairy industry. He studied how Wells Dairy uses RFID in its production operations and examines how why tag each case and pallet while running through the production line. Once tagged they are sent to the freezer where Wells ran into problems with the extreme temperature changes the tags were experiencing. Because of this, Wells had to install a verification station in order to ensure that no damage was done to either the cases or tags prior to the pallets leaving the warehouse. However, even with these increased costs, Wells reported great success with the project in that management has a better grasp on their inventory and has been able to make better informed decisions. Due to increased use of RFID tagging during the manufacturing stage, they have seen great efficiencies by being able to track inventory at any stage in the supply chain and understand what percentage is delivered to the final customer versus being returned or destroyed for any reason.

With this long list of advantages that RFID brings with it, there must be just as long a list of disadvantages, right? Not exactly. While it is true that every system you use, there will inherently always be downsides to that system. It is not so simple with RFID tags. RFID is simply a tool, so explaining the disadvantages becomes more difficult. Like a hammer can be used to build a house, so can RFID by used to identify and track objects in real time and improve upon ones supply chain. In other words, RFID is efficient in what it is designed to do, it will not guarantee increased sales or even fix a defunct supply chain, but it should help in identifying what and where certain objects are and help you move towards a more efficient supply chain by having goods on the shelf when customers want them.

What is Radio Frequency Identification (RFID) Technology?

Supply chain management (SCM) has been one of the most difficult and necessary parts of a modern and functional economy. The global market demands that isolationism cannot exist and most all businesses and companies, large and small, foreign and domestic, new and old, have to have a functional and comprehensive supply chain. The advent of new technologies like seafaring freighters, ground transportation, third party suppliers, and outsourcing labor has really changed the face of the profession. Of the many new technologies and adverts, one of the most relevant changes to not only the SCM industry but to a dozen broad sectors is the RFID technology. RFID technology promises revolutions in areas such as supply chain management (Lee & Park, 2008). It is essentially a miniaturized electromagnetic radar that allows some real time tracking of goods, services, persons, or really anything that can be given a transponder and is connected to a receiver.

How is RFID used?

RFID technology can come in many forms and the style, usage, and overall functionality has changed very drastically since the creation around 1980s and further development through 1990s and 2000s. In its modern incarnation, the RFID is a small node with a self-contained power source and transponder, similar to that of an aircraft, which is encoded specifically for the particular receiver. The information that is received at the supply chain manager's computer can track where a tagged good or product is, as a location confirmation or in an assembly line, or in a specific location within a smaller local. According to EEEI "A recent Aberdeen Group survey of 200 companies found that more than half of the companies with RFID systems were using the technology in asset tracking" (Michael and Caine, 2005) shows that many of the companies use RFID for asset tracking in real time. This is the most well-known usage but as this research study will show, the usage of RFID has expanded vastly. This chapter will be covering information about the RFID, including what it is, the history of the RFID, and some pros and cons currently of the technology. The chapter will include a discussion of some of the business sectors that are most familiar with RFID technology in one form or another, as well as what they use, how they use that technology, and how it may be changing the field. The chapter will end with the summary and conclusions including a recap, the results, and the researcher's conclusions, followed by the references and a sample of the questionnaire.

RFID Technology

How does RFID work?

Radio Frequency Identification (RFID) technology, as it is generally accepted, as evolved vastly since the creation in the early 1980s. The technology is based strongly on the Radar technology developed during World War II. However, around 1970, Mario Cardullo thought of and developed the idea for the original RFID, which was a simple versatile tag that consisted of a transponder and receiver system. Though the original was a simple 16-bit interfacing tag, the 1990s saw the technology really pick up. As it is now, the RFID is far more than a simple transponder that can broadcast and receive a signal. Much of the early RFID technology was limited by barcodes in order to confirm an assets location while in transportation, but today, a tag is much cheaper and far more versatile, not even needing an active scan or anything. A modern tag can be registered through a "gate" or a receiver even if the tag is embedded within a box, in metal, or not at all visible The gate, be it an actual tunnel or a within house monitoring system, then sends the information in real time to the supply chain manager. This kind of real time tracking is a massive benefit for any supply chain manager and today, at some large companies, it is simply mandatory as no number of humans could watch thousands of products move every second.

Historical Aspects of RFID

As briefly mentioned above, the RFID was the grandchild of radar technology developed during World War II. The radar originally used electromagnetic waves and time to measure an objects distance from the apex of the radar. The development of RFID was done concurrently between private technology firms and the US government. The original RFID had a very low frequency signal, around 125 kHz, and increased over time up to 13.56 MHz and UHF level tags, which had far more range and usability than the original, which only worked, within a small space. The true game changer, however, was the integration of the RFID tag from a private network system to the internet connectivity. This, combined with the rise of the WiFi networks and satellite GPS technology, toke the RFID global, allowing a supply chain manager to monitor any given good from step one, where the tag is attached, to the final destination with corroborated checkpoints for each partner who has a hand in the process.

Pros of RFID

The obvious benefit and primary usage of the RFID is the real-time location tracking of assets. This can come in the form of many, many different industries tracking their products at different sizes and speeds in order to get an actual monitor of a supply. This could mean, for instance, a shop could watch how much of a certain product is in the store or warehouse, or an agency could watch the "hits" of a certain product, like a passport for instance, where people are showing up and write that information into a database to follow people. With the advent of more sophisticated applications of automation in manufacturing and logistics, such as VAT, the potential benefits of RFID-related technologies are too numerous to list in a comprehensive fashion.

As well, in the instance of a massive assembly line, the captain or manager could see where the product being built is in the "assembly line" and if the KPI are being hit or not. This kind of asset tracking during construction means that companies, which survive on massive contracts, can know whether they are on schedule or not to meet their goals and deadlines. Finally, RFID can be connected in most everywhere today, allowing for a very widespread real time tracking, much like an aircraft's transponder allows for an air traffic controller to see where they are in the sky from takeoff to landing, an individual could watch where the good or service was, being tracked in real time, across the global. Obviously, this technology is becoming integral to supply chain managers for their work, even in small and large chains across many partners due to fact that the RFID has not only gotten more advanced, but they are much cheaper, less than a dime per tag.

Cons of RFID

RFID can be a very handy tool to use but it is not without a few hang-ups. As it stands now, depending on the size of the supply chain that the manager is trying to get tagged up, several things are needed. One is a complete and total commitment from all the supply chains partners, meaning that everyone has to invest in one tag, one software, and one overall system completely. While the tags themselves are not particularly expensive, the setup of the system can be very expensive to get up and running. As one research study states: "By adopting RFID technology, companies will be confronted with a huge amount of data generated by RFID tags" (Lee & Park, 2008). RFID system requires that, as mentioned before, every supply partner and involved distributor, retailer, and raw material constructor, need to be in on the "plan." This means that, for example, if one-step in the supply chain chooses not to get involved or rejects the idea of an RFID system, the entire system is effectively moot. This can hurt relationships between supplier and distributor or retailer and could even demand that a supply chain manager must find new partners to work, which could really hurt or even stop production.

BUSINESS SECTORS

Who Uses RFID?

In this chapter, we want to see how people in the real world choose to utilize and how much they like or dislike the actual technology. However, a known limitation of this project is that it is impossible for me to know literally every single use of RFID technology, in and out of supply chain management. So for the sake of having a cohesive research project, we will focus not on every use of RFID, but of the more popular uses in sectors and determine at what size of a company, perhaps, uses an RFID technology in some form, and try to determine if they are really worth it or not. The above discussed several instances of this section of the chapter will be discussing some of the known uses. The order listed is in no particular order but will be the business sectors that this chapter.

Retail

Retail traditionally has been one of the most notable sectors to adopt RFID technology across the board. Most people know the common use of tags, for instance, on clothing as security tags, to deter people from shop lifting the tagged clothing that will set off a gate if the tag goes through it. While most people thing that this is the most popular use of RFID, another less well-known usage is actual pallet tracking (Thrasher, 2013). When a big box supplier needs to flow what is coming any given week, how much or little of X product is on the way, a company can see that, using gate tracking, assets are being tracked both in-bound, upon arrival, and precisely how far across the supply chain these products actually travel. According to one study "...through its capabilities to uniquely identify, track and trace consumer products along the entire supply chain requiring neither direct human contact nor line of sight" (Bardaki, Pramatari, & Doukidis, 2007, p. 1). This kind of automation is a major strength to retails from small to large since not only does this save work hours but also it helps remove some of the human element with regards to making a mistake.

Financial

Much the same way that other industries use RFID for asset tracking, this fact, is especially important in financial sectors for tracking money transfer and related financial documents. The way this is most often used is with banks, who use tags on large sums of money in order to manage asset tracking. As well, despite how important it is for a bank to keep track of their money, this saves dozens of man hours' worth of having to have a teller or accountant count the money between locations, as well as financial firms like large banks being able to track their IT assets.

Information Technology (IT)

Dealing with IT asset tracking, this has become one of the more behind the scenes and prevalent uses of RFID technology. Like in the instance of datacenters and server farms, RFID have changed how high-tech firms manage their equipment. According to one expert on RFID, "A full inventory often took days to complete. With RFID, some financial institutions are accomplishing the task in hours" (Pleshek, 2011, p. 1). Firms who live and die by their technology and database functionality can have much shorter maintenance times and more active time so long as a supply chain manager is able to watch their expensive IT parts in a collaborated database. Information technology uses RFID in other instances as well, for example with GPS connects and US passport tagging to track where people have checked into when traveling. Finally, one of the more innovative technologies that are being implemented is real time dynamic advertising, where objects like phones will receive an ad or message based on a real time location with information received from a nearby store or kiosk.

Healthcare

One of the larger trends we have seen growing according to several studies is the use of RFID in the healthcare system (Rodger, 2017). Healthcare system are the involved hospitals, who are the consumers in this supply chain, and the associated retailers, distributors, and such, that have been benefitting from asset tracking of such important, expensive and specific tools. According to one research article: "Potential benefits that are associated with intelligent healthcare information systems include improved patient safety through reduced medication errors and adverse events, improved medication/test ordering, improved quality of care, and improved efficiency in healthcare delivery" (Tua, Zhoub, & Piramuthub, 2009, p. 587). Hospitals can keep an active tracking of their limited and specific supplies in real time in the instance that a situation arises that requires some equipment within seconds. Hospitals are gaining the ability to track their ambulances with RFID and GPS in order to read traffic and location and help expedite getting a critical patient to the hospital as soon as possible.

Aerospace

While most everyone assumes that RFID in aerospace is mostly used in baggage handling, the technology is evolving very quickly and finding its footing in a new functionality. The normal baggage tag, used at the usual large, commercial airports, allows airliners to track the flow on and off baggage in an aircraft along with information related to that baggage such as size and weight in order to create the most balanced baggage situation on a flight. As well, one of the new techniques being used is from large manufacturers like Boeing or Airbus can track the construction of a new aircraft in real time (Pleshek, 2011). A commercial aircraft is made of so many parts that all have to come together in a timely fashion and the construction of an aircraft is so complex that applying RFID tags to different parts can let a manager monitor the situation.

RFID and VMI Implementation Strategies for a Green Supply Chain

The following is a set of guidelines managers can use as they seek to implement RFID into their sustainable supply chain. There is little doubt from the many readings in SCM; a well-documented purchasing portfolio has many admirable characteristics that has the potential for great benefits and profitability. The following sections will present some collaborating evidence for combining these approaches via successful practice of VMI (vendor-managed inventory) with retailer-managed inventory systems.

For example, Mishra and Raghunathan (2004) offered details as to why retailers may want manufacturers to manage their inventories. The authors also present the argument "that VMI intensifies the competition between manufacturers of competing brands" (p. 445). These relationships encourage a collaboration that is not established in the traditional retailer-managed inventory (RMI) system. The type of collaboration that is essential to VMI is information sharing. The authors suggested "information sharing reduces the 'bullwhip' effect" (p. 445). Perhaps, their greatest argument is not about bullwhip effect, but that VMI increases competition. Out-of-stocks lead to brand switching, and brand switching over time, can affect market share. Personally, a purchase portfolio concentrates on normal aspects of costs, but not on more creative problems that result in brand switching and vender selection, product substitution, demand models, and order quantities and profits. Mishra and Raghunathan discuss the role of product substitution as regards to retailer competition. This was an interesting concept, since companies I consulted for that sells to Walmart and all our other customers would consider Walmart to be one of their competitors, if not their biggest competitor. They completed an experiment at 2 items made by two different manufacturers that were considered substitutable. They wanted to test what the customer would do when the preferred brand was out of stock. The customer could buy either the substitute brand or backorder the preferred brand. They used derivatives to combine the price and stocking levels to see how it would affect demand. Some of these discussions were slightly irrelevant to what I do as a VMI analyst/consultant, as many SCM professionals are not typically aware of stocking levels or profit margins of the retailers. With VMI, the opportunity costs of stocking decisions are both the profit lost if out of stocks occur and the profit that could be realized if a competitor takes out of stocks.

Mishra and Raghunathan (2004) and Waller, Johnson, and Davis (1999) summarized the need to fixed prices, the possible benefits of VMI almost seem irrelevant if the retailer is making stocking-level decisions. This is an area that there is much agreement (Rodger, 2017). Mishra and Raghunathan (2004) continued with their experiment using endogenous prices, by describing a backward induction procedure that they use to determine that the retailer would not adjust prices, but they would adjust the stocking level. With regards to VMI, the profits are higher because the stocking levels are higher and considerations of uniformly distributed demand. In their conclusion, they state that competition can be a benefit of VMI. They also believe that the higher stocking results in higher profits for the retailer. Interesting enough, that although the retailer may encourage VMI, they remain in control of stocking levels, which may not necessarily be good for competition. What is good for the retailer is the demand data that is received from the retailer. That alone can be benefit enough for the manufacturer to take up VMI.

Waller, et al. (1999), further suggested that VMI seems to work well for food manufacturers considering how long Proctor and Gamble, Campbell Soup, and Barilla pasta has been practicing it. VMI and related SCM activities may result in the retailer giving up control in exchange for the manufacturer to hit a targeted service level. VMI can save money and the technology required to do so. They discuss the variables that affect VMI and some pitfalls of the process, reduced costs and improved service, which are of no surprise. However, the idea of a smoother demand signal is important to modern SCM systems. Costs are reduced because of the visibility of demand, and the better use of production, warehousing, and transportation. VMI can provide safeguards against buyer calendars which may be difficult to interpret. The authors believe service is based off of product availability. Improved service may lead to more shelf space and more shelf space may lead to higher revenues. VMI also seems to be the answer to better service during difficult situations, such as product shortages, the introduction of replacement products, and shipment optimization. They touch on EDI, which all of our VMI customers typically use. It would be difficult to imagine doing SCM transactions job without EDI.

Using a simulation of Hewlett-Packard, the authors evaluated the VMI approach. In this section of the paper, the authors specifically call out the effect of demand variability, the effect of VMI adoption rates, and the effect of limited manufacturing capacity. In regard to demand variability, the authors used three measurements: low, medium, and high. Benefits arise from a shorter review period, which may lead to more frequent shipments, however order frequency was not changed. In this respect, the manufacturer was better able to serve all its customers. With VMI, adoption rates the authors looked at light adoption and widespread adoption, while their VMI candidates made up 30% of their total demand. Overall, widespread adoption offers the greatest benefit, but even bringing key customers onto VMI with light adoption is a step in the right direction.

In looking at the effect of limited manufacturing capacity, the authors construct five scenarios. The main learning was that "VMI is even more important for manufacturers with little excess capacity" (Waller, et al., 1999, p. 196). Hence, VMI leads to greater production efficiencies and the "operational benefits of VMI are very compelling" (p. 198). Those benefits include cost reductions and increased service. These benefits are also being received at lower costs due to the declining price of the technology needed. Interesting enough, the authors also admit that customers who are not VMI are still benefiting from the manufacturers who are offering that service to other customers. However, VMI may not be beneficial if the company does not consider the planning and relationships that go into creating a successful partnership. Teamwork, trust, and goals are all needed for the system to be successful.

Does not the need for continuous planning and relationships that go into creating a successful partnership must be developed for any supply collaborating to occur? Many managerial consultants may use the VMI example as a way to emphasize that teamwork, trust and mutually obtainable goals are essential to the overall success of such partnering activities. These goals cannot be successfully attained by using only one analytical approach. The following are suggested approaches to promote these mutually sustainable goals.

1. Top management needs to be involved with the pursuit of sustainability.

According to Case (2007), he found that executives and supply chain managers need to cooperate in establishing rules of engagement for interaction with suppliers, establish a sustainability statement to suppliers, making the decision if green criteria should be included in the certification of the supplier, and deciding the rollout of a "supplier code of conduct" for supporting sustainability practices.

2. Having a strong business case for going green.

Case (2007) suggested that top management must provide a strong business case for implementing a sustainability strategy. Typically, green supply chains are implemented and justified by way of cost savings and gains in efficiency. When you pair that up with the reduction in waste and enabling JIT manufacturing, there are significant gains in sustainability to be achieved.

3.   Outline a plan for pursuing a sustainable supply chain.

In Hershauer (2008) suggested that there needs to be a top tier executive or cross functional team that oversees the initiatives will ensure continuity in pursuing these initiatives. There are several supply chain management tools available in assisting with these initiatives and will help the team in developing a supplier code of conduct, supplier scorecards, to name a few.

4.   Outline Opportunities using RFID in the business processes.

Hershauer (2008) further pointed out that the focus of the implementation will be promoting the green supply chain, while cutting costs and increasing performance of production. Managers need to identify all business process problems that would benefit with RFID deployment.

5.   Identify RFID issues in the IT department.

Case (2007) established that a companywide roll out of RFID initiatives would undoubtedly involve the setup of new enterprise systems to handle the increased data flow. An IT department needs to ensure that users of the data can access it reliably and effortlessly. One such way of achieving this, would be to offer web services in the delivery of this information. Web-based services give suppliers access to the information without giving them access to the company's internal database.

Rallying Suppliers to Support the Green Initiatives

Hershauer (2008), Mishra and Raghunathan (2004), and Waller, et al. (1999) all suggested that there needs to be incentives and penalties tied to the suppliers' participation of this green initiatives. By utilizing the scorecard created in an earlier step, there needs to be continuity across the board and suppliers need to feel that they are treated fairly when rolling out this initiative.

Proposition 1: RFID technology may not be universally applied with the same benefits. While the subject matter that we are testing is inherently quantitative, the questionnaire gives the research study data a degree qualitative merit to see. We believe that in some sectors, the use of RFID technology may be done across the board, hands down but may not be as universally loved due to technical limitations with third party supply partners.

Proposition 2: This proposition suggest that only very large companies have access to the realist, broad margin use of RFID technology in whatever sector they are involved with. For instance, in retail, only the kind of "mega stores" like Walmart, Kroger, Costco, etc. Using correlations between dollar values of the responding subject's business/company and their familiarity with RFID will provide insight into the limit of RFID, whether or not anyone smaller than a massive retail chain or heavy manufacturer like Boeing bother with RFID. The concept behind this proposition is that though much of the RFID system is and has become more affordable, the ceiling placed on supply chain managers and their partners stops most attempts.

Null Hypothesis: The null hypothesis is that RFID technology is, in fact, as popular and widely acknowledged as many research articles and studies indicate. This would be a reversal of the prior two hypothesize that did not completely acknowledge the value of RFID technology. The null hypothesis assumes that all sectors and all sizes have generally positive feelings regarding RFID technology and use them in some aspect.

GENERAL CONCLUSIONS AND IMPLICATIONS

14

Chapter Summary

This chapter deals with the usages and popularity of RFID-embedded technology. This study aims to discover what the situation is in the modern supply chain in a wide array of sectors. Using previous RFID literature that have referenced the use of RFID-based technology in other sectors, this research study sought to, colloquially, find the "temperature" of how people are feeling and more importantly, using RFID in their business. While some RFID usages are obvious, this research study can find if there are new, more cutting edge uses of RFID that not even any of the previous literature has touched on. This chapter is reminiscent of a professional survey, seeks to add to the conversation about what is possibly working, what is not working, and what people are really thinking ideally.

Strategic Conclusions

Though the proposed empirical study has not yet been conducted, the conclusions that are expected to be reached will be reviewed by all associated peers in the immediate vicinity and academy structure to double check all of the data and reading. If the majority of the reviewers positively review both the study methodology and the study itself, the study will be distributed to other university professionals in the area in order to continue to receive reviewing. Testing these propositions should place a spotlight on the usefulness of RFID-embedded technologies with the SCM industry and help make the situation clearer to other supply chain professionals.

DIRECTIONS FOR FUTURE RESEARCH

Forward-looking companies and supply chains partners need to take a closer look at RFID tagging and the current/future sustainability initiatives that they enable. RFID tagging can help these firms improve their impact on the environment by utilizing the information flow RFID enables, improving logistic assets, and reducing reliance on disposable packaging. Couple these initiatives with the impact that RFID tagging can have in improving business processes and production methods, and your company can cement a solid plan as to why RFID tagging may be instrumental in the implementation of your sustainable supply chain.

REFERENCES

Ashenbaum, B. (2008). *Critical Issues Report: Green Corporate Strategies: Issues and Implementation from the Supply Management Perspective. CAPS Research*. Institute for Supply Management.

Bardaki, C., Pramatari, K., & Doukidis, G. I. (2007). RFID-enabled supply chain collaboration services in a networked retail business environment. *Association for Electronic Information*. Retrieved April 19, 2019 from http://aisel.aisnet.org/cgi/viewcontent.cgi?article=1008&context=bled2007

Bhattacharya, M., Chu, C., Hayya, J., & Mullen, T. (2010). An exploratory study of RFID adoption in the retail sector. *Operations Management Research*, 3(1), 80–89. doi:10.100712063-010-0029-z

Cardullo, M. (2003). Genesis of the versatile RFID tag. *RFID Journal*. Retrieved July 11, 2019 from http://www.rfidjournal.com/articles/view?392

Case, S. (2007). Socially responsible purchasing. *Inside Supply Management, 18*(1), 8-12.

Cooling, L. (2008) Scorecards for sustainability. *Inside Supply Management, 19*(10), 23-25.

Goldenhersh, L. (2009). *Supply Chain Environmentalism. Inside Supply Management, 20*(3), 30–31.

Gordon, M., & Levin, M. (2009) Working with suppliers to achieve CSR goals. *Inside Supply Management, 20*(6), 30-33.

Granneman, S. (2003). RFID chips are here. *The Register.* Retrieved July 21, 2019 from https://www.theregister.co.uk/2003/06/27/rfid_chips_are_here/

Greengard, S. (2007) Wells' dairy milks RFID for benefits. *RFID Journal.* Retrieved July 21, 2018 from https://www.rfidjournal.com/purchase-access?type=Article&id=2907&r=%2Farticles%2Fview%3F2907

Hershauer, J. (2008). *Process Guide for Supply Management Environmental Sustainability.* CAPS Research. Retrieved July 21, 2019 from https://www.instituteforsupplymanagement.org/content.cfm?ItemNumber=4769&SSO=1

Kumar, R. (2003). Interaction of RFID technology and public policy. *WIPRO.* Retrieved July 21, 2019 from http://citeseerx.ist.psu.edu/viewdoc/download?doi=10.1.1.67.3466&rep=rep1&type=pdf

Landt, J. (2001). *Shrouds of time: The history of RFID. The Association for Automatic Identification.* AIM, Inc. Retrieved April 14, 2019 from http://www.sepaco-tech.com/modules/Manager/Articles/the%20history%20of%20rfid.pdf

Lee, D., & Park, J. (2008). RFID-based traceability in the supply chain. *Industrial Management & Data Systems, 108*(6), 713–725. doi:10.1108/02635570810883978

Michael, K., & McCathie, L. (2005). The pros and cons of RFID in supply chain management. *IEEE Computer Society*, 1-7. Retrieved April 19, 2019 from https://ieeexplore.ieee.org/stamp/stamp.jsp?tp=&arnumber=1493672&tag=1

Mishra, B. K., & Raghunathan, S. (2004). Retailer- vs. Vendor-managed inventory and brand competition. *Management Science, 50*(4), 445–457. doi:10.1287/mnsc.1030.0174

Pleshek, J. (2011). RFID technology: use cases in almost every industry. *WTN News.* Retrieved July 6, 2019 from http://wtnnews.com/articles/8215/

Rodger, J. A. (2017). Forecasting of radio frequency identification entropy viscosity parking and forwarding algorithm flow risks and costs: Integrated supply chain health manufacturing system (ISCHMS) approach. *IEEE Journal of Radio Frequency Identification, 1*(4), 267-278.

Smith, A. A., & Smith, A. D. (2017). Radio frequency identification technologies and issues in healthcare. In *Encyclopedia of Information Science and Technology, 4th Ed.* Information Resources Management Association. https://www.igi-global.com/chapter/radio-frequency-identification-technologies-and-issues-in-healthcare/184293

Smith, A. D. (2017). Inventory Management, Shrinkage Concerns, and Related Corrective RFID Strategies. In I. Lee (Ed.), *RFID Technology Integration for Business Performance Improvement* (pp. 218–246). IGI Global. doi:10.4018/978-1-4666-6308-4.ch011

Song, J.-S., Xiao, L., Zhang, H., & Zipkin, P. H. (2017). Optimal policies for a dual-sourcing inventory problem with endogenous stochastic lead times. *Operations Research*, *65*(2), 379–395. doi:10.1287/opre.2016.1557

Thrasher, J. (2011). How is RFID used in real world applications? In *RFID Insider*. Retrieved July 6, 2019 from https://blog.atlasrfidstore.com/what-is-rfid-used-for-in-applications

Tu, Y., Zhou, W., & Piramuthu, S. (2009). Identifying RFID-embedded objects in pervasive healthcare applications. *Decision Support Systems*, *46*(2), 586–593. doi:10.1016/j.dss.2008.10.001

Waller, M., Johnson, E., & Davis, T. (1999). Vendor managed inventory in the retail supply chain. *Journal of Business Logistics*, *20*(1), 183–203.

Zhong, R. Y., Huang, G. Q., Lan, S., Dai, Q. Y., Zhang, T., & Xu, C. (2015). A two-level advanced production planning and scheduling model for RFID-enabled ubiquitous manufacturing. *Advanced Engineering Informatics*, *29*(4), 799–812. doi:10.1016/j.aei.2015.01.002

ADDITIONAL READING

Afsharian, S. P., Alizadeh, A., & Chehrehpak, M. (2016). Effects of applying radio frequency identification in supply chain management: An empirical study of manufacturing enterprises. *International Journal of Business Information Systems*, *23*(1), 97–115. doi:10.1504/IJBIS.2016.078026

Fan, T., Tao, F., Deng, S., & Li, S. (2015). Impact of RFID technology on supply chain decisions with inventory inaccuracies. *International Journal of Production Economics*, *159*, 117–125. doi:10.1016/j.ijpe.2014.10.004

Fan, T.-J., Chang, X.-Y., Gu, C.-H., Yi, J.-J., & Deng, S. (2014). Benefits of RFID technology for reducing inventory shrinkage. *International Journal of Production Economics*, *147*, 659–665. doi:10.1016/j.ijpe.2013.05.007

Hu, G., Wang, L., Fetch, S., & Bidanda, B. (2008). A multi-objective model for project portfolio selection to implement lean and Six Sigma concepts. *International Journal of Production Research*, *46*(23), 6611–6648. doi:10.1080/00207540802230363

Jain, V., Benyoucef, L., & Deshmukh, S. G. (2008). What's the buzz about moving from 'lean' to 'agile' integrated supply chains? A fuzzy intelligent agent-based approach. *International Journal of Production Research*, *46*(23), 6649–6678. doi:10.1080/00207540802230462

Kamhawi, E. M. (2008). System characteristics, perceived benefits, individual differences and use intentions: A survey of decision support tools of ERP systems. *Information Resources Management Journal*, *21*(4), 66–83. doi:10.4018/irmj.2008100104

Ngai, E. W. T., Cheung, B. K. S., Lam, S. S., & Ng, C. T. (2014). RFID value in aircraft parts supply chains: A case study. *International Journal of Production Economics, 147*, 330–339. doi:10.1016/j.ijpe.2012.09.017

Okoniewska, B., Graham, A., Gavrilova, M., Wah, D., Gilgen, J., Coke, J., Burden, J., Nayyar, S., Kaunda, J., Yergens, D., Baylis, B., & Ghali, W. A. (2010). Multidimensional evaluation of a radio frequency identification Wi-Fi location tracking system in an acute-care hospital setting. *Journal of the American Medical Informatics Association, 19*(4), 674–679. doi:10.1136/amiajnl-2011-000560 PMID:22298566

Song, J.-S., Xiao, L., Zhang, H., & Zipkin, P. H. (2017). Optimal policies for a dual-sourcing inventory problem with endogenous stochastic lead times. *Operations Research, 65*(2), 379–395. doi:10.1287/opre.2016.1557

Ustundag, A. (2010). Evaluating RFID investment on a supply chain using tagging cost sharing factor. *International Journal of Production Research, 48*(9), 2549–2562. doi:10.1080/00207540903564926

Visich, J. K., Li, S., Khumawala, B. M., & Reyes, P. M. (2009). Empirical evidence of RFID impacts on supply chain performance. *International Journal of Operations & Production Management, 29*(12), 1290–1315. doi:10.1108/01443570911006009

Zhou, H., & Piramuthu, S. (2013). Remanufacturing with RFID item level information: Optimization, waste reduction and quality improvement. *International Journal of Production Economics, 145*(2), 647–657. doi:10.1016/j.ijpe.2013.05.019

KEY TERMS AND DEFINITIONS

Automatic Identification and Data Capture Technologies (AIDC): Types of AIDC-related technologies to leave the human element out of the data collection and storage functions of information derived from manufacturing, integrated through the manufacturing process, types of authentication concerns and/or e-security strategies, and relationship links to customer profiles. Typical types of AIDC include, bar coding, RFID, magnetic strips, touch memory, and smart cards.

Barcoding Technology: A long-term and very reliable type of AIDC technology, it is known for its very accurate and economical approaches to identity products and machine-readable information from a variety of manufactured goods and services. Most barcodes use a type of standardized bars and spacing coding or symbology that is certified by an international standards body (GS1 System). This system provides for the universal global acceptance of many types of barcodes designed for a variety of shipping and identification applications. Example barcode formats that are in common use today include EAN/UPC, GS1 DataBar, GS1-128, ITF-14, GS1 DataMatrix, GS1 QR Code and Composite Components.

Inventory Control: Inventory control is the concept by which the negative aspects of maintaining inventories (i.e., less capital to invest elsewhere, costs associated with shrinkage and storage) are balanced with its positive aspects (i.e., having goods and services available in a JIT fashion). A number of traditional models are used to optimize levels of inventory (i.e., Minimum Stock, Economic Order Quantity (EOQ), and Safety Stock methods) that help determine minimum stock necessary to adequately maintain production levels.

JIT: JIT methodologies are intended to maximize the ability to respond to consumer preferences but simultaneously reduce levels of inventories via lean or cost-sensitive approaches. It is hoped by the eliminating any wasteful or non-value-added activities, a firm can strategically level automation and its highly skilled.

Radio Frequency Identification (RFID): RFID technologies are types of automatic data capture techniques that use a combination of active and passive senders and receivers to collect and store codified information for further uses. The implementation of such technologies should lead to improved managerial and/or supply chain performance. On the surface, there appears to be few drawbacks to implementing such technology into a production process, assuming it enhances performance and improves output of the product. The main issues surrounding the RFID applications are whether the initial costs and labor required to utilize this technology are worth it and will result in a positive outcome of revenues.

Supply Chain Management (SCM)/Performance: In basic terms, supply chain is the system of organizations, people, activities, information and resources involved in moving a product or service from supplier to customer. The configuration and management of supply chain operations is a keyway companies obtain and maintain a competitive advantage. The typical manufacturing supply chain begins with raw material suppliers, or inputs. The next link in the chain is the manufacturing, or transformation step; followed the distribution, or localization step. Finally, customers as outputs purchase the finished product or service. Service and Manufacturing managers need to know the impact of supply on their organization's purchasing and logistics processes. However, supply chain performance and its metrics are difficult to develop and actually measure.

Vendor-Managed Inventory Systems (VMI): VMI-based systems are designed to transfer the control of inventory and its planning activities to a manufacturer or distributor in order to provide a beneficial relationship to promote a more transparent and seamless flow of goods and services at lower costs. As in many recent retailer applications, the supplier/vendor assumes responsible for replenishing and stocking inventory at appropriate levels to minimize inconvenience to the ultimate customer.

Virtual Asset Trackers (VAT): Increased transparency in supply chains and the need to track personal as well as physical assets has led to the development of Virtual Asset Trackers (VAT). VAT-based technologies allow for hosted users to automatically received updates on inventories on their RFID handhelds and Web Asset Managers. VAT is a type of application of active RFID tagging that allows healthcare practitioners to enhance security to patients, residents, and hospital staff while providing better patient and resident-care services. Ideally, proper leveraging of VAT-based technologies allow management within the healthcare setting to simultaneously improve regulatory compliance, preventing or reducing inventory shrinkage, reduce labor intensive staff assignments, and lessen spoilage of perishables. These are mainly operational advantages that are commonly associated with active RFID applications.

APPENDIX

RFID by Sectors and Real-World Usage Questionnaire

Radio Frequency Identification (RFID) technology has been one of the most talked about and least understood pieces of supply chain management since the rise of the internet age. Virtually every individual business and supply chain uses RFID differently for mostly tracking and observing small transponders in real time. **Please spend a few moments to answer the following questions regarding your RFID technology usage. Please check the single best answer.**

Business Experience and RFID Familiarity

For the following questions, please check the appropriate response concerning your business/companies experience with RFID. Please note that the questions should be answered on a 1-4 scale.

Strongly Disagree Agree Strongly Disagree Agree

My business/company uses RFID technology ☐ ☐ ☐ ☐
My business/company is very familiar with RFID ☐ ☐ ☐ ☐
My business/company has only recently
(<5 years) started using RFID technology ☐ ☐ ☐ ☐
My business/company has experience ☐ ☐ ☐ ☐
(>5 years) using RFID technology
My business/company is in the (Retail/IT/
Healthcare/Aerospace/Manufacturing) industry ☐ ☐ ☐ ☐
RFID technology has proven to be effective at my workplace ☐ ☐ ☐ ☐
RFID technology has had no problems with implementation/maintenance ☐ ☐ ☐ ☐

Current and/or Past RFID Usage / Primary Uses of RFID Technology

For the following questions, please check the appropriate response concerning the previous/current usage of RFID technology. Please note that the questions should be answered on a 1-4 scale.

Strongly Disagree Agree Strongly Disagree Agree

1. My business/company has previously/currently implemented RFID technology ☐ ☐ ☐ ☐
2. My business/company has plans to implement/expand RFID technology in some form ☐ ☐ ☐ ☐
3. My business/company is, in my opinion, overall happy with RFID technology ☐ ☐ ☐ ☐
4. My business/company uses RFID primarily for purposes ☐ ☐ ☐ ☐
5. My business/company uses RFID primarily for security purposes ☐ ☐ ☐ ☐
6. My business/company uses RFID for logistics purposes ☐ ☐ ☐ ☐
7. My business/company uses RFID for Supply Chain Management (SCM) purposes ☐ ☐ ☐ ☐
8. My business/company has partner(s) that use RFID technology ☐ ☐ ☐ ☐

Ease of Use of RFID Technology

For the following questions, please check the appropriate response concerning the ease of use of RFID technology. Please note that the questions should be answered on a 1-4 scale.
    Strongly Disagree Agree Strongly Disagree Agree

1. RFID technology was easy to purchase/implement ☐ ☐ ☐ ☐
2. RFID technology has, generally, worked without error ☐ ☐ ☐ ☐
3. My business/company has continued to commit to RFID usage ☐ ☐ ☐ ☐
4. In general, RFID works as intended for your business's specific need ☐ ☐ ☐ ☐
5. RFID technology is easy to update and expand ☐ ☐ ☐ ☐
6. RFID technology is, generally, well received among all involved supply partners ☐ ☐ ☐ ☐
    My business/company hired/contracted a third party for RFID implementation ☐ ☐ ☐ ☐
        1. My business/company hired/contracted a third party for RFID technology maintenance/troubleshooting ☐ ☐ ☐ ☐

Future Development/Implementation of RFID

For the following questions, please check the appropriate response concerning the future of RFID technology at your business/company. Please note that the questions should be answered on a 1-4 scale.
    Strongly Disagree Agree Strongly Disagree Agree

1. My business/company has plans to expand their RFID technology ☐ ☐ ☐ ☐
2. My business/company has plans to implement new RFID technologies ☐ ☐ ☐ ☐
3. My business/company has expressed interest in keeping their current RFID technology ☐ ☐ ☐ ☐
4. My business/company has expressed interest in stopping/removing any existing RFID technology ☐ ☐ ☐ ☐
5. My business/company's supply partners have expressed interest in RFID technology ☐ ☐ ☐ ☐
6. My business/company's supply partners have expressed disdain with RFID technology ☐ ☐ ☐ ☐

Final Questions*

For the following questions, please check the appropriate response concerning your personal opinions on RFID technology. Please note that the questions should be answered on a 1-4 scale.
    *These answers represent only the individual filling out the survey and do not reflect the feelings of any other entities.
    Strongly Disagree Agree Strongly Disagree Agree

1. I like Radio Frequency Identification Technology (RFID) ☐ ☐ ☐ ☐
2. RFID has made supply chain management easier overall ☐ ☐ ☐ ☐
3. RFID technology was implemented properly and works well ☐ ☐ ☐ ☐

Demographic Information

For the following questions, please check the appropriate response:

1. Please state your gender:
   - Male ☐ Female
2. Please state your age group:
   - 18-24
   - 25-34
   - 35-44
   - 45+
3. Please state your level of education:
   - No education
   - High School or equivalent
   - Associate Degree or some college
   - Bachelors' Degree
   - Masters' Degree
   - Doctorate Degree
4. Please state your professional industry:
   - Retail Services
   - Financial Services
   - Healthcare Services
   - Manufacturing/Production
   - Aerospace
   - Computer Information Systems (IT)
   - Other: _____
5. Please state your years of professional experience in your sector (years):
   - 1-3 ☐ 4-6 ☐ 7-10 ☐ 11-15 ☐ 16-25 ☐ 25+

Environmental Friendliness in Low Carbon Supply Chain and Operations

14

Muhammad Shabir Shaharudin
https://orcid.org/0000-0002-3453-7813
Universiti Malaysia Pahang, Malaysia

Yudi Fernando
https://orcid.org/0000-0003-0907-886X
Universiti Malaysia Pahang, Malaysia

INTRODUCTION

Increasing environmental concerns has compelled manufacturing firms to reconsider their operation strategy. Rethinking of manufacturing firm's operations to meet customer requirements and to achieve performance in operations, economy, social and environment are necessary (Fernando, Jasmi, & Shaharudin, 2019). Nowadays, environmental issue such as climate change due to carbon emissions from manufacturing industry has become a popular topic among firms, customers and society. Evolution of shifting customer requirements from cost reduction to include more product features to product that not harmful to the environment have demand firms to change its operation management. For instance, manufacturing firms have evolved from mass production to mass customization and now towards energy management and environmental principle (Fernando, Shaharudin, Ismail, Yew, & Ganesan, 2018; Fernando, Shaharudin, Haron, Karim, & Ganesan, 2018). These shifting in strategies have seen manufacturing firms practicing just-in-time (JIT) strategy, total quality management (TQM), flexible manufacturing system (FMS), agile manufacturing (AM) strategy, lean production (LP) and supply chain management (SCM) (Gunasekaran & Ngai, 2012). These strategies are practiced by firms to achieve performances such as economic (Schandl et al., 2016), social (Beitzen-Heineke, Balta-Ozkan, & Reefke, 2017), operations (Mirkouei, Mirzaie, Haapala, Sessions, & Murthy, 2016) and environment (Nouira, Frein, & Hadj-Alouane, 2014).

Nowadays, manufacturing firms are expected to reduce environmental impacts in its supply chain and operations (Willersinn, Möbius, Mouron, Lansche, & Mack, 2017). The importance of reducing environmental impacts and threats has been studied across manufacturing sectors such as in food sector (Camanzi, Alikadic, Compagnoni, & Merloni, 2017), medical sector (Unger & Landis, 2016), automotive sector (Bechtsis, Tsolakis, Vlachos, & Iakovou, 2017), aerospace sector (Ruiz-Benitez, López, & Real, 2018), furniture sector (Fernando, Shaharudin, & Wahid, 2016) and energy sector (Fernando & Hor, 2017). These sectors need to address environmental issues especially in regard to carbon emission. Increasing carbon emission from manufacturing firms' supply chain and operations activities are highlighted as critical issue that need attention from every stakeholder (Shaharudin & Fernando, 2015). Thus, manufacturing firms need to adopt environmental friendliness criteria to appease its stakeholders. Environmental friendliness criteria can be defined as firm's operations that will not harm the environment through energy efficient and clean energy (Gunasekaran & Ngai, 2012).

DOI: 10.4018/978-1-7998-3473-1.ch167

Nevertheless, literature on environmental management are divisive for supply chain cluster and operations cluster. Most articles in the literature recognized that green supply chain management (GSCM) (Kamal & Fernando, 2015), low carbon supply chain management (LCSCM) (Shaharudin & Fernando, 2017) and sustainable supply chain management (SSCM) (Balaman, Matopoulos, Wright, & Scott, 2017) have acknowledged the importance of environmental friendliness criteria. Yet, operations cluster has fallen behind in recognizing environmental friendliness criteria (Shaharudin, Fernando, Jabbour, Sroufe, & Jasmi, 2019). While Gunasekaran and Ngai (2012) introduced the concept in operations and Balfaqih, Nopiah, Saibani and Al-Nory (2016) highlighted of its importance, an investigation on environmental friendliness criteria is still limited. Furthermore, an in-depth walkthrough of this criteria such as its definition, features and previous studies discussion should be undertaken by scholars.

Since low carbon operations has been sought after by customers (Böttcher & Müller, 2015), manufacturing firms need to ensure it can meet the customer environmental requirements (Fernando, Wah, & Shaharudin, 2016). Environmental friendliness criteria are based on customer requirement for low carbon operations where it is emphasis on energy and green criteria. The reason for environmental friendliness is critical for manufacturing operations because energy is one of the highest contributor to environmental degradation and pollution (Chang, Hu, & Jan, 2016). As recorded, 49 percent of the carbon emissions come from energy and heat production (World Bank, 2014). Furthermore, firms that failed to record its energy use or adopt energy efficient technology will lag behind firms that have energy management practice in reducing carbon emissions and realising environmental friendliness (Fernando & Hor, 2017). A recent life cycle analysis study in China manufacturing industry has found that 37 percent of carbon emissions come from heating process of energy generation (Ma, Du, Zhang, Wang, & Xie, 2017). These statistical numbers show that energy efficient and low energy consumption have greater impact on operations of firms to reduce carbon emissions. Therefore, manufacturing firms should adopt environmental friendliness principles and energy efficient criteria in its operations.

As environmental friendliness is operations performance measure, this study is bound to generate interest for low carbon operations criteria and contributing to the literature. The insight of this study will prompt future studies in developing environmental friendliness, distinguishing environmental friendliness criteria with other performance measure and addressing literature gaps in regard to understanding the concept of environmental friendliness criteria. Thus, research questions for this study:

1. What is the current knowledge of environmental friendliness from the perspective of supply chain and operations?
2. What is environmental friendliness performance indicator?

BACKGROUND

Environmental Friendliness can be defined as operational performance without harming the environment using less energy consumption, clean energy, has green value and use life cycle assessment to support environmental friendliness principles. This definition is established through understanding several underlying concepts of environmental friendliness by scholars as shown in Table 1.

Features of environmental friendliness for operations in manufacturing industry are shown in Table 2. In regard to environmental friendliness, there are several main features that manufacturing firms can consider. Green value, which consist of recycling, green image, green product features and green materials are critical environmental friendliness features. These features are widely practiced and implemented by

Table 1. Definition of environmental friendliness

Author	Sector	Definition
(Gunasekaran & Ngai, 2012)	Manufacturing	Better performance with no harm to the environment through energy efficient and low energy consumption.
(Ribeiro et al., 2016)	Manufacturing	A method and strategy to reduce environmental impacts incorporated in product.
(Su et al., 2016)	Manufacturing	Communicating, encouraging or promoting environmentally friendly concern to stakeholders.
(Goossens et al., 2017)	Manufacturing	Refers to label of environmental management practice.
(Kushwaha & Sharma, 2016)	Manufacturing	A symbol of green image which includes recycling, eco-friendly, green features of product.
(Carter & Carter, 1998)	Manufacturing	Features of green product.
(Garg, Kannan, Diabat, & Jha, 2015)	Manufacturing	Low greenhouse gasses and less fuel consumption.
(Zailani, Jeyaraman, Vengadasan, & Premkumar, 2012)	Manufacturing	Green features of a product and packaging of product.
(Madu, Kuei, & Madu, 2002)	Manufacturing	Product life cycle with green consideration of a product.

manufacturing firms. In addition, life cycle analysis has been used by scholars and firms to assess product or process. The analysis aids scholars and firms to categorize and analyse green criteria of a product or process. Thus, life cycle analysis should be incorporate in environmental friendliness performance measure as it has proven to be important for reducing environmental impacts (Feitó-Cespón, Sarache, Piedra-Jimenez, & Cespón-Castro, 2017; Goossens et al., 2017; Low, Tjandra, Lu, & Lee, 2016; Palmieri, Forleo, & Salimei, 2017; Prosman & Sacchi, 2017; Rodrigues et al., 2016; Tasca, Nessi, & Rigamonti, 2017; Unger & Landis, 2016; Vasilaki, Katsou, Ponsá, & Colón, 2016; Xing, Qian, & Zaman, 2016). Since energy efficient and energy consumption have greater impacts on the environment, both performance indicators are recommended by scholars for environmental friendliness criteria (Gunasekaran & Ngai, 2012). There are other performance indicators that can be included in this criterion, however these four indicators are found to be relevant in supply chain and operations studies.

Previous studies in regard to environmental friendliness in operations management and supply chain have pointed that environmental criterion is critical for operational performance success. As shown in Table 3, several scholars have underlined the importance of environmental friendliness in manufacturing industry. Moreover, cost reduction that has been one of the main operational performance indicators is still relevant to the industry (Balfaqih et al., 2016; Beamon, 1999). Therefore, operations management and supply chain scholars have tried to relate cost reduction with environmental friendliness so that firms will be able to achieve both objectives (Shanmugan, Shaharudin, Ganesan, & Fernando, 2019). A study by Zhu, Sarkis, and Lai (2013) has found that firms that achieve environmental and operational performance will be able to realise economic benefits. In that sense, firms achieving environmental friendliness in its operations will be able to achieve higher economic and environmental performance. This is the reason why environmental friendliness is critical for operations and for firms to achieve low carbon emissions.

Table 2. Criteria of environmental friendliness

Author	Energy Consumption	Energy Efficiency	Life Cycle Analysis	Eco-Labelling	Green Value	Nanomaterials	Clean Energy Fuel	Green Design	Green Process	Green Package
(Gunasekaran & Ngai, 2012)	✓	✓				✓	✓			
(Ribeiro et al., 2016)					✓			✓	✓	
(Su et al., 2016)					✓					
(Laroche et al., 2001)					✓					
(Goossens et al., 2017)			✓		✓					
(Kushwaha & Sharma, 2016)			✓	✓	✓			✓		✓
(Carter & Carter, 1998)			✓					✓		✓
(Garg et al., 2015)	✓	✓							✓	
(Madu et al., 2002)			✓		✓					

Methods

This study investigates environmental friendliness criterion for operational performance in manufacturing industry to achieve low carbon operations. This is due to the environmental friendliness concept has not been widely discussed in the literature even through environmental management literature from supply chain and operations discipline is rich with environmental management concepts. Therefore, this study

Table 3. Previous studies on environmental friendliness

Author	Methodology	Investigation	Findings
(Gunasekaran & Ngai, 2012)	Conceptual	Future performance objectives for operations	Responsiveness, flexibility, dependability, quality, price, safety and environmental friendliness
(Ribeiro et al., 2016)	Case study	Sustainable manufacturing technologies	Environmental friendliness and cost
(Su et al., 2016)	Simulation	Improving sustainable supply chain	Environmental friendliness, cost and responsiveness
(Laroche et al., 2001)	Quantitative	Municipals study on consumer environmental willingness	Environmental friendliness and safety
(Goossens et al., 2017)	Quantitative	Eco-labels of supply chain	Environmental friendliness
(Kushwaha & Sharma, 2016)	Quantitative	Green initiatives for firm's performance	Environmental friendliness, cost and delivery
(Carter & Carter, 1998)	Quantitative	Determinants of environmental purchasing	Environmental friendliness, flexibility and quality
(Garg et al., 2015)	Case study	Optimization of closed loop supply chain	Environmental friendliness and cost
(Zailani et al., 2012)	Quantitative	Sustainable supply chain	Environmental friendliness
(Madu et al., 2002)	Experimental design	Integration of green issues in manufacturing	Cost and environmental friendliness

Figure 1. Content analysis process
Source: *(Shaharudin & Fernando, 2017)*

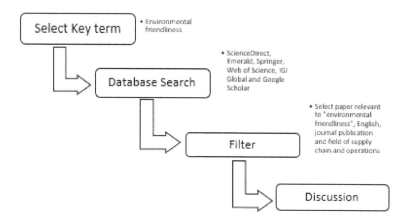

has undertaken a review of previous studies in regard to environmental friendliness. The purpose of the investigation is to understand current knowledge of environmental criterion in operations of manufacturing industry and develop a certain performance indicator for environmental friendliness in support of low carbon operations.

In order to perform the investigation, this study followed content analysis method as proposed by Shaharudin and Fernando (2017). To do that, the keyword used for this study is environmental friendliness as this is related to the objectives of this study. Next, the publishers for data collection used for this study are ScienceDirect, Emerald and Springer. In addition, this study also extracts journal articles and review articles from reputable databases such as Web of Science, IGI Global and Google Scholar. The reason for combining publishers and databases for data collection is because even though there will be a duplicate in search, the coverage of articles extraction will be more wide and complete. After data collection through database search, this study then applies filters such as selecting relevant articles in regard to environmental friendliness, considering only research article and review article, selecting only English language article and removing duplicates. This study only interested in the findings for current published journal articles in regard to environmental friendliness and developing performance measure indicators for environmental friendliness. Thus, only articles in the field of supply chain and operations were selected. After completion of selection of key term, database search and filter, this study proceeds with discussion to answer the research questions on environmental friendliness.

FUTURE RESEARCH DIRECTIONS

Current knowledge for environmental friendliness based on content analysis shows that there is limited number of articles discussing greening of operations in manufacturing industry. In the literature, green value that take into consideration of green design, green process, green packaging and eco-labelling are regards as performance indicator for environmental friendliness. Yet, every manufacturing firm might have different performance indicator for environmental friendliness. Therefore, scholars should develop a model or specific criterion for performance measure in regard to environment so that firms can assess its manufacturing or supply chain performance. In addition, standardise performance indicator is able to help scholar and firms to benchmark operational performance with other firms in the industry.

Early study by Gunasekaran and Ngai (2012) has suggested several operational performance indicators that is critical for firms to sustain its operations. The criteria of performance measure include responsiveness, flexibility, dependability, quality, price, safety and environmental friendliness. There are some articles in the literature that suggested the importance of responsiveness, flexibility and cost reduction. Therefore, future studies should look into developing model that combine critical operational performance indicators with environmental friendliness. This is because environmental friendliness is not only for achieving environmental performance such as low carbon operations but also economic performance (Zhu et al., 2013).

Environmental friendliness indicator to realise operational excellence and low carbon operations should incorporate green value, life cycle analysis, environmental friendliness principle, energy efficiency and low energy consumption. These indicators are found to be widely discussed in the literature of supply chain and operational studies. Furthermore, with climate change becoming an important issue need to be addressed, manufacturing firms should not neglect energy efficiency and substituting towards low energy consumption. In addition, green value that is part of green features in product starting from design, process and packaging should also become part of environmental friendliness indicator. Other than that, life cycle analysis is critical for supply chain and operations management to assess product, process and achieving environmental objectives. Therefore, life cycle analysis and environmental friendliness principles should be incorporated as well. Environmental friendliness principles include other green practice that is appropriate for the manufacturing industry.

Through standardisation of environmental friendliness indicators, manufacturing firms are able to evaluate its operational performance and able to achieve better environmental objective. Future studies should test the relevancy of environmental friendliness with empirical findings and strengthening the principles of environmental friendliness.

CONCLUSION

Generally, environmental management studies are aplenty in supply chain and operations management literature. Nevertheless, operations management field is lacking in producing copious studies in regard to current environmental management. In operations management cluster, green features are considered as important while lacking in current issues such as low carbon emission, energy management, energy consumption and issues related to safety and security. This study proposed operational indicators of environmental friendliness to help firms to assess its operational performance in meeting environmental objectives such as low carbon operations. Furthermore, this study also develops an interest in management scholars to strengthening the understanding of environmental friendliness. Future studies should delve more on this topic especially on defining the principle of environmental friendliness and testing the relevancy of its indicators with empirical data.

REFERENCES

Balaman, Ş. Y., Matopoulos, A., Wright, D. G., & Scott, J. (2017). Integrated optimization of sustainable supply chains and transportation networks for multi technology bio-based production: A decision support system based on fuzzy ε-constraint method. *Journal of Cleaner Production*. Advance online publication. doi:10.1016/j.jclepro.2017.11.150

Balfaqih, H., Nopiah, Z. M., Saibani, N., & Al-Nory, M. T. (2016). Review of supply chain performance measurement systems: 1998-2015. *Computers in Industry*, *82*, 135–150. doi:10.1016/j.compind.2016.07.002

Beamon, B. M. (1999). Measuring Supply Chain Performance. *Industrial Engineering*.

Bechtsis, D., Tsolakis, N., Vlachos, D., & Iakovou, E. (2017). Sustainable supply chain management in the digitalisation era: The impact of Automated Guided Vehicles. *Journal of Cleaner Production*, *142*, 3970–3984. doi:10.1016/j.jclepro.2016.10.057

Beitzen-Heineke, E. F., Balta-Ozkan, N., & Reefke, H. (2017). The prospects of zero-packaging grocery stores to improve the social and environmental impacts of the food supply chain. *Journal of Cleaner Production*, *140*, 1528–1541. doi:10.1016/j.jclepro.2016.09.227

Böttcher, C. F., & Müller, M. (2015). Drivers, Practices and Outcomes of Low-carbon Operations: Approaches of German Automotive Suppliers to Cutting Carbon Emissions. *Business Strategy and the Environment*, *24*(6), 477–498. doi:10.1002/bse.1832

Camanzi, L., Alikadic, A., Compagnoni, L., & Merloni, E. (2017). The impact of greenhouse gas emissions in the EU food chain: A quantitative and economic assessment using an environmentally extended input-output approach. *Journal of Cleaner Production*, *157*, 168–176. doi:10.1016/j.jclepro.2017.04.118

Carter, C. R., & Carter, J. R. (1998). Interorganizational Determinants of Environmental Purchasing: Initial Evidence from the Consumer Products Industries. *Decision Sciences*, *29*(3), 659–684. doi:10.1111/j.1540-5915.1998.tb01358.x

Chang, M.-C., Hu, J.-L., & Jan, F.-G. (2016). Performance estimation of energy consumption and carbon dioxide emissions for sustainable development in Baltic Sea countries. *Journal of Cleaner Production*, *139*, 1370–1382. doi:10.1016/j.jclepro.2016.09.006

Feitó-Cespón, M., Sarache, W., Piedra-Jimenez, F., & Cespón-Castro, R. (2017). Redesign of a sustainable reverse supply chain under uncertaintyA case study. *Journal of Cleaner Production*, *151*, 206–217. doi:10.1016/j.jclepro.2017.03.057

Fernando, Y., Shaharudin, M. S., Ismail, I., Yew, S. Q., & Ganesan, Y. (2018). A Mediating Model of Resource Commitment, Reverse Logistics and Financial Performance: Importance-Performance Map Analysis. *8th International Borneo Business Conference*, 20–30.

Fernando, Y., Shaharudin, M. S., Haron, H., Karim, N. A., & Ganesan, Y. (2018). A Moderating Impact of ISO 14001 Certified Firms on Reverse Logistics Implementation: Analysis of A Second-Order Model. *8th International Borneo Business Conference*, 31–43.

Fernando, Y., & Hor, W. L. (2017). Impacts of energy management practices on energy efficiency and carbon emissions reduction: A survey of malaysian manufacturing firms. *Resources, Conservation and Recycling*, *126*, 62–73. doi:10.1016/j.resconrec.2017.07.023

Fernando, Y., Jasmi, M. F. A., & Shaharudin, M. S. (2019). Maritime green supply chain management: Its light and shadow on the bottom line dimensions of sustainable business performance. *International Journal of Shipping and Transport Logistics*, *11*(1), 60–93. doi:10.1504/IJSTL.2019.096872

Fernando, Y., Shaharudin, M. S., & Wahid, N. A. (2016). Eco-innovation practices: A case study of green furniture manufacturers in Indonesia. *International Journal of Services and Operations Management*, *23*(1), 43–58. doi:10.1504/IJSOM.2016.073289

Fernando, Y., Wah, W. X., & Shaharudin, M. S. (2016). Does a firm's innovation category matter in practising eco-innovation? Evidence from the lens of Malaysia companies practicing green technology. *Journal of Manufacturing Technology Management*, *27*(2), 208–233. doi:10.1108/JMTM-02-2015-0008

Garg, K., Kannan, D., Diabat, A., & Jha, P. C. (2015). A multi-criteria optimization approach to manage environmental issues in closed loop supply chain network design. *Journal of Cleaner Production*, *100*, 297–314. doi:10.1016/j.jclepro.2015.02.075

Goossens, Y., Berrens, P., Charleer, L., Coremans, P., Houbrechts, M., Vervaet, C., De Tavernier, J., & Geeraerd, A. (2017). Qualitative assessment of eco-labels on fresh produce in Flanders (Belgium) highlights a potential intention–performance gap for the supply chain. *Journal of Cleaner Production*, *140*, 986–995. doi:10.1016/j.jclepro.2016.05.063

Gunasekaran, A., & Ngai, E. W. T. (2012). The future of operations management: An outlook and analysis. *International Journal of Production Economics*, *135*, 687–701.

Kamal, A. N., & Fernando, Y. (2015). Review of supply chain integration on green supply chain management (GSCM). Promoting Sustainable Practices through Energy Engineering and Asset Management, 348–368.

Kushwaha, G. S., & Sharma, N. K. (2016). Green initiatives: A step towards sustainable development and firm's performance in the automobile industry. *Journal of Cleaner Production*, *121*, 116–129. doi:10.1016/j.jclepro.2015.07.072

Laroche, M., Bergeron, J., Barbaro-Forleo, G., Laroche, M., Bergeron, J., & Barbaro-Forleo, G. (2001). Targeting consumers who are willing to pay more for environmentally friendly products. *Journal of Consumer Marketing*, *18*(6), 503–520. doi:10.1108/EUM0000000006155

Low, J. S. C., Tjandra, T. B., Lu, W. F., & Lee, H. M. (2016). Adaptation of the Product Structure-based Integrated Life cycle Analysis (PSILA) technique for carbon footprint modelling and analysis of closed-loop production systems. *Journal of Cleaner Production*, *120*, 105–123. doi:10.1016/j.jclepro.2015.09.095

Ma, J. J., Du, G., Zhang, Z. K., Wang, P. X., & Xie, B. C. (2017). Life cycle analysis of energy consumption and CO_2 emissions from a typical large office building in Tianjin, China. *Building and Environment*, *117*, 36–48. doi:10.1016/j.buildenv.2017.03.005

Madu, C. N., Kuei, C., & Madu, I. E. (2002). A hierarchic metric approach for integration of green issues in manufacturing : A paper recycling application. *Journal of Environmental Management*, *64*(3), 261–272. doi:10.1006/jema.2001.0498 PMID:12040959

Mirkouei, A., Mirzaie, P., Haapala, K. R., Sessions, J., & Murthy, G. S. (2016). Reducing the cost and environmental impact of integrated fixed and mobile bio-oil refinery supply chains. *Journal of Cleaner Production, 113*, 495–507. doi:10.1016/j.jclepro.2015.11.023

Nouira, I., Frein, Y., & Hadj-Alouane, A. B. (2014). Optimization of manufacturing systems under environmental considerations for a greenness-dependent demand. *International Journal of Production Economics, 150*, 188–198. doi:10.1016/j.ijpe.2013.12.024

Palmieri, N., Forleo, M. B., & Salimei, E. (2017). Environmental impacts of a dairy cheese chain including whey feeding: An Italian case study. *Journal of Cleaner Production, 140*, 881–889. doi:10.1016/j.jclepro.2016.06.185

Prosman, E. J., & Sacchi, R. (2017). New environmental supplier selection criteria for circular supply chains: Lessons from a consequential LCA study on waste recovery. *Journal of Cleaner Production*. Advance online publication. doi:10.1016/j.jclepro.2017.11.134

Ribeiro, I., Kaufmann, J., Schmidt, A., Peças, P., Henriques, E., & Götze, U. (2016). Fostering selection of sustainable manufacturing technologies - A case study involving product design, supply chain and life cycle performance. *Journal of Cleaner Production, 112*, 3306–3319. doi:10.1016/j.jclepro.2015.10.043

Rodrigues, J., Houzelot, V., Ferrari, F., Echevarria, G., Laubie, B., Morel, J. L., Simonnot, M.-O., & Pons, M. N. (2016). Life cycle assessment of agromining chain highlights role of erosion control and bioenergy. *Journal of Cleaner Production, 139*, 770–778. doi:10.1016/j.jclepro.2016.08.110

Ruiz-Benitez, R., López, C., & Real, J. C. (2018). Environmental benefits of lean, green and resilient supply chain management: The case of the aerospace sector. *Journal of Cleaner Production, 167*, 850–862. doi:10.1016/j.jclepro.2017.07.201

Schandl, H., Hatfield-Dodds, S., Wiedmann, T., Geschke, A., Cai, Y., West, J., Newth, D., Baynes, T., Lenzen, M., & Owen, A. (2016). Decoupling global environmental pressure and economic growth: Scenarios for energy use, materials use and carbon emissions. *Journal of Cleaner Production, 132*, 45–56. doi:10.1016/j.jclepro.2015.06.100

Shaharudin, M. S., Fernando, Y., Jabbour, C. J. C., Sroufe, R., & Jasmi, M. F. (2019). Past, Present, and Future Low Carbon Supply Chain Management: A Content Review Using Social Network Analysis. *Journal of Cleaner Production*. Advance online publication. doi:10.1016/j.jclepro.2019.02.016

Shaharudin, M.S., & Fernando, Y. (2015). Low Carbon Footprint: The Supply Chain Agenda in Malaysian Manufacturing Firms. *Promoting Sustainable Practices through Energy Engineering and Asset Management*, 324–347.

Shaharudin, M. S., & Fernando, Y. (2017). Measuring Low Carbon Supply Chain. In M. Khosrow-Pour (Ed.), *Measuring Low Carbon Supply Chain*. IGI Global.

Shanmugan, M., Shabir Shaharudin, M., Ganesan, Y., & Fernando, Y. (2019). Manufacturing Outsourcing to Achieve Organizational Performance through Manufacturing Integrity Capabilities. *KnE Social Sciences, 2019*, 858–871. doi:10.18502/kss.v3i22.5092

Su, C.-M., Horng, D.-J., Tseng, M.-L., Chiu, A. S. F., Wu, K.-J., & Chen, H.-P. (2016). Improving sustainable supply chain management using a novel hierarchical grey-DEMATEL approach. *Journal of Cleaner Production, 134*, 469–481. doi:10.1016/j.jclepro.2015.05.080

Tasca, A. L., Nessi, S., & Rigamonti, L. (2017). Environmental sustainability of agri-food supply chains: An LCA comparison between two alternative forms of production and distribution of endive in northern Italy. *Journal of Cleaner Production, 140*, 725–741. doi:10.1016/j.jclepro.2016.06.170

Unger, S., & Landis, A. (2016). Assessing the environmental, human health, and economic impacts of reprocessed medical devices in a Phoenix hospital's supply chain. *Journal of Cleaner Production, 112*, 1995–2003. doi:10.1016/j.jclepro.2015.07.144

Vasilaki, V., Katsou, E., Ponsá, S., & Colón, J. (2016). Water and carbon footprint of selected dairy products: A case study in Catalonia. *Journal of Cleaner Production, 139*, 504–516. doi:10.1016/j.jclepro.2016.08.032

Willersinn, C., Möbius, S., Mouron, P., Lansche, J., & Mack, G. (2017). Environmental impacts of food losses along the entire Swiss potato supply chain – Current situation and reduction potentials. *Journal of Cleaner Production, 140*, 860–870. doi:10.1016/j.jclepro.2016.06.178

World Bank. (2014). *CO2 emissions from electricity and heat production, total (% of total fuel combustion).* Retrieved from IEA Statistics website: https://data.worldbank.org/indicator/EN.CO2.ETOT.ZS?end=2014&start=1960&view=chart

Xing, K., Qian, W., & Zaman, A. U. (2016). Development of a cloud-based platform for footprint assessment in green supply chain management. *Journal of Cleaner Production, 139*, 191–203. doi:10.1016/j.jclepro.2016.08.042

Zailani, S., Jeyaraman, K., Vengadasan, G., & Premkumar, R. (2012). Sustainable supply chain management (SSCM) in Malaysia : A survey. *International Journal of Production Economics, 140*(1), 330–340. doi:10.1016/j.ijpe.2012.02.008

Zhu, Q., Sarkis, J., & Lai, K. (2013). Institutional-based antecedents and performance outcomes of internal and external green supply chain management practices. *Journal of Purchasing and Supply Management, 19*(2), 106–117. doi:10.1016/j.pursup.2012.12.001

KEY TERMS AND DEFINITIONS

Environmental Friendliness: Defined as operational performance without harming the environment using less energy consumption, clean energy, has green value and use life cycle assessment to support environmental friendliness principles.

Environmental Management: Firm's management practices reducing environmental degradation.

Low Carbon Performance: Performance of firm in reducing carbon emissions through reducing per output carbon emission, substitute or minimization of carbon-intensive materials and reduction of energy use.

Manufacturing Performance: Performance of manufacturing or operations through cost reduction and efficiency of operations such as flexible production, responsive to customer demand and quality improvements.

Supply Chain Management: Firm's management of product or service, information and financial flow throughout the process of supply chain starting from procurement, product design, production process, distribution channel and network and logistics.

A Review of Future Energy Efficiency Measures and CO2 Emission Reduction in Maritime Supply Chain

14

Muhamad Fairuz Ahmad Jasmi

https://orcid.org/0000-0003-0171-2125

Faculty of Business and Management, Universiti Teknologi MARA (UiTM), Puncak Alam, Malaysia

Yudi Fernando

https://orcid.org/0000-0003-0907-886X

Faculty of Industrial Management, Universiti Malaysia Pahang, Malaysia

INTRODUCTION

As the world's largest industry, the maritime supply chain sector is a significant contributor to global CO2 emissions. Based on the recent report (see Figure 1) by the International Maritime Organization (IMO), the maritime supply chain sector currently accounts for approximately 3% of global CO2 emissions, projected to double or triple by 2050 (Buhaug et al., 2009). Conversely, it is also projected that 25-70 per cent of CO_2 emission can also be lessened with appropriate strategies through better energy efficiency practice, adoption green technologies and improved logistics system (Johnson & Styhre, 2015). However, the implementation of all current cost-efficient technologies aiming at reducing fuel consumption and curbing emissions have proved to be inadequate to counteract the effects of rapid growth of maritime supply chain sector (Eide, Longva, Hoffmann, Endresen, & Dalsøren, 2011).

Due to this concern, numerous studies have been taken in the field of substitute power sources and energy-saving measures for shipping operation to reduce CO_2 emission. Nevertheless, the gaps remain between existing knowledge and the execution of energy efficiency measures by maritime supply chain organizations (Styhre & Winnes, 2013). As in other numerous sectors, several measures that would improve fuel efficiency and CO_2 emission in the maritime supply chain have yet to be implemented despite their known cost efficiency. This situation is known as energy efficiency gap in the literature. This situation is generally occurred due to lack of understanding/awareness, low capital, weak policies and slow technology adoption. While Sorell, Mally, Schleich and Scott (2004) underpin this problem through recognition of organizational barriers such as organizational risk, asymmetrical of information, hidden costs, higher capital, split incentives and bounded rationality.

From the legislator viewpoint, these problems call for proactive policy intervention in this sector. IMO as a sole global legislator has been implementing a few chapters in its MARPOL Annex VI in achieving a comprehensive goal to reduce GHG emission in shipping operation (Kader, 2013). Current IMO declarations such as Energy Efficiency Design Index (EEDI), Ship Energy Efficient Management Plan (SEEMP) and Energy Efficiency Operational Indicator (EEOI) are to collect data on energy consumption and emission so that reliable measures can be implemented. IMO also is in the ongoing discussion on the possible implementation of sector-specific market-based measures (MBM) to further curb specific CO2 reduction within this sector (Hannes Johnson & Andersson, 2016). This annex will

DOI: 10.4018/978-1-7998-3473-1.ch168

Figure 1. CO$_2$ emission projection for maritime transportations
Source: International Maritime Organization (IMO)

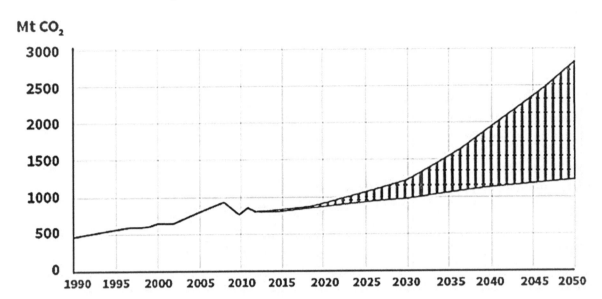

eventually become a blueprint for many maritime organizations to abide as it is obligatory to follow suit these regulations in order to fulfil the global requirement for trade in the future. However, as the volume of trade is predicted to rise over the year, total reductions in fuel consumption and CO2 emissions from the sector are not expected to lower despite these new regulations (Anderson & Bows, 2012).

Currently, it is more important to focus on what prevents energy efficiency and emission improvements within the maritime organization and what can be done to overcome the current barriers. Overcoming energy efficiency gaps should be a priority since direct fuel costs are expected to rise in the future. The role of energy efficiency should be considered as a critical success factor for any maritime organization to be profitable and to achieve long-term sustainability. Thus addressing this need, this paper provides an overview of measures that can be considered for future energy efficiency and emission reduction in the maritime supply chain. In addition, the current stage of adoption, barriers, overcoming the barriers and potential research direction is discussed through the remaining of the paper.

BACKGROUND

The Future Potential of Energy Efficiency Measure and CO$_2$ Emission Reduction

The energy in maritime supply chain can be defined as a source of power necessary to carry out logistics and transportation activities. While maritime transport can be powered by various sources of energy (e.g. fossil fuels, biofuels, nuclear electricity, or alternative energy), fossil fuels are still the most common form of energy source used in this sector (M. F. A. Jasmi & Fernando, 2018). However, as the scarcity of fossil fuels and concern on climate change increased, there is an urgent need for proper technical and managerial measures within maritime supply chain sector. Additionally, as maritime supply chain is an energy-intensive sector, energy costs contribute a large share of total operating costs. This is a substantial

Figure 2. Emissions NOx and SOx from the year 1990–2030 (projected number) from land-based sources and international shipping
Source: Komar and Lalić (2015)

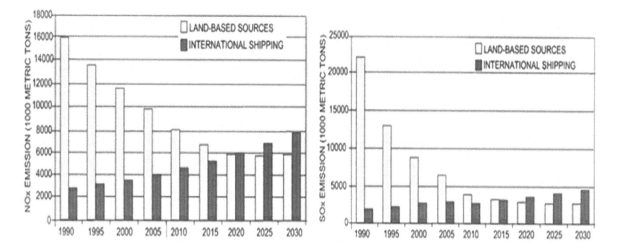

ratio by nature since other industries only constitute around 5% to 20% of energy cost (Thollander & Ottosson, 2010). Even though this sector is considered most efficient mode of commercial transportation compare to other modes of transportation (such as air freight or land trucking), the efficiency of shipping as opposed to land-based transportation has been lately questioned, with respect to nitrogen oxide (NOx) and sulphur oxide (SOx) emissions per transportation work (see Figure 2) and also when it comes to energy efficiency (Hjelle, 2010). Addressing these problems several measures of energy efficiency measure and CO2 emission reduction in maritime supply chain can be considered in the future consisting of:

Greener Ship Design

IMO estimates that greener ship design measures could potentially reduce CO_2 emissions by 10% to 50% per transport work. The current technical ship design measures related to improvement on hull and propeller geometry, hull construction, propulsion machinery, auxiliary machinery and equipment, heat recovery and cargo handling are intensive to ensure efficient usage of energy consumption in shipping operation (Chang, 2012). Newer hull cleaning system and paint technology to reduce resistance are further explored to enhance the general efficiency of the ships. New technologies such as a hybrid system for propulsion system (Dedes, Hudson, & Turnock, 2012), solar technology (Chambliss, 2015), autopilot upgrade and wind power (Nuttall, Newell, Prasad, Veitayaki, & Holland, 2014) have also been proposed for consideration to be implemented in new ships. From policy standpoint, IMO has also outlined the EEDI for adoption to new and latest ships starting from the year 2013 onwards. EEDI functions as a technical measurement indicator with the major objective of encouraging the utilization of efficient energy and less polluting types of equipment as well as the more environmentally engines in designation and production phase. Additionally, the design of greener engine is also being considered for future consideration of cleaner usage of biofuel and alternative energy (Bengtsson, Fridell, & Andersson, 2012).

Cleaner Fuels

There are few alternative fuels currently in various stages of development for commercial implementation. For example liquefied natural gas (LNG) is a potential candidate to replace fossil oil in the fleet due to lower production of SOx and NOx and abundance in reserve compare to existing fossil fuel. It is currently in the commercialization stage where IMO has forecasted current fossil fuel will be entirely replaced by distillate oils and LNG by 2020. Biofuel such as methane is also considered since it is a renewable energy resource produced from biomaterial waste from the fermentation process. A new option is the development of synthetic diesel, which is produced from natural gas, biogas, coal or biomass by the Fischer-Tropsch method. However since the cost exceeds the benefit it is only an option based on current technology development (Bengtsson et al., 2012). Other alternative fuel suggested is the usage of dimethyl ether (DME) for diesel engine which is cleaner than current diesel fuel (Fridell, Winnes, & Styhre, 2013).

Managerial Measures

Recently, green managerial practices aim at improving operational efficiency has emerged extensively. The concept of green supply chain management (GSCM) (Caniëls, Cleophas, & Semeijn, 2016), green shipping practice (GSP) (Lai, Lun, Wong, & Cheng, 2011), maritime green supply chain management (MGSCM) (Jasmi & Fernando, 2018) and sustainable maritime supply chain (Lam, 2014) have been discussed in maritime literatures to increase efficiency and decrease environmental impact. All of these concepts aim at achieving three bottom lines of sustainability; to improve economy, environment and social dimension. Among suggested managerial criteria proposed in the literature are (the lists are not exhaustive):

i.   Streamlining IT system using the green information system to improve paperless transaction, reduce waiting time and information sharing and streamlining production schedule, inventory and demand forecasting for increase efficiency.

ii. Integrative solution through green integration practice where green collaboration among supply chain partners can be enhanced; through close integration and information sharing related to green practices to streamline the process flow.

iii. Green financial flow where the monetary allocation of green practice can be tracked and allocated accordingly to certain operation measure where efficiency is mostly needed.

iv. Enhancing company policy and procedure to be aligned with external environmental policy through corporate commitment and managerial support

v.   Enhancing shipping equipment and activities that include reuse, recycling and material recovery to comply with environmental compliance.

Onshore Power Supply

In general, the fuel consumed by idle ships at the port is mostly used to produce electricity in order to run general facilities onboard such as ship system, air conditioning and lighting. This activity is not efficient since the ships still consume considerable quantity of fuel in static condition. Using onshore power supply or port electricity might be an alternative solution to reduce emission released from idle ships (Fridell et al., 2013). The technology is relatively new but several port system equipped with this innovation, prove to be feasible. However, practical issues concerning with development cost, expert crew dealing with electrical connection and variation of ship voltage have hampered further development. The cost of low bunker fuel (onboard ship's fuel storage or container) usage which is relatively low to produce electricity onboard makes this innovation currently stagnant for now. Nonetheless, with increasing fuel price versus operation cost in the future might cultivate the development of onshore power supply in the years to come.

Operational Measures

Many operational measures have been suggested in maritime literature. The most common method to achieve energy efficiency is through decrease time in port (Hannes Johnson & Styhre, 2015) and slow steaming practice (Corbett, Wang, & Winebrake, 2009). The relationship between speed and time with fuel consumption per unit time is relatively cubical; for this reason, a speed reduction or consistent speed and less time in port can have a significant impact on fuel consumption which reflects in energy efficiency. Fuel consumption monitoring and weather routing are also common methods which are more cost-effective operational measures to increase energy efficiency (Takashima, Mezaoui, & Shoji, 2009). Another significance measure is to improve port efficiency, which can improve turnaround time in port. Shorter time in port can relatively reduce the speed at sea while maintaining the tight transport service time/schedule. A study by Johnson and Styhre (2013) denote that speed at sea for short sea bulk shipping can be reduced substantially by decreasing idle waiting time (due to port close or early arrival) in port system. The potential for increased energy efficiency through this measure is substantial and can add up to 2%-8% of energy saving.

Policy Measures

Environmental sustainability has appeared on the political agenda for decades. The current inclination towards climate change, conservation and environmental sustainability have been extensively discussed by industry players, stakeholders, as well as worldwide political leaders that helped to shape the required policy and incentive measures. International conventions such as the Kyoto Protocol to the United Nations Framework Convention on Climate Change (UNFCCC) have been established following collaboration between several nations containing provisions for reducing GHG emissions from aviation and shipping operation. Currently, the central agreement of policies and protocols in regards to shipping operation is regulated through involvement from IMO. IMO acts as the major source of more than 60 legal mechanisms that funnel the laws and regulatory development of its member states to develop a comprehensive safety and security dimension at sea as well as facilitate trade among maritime states and keep the marine environment protected. The most critical regulations include the International Convention for the Safety of Life at Sea (SOLAS), International Convention for the Prevention of Pollution from Ships (MARPOL 73/78) as well as International Convention on Oil Pollution Preparedness, Response and Co-operation (OPRC) (the lists are not exhaustive).

In recent years, IMO has shifted its focus to new policy options for increasing fuel efficiency and lowering GHG emissions such as EEDI, SEEMP and EEOI. The EEDI is established to put pressure on ship design to become more energy efficient in the future. According to a study by Organisation for Economic Co-operation and Development (OECD) 2017, full compliance with the EEDI regulation will reduce total CO_2 emissions by approximately 115 million tons from bulkers, tankers and container ships in 2035 compared to a scenario where such regulation does not exist and where there is no endogenous

Figure 3. CO$_2$ emissions with and without EEDI
Source: OECD (2017)

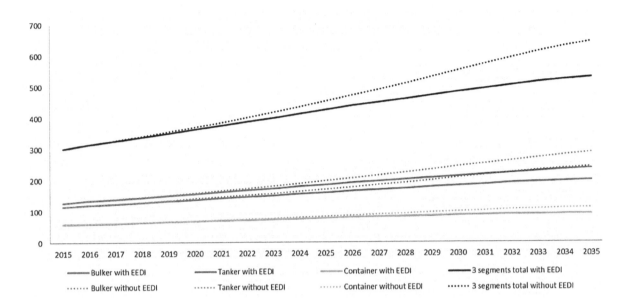

improvement in fuel efficiency (i.e. due to reactions to bunker fuel prices). Given that this reduction represents 38 percent of the 2015 CO$_2$ emissions from bulkers, tankers and container ships, the EEDI regulations have a significant impact on limiting the increase in shipping sector CO$_2$ emissions and energy usage under these assumptions (see Figure 3).

Meanwhile, SEEMP establishment aims at improving operational measures for better energy efficiency and an approach to monitoring the performance of ships and fleets over time and forces responsible persons and entities to consider new technologies and practices in order to optimize ship performance

Table 1. SEEMP related measures

Energy Efficiency Measure	Description
Engine tuning and monitoring	Engine operational performance and condition optimization.
Hull condition	Hull operational fouling and damage avoidance.
Propeller condition	Propeller operational fouling and damage avoidance.
Reduced auxiliary power	Reducing the electrical load via machinery operation and power management.
Speed reduction (operation)	Operational slow steaming.
Trim/draft	Trim and draft monitoring and optimisation.
Voyage execution	Reducing port times, waiting times, etc. and increasing the passage time, just in time arrival
Weather routing	Use of weather routing services to avoid rough seas and head currents, to optimize voyage efficiency.
Advanced hull coating	Re-paint using advanced paints.
Propeller upgrade and aft body flow devices	Propeller and after-body retrofit for optimisation. Also, addition of flow improving devices (e.g. duct and fins).

Source: International Maritime Organization (IMO)

(see Table 1 for SEEMP related measures). The Second IMO GHG Study 2009 shows that a 20 percent reduction on a ton-mile basis is possible due mainly to operational measures and would be cost-effective even with the current fuel prices, and the SEEMP will help the shipping industry to achieve this potential.

Finally, EEOI is an operational indicator tool for assessing the ship energy efficiency and CO_2 emission to the environment. Guidelines for the voluntary use of the EEOI ship have been developed to establish a consistent approach for measuring the energy efficiency of ships on each journey or over a certain period of time to assist shipowners and ship operators in assessing their fleet's operational performance. Since the amount of CO_2 emitted by ships is directly related to bunker fuel oil consumption, EEOI can also provide useful information about the fuel efficiency performance and energy usage of a ship. All of these regulations are expected to be implemented on new ships starting from the year 2013 which increase in stringency every five years up until 2030 onwards to further improve energy efficiency measure and CO_2 emission reduction (Rehmatulla, Calleya, & Smith, 2017).

Current Adoption and Major Barriers

According to Rehmatulla et al. (2017), current adoption in general finds lower levels of implementation for the different categories of energy efficiency measures and CO_2 reducing technologies. They noted that certain energy efficiency measures are relatively average across different type of measures. Some measure such as the use of alternative fuel is noted to be lowest in implementation whereas ship design measure is relatively higher in implementation. This uneven spread of implementation suggests inherent barriers are facing this sector to implement specific energy efficiency measures.

In general, institutional barriers are considered the major inherent barrier in the maritime supply chain. The maritime supply chain system is a part of global distribution chain which consists of different players and stakeholders (domestic and global players) from diverse organizations with each player have their own organisational functions, goals and needs. This complex nature of successive multiple phases of the distribution chain adding up to interconnected operation where the reality of this chain goes beyond diverse interests and priorities of involving players in each phase of the maritime supply chain. The different views of each player in this chain may influence the implementation of energy efficiency measures. Due to the complex nature of this sector, it is challenging to develop and implement energy efficiency measures that meet all the player's requirement collectively (Fridell et al., 2013).

According to Johnson and Andersson (2016) from the maritime supply chain market viewpoint, imperfect information or information asymmetries seem to be a significant barrier in this sector. The theoretical underpinning is that since information is naturally underprovided by ordinary market activity, maritime players lack adequate knowledge and basis for taking important economically efficient decisions due to multiple phases of the organizational level. For example, various players can be involved in providing a shipping service, with separated geographically and managerially differences that potentially opening up for many problems related to misinformation, and communication problems related to the adoption of energy efficiency measures. In this context, the slow and low implementation of energy efficiency measures is a natural consequence of information asymmetries.

Another major barrier that influences the implementation of energy efficiency measures concerns transaction costs and the difficulties of allocating appropriate costs and profits among diverse business organizations for an investment that can benefit multiple stakeholders (Kesicki & Strachan, 2011). Furthermore, the existence of additional cost, concerning non-negligible cost associated with the measures, which can mean that capital might be not appropriately allocated to the maritime operation where it is most needed. However, it is forecasted that hike in future fuel prices can become an effective driver of energy efficiency efforts among maritime supply chain companies (Smith, 2012). This partly explains the recent increased interest in energy efficiency amongst shipping organizations lately.

Overcoming the Barriers

To achieve energy efficiency measure and CO_2 emission reduction agenda, the difficulty of managing the complicated inter-relationship among players (institutional barriers) in maritime supply chain system should be first acknowledged and taken into consideration when tackling with specific measures. In order to successfully achieve this agenda, maritime supply chain players require well-ordered, integrated and efficient administrative action through close collaboration with the global and domestic partner. It can be achieved via the fulfillment of outlined compliance with international standards, supported by relevant institutions and technical know-how expertise. Maritime supply chain organizations and stakeholders must collectively involve in synchronized and coordinated support from the government, policymakers as well as the shore-side entity (such as port facilities, cargo-handling infrastructure and land logistics systems) to ensure transparent and holistic adoption of sustainability measures in its operation. This close collaboration of shore-side players from both industry and governmental entities, for example, could provide proper sustainable provision and evaluation for both maritime operations and environmental protection in order to ensure that the entire maritime supply chain integrity and energy efficiency measures do not become stagnant in progress.

In regards to imperfect information barriers, the qualified, skilled and competent workforce is important to be considered in the maritime supply chain. In the maritime context, the current challenging issue facing this sector is how to draw and maintain adequate people of sufficiently trained and qualified workforce with the right expertise and understanding of "green" concept, motivation, information and skills for sustainable application of developing energy efficiency measures. The challenges of maintaining a well-informed workforce will increase drastically further as rapid global trade and technology advancement continues to develop in the future. With this kind of backdrop, an all-inclusive approach and strategy for the advancement of maritime supply chain operation are therefore indispensable in order to accomplish energy efficiency measure and CO_2 emission reduction.

In addition, all players in the maritime supply chain system are subjected to peripheral and transaction costs. Nevertheless, several of these costs will eventually involve all players. In this sense, if the costs affect specific parts within the maritime supply chain system, inevitably it will also affect the whole maritime supply chain system or just a link in the respective maritime supply chain system. A coherent approach is needed to overcome this problem through comprehensive regulation and policies as well as educating the players by overseeing governmental bodies regarding this predicament issue. Maritime supply chain operations must be cautiously planned and well-managed in an organized, systematic and integrated approach among maritime players to ensure level playing field among them. Besides the contemplations concerning the equilibrium between expenditure (cost) and benefit, it is imperative that value creation which contains a chain of industry players all of whom must allocate and distribute values should be protected. In this sense, if each and every player in the maritime sector fulfil their diverse functions, and work collectively in mutual support of this value chain, the maritime supply chain will not only operate efficiently for the entire stakeholders concerned but also to the general stakeholders as a whole. Addressing the underlying said barriers, a universal and coherent plan suggested in this paper should include the subsequent approaches:

i. Suitable policies, regulations, conventions, set of laws and plans must be comprehensively set up and research accordingly to support the development of energy efficiency measures in specific comportment that could concentrate on that particular needs and adjust to distinctive developments in specific unique sectors that require certain attention.

ii. Assisting diverse governmental bodies, agencies, organizations and institutions involved in maritime supply chain activities to focus their attention, information, effort and share their existing knowledge with each another and with other related sectors of the maritime supply chain.

iii. Constructing efficient, transparent and effective measurement approaches in assessing the energy efficiency measures of maritime supply chain operation.

iv. Amplifying the existing collaboration and cooperation amongst the maritime supply chain stakeholders including individual players, private enterprises, NGOs, communities as well as governmental bodies involved in maritime sectors. It is also important for these entities to expand the valuable relationship with international maritime agencies to align its operation with global standard and needs.

v. Financial support by financial sectors or government entities should be properly considered in supporting the evolving nature of the maritime supply chain to permit for long-term efficiency of resources allocation to progress the entire three pillars aspect of sustainability.

vi. Engaging close collaboration with academic institutions and other researchers and development entities to align the current understanding with new evolving green technologies and new operational practices that will allow the industries to continually progress towards this sustainable and energy efficiency agenda.

vii. Greater emphasis on monitoring and follow-up of performance should be in place, both internally and externally within the maritime organizations and with respect to external contracts and global standards.

FUTURE RESEARCH DIRECTION

The scope of this article is limited to an overview of future potential energy efficiency measure in maritime supply chain and its organization. It is thus limited in the sense that it does not provide an empirical assessment of discussed energy efficiency measure. Future studies might extend this limitation by providing each of energy efficiency measure an in-depth empirical study to understand the measures further and the measurement can also be extending in other industry as well. The low current adoption in certain specific energy efficiency measures also become an intriguing research question that can be investigated further in future research. Overcoming the barriers is also an interesting direction in future research especially addressing the problem regarding the regional, organizational and geographical context of information asymmetries and institutional barriers in maritime supply chain context.

CONCLUSIONS

Pressure on the maritime supply chain sector to reduce its environmental impacts will increase substantially, and without a doubt, the most cost-efficient route to CO_2 emission reduction will be through increased energy efficiency. Current assessments have shown that several measures when it comes to energy efficiency are the only way to reach emission reductions in the short term while certain energy efficiency measures may take longer than others. This is expected since the maritime supply chain is a complex system which requires intricate assessment on each link of its value chain to understand the specific potential of energy efficiency measures that can be implemented. On the other note, the diverse possibilities for potential future energy efficiency measures covered in this paper demonstrate how maritime and shipping organizations could move towards greater efficiency of the overall maritime supply chain system. Concurrently, however, there seem to be various barriers that hinder maritime organizations from realizing this potential.

For this reason, greater importance in the planning, coordination, management, execution and monitoring of maritime supply chain operations in this sector must be materialized first before all the energy efficiency measures can be implemented successfully. Further research is thus essential to further understand the role of energy use and efficiency internally in a maritime organization as well as in its relationship with other organizations in this sector. A dynamic integration between all maritime supply chain players must be well cultivated to motivate efficient decision making and effective collaboration among them to provide a concrete platform for energy efficiency measures to function successfully in the future.

REFERENCES

Anderson, K., & Bows, A. (2012). Executing a Scharnow turn: Reconciling shipping emissions with international commitments on climate change. *Carbon Management*, *3*(6), 615–628. doi:10.4155/cmt.12.63

Bengtsson, S., Fridell, E., & Andersson, K. (2012). Environmental assessment of two pathways towards the use of biofuels in shipping. *Energy Policy*, *44*, 451–463. doi:10.1016/j.enpol.2012.02.030

Buhaug, O., Corbett, J. J., Eyring, V., Endresen, O., Faber, J., Hanayama, S., … Markowska, A. Z. (2009). Prevention of Air Pollution from Ships: second IMO GHG Study. International Maritime Organization.

Caniëls, M. C. J., Cleophas, E., & Semeijn, J. (2016). Implementing green supply chain practices: An empirical investigation in the shipbuilding industry. *Maritime Policy & Management*, *43*(8), 1005–1020. doi:10.1080/03088839.2016.1182654

Chambliss, S. (2015). International Council on Clean Transportation. *Electric Vehicle Incentives, Chargers, and Sales: What We See and What We Don't (Yet), 25.*

Chang, C.-C. (2012). Marine energy consumption, national economic activity, and greenhouse gas emissions from international shipping. *Energy Policy*, *41*, 843–848. doi:10.1016/j.enpol.2011.11.066

Corbett, J. J., Wang, H., & Winebrake, J. J. (2009). The effectiveness and costs of speed reductions on emissions from international shipping. *Transportation Research Part D, Transport and Environment*, *14*(8), 593–598. doi:10.1016/j.trd.2009.08.005

Dedes, E. K., Hudson, D., & Turnock, S. R. (2012). Assessing the potential of hybrid energy technology to reduce exhaust emissions from global shipping. *Energy Policy*, *40*, 204–218. doi:10.1016/j.enpol.2011.09.046

Eide, M. S., Longva, T., Hoffmann, P., Endresen, Ø., & Dalsøren, S. B. (2011). Future cost scenarios for reduction of ship CO2 emissions. *Maritime Policy & Management*, *38*(1), 11–37. doi:10.1080/03088839.2010.533711

Fridell, E., Winnes, H., & Styhre, L. (2013). *Measures to improve energy efficiency in shipping.* Academic Press.

Hjelle, H. M. (2010). Short sea shipping's green label at risk. *Transport Reviews, 30*(5), 617–640. doi:10.1080/01441640903289849

Jasmi, F., & Fernando, Y. (2018). Notions of Maritime Green Supply Chain Management. In *Encyclopedia of Information Science and Technology* (4th ed., pp. 5465–5475). IGI Global. doi:10.4018/978-1-5225-2255-3.ch475

Jasmi, M. F. A., & Fernando, Y. (2018). Drivers of maritime green supply chain management. *Sustainable Cities and Society, 43*, 366–383. doi:10.1016/j.scs.2018.09.001

Johnson, H., & Andersson, K. (2016). Barriers to energy efficiency in shipping. *WMU Journal of Maritime Affairs, 15*, 79–96.

Johnson, H., & Styhre, L. (2013). *Increased energy efficiency in short sea shipping through increased port efficiency.* De Próxima Publicación.

Johnson, H., & Styhre, L. (2015). Increased energy efficiency in short sea shipping through decreased time in port. *Transportation Research Part A, Policy and Practice, 71*, 167–178. doi:10.1016/j.tra.2014.11.008

Kader, A. S. A. (2013). *Pilot Study for Quantification of Emissions of Green House Gas for Decision Support towards International Maritime Organization (IMO) Rule Making, 13.* Academic Press.

Kesicki, F., & Strachan, N. (2011). Marginal abatement cost (MAC) curves: Confronting theory and practice. *Environmental Science & Policy, 14*(8), 1195–1204. doi:10.1016/j.envsci.2011.08.004

Komar, I., & Lalić, B. (2015). *Sea transport air pollution. In Current Air Quality Issues.* InTech.

Lai, K.-H., Lun, V. Y. H., Wong, C. W. Y., & Cheng, T. C. E. (2011). Green shipping practices in the shipping industry: Conceptualization, adoption, and implications. *Resources, Conservation and Recycling, 55*(6), 631–638. doi:10.1016/j.resconrec.2010.12.004

Lam, J. S. L. (2014). Designing a sustainable maritime supply chain: A hybrid QFD–ANP approach. *Transportation Research Part E, Logistics and Transportation Review.* Advance online publication. doi:10.1016/j.tre.2014.10.003

Nuttall, P., Newell, A., Prasad, B., Veitayaki, J., & Holland, E. (2014). A review of sustainable sea-transport for Oceania: Providing context for renewable energy shipping for the Pacific. *Marine Policy, 43*, 283–287. doi:10.1016/j.marpol.2013.06.009

OECD. (2017). *Analysis of Selected Measures Promoting the Construction and Operation of Grenner Ships, 67.* OECD.

Rehmatulla, N., Calleya, J., & Smith, T. (2017). The implementation of technical energy efficiency and CO2 emission reduction measures in shipping. *Ocean Engineering, 139*, 184–197. doi:10.1016/j.oceaneng.2017.04.029

Smith, T. W. P. (2012). Technical energy efficiency, its interaction with optimal operating speeds and the implications for the management of shipping's carbon emissions. *Carbon Management, 3*(6), 589–600. doi:10.4155/cmt.12.58

Sorell, S., O'Mally, E., Schleich, J., & Scott, S. (2004). *The economics of energy efficiency*. Elgar. Google Scholar.

Styhre, L., & Winnes, H. (2013). Energy efficient shipping–between research and implementation. In *Proceedings of the IAME2013 Conference* (pp. 3–5). Academic Press.

Takashima, K., Mezaoui, B., & Shoji, R. (2009). On the fuel saving operation for coastal merchant ships using weather routing. In *Proceedings of Int. Symp. TransNav* (*Vol. 9*, pp. 431–436). Academic Press.

Thollander, P., & Ottosson, M. (2010). Energy management practices in Swedish energy-intensive industries. *Journal of Cleaner Production*, *18*(12), 1125–1133. doi:10.1016/j.jclepro.2010.04.011

ADDITIONAL READING

Chang, C.-C., & Wang, C.-M. (2012). Evaluating the effects of green port policy: Case study of Kaohsiung harbor in Taiwan. *Transportation Research Part D: Transport and Environment, Elsevier*, *17*(3), 185–189. doi:10.1016/j.trd.2011.11.006

Jafarzadeh, S., & Utne, I. B. (2014). A framework to bridge the energy efficiency gap in shipping. *Energy*, *69*, 603–612. doi:10.1016/j.energy.2014.03.056

Ren, J., Lützen, M., & Rasmussen, H. B. (2018). Identification of Success Factors for Green Shipping with Measurement of Greenness Based on ANP and ISM. In *Multi-Criteria Decision Making in Maritime Studies and Logistics* (pp. 79–103). Springer. doi:10.1007/978-3-319-62338-2_4

Zhongxiong, B. Q. H. X. G., & Wei, J. X. G. (2009). Plan Proving of the Onshore Power Supply Trial Project in Shanghai Port Waigaoqiao Terminal. *Science & Technology of Ports*, *12*, 4.

KEY TERMS AND DEFINITIONS

Energy Efficiency: It refers the goal of reducing the amount of energy required to provide products and services. The energy definition in this context can be fossil fuel or electricity.

Energy Efficiency Gap: It refers to the difference cost potential improvement of energy efficiency and the level of energy efficiency actually realized. For example, although cost-effective technologies that can improve energy efficiency are recognized, they are not always implemented due to this 'energy efficiency gap'.

Maritime Supply Chain: It refers to entire shipping industry consisting of shipping lines, port terminal operators, freight forwarders and land-based logistic system. It is a part of comprehensive worldwide logistics systems of moving cargoes between places.

Sustainability: It refers to the ability of the organization to maintain a certain rate or level especially in term of natural resources or ecological balance. In most literature, sustainability also constitutes the three bottom line concept of sustainable development which emphasizes improving the economy, environment, and social dimension.

Big Data Analytics in Supply Chain Management

Nenad Stefanovic

(iD) https://orcid.org/0000-0002-0339-3474

Faculty of Science, University of Kragujevac, Serbia

INTRODUCTION

During the last several years there was an amazing progression in the amount of data produced within the supply chain information systems, but also externally. This poses many challenges related to data analysis specifically in terms of know-how, technology, infrastructure, software systems and development methods. The current business climate demands real-time analysis, faster, collaborative and more intelligent decision making.

The current approach to supply chain intelligence has some fundamental challenges when confronted with the scale and characteristics of big data. These include not only data volumes, velocity and variety, but also data veracity and value (Arunachalam, 2018).

The best way to effectively analyze these composite systems is the use of business intelligence (BI). Traditional BI systems face many challenges that include processing of vast data volumes, demand for real-time analytics, enhanced decision making, insight discovery and optimization of supply chain processes. Big Data initiatives promise to answer these challenges by incorporating various methods, tools and services for more agile and flexible analytics and decision making. Nevertheless, potential value of big data in supply chain management (SCM) has not yet been fully realized and requires establishing new BI infrastructures, architectures, models and tools (Marr, 2016).

Supply chain BI system proved to be very useful in extracting information and knowledge from existing enterprise information systems, but in recent years, organizations face new challenges in term of huge data volumes generated through supply chain and externally, variety (different kind of structured and unstructured data), as well as data velocity (batch processing, streaming and real-time data). Most of the existing analytical systems are incapable to cope with these new dynamics (Larson & Chang 2016).

On the other hand, we have seen tremendous advancements in technology like in-memory computing, cloud computing, Internet of Things (IoT), NoSQL databases, distributed computing, machine learning, etc. Big data is a term that underpins a raft of these technologies that have been created in the drive to better analyze and derive meaning from data at a dramatically lower cost and while delivering new insights and products for organizations in the supply chain.

The key challenges for modern supply chain analytical systems include (Wang et al., 2016):

§ Data explosion – supply chains need the right tools to make sense of the overwhelming amount of data generated by a growing set of data internal and external sources.
§ Growing variety of data – most of the new data is unstructured or comes in different types and forms.
§ Data speed – data is being generated at high velocity which makes data processing even more challenging.

DOI: 10.4018/978-1-7998-3473-1.ch169

§ Real-time analysis - in today's turbulent business climate the ability to make the right decisions in real-time brings real competitive advantage. Yet many supply chains do not have the infrastructure, tools and applications to make timely and accurate decisions.

§ Achieving simplified deployment and management – despite its promise, big data systems can be complex, costly and difficult to deploy and maintain. Supply chains need more flexible, scalable and cost-effective infrastructure, platforms and services, such as those offered in cloud

In this chapter, challenges and new trends in supply chain big data analytics are discussed and background research of big data initiatives related to SCM is provided. The chapter also describes the main technologies, methods and tools for big data analytics. The methodology and the unified model for supply chain big data analytics which comprises the whole BI lifecycle is presented. Architecture of the model is scalable and layered in such a way to provide necessary agility and adaptivity. The proposed big data model encompasses supply chain process model, data and analytical models, as well as insights delivery. It enables creation of the next-generation cloud-based big data systems that can create strategic value and improve performance of supply chains. An example of supply chain big data solution that illustrates applicability and effectiveness of the model is presented. Finally, future trends, directions and technologies are presented.

BACKGROUND

As the globalized business environment is forcing supply chain networks to adapt to new business models, collaboration, integration and information sharing are becoming even more critical for the ultimate success. Supply chains enterprise systems are experiencing a major structural shift as more organizations rely on a community of partners to perform complex supply chain processes. While supply chains are growing increasingly complex, from linear arrangements to interconnected, multi-echelon, collaborative networks of companies, there is much more information that needs to be stored, processed and analyzed than there was just a few years ago (Tiwari et al., 2018).

Supply chain business intelligence is a collection of activities to understand business situations by performing various types of analysis on the organization data as well as on external data from supply chain partners and other data sources (devices, sensors, social networks, etc.) to help make strategic, tactical, and operational business decisions and take necessary actions for improving supply chain performance. This includes gathering, analyzing, understanding, and managing high volumes of variety data about operation performance, customer and supplier activities, financial performance, production, competition, regulatory compliance, quality controls, device data and Internet (Stefanovic & Milosevic, 2018).

Over the past few decades, the way in which companies need to collate, analyze, report and share their data has changed dramatically. Organizations need to be more adaptive, have increased access to information for decision-making, and effectively deal with a rapidly growing volume of data. Today's business environment demands fast supply chain decisions and reduced time from raw data to insights and actions. Typically, supply chains are capturing enormous data volumes - including vast amounts of unstructured data such as files, images, videos, blogs, clickstreams and geo-spatial data, as well as data coming from various sensors, devices, and social networks (Stefanovic & Milosevic, 2017).

During the past two decades organizations have made large investments in SCM information systems in order to improve their businesses. However, these systems usually provide only transaction-based functionality and mostly maintain operational view of the business. They lack sophisticated analytical capabilities required to provide an integrated view of the supply chain. On the other hand, organizations that implemented some kind of enterprise business intelligence systems still face many challenges related to data integration, storage and processing, as well as data velocity, volume and variety. Additional issues include lack of predictive intelligence features, mobile analytics and self-service business intelligence capabilities (Harvey, 2017).

Sixty-four percent of supply chain executives consider big data analytics a disruptive and important technology, setting the foundation for long-term change management in their organizations (Renner, 2016). Ninety-seven percent of supply chain executives report having an understanding of how big data analytics can benefit their supply chain. Nonetheless, only 17 percent report having already implemented analytics in one or more supply chain functions (Accenture, 2014).

Another survey shows that 68% of supply chain leaders believe that supply chain analytics are critical to their operations. However, a key ingredient for the success of supply chain analytics is consolidating data from all participants and flows in the system, essentially breaking the boundaries between them. 66% of supply chain leaders say advanced supply chain analytics are critically important to their supply chain operations in the next 2 to 3 years. While 94% of supply chain leaders say that digital transformation will fundamentally change supply chains in 2018, only 44% have a strategy ready (Columbus, 2018).

Running a global supply chain demands intricate planning, sourcing, delivery and measurement. This requires big data strategy and governance, as well as investing in education of supply chain professionals. The general guidelines include (Morley, 2017):

- Starting with business objectives
- Break down the communication silos between different teams
- Define reasonable and achievable goals
- Plan globally, but start with small projects
- Prioritize and streamline analytical reports
- Turn data into concrete decision
- Evaluate and improve

The current approaches to BI have some fundamental challenges when confronted with the scale and characteristics of big data: types of data, enterprise data modeling, data integration, costs, master data management, metadata management, and skills (Chen et al., 2016).

The big data phenomenon, the volume, variety, and velocity of data, has impacted business intelligence and the use of information. New trends such as real-time and predictive analytics and data science have emerged as part of business intelligence (Schoenherr & Speier-Pero, 2015). In its essence, Data Science is simply a new term for Business Intelligence. It is a multi-disciplinary field that uses scientific methods, processes, algorithms and systems to extract knowledge and insights from structured and unstructured data (Frankenfield & Banton, 2019). is the concept that utilizes scientific and software methods, IT infrastructure, processes and software systems in order to gather, process, analyze and deliver useful information, knowledge and insights from various data sources.

Some of the supply chain challenges that data science is helping to solve include (Prokle, 2019):

- Making the supply chain greener to minimize the environmental impact of global sourcing (e.g., shorter distances or consolidated shipments)
- Increasing visibility into the supply chain and response time (e.g., through blockchain)
- Adapting to demographic changes and customer expectations (e.g., free same day deliveries)

- Allowing manufacturers to decrease their product life-cycle times (e.g., through better market insights and smart sourcing) to react to trends and demand more quickly
- Increasing the product portfolio to serve not only the mass market but the entire demand curve (e.g., through mass-customization)

While data science, predictive analytics, and big data have been frequently used buzzwords, rigorous academic investigations into these areas are just emerging. Even though a hot topic, there is not many researches related to big data analytics in SCM. Most of the papers deal with big data potential, possible applications and value propositions.

Fosso Wamba and Akter (2015) provide a literature review of big data analytics for supply chain management. They highlight future research directions where the deployment of big data analytics is likely to transform supply chain management practices. Waller and Fawcett (2013) examine possible applications of big data analytics in SCM and provide examples of research questions from these applications, as well as examples of research questions employing big data that stem from management theories.

Identifying specific ways that big data systems can be leveraged to improve specific supply chain business processes and to automate and enhance performance becomes crucial for ultimate business success. The information and analytics delivered would be used to improve supply planning, vendor negotiations, capacity planning, warehousing and transportation performance, productivity, shop floor performance, materials requirements planning, distribution and customer service.

Organizations can apply big data and BI in the following supply chain areas (Stefanovic, 2014):

- Plan Analytics — balancing supply chain resources with requirements.
- Source Analytics — improving inbound supply chain consolidation and optimization.
- Make Analytics — providing insight into the manufacturing process.
- Deliver Analytics — improving outbound supply efficiency and effectiveness.
- Return Analytics — managing the return of goods effectively and efficiently.

Big Data technologies are opening a range of possibilities for capitalizing on big data in logistics, and the use cases, as well as the benefits, continue to roll in (Feliu, 2019). These efforts can be classified into the following categories: visibility improvement, better form of demand and supply synchronization, optimization of fulfillment channels, building a smart and connected products, increased asset intelligence, and better work safety and productivity (Lopez, 2017).

Logistics companies such as DHL, are using big data analytics for flexible routing and optimization, as well as for capacity planning. Others use data-collecting sensors within vehicles to track the status of every vehicle to provide updates and make optimal decisions. Some airline companies are using big data analytics to improve the bottom line by predicting demand and performing dynamic pricing strategies (Eleks, 2019).

The supply chain economy is a web of multiple industries, and big data analytics has made an impact on most of them. McDaniel (2019) describe practical application of big data analytics in manufacturing (i.e. collecting telemetry data for predictive equipment maintenance, gathering contextual intelligence to eliminate bottlenecks for high throughput, or forecasting demand), consumer goods (i.e. plan for what-if scenarios and answer questions on whether strategies, such as marketing spends, are bringing in expected returns), and agriculture (i.e. combining past and real-time data to enhance operational efficiencies and reduce delivery cycles).

Some of the most important data-driven supply chain management challenges can be summarized as follows (Columbus, 2015):

- Meet rising customer expectations on supply chain management.
- Increase costs efficiency in supply chain management.
- Monitor and manage supply chain compliance & risk.
- Make supply chain traceability and sustainability a priority.
- Remain agile and flexible in volatile times and markets.

Supply chains which implemented certain big data systems have achieved the following benefits (Howard, 2016):

- Improvement in customer service and demand fulfillment.
- Faster and more efficient reaction time to supply chain issues.
- An increase in supply chain efficiency.
- Integration across the supply chain.
- Optimization of inventory and asset productivity.

Leading SCM and ERP solution vendors have incorporated analytical features into their latest information systems. There are many companies offering various software systems, platforms and services

As data analytics becomes critical in supply chain operations and management, supply chain analytics software solutions and tools have become must-have technologies. Many supply chain analytical tools feature improved forecasting and sales and operations planning to give supply chain managers the business intelligence they need to streamline operations, lower costs, and improve customer service. Leading SCM and ERP solution such as SAP, Microsoft, Oracle, and others, have incorporated some analytical features into their latest SCM information systems (Pontius, 2019). However, these analytics solutions usually relay on the own databases and data sources, thus requiring additional systems, services and tools to integrate and process large volumes of data from various departments and organizations across the supply network.

Despite new business requirements and technology innovations, big data methods, models and applications in SCM still need to be researched, studied and developed. In the subsequent sections, the supply chain big data model, software architecture and example of big data analytical system are presented.

BIG DATA AND SUPPLY CHAIN MANAGEMENT

Big data analytics uncovers patterns in a wide variety of data and associates the patterns with business outcomes. Analysts use analytical techniques and tools to detect unusual, interesting, previously unknown, or new patterns in data. Big data is a result of interaction of four dimensions of scale (increasing data volumes, high velocity of data creation, increasing complexity of data types, and extreme time sensitivity of data diminishing its value if not treated at that moment) thereby posing different challenges to manage, not to mention applying analytics techniques to find new insights. Big data does not behave the same as other data. The challenges associated with analytics on big data require a different approach from traditional data analytics processes (Nguyen et al., 2018).

Big data analytics has to do more with ideas, question and value, than with technology. Therefore, the big data analytics methodology is a combination of sequential execution of tasks in certain phases and highly iterative execution steps in certain phases.

The big data analytics process lifecycle is a combination of sequential execution of tasks in certain phases and highly iterative execution steps in certain phases. Because of the scale issue associated with supply chain big data system, an incremental and agile approach is recommended, which include modifying and expanding processes gradually across several activities as opposed to designing a system all at once (Mohanty, 2013).

In this section, an agile, iterative big data analytical process model to deliver supply chain predictive analytics solutions and intelligent applications efficiently is presented. The complete process model should encompass the lifecycle (phases, tasks, and workflows), roles, infrastructure, tools, and artifacts produced.

The proposed model is comprised of the following key components:

- A big data lifecycle.
- A standardized project structure.
- Infrastructure and resources for big data projects.
- Tools and utilities for project execution.

Figure 1 shows a proposed analytical lifecycle that can used to structure and execute various big data analytics projects (Ericson et al., 2017).

The lifecycle outlines the steps, from start to finish, that projects usually follow when they are executed. The process model includes the following stages that analytical projects typically execute, often iteratively:

1. Business understanding
2. Data acquisition and understanding
3. Modeling
4. Deployment
5. Customer acceptance

The lifecycle defines goals, tasks, and documentation artifacts for each stage of the lifecycle. These tasks and artifacts are associated with project roles such as: project manager, solution architect, data scientist, project lead, IT manager, business analyst, DevOps specialist, application developer, tester, etc.

The goal of the business understanding phase is to specify the key variables that are to serve as the model targets and whose related metrics are used determine the success of the project, and to identify the relevant data sources that the supply chain has access to or needs to obtain.

The second phase includes the three main tasks:

- Data ingestion from various supply chain data sources into the target analytic environment.
- Data exploration in order to determine if the data quality is adequate to answer the question.
- Solution architecture development of the data pipeline that refreshes and scores the data regularly.

The modeling phase addresses the following tasks:

Figure 1. Big Data Analytic Lifecycle

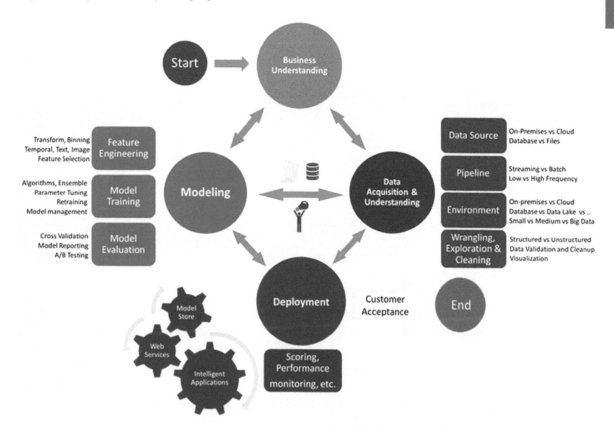

- Feature engineering - Create data features from the raw data to facilitate model training.
- Model training - Find the model that answers the question most accurately by comparing their success metrics.
- Model evaluation - Determine if the model is suitable for production.

Deployment phase refers to deploying the models with a data pipeline to a production or production-like environment for final user acceptance and application usage. The final phase includes system validation (confirming that the deployed model and pipeline meet the customer's needs) and project delivery (hand the project off to the entity that's going to run the system in production.

The model also includes the standardized project structure so that projects share a common directory structure and use templates for project documents. This makes it easy for the team members to find information about their projects. All code and documents are stored in a version control system to enable more effective and efficient team collaboration. Tracking tasks and features in an agile project tracking system allows closer tracking of the code for individual features. The standardized structure for all projects helps build institutional knowledge across the supply chain.

The proposed big data process model also provides recommendations for managing shared analytics and storage infrastructure such as: cloud file systems for storing datasets, databases, big data (Hadoop or Spark) clusters, machine learning service, etc. Tools provided to implement the big data process and lifecycle help lower the barriers to and increase the consistency of their adoption. They are used to pro-

Figure 2. Supply chain analytical lifecycle model

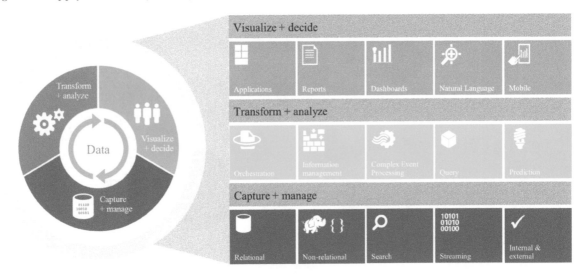

vision the shared resources, manage them, and allow each team member to connect to those resources securely. Tools also helps automate some of the common tasks in the data science lifecycle such as data exploration and baseline modeling.

The real users of the analytics outcomes are business users, but they often do not understand the complex mathematical formulae, statistical analysis models, etc. Therefore, it is extremely important to equip the business users with easy-to-understand and highly intuitive tools through which they will understand what actions are to be performed.

The proposed model and the lifecycle offer several advantages over existing supply chain analytical systems. They take into account the specifics of the big data analysis and provide unified framework for designing, developing, and deploying big data analytical solutions. The model can be applied to various analytical projects, regardless of technology and platforms. This enables faster development and implementation with high level of agility comparing to existing approaches.

SOLUTIONS AND RECOMMENDATIONS

In order to overcome main challenges of modern analytics and deficiencies of existing BI supply systems we propose a comprehensive multi-layered supply chain big data BI model that utilizes cloud-based big data services and tools for data extraction, transformation and loading (ETL), analysis, and reporting. Figure 2 shows the architecture with layers and services.

The proposed big data model unifies processes, methodologies and tools into a single business solution. The model has been developed in such a way to seamlessly integrate within overall BI and collaboration framework (Stefanovic et al., 2011). It is process-centric, metrics-based and modular. It introduces the new supply network and data modeling approaches, as well as layered application architecture which enables creation of composite BI systems.

The data integration layer supports various data types (relational, unstructured, streaming, OLAP, etc.) via cloud ETL services. The data management layer is based on the Hadoop engine but with additional services which provide more flexible data models and querying. The analytical layer hosts various analytical models and schemas. These can be exploration, data mining, or performance monitoring models. The final insights layer provides insights to all users such as self-service BI, data search, collaboration and performance monitoring. The central component of this layer is specialized supply chain BI portal as the unifying component that provides integrated analytical information and services, and also fosters collaborative decision making and planning (Stefanovic & Stefanovic, 2011).

This approach utilizes various cloud data management services such as ETL jobs for data extraction, cleansing and import, as well as event hubs that acts as a scalable data streaming platform capable of ingesting large amounts of high-velocity data form sensors and IoT devices throughout supply chain.

Additionally, the supply chain-wide data catalog was created in the cloud. It is fully managed cloud service that enables users to discover, understand, and consume data sources. The data catalog includes a crowdsourcing model of metadata and annotations, and it allows all supply chain participants to contribute their knowledge to build a various data models which can be integrated into specific applications and services.

In order to provide more flexibility, two big data stores are designed: supply chain enterprise multi-dimensional data warehouse and special in-memory tabular model for processing large amount of data. Combined with specific cloud analysis services, it is possible to design different analytical models. For example, stream analytical services can be used to set up real-time analytic computations on data streaming from devices, sensors, e-commerce sites, social media, information systems, infrastructure systems, etc. Another example is cloud machine learning service that enables supply chain participants to easily build, deploy, and share predictive analytics solutions (i.e. forecasting sales or inventory data) (Stefanovic & Stefanovic, 2015).

Finally, information derived from such analytical models need to be delivered to decision makers in timely and user-friendly way. For this purpose, a special web portal is used. It acts as a single point of data analysis, collaborative decision making.

In order to demonstrate our approach, we have designed a supply chain BI solution for analysis of supplier quality within the supply chain. Data from different sources (relational database, files, and web feeds) is integrated via cloud ETL job into the in-memory tabular data store.

Various analytical reports are designed using different technologies and services. All these BI artifacts (reports, charts, maps, etc.) are than integrated in the web dashboards as shown in Figure 3.

Supplier quality analysis is a typical supply chain task. Two primary metrics in this analysis are: total number of defects and the total downtime that these defects caused. This sample has two main objectives:

- Understand who the best and worst supply chain suppliers are, with respect to quality.
- Identify which plants do a better job finding and rejecting defects, to minimize downtime.

Each of the analytical segments on the dashboard can be further investigated by using various drill-down reports. For example, if user wants to analyze how plants deal with defective materials and the downtime, by clicking on the map segment, it opens supplier analysis dashboard that can be used for deeper analysis and filtering in order to derive meaningful knowledge about supplier management processes and take corrective actions.

The presented solution demonstrates the effectiveness and applicability of the proposed big data analytical model and the lifecycle. It encompasses the complete analytical lifecycle, from data capture and transformation, to storage, processing and visualization. This innovative approach enables better supply chain integration and coordination, as well as more informed decision making based on the advanced analytical services based on machine learning and visualization.

Figure 3. Supplier quality dashboard page

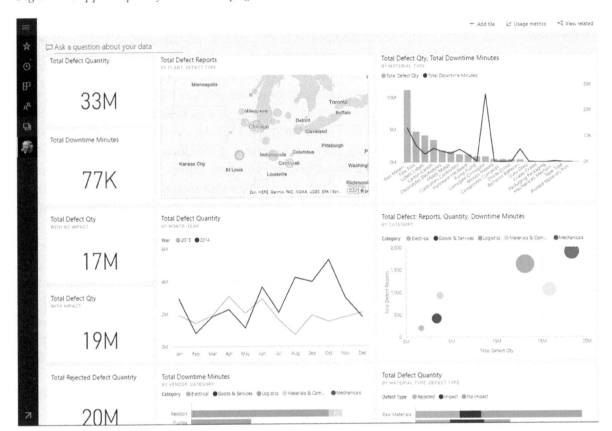

FUTURE RESEARCH DIRECTIONS

Supply chain management has been a highly researched area during the past twenty years, and it was seen as the key approach and enabler for organizational success and sustainability. Today's increased globalization, market pressures, uncertainty, shorter product lifecycles, tough competition and technological advancement make SCM critical in the years to come. Efficient decision making based on produced information and knowledge derived from vast supply chain data sources is the key for successful supply chain management (Pettey, 2019).

The impact of advanced analytics on supply chain is significant. Big data analytics is increasingly being deployed in real time or near-real time in various supply chain areas, from planning, sourcing and making, to delivery and return. The growth of data analytics has been particularly dramatic. In 2018 alone, big data adoption increased to 59% from 17% in 2015 (Keary, 2019).

The research show that supply chain leaders are using advanced analytics and artificial intelligence (AI) to augment and automate supply chain decision making. Within advanced supply chain companies, defined as those using two or more of the three advanced analytics techniques — predictive analytics, prescriptive analytics and artificial intelligence — 96% of respondents use predictive analytics, 85% use prescriptive analytics and 64% use AI (Van der Meulen, 2018).

Big data will certainly continue to play a crucial role in supply chain analytics and SCM in overall. Besides advancements directly related to big data systems, it is expected that big data will be combined with other technologies such as IoT, blockchain, augmented reality, cloud computing and many others. The main big data trends and research directions will be related to (Elliot, 2019):

- Cloud analytics
- Internet of Things (IoT)
- Predictive analytics
- Augmented analytics
- Artificial Intelligence
- Quantum Computing
- Digital assistants and chatbots
- Visualization and user experience
- Mobile analytics

CONCLUSION

During the last several years there was an amazing progression in the amount of data produced within the supply chain information systems, but also externally. This poses many challenges related to data analysis specifically in terms of technology, infrastructure, software systems and development methods. The current business climate demands real-time analysis, faster, collaborative and more intelligent decision making.

The current approach to supply chain intelligence has some fundamental challenges when confronted with the scale and characteristics of big data. These include not only data volumes, velocity and variety, but also data veracity and value. One of the key aspects of leveraging big data is to also understand where it can be used, when it can be used, and how it can be used - how the value drivers of big data are aligned to supply chain strategic objectives.

Big data is starting to make inroads into logistics and supply chain management – large steps have certainly been taken over the past several years – but there is still a long way to go. Opportunities to create efficiency and savings through smart use of data are evident and concerted effort is being put into finding them. Big data and advanced analytics are being integrated successfully as logistics management solutions such as: optimization tools, demand forecasting, integrated business planning, supplier collaboration and risks analytics.

The proposed layered supply chain big data model and architecture allows construction of the next-generation loosely-coupled analytical systems that combine different services, data sources, analytical models and reporting artifacts into a unified analytical. This will enable collaborative, efficient, responsive, and adaptive supply chains.

ACKNOWLEDGMENT

Research presented in this paper was supported by Ministry of Science and Technological Development of Republic of Serbia, Grant III-44010, Title: Intelligent Systems for Software Product Development and Business Support based on Models.

REFERENCES

Accenture. (2014). *Big Data Analytics in Supply Chain: Hype or Here to Stay?* https://www.accenture.com/t20160106T194441__w__/fi-en/_acnmedia/Accenture/Conversion-Assets/DotCom/Documents/Global/PDF/Digital_1/Accenture-Global-Operations-Megatrends-Study-Big-Data-Analytics-v2.pdf

Arunachalam, D., Kumar, N., & Kawalek, J. P. (2018). Understanding big data analytics capabilities in supply chain management: Unravelling the issues, challenges and implications for practice. *Transportation Research Part E, Logistics and Transportation Review*, *114*, 416–436. doi:10.1016/j.tre.2017.04.001

Chen, D. Q., Preston, D. S., & Swink, M. (2016). How the Use of Big Data Analytics Affects Value Creation in Supply Chain Management. *Journal of Management Information Systems*, *32*(4), 4–39. doi:10.1080/07421222.2015.1138364

Columbus, L. (2015, July 13). *Ten Ways Big Data Is Revolutionizing Supply Chain Management*. Retrieved from https://www.forbes.com/sites/louiscolumbus/2015/07/13/ten-ways-big-data-is-revolutionizing-supply-chain-management/#3edf715f69f5

Columbus, L. (2018, January 15). *Analytics Will Revolutionize Supply Chains In 2018*. Retrieved from https://www.forbes.com/sites/louiscolumbus/2018/01/15/analytics-will-revolutionize-supply-chains-in-2018/#342dc94b6127

Eleks. (2019, October 13). *3 Winning Use Cases for Big Data in Logistics and Transportation*. Retrieved from https://eleks.com/blog/use-cases-for-big-data-in-logistics-and-transportation/

Elliot, T. (2019, January 29). *Top 10 Analytics Trends For 2019*. Retrieved from https://www.digitalist-mag.com/cio-knowledge/2019/01/29/top-10-analytics-trends-for-2019-06196108

Ericson, G., Rohm, W. A., Martens, J., Sharkey, K., Casey, C., Harvey, B., … Schonning, N. (2017, October 20). *Team Data Science Process*. Retrieved from https://docs.microsoft.com/en-us/azure/machine-learning/team-data-science-process

Feliu, C. (2019, October 14*). 4 relevant Big Data case studies in Logistics*. Retrieved from https://blog.datumize.com/4-relevant-big-data-case-studies-in-logistics#smooth-scroll-top

Fosso Wamba, S., & Akter, S. (2015). Big Data Analytics for Supply Chain Management: A Literature Review and Research Agenda. In Enterprise and Organizational Modeling and Simulation. Springer. doi:10.1007/978-3-319-24626-0_5

Frankenfield, J., & Banton, C. (2019, May 30). *Data Science*. Retrieved from https://www.investopedia.com/terms/d/data-science.asp

Harvey, C. (2017, June 5). *Big Data Challenges*. Retrieved from https://www.datamation.com/big-data/big-data-challenges.html

Howard, F. (2016, July 13). *Top Challenges for Big Data in the Supply Chain Management Process*. Retrieved from http://en.advancedfleetmanagementconsulting.com/2016/07/13/1199/

Keary, T. (2019, March 26). *A look at data analytics trends for 2019*. Retrieved from https://www.information-age.com/data-analytics-trends-2019-123481163/

Larson, D., & Chang, V. (2016). A review and future direction of agile, business intelligence, analytics and data science. *International Journal of Information Management, 36*(5), 700–710. doi:10.1016/j. ijinfomgt.2016.04.013

Lopez, E. (2017, February 13). *How do supply chains use Big Data?* Retrieved from https://www.supplychaindive.com/news/how-big-data-application-supply-chain-Deloitte-digital-stack/435866/

Marr, B. (2016, April 22). *How Big Data And Analytics Are Transforming Supply Chain Management.* Retrieved from https://www.forbes.com/sites/bernardmarr/2016/04/22/how-big-data-and-analytics-are-transforming-supply-chain-management

McDaniel, S. (2019, August 22). *Big Data for Supply Chain Management.* Retrieved from https://www.talend.com/resources/big-data-supply-chain/

Mohanty, S., Jagadeesh, M., & Srivatsa, H. (2013). *Big Data Imperatives - Enterprise Big Data Warehouse, BI Implementations and Analytics.* Apress.

Morley, M. (2017). Supply Chain Analytics. John Wiley & Sons.

Nguyen, T., Yhou, L., Spiegler, V., Ieromonachou, P., & Lin, Y. (2018). Big data analytics in supply chain management: A state-of-the-art literature review. *Computers & Operations Research, 98,* 254–264. doi:10.1016/j.cor.2017.07.004

Pettey, C. (2019, April 22). *Gartner Top 8 Supply Chain Technology Trends for 2019.* Retrieved from https://www.gartner.com/smarterwithgartner/gartner-top-8-supply-chain-technology-trends-for-2019/

Pontius, N. (2019, October 21). *Top Supply Chain Analytics: 50 Useful Software Solutions and Data Analysis Tools to Gain Valuable Supply Chain Insights.* Retrieved from https://www.camcode.com/asset-tags/top-supply-chain-analytics/

Prokle, M. (2019). *How data science is disrupting supply chain management.* Retrieved from https://www.northeastern.edu/graduate/blog/data-science-supply-chain-management/

Renner, A. (2016, February 19). *Overcoming 5 Major Supply Chain Challenges with Big Data Analytics.* Retrieved from https://www.computerworld.com/article/3035144/data-center/overcoming-5-major-supply-chain-challenges-with-big-data-analytics.html

Schoenherr, T., & Speier-Pero, C. (2015). Data Science, Predictive Analytics, and Big Data in Supply Chain Management: Current State and Future Potential. *Journal of Business Logistics, 36*(1), 120–132. doi:10.1111/jbl.12082

Stefanovic, N. (2014). Proactive Supply Chain Performance Management with Predictive Analytics. *The Scientific World Journal.* doi:10.1155/2014/528917

Stefanovic, N. (2015). Collaborative predictive business intelligence model for spare parts inventory replenishment. *Computer Science and Information Systems, 12*(3), 911–930. doi:10.2298/CSIS141101034S

Stefanovic, N., & Milosevic, D. (2017). Model for Big Data Analytics in Supply Chain Management. In M. Zdravkovic, Z. Konjovic, & M. Trajanovic (Eds.), *Proceedings of the 7th International Conference on Information Society and Technology.* Belgrade: Society for Information Systems and Computer Networks.

Stefanovic, N., & Milosevic, D. (2018). A Review of Advances in Supply Chain Intelligence. In M. Khosrow-Pour, D.B.A. (Ed.), Encyclopedia of Information Science and Technology, Fourth Edition (pp. 5538-5549). Hershey, PA: IGI Global. doi:10.4018/978-1-5225-2255-3.ch481

Stefanovic, N., & Stefanovic, D. (2011). Supply Chain Performance Measurement System Based on Scorecards and Web Portals. *Computer Science and Information Systems*, *8*(1), 167–192. doi:10.2298/CSIS090608018S

Stefanovic, N., Stefanovic, D., & Radenkovic, B. (2011). Integrated Supply Chain Intelligence through Collaborative Planning, Analytics and Monitoring. In S. Mohhebi, I. Mahdavi, & N. Cho (Eds.), *Electronic Supply Network Coordination in Intelligent and Dynamic Environment: Modeling and Implementation* (pp. 43–92). IGI Global. doi:10.4018/978-1-60566-808-6.ch003

Tiwari, S., Wee, H. M., & Daryanto, Y. (2018). Big data analytics in supply chain management between 2010 and 2016: Insights to industries. *Computers & Industrial Engineering*, *115*, 319–330. doi:10.1016/j.cie.2017.11.017

Van der Meulen, R. (2018, July 13). *Improve the Supply Chain With Advanced Analytics and AI*. Retrieved from https://www.gartner.com/smarterwithgartner/improve-the-supply-chain-with-advanced-analytics-and-ai/

Waller, M. A., & Fawcett, S. E. (2013). Data Science, Predictive Analytics, and Big Data: A Revolution That Will Transform Supply Chain Design and Management. *Journal of Business Logistics*, *34*(2), 77–84. doi:10.1111/jbl.12010

Wang, G., Gunasekaran, A., Ngai, E. W. T., & Papadopolous, T. (2016). Big data analytics in logistics and supply chain management: Certain investigations for research and applications. *International Journal of Production Economics*, *176*, 98–110. doi:10.1016/j.ijpe.2016.03.014

ADDITIONAL READING

Moshirpour, M., Far, B., & Alhajj, R. (2018). *Highlighting the Importance of Big Data Management and Analysis for Various Applications*. Springer International Publishing AG. doi:10.1007/978-3-319-60255-4

Pyne, S., Rao, P., & Rao, S. B. (2016). *Big Data Analytics: Methods and Applications*. Springer India.

KEY TERMS AND DEFINITIONS

BI Portal: A specialized web portal that provide a range of analytical services and which enables collaborative decision-making.

Big Data: The evolving term that describes a large volume of structured, semi-structured and unstructured data that has the potential to be mined for information and used in machine learning projects and other advanced analytics applications.

Business Intelligence: A set of processes, technologies and tools comprising data warehousing, On-Line Analytical Processing, and information delivery in order to turn data into information and information into knowledge.

Cloud Analytics: Cloud analytics is a type of cloud service model where data analysis and related services are performed on a public or private cloud.

Data Science: The concept that utilizes scientific and software methods, IT infrastructure, processes, and software systems in order to gather, process, analyze and deliver useful information, knowledge and insights from various data sources.

Machine Learning (Data Mining): Set of knowledge discovery techniques for intelligent data analysis in order to find hidden patterns and associations, devise rules and make predictions.

Supply Chain: Dynamic, interconnected, and collaborative group of companies working jointly on planning, management and execution of cross-company business processes spanning from the first-tier suppliers to the end-customers.

Supply Chain Intelligence: Process of integrating and presenting supply chain information in order to provide collaborative planning, monitoring, measurement, analysis and management of the supply network.

Critical Success Factors of Analytics and Digital Technologies Adoption in Supply Chain

Debasish Roy

(iD) https://orcid.org/0000-0003-1883-0435

AIMA AMU, India

INTRODUCTION

The digital economy has brought into focus the importance of Supply chain as a competitive advantage. (Li et al, 2006). Competition has evolved from firm vs firm to supply chain vs supply chain (Ketchen & Hult, 2007). This has encouraged firm to adopt analytics to improve supply chain performance. Impact of analytics, on supply chain performance, is an important topic of research (Kohavi et al. 2002).

The supply chain is a bidirectional flow of information products and money between the initial suppliers and final customers through different firms. Supply chain management includes planning, implementing and controlling this flow. Management scholars and practitioners' agree that analytics has the potential of working on all areas of supply chain management to provide insights thereby improving supply chain performance. As demand and supply volatility has increased, the need for data and analytics has grown. A holistic analytics strategy may be the answer to many of the pains ailing the supply chain today (Cecere, 2016).

At a firm level, it is of interest to the Chief Executive Officer and Chief Supply Chain Officer, supported by the Chief Information Officer to explore what are the strategies to improve effectiveness of analytics in the supply chain. Research need to explore the effect of analytics on individual firm performance, an important factor that all firms are concerned about (Maskey et al. 2015). Harrington and Gooley (2017) opined that it is important to demonstrate the business benefits of analytics in supply chain initiatives to firms' leadership.

Acceptance and use of technology by an individual or a firm is one of the most mature stream of information system research (Benbasat & Barki, 2005; Venkatesh et al., 2007; Venkatesh et al., 2012). Better means for predicting and explaining information system acceptance and use have great practical value (Davis, 1989). Identifying the facilitators to improve adoption of analytics in supply chain, using validated framework of acceptance and use of information technology, has both practical and theoretical value.

The Research questions are:

- What are the facilitating factors for adoption of analytics in supply chain?
- What are the perceived benefits of use of analytics on supply chain?

DOI: 10.4018/978-1-7998-3473-1.ch170

BACKGROUND: LITERATURE SURVEY

The existing research frameworks were perused for their applicability in this research and have been presented.

Technology Adoption model: Various theoretical models of Technology adoption have been proposed by researchers (Fishbein & Ajzen, 1975; Bandura, 1986; Compeau, 1999; Davis, 1989; Ajzen, 1991; Moore & Benbasat, 1991; Venkatesh & Davis, 2000) that specifies factors which influence technology adoption. The constructs of Technology adoption have been specified as performance expectancy i.e. perceived benefits on adopting the technology, effort expectancy or ease of use of adopting the technology, *social influence* to adopt or not adopt the technology, facilitating conditions, which positively or negatively influence adoption and behavioral intention to adopt the technology (Venkatesh et al., 2003).

SCOR model: SCOR model provides a systematic approach to identifying, evaluating and monitoring supply chain performance, covering the four core supply chain processes of Plan, Source, Make and Deliver (Jamehshooran et al, 2015; Stephens, 2001). In Plan, data is analysed to forecast the market trends for the products and services (Azvine et al, 2005). In Source, agent based information systems are studied that include evaluation, search, selection and price negotiation (Lee et al, 2009; Trkman et al, 2007). In Make, factors that facilitate production to be within specification and on time are perused (Ranjan, 2008). In Deliver, analytics used in logistics management to reach products on time are investigated (Reyes, 2005). Trkman et al, (2010) used the SCOR model to study Supply chain performance and introduced Process Orientation and Information Systems as moderators.

Literature survey on use of Analytics and Big Data in supply chain- Hahn & Packowski (2015) described four types of use cases of analytics in supply chain (i) monitor and navigate (ii) sense and respond (iii) predict and act (iv) plan and optimize. Business analytics may help in increasing organization efficiency, using different analytical methods to forecast market trends, reduce the operating cost and increase the profits by using mature supply chain systems (Hoole, 2005; Hedgebeth, 2007). Analytics may produce breakthrough insights that can help supply chains reduce costs and risks whilst improving operational agility and service quality (Deloitte & MHI, 2014).

Fawcett & Wallet (2013) found an increase in Big data in Supply Chain. Garmaki et al (2016) found that Big data analytics is being used to create actionable insights for sustained competitive advantage. There is increased demand of Volume of data from Sales (details of price, quantity, time of day, date), Consumer (more details of purchasing behaviour, browsing history, frequency, value, timing), Inventory (perpetual inventory at more locations with more details e.g. style/color/size), Location and time (sensor data to detect location in stores/distribution center / transit). They also found that the Velocity of data is increasing from monthly / weekly to hourly, from consumer card usage to click history. The Variety of data is also increasing, from firms' sale to competitors sales, international sales, consumers identification to eye tracking, emotion detection, sentiment based on tweets and likes, inventory in warehouses to that with online retailer, location of product to who is moving it, nearby locations, path being taken etc.

Studies on the benefits of analytics on Supply chain- As Kwan (1999) found that information technologies allow firms to quickly and accurately share demand data, sales projections and production schedules, which provides adopting firms greater flexibility and responsiveness in the face of a constantly changing environment. Luu et al. (2017), in the Annual Forrestor Data Analytics survey, found that digitising the supply chain enables firms to integrate, embed intelligence and visualise all supply chain processes from supplier to customer. This opens the door to live inventory management that provides true transparency on inventory flows. Manufacturing costs are reduced as detailed planning and scheduling enables agility within the supply chain and optimises the efficient use of capacity. Gstettner et al (2016) referred a study by 'The Boston Consulting Group' that shows that the leaders in digital supply chain management are enjoying increase in product availability of up to 10% points, more than 25% faster response time to changes in market demand, and 30% better realization of working-capital reductions than the laggards. They have 40% to 110% higher operating margins and 17% to 64% fewer cash conversion days. They have reported that analytics is helping help managers to dynamically calculate optimal inventory allocations and forecast demand more accurately. Depending on the analytics of customer clicks on the website in a country or region, firms are adjusting inventories even though customers have not yet placed orders, holding more stock in the right locations, thereby decreasing the lead time promised to customers and increase their willingness to buy. Harrington and Gooley (2017), in their research, reported the perceived benefits from applications of supply chain analytics are customer service, profitability, visibility to cost-to-serve, inventory management, risk and resiliency management, demand planning and end-to-end supply chain collaboration.

Studies on adoption of analytics in supply chain- Various studies (Irani, 2010; Roach et al 1987; Sharif & Irani, 2006) have argued that Information systems (IS) investments have not resulted in business value. Studies in IS and business value have concluded that the results may be mediated by a number of intermediate variables (Mooney et al, 1996). Researchers have also proposed that multi-dimensional perspective of business value need to be studied to understand the impact of IS capabilities (Bharadwaj, 2000; Bhatt & Grover, 2005; Santhanam & Hartono, 2003).

Study by Schoenherr and Speier-Pero (2015) has highlighted factors which act as barriers to adoption of supply chain like inability to identify most suitable data, security concerns, lack of top management support, unclear business case or value, cost of currently available solutions, employees are inexperienced (need for training), current applications unable to meet business needs etc.

Harrington and Gooley (2017) similarly reported major impediments as lack of integration of data warehousing initiatives, need to invest in software and hardware, analytical tools' level of difficulty for users, acquisition of talent and expertise, difficulty of using analytical tools, management commitment and support, uncertainty about return on investment or value.

Patterson et al. (2003) found that firms subjected to greater pressure from supply chain partners would be more likely to adopt supply chain technology. Further firms with a more favourable transaction climate with supply chain members will be more likely to adopt supply chain technology.

Greater environmental uncertainty would lead to greater technology adoption as uncertainty creates the need for more accurate information in order to respond as environmental conditions necessitate (Ahmad and Schroeder, 2001). Firms facing higher environmental uncertainty will be more likely to adopt supply chain technology.

To have a broader and more multidimensional view of impact of Analytics on Supply chain performance, related management and technology initiatives were also studied.

Digital Technologies IoT through use of Big Data and analytics has led to supply chain innovations (Li & Li, 2017), servitization (Fichman et al 2014) and Multimodal delivery (Ganesan et al, 2016). Additive Manufacturing is disrupting the Supply chain models by a dramatic reduction in transportation volumes and bringing manufacturing closer to the customer (Chen, 2016; Mohr & Khan, 2015). Amazon has filed a patent for a mobile 3-D-printing delivery truck that would make it possible to print out a customer's order from a data file sent to the nearest vehicle. This innovation would let the company get items to shoppers much more quickly and reduce its warehouse space. Autonomous vehicles or drone technology is a supply chain design inflection point (Fawcett & Waller, 2014). Block Chain is a ledger based technology with decentralized data design and data recording, which improves transaction execution and transaction validation capabilities in supply chain (Korpela et al, 2017; Kshetri, 2018).

Information System (IS) Capability Pervious studies (Lin, 2007; Lu & Ramamurthy, 2011; Chen et al, 2014) have brought out a positive relationship between IS capability and firms performance. Wamba et al. (2016) and Kim et al. (2012) in their research have further refined IS capability and concluded that Business Data Analytics infrastructure capability, management capability and personnel capability have an impact on Supply chain performance.

Extended supply chain: With the advent of unstructured data, firms need to redesign business processes to be able to extract actionable insights from unstructured data (Jha et al, 2016).The inclusion of cross-functional business processes may be needed to exploit the advantages of analytics based supply chain planning. The extended supply chain also involves collaboration with external supply chain partners.

Supply chain visibility across the extended supply chain is a core issue involving interaction of people, processes, technologies and information flow (Hearney, 2013).

Kiron et al (2013) reported that, i) respondents who agree that analytics is helping their firms innovate are much more likely to say they collaborate with partners and suppliers through use of analytics (ii) are reaching beyond their own data to feed their analytics process. Studies have highlighted the importance of achieving a high level of inter and intra organizational processes and information systems (Wamba & Akter, 2015). With collaborative business processes and the seamless integration of processes of different firms, dynamic and flexible collaborations can be created in order to improve performance (Liu et al, 2009).

Perusal of literature also gave the perspective of the Gaps in literature. Feki et al (2016) concluded that the research challenge is determining the theories that can be mobilized and developing metrics to measure supply chain performance in big data and analytics settings. Schoenherr & Speier-Pero (2015) found that there is a research gap and need of more formal investigation into adoption and infusion of analytics.

This research tries to address this research gap by mobilizing the construct "Facilitators" and "Performance expectancy" of Unified model of Adoption and Use of Technology (UTAUT) to study critical success factors adoption of analytics in supply chain. Further, it uses the SCOR model, widely used by the practitioners of supply chain, to develop metrics, which align "performance expectancy" of analytics to the key parameters of supply chain.

RESEARCH FRAMEWORK

Data collection was done by a questionnaire. The questionnaire was pre tested by a panel of experts, before it was administered to respondents across manufacturing, infrastructure, consumer goods, ecommerce and third party logistics industries in face to face interviews.

Profile of the Respondents: The feedback from fourteen Chief Executive officers, thirty-five Chief Supply chain officers and eighteen Chief Information officers from firms of various sizes across India, was compiled.

The measurement models for constructs "Facilitating Factors" and "Performance Expectancy" have been subjected to confirmatory factor analysis with data from the questionnaire survey. Structural equation modeling package AMOS 18.0 has been used for this purpose. The standardized regression weights of the measurement items with the corresponding construct has been evaluated along with the critical ratio. The critical ratio of over 1.96 and the standardized regression weight of over 0.3 is considered acceptable. Based on this criterion, measurement items were dropped from each of the constructs due to poor loading.

The revised measurement models for constructs were again subject to confirmatory analysis. The acceptance criterion was that the chi square value of the measurement model should be between 1 to 3 and the p value greater than 0.05. It was recommended that standardized regression weight will be over 0.3 and the corresponding critical ratio over 1.96 for the measurement items.

The composite reliability and variance extracted for each measurement model has been computed separately. The construct reliability values are above the threshold of 0.70 (Nunnaly, 1978) and the convergent validity (Average variance extracted) is higher than 0.50 which is the accepted value (Hair et al, 1998). This analysis has been done on the revised measurement models that have been accepted by confirmatory analysis. The interpretation of the revised measurement models have been also taken up for discussion next.

RESULTS AND DISCUSSIONS

Facilitating factors: This construct discusses the factors which facilitate adoption.

Figure 1. Measurement Model of Facilitating factors of adoption of Analytics in supply chain

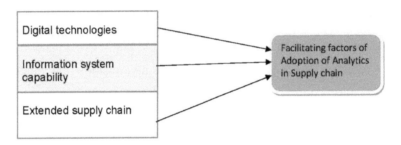

In the context of adoption of analytics in supply chain, the measurement parameters and related hypothesis are defined as follows:

H1: Digital technologies have a positive influence on adoption of Analytics. The findings of the study support this hypothesis.

Digital technologies, which facilitate the adoption of analytics in the Supply chain, are *Additive manufacturing* (3 D printing) which is enabling businesses to station local manufacturing centres closer to strategic markets. This along with insights from analytics is making supply chains become agile and able to cope with faster product design and production cycles.

Oettmeier & Hofmann (2016) found that adoption of Additive manufacturing in customized products is helping analytics to speed up complaint processing, increase material utilization and reducing order lead time. They also found that Additive manufacturing is improving quality management and influencing vendor management.

Another Digital technology, *Internet of Things* (IoT) information is being used to generate analytics across the value chain and reducing manual intervention, improving visibility and decision making. Objects moving through the value chain are producing unprecedented supply chain visibility. Stationary objects connected over the Internet of Things are monitoring the surrounding environment, reporting conditions, altering their state depending on predefined parameters, enabling firms to come closer to the customer.

Li & Li (2017) reported that adoption of IoT along with analytics is leading to sourcing innovation by optimizing inventory levels and by building trust between the firm and the vendor. They also reported that IoT is helping analytics to bring innovation in logistics by improving information transparency of transportation.

Drones and vehicle automation are disrupting the supply chain by enabling automation in the world of supply chain logistics and materials handling. The scope is enormous from Self driving trucks and cargo ships, loading / unloading of parcels, last mile delivery drones as being tested by UPS and Amazon.

Block Chain can disrupt supply chain by improving traceability, increasing trust and speed up transaction through smart contracts (Fransisco & Swanson, 2018; Pruitt, 2017).

H 2: Information system capability influences adoption of Analytics. The findings of the study support this hypothesis

Jha et al (2016) concluded that Big Data analytics requires business processes to change and it must align with the firms IS infrastructure to support the business initiatives. New ways of doing data analytics and business intelligence depend on information system capability. Firms need to focus on this now than later to gain competitive advantage in the market place. Raguseo (2018) found that lack of Information System and infrastructure support is a strong barrier to adoption of analytics in supply chain.

H 3: Extended supply chain has a positive impact on adoption of Analytics. The findings of the study support this hypothesis.

Research findings strongly support these. Respondents opined that analytics can be, over time, copied by rivals eroding the competitive advantage. To sustain the competitive advantage of analytics adoption, realignment of business processes is being undertaken. Firms reengineering their Supply chains to Extended supply chain agree that analytics is helping their firms innovate. The supply chain visibility is helping firms to collaborate with logistic partners and vendors through the use of analytics. However firms also agree that internal integration is a prerequisite for extended supply chain.

This is supported by Rozados & Tjahjno (2014), who states that an extended supply chain is a multi-echelon system that connects organisations, allowing collaboration and integration. Sanders (2014) supported by stating that the exchange and sharing of data across the extended supply chain has provided transparency and enabled coordinated cross-enterprise efforts.

"Perceived Benefits" refers to the expected benefits of adoption and use of technology.

The measurement items of the construct "Perceived Benefits" of Analytics and the related hypothesis in Supply chain is presented in a Tabular form.

Overall there is a strong correlation between performance expectancy and intention to adopt analytics. This is in line with study of Jamehshooran et al (2015), which proved that Analytics in Plan, Source, Make and Delivery has positive and significant impact on performance. Chen et al (2016) found a strong relation between expected benefits and adoption of analytics in supply chain. Aronow & Johnson (2016) has reported Gartner research that states 29% of companies have achieved a high return on investment (ROI) from putting data analytics programs in place, while only 4% said they have not achieved an ROI from their analytics investment. The data also shows that the ROI from data analytics investments consistently increases in correlation with maturity level. For example, of the high-maturity companies that deployed data analytics, 50% noted improved product quality as a benefit, as compared to only 24% of low-maturity organizations. Accenture (2015) reported that Big data and analytics is having an impact on organizations' reaction time to supply chain issues (41%), increased supply chain efficiency of 10% or greater (36%), and greater integration across the supply chain (36%).

Figure 2. Measurement Model of Perceived Benefits of adoption of Analytics in supply chain

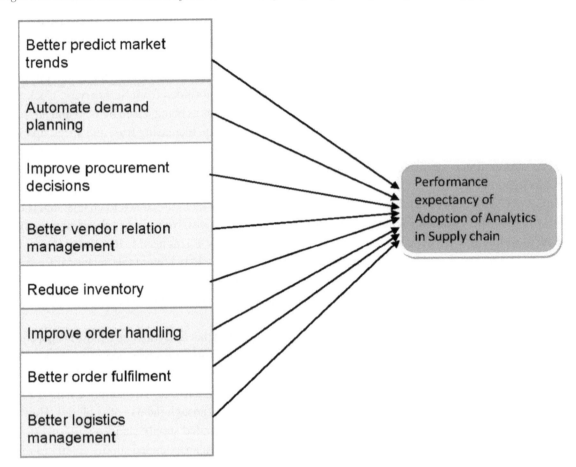

CONCLUSION

The results of the discussion contributes to a systematic review of impact of analytics on supply chain performance. The use of a Framework developed on the universally accepted SCOR Model has given an opportunity to do a structured inquiry on perceived benefits of analytics in various aspects of supply chain. This may provide actionable insights to practitioners on perceived impact of analytics in various functions of Supply chain.

The study of the impact of facilitating factors, i.e. Digital Technologies, Extended supply chain and IS capability on supply chain performance, reemphasises that analytics in isolation will not have its intended benefits, if these facilitating conditions are absent.

The perceived impact of the adoption of analytics on the supply chain performance has come out very strongly and emphatically in the research. It is crucial that firms have the facilitating factors (i.e. Digital technologies Extended supply chain and IS capability) to reap the full potential of analytics in supply chain performance.

This is of particular importance in a developing country like India, where Information System infrastructure and availability of trained personnel across all the supply chain partners is a challenge. It is important that the Industry leaders and Industry trade bodies take particular attention to improve the whole supply chain and have innovative solutions wherever needed. Saldhana et al (2015) pointed that

Table 1. Measurement model of perceived benefits of adoption of analytics in supply chain

Measurement items- Hypothesis	Key Conclusions	Previous results
Analytics will improve planning by better predicting market trends -*Supported*	Firms are adopting predictive analytics for planning Supply chain practitioners use analytics for contingency planning	DeAngelis (2017), Hanesbrands uses analytics to sense supply chain issues in time.
Analytics will improve planning by automating demand planning - *Supported*	Firms monitor demand upto the stock keeping unit level, at point of sale and during promotional events, track lost sales.	Leveling & Otto (2014) - analytics is resulting in automatic ordering if demand is recognized.
Analytics will impact Sourcing by improving procurement decisions-*Supported*	Adoption of Analytics has led to decrease in Total cost of ownership and more effective supplier negotiation	Innamarto et al (2017) - analytics support better sourcing decisions. Rozados & Tjahjno (2014) - analytics is providing visibility on aggregated procurement patterns.
Analytics will improve Sourcing by leading to better vendor relation management - *Supported*	Firms are using analytics for annual vendor scorecard and product sourcing process. This has reduced the 'Request for Quote' process and at the same time allow real-time benchmarking.	Panchmatia (2015) - analytics gives information on firms spending pattern and return on investment. Ahlawat & Martinez (2016)- analytics helps to monitor quality
Analytics will improve Make by reducing inventory - *Supported*	Analytics has led to finished Inventory optimizations (Inventory carrying cost optimization, decreasing bullwhip effect, customized fulfilment level based on customer segmentation).	Hoffman (2017) - relation between adoption of analytics and reduction of bullwhip effect.
Analytics will improve Make by improving order handling- *Supported*	Analytics is helping in processing data available through sensors and digital machines in shop floors, production lines and factories to improve order handling.	Zhong, Huang, and Lan (2014) - analytics support shop floor logistics planning and scheduling. Zhong, Xu, Chen, & Huang, 2017; Zhong et al., 2015 - Analytics is supporting in building intelligent shop floor logistics system Rozados & Tjahjno (2014) analytics has led to better inventory sensing capability and material handling and packaging.
Analytics will improve Delivery by better order fulfilment - *Supported*	Analytics in supply chain has improved network planning and optimization	Aronow & Johnson (2016) 26% of the respondents say that better customer service is a driver of adoption of analytics. Sanders (2014)- analytics has optimized supply chain segments and made it focussed to meet customer demands
Analytics will improve Delivery by better logistics management-Supported	Analytics may facilitate hyper-scale, real-time improving logistics efficiency and utilitization Analytics can help in prior shipment using lower cost transportation Analytics has improved traceability of products.	Bubner et al (2014)- analytics could speed up delivery times of goods and increase the utilization ratio of distribution capacities. Spiegel et al (2013) - predictive analytics can help to ship goods prior to the customers' order to reduce delivery time

Source: Developed for this Research

in India language differences, low accessibility of internet, purely transactional relationship with channel, lack of IS expertise of logistics partners, lack of information sharing with suppliers are constraints in supply chain. The extended supply chain needs to provide benefits to the entire supply chain, rather than be internally-focused and transaction-oriented. In transaction oriented, firms acts solely for its own benefit, regardless of the potential detriment or constraints to the rest of the supply network (Rice & Hoppe, 2001).

FUTURE SCOPE OF THE STUDY

The research helped firm up the measurement items of the constructs "Facilitators" and "Performance expectancy". Additionally similar study needs to be done to identify the measurement items of the other constructs "Effort expectancy" and "Social influence". Further, the final model need to be statistically validated using Structural Equation modelling. This will lead to operationalizing UTAUT to study adoption issues of analytics in supply chain and may be used to predict adoption of analytics in supply chain, across industries, countries and firms size. This is an important subject of management research.

REFERENCES

Accenture. (2015). *Big Data Analytics in Supply Chain: Hype or Here to Stay?* Accenture Global Operations Megatrends Study. Retrieved from https://www.accenture.com/t20160106T194441_w_/fi-en/_acnmedia/ Accenture/ Conversion-Assets/DotCom/ Documents/Global/PDF/Digital_1/Accenture-Global-Operations-Megatrends-Study-Big-Data-Analytics-v2.pdf

Ahlawat, V., & Martinez, D. (2016). *Improving Supply Chain Performance Using Analytics*. MIT Global SCALE Network, Research Report: ZLC-2016-2. Retrieved from http://dspace.mit.edu/bit-stream/1721.1/102948/1/2016_2_Ahlwat_Martinez.pdf

Ajzen, I. (1991). The Theory of Planned Behavior. *Organizational Behavior and Human Decision Processes, 50*(2), 179–211.

Aronow, S., & Johnson, J. (2016). *Supply chain trends in the Digital edge.* Gartner. Retrieved from https://www.gartner.com/doc/3211627/supply-chain-trends-digital-age

Azvine, B., Nauck, D., & Cui, Z. (2005). Towards real time business intelligence. *BT Technology, 23*(3), 214–225.

Bandura, A. (1986). *Social Foundations of Thought and Action: A Social Cognitive Theory.* Prentice Hall.

Benbasat, I., & Barki, H. (2007). Quo Vadis, TAM? *Journal of the Association for Information Systems, 8*(4), 212–218.

Bharadwaj, A. S. (2000). A resource-based perspective on information technology capability and firm performance: An empirical investigation. *Management Information Systems Quarterly, 24*(1), 169–197.

Bhatt, G. D., & Grover, V. (2005). Types of information technology capabilities and their role in competitive advantage, an empirical study. *Journal of Management Information Systems, 22*, 253–277.

Bouchard, L. (1993). Decision criteria in the adoption of EDI. *Proceedings of the Thirteenth International Conference on Information Systems*, 365–376.

Bowersox, D. J., & Daugherty, P. J. (1995). Logistics paradigms: The impact of information technology. *Journal of Business Logistics, 16*(1), 65–80.

Bubner, N., Bubner, N. I., Helbig, R., & Jeske, M. (2014). *Logistics trend radar: Delivering insight today. Creating value tomorrow.* DHL Customer Solutions & Innovation.

Cecere, L. (2016). Putting Together the Pieces: Supply Chain Analytics: Insights on Technology Options. *Supply Chain Insights*.

Chen, D. Q., Preston, D. S., & Swink, M. (2015). How the use of big data analytics affects value creation in supply chain management. *Journal of Management Information Systems*, *32*(4), 4–39.

Chen, Y., Wang, Y., & Nevo, S. (2014). IT Capability and Organizational Performance: The Roles of Business Process Agility and Environmental Factors. *European Journal of Information Systems*, *23*(3), 326–342.

Chen, Z. (2016). Research on the Impact of 3D Printing on the International Supply Chain. *Advances in Materials Science and Engineering*, 1-17.

DeAngelis, S. (2017). Supply Chain transformation and Digitisation. *Supply Chain Insights*. http://beetfusion.com/blogs/stephen-deangelis/supply-chain-transformation-and-digitization

Deloitte & MHI. (2014). *The 2014 MHI Annual Industry Report – Innovations that drive supply chains*. MHI.

Fawcett, S., & Waller, M. (2014). Supply Chain Game Changers. *Journal of Business Logistics*, *35*(3), 157–164.

Feki, M., Boughzala, I., & Wamba, S. F. (2016). Big data analytics-enabled supply chain transformation: A literature review. *Proceedings of 49th International conference on system sciences*.

Fichman, R. G., Dos Santos, B. L., & Zheng, Z. E. (2014). Digital Innovation as a Fundamental and Powerful Concept in the Information Systems Curriculum. *Management Information Systems Quarterly*, *38*(2), 329–353.

Fishbein, M., & Ajzen, I. (1975). *Belief, Attitude, Intention and Behavior: An Introduction to Theory and Research*. Addison-Wesley.

Fransisco, K., & Swanson, D. (2018). The supply chain has no clothes: Technology Adoption for Supply chain transparency. *Logistics*, *2*(1), 2–13.

Ganesan, V., Maragatham, G., & Lavanya, U.S. (2016). *A study of IoT and its nodes in Multimodal Business Process*. Academic Press.

Garmaki, M., Boughzala, I., & Wamba, S. F. (2016). The effect of big data analytics capability on firm performance. *Proceedings of Pacific Asia Conference on Information Systems PACIS 2016*.

Gettens, D., Jauffred, F., & Steeneck, D. W. (2016). IoT Can Drive Big Savings in the Post-Sales Supply Chain. *MIT Sloan Management Review*. Retrieved from https://sloanreview.mit.edu/article/iot-can-drive-big-savings-in-the-post-sales-supply-chain/

Hahn & Packowski. (2015). A perspective on applications of in-memory analytics in supply chain management. *Decision Support Systems*, *76*, 45–52.

Hair, J. F., Anderson, R. E., Tatham, R. L., & Black, W. C. (1998). *Multivariate Data Analysis with Readings* (5th ed.). Prentice Hall.

Harrington, L., & Gooley, T. (2017). Big data analytics in Supply Chain tackling the tidal wave. *Supply Chain Quarterly*. Retrieved from www. supplychainquarterly.com /20171030-big-data-analytics-in-supply- chain-tackling-the-tidal-wave/

Hearney, B. (2013). *Supply chain visibility – A critical strategy to optimize cost and service*. Retrieved from online http://aberdeen.com/8509

Hedgebeth, D. (2007). Data driven business decision making for the enterprise – an overview of Business Intelligence applications. *Vine, 37*(4), 414–420.

Hofmann, E. (2017). Big data and supply chain decisions: The impact of volume, variety and velocity properties on the bullwhip effect. *International Journal of Production Research, 55*(17), 5108–5126.

Hoole, R. (2005). Five ways to simplify your supply chain Management. *International Journal (Toronto, Ont.), 10*(1), 3–6.

Innamorato, T., Prilepok, M., & Schillinger, I. (2017). *The Era of Advanced Analytics In Procurement-has begun*. Retrieved from https://operations-extranet. mckinsey.com/article/the-era-of-advanced-analytics-in-procurement- has-begun/

Irani, Z. (2010). Investment evaluation within project management: An information systems perspective. *The Journal of the Operational Research Society, 61*(6), 917–928.

Ittmann, H. W. (2015). The impact of big data and business analytics on supply chain management. *Journal of Transport and Supply Chain Management, 9*(1), 1-9.

Jamehshooran, B. G., Shaharoun, A. M., & Haron, H. N. (2015). Assessing Supply Chain performance through applying the SCOR model. *International Journal of Supply Chain Management, 4*(1), 1–9.

Jha, M., Jha, S., & Obrien, L. (2016). Combining Big Data Analytics with Business Process using Re-engineering. *Conference Proceedings, IEEE 10th International Conference on Research Challenges in Information Science.*

Ketchen, D., & Hult, G. (2007). Bridging organizing theory and supply chain management: The case of best value supply chain. *Journal of Operations Management, 25*, 573–580.

Kim, G., Shin, B., & Kwon, O. (2012). Investigating the Value of Socio-materialism in Conceptualizing IT Capability of a Firm. *Journal of Management Information Systems, 29*(3), 327–362.

Kiron, D., Ferguson, R. B., & Prentice, P. K. (2013). Innovating with analytics. *MIT Sloan Management Review, 54*(1), 47–52.

Kohavi, R., Rothleder, N., & Simoudis, E. (2002). Emerging trends in business analytics. *Communications of the ACM, 45*(8), 45–48.

Korpela, K., Halikus, J., & Dahlberg, T. (2017). Digital Supply Chain Transformation toward Blockchain Integration. *Proceedings of the 50th Hawaii International conference on system sciences.*

Kshetri, N. (2018). Blockchain's role in meeting supply chain objectives. *International Journal of Information Management, 39*, 80–89.

Lee, C.K.M., Lau, H.C.W., Ho, G.T.S., & Ho, W. (2009). *Design and development of agent-based procurement system to enhance business intelligence, expert systems with applications*. Academic Press.

Leveling, J., Edelbrock, M., & Otto, B. (2014). Big data analytics for Supply Chain Management. *Proceedings IEEE International conference on Industrial Engineering and Engineering Management.*

Li, B., & Li, Y. (2017). Internet of things drives supply chain innovation: A research framework. *The International Journal of Organizational Innovation*, *9*(3B), 71–86.

Li, S., Ragu-Nathan, B., & Ragu-Nathan, T. S., & SubbaRao, S. (2006). The impact of supply chain management practices on competitive advantage and organizational performance. *Omega*, *34*(2), 107–124. PMID:17876965

Lin, B. W. (2007). Information technology capability and value creation: Evidence from the US Banking Industry. *Technology in Society*, *29*, 93–106.

Liu, C., Li, Q., & Zhao, X. (2009). Challenges and opportunities in collaborative business process management: Overview of recent advances and introduction to the special issue. *Information Systems Frontiers*, *11*(3), 201–209.

Lu, Y., & Ramamurthy, K. (2011). Understanding the Link Between Information Technology Capability and Organizational Agility: An Empirical Examination. *Management Information Systems Quarterly*, *35*(4), 931–954.

Luu, B., McDaniel, T., Reitsma, R., Duan, X., & Hart, C. (2017). *Global Business Technographics Data Analytics Survey 2017 Overview*. Retrieved from https://www.forrester.com/report/Global+Business+Technographics+Data+ Analytics+Survey+2017+Overview/

Mohr, S., & Khan, O. (2015). 3D Printing and its disruptive impacts on Supply chains of the future. *Technology Innovation Management Review*, *1*(1), 20–25.

Mooney, J. G., Gurbaxani, V., & Kraemer, K. L. (1996). A process oriented framework for understanding the Business Value of Information Technology. *SIGMIS Database*, *27*, 68–81.

Moore, G. C., & Benbasat, I. (1991). Development of an Instrument to Measure the Perceptions of Adopting an Information Technology Innovation. *Information Systems Research*, *2*(3), 192–222.

Norris, R. C. (1988). The ADL grocery report revisited. *EDI Forum*, 44–48.

Nunnally, J. C. (1978). *Psychometric Theory* (2nd ed.). McGraw-Hill.

Oettmeier, K., & Hofmann, E. (2016). Impact of Additive Manufacturing Technology Adoption on Supply Chain Management Processes and Components. *Journal of Manufacturing Technology Management*, *27*(8), 944–968.

Panchmatia, M. (2015). *Use big data to help procurement make a real difference*. Retrieved from http://www.4cassociates.com

Patterson, K. A., Grimm, C. M., & Corsi, T. M. (2003). Adopting new technology for supply chain management. *Journal of Transportation Research*, *39*, 95–121.

Pruitt, L. (2017). *What does Block Chain technology mean for the procurement industry?* IDG Connect. Retrieved from https://www.idgconnect.com

Raguseo, E. (2018). Big data technologies: An empirical investigation on their adoption, benefits and risks for companies. *International Journal of Information Management*, *38*, 187–195.

Ranjan, J. (2008). Business justification with business intelligence. *The Journal of Information and Knowledge Management Systems, 38*(4), 461-475.

Reyes, P. M. (2005). Logistics networks: A game theory application for solving the trans shipment problem. *Applied Mathematics and Computation, 168*(2), 1419–1431.

Rice, J.B., & Hoppe, R.M. (2001). Supply chain vs supply chain, hype vs reality. *Supply Chain Management Review*, 47-54.

Roach, S. S., & Stanley, M. (1987). Americas Technology dilemma; A profile of the information economy. Morgan Stanley Publication.

Rozados, I. V., & Tjahjno, B. (2014). Big Data analytics in supply chain management: Trends and related research. *Proceedings of 6th International conference on Operations and Supply Chain Management.*

Saldanha, J., Mello, J., Knemeyer, A., & Vijayaraghavan, T. A. S. (2015). Coping Strategies for Overcoming Constrained Supply Chain Technology: An Exploratory Study. *Transportation Journal, 54*, 368–404.

Sanders, N.R. (2014). *Big Data Driven Supply Chain Management A Framework for Implementing Analytics and Turning Information into Intelligence.* Pearson Education.

Santhanam, R., & Hartono, E. (2003). Issues in linking information technology and capability to firms performance. *Management Information Systems Quarterly, 27*, 125–153.

Schoenherr, T., & Speier-Pero, C. (2015). Data Science, Predictive Analytics, and Big Data in Supply Chain Management: Current State and Future Potential. *Journal of Business Logistics, 36*(1), 120–132.

Sharif, A., & Irani, Z. (2006). Exploring fuzzy cognitive mapping for IS evaluation- A research note. *European Journal of Operational Research, 173*(3), 1175–1187.

Spiegel, J. R., McKenna, M. T., Lakshman, G. S., & Nordstrom, P. G. (2013). *Amazon US Patent Anticipatory Shipping.* Amazon Technologies Inc.

Stephens, S. (2001). Supply chain operations reference model version 5.0: A new tool to improve supply chain efficiency and achieve best practice. *Information Systems Frontiers, 3*(4), 471–476.

Tiwari, S., Weeb, H. M., & Daryanto, Y. (2018). Big data analytics in supply chain management between 2010 and 2016: Insights to industries. *Computers & Industrial Engineering, 115*, 319–330.

Trkman, P., McCormack, K., de Oliveira, M. P. V., & Ladeira, M. B. (2010). The impact of business analytics on supply chain performance. *Decision Support Systems, 49*(3), 318–327.

Trkman, P., Stemberger, I., Jaklic, M., & Groznik, A. (2007). Process approach to supply chain integration. *Supply Chain Management, 12*(2), 116–128.

Truman, G. E. (2000). Integration in electronic exchange environments. *Journal of Management Information Systems, 17*(1), 209–244.

Venkatesh, V., & Davis, F. D. (2000). A Theoretical Extension of the Technology Acceptance Model: Four Longitudinal Field Studies. *Management Science, 46*(2), 186–204.

Venkatesh, V., Davis, F. D., & Morris, M. G. (2007). Dead or Alive? The Development, Trajectory and Future of Technology Adoption Research. *Journal of the Association for Information Systems, 8*(4), 268–286.

Venkatesh, V., Morris, M. G., Davis, G. B., & Davis, F. D. (2003). User acceptance of information technology - towards a unified view. *Management Information Systems Quarterly*, *27*(3), 425–478.

Venkatesh, V., Thong, J., & Xu, X. (2012). Consumer acceptance and use of information technology: Extending the unified theory of acceptance and use of technology. *Management Information Systems Quarterly*, *36*(1), 157–178.

Wamba, S. F., & Akter, S. (2015). Big data analytics for supply chain management: A literature review and research agenda. *Proceedings of Enterprises and Organizational modelling and Stimulation workshop*.

Wamba, S. F., Akter, S., Edwards, S., Chopin, G., & Gnannzou, D. (2015). How big data can make big impact, findings from a systematic review and a longitudinal case study. *International Journal of Production Economics*, *165*, 234–246.

Wamba, S. F., Gunasekaran, A., Akter, S., Ren, S. J., Dubey, R., & Childe, S. J. (2016). Big data analytics and firm performance: Effects of dynamic capabilities. *Journal of Business Research*, *70*, 356–365.

Zhong, R. Y., Huang, G. Q., & Lan, S. L. (2014). Shop floor logistics management using RFID-enabled big data under physical internet. *Proceedings of 1st International Physical Internet Conference*.

Zhong, R. Y., Huang, G. Q., Lan, S. L., Dai, Q. Y., Xu, C., & Zhang, T. (2015). A big data approach for logistics trajectory discovery from RFID-enabled production data. *International Journal of Production Economics*, *165*, 260–272.

Zhong, R. Y., Xu, C., Chen, C., & Huang, G. Q. (2017). Big data analytics for physical internet-based intelligent manufacturing shop floors. *International Journal of Production Research*, *55*(9), 2610–2621.

KEY TERMS AND DEFINITIONS

Analytics in Supply Chain: Analytics can be defined as tools and techniques that are dedicated to harnessing external and internal data to improve supply chain efficiency.

Big Data: Refers to the 3Vs (i.e., Volume, Velocity, Variety) of data which is captured for actionable insights.

Business Process Reengineering (BPR): Involves the analysis and redesign of firms' processes and workflows to achieve sustainable improvements in quality of response and cost competitiveness.

Digital Technologies: Relevant to supply chain are Additive manufacturing (3D Printing), Internet of things (Machine to machine communication between devices that belong to different systems, including public infrastructure), Drone technology for logistics and Block Chain for transactions.

Extended Supply Chain: Is the BPR initiative, which assists in maximizing the impact of analytics in supply chain. Extended supply chain proposes a close integration with other lines of business units that are key in the supply chain such as product development, manufacturing, sales, and operations.

SCOR Model: Is the framework used for analysis and insights of Supply chain performance. It is used in this research for measuring the impact of Business analytics in supply chain.

Unified Model of Adoption and Use of Technology (UTAUT): It is a consolidated model to study Technology adoption, proposed by Venkatesh et al. (2003).

Blockchain for Supply Chain Management:
Opportunities, Technologies, and Applications

Nenad Stefanovic

(iD) https://orcid.org/0000-0002-0339-3474

Faculty of Technical Sciences Cacak, University of Kragujevac, Serbia

INTRODUCTION

Over the past decades, digital technologies empowered more efficient, effective and connected supply chains. Many organizations have invested a significant amount of resources in various supply chain management (SCM) in order to improve performance and profitability. However, as supply chain complexity continues to increase, organizations face new challenges of maintaining visibility into origin, authenticity, and asset handling as they cross organizational boundaries (Stefanovic, 2015). The existing SCM information systems and apps usually cannot provide required visibility, traceability, automation, provenance, and efficiency.

Blockchain technology is considered to be a game-changer for decentralizing infrastructure and building a trust layer for business logic. It is envisioned to be a technology that could drive us into the next industrial revolution, with new paradigms for doing business in supply chain, transportation, manufacturing, finance and many other industries (Vorabutra, 2016).

It has a potential impact on most documentation processes, but it adds value through the ability to track purchase orders, assign and verify certifications, link physical goods to IoT (Internet of Things)-enabled devices, such as digital tax, barcodes, and serial numbers, and sharing such information with suppliers, vendors, and other supply chain partners (Robinson, 2019).

Blockchain is a transparent and verifiable system that will change the way supply chain partners exchange value and assets, manage contracts, and share data. The technology is a shared, secure ledger of transactions distributed among a network of computers, rather than resting with a single provider. Blockchain can be used as a common data layer to enable a new class of SCM applications. Thus, business processes and data can be shared across multiple organizations, which eliminates waste, reduces the risk of fraud, and creates new revenue streams.

Blockchain-based supply chain solutions are changing the way industries do business by offering end-to-end decentralized processes via the distributed and digital public ledger (Miaoulis, 2019).

Blockchain within the supply chain provides supply chain participants with a decentralized ledger that can store an entire history of transactions across a shared database — an ideal solution for multi-tier collaboration within the context of a dynamic and digital supply chain ecosystem (Doubleday, 2019).

Certain supply chains are already using the blockchain technology, and literature suggests blockchain could soon become a universal "supply chain operating system" (Spend Matters, 2015). Blockchain technology could improve the following supply chain tasks:

- Recording the quantity and transfer of assets - like pallets, trailers, containers, etc. - as they move between supply chain nodes (Gonzalez, 2016)

DOI: 10.4018/978-1-7998-3473-1.ch171

14

- Tracking purchase orders, change orders, receipts, shipment notifications, or other trade-related documents
- Assigning or verifying certifications or certain properties of physical products; for example, determining if a food product is organic or fair trade (Herzberg, 2015)
- Linking physical goods to serial numbers, bar codes, digital tags like RFID, etc.
- Sharing information about manufacturing process, assembly, delivery, and maintenance of products with suppliers and vendors

Supply chain organizations must can achieve significant benefits from blockchain in core areas of supply chain operations (Francis, 2018):

- Removing paperwork - by using blockchain to create a tamper-proof "master ledgers" between trading parties
- Creating "smart contracts" - that check when new records are written, ensure there are no out of balance conditions, and remove the existence of 'bad' invoices
- Having a single system of record - replicated across all partners to a transaction, which enables the impartial enforcement of contract terms

With the power to bring transparency and accountability to even the most complex supply chains, blockchain is poised to transform the way suppliers, retailers, and consumers interact with one another and their goods. Blockchain has the potential to replace complicated, error prone processes such as look-back auditing with streamlined smart contracts. As the technology grows and matures, it will be used to open new doors for cross-organizational collaboration and enable new business models along the supply chain (Microsoft, 2018).

Supply chain blockchain is taking ground at a rapid pace. Most of the key technological components needed to create robust supply chain blockchain networks are available or in a mature development stage. However, radical change will truly start to take shape through the integration of blockchain with other innovative technologies like AI and IoE (XChain2, 2018).

In this chapter, we discuss the various opportunities blockchain provides for SCM, as well as the main technologies including infrastructure and services. The main applications and benefits of blockchain for SCM are described including smart contracts, payments, transaction recording, dispute resolution, environmental monitoring, and security. We also introduce the multi-layered and cloud-based hybrid blockchain model that combines various data, integration, blockchain, and security services.

BACKGROUND

Supply chains are definitely critical for the overall success of today's organizations. Supply chain management includes integrated planning as well as the execution of different processes within the supply chain such as planning, sourcing, making, delivering, end returning. These processes include material, information and financial flows (Stefanovic & Stefanovic, 2013).

Supply chains are currently managed on centralized software platforms, and the chain activities rely on human paper-and-pen processes to ensure certified products are delivered as intended to final consumers. The current supply chain management system as it exists today is outdated and unable to keep up with growing interconnectedness that the global industry presently demands. Some of the main challenges that existing supply chain systems face are related to (Miaoulis, 2019):

- **Speed:** The speed of the current supply chain is very slow due to the presence of intermediary heavy authentication processes, doing business across time zones, and logistics management inadequacies. Transacting across time zones is a slow process that requires third-party financial services that are expensive and multi-day.
- **Counterfeiting and Fraud:** Counterfeiting not only damages organization' reputations, but it can also potentially endanger lives (i.e., frauds in pharmaceutical, food or electronic supply chains). Fraud is so widespread because global supply chains are not able to know for sure the volume of every item stored in every location.
- **Costs:** Frauds, slow processes, and intermediaries all add to costs for everyone in the supply chain. Consumers end up paying for these added expenses and companies take their fair share out of their revenue.
- **Trust:** Centralized supply chains require that all players trust that the others are operating honestly and will be on schedule. Without automation and better technological infrastructure, all processes hinge on trust or costly third-party verification.
- **Reliability and Data Security:** Data analytics help to improve supply chain management, when data is inaccurate this data is less likely to be useful and work towards a more robust chain. Additionally, insecure customer data leaves consumers vulnerable to identity theft.

Managing today's supply chains—all the links to creating and distributing goods—is extraordinarily complex. There are many challenges with the existing supply chain organization and technologies that are related to transactions efficiency, transparency, traceability, trust, and security. One of the studies found that 408 organizations from 64 countries were facing consistent supply chain visibility challenges (RiskMethods, 2019):

- 69% do not have full visibility into their supply chains
- 65% experienced at least one supply chain disruption
- 41% still rely on spreadsheets to keep track of supply chain disruptions

There is a significant amount of locked in value in SCM, largely stemming from the fragmented and competitive nature of the logistics industry. Hence, there is an increased interest in how blockchains might transform the supply chain and logistics industry (Marr, 2018).

Blockchain is a transparent and verifiable system that will change the way organizations think about exchanging value and assets, enforcing contracts, and sharing data. The technology is a shared, secure ledger of transactions distributed among a network of systems, rather than resting with a single centralized provider. Supply chain organizations are using blockchain as a common data layer to enable a new class of applications. Now, business processes and data can be shared across multiple organizations, which eliminates waste, reduces the risk of fraud, and creates new revenue streams (Microsoft, 2019a).

The three properties of the blockchain technology that is going to help disrupt the supply chain management system are (Mitra, 2019):

- **Decentralization:** What it essentially means is that any data that is stored inside the blockchain is not owned by one centralized entity but shared by everyone who is part of that blockchain's network.
- **Immutable:** Immutability basically means non-tamperable. Any data put inside the blockchain cannot be tampered with.
- **Transparency:** Every single operation that will ever take place in the supply chain will be recorded in the blockchain for authorized parties to see.

Blockchain is a top 10 strategic technology trend in 2018 according to Gartner. By 2030, it is predicted it will provide $3.1tr of added value to businesses worldwide (Pettey, 2017). It is likely to affect key supply chain management objectives such as cost, quality, speed, dependability, risk reduction, sustainability and flexibility (Kshetri, 2018). Blockchain can make tracking items and transactions in the supply chain radically faster and simpler when used in conjunction with IoT technology, cutting administrative and logistics timelines in shipping by an estimated 85% (Deloitte, 2017). Where the movement of goods involves dozens of individuals and organizations communicating with each other, blockchain can dramatically simplify record keeping (Lehmacher, 2017). Blockchain is more than a pure electronic data interchange (EDI) – it is the backbone of digital supply chains, offering distinct advantages over today's conventional supply chain IT infrastructure and analytics capabilities (Lierow et al., 2017).

Blockchain is scalable, thus any number of supply chain members may be seamlessly integrated into the blockchain without losing data consistency. Blockchain is independent of adjacent and legacy systems, making implementation quick. Every participant along the chain holds a complete copy of the data. But, by defining specific access rights, participants can ensure that confidential corporate information is kept private. While the blockchain record possesses a high degree of integrity, organizations will need to ensure that they are vigilant to cyber-security threats given that entries on the ledger are distributed immediately and are then permanent (Lin & Liao, 2017).

For blockchain to be deployed successfully across the supply chain the following prerequisites are needed (InsightBrief, 2018):

- Joint standards (covering terminology, development, security and more).
- The technical ability to handle large transaction volumes must be enhanced.
- Smooth and easy interface with legacy systems.
- Broad stakeholder buy-in.

True blockchain-led transformation of business and supply chain is still in progress and in its early stages. It is a hot topic among academic researchers, industry experts and enterprise software vendors. Even though there are certain research projects related to blockchain technologies and SCM, available software platforms, services and apps, as well as successful real-world implementations, presently academic and managerial adoption of blockchain technologies is quite limited (Swanson & Francisco, 2018).

Peterson et al. (2018) explore benefits, challenges and opportunities of blockchain applications in SCM. Other studies report blockchain applications in pharmaceutical (Bocek et al., 2017), food (Caro et al., 2018), and healthcare (Clauson, 2018) supply chains.

For blockchain to add true value to the supply chain, it will generally require extensive use of IoT, AI (Artificial Intelligence), cloud technologies and analytics (Stefanovic, 2014). Furthermore, every stage of the supply chain must be digitized and integrated, presenting a logistical challenge at the launch phase (De Meijer, 2018).

Even though surveys show that supply chain organizations have quite positive stand about blockchain technology and possible benefits, they still have a strong reserve against concrete implementations. The benefits over existing IT solutions must be elaborated more carefully and use cases must be further explored (Hackius & Petersen, 2017). This requires an additional research and studies about concrete blockchain applications in supply chain processes, as well as adequate software systems, platforms, services and apps capable to support decentralized, distributed and heterogenous SCM software systems, all with necessary scalability, flexibility, security and compliance.

In the following chapters, the main blockchain SCM use cases and benefits, system architectures, concrete solutions, and future research directions and trends are described.

BLOCKCHAIN APPLICATIONS IN SUPPLY CHAIN MANAGEMENT

Blockchain promises real long-term potential for the global transformation of economies and industries that, over time, will lead to the era of the "programmable economy" (Prentice et al., 2015).

A practical approach to blockchain development and implementation demands a clear understanding of the business opportunity, the capabilities and limitations of blockchain technology, a trust architecture, and the necessary IT to implement the technology (Furlonger, 2017). Blockchain's key attributes and potential benefits are:

- Improved cash flow
- Lower transaction costs
- Asset provenance
- Native asset creation
- New trust models

In general, blockchain technologies can be utilized at three levels (Piscini et al., 2017):

1. Storage of digital records – blockchain can be used to store digital identities of supply chain organizations, assets, documents, events, transactions, and essentially everything that can be represented digitally.
2. Exchange of digital assets – blockchain can execute P2P (peer-to-peer) transactions without trusted intermediaries, thus reducing clearing and settlement, human work, and related costs
3. Creation and execution of smart contracts – they are kind of digital codes which enable automated execution of specified actions based on contractual conditions as validated by all the supply chain participants.

To assess the value of blockchain technologies for the supply chain domain, the three main areas where it could add value can be observed (Alicke et al., 2017):

- Replacing slow, manual processes. Although supply chains can currently handle large, complex data sets, many of their processes, especially those in the lower supply tiers, are slow and rely entirely on paper.
- Strengthening traceability. Increasing regulatory and consumer demand for provenance information is already driving change.

- Reducing supply-chain IT costs. This often means lower data storage, transaction, integration, exchange and analytical costs.

14

Blockchain can definitely improve the following supply chain processes (Mitra, 2019):

- Recording the quantity of the products and its transfer through different participants.
- Tracking all the purchase orders, change orders, receipts, trade-related details, etc.
- Verifying the validity of the certification of the products. For example, this can be used to track whether a particular item meets certain quality standards or not.
- It can link various physical items to serial numbers, barcodes, and tags like RFID etc.
- Helps in the sharing all the information about the manufacturing process, assembly, delivery, and maintenance of products with the different participants in the supply chain.

Additional benefits of blockchain in the supply chain for visibility include (Robinson, 2019):

- The creation of smart contracts to hold vendors and suppliers accountable, maintaining adherence to duties and responsibilities defined within service level agreements (SLAs).
- Integrated payment solutions, reducing the time between ordering and payment processing, ensuring the proper, timely movement of products. Payment processing also has major ramifications for avoiding violations of international and domestic trade agreement, preventing illicit payments from countries and entities that are sanctioned from doing business with other parts of the world.
- Ability to create public and private blockchains, protecting proprietary, if not private, information from unauthorized parties.
- Recording all activities throughout the supply chain, including the quantity and transfer of assets, regardless of the motive transit. This will grow more important as new technologies, including unmanned, autonomous trucks, drones, and even Amazon's proposed floating fulfillment center, emerge.
- Better customer service levels and far-reaching scalability, resulting from the ability to provide more information regarding a product's manufacturer, origin, transfer, and use.

Regardless of the application, blockchain offers shippers the following advantages (Vorabutra, 2016):

- Enhanced Transparency. Documenting a product's journey across the supply chain reveals its true origin and touchpoints, which increases trust and helps eliminate the bias found in today's opaque supply chains. Manufacturers can also reduce recalls by sharing logs with OEMs (Original Equipment Manufacturers) and regulators (Gonzalez, 2016).
- Greater Scalability. Virtually any number of participants, accessing from any number of touchpoints, is possible (Chester, 2016).
- Better Security. A shared, indelible ledger with codified rules could potentially eliminate the audits required by internal systems and processes (Spend Matters, 2015).
- Increased Innovation. Opportunities abound to create new, specialized uses for the technology as a result of the decentralized architecture.

Blockchain can add a great deal of value when combined with IoT devices, tracking real-world events and uploading the information to the chain. Applications include (InsightBrief, 2018):

- Automating payments on completion of delivery
- Detecting temperature changes and voiding products that have been adversely affected
- Recording security logs for items in transit

If applied correctly, blockchain technology can assure provenance tracking and traceability across the supply chain. This, in turn, will lead to fewer counterfeiters and ensured safety in the processes. Blockchain in the supply chain will also allow manufacturers, transporters, and end-users to collect data, study trends, and apply predictive monitoring process for better product experience (Pratap, 2018).

Besides many proven and promising advantages and benefits, application and utilization of blockchain technologies is still at its nascent stage and have some challenges (Queiroz & Fosso Wamba, 2019). The main challenges include (Lawton, 2019):

- Higher computational overhead
- Managing decentralized systems
- Data complexity
- Buy-in with multiple parties
- Readiness of participants
- Integration with existing ERP (Enterprise Resource Planning) systems
- Application development complexity

Supply chain managers, as well as IT managers need to be aware of these challenges and to take the right preparations and actions to successfully carry out blockchain project.

SOLUTIONS AND RECOMMENDATIONS

In this section, cloud-based blockchain reference architecture for supply networks is presented. Furthermore, architectures of the two characteristic supply chain use cases are described. They are based on the blockchain-as-a-service (BaaS) cloud platform that is used to create and deploy blockchain applications, and to share business processes and data among supply chain organizations.

Successful supply chain blockchain implementations support multi-level confidentiality and privacy which is achieved through multichannel or subchain communication, multiple sub-ledgers, and multiple stakeholders for transaction visibility based on a need-to-know-basis. There are several characteristics that apply to blockchain systems that affect their architecture and implementation: cryptography, immutability, provenance, decentralized computing infrastructure, distributed transaction-processing platform, decentralized database, shared and distributed accounting ledger, software development platform, cloud computing, peer-to-peer network, and digital wallet (OMG, 2017).

Figure 1 shows the SCM blockchain reference architecture with typical capabilities needed for a node (organization) or the supply chain participating in the blockchain system. The reference architecture is expressed across three networks – public, cloud, and enterprise. The technical implementations of blockchains vary depending on the type of blockchain that is chosen. They can use different methods to establish the network topology, manage participation, execute smart contracts, and manage growth.

Figure 1. Blockchain reference architecture capabilities and runtime flow

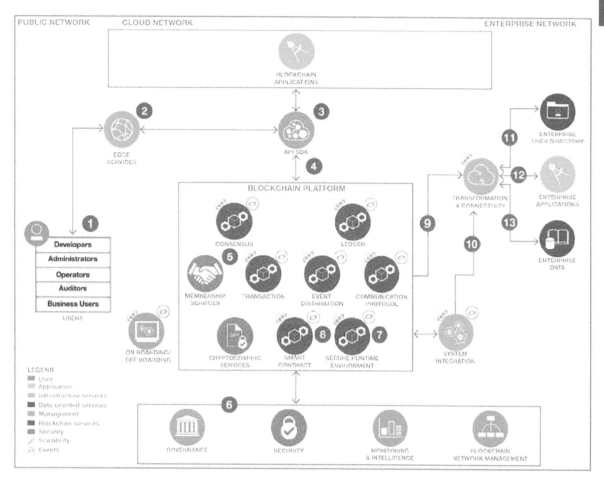

1. A blockchain user accesses the blockchain platform to perform a transaction. Business users are likely to access the blockchain network through blockchain applications running on the cloud network. Other users may access the blockchain network from within the environment for administrative and operational purposes.

2. Upon receiving the request to access the blockchain network, edge services route the request to the security gateway.

3. Business users may access the application using a browser client that passes the request to the blockchain platform.

4. The request passes through the API SDK to the blockchain platform for authentication, authorization and execution.

5. Blockchain membership services, which provides security, privacy and protection for blockchain users, authenticates the user and authorizes the action requested by the user based on their role.

6. Security services enable the blockchain membership services to establish the user's identity and provide authentication, authorization and integration capabilities.

7. A secure environment is spawned to execute server-side blockchain business logic.

8. Based on various triggers, smart contract business logic enforces contract terms between the supply chain participants.

9. The validation of the smart contract may necessitate access to enterprise data. The request goes through the transformation and connectivity service which transforms the data and ensures secure and reliable delivery.

10. In addition, external events may trigger a blockchain transaction such as the creation of business documents (i.e. by uctoms or a bank) through their legacy systems.

11. Before any processing is performed by the enterprise application, the blockchain service instance may authenticate the user via the enterprise user directory.

12. The enterprise application may leverage data used by the client app as well as logs and context data for analytics. If the client application updates the data then the enterprise application may process those changes.

13. Enterprise Data is the data store for the Enterprise Application.

Blockchain Workflow Application

Businesses use blockchain to digitize workflows they share with other organizations, such as moving physical assets across supply chains. The anatomy of blockchain apps is similar across supply chain use cases. Here, Azure Blockchain Service as the foundational managed blockchain network is used, and a consortium application that can ingest signals from relevant user interfaces and communicate ledger data to consuming apps across the consortium is built (Microsoft, 2019b).

Figure 2. Blockchain workflow application architecture

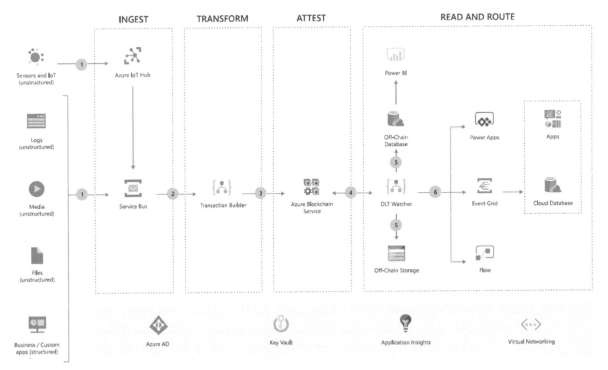

1. Relevant apps, devices, and data sources send events or data to a message broker (Azure Service Bus).
2. The distributed ledger technology (DLT) consumer Logic App fetches the data from the Service Bus and sends to transaction builder which builds and signs the transaction.
3. The signed transaction gets routed to Azure Blockchain Service (fully managed Ethereum consortium network) via a ledger-specific Logic App connector.
4. The DLT watcher Logic App gets confirmation of the transaction commitment to the blockchain and sends the confirmed blockchain transactions to off-chain databases and storage.
5. Information is analyzed and visualized using tools such as Power BI by connecting to off-chain database
6. Message broker sends ledger data to consuming business process applications.

Tracking and Tracing Throughout Supply Chain

A common blockchain pattern is IoT-enabled monitoring of an asset as it moves along a multi-echelon supply chain. A great example of this pattern is the refrigerated transportation of perishable goods like food or pharmaceuticals where certain compliance rules must be met throughout the duration of the transportation process. In this scenario, an initiating company (such as a retailer) specifies contractual conditions, such as a required humidity and temperature range, that the custodians on the supply chain must adhere to. At any point, if the device takes a temperature or humidity measurement that is out of range, the smart contract state will be updated to indicate that it is out of compliance, recording a transaction on the blockchain and triggering remediating events downstream (Microsoft, 2019c).

Figure 3. Architecture of blockchain IoT tracking system

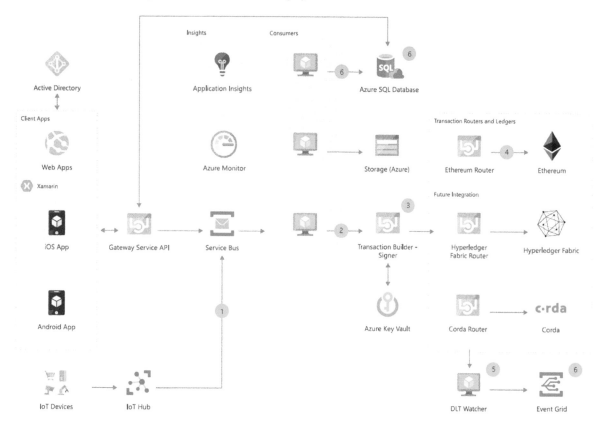

1. IoT devices communicate with IoT Hub. IoT Hub as a route configured that will send specific messages to a Service Bus associated with that route. The message is still in the native format for the device and needs to be translated to the format used by Azure Blockchain Workbench. An Azure Logic App performs that transformation. It is triggered when a new message is added to the Service Bus associated with the IoT hub, it then transforms the message and delivers it to the Service Bus used to deliver messages to Azure Blockchain workbench. The first service bus effectively serves as an "Outbox" for IoT Hub and the second one serves as an "Inbox" for Azure Blockchain Workbench.

2. DLT Consumer fetches the data from the message broker (Service Bus) and sends data to Transaction Builder - Signer.

3. Transaction Builder builds and signs the transaction.

4. The signed transaction gets routed to the Blockchain (Private Ethereum Consortium Network).

5. DLT Watcher gets confirmation of the transaction commitment to the Blockchain and sends the confirmation to the message broker (Service Bus).

6. DB consumers send confirmed blockchain transactions to off-chain databases (Azure SQL Database).

7. Information analyzed and visualized using tools such as Power BI by connecting to off-chain database (Azure SQL Database).

8. Events from the ledger are delivered to Event Grid and Service Bus for use by downstream consumers. Examples of "downstream consumers" include logic apps, functions or other code that is designed to take actions on the events. For example, an Azure Function could receive an event and then place that in a datastore such as SQL Server.

FUTURE RESEARCH DIRECTIONS

Supply chain management has been one of the top five organizational initiatives and highly researched topic within academia for last two decades and it is expected to continue so. Blockchain is seen as a disruptive technology with high potential to improve supply chain operations. Incorporating blockchain into supply chains has the potential to transform everything from warehousing and delivery to order tracking and payment (Exegistics 2019).

Blockchain is aligned to potentially fulfill critical and long-standing challenges presented across dynamic and complex global supply chains that traditionally have held centralized governance models. Current capabilities offered by blockchain solutions for supply chain include a loose portfolio of technologies and processes that spans middleware, database, verification, security, analytics, and contractual and identity management concepts. Blockchain is also increasingly being offered as a service or development option across supply chain solutions that target closely aligned objectives such as automation, traceability and security. A critical aspect of blockchain technology today is the unregulated, ungoverned verification of successful transactions, as well as immutability. These capabilities currently fund much of blockchain development for supply chain (Pettey, 2019).

This chapter introduces some new SCM blockchain architecture patterns, and the concrete solutions for workflow automation and tracking and traceability. Further research that will be carried out includes integration of blockchain data with cloud analytical systems and machine learning services in order to provide better insights and business decisions.

Blockchain in the future will revolutionize business processes in many supply chain industries, but its adoption requires time and efforts. Nevertheless, in the near future, it is expected that governments will finally accept blockchain benefits and begin to use it for improving financial and public services. Though some blockchain startups will fail, people will get more experience and knowledge on how to use this technology. Blockchain will stimulate people to acquire new skills, while traditional business will have to completely reconsider their processes (Gogan, 2018).

Many IoT companies are considering the implementation of blockchain technology in their solutions. The reason for this is that blockchain technology can provide a secure and scalable framework for communication between IoT devices.

The market potential for blockchain is immense. In a recent survey by PwC of 600 executives, 84% of organization are already involved in some way with blockchain technology (PWC, 2019).

International Data Corporation (IDC) forecasts worldwide spending on blockchain will reach $11.7 billion by 2022, with the United State leading the way accounting for 36% of the investment, followed by Western Europe, China and Asia Pacific (Goepfert & Shirer, 2018). Gartner predicts that blockchain's business value-add will grow to more than $3.1 trillion by 2030 and that 10-20% of the global infrastructure will be running on blockchain technology by 2030 (Gartner, 2017).

CONCLUSION

Today's modern global distributed supply chain is incredibly complex, with blockchain having the potential to transform how business is done. With its distributed digital ledger, blockchain has many potential applications in the supply chains for any type of transaction, contract, tracking item, payment and more.

Blockchain technology has the potential to significantly boost the global economy. By accelerating the flow of information in the supply chain, increasing efficiency and enabling the faster turnaround of goods, blockchain could drive trillions of dollars of trade over the next decade.

In this chapter, the main challenges, benefits and use cases of blockchain supply chain systems are identified and discussed. The blockchain reference architectures along with typical supply chain scenarios are presented. They can be used as a blueprints or patterns of how to design and deploy scalable, flexible, and secure could-based blockchain system integrated with other enterprise IT services and systems.

The presented SCM blockchain scenarios provide cloud-based architectures for typical supply chain processes. By utilizing the blockchain-as-a-service platform, it is possible to create, deploy, manage and automate blockchain networks more efficiently and with greater level of scalability and security.

Application of blockchain holds promises to increase visibility, renew viability, reduce inconsistency, increase payment processing accuracy, and eliminate compliance problems. Even though the technology is still new, its potential cannot be ignored, and supply chain executives, managers and IT experts need to know how to best utilize blockchain technologies in order to improve supply chain processes and cut costs.

In the near future, blockchain has the power to replace complicated, error prone supply chain processes with streamlined smart contracts. As the technology grows and matures, it will be used to open new doors for cross-organizational collaboration and enable new business models along the supply chain.

REFERENCES

Alicke, K., Davies, A., Leopoldseder, M., & Niemeyer, A. (2017). *Blockchain technology for supply chains—A must or a maybe?* Retrieved from https://www.mckinsey.com/business-functions/operations/our-insights/blockchain-technology-for-supply-chainsa-must-or-a-maybe

Bocek, T., Rodrigues, B. B., Strasser, T., & Stiller, B. (2017). Blockchains everywhere - a use-case of blockchains in the pharma supply-chain. *IFIP/IEEE Symposium on Integrated Network and Service Management (IM)*, 772-777. 10.23919/INM.2017.7987376

Caro, M. P., Ali, M. S., Vecchio, M., & Giaffreda, R. (2018). *Blockchain-based traceability in Agri-Food supply chain management: A practical implementation. IoT Vertical and Topical Summit on Agriculture - Tuscany.* IOT Tuscany. doi:10.1109/IOT-TUSCANY.2018.8373021

Chester, J. (2016, January 11). *Why Innovative Companies Are Using The Blockchain.* Retrieved from https://www.forbes.com/sites/jonathanchester/2016/01/11/why-innovative-companies-are-using-the-blockchain/

Clauson, K. A., Breeden, E. A., Davidson, C., & Mackey, T. K. (2018). Leveraging Blockchain Technology to Enhance Supply Chain Management in Healthcare: An exploration of challenges and opportunities in the health supply chain. *Blockchain in Healthcare Today, 2*. Advance online publication. doi:10.30953/bhty.v1.20

De Meijer, C. R. W. (2018, January 29). *IBM-Maersk Blockchain Platform: Breakthrough for Supply Chain?* Retrieved from https://www.finextra.com/blogposting/14975/ibm-maersk-blockchain-platform-breakthrough-for-supply-chain

Deloitte. (2017). *Using blockchain to drive supply chain transparency - Future trends in supply chain.* Retrieved from https://www2.deloitte.com/us/en/pages/operations/articles/blockchain-supply-chain-innovation.html

Doubleday, K. (2019). *Why Blockchain Within The Supply Chain Makes Perfect Sense.* Retrieved from https://cerasis.com/blockchain-within-the-supply-chain/

Exegistics. (2019). *10 Supply Chain Trends.* Retrieved from https://exegistics.com/blockchain-and-9-more-trends-transforming-supply-chain/

Francis, J. (2018). *Closing the Hall of Mirrors – How Blockchain Will Simplify and Transform Supply Chain.* Accenture.

Furlonger, D. (2017, March 3). *Practical Blockchain: A Gartner Trend Insight Report.* Retrieved from https://blockcointoday.com/wp-content/uploads/2018/04/Practical-Blockchain_-A-Gartner-Trend-Insight-Report.pdf

Gartner. (2017, March 2). *Forecast: Blockchain Business Value, Worldwide, 2017-2030.* Retrieved from https://www.gartner.com/en/documents/3627117/forecast-blockchain-business-value-worldwide-2017-2030

Goepfert, J., & Shirer, M. (2018, July 19). *IDC Spending Guide.* Retrieved from https://www.idc.com/getdoc.jsp?containerId=prUS44150518

Gogan, M. (2018, August 17). *Blockchain Technology in the Future: 7 Predictions for 2020.* Retrieved from https://aithority.com/guest-authors/blockchain-technology-in-the-future-7-predictions-for-2020/

Gonzalez, A. (2016). *One More Prediction For 2016: Blockchain Technology Will Make Its Debut In Supply Chain Management.* Retrieved from https://talkinglogistics.com/2015/12/21/one-more-prediction-for-2016-blockchain-technology-will-make-its-debut-in-supply-chain-management/

Hackius, N., & Petersen, M. (2017). Blockchain in logistics and supply chain: trick or treat? In K. Wolfgang, B. Thorsten, & R. Christian (Eds.), *Proceedings of the Hamburg International Conference of Logistics (HICL)* (pp. 3-18). Hamburg, DE: Logistik und Unternehmensführung W-2. doi: 10.15480/882.1444

Herzberg, B. (2015, November 21). *Blockchain: the solution for transparency in product supply chains.* Retrieved from https://www.provenance.org/whitepaper

InsightBrief. (2018). *Blockchain in the Supply Chain – Driving End-to-End Change.* Retrieved from https://www.insightbrief.net/blockchain/supply-chain/blockchain-in-the-supply-chain-driving-end-to-end-change/

Kshetri, N. (2018). 1 Blockchain's roles in meeting key supply chain management objectives. *International Journal of Information Management, 39,* 80–89. doi:10.1016/j.ijinfomgt.2017.12.005

Lawton, G. (2019). *10 blockchain problems supply chains need to look out for.* Retrieved from https://searcherp.techtarget.com/feature/10-blockchain-problems-supply-chains-need-to-look-out-for

Lehmacher, W. (2017, May 23). *Why blockchain should be global trade's next port of call.* Retrieved from https://www.weforum.org/agenda/2017/05/blockchain-ports-global-trades/

Lierow, M., Herzog, C., & Oest, F. (2017). *Blockchain: The Backbone Of Digital Supply Chains.* Retrieved from https://www.oliverwyman.com/our-expertise/insights/2017/jun/blockchain-the-backbone-of-digital-supply-chains.html

Lin, I.-C., & Liao, T. C. (2017). A Survey of Blockchain Security Issues and Challenges. *International Journal of Network Security, 19*(5), 653–659.

Marr, B. (2018, March 3). *How Blockchain Will Transform the Supply Chain and Logistics Industry.* https://www.forbes.com/sites/bernardmarr/2018/03/23/how-blockchain-will-transform-the-supply-chain-and-logistics-industry/#3d16d81c5fec

Miaoulis, C. (2019). *Blockchain Applications in Supply Chain.* Retrieved from https://www.blockchaintechnologies.com/applications/supply-chain/

Microsoft. (2018). *How blockchain will transform the modern supply chain.* Microsoft.

Microsoft. (2019a). *Blockchain - Develop, test, and deploy secure blockchain apps.* Retrieved from https://azure.microsoft.com/en-us/solutions/blockchain/

Microsoft. (2019b). *Blockchain workflow application.* Retrieved from https://azure.microsoft.com/en-us/solutions/architecture/blockchain-workflow-application/

Microsoft. (2019c). *Supply Chain Track and Trace.* Retrieved from https://azure.microsoft.com/en-us/solutions/architecture/supply-chain-track-and-trace/

Mitra, R. (2019). *Blockchain And Supply Chain: A Dynamic Duo.* Retrieved from https://blockgeeks.com/guides/blockchain-and-supply-chain/

OMG. (2017). *Cloud Customer Architecture for Blockchain.* Retrieved from https://www.omg.org/cloud/deliverables/CSCC-Cloud-Customer-Architecture-for-Blockchain.pdf

Petersen, M., Hackius, N., & Von See, B. (2018). Mapping the sea of opportunities: Blockchain in supply chain and logistics. *Information Technology - Methods and Applications of Informatics and Information Technology, 60*(5-6). doi:10.1515/itit-2017-0031

Pettey, C. (2017, October 4). *Gartner Identifies the Top 10 Strategic Technology Trends for 2018*. Retrieved from https://www.gartner.com/en/newsroom/press-releases/2017-10-04-gartner-identifies-the-top-10-strategic-technology-trends-for-2018

Pettey, C. (2019, April 22). *Gartner Top 8 Supply Chain Technology Trends for 2019*. Retrieved from https://www.gartner.com/smarterwithgartner/gartner-top-8-supply-chain-technology-trends-for-2019/

Piscini, E., Hyman, G., & Henry, W. (2017). Blockchain: Trust Economy. *TechTrends*.

Pratap, M. (2018, August 8). *How is Blockchain Disrupting the Supply Chain Industry?* Retrieved from https://hackernoon.com/how-is-blockchain-disrupting-the-supply-chain-industry-f3a1c599daef

Prentice, S., Valdes, R., & Furlonger, D. (2015, October 19). *Maverick Research: The Programmable Economy Is the Ultimate Destination for Digital Business*. Retrieved from https://www.gartner.com/en/documents/3152917

PWC. (2019). *Blockchain is here. What's your next move?* Retrieved from https://www.pwc.com/gx/en/issues/blockchain/blockchain-in-business.html

Queiroz, M. M., & Fosso Wamba, S. (2019). Blockchain adoption challenges in supply chain: An empirical investigation of the main drivers in India and the USA. *International Journal of Information Management, 46*, 70–82. doi:10.1016/j.ijinfomgt.2018.11.021

RiskMethods. (2019). *A Beginner's Guide to Supply Chain Risk Management*. Retrieved from https://www.riskmethods.net/resources/beginners-guide/#

Robinson, A. (2019). *Why Blockchain in the Supply Chain Is an Absolute Game Changer*. Retrieved from https://cerasis.com/blockchain-in-the-supply-chain/

Spend Matters. (2015, November 9). *Why Bitcoin's Blockchain Technology Could Revolutionize Supply Chain Transparency*. Retrieved from https://spendmatters.com/2015/11/09/why-bitcoins-blockchain-technology-could-revolutionize-supply-chain-transparency/

Stefanovic, N. (2014). Proactive Supply Chain Performance Management with Predictive Analytics. *The Scientific World Journal*. doi:10.1155/2014/528917

Stefanovic, N. (2015). Collaborative predictive business intelligence model for spare parts inventory replenishment. *Computer Science and Information Systems, 12*(3), 911–930. doi:10.2298/CSIS141101034S

Stefanovic, N., & Stefanovic, D. (2013). Integrated and interactive software solution for knowledge-based supply network design. *Computer Systems Science and Engineering, 28*(1), 5–23.

Swanson, D., & Francisco, K. (2018). The Supply Chain Has No Clothes: Technology Adoption of Blockchain for Supply Chain Transparency. *Logistics, 2*(1), 2. doi:10.3390/logistics2010002

Vorabutra, J.-A. (2016, October 3). *Why Blockchain is a Game Changer for Supply Chain Management Transparency*. Retrieved from https://www.supplychain247.com/article/why_blockchain_is_a_game_changer_for_the_supply_chain

XChain2. (2018). *XChain2: Blockchain for Supply Chain and Logistics Forum*. Retrieved from https://blockchainsupplychain.io/?r=blockchain_technology_initiatives

ADDITIONAL READING

Asharaf, S., & Adarsh, S. (2017). *Decentralized Computing Using Blockchain Technologies and Smart Contracts: Emerging Research and Opportunities*. IGI Global. doi:10.4018/978-1-5225-2193-8

Blokdyk, C. (2019). Blockchain and Supply Chain Management A Complete Guide - 2019 Edition. Emereo Pty Limited.

Shi, N. (2019). *Architectures and Frameworks for Developing and Applying Blockchain Technology*. IGI Global. doi:10.4018/978-1-5225-9257-0

Vyas, N., Beije, A., Krishnamachari, B. (2019). Blockchain and the Supply Chain: Concepts, Strategies and Practical Applications. Kogan Page.

KEY TERMS AND DEFINITIONS

Blockchain: Blockchain is a type of public/private, immutable and distributed ledger for maintaining a permanent and tamper-proof record of transactional data.

Blockchain as a Service (BaaS): It is an offering that allows customers to leverage cloud-based solutions to build, host and use their own blockchain apps, smart contracts and functions on the blockchain while the cloud-based service provider manages all the necessary tasks and activities to keep the infrastructure agile and operational.

Distributed Ledger: It is a database that is consensually shared and synchronized across multiple sites, organizations or geographies.

Ethereum: It is an open source, distributed software platform and cryptocurrency built on the blockchain technology that enables creation of smart contracts.

Hyperledger: Hyperledger is an umbrella project, which offers the necessary framework, standards, guidelines, and tools, to build open source blockchains and related applications for use across various industries.

Mining: In the context of blockchain technology, mining is the process of using computer resources for adding transactions to the large distributed public ledger of existing transactions.

Node: It is a copy of the ledger operated by a participant of the blockchain network, which enables establishing trust in the network, as well as cryptographic and transaction clearing.

Smart Contract: Smart contracts are self-executing contracts with the terms of the agreement between business parties being directly written into lines of code and hosted in the blockchain.

Supply Chain: The evolving term that describes a large volume of structured, semi-structured and unstructured data that has the potential to be mined for information and used in machine learning projects and other advanced analytics applications.

Supply Chain Management (SCM): The management of the flow of goods, services, financials and information across the interconnected business network of companies.

Adoption of Blockchain Technology to Improve Integrity of Halal Supply Chain Management

Yudi Fernando

(iD) https://orcid.org/0000-0003-0907-886X

Faculty of Industrial Management, Universiti Malaysia Pahang, Malaysia

Mohd Ridzuan Darun

Faculty of Industrial Management, Universiti Malaysia Pahang, Malaysia

Ahmed Zainul Abideen

Faculty of Industrial Management, Universiti Malaysia Pahang, Malaysia

Daing Nasir Ibrahim

Faculty of Industrial Management, Universiti Malaysia Pahang, Malaysia

Marco Tieman

Faculty of Industrial Management, Universiti Malaysia Pahang, Malaysia

Fazeeda Mohamad

Faculty of Industrial Management, Universiti Malaysia Pahang, Malaysia

INTRODUCTION – "EVOLUTION OF BLOCKCHAIN TECHNOLOGY"

Blockchain technology was invented by Satoshi Nakamoto along with a few others which still remains a mystery (Kersten, Blecker, Ringle, Hackius, & Petersen, 2017). This technology can help company protect assets, initiate transactions and maintain records between parties in verified chronical events without being hacked or tampered. Blockchain has the potential to change any nation into a cashless entity. A verifiable distributed ledger that records transactions are one of the major concepts of blockchain phenomena (Iansiti, Lakhani, & Mohamed, 2017).

The Blockchain is a chain of orphaned divergent blocks to bring equilibrium inside any digital system (Biais, Bisiere, Bouvard, & Casamatta, 2018). Much focus is now being paid to electronic agreements. Public blockchains applications are constructed into a full digital framework for converting acts and registries. Many governments, personal and economic sector industries are now exploring the possibilities of smart contracts depending on blockchain (Bocek & Stiller, 2018). The success and failure of a key party to handle inter-agency business transactions are no longer necessary. In companies that request safe economic operations, Blockchains are now beginning to affect business management procedures (Mendling et al., 2018).

DOI: 10.4018/978-1-7998-3473-1.ch172

Blockchain Based Smart Contracts

14

Smart contracts based on Blockchain offer a decentralized consensus and conduct algorithms that cannot be readily altered. The manner in which any organization functions is entirely reorganized by incredible quintessence and helps create and build better platforms for records and databases with advanced features (Cong & He, 2018). The installation of blockchain-based tracking improves supply chain provenance. The ability to trace and trace the vanity amount of any products can be seen. Counterfeiting and manipulation in global supply chains have now become very simple (Kim & Laskowski, 2018).

Blockchain's backbone with respect to any smart contracts financial transactions is cryptocurrencies. Pseudonymous payments can be made online using cryptocurrency. They can be used to exchange currencies through a smart contract but somehow exhibit few drawbacks regarding throughput and latency (Eyal et al., 2016). Cryptocurrencies are decentralized currencies which can be used to design and develop a smart property over an internet platform without human interventions. Self-administrating regulations if established could deploy law-abiding self-executing smart contracts. Government and multinational corporates could find it difficult to regulate activities through old means. Hence, there is great need to still refine and fine-tune this cryptocurrency technology (Wright & De Filippi, 2015). Social world can be mediated by decentralized technologies that has the capability to completely transform bureaucratic government models (Reijers & Coeckelbergh, 2018). Cryptocurrency is an irreversible virtual currency that has become more flexible, private and less amenable when compared to other transaction procedures (Böhme, Christin, Edelman, & Moore, 2015).

Background of Study - Halal Supply Chain Management

Conventional supply chain management (SCM) focusses on the integration of the business process from the original suppliers that provide products, services, and information until it reaches the end-user. According to Halal Industry Development Corporation (HDC), Halal SCM, on the other hand, makes the conventional SCM becoming more meaningful by addressing the details of supply chain management which has to comply with the Islamic law (Syariah Law) by addressing few details as follows:

- Does not contain any parts or products of non-halal animals or animal products that are not slaughtered under Islamic law,
- Does not contain any material that Najs according to Sharia law,
- Safe and harmless
- Not prepared, processed or manufactured using equipment contaminated with Najs matter (dirt or impurities) in accordance with Sharia law,
- The food or ingredients used do not contain any portion or derivative of human beings which is not permitted by Shariah law, and
- And during preparation, processing, packaging, storage or transportation, meals are physically separated from other foods that do not qualify as aforementioned or any other matter that has been designated as Najs by Shari 'ah Law (Halal Industry Development Corporation - Halalan Toyyiban).

The word halal comes from Arabic words which are halla, yahillu, hillan, wahalalan which mean allowed or permitted according to Islamic Law. It covers the entire processes from the method of preparation (including the equipment), processing, storage, packaging and environmental areas that must be free from Najs and comply with hygiene practices (Soon, Chandia, & Regenstein, 2017). While conventional supply chain focusses on maximizing profitability, reducing costs and meeting consumer demand, the halal supply chain main objective is to protect the integrity of halal food to ensure that Muslim consumers eat only halal and toyyib. This is important as Islam ensures its people to eat only acceptable, nutritious, healthy and quality foods.

The Halal SCM integrity has become an important issue and the biggest challenge that need to be tackled in the Halal industry. Halal food integrity can only be protected by ensuring that there is no direct contact between halal products and non-halal products across the supply chain. In addressing the growing demand for Halal food from around the world, the need for a comprehensive and well-managed integrity supply chain management approach has to be emphasized. This is to ensure the availability of halal food products in the market is entirely based on integrity concept and practices (Abd Rahman, Singhry, Hanafiah, & Abdul, 2017; Roslan Mohd Nor, Latif, Nazari Ismail, & Nazri Mohd Nor, 2016; Soon et al., 2017).

Halal Supply Chain Issues

A stronger scheme must be created continually to track and trace Halal products in any stage of the supply chain. Some of the Halal producers are not complying with the regulations established by the Halal bodies and are therefore acting as loophole for communication transparency in a negative way within the supply chain network (Zailani, Arrifin, Wahid, Othman, & Fernando, 2010). In order to satisfy the demands of Muslims, Halal supply chain and logistics norms play a dominant role. Not every Halal manufacturer is including Halal methods in their entire supply chain. The adoption rate for Halal in the supply chain is also too low among many foreign manufacturers. A separate body of Halal supply chain providers needs to be established to help overcome competitive pressure, lack of awareness and stringent governmental regulations (Ngah, Zainuddin, & Thurasamy, 2014).

Supply chain of Halal products needs to meet specific objectives and goals with respect to Halal standards and policies set by the government agencies which primarily differ from traditional supply chain practices right from the design of the supply chain network to business processes for logistics control (Tieman, van der Vorst, & Che Ghazali, 2012). Therefore, consumer's purchase intention not only depends on Halal slaughtering but also on storage and packaging methods (Adura et al., 2015; Tieman, 2011). Halal consumer market directly depends on Halal storage and packaging standards implemented by Halal supply chain service providers to provide higher assurance to the customers and increase integrity and help design robust and flexible requirements (Bahrudin, Illyas, & Desa, 2011). Nowadays, some customers tend to ask even what type of feed was given to slaughtered animals (Omar & Jaafar, 2011).

Halal containerization and coding is another major challenge. Some sections of the supply chain of Halal are still susceptible to cool / ambient and bulk/unit contamination. Some Muslim and non-Muslim countries ' business demands also differ, which have to be monitored constantly to guarantee regulated operations and to decrease vulnerabilities (Tieman & Ghazali, 2014). A specialized transport and retention of Halal are needed for cold-chain products such as meat and fish which are imports from other nations or distinct parts of the same nation and must be specifically devoted to a transport port and airport system with Halal standards. Efforts should be made for the eradication of Halal ambient products from the adulteration of Non-Halal products (Tieman & van Nistelrooy, 2014). In attempt to obtain Halal consistency without cross-contamination from raw material to finished goods, presentable data on Halal status should be created available to the public (Soon et al., 2017).

Future Scope for Blockchain-based Halal Supply Chain Smart Contracts

High-end supply chain technology related software is booming with the help IT in manufacturing sectors to enhance supply chain security that is assisted by blockchain technology. This concept's major advantage is to help us to trace every item's origin. It saves IoT (Internet of Things) linked devices from cyber-attacks. It is very apt in handling complex workflows in supply chain and logistics (Kshetri, 2017). The blockchain technology acts as a foundation for distributed ledgers and an innovative platform for establishing businesses. Transaction of any goods and services can be made possible by the help of inherited transparency and traceability characteristics of blockchain software.

Key product information is collected, managed and stored in a smart contract that operates with a decentralized distributed ledger. This process can be repeated throughout the life cycle of the product creating a shared and secured record combining all the specific information of the product. A product normally passes through many actors like producers and manufacturers, suppliers and distributors and retailers and finally end customers. A unique digital profile can be generated to each and every product in the supply chain network to preserve its identity at any given level. A Barcode, RFID or QR code shall be used to attach a product to the network along with all of its information. A unique cryptographic spotter helps to connect a physical product to its virtual identity on the network. Owners of every echelon of the supply chain will possess their own digital profile that portrays the location, product description, certifications and association of other products linking the player profile and the product profile. Every stage of the contract can be privacy protected (Abeyratne & Monfared, 2016). The blockchain features allow consumers to monitor each high-value object from the origin. And all private data would be driven into strings that can prevent some privacy issues (Xu et al., 2019). Hyperconnected logistical ideas ensure that the supply chain of products is accessible, more effective and environmentalism. Increasingly, Blockchain and IoT techniques are considered as key enablers of progress in this field (Betti, Khoury, Hallé, & Montreuil, 2019).

Figure 1. Conceptual framework

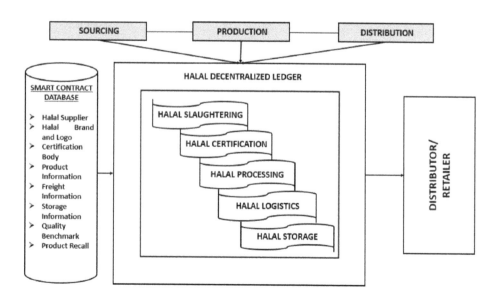

A lot of paperwork is done when containers carrying goods are shipped globally also incurring a lot of money and time. Documents and files, in particular the high-profile goods, are susceptible to falsification and cheating. The food chain where foodborne outbreaks are caused by counterfeit products is one of the worst impacted. Through source monitoring systems which can be efficiently processed through blockchain technology, the identification of the products should, therefore, be monitored and identified at all stage of the supply chain. All information is collected and collected in an affordable and immutable form (Kersten et al., 2017). Blockchain technology has a prospective impact on supply chain management (Chang, Chen, & Lu, 2019). Drug supply chains can be made secure with a Hyper-ledger fabric based on blockchains (Jamil, Hang, Kim, & Kim, 2019). Blockchains have the capability to create a disruptive global sustainable supply chain (Saberi, Kouhizadeh, Sarkis, & Shen, 2019). However, the heavy costs of developing this technology require thorough consideration and an awareness of its advantages and results (Kumar, Liu, & Shan, 2019).

Blockchain Based Halal Supply Chain – A Conceptual Framework

The above Blockchain-based Halal framework (Figure 1) is designed and proposed based on the various Halal requirements that need to be fulfilled to meet customer satisfaction in Halal Food supply chain in a Halal context. Time-Consuming and tiring constraints and requirements can be made easy by imparting them into a distributed decentralized ledger as shown in the figure above. The main aim is to interconnect all the constraints together and retrieve Halal data and information at any point of the business process and financial transactions. The Halal certifications and governmental norms are made online to reduce a huge amount of time. Maintaining security and integrity of Halal manufacturing, storage and transportation can be made easy by adopting blockchain-based Halal Supply chain.

An asymmetric encryption mathematical modules which need a matching key to decrypt the blockchain cannot be falsified at any point in the procedure. With the decryption technique, the buyer can track the vendor and the route of delivery. His real source, certification, or process cannot be hidden by anyone or changed. When used in the Halal supply chain, this technology can demonstrate unthinkable benefits, especially for the Halal food industry as stronger traceability is required throughout the value chain enabling more robust trading is feasible.

LIMITATIONS

A blockchain is faster for economic operations, but more sophistication is needed for products like inventory quality check, registrations, certifications, documents, and taxes. But there are real-time issues to overcome traditional supply chain transactional features. Sometimes the miners could pose a threat in hacking transactional processes like over-invoicing, changing document quality and content, certification, contracts and protocols, supplier preferences and logistics details. Quality audits with human interventions are also a major issue which can prove disastrous if not done properly especially in pharmaceuticals and perishable food chains (Apte & Petrovsky, 2016).

CONCLUSION

Scholars argue that this technology can bring reliable, robust and speedy financial transactions without changing hands of any physical goods. Blockchain-powered platforms can take care of business process of stock market, insurance and taxation, land-registry and medical records. Several ways are being explored and experimented to apply this technology to suffice the requirements for secure and safe physical transportation of goods. This technology has a great potential to revolutionize the existing system and make it a transparent and secure one (Iansiti et al., 2017; Spend Matters Team, 2015). With a high-end supply chain technology the primary advantage of tracing the origin of each element is identified. It avoids cyber-attacks of linked devices IoT (Internet of Things). It can be used to manage complex supply chain and logistics workflows (Kshetri, 2017).

Halal supply chains are susceptible in view of the credence quality attributes, and to preserve the integrity of halal in the entire supply chain, the suspicion must be avoided, food standards are to be monitored to tackle the Muslim consumers who are sensitive to Halal standards (Tieman & Darun, 2017). Brand holders are facing many difficulties with regard to the development of complete halal supply chains and the governance of halal issues. To this purpose, major Halal Certification Bodies (HCBs) put up a panel of discussions on the prospective position of halal blockchain technology. The problems of Halal can be split into three main fields: contamination, failure to comply and perception. Higher flaws are expected to happen in Non-Muslim countries and can be handled with effective communication, whereby the term 'halal supply chain' is encoded in freight documents, on freight labels and within the ICT system (Tieman, Darun, Fernando, & Ngah, 2019).

FURTHER RESEARCH DIRECTIONS

Pros of this technology can be used in production and supply chain business for the implementation of financial, social and legal processes. Blockchain presents special features such as longevity, easiness, immutability and process sincerity. The future study can include the features of blockchain technology and the enablers of adoption. It is also worth to consider the security aspect in blockchain technology. Unlike distributed systems, the risk of error is totally prevented. Any individual node in a supply chain shall be retained with the same copy, which is practically unchanged and needs other nodes to be validated. Very soon, the supply chain will be fully controlled by decentralized systems, bridging the division between organizations and countries and building a revolutionary worldwide chain. Blockchain technology has a much broader range in the Halal supply chain because of its tiring accreditation and reliability obligations. Countries like Malaysia, Saudi Arabia are considered to be the Halal hubs of the world. It would be a great revolutionary change in the Halal business if the Halal Global Supply chain is integrated and connected together by sophisticated high-end blockchain platforms.

ACKNOWLEDGMENT

The authors convey their appreciation to the Division of Research & Innovation, Universiti Malaysia Pahang for funding this study (RDU grant no: 172208 & UIC181505).

REFERENCES

Abd Rahman, A., Singhry, H. B., Hanafiah, M. H., & Abdul, M. (2017). Influence of perceived benefits and traceability system on the readiness for Halal Assurance System implementation among food manufacturers. *Food Control, 73*, 1318–1326. doi:10.1016/j.foodcont.2016.10.058

Abeyratne, S. A., & Monfared, R. P. (2016). Blockchain ready manufacturing supply chain using distributed ledger. *International Journal of Research in Engineering and Technology, 5*(9), 1–10. doi:10.15623/ijret.2016.0509001

Adura, F., Yusoff, M., Nerina, R., Yusof, R., Siti, A., & Hussin, R. (2015). Halal Food Supply Chain Knowledge and Purchase Intention. *Int. Journal of Economics and Management International Journal of Economics and Management, 9*, 155–172. http://www.econ.upm.edu.my/ijem

Apte, S., & Petrovsky, N. (2016). Will blockchain technology revolutionize excipient supply chain management? *Journal of Excipients and Food Chemicals, 7*(3), 910. https://jefc.scholasticahq.com/article/910-will-blockchain-technology-revolutionize-excipient-supply-chain-management

Bahrudin, S. S. M., Illyas, M. I., & Desa, M. I. (2011). Tracking and tracing technology for halal product integrity over the supply chain. *Proceedings of the 2011 International Conference on Electrical Engineering and Informatics, ICEEI 2011.* 10.1109/ICEEI.2011.6021678

Betti, Q., Khoury, R., Hallé, S., & Montreuil, B. (2019). *Improving Hyperconnected Logistics with Blockchains and Smart Contracts.* ArXiv Preprint ArXiv:1904.03633

Biais, B., Bisiere, C., Bouvard, M., & Casamatta, C. (2018). *The Blockchain Folk Theorem.* SSRN Electronic Journal. doi:10.2139srn.3108601

Bocek, T., & Stiller, B. (2018). Smart Contracts – Blockchains in the Wings. In *Digital Marketplaces Unleashed* (pp. 169–184). Springer Berlin Heidelberg. doi:10.1007/978-3-662-49275-8_19

Böhme, R., Christin, N., Edelman, B., & Moore, T. (2015). Bitcoin: Economics, Technology, and Governance. *The Journal of Economic Perspectives, 29*(2), 213–238. doi:10.1257/jep.29.2.213

Chang, S. E., Chen, Y.-C., & Lu, M.-F. (2019). Supply chain re-engineering using blockchain technology: A case of smart contract based tracking process. *Technological Forecasting and Social Change, 144*, 1–11. doi:10.1016/j.techfore.2019.03.015

Cong, L. W., & He, Z. (2018). *Blockchain Disruption and Smart Contracts.* doi:10.3386/w24399

Eyal, I., Gencer, A. E., Sirer, E. G., Van Renesse, R., Efe, A., Emin, G., & Sirer, G. (2016). Bitcoin-NG: A Scalable Blockchain Protocol Bitcoin-NG: A Scalable Blockchain Protocol. *Proceedings of 13th USENIX Symposium on Networked Systems Design and Implementation (NSDI'16)*. Retrieved from https://www.usenix.org/conference/nsdi16/technical-sessions/presentation/eyal

Halal Industry Development Corporation - Halalan Toyyiban. (n.d.). Retrieved August 31, 2019, from http://www.hdcglobal.com/publisher/bdh_halalan_toyyiban

Iansiti, M., Lakhani, K. R., & Mohamed, H. (2017). It will take years to transform business, but the journey begins now. *Harvard Business Review.* Retrieved from https://enterprisersproject.com/sites/default/files/the_truth_about_blockchain.pdf

14

Jamil, F., Hang, L., Kim, K., & Kim, D. (2019). A Novel Medical Blockchain Model for Drug Supply Chain Integrity Management in a Smart Hospital. *Electronics (Basel)*, 8(5), 505. doi:10.3390/electronics8050505

Kersten, W., Blecker, T., Ringle, C. M., Hackius, N., & Petersen, M. (2017). *Digitalization in Supply Chain Management and Logistics Blockchain in Logistics and Supply Chain: Trick or Treat?* Retrieved from https://tubdok.tub.tuhh.de/bitstream/11420/1447/1/petersen_hackius_blockchain_in_scm_and_logistics_hicl_2017.pdf

Kim, H. M., & Laskowski, M. (2018). Toward an ontology-driven blockchain design for supply-chain provenance. *Intelligent Systems in Accounting, Finance & Management*, 25(1), 18–27. doi:10.1002/isaf.1424

Kshetri, N. (2017). Can Blockchain Strengthen the Internet of Things? *IT Professional*, 19(4), 68–72. doi:10.1109/MITP.2017.3051335

Kumar, A., Liu, R., & Shan, Z. (2019). Is Blockchain a Silver Bullet for Supply Chain Management? Technical Challenges and Research Opportunities. *Decision Sciences*.

Mendling, J., Dustdar, S., Gal, A., García-Bañuelos, L., Governatori, G., Hull, R., ... Dumas, M. (2018). Blockchains for Business Process Management - Challenges and Opportunities. *ACM Transactions on Management Information Systems*, 9(1), 1–16. doi:10.1145/3183367

Ngah, A. H., Zainuddin, Y., & Thurasamy, R. (2014). Adoption of Halal Supply Chain among Malaysian Halal Manufacturers: An Exploratory Study. *Procedia: Social and Behavioral Sciences*, 129, 388–395. doi:10.1016/j.sbspro.2014.03.692

Omar, E. N., & Jaafar, H. S. (2011). Halal supply chain in the food industry - A conceptual model. In *ISBEIA 2011 - 2011 IEEE Symposium on Business, Engineering and Industrial Applications* (pp. 384–389). 10.1109/ISBEIA.2011.6088842

Reijers, W., & Coeckelbergh, M. (2018). The Blockchain as a Narrative Technology: Investigating the Social Ontology and Normative Configurations of Cryptocurrencies. *Philosophy & Technology*, 31(1), 103–130. doi:10.100713347-016-0239-x

Roslan Mohd Nor, M., Latif, K., Nazari Ismail, M., & Nazri Mohd Nor, M. (2016). Predominant factors of Malaysia–Middle East religious and cultural relations from the perspective of halal food supply chain. *Arabian Journal of Business and Management Review*, 6(1). Retrieved from www.arabianjbmr.com

Saberi, S., Kouhizadeh, M., Sarkis, J., & Shen, L. (2019). Blockchain technology and its relationships to sustainable supply chain management. *International Journal of Production Research*, 57(7), 2117–2135. doi:10.1080/00207543.2018.1533261

Soon, J. M., Chandia, M., & Mac Regenstein, J. (2017). Halal integrity in the food supply chain. *British Food Journal*, 119(1), 39–51. doi:10.1108/BFJ-04-2016-0150

Spend Matters Team. (2015). *Why Bitcoin's Blockchain Technology could revolutionize supply chain transparency.* Retrieved from https://spendmatters.com/2015/11/09/why-bitcoins-blockchain-technology-could-revolutionize-supply-chain-transparency/

Tieman, M. (2011). The application of *Halal* in supply chain management: In-depth interviews. *Journal of Islamic Marketing*, 2(2), 186–195. doi:10.1108/17590831111139893

Tieman, M., & Darun, M. R. (2017). Leveraging blockchain technology for halal supply chains. *Islam and Civilisational Renewal*, 8(4), 547–550. doi:10.12816/0045700

Tieman, M., Darun, M. R., Fernando, Y., & Ngah, A. B. (2019). Utilizing Blockchain Technology to Enhance Halal Integrity: The Perspectives of Halal Certification Bodies. In *World Congress on Services* (pp. 119–128). Springer. 10.1007/978-3-030-23381-5_9

Tieman, M., van der Vorst, J. G. A. J., & Che Ghazali, M. (2012). Principles in halal supply chain management. *Journal of Islamic Marketing*, 3(3), 217–243. Advance online publication. doi:10.1108/17590831211259727

Tieman, M., & van Nistelrooy, M. (2014). Perception of Malaysian Food Manufacturers Toward Halal Logistics. *Journal of International Food & Agribusiness Marketing*, 26(3), 218–233. doi:10.1080/08974438.2013.833572

Wright, A., & De Filippi, P. (2015). *Decentralized Blockchain Technology and the Rise of Lex Cryptographia*. SSRN Electronic Journal. doi:10.2139srn.2580664

Xu, Z., Jiao, T., Wang, Q., Van, C. B., Wen, S., & Xiang, Y. (2019). An Efficient Supply Chain Architecture Based on Blockchain for High-value Commodities. In *Proceedings of the 2019 ACM International Symposium on Blockchain and Secure Critical Infrastructure* (pp. 81–88). ACM. 10.1145/3327960.3332384

Zailani, S., Arrifin, Z., Wahid, N. A., Othman, R., & Fernando, Y. (2010). Halal Traceability and Halal Tracking Systems in Strengthening Halal Food Supply Chain for Food Industry in Malaysia (A Review). *Journal of Food Technology*, 8(3), 74–81. doi:10.3923/jftech.2010.74.81

ADDITIONAL READING

Fernando, Y., Achmad, S., & Gui, A. (2019). Leveraging business competitiveness by adopting cloud computing in Indonesian creative industries. *International Journal of Business Information Systems*, 32(3), 364–392. doi:10.1504/IJBIS.2019.103082

Fernando, Y. & Zhengxiaoming, A. (2019). Why Does Theory of Inventive Problem Solving Matter in Malaysian Food and Beverage industry? *KnE Social Sciences*, 746-757.

Role of Smart Contracts in Halal Supply Chain Management

Yudi Fernando

https://orcid.org/0000-0003-0907-886X
Faculty of Industrial Management, Universiti Malaysia Pahang, Malaysia

Mohd Ridzuan Darun
Faculty of Industrial Management, Universiti Malaysia Pahang, Malaysia

Basheer Al-haimi
Faculty of Industrial Management, Universiti Malaysia Pahang, Malaysia

Daing Nasir Ibrahim
Faculty of Industrial Management, Universiti Malaysia Pahang, Malaysia

Marco Tieman
Faculty of Industrial Management, Universiti Malaysia Pahang, Malaysia

Fazeeda Mohamad
Faculty of Industrial Management, Universiti Malaysia Pahang, Malaysia

INTRODUCTION

The technologies and its advancement have brought many solutions to various complex aspects of our life. Blockchain technology is a new revolution in the era of technology that called the Fourth Industrial Revolution (Tieman and Darun 2017). The basic idea behind this technology is that, its "an open, distributed ledger that stores transactions between two parties on distributed servers located in different places around the world and this make it more secure and trustable (Iansiti and Lakhani 2017, Tapscott and Tapscott 2017). The blockchain system has the ability to improve traceability and the transparency of the supply chain operations (Tieman et al., 2019). Hence, Blockchain technology had provided solutions and had enormous values in streamlining agreements, transactions and industry workflows inside and among the organizations. For instance, varied number of industries such as energy sector, robotics systems industries, finance, medical, insurance and supply chain can potentially apply this technology and provide solutions to overcome challenges and being greater benefits to all these sectors (Burger, Kuhlmann et al. 2016, Engerati 2017) (Gatteschi, Lamberti et al. 2018).

In the energy sector, Blockchain technologies has confirmed its great potentials to enhance the existing processes and practices in this field. Blockchain technologies can offer a great benefits to this industry in various ways such as: reduce costs, enhance energy security and foster sustainability (Andoni, Robu et al. 2019). Similarly, Blockchain technologies shows its potentials and promises in the robotic systems industries. (Ferrer 2018, Lopes and Alexandre 2018, Afanasyev, Kolotov et al. 2019, Lopes, Alexandre et al. 2019) emphasized the benefits and outcomes of the integration of Blockchain and robotic systems

DOI: 10.4018/978-1-7998-3473-1.ch173

whereby it will offer an essential capabilities to enable the operation of robotic swam systems, rise the efficiency between agents.

Other field and sectors such as business sector, Blockchain technologies has offered numerous types of applications to facilitate the operations and business processes. (Andoni, Robu et al. 2019) summarized those applications as a use cases by Blockchain technologies in the business field. Billing, Sales and marketing, Trading and market, Automations, Smart grid applications, and Grid Management are among the potential applications in the field of business offered by Blockchain technologies (Grewal-Carr V 2016, Arsenjev, Baskakov et al. 2019)

On the other hand, with the invention of smart contracts within the Blockchain technology, the overall Supply Chain Management (SCM) will become more efficient as well as the transaction and traceability will be better in the supply chain process (Catallini 2017, Law 2017). To elaborate this, Blockchain offers capabilities such as tamper data saved in Blockchain, providing a single source of the truth, and smart contracts that automatically execute agreement terms. In combination, these capabilities promote the supply chain traceability, trust and veracity that are vital to the industry's future competitiveness (Casey and Vigna 2018) .

Likewise, Tieman and Darun (2017) argued that Halal Supply Chains Management (HSCM) are susceptible and due that becomes more difficult to design, manage and optimize. As a result, a combination of Blockchain technology and smart contracts that help in transparency is needed to ensure trust, reputation and originality of Halal supply chains products. Thus, this study aims to provide a comprehensive review on the role, benefits, and promises of utilizing the smart contracts in the domains of SCM, and HSCM.

Moreover, to the best of our awareness, till date, there has been no review study specifically focused on the implementation impact of the smart contract on the SCM and HSCM. Hence, this chapter will add new value to the intended researchers and practitioners by providing a clear view and critical discussion on smarts contracts in term of its roles and benefits to the HSCM.

This paper is organized into the two main sections: Section 2 (Background) elaborates the smarts contracts with SCM along with providing a detailed discussion on the roles, benefits, and promises of utilizing the smarts contracts in SCM domain. Section 3 discusses further the application of smart contracts in HSCM with presenting its roles, benefits, and promises. Section 4 concludes this study.

BACKGROUND

Benefits and Promises of Smart Contracts with Supply Chains Management

Smart contracts are not a word to do with artificial intelligence but it's a term used to define an automated computer program that is capable of facilitating, executing and enforcing an agreement without interference of third party. The idea back to the mid-90s when scholar Nik Szabo has introduced this term explaining its uses and potentials (Botsman 2017). Hence, since the required technological infrastructure was not existed, Nik Szabo innovation was not recognized. But and due to the advent of Blockchain and crypto protocols, many things are changing and smart contracts starts its revolution.

In our global society, traditional contracts require a middle man for enforcement such as bank, lawyer, ebay and etc. On the other hand, smart contracts are segments of code that build upon Blockchain technology to verify or enforce the performance of contracts. Moreover, smart contracts have many advantages over traditional contracts. Simple computer programs to replace enforcers, easy to understand, immutable, transparent, accurate, verification, visibility, lower costs, self-execution, clarity of

Table 1. Current usage fields of smart contracts

Fields	How smart contracts being used
Management	Smart contracts improves security, communication and efficiency through the transparent, accurate, and automated system of Blockchain technology. .
Government	An obvious example in how smart contracts being used in government is the vital role that smart contracts play in securing the voting system.
Automobile	Smart contracts can be a boon for the automobile industry. They could help in detecting the culprit of a crash. This could also help the automobile insurance companies to charge the rates on the bases of the conditions under which the customer operates their automobiles.
Supply chain	In paper-based systems of supply chains, the forms go through many processes for approval. This increases the susceptibility to fraud and loss. This common and sensitive issue has long been countered by the use of Blockchain technology. The use of smart contracts in Blockchain offers tremendous security and accessibility to all the associated parties. This automates tasks as well as payment. The transparency offered by incorporating Blockchain in the supply chain also helps in building trusts between the involved parties.
Real Estate	By using smart contracts, all the additional cost to be paid to the third party and others will be cut off and this lead to increase the revenues. Because, by using smart contracts, the payment is only through bitcoin and encode the contract on the ledger. As a result, this will benefit the real estate agent.
Healthcare	It makes the healthcare management simpler such as regulation compliance, administering drugs, regulating the healthcare supplies and testing results.(Griggs, Ossipova et al. 2018)
Transportation	Making the flight more saver and to avoid flight data confliction, storing the flight data and uses of smart analysis can achieve this goal.
Banking	It assists the clients in sharing and exchange money and properties. It also bring more transparency, trusts and efficiency in the working process.

Source: Zfort Group (2018)

agreement terms, fraud protection and connectivity are among the advantages of smart contract over traditional one (Cottrill 2017).

Furthermore, as mentioned earlier, smart contract is a new technological storm that being used in various fields and industries. Table 1 shows some examples of current fields used by smart contracts.

ISSUES

According to John et al., 2017), *"smart contracts represent a next step in the progression of blockchains from a financial transaction protocol to an all-purpose utility,"*. Noticeably, smart contracts have affected businesses whether directly or indirectly. This can be seen in many smart contracts applications such as insurance products, copyright protection, company recordkeeping and smarter voting as well as in supply chain management. Peter Harris, co-founder and research principal at Chain Business Insights stated that " Numerous firms realized the capabilities of smart contracts to the supply chains field". Similarly, in supply chains management, smart contracts can provides many benefits and promises to this particular field. Figure 1 presents the summary of the smart contracts benefits provided to the supply chains management.

Figure 1 illustrates the benefits of smarts contracts to supply chains management in terms of transparency, traceability and efficiency. These three major benefits are discussed further in the following points:

Figure 1. Smart contracts benefits to supply chains management
Source: (Law 2017).

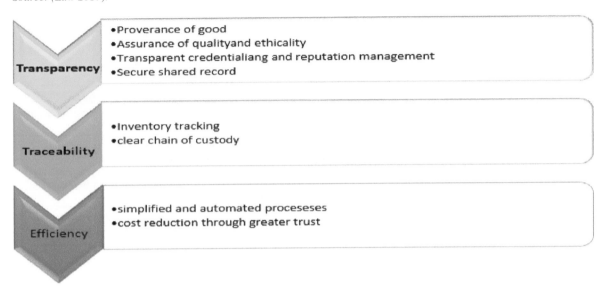

Transparency

Smart contracts can play an important role in building trust and confidence among the manufacturers and the consumers. The ability to save all the goods' information such as origins, date, location and quality on the Blockchain will result to improve transparency of SCM. Therefore, when these information are available, secured and can't be changed, the products can be easily proved and as a result, manufacturers and consumers can be more confident and assured about the originality and legitimacy of the products. Likewise, HSCM can benefited a lot of this technology in terms of transparency.

Traceability

Tieman and Darun (2017) stated that one of the challenges facing Halal supply chain management is the traceability or the ability of verifying the location and the product. Therefore, traceability can be a second benefit of smart contracts for SCM. The benefit can be represented by allowing the inventory to be checked and tracked along the way of the SCM processes. With advent technology such as IoT, real-time systems and connected devices, smart contracts can enhance the traceability even more in SCM. The sensors embedded on those devices will help to provide the necessary data such as location m, environmental condition which will be bases for supply chain mangers for taking faster decisions.

Efficiency

One of the smart contract features is that it's generally faster and convenient which help the processes efficiently. The efficiency of smart contracts can be represented by two main aspects: process and cost (Law 2017). The ease of use make the process of smart contract faster and available at any time comparing to traditional contracts in supply chain management. The second aspect that how supply chain management can be facilitated through efficiency is through cost reduction. As we know that typical supply chain process required many physical documents and middlemen to handle all these processes, smart contracts can shorten these and reduce the cost.

14

FUTURE RESEARCH DIRECTIONS

To claim that product is a Halal product, a number of structured stages in HSC are needed and have to be tracked accordingly. The first stage is slaughterhouses and processing plants. In this stage, the materials are shipped to production/manufacturing place where a Halal certificate is issued and transported to the storage facility. The second stage is to distribute and transport to retailers/wholesalers. This stage need to be tracked by barcoding technology which is expensive to deploy (Supply Chain, 2018). As a result, when the items are delivered, there is no ways to track back product origins. Thus, any failures occurs in any of these processing parts, product is no longer classified as Halal. Above all, the current traceability system, for instance, in Malaysia, is manual and has no real-time tracking as well as its not widely trusted (Supply Chain, 2018).

BENEFITS AND PROMISES OF SMART CONTRACTS WITH HALAL SUPPLY CHAINS MANAGEMENT

Halal concept has become a popular and increasingly grabbed the attention of many Muslims and non-Muslims countries. The wide distribution of Halal food around the world, the increase in demands, rising population of the Halal food consumers and the huge revenues are among the reasons behind the popularity of this concept (Omar and Jaafar 2011). Therefore, the Halal supply chain is very sensitive matter towards Muslim consumers which make it more sophisticated and required special attention.

In other word, Halal supply chain is very complex that needs more commitment and rigor of the trading partners in terms of product isolation practices. Sometimes, the failure of these practices lead to the diminish of the consumer trust. To avoid all the above mentioned consequences and obtained the consumers trust and confidence, smart contracts in Blockchain technology is the promise solutions to Halal traceability issues and overcome many drawbacks. The reason behind that is, smart contracts using Blockchain technology can engender trust as the bases of this technology is designed with immutable tamper-proof database. Likewise, it can remove third parties to verify sources of products.

CONCLUSION

The aim of this chapter was to investigate the roles, benefits and promises of smarts contracts on Halal supply chains management. The smart contracts applications on Blockchain technology are going to be used widely while the traditional contracts are nearing its end. The features that smart contracts possesses and because of the complexity and sensitivity of the Halal supply chains management processes, smart contracts can be a useful solution. Among the promises and benefits that smart contracts can affords to Halal supply chain management are: increase the trust among manufacturers and consumers, security and ease of use, reduce the payment for lawyers and eliminate middlemen. Finally, smart contracts is a new promises applications of Blockchain technology that will change the business world and bring it to a new business model.

REFERENCES

Afanasyev, I. (2019). *Towards blockchain-based multi-agent robotic systems: Analysis, classification and applications.* arXiv preprint arXiv:1907.07433

Andoni, M., Robu, V., Flynn, D., Abram, S., Geach, D., Jenkins, D., McCallum, P., & Peacock, A. (2019). Blockchain technology in the energy sector: A systematic review of challenges and opportunities. *Renewable & Sustainable Energy Reviews, 100*, 143–174. doi:10.1016/j.rser.2018.10.014

Arsenjev, D. (2019). Distributed Ledger Technology and Cyber-Physical Systems. In *Multi-agent Systems. Concepts and Trends. International Conference on Computational Science and Its Applications.* Springer.

Botsman, R. (2017, Oct. 21). Big data meets Big Brother as China moves to rate its citizens. *Wired.*

Burger, C. (2016). *Blockchain in the energy transition. A survey among decision-makers in the German energy industry.* DENA German Energy Agency.

Casey, M. J., & Vigna, P. (2018). *The Truth Machine: The Blockchain and the Future of Everything.* HarperCollins.

Catallini, C. (2017). How blockchain applications will move beyond finance. *Harvard Business Review, 2.*

Cottrill. (2017). *Smart Contracts in Supply Chain: Making Sense of a Potential Game Changer.* Academic Press.

Engerati. (2017). *Blockchain Europe: Utilities pilot peer-to-peer energy trading.* Retrieved 25 November, 2019, from www.engerati.com/article/blockchain-europe-utilities-pilot-peer-peer-energytradingñ.

Ferrer, E. C. (2018). The blockchain: a new framework for robotic swarm systems. In *Proceedings of the Future Technologies Conference.* Springer.

Gatteschi, V., Lamberti, F., Demartini, C., Pranteda, C., & Santamaría, V. (2018). Blockchain and smart contracts for insurance: Is the technology mature enough? *Future Internet, 10*(2), 20. doi:10.3390/fi10020020

Grewal-Carr, V. M. S. (2016). *Blockchain enigma paradox opportunity.* Retrieved 25 November, 2019, from https://www2.deloitte.com/content/dam/Deloitte/uk/Documents/Innovation/deloitteuk-blockchain-full-report.pdf

Griggs, K. N., Ossipova, O., Kohlios, C. P., Baccarini, A. N., Howson, E. A., & Hayajneh, T. (2018). Healthcare blockchain system using smart contracts for secure automated remote patient monitoring. *Journal of Medical Systems, 42*(7), 130. doi:10.100710916-018-0982-x PMID:29876661

Iansiti, M., & Lakhani, K. R. (2017). The truth about blockchain. *Harvard Business Review, 95*(1), 118–127.

Law, A. (2017). *Smart contracts and their application in supply chain management.* Massachusetts Institute of Technology.

Law, A. (2017). *Smart contracts and their application in supply chain management.* Massachusetts Institute of Technology.

Lopes, V. (2019). *Controlling robots using artificial intelligence and a consortium blockchain.* arXiv preprint arXiv:1903.00660

Lopes, V., & Alexandre, L. A. (2018). *An overview of blockchain integration with robotics and artificial intelligence.* arXiv preprint arXiv:1810.00329

Omar, E. N., & Jaafar, H. S. (2011). Halal supply chain in the food industry-A conceptual model. In *Business, Engineering and Industrial Applications (ISBEIA), 2011 IEEE Symposium on.* IEEE. 10.1109/ISBEIA.2011.6088842

Supply Chain. (2018). *Is Blockchain the Missing Link in the Halal Supply Chain?* Retrieved from: http://supplychainmit.com/2018/05/10/is-blockchain-the-missing-link-in-the-halal-supply-chain/

Tapscott, D., & Tapscott, A. (2017). How blockchain will change organizations. *MIT Sloan Management Review, 58*(2), 10.

Tieman, M., & Darun, M. R. (2017). Leveraging Blockchain Technology for Halal Supply Chains. *Islam and Civilisational Renewal, 8*(4), 547–550. doi:10.12816/0045700

Tieman, M., Darun, M. R., Fernando, Y., & Ngah, A. B. (2019, June). Utilizing Blockchain Technology to Enhance Halal Integrity: The Perspectives of Halal Certification Bodies. In *World Congress on Services* (pp. 119-128). Springer. 10.1007/978-3-030-23381-5_9

Zfort Group. (2018). *Blockchain: smart contract benefits and vulnerabilities.* Retrieved from: https://medium.com/swlh/blockchain-smart-contract-benefits-and-vulnerabilities-7543b3955ac9

ADDITIONAL READING

Afanasyev, I., Kolotov, A., Rezin, R., Danilov, K., Kashevnik, A., & Jotsov, V. (2019, April). Blockchain solutions for multi-agent robotic systems: Related work and open questions. In *Proceedings of the 24th Conference of Open Innovations Association FRUCT* (p. 76). FRUCT Oy.

Andoni, M., Robu, V., Flynn, D., Abram, S., Geach, D., Jenkins, D., McCallum, P., & Peacock, A. (2019). Blockchain technology in the energy sector: A systematic review of challenges and opportunities. *Renewable & Sustainable Energy Reviews, 100,* 143–174. doi:10.1016/j.rser.2018.10.014

Arsenjev, D., Baskakov, D., & Shkodyrev, V. (2019, July). Distributed Ledger Technology and Cyber-Physical Systems. Multi-agent Systems. Concepts and Trends. In *International Conference on Computational Science and Its Applications* (pp. 618-630). Springer.

Burger, C., Kuhlmann, A., Richard, P., & Weinmann, J. (2016). *Blockchain in the energy transition. A survey among decision-makers in the German energy industry.* DENA German Energy Agency.

Grewal-Carr, V., & Marshall, S. (2016). *Blockchain: Enigma. Paradox. Opportunity.* Tech. Rep.

KEY TERMS AND DEFINITIONS

Blockchain: A list of records namely blocks, that are tied with cryptography.

Blockchain Technologies: Technologies that stored everything of value and prevent corruptions in many aspects of daily work and transactions.

Halal: Word originated from Arabic language that describe any food, deal with others based on Islamic law.

Halal Supply Chain Management: Sha'riah compliance of management of goods and services movement which transform raw materials into final products and distribute it to the end users.

Smart Contracts: Blockchain-based technology that make many parties to deal electronically based on prior sets of rules and agreements.

Wasta Effects on Supply Chain Relationships in the Middle East Region

14

Noor Al-Ma'aitah
Mutah University, Jordan

Ebrahim Soltani
Hamdan Bin Mohammed Smart University, UAE

Ying-Ying Liao
Hamdan Bin Mohammed Smart University, UAE

INTRODUCTION

Globalization and new rules of competition have forced many firmsto revisit their relationship-building strategies for achieving a competitive position over their rivals in the global marketplace (Cannon, Doney, Mullen, & Petersen, 2010; Rita &Krapfel, 2015; Wiengarten, Fynes, Pagell, & de Búrca, 2011). The globalization of markets requires individual firms to build mutual trust and long-lasting business relationships withfirms from different countries, eachwith its own unique and distinguishable culture (Hofstede, 1980).The accelerating expansion of supply chains beyond national boundariescoupled with the rise in product recalls in the global supply chain have encouraged management scholars to examine the effects of culture on trustworthy supply chain relationships (Carter et al., 2015; Choi & Wacker, 2011; Halldórsson et al., 2015; Hunt &Davis, 2012; Miles &Snow, 2007;Steven et al., 2014).Overall, prior supply chain relationships research has theorized cultural effects on supply chain relationships and trust as having a mediating or moderating effect on the long-term stability of a supply chain relationship (see Chandra & Kumar, 2001; Peters &Hogensen, 1999).

Although the extant research has made substantial contributions to knowledge, the research on cultural effects on long-term supply chain relationships is still patchy. A common concern relates to existing conceptualization and empirical scrutiny of cultural effects on supply chain that has largely relied on Western-driven cultural frameworks(e.g., Hofstede's cross-cultural paradigm) with a focus on highly advanced Anglo-American (e.g. USA, UK, Germany) and several other developed and emerging economies (e.g. Japan, South Korea, China, Singapore). Whereas the homogeneity of cultural formworks in the context of developed Western economies is assumed to function asfundamental universal assumptions concerning nationalculture and supply chains, recent research has viewed such generalizations as unhelpful in explaining cultural orientations in the context of (non-Western) developing economies such as the Arab Middle East region(see Cannon et al., 2010;Graca, Barry&Doney, 2015; Soni &Kodali, 2011; Soltani et al., 2018). In this respect, Meyer (2006) has arguedthat "Asian management research should be able to make major contributions, for instance by explaining context-specific variables and effects, and by drawing on traditional Asian thought in developing new theories" (p. 119).

The research presented in this chapter is a quantitative study of the impact of Arab Middle East cultural values on long-term supply chain relationships in Jordon. The aim is to examine the impact of *Wasta*(الواسطة network) on the long-term supply chain relationship as well as the moderating effect of

DOI: 10.4018/978-1-7998-3473-1.ch174

theqa(trustثقة)in this relationship in the Jordanian manufacturing sector. Jordan is an ideal locus for such research because, not only does it share almost the same cultural norms and attitudes with other countries in the region, but it has also been recognized as the most globalized country in the region (Abu Tahun, 2012). Focusing on privatization, it has adopted an open economy strategy to attract foreign investment. Globalization, low purchasing power in the Jordanian manufacturing sector coupled with limited natural resources have made Jordon an interesting research site for studying the effects of culture on supply chain relationships (see Noor, 2014).

The chapter starts with a review of the literature pertinent to national culture and supply chain relationships. It will then discuss the proposed research framework and development of research hypotheses. Next, itwill describe the adopted research methodology followed by a presentation of the research findings. The chapterconcludes with a discussion of research implications.

CONCEPTUAL FRAMEWORK AND HYPOTHESES DEVELOPMENT

As Figure 1 shows, the proposed research framework suggests that national cultural norms (i.e. wasta) have effects on the long-term supply chain relationships and that trust moderates the effects of national culture on supply chain relationships. In addition, trust could also have a direct effect on long-term supply chain relationships.

Figure 1. Conceptual framework

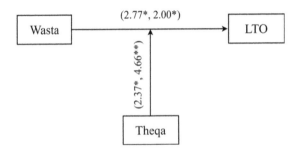

NATIONAL CULTURE AND SUPPLY CHAIN RELATIONSHIPS

A great deal of research has been undertaken to determine just what culture is and how various national cultures differ. Space does not permit a full review of this literature here. It must suffice to say that culture is best reflected in Hofstede and Hofstede's (2005) definition: "the collective programming of the mind that distinguishes the members of one group or category of people from others" (p. 4). In addition, while "cultural dimensions" have no limited list, the extant literature has identified a number of dimensions (Hall &Hall, 1990; Hofstede, 1980; Morden, 1999; Trompennars &Hampden-Turner, 1997; Schwartz, 1999).

Although the role of national culture has been investigated in various human behaviours such as consumer behavior, marketing, and human resources, operations and supply chain management has relatively little researchon culture. For example, Hope and Mühlemann (2001) stated that production and operations management (POM) researchers have been relatively slow in examining the inter-relationships between POM practices and culture. Pagell, Katz, and Sheu, (2005) examined the influence of national culture

14

on operational decision-making. While their study found that national culture explains some variance related to the decisions with regard to the number of suppliers, extending the relationships, outsourcing percentage, the level of export, and the time horizon of forecasting, it did not show how and why culture is a factor influencing Operations Management (OM) decisions. Metters, Zhao, Bendoly, Jiang, and Young's (2010) studied national cultural effects on OM decision making, indicating that culture plays a role in a range of OM decisions in Asia such as location, shift scheduling, revenue management, and total quality management (TQM). Kull and Wacker (2010) examined whether cultural values in Asian (China, Korea and Taiwan) and non-Asian countries moderated TQM practices and evaluated how effective they were in improving quality performance. They found that implementing TQM practice is accomplishable, but such practice assumes specific cultural values in certain Asian cultures. Power, Schoenherr, and Samson (2010) concluded that the Western individualistic and industrialized countries invest more in structural resources such as physical and capital assets, and collectivist emerging Asian economies invest more in infrastructure assets such as team-based improvement programs. Wiengarten et al. (2011) reported that cultural dimensions influence investments in OM practices and operational performance. Graca et al. (2015) examined the impact of relationship capital and exchange climate on performance satisfaction between Brazilian buyers and USA suppliers and find that individualism moderates the relationship between trust and exchange climate (i.e. communication and conflict resolution). Metters (2008) studied the impact of national culture on off-shoring services in airline companies and argues that managers should modify their operational practices in light of the local culture. In a similar vein, Hope (2004) reportsthat national culture influencessuccessful best practices among hotels in St. Lucia. Altogether, these bodies of literature suggest that national culture has important implications for the nature and scope of long-term supply chain relationships (see alsoRunyan, Sternquist, and Chung, 2010; Cannon et al., 2010)

In light of globalization and the emergence of a global marketplace, recent studies of operations and supply chain management has shifted the focus from Western settings to non-Western organizational and cultural contexts.For example, Fang and Kriz (2000) offered evidence from the Chinese culture by arguing that industrial marketing and purchasing (IMP) paradigm is not a universal paradigm. Instead,it needs to be modified to incorporate all cultures. Lee, Pae, and Wong (2001) developed a *guanxi* (i.e. personal relationship) model and examined its influence on relationship performance in Hong Kong and mainland China. In the same vein, Chung, Sternquist, and Chen (2006) studied Japanese retailer buyers' relationships with their suppliers and find that long-term orientation is an antecedent of trust and dependence, not an outcome. Jia and Lamming (2013) arguesthat cultural adaptation eliminates the negative impact of cultural differences on cross-cultural supply chain relationships between Western buyers and Chinese suppliers. Wiegel and Bamford (2015) found that *guanxi* plays an important role in buyer-supplier relationships in SMEs in China both as an organizational source and as a strategic tool to achieve organizational goals in approaching new and existing customers and suppliers.

The preceding review of the extant literature suggests that most of previous cross-border operations and supply chain management studies havefocused onWestern and developed countries and that Hofstede's cross-cultural paradigm has often been used as a theoretical lens for the evaluation of cultural effects on operationsand supply chain decision making. Hence, few studies have tried to integrate various aspects of non-Western cultural norms to reach a better understanding of organisational decision making. More specifically, emerging Arab Middle East nations have been overlooked in past cross-cultural operations and supply chain management research (Soni &Kadoli, 2011). Consequently, there has been call for more research into the role of cultural values in buyer-supplier relationships in the Arab Middle East region – largely owing to the distinct religious culture and geo-strategic importance of the Middle East to the global economy (Cannon et al., 2010; Doney et al., 1998; Friman, Gärling, Millett, Mattsson, & Johnston, 2002; Graca et al., 2015). As Fang (2010) observes, "The Hofstede paradigm with its focus on cultural differences can hardly capture today's new cross-cultural management environment characterized by change and paradox in borderless and wireless cultural learning, knowledge transfer, and synchronized information sharing" (p. 155). Fang (2010) takes the argument further by asserting that:

in the twenty-first century, management faces new challenges because people in the twenty-first century are increasingly no longer bipolarized and isolated creatures but of multicultural identities and multi-cultural minds" and that scholars from developing economies such as Asia "need to learn from the West but at the same time need to have self-confidence and courage in using indigenous knowledge to make contributions to theory building with global relevance. (p. 155).

In light of the critiques of Hofstede's (and several others) cross-cultural paradigms which have their roots in the West, coupled with their inability to capture the richness of distinct cultural traditions of non-Western societies (Javidan, House, Dorfman, Hanges& De Luque, 2006; Liao, Soltani, &Petrovici, 2010), this study uses the Arab Middle East cultural values as a theoretical lens to study national cultural effects on supply chain relationships. More specifically, the aim of this studyis two-fold: (a) to explorethe impact of Arab Middle Eastern cultural values (i.e., Wasta) on building long-term supply chain relationships, and (b) to examine the moderating effect oftheqa(trust)on the relationship between *wasta* and long- term supply chain relationships from the perspectives of both buying and supplying firms.

Long-Term Buyer-Supplier Relationship

Long-term business relationships allow firms to move beyond short-term benefits and improve financial and non-financialperformance of all members of the entire supply chain. Lambert, Emmelhainz, and Gardner define (1996)long-term relationship between supply chain partners as "business relationships based on mutual trust, openness, shared risk and shared rewards that yield a competitive advantage, resulting in business performance greater than would be achieved by the firms individually" (p. 2). The literature on long-term buyer-supplier relationships includes several constructs, including relationship continuity (Jena et al., 2011), commitment (Grayson &Ambler, 1999), and long-term orientation (Cannon et al., 2010). While these constructs differ, each enhances the relationship between buying and supplying firms. Given the paramount importance of the role of long-term relationship in fulfilling the goals of the all supply chain parties, the current study adopts Lambert et al. (1996) definition of long-term supply chain relationship and uses items largely adapted from Cannon et al.'s (2010) study of buyer–supplier relationships in international markets

Wasta and Long-Term Buyer-Supplier Relationship

Wasta or *Wasata* (وَاسِطَة) is an Arabic word which refers to using one's connections and/or influence to cement a business deal and grow long-term business relationships. El-Said and Harrigan (2009) view *Wasta* as "to employ a middle man, a broker, ago-between or an intermediary (usually a person of high social status and accepted rank) to achieve one's end" (p. 1238).Alwerthan, Swanson, and Rogge (2017) defined it as "broad set of practices in which an individual is expected to extend favors to family, friends and people from their tribe" (p. 1). *Wasta* overlaps in meaning with nepotism in English and *guanxi* in Chinese, amounting to the use of personal connections to gain something or getting something through favoritism rather than merit.*Wasta* is a way of life in the MENA region and frequently practiced by both local and international businesses who use their connections as *wasta*. In the absence of a "no-nepotism" policy, *Wasta*has always been a mechanism for developing strong,productive, and enduring relationships in Arab countries, and its importance has only become more pronounced with the widespread ubiquity of cultural diversity and the desire for the establishment of a long-term harmonious business relationship. Loewe et al. (2008) studied the business climate and investment activities in Jordan, finding that 86% of the interviewees perceived*wasta*to be of paramount importance in all kinds of interactions, and some 56% of the respondents admitted that they usedtheir various means of personal connections to reach their goals.

Cunningham and Sarayrah (1993),Tlaiss and Kauser (2011) and Hooker (2008)noted that *wasta* was an important determinant of business decision making.Solberg (2002) observed that *wasta*in its multitudes of forms (e.g., family relationships, social networks) accelerates the process of handling a document through an organization by accessing decision-makers inside the organization. Similarly, Barnett, Yandle, and Naufal(2011) viewed*wasta* as a tool that plays a part in facilitating the flow of business in Middle Eastern countries wherein a partner has a family member or a close friend with a high power status and is able to help speed up business transactions and support projects.Overall, the existing research highlights the paramount importance of *wasta* as an intrinsic part of the MENA culture and a morally accepted business practice that serves as the beginning and sets the tone for a successful long-term business relationship (see Aljbour &Hanson, 2015;Berger et al., 2015). In fact, recent research identified*wasta* as the cornerstone in a social organization and serves as a basis for the continuation of a business relationship in the future (Brandstaetter, Bamber, & Weir, 2016; Weir, David, Nabil Sultan, &Van De Bunt, 2016). Recent evidence has shownthat using *wasta* through politico-business networks is important since it enables access to current information that is crucial for the success of SMEs. The concept of *wasta*h has also been mentioned in relation to financial resources and suppliers. Findings revealed that strong relationships with suppliers enable firms to get financial resources in the form of trade credits (Sefiani, Davies, Bown, & Kite, 2018).Despite the prevalence of *wasta* across the Arab World as an intrinsic part of the culture and a way of conducting business, it has also been cited as one of the main obstacles to good governance and economic development in the MENA countries. While *wasta* or favoritism has recently received growing attention in the Asian cultural studies, very little research focused on the use of *wasta* and its effects on business climate in MENA countries (Hutchings &Weir, 2006). Therefore, it is hypothesized that:

H1a: *Wasta*is positively related to long-term buyer-supplier relationships in the Jordanian manufacturing sector.

Moderating Effect of Theqa (Trust)

Theqa is equivalent to "trust" in the Western context. Trust has been extensively studied in the literature, which has demonstrated trust as a critical factor for developing successful long-termrelationships. Several model studies have posited trust as a mediating variable (e.g.,Chandra & Kumar 2001; Ferro et al., 2016; Morgan &Hunt, 1994; Nyaga et al., 2010; Peters &Hogensen, 1999). Furthermore, researchers have distinguished between in-group and external trust (Huff &Kelly, 2003). In the Middle East, people are very trusting and empathetic towards their in-group members and subordinate personal goals to achieve the group goal (Elahee, Kirby, & Nasif 2002; Power et al., 2010). Moreover, there is a great level of integration between members, which enhances the building of trust via a transfer process (i.e.,*wasta*) (Doney et al., 1998).Solberg (2002) found that the purchasing process in Arab countries followed the

Western model, except that developing trust between exchange parties takes longer, which was evident in the slow decision processes within Arabic organizations.Doney and Cannon (1997) identified five processes of building trust, noting the transfer process as one of these whereby a third party facilitates the initial meetings (i.e., *ta'arof*) and conversations between parties (Javidan &Dastmalchian, 2003) and helps to transfer *theqa* (i.e., trust) from the *wasta* as a "proof source" to another party to build a friendly environment. Therefore, *wasta* (i.e., *waseet*) works as a mechanism to transfer *theqa* and friendship between exchange parties. *Waseet* is a helpful component in facilitating the joining of a party in *wasta*-closed circles, which provides access to advantages and builds business relationships (Loewe et al., 2008; Tlaiss &Kauser, 2011).Therefore, it is hypothesized that:

H1b: Theqa moderates the positive relationship between wasta and buyer-supplier relationships in the Jordanian manufacturing sector.

Research Context

The Middle East and North Africa (MENA)region generally and the Arab Middle East region in particular offer great opportunities for international business and foreign investment on several fronts. The young population, averaging 25 years old, less than any other region, presents a great opportunity both as a market and a source of labor. Renewable energy has become an important opportunity for investment in non-oil trade in the MENA region. With 60% of the oil and 45% of the gas reserves in the world, the resource-rich countries in the region still represent great assets for many countries. Overall, the MENA region offers a significant market in terms of tourism, manufacturing, services, and agribusiness (O'Sullivan, Rey& Mendez, 2011). While companies around the world have recognized the long-term economic potential in the region and are willing to invest outside the oil and gas sector, cultural issues have been cited as having a major impact on their decisions to operate in the region (Economist Intelligence Unit, 2011). The region is becoming a home base for many multinational corporations (MNCs) that are dominant players and control a significant market share in almost all region countries in different sectors (Soltani &Wilkinson, 2011). Local companies could benefit from the MNCs and act as active partners of the supply chain for these MNCs. Multinational corporations bring new technology into the market that can help local companies become innovators rather than imitators. This in turn shapes managerial thinking and practice and assist local business partners to catch up with international standards (Zahra, 2011). Altogether, the MENA non-oil export potential, its potential to be a profitable emerging consumers market for international firms, and the need for local business partners to establish a trustworthy long-lasting business relationships have motivated the current study.

Research Design

Sampling and Data Collection

Data for this study emerged from questionnaires distributed across two samples: buying firms and supplier firms. The questionnaires were translated and back-translated using standard procedure (Ralston et al., 2012). Questionnaires were administered in Arabic as this was the country's and the respondent's language. To ensure that a wide range of industries were included in the response base, the Amman Chamber of Industry (ACI) database was used to select the buyer firms. Then the buyers were asked to provide the researchers with the supplier contact details. Due to the challenges in random sampling and respondent access in the Middle East, we employed a drop-off and pick-up method commonly used in this region (Ralston et al., 2012). This technique resulted in a high response rate compared to previous results in the literature (e.g., Cannon et al., 2010; Chung et al., 2006; Jena et al., 2011). Overall, a total number of 652 completed questionnaires from both buying (n = 350) and supplying firms (n = 302) were collected within a five-month time period (January to May 2013).

Measurement

To measure the respondents' perspective, researchers adopted survey measurement items from past studies where appropriate. Each survey contained items representing three constructs. The constructs were *wasta* (Al-Ali, 2008; Coyne&Collins, 2009), *theqa* (Cannon et al., 2010; Doney &Cannon, 1997; Jean et al., 2010), and long-term orientation relationship (Cannon et al., 2010). All measures used a five point Likert scale (where 1= "strongly disagree" and 5= "strongly agree").

Sample analysis

The majority of respondents (34.3% for buyers and 39.40% of suppliers) were general or sales managers. While 50% of respondents in the buying sample had a business relationship up to five years with their suppliers, 37.7% of suppliers had 6 to 11 years of business relationship with their buyers. Table 1 provides a summary of descriptive analysis of the sample organizations in terms of length of business operations, size and market share.

Table 1. Descriptive analysis of the sample organizations

Category	Buyers	Suppliers
Company's age (0-11) years	58%	52%
Number of employees (1-300) employees	90.9%	86.4%
Market share (0%-10%)	40%	38.4%

Analysis procedure and results

The Statistical Package for the Social Sciences 20 (SPSS) program was used to test the hypothesized model. The completed questionnaires were used to test the construct's reliability and validity as well as the research hypotheses.

Assessment of validity and reliability

To assess the validity and reliability of scale measures, we conducted principle component analysis (PCA) and Cronbach's alpha statistic. For the total sample, the scale reliabilities (Cronbach's α) for the dimensions exceeded the recommended value of 0.70 (see appendix) (Jena et al., 2011).To assess the validity of scale, a number of steps were taken as follows. First, we reviewed the literature pertinent to research phenomena and gained feedback from academics during the course of pilot study. Second, we performed an exploratory factor analysis (EFA) to explore the validation of the construct using varimax rotation (Wiengarten et al., 2011). Principle component analysis (PCA) resulted in dropping 10 items from the buyer's survey and 11 items from the supplier's survey– largely due to low factor loading (<0.40) or cross loading. The retained measures had high factor loading, and all Kaiser-Meyer-Oklin (KMO) values for all constructs exceeded the recommended value of 0.60 (Gray &Kinnear 2012). Bartlett's Test of Sphericity reached statistical significant (p < 0.05).

Hypothesis Testing

Multiple regression analysis was used to test the research hypotheses. Prior to testing the hypotheses, the data were tested for linearity and multi-co-linearity (Wiengarten et al., 2011). Since none of the cultural dimensions werehighly correlated, the likelihood of multi-co-linearity waslow (Wiengarten et al., 2011). Moreover, the variance inflation factors (VIFs) were calculated to detect any possible threats. Results indicated that VIFs were all less than 2(i.e. less than the commonly used threshold of 10)– an indication that multi-co-linearity was not a concern (Field, 2005; Wiengarten et al., 2011). As Table 2 seeks to suggest, the results provide support for the hypotheses meaning that both hypotheses were significant at l 0.05 and 0.01 levels from buyers and suppliers perspectives, accordingly.

Table 2. Wasta regression analysis (H1a and H1b)

Independent variable	Dependent variable LTO			
	Buyers Model		Suppliers Model	
	β	t-test	B	t-test
Wasta	0.147	2.770**	0.089	2.00*
Theqa	0.682	17.288**	0.741	19.120**
WastaXTheqa	0.096	2.370*	0.176	4.666**
R²	0.483		0.584	

* P < 0.05, ** P < 0.01

DISCUSSION ANDFUTURE RESEARCH DIRECTIONS

The role of cultural values in business relationships is a field of growing potential and importance due to several reasons namely, (i) the trend for increasing international trade across national boundaries and (ii) the shift in the global economic balance of power from homogeneous Western industrialized nations to the developing and emerging markets across Southeast Asia and the MENA region driven by unique religious cultural norms and traditions. The current study contributes to this debate through analyzing the cultural effects on long-term supply chain relationships in the Jordanian manufacturing sector.

In accordance with previous research(e.g. Cannon et al., 2010; Hope & Mühlemann, 2001; Metters, 2008; Pagell et al., 2005; Wiengarten et al., 2011), the results of the current study provide support for cultural effects on supply chain relationships from the perspective of buying and supplying firms. Both perspectives support wasta as a widespread cultural norm in the Middle East region. Wasta works as a loyalty system for the in-group members. It also facilitates the paperwork for the in-group members with the government. In the Middle East business environment,business partners (buyer or supplier) prefer to keep working relationships with their business counterparts(supplier or buyer) organization who has wasta. Solberge (2002) views wasta as an influential factor in handling the paperwork by giving access to the decision-makers inside the organization.Wasta in the MENA region is connected to a person with high reputation, status, or power between the in-group and out-group people. Because of this high reputation, the exchange partners has theqa(trust) in the wasta person and a person from the wasta's side. Therefore, the exchange partner accepts the business process and contract terms with the partner after negotiation because both of them respect the wasta and work closely to save face. This is consistent with Doney and Cannon's (1997) study of the process of building trust which is transferred through a proof source. The findings have also close affinity with the results of cultural studies in other developing economies (e.g. China) in a sense that personal connection has been reported to influence the nature, scope and length of business relationships (see Lee et al., 2001).

The results of the current study suggest a need to revisit and integrate theories of culture into buyer-supplier relationship research. In contrast to previous Western-dominated cross-cultural studies of long-term business relationships, the current study contributes to the debate on conceptualization of supply chain relationships with a focus on distinctive religious culture of the Arab middle East region(see Cannon et al., 2010; Jia & Lamming, 2013; Matters et al., 2010; Metters 2008; Pagell et al., 2005; Power et al., 2010;).

The findings can assist the management of regional and multinational firms operating in the MENA region to better understand context-sensitive and culture-specific issues that are deemed essential in optimizing supply chain relationships. The successful implementation of supply chain strategy in the long-term hinges on the ability of exchange partners to develop and maintain trusting relationships as well as a willingness to accept cultural differences and embrace and promote cultural awareness.International managers should recognize thatArab Middle East nations (in particular Gulf Cooperation Council or GCC countries) have recently undergone a number of structural changes in a bid to spur capital influx and stimulate their oil-reliant economies. Ease of setting up and doing business, improving procedures to access credit locally, reducing bureaucratic interruptions, and launching processes to improve transparency are examples of recent mechanisms by the GCC countries for integrating into the global economy and making the Arab countries the preferred investment destination in the region. To reap the benefits of globalization and penetrate this largely untapped market of the Arab Middle East economies, international managers from both individualist and collectivist cultures should make concerted efforts to minimize the cultural differences with their MENA-based business partners. Managers from individualist Western cultures as well as from collectivist, Muslim minority, Eastern countries (e.g., China, India, Southeast Asia) need to appreciate the extent to which Islamic doctrine and thinking (religious culture) are intertwined and permeate all levels of society (Vogel, 2002, cited in Lagace, 2002). In essence, our findings instruct international managers interested in long-term business relationships in the Arab world to recognize and assimilate the peculiar cultural traits of the Arab world. As Mahajan (2013) succinctly put it, "Companies that gloss over the interplay between culture and religion ignore a critical factor for success in the region". In a similar vein, Hays (2002) observed that "Executives who understand the basic tenets of the Islamic religion as it relates to commerce will have an easier time abroad".

In international businesses, the MENA region's strategic location positions it as a global hub, a candidate for becoming the most important developing economy for global opportunities. These opportunities to invest in different sectors in the MENA region still need a suitable entry method on the part of international businesses. International firms need to find a local partner and hire local staff. This requires foreign businesses to concentrate on understanding the unique cultural norms of the region and minimize the cultural differences for fostering global integration. Effective and feasible solutions to cultural differences in international business relationships require policy makers to take proactive steps to further boost foreign investment in the region. Policymakers need to focus on reforms that help their countries catch up with their peers on issues such as investor-friendly and free trade policies, establishment of new free zones, and state-of-the-art infrastructure (Abbas, 2018).The Arab Middle East governments need to play the linking role among the parties involved in business relationships. They need to focus on strengthening the relationship between the parties to ensure business continuity through effective buyer-supplier relations policies.

CONCLUSION

The aim of the study was to explore the implications of Arab Middle East cultural values (i.e.,*wasta* and *theqa*)for long-term buyer-supplier relationships and the manners in which *theqa*interplay between *wasta* and supply chain relationship. Unlike a majority of previoussimilarresearch that adopted Hofstede cultural paradigm as their theoretical lens, the current study examinesthe buyer-supplier relationships through the unique cultural values of the Arab Middle East region. Using survey data gathered from both buying and supplying firms operating in the Jordanian manufacturing sector, this study shows a general consensus that long-term buyer-supplier relationship is significantly affected by the religious cultural norms of the Arab world and that the moderating effect of *theqa* appears to vary between buying and supplying firms.

REFERENCES

Abbas, W. (2018). *UAE top Arab world's 15th largest exporter*. Retrieved from https://www.khaleejtimes. com/business/economy//uae-top-arab-exporter-worlds-15th-largest

Abu Tahun, I. (2012). Report from the Jordanian Endodontic Society. *Australian Endodontic Journal*, *38*(2), 87–88. doi:10.1111/j.1747-4477.2012.00364.x

Al-Ali, J. (2008). *Structural barriers to Emiratisation: Analysis and policy recommendations* (Doctoral dissertation). Victoria University.

Al-Ma'aitah, N. (2014). *An examination of supply chain relationships in Jordanianmanufacturing context: A cultural perspective* (Unpublished PhD Thesis). University of Kent, UK.

Aljbour, R. H., & Hanson, R. J. (2015). Task complexity and non-Arab expatriates' *wasta* performance in Arab markets. *Middle East Journal of Management*, *2*(1), 1–20. doi:10.1504/MEJM.2015.069005

Aljbour, R. H., Hanson, R. J., & El-Shalkamy, M. M. (2013). Cultural training impact on non-Arab leaders' network performance in Arab markets. *Middle East Journal of Management*, *1*(1), 3–27. doi:10.1504/MEJM.2013.054063

Alwerthan, T. A., Swanson, D. P., & Rogge, R. D. (2017). It's better to give than to receive: Psychological need satisfaction mediating links between *wasta* (favouritism) and individuals' psychological distress. *International Journal of Psychology*, *53*, 11–20. doi:10.1002/ijop.12419 PMID:28547913

Balakrishnan, M. (2013). Featured commentary: Special Issue on the Middle East North Africa Region. *AIB Insight, 13*(2), 3-4. Retrieved from http://documents.aib.msu.edu/publications/insights/v13n2/v13n2_Article1.pdf

Barnett, A., Yandle, B., & Naufal, G. (2013). Regulation, trust, and cronyism in Middle Eastern societies: The simple economics of "wasta." *Journal of Socio-Economics*, *44*, 41–46. doi:10.1016/j.socec.2013.02.004

Berger, R., Silbiger, A., Herstein, R., & Barnes, B. R. (2015). Analyzing business-to-business relationships in an Arab context. *Journal of World Business*, *50*(3), 454–464. doi:10.1016/j.jwb.2014.08.004

Brandstaetter, T., Bamber, D., & Weir, D. (2016). 'Wasta': Triadic trust in Jordanian business. In *The Political Economy of Wasta: Use and Abuse of Social Capital Networking* (pp. 65–78). Springer. doi:10.1007/978-3-319-22201-1_5

Cannon, J. P., Doney, P. M., Mullen, M. R., & Petersen, K. J. (2010). Building long-term orientation in buyer–supplier relationships: The moderating role of culture. *Journal of Operations Management*, *28*(6), 506–521. doi:10.1016/j.jom.2010.02.002

Chandra, C., & Kumar, S. (2001). Enterprise architectural framework for supply-chain integration. *Industrial Management & Data Systems*, *101*(6), 290–304. doi:10.1108/EUM0000000005578

Chung, J. E., Sternquist, B., & Chen, Z. (2006). Retailer–buyer supplier relationships: The Japanese difference. *Journal of Retailing*, *82*(4), 349–355. doi:10.1016/j.jretai.2006.08.008

Clark, J. M. (1940). Toward a concept of workable competition. *The American Economic Review*, 241–256.

Coyne, A., & Collins, M. (2009). *Integrating electronic reverse auctions into defense procurement: Exploratory research on opportunities, issues, processes, risks and cultural implications*. Naval Postgraduate School. doi:10.21236/ADA529419

Cunningham, R. B., & Sarayrah, Y. K. (1993). *Wasta: The hidden force in Middle Eastern society*. Praeger Publishers.

Doney, P. M., & Cannon, J. P. (1997). An examination of the nature of trust in buyer-seller relationships. *Journal of Marketing*, *61*(2), 35–51.

Doney, P. M., Cannon, J. P., & Mullen, M. R. (1998). Understanding the influence of national culture on the development of trust. *Academy of Management Review*, *23*(3), 601–620. doi:10.5465/amr.1998.926629

Dyer, J. H. (1996). Specialized supplier networks as a source of competitive advantage: Evidence from the auto industry. *Strategic Management Journal*, *17*(4), 271–291. doi:10.1002/(SICI)1097-0266(199604)17:4<271::AID-SMJ807>3.0.CO;2-Y

Dyer, J. H., & Chu, W. (2000). The determinants of trust in supplier-automaker relationships in the US, Japan and Korea. *Journal of International Business Studies*, *31*(2), 259–285. doi:10.1057/palgrave.jibs.8490905

El-Said, H., & Harrigan, J. (2009). "You reap what you plant": Social networks in the Arab world— The Hashemite Kingdom of Jordan. *World Development*, *37*(7), 1235–1249. doi:10.1016/j.worlddev.2008.12.004

Elahee, M. N., Kirby, S. L., & Nasif, E. (2002). National culture, trust, and perceptions about ethical behavior in intra-and cross-cultural negotiations: An analysis of NAFTA countries. *Thunderbird International Business Review*, *44*(6), 799–818. doi:10.1002/tie.10049

Fang, T., & Kriz, A. (2000, September). Cross-cultural challenges to the IMP paradigm: Evidence from Chinese markets. *Proceedings of the IMP 16th Annual International Conference.*

Ferro, C., Padin, C., Svensson, G., & Payan, J. (2016). Trust and commitment as mediators between economic and non-economic satisfaction in manufacturer-supplier relationships. *Journal of Business and Industrial Marketing, 31*(1), 13–23. doi:10.1108/JBIM-07-2013-0154

Field, A. (2005).Discovering statistics using SPSS (and sex, drugs and rock 'n' roll (2nd ed.). Sage Publications Limited.

Friman, M., Gärling, T., Millett, B., Mattsson, J., & Johnston, R. (2002). An analysis of international business-to-business relationships based on the Commitment–Trust theory. *Industrial Marketing Management, 31*(5), 403–409. doi:10.1016/S0019-8501(01)00154-7

Graca, S. S., Barry, J. M., & Doney, P. M. (2015). Performance outcomes of behavioral attributes in buyer-supplier relationships. *Journal of Business and Industrial Marketing, 30*(7), 805–816. doi:10.1108/JBIM-04-2014-0072

Grayson, K., & Ambler, T. (1999). The dark side of long-term relationships in marketing services. *JMR, Journal of Marketing Research, 36*(1), 132–141. doi:10.1177/002224379903600111

Hofstede, G., & Hofstede, G. J. (2005). *Cultures and organizations: Software of the mind: Intercultural cooperation and its importance for survival.* McGraw-Hill.

Hooker, J. (2009). Corruption from a cross-cultural perspective. *Cross Cultural Management, 16*(3), 251–267. doi:10.1108/13527600910977346

Hope, C. A. (2004). The impact of national culture on the transfer of "best practice operations management" in hotels in St. Lucia. *Tourism Management, 25*(1), 45–59. doi:10.1016/S0261-5177(03)00059-1

Hope, C. A., & Mühlemann, A. P. (2001). The impact of culture on best-practice production/operations management. *International Journal of Management Reviews, 3*(3), 199–217. doi:10.1111/1468-2370.00064

Huff, L., & Kelley, L. (2003). Levels of organizational trust in individualist versus collectivist societies: A seven-nation study. *Organization Science, 14*(1), 81–90. doi:10.1287/orsc.14.1.81.12807

Hutchings, K., & Weir, D. (2006). *Guanxi* and *wasta*: A comparison. *Thunderbird International Business Review, 48*(1), 141–156. doi:10.1002/tie.20090

Javidan, M., & Dastmalchian, A. (2003). Culture and leadership in Iran: The land of individual achievers, strong family ties, and powerful elite. *The Academy of Management Perspectives, 17*(4), 127–142. doi:10.5465/ame.2003.11851896

Javidan, M., House, R. J., Dorfman, P. W., Hanges, P. J., & De Luque, M. S. (2006). Conceptualizing and measuring cultures and their consequences: A comparative review of GLOBE's and Hofstede's approaches. *Journal of International Business Studies, 37*(6), 897–914. doi:10.1057/palgrave.jibs.8400234

Jena, S., Guin, K. K., & Dash, S. B. (2011). Effect of relationship building and constraint-based factors on business buyers' relationship continuity intention: A study on the Indian steel industry. *Journal of Indian Business Research, 3*(1), 22–42. doi:10.1108/17554191111112451

Jia, F., & Lamming, R. (2013). Cultural adaptation in Chinese-Western supply chain partnerships: Dyadic learning in an international context. *International Journal of Operations & Production Management, 33*(5), 528–561. doi:10.1108/01443571311322715

Kull, T. J., & Wacker, J. G. (2010). Quality management effectiveness in Asia: The influence of culture. *Journal of Operations Management, 28*(3), 223–239. doi:10.1016/j.jom.2009.11.003

Lagace, M. (2002). *How to do business in Islamic countries.* Harvard Business School. Retrieved from https://hbswk.hbs.edu/item/how-to-do-business-in-islamic-countries

Lambert, D. M., Emmelhainz, M. A., & Gardner, J. T. (1996). Developing and implementing supply chain partnerships. *International Journal of Logistics Management, 7*(2), 1–18. doi:10.1108/09574099610805485

Lee, D. J., Pae, J. H., & Wong, Y. H. (2001). A model of close business relationships in China (*guanxi*). *European Journal of Marketing, 35*(1/2), 51–69. doi:10.1108/03090560110363346

Liao, Y. Y., Soltani, E., & Petrovici, D. (2010).Service quality through the lens of Chinese cultural values: Setting the agenda for future research. *Proceedings of the 21st Production and Operations Management Society (POMS) Conference: Operations in Emerging Economics.*

Loewe, M., Blume, J., & Speer, J. (2008). How favoritism affects the business climate: Empirical evidence from Jordan. *The Middle East Journal, 62*(2), 259–276.

Mahajan, V. (2013). Understanding the Arab consumer. *Harvard Business Review, 91*(5).

Metters, R. (2008). A case study of national culture and offshoring services. *International Journal of Operations & Production Management, 28*(8), 727–747. doi:10.1108/01443570810888616

Metters, R., Zhao, X., Bendoly, E., Jiang, B., & Young, S. (2010). "The way that can be told of is not an unvarying way": Cultural impacts on operations management in Asia. *Journal of Operations Management, 28*(3), 177–185. doi:10.1016/j.jom.2009.10.004

Meyer, K. E. (2006). Asian management research needs more self-confidence. *Asia Pacific Journal of Management, 23*(2), 119–137. doi:10.100710490-006-7160-2

Morden, T. (1999). Models of national culture–a management review. *Cross Cultural Management, 6*(1), 19–44. doi:10.1108/13527609910796915

Morgan, R. M., & Hunt, S. D. (1994). The commitment-trust theory of relationship marketing. *Journal of Marketing, 58*(3), 20–38. doi:10.1177/002224299405800302

Nishiguchi, T. (1994). *Strategic industrial sourcing: The Japanese advantage.* Oxford University Press on Demand.

Noordewier, T. G., John, G., & Nevin, J. R. (1990). Performance outcomes of purchasing arrangements in industrial buyer-vendor relationships. *Journal of Marketing, 54*(4), 80–93. doi:10.1177/002224299005400407

Nyaga, G. N., Whipple, J. M., & Lynch, D. F. (2010). Examining supply chain relationships: Do buyer and supplier perspectives on collaborative relationships differ? *Journal of Operations Management, 28*(2), 101–114. doi:10.1016/j.jom.2009.07.005

O'Sullivan, A., Rey, M. E., & Mendez, J. G. (2011). Opportunities and challenges in the MENA region. *Arab World Competitiveness Report, 2012,* 42–67.

Pagell, M., Katz, J. P., & Sheu, C. (2005). The importance of national culture in operations management research. *International Journal of Operations & Production Management, 25*(4), 371–394. doi:10.1108/01443570510585552

Peters, J. E., &Hogensen, A. J. (1999). New directions for the warehouse. *Supply Chain Management Review*, 23-25.

Power, D., Schoenherr, T., & Samson, D. (2010). The cultural characteristic of individualism/collectivism: A comparative study of implications for investment in operations between emerging Asian and industrialized Western countries. *Journal of Operations Management, 28*(3), 206–222. doi:10.1016/j.jom.2009.11.002

Ralston, D. A., Egri, C. P., Riddle, L., Butt, A., Dalgic, T., & Brock, D. M. (2012). Managerial values in the greater Middle East: Similarities and differences across seven countries. *International Business Review, 21*(3), 480–492. doi:10.1016/j.ibusrev.2011.05.007

Rita, P., & Krapfel, R. (2015). Collaboration and competition in buyer-supplier relations: the role of information in supply chain and e-procurement impacted relationships. In *Assessing the different roles of marketing theory and practice in the jaws of economic uncertainty* (pp. 98–105). Springer. doi:10.1007/978-3-319-11845-1_37

Rogmans, T. (2013). Building political risk management skills in the Middle East. *AIB Insight, 13*(2), 2-15. Retrieved from http://documents.aib.msu.edu/publications/insights/v13n2/v13n2_Article4.pdf

Runyan, R. C., Sternquist, B., & Chung, J. E. (2010). Channel relationship factors in cross-cultural contexts: Antecedents of satisfaction in a retail setting. *Journal of Business Research, 63*(11), 1186–1195. doi:10.1016/j.jbusres.2009.10.015

Sefiani, Y., Davies, B. J., Bown, R., & Kite, N. (2018). Performance of SMEs in Tangier: The interface of networking and wasta. *EuroMed Journal of Business, 13*(1), 20–43. doi:10.1108/EMJB-06-2016-0016

Solberg, C. A. (2002, September). Culture and industrial buyer behavior: The Arab experience. *Proceedings of the 18th IMP Conference*. Retrieved from http://impgroup. org/uploads/papers/522. pdf

Soltani, E., Ahmed, P., Liao, Y. Y., & Anosike, P. (2013). Qualitative research in operations and supply chain management: The need for theory-driven empirical inquiry. *International Journal of Operations & Production Management, 34*(8), 1003–1027. doi:10.1108/IJOPM-11-2012-0486

Soltani, E., Liao, Y. Y., Gholami, A., & Abdullah, I. (2018). Saying it without words: A qualitative study of employee voice in the Iranian building sector. *International Journal of Human Resource Management, 29*(5), 1015–1055. doi:10.1080/09585192.2017.1369447

Soltani, E., & Wilkinson, A. (2011). The razor's edge: Managing MNC affiliates in Iran. *Journal of World Business, 46*(4), 462–475. doi:10.1016/j.jwb.2010.10.007

Soni, G., & Kodali, R. (2011). A critical analysis of supply chain management content in empirical research. *Business Process Management Journal, 17*(2), 238–266. doi:10.1108/14637151111122338

Syed, J., Hazboun, N. G., & Murray, P. A. (2014). What locals want: Jordanian employees' views on expatriate managers. *International Journal of Human Resource Management, 25*(2), 212–233. doi:10.1080/09585192.2013.812975

Tlaiss, H., & Kauser, S. (2011). The importance of wasta in the career success of Middle Eastern managers. *Journal of European Industrial Training, 35*(5), 467–486. doi:10.1108/03090591111138026

Weir, D., Sultan, N., & Van De Bunt, S. (2016). Wasta: A scourge or a useful management and business practice? In *The political economy of wasta: Use and abuse of social capital networking* (pp. 23–31). Springer. doi:10.1007/978-3-319-22201-1_2

Wiegel, W., & Bamford, D. (2015). The role of guanxi in buyer–supplier relationships in Chinese small- and medium-sized enterprises–a resource-based perspective. *Production Planning and Control, 26*(4), 308–327.

Wiengarten, F., Fynes, B., Pagell, M., & de Búrca, S. (2011). Exploring the impact of national culture on investments in manufacturing practices and performance: An empirical multi-country study. *International Journal of Operations & Production Management, 31*(5), 554–578. doi:10.1108/01443571111126328

Wonga, W. Y., Sanchaband, C., & Thomsen, C. (2017). A national culture perspective in the efficacy of supply chain integration practices. *International Journal of Production Economics, 193*, 554–565. doi:10.1016/j.ijpe.2017.08.015

Zahra, S. A. (2011). Doing research in the (new) Middle East: Sailing with the wind. *The Academy of Management Perspectives, 25*(4), 6–21. doi:10.5465/amp.2011.0128

ADDITIONAL READING

Al-Faleh, M. (1987). Cultural influences on Arab management development: Aa case study of Jordan. *Journal of Management Development, 6*(3), 19–33. doi:10.1108/eb051643

Al-Jabri, S. H. (2010).,*Trust in supply chain relationships and its impact on organisation and supply chain performance* (PhD dissertation). University of Hull, UK.

Ali, S., Raiden, A., & Kirk, S. (2013). Wasta in the Jordanian cCulture: A study in the Bbanking sSector. *International Journal of Innovations in Business, 2*(6), 529–550.

Aljbour, R. H., Hanson, R. J., & El–Shalkamy, M. M. (2013). Cultural training impact on non–Arab leaders' network performance in Arab markets. *Middle East Journal of Management, 1*(1), 3–27. doi:10.1504/MEJM.2013.054063

Hutchings, K., & Weir, D. (2006). Guanxi and wasta: A comparison. *Thunderbird International Business Review, 48*(1), 141–156. doi:10.1002/tie.20090

Kaako, A. (2019). Promoting an academic culture in the Arab world: Correspondence. *Avicenna Journal of Medicine, 9*(1), 39. PMID:30697527

Marktanner, M., & Wilson, M. (2018). 14. Wasta in the Arab world: an overview. In B. Warf (Ed.), *Handbook on the gGeographies of cCorruption* (p. 228). Elgar publishing. doi:10.4337/9781786434753.00020

Soltani, E., & Wilkinson, A. (2011). The Razor's Edge: Managing MNC Affiliates in Iran. *Journal of World Business, 46*(4), 462–475. doi:10.1016/j.jwb.2010.10.007

KEY TERMS AND DEFINITIONS

Guanxi: Is personal connection in Chinese culture.

National Culture: A set of norms, values, attitudes, and behaviors.

Supply Chain Relationships: On-going relationships between two firms with, at a minimum, a commitment from each party to engage in long-term business projects.

Theqa: Is equivalent to "trust" in the Western context.

Wasta: Is a social behavior based on whom one knows or networks.

Section 15

Organizational Management and Communications

Types and Challenges of Expatriation

Carla Freitas Morence
University of Aveiro, Portugal

Marta Ferreira Esteves
University of Aveiro, Portugal

Núria Rodrigues Silva
University of Aveiro, Portugal

António Carrizo Moreira
ⓘ https://orcid.org/0000-0002-6613-8796
University of Aveiro, Portugal

INTRODUCTION

Based on the Latin etymological root (*expatria*, outside of the mother land), expatriation comprises all individuals residing temporarily or permanently in a country other than the one in which they were born (González & Oliveira, 2011). However, the management literature clearly differentiates terms as expatriate and immigrant, in which the former is associated with individual sent abroad by the firms they work for, and the latter with individuals that left their countries, normally for socio-economic conditions (González & Oliveira, 2011).

The thriving economic globalization process has led to a clear increase in the number of migrants, expatriates and mobile employees, which has led the academic community to focusing on the expatriation phenomenon, especially in the process of adaptation of those expatriates to the countries of destination (Black & Mendenhall, 1991; González & Oliveira, 2011; Shaffer, Harrison, & Gilley, 1999; Wang, 2002).

Expatriation has been studied based on the interest of many multinationals in sending their managers/ executives abroad, since qualified and skilled expatriates are major intangible assets to their companies when it comes to compete in the global market. (Black & Mendenhall, 1991; Shaffer, Harrison, & Gilley, 1999; Wang, 2002; Bonache, Brewster, Suutari, & Cerdin, 2018; Tahir, 2018). However, expatriation has also been studied from the point of view of small and medium-sized enterprises, although with less intensity (Ribau, Moreira, & Raposo, 2018). From the managerial point of view, the expatriate lives temporarily in a foreign country. Expatriation is the act of transferring an executive, eventually his/her family and children, to another subsidiary of the company, located in a different country and culture (Bonache et al., 2018).

When internationalizing a company, expatriation works as a way to solve the problems of lack of professionals with technical and managerial skills. Expatriates are also of added value to the company in the implementation of new projects.

When one experiences times of crisis, the tendency is to seek a better life in another country, yet expatriates tend to do it in ways different from what the ordinary migrants do. They are more adventurous, fearless, and willing to take more risks, bearing in mind that expatriation is seen initially as a temporary experience, something enriching and less like a necessity. Expatriates' performance is a multidimensional

DOI: 10.4018/978-1-7998-3473-1.ch175

15

construction that encompasses the dimensions of cross-cultural adaptation and requires success of the international mandate, i.e. achieving the goals proposed, managing local employees, leading the foreign affiliate, scanning the economic environment and appropriately dealing with important international counterparts.

With the globalization process, expatriation has been growing and tends to be seen as an important step in the development of an international professional career. As a worldwide phenomenon, expatriation is guided by a constantly dynamic working relationship between employer and employee (Jokinen, Brewster, & Suutari, 2008).

Although there is extant research on expatriates, it addresses career-based and business-based expatriation as *"business expatriates, defined as, legally working individuals who reside temporarily in a country of which they are not a citizen in order to accomplish a career-related goal, being relocated abroad either by an organization, by self-initiation or directly employed within the host-country"* (Selmer et al., 2018, p. 136).

The expatriation process ends with repatriation and means that the international assignee returns to his/her home country with family members with whom he/she had expatriated in first place. Regarding this final phase of expatriation, that can be alone a very complicated process, there are already many studies trying not only to understand its complexity but also seeking improved strategies to solve difficulties that the repatriates may face (Chiang, Van Esch, Birtch, & Shaffer, 2018).

In this chapter expatriation is scrutinized in depth in its several dimensions, due to the complexity of the concept and bearing in mind the singularity of the different terms and concepts. This chapter also addresses the impact they might have in the economy and other variables such as gender, social class, or country of origin. This chapter focuses on differentiating five major realities: migration; assigned expatriates (AEs); self-initiated expatriates (SIEs); lifestyle expatriates; and expat-preneurs. The former focuses on survival, whereas the latter are more related to personal realization. Clearly, the expat-preneurs concept combines expatriation with entrepreneurship.

This chapter is divided in six different sections. After this introduction, that comprises the first section, the research method is lain drown in the second section. The literature review is presented in section three and covers several types of expatriation. The discussion and conclusions are addressed in section four. Finally, section five presents the future research direction.

RESEARCH METHOD

In order to prepare this chapter a research was carried out in the SCOPUS database. Eight articles were analyzed taking into account differences in approaches of the expatriates. The objective was not to analyze in depth the articles, nor the variables / constructs that compose them, but to explore the most important different perspectives embracing the terms covering expatriation. As such, as referred to in the introduction section it was decided to embrace the analysis of five peculiar but complementary approaches: migration; assigned expatriates (AEs); self-initiated expatriates (SIEs); lifestyle expatriates; and expat-preneurs.

Expats profiles are presented and explained according to the reasons of their expatriation and behaviors taken abroad. The main reasons that motivate leaving the country of origin determine the enrolment in the new country with positive interaction and sharing of common interests, stimulating cooperation and good performance, as well as diminishing situations of bias and stress. The inverse also happens.

In order to analyze the findings regarding expats, the eight articles were analyzed, their information compiled and crossed-over, and subsequently their differences discussed.

LITERATURE REVIEW

The concept of expatriation encompasses other associated concepts, taking into account the role of the expatriate. Although there are several typologies associated to expatriation (Guttormsen, 2018), one can claim that there are two large expatriate groups (Selmer et al., 2017): self-initiated expatriates (SIE) and company assigned expatriates (AEs). AEs are expatriated through the organizations they represent and for which they will perform a particular function outside their country of origin. According to Selmer et al. (2012, p.1286), SIEs *"initiate and usually finance their own expatriation and are not transferred by organizations; they relocate to a country of their choice to pursue cultural, personal, and career development experiences, often with no definite time frame in mind."* As referred by Selmer et al. (2017) and Tharenou (2013), the introduction of SIE research was very important in understanding the different roles of expatriates, which includes those who go abroad primarily for the perceived value of international work experience, and those who seek a long-term personal and professional development. Selmer and Lauring (2012) analyze the work outcomes and the reasons for expatriation by SIEs. This study is based on a category proposed by Richardson and McKenna (2002), where they categorize people for the reasons that lead them to leave the country by themselves and not by a company. This typology is divided into four categories: the Refugee; the Mercenary; the Explorer; and the Architect.

The refugee is normally associated to people that leave the country because they want to escape their routine. The refugee is simply motivated by changes related to her/his life. Secondly, the mercenary is a person who is motivated by financial incentives, i.e. for opportunities to make more money than in his/her home country. Thirdly, the explorers are people who expatriate by the sense of adventure and the curiosity to know new places and cultures. Finally, the architects are individuals looking to develop their careers seeking better career opportunities (Richardson & McKenna, 2002; Selmer & Lauring, 2012).

To ascertain the relationship between these categories and work outcomes, Selmer and Lauring (2012) divided the results in three variants: work performance, work effectiveness and job satisfaction – and applied a questionnaire to academics in 34 universities in Nordic countries and in the Netherlands. The results of this study showed that all individuals, regardless of the category, perceived their performance as valid and considered themselves to be effective in their work, which they were satisfied with. According to the reasons for expatriation, the Explorers and Architects had a higher score, which infers that Explorers have a better job satisfaction and that Architects look for a higher job performance and superior effectiveness (Selmer & Lauring, 2012).

Although there are many more studies on AEs than about SIEs, Jokinen, Brewster, and Suutari (2008), under the premise that SIEs are a significant number when compared with the number of AEs, intended to contribute to greater information about SIEs. So, the authors conducted a study in order to compare the performance of the two groups, considering three variables relevant to the analysis of the employment status as an individual and as an expatriate: knowing-how, knowing-why, and knowing-whom. Taking into account those variables, they drew up the questionnaire, which was directed only to Finns on a range from minimal qualifications up to masters' level in economics and management. The sample consists of 222 surveys considered valid for analysis.

The knowing-how sets essentially the skills and knowledge of the work performed. Jokinen et al. (2008) consider that work experiences on an international level reinforce the knowledge already acquired in the country of origin and allow the acquisition of new skills that stimulate the confidence of the individuals, since in an international environment the expatriates felt a greater demand on themselves. The results obtained with the questionnaire are in line with these assumptions, since there is no great difference between the two groups. However, those results do not reveal an increase in the business knowledge as originally expected.

When discussing the knowing-why variable, i.e. the reasons for the performance of the various tasks that are related to self-confidence and motivation towards a particular career path, both groups had positive and very similar results. These skills are seen as essential for a good performance of the individual in her/his tasks. About the international work experience, individuals believe to be stimulating their skills, increasing their self-confidence and their value as professionals, being seen as a future investment. The knowing-whom is connected to social and professional relationships, both inside and outside the company, i.e., to the individuals network of contacts. With international experience, there is an expansion of this network, especially for expatriates through companies with which they are related, with a multiplicity of types of more or less formal relations. This premise was also clear in this study, in which it is noted that, although most claim their social skills increased, there are differences between SIEs and AEs in the connoisseurship of the organization, being naturally lower for the SIEs. By definition, as SIEs have no previous connections with the company where they are working for, they are expected to experience lower mobility.

In terms of career progression, AEs show higher values than SIE, which can be justified by the fact that the expatriation of the AEs is due to promotions in their careers, while the SIEs start their expatriation on a significantly lower level when compared with AEs. In this group, and for the variables analyzed, public sector workers showed significantly lower values of development when compared with those who performed functions in the private sector. Thus, the main conclusions of the study are clear: the performance of a professional activity outside of the country of origin improves the general professional skills of the individual, for both groups of expatriates. The individuals are not dependent on the employer as they and can autonomously create their experiences and be successful within them (Jokinen et al., 2008).

Related with the concept of expatriates, it is the concept of expat-preneurs as *"being defined as an individual temporarily living abroad who initiates an international new venture (self-employment) opportunity in the host country"* (Selmer, McNulty, Lauring, & Vance, 2017, p. 137). This notion of expat-preneurs evolved recently to be considered a subtype of expatriates on its own (SIEs), although this simplification could impoverish both the debate on the subject and on the general knowledge of this specific subtype. The growing importance given to entrepreneurship as the engine of local economic development cannot be ignored as well as the growing immigrant and entrepreneur population, substantially more efficient than the resident population in terms of success at undertaking new businesses. As such, it becomes relevant to analyze with greater attention this subtype.

Without disregarding migratory fluxes and economic and institutional general circumstances, Selmer et al. (2017) present several important individual factors in the analysis of this subtype of expatriates, educational level, gender, marital status, position, time in current job in host location, time the expatriate and time in host location.

The authors also distinguish expat-preneurs from expatriates who leave their country seeking better living conditions. As such expat-preneurs tend to move to a new country and there establish themselves as citizens. Expat-preneurs define themselves as expats on their own account because they only intend to stay temporarily in the host country since they invest in their career and feel free to take up any better proposal. They are portrayed as people gifted with the capability to recognize the potential of the host country and are particularly keen on taking risks. On the other hand, the capability to be involved in social and relational engagement with people in the host country emphasizes this phenomenon. Expat-preneurs may have initially started their path as AEs or SIEs but when facing new opportunities and possibilities in terms of network contacts, they embrace a new challenge. They are also characterized as having better market assessment skills, which allows them to embrace advantageous opportunities in the host country (Selmer et al., 2017).

To find the key factors that could define the differences between expat-preneurs and the other self-initiated expatriates, Selmer et al. (2017) sent a survey to several expatriates living on China, Hong Kong, and Singapore. Based on 268 answers SIEs and 57 from expat-preneurs, the results showed that, when compared to SIEs, expat-preneurs were older, had longer experience as expatriates and had higher corporate positions, which highlights the importance of time and experience for individuals to self-develop and self-employ themselves. Aware of these differences, it became clear the need to differentiate the multiple expatriates' profiles, not only to understand but also to better apply the several procedures when hiring and managing expatriates with clear consequences for corporate human resources management policies (Selmer et al., 2017).

Following a different perspective, Vance et al. (2016) analyze the shared and unshared features among SIEs distinguishing expatriates and migrants in specific scenarios, in the European Union. It is important to refer to the visible goal to have a different citizenship and its relation with migration, especially in the European Union, where there are incentives for the freedom of movement of European citizens in European space. Expatriation tends to be seen as more temporary compared to migration, as expatriation is normally sought after by those seeking personal and professional development who want to achieve specific goals and adventure in a certain period of time of their lives. Specifically, the SIEs seek for international professional experience and the development of leadership competences. As a result, the organizations they are part of tend to be more positive and the host countries benefit largely from the knowledge and know how transfer, providing a sustainable growth and development of the economy where SIEs are settled. This phenomenon tends to increase stimulated by the current technological advances, by a more globalized world, by the free movement of people and goods and by the encouragement of foreign direct investment (Vance et al., 2016).

Eisenberg et al. (2015) presents the case of Poland, an Eastern European country with a specific social, economic, and political reality that only recently became a member of the European Union. They analyze the case of expatriates in Poland. Eisenberg et al. (2015) starts by highlighting the fact that as an Eastern European country, with all its defining traits, its integration on the EU led to an inevitable change in the national economy, which is now considered a market-based economy. Considering the Polish economic framework and its differences to the EU economy, it became a necessity to change and adapt the management style of Polish managers. Since the Polish management leadership style was very autocratic, the Western Europe expatriates were fundamental to Poland to adjust and be successful before this new social, economic and political reality. Eisenberg et al. (2015) analyze how Western expatriates have taken part of the changing paradigm at the economic scenario and how this was perceived by the Polish workers (Eisenberg et al., 2015).

To understand the effects of these expatriates in Poland, a survey was applied to a sample of Polish workers led by Western European expatriates. Some interviews were afterwards carried out to a sample of these expatriates. The results show that the Western Europe leaders were perceived as more honest, more able to motivate and inspire, more capable to communicate, relate and more tolerant, when compared to the general Polish leaders, who were described as more authoritarian, evasive, egocentric, and more oriented to administrative labor. The respondents also perceive the Western leadership and management style as being three times more efficient, although the adjustment takes time and the general Polish workers still felt they work better with Polish leaders, with its authoritarian performance, which is typical from countries that were under the soviet influence. The ones with working experience with foreigner leaders felt more open and prepared to work with them. The foreign managers were encouraged to adapt their leadership style, actions, and decisions to the host country as a way to prevent cultural crash, however without disregarding the necessary and desired change. Analyzing the role of expatriates in Poland, one can argue that their work was crucial to bring Poland closer to the European Union. Nowadays it is possible to see a balance between the Polish leadership profile and the Western leadership style as more people oriented. The merge of those different leadership approaches leads to more global and open organizations, which is very important in the current globalized world.

Expatriation is a complex phenomenon that not always reaches the intended goals. Therefore, many companies may face some problems with their expatriate employees, as some of them quit their jobs, while other underperform, way below from original expectations, and in some cases they are recalled back home or resign, which in fact also signifies losses of Million Dollars to the firms for each unsuccessful expatriation. Thereby, the selection procedure and preparation must be carefully considered as well as the adjustment process, which must be also seen as multidimensional concept involving several variables (Tahir, 2018). Considering these situations, Nunes, Felix, and Prates (2017) analyzed how cross-cultural adaptation and cultural intelligence could promote a positive expatriate performance. For that they analyzed a sample of 217 expatriates from different nationalities living in Brazil.

Based on the contact theory, Nunes et al. (2017) argue that the closer the interpersonal relationships of the individuals, the greater will be their level of happiness. Although the proximity of personal relationships is more typical of individuals with similar characteristics, one can infer that this factor has relevance among expatriates and interferes in their performance, since their level of happiness is directly proportional to the level of general performance of the individual, as well as their self-evaluation. Positive interactions and sharing of interests encourage cooperation and good performance and decrease situations of prejudice and stress. The reverse is also valid: negative experiences regarding personal relationships negatively affect the cognitive performance of the individual. For interactions to be successful, it is necessary for the individual to self-regulate and adapt his/her emotional intelligence. In this regard, and taking into consideration the universe of expatriates, the interpersonal relationships that expatriates develop in the host country influence their degree and ability to adapt to the requirements of the new culture.

In this sense, cross-cultural adaptation is seen as an important antecedent in the performance of the expatriates' tasks and presupposes a positive impact in the quality of the integration of the expatriate in their host country and, consequently, in the performance of the task performed (Agha-Alikhani, 2018). This concept is associated with cultural intelligence, a multidimensional construct that links cognitive, meta-cognitive, motivational and behavioral dimensions, i.e. the ability of the individual to interact satisfactorily in different cultural contexts. Cultural intelligence is understood as a capability to successfully adapt to non-familiar cultures and to be successful in situations characterized by cultural diversity. As such, it is expected from an individual with a high level of cultural intelligence to have a better capability to relate with different cultures, while cross-cultural adaptation is the degree of comfort towards situations of greater or lesser degree of difficulty with which the individual is confronted in the host country. Cross-cultural adaptation can be divided in general, labor, and interactive adaptation (Nunes et. al., 2017).

Although the research results show a correlation between cultural intelligence and cross-cultural adaptation, no correlation was found between cultural intelligence and the expatriates' performance, but the correlation between cross-cultural adaptation and the expatriates' performance was found to be significant. As such, it is possible to infer that individuals with high cultural intelligence do not necessarily have a satisfactory performance. This will only happen if the cultural intelligence leads to a better cross-cultural adaptation, which will effectively contribute to a better performance.

Relating to the concept of expat-preneurs, Stone and Stubbs (2007) studied the relation between "lifestyle migration" and entrepreneurship in rural areas of France and Spain. They begin by explaining entrepreneurship associated with migration aiming to study the connection between lifestyle migration, entrepreneurship, and the specificity of the location in order to put forward a conceptual framework relating these three concepts. However, this study focuses on the self-employed, within entrepreneurship.

Stone and Stubbs (2007) conducted a field study about entrepreneurship within the expatriates' community in four rural locations in France and Spain. To do this, they did interviews, combining with open and closed questions, as well as observation techniques to gather information about processes, attitudes, and interactions. The results indicate that almost all the interviewees chose the residential and migration location based on the climate and scenery, having often been visited them in previous vacations. Few of the interviewees migrated with ideas and business plans to begin their start-ups. Furthermore, even a smaller number of the interviewees stated that they would go to the chosen location because it was a good opportunity for a business (Stone & Stubbs, 2007).

Different levels of qualifications and education were found between the two countries. In France, most of the expatriates had higher education and some of them had tertiary education. Likewise, half of the expatriates in France had experience working abroad before the expatriation decision, with half of the interviewees having experience as entrepreneurs. On the contrary, in Spain, most of them did not have qualifications and skills (Stone & Stubbs, 2007).

The greatest contrast was the ability to speak the local language. In France, all expatriates self-evaluated themselves as fluent (Stone & Stubbs, 2007), while in Spain the expatriates showed difficulties with the language. This situation can be explained by the difference between the level of education and the previous experience working abroad (Stone & Stubbs, 2007).

The study also looked at which motivations made the expatriates want to build their own start-ups. The most common reason was that a start-up was a way to continue with their lifestyles and that they did not want to work for others or have the same kind of job that they had before the expatriation. Few of the interviewees chose the location to where they were going based on business opportunities, meaning that the ideas about start-ups were only advanced after the interviewees reallocated themselves and engaged in the following solutions: a way to have funds to continue their lifestyles; as an idea of fun; as a challenge; or to have something to do (Stone & Stubbs, 2007).

It is important to mention that business was a very positive to revive the rural areas of France and Spain, where there was a positive local impact for employment, but also the sharing of culture because of these start-ups.

One can conclude that self-employment can be considered a result of migration, even if expatriates did not have the idea of starting a business, since they could spot the business opportunities in the areas where they were and, regardless of the reasons that have led them to grab these opportunities and to create their own businesses, it is always seen as positive point because it can lead to the best use and revival of those rural areas and bring benefits both to the people living there and to the expatriates.

When analyzed following a gender-based perspective, expatriation seeks to find an explanation to understand what leads women to follow a SIE-perspective and not a company-assigned perspective. Apparently this occurs as most of the companies do not select women for their expatriate roles, contrary to what happens with men. Based on this gender discrimination, women end up opting for SIE roles. In addition to this, according to Tharenou (2010, p. 75) there are also "(...) *disadvantage, gender bias, and inequality of opportunity.*" These reasons lead women to leave their country and seek better working conditions and better opportunities for developing their careers, which they often do not get in their home country. On the other hand, there are situations where women want to flee oppressive cultures and societies and seek freedom. Socially accepted gender roles often prevent women from seeking employment abroad and have to relocate. In this context, expatriation is best seen for single and childless women (Tharenou, 2010).

Complementarily, Tharenou (2010) points out that expatriation may not always bring positive outcomes, since the same treatment that women suffer in the country of origin may also be felt in the host (or relocation) country. In her article, she points out that some studies on the subject indicate that women who go abroad benefit from career development. However, when they are about to return to their home country they do not receive as many benefits as men do. Tharenou (2010) concludes that for women to be able to secure the best conditions and job opportunities and to benefit their careers they must be proactive in finding options and career opportunities and that, despite expatriation, SIE can be a response to some careers, although it is not a solution to the unfair treatment women are subjected to.

DISCUSSION AND CONCUSION

Expatriation is not a fully delineated phenomenon. Its definition has undergone constant mutations over time. As the world changes, so expatriation does, as it adapts to new challenges and evolves. If the definition initially encompassed only individuals leaving their country, the profile of expatriates has been changing over time showing distinctions between groups of individuals as well as differences within the same groups.

Self-initiated expatriates and company assigned expatriates are the two largest groups and within these, mainly within the SIEs group, we have several sub-types, such as expat-preneurs, refugees, mercenaries, explorers, and architects, according to the concepts outlined in the literature review. This clearly indicates that this type of expatriation can be seen differently.

Expat-preneurs, by their characteristics, were the sub-type on which this work was most related. One can conclude that its definition is more or less constant in all the articles analyzed on the subject, although there may not be a line that completely separates them from the profile of an immigrant. It is probably the most complex sub-type because of the broad perspectives in which expat-preneurs can be studied. This is related to its recent development and to its specificity in the global world in which we live today, which creates new specificities and challenges to the global labor market.

In general, the concept of expatriate reports positive consequences for expatriates and the communities where they live, as well as for the development of the areas where they live, showing the complexity of the effects they can bring to all those involved in this process. It was possible to realize that the cognitive, psychological and sociological processes have an effect on the success or failure of the expatriate, both professionally and personally.

Expatriation brings some light to certain phenomena regarding cultural and gender discrimination perspectives. In fact, this is particularly true in the case of the AEs, where women, on one hand, for cultural reasons are discouraged to embrace expatriation, which leads them to embrace expatriation at their own risk and, on the other hand, to feel difficulties when they return to their country of origin, encountering many more obstacles than men do during the expatriation and repatriation processes.

Lifestyle expatriation involves a different perspective of expatriation, as the creation of their start-ups was the main motivation of those expatriates. One particular aspect is that those expatriates decided to start-up their businesses after choosing the places they wanted to live in, but based on the type of employment before expatriation. Moreover, the place they relocated to was decided based on the business opportunity they had in mind previous to their relocation. The business ideas were based on the way they could figure out to generate their funds to continue their lifestyle, the idea of lifestyle they had in mind as well as the challenge they wanted to face.

There is no doubt that expatriation is not a simple phenomenon confined to the classical view of immigration, or only associated with the multinational companies that sent their employees/managers abroad. With the ongoing globalization process, expatriation developed new contours that traditionally were not envisaged. Nowadays, it involves more entrepreneurial, cultural, knowledge-based and gender-based contours based on global situations, which address challenges around the globe.

Expatriation is moderately normal in the EU, based on policies that promote free movement of citizens and labor market liberalization. This reality is not present in all countries. However, the resilience of human beings and their instinct for survival allow them to overcome great adversities and continue to seek comfort and happiness, which can happen through expatriation, both as AEs and SIEs, often giving rise to new phenomena as we have seen in the literature review. Today's expats will make all the difference in tomorrow's future as they contribute to multicultural wealth while having a positive impact on the economy, often changing paradigms and opening doors to new experiences.

FUTURE RESEARCH DIRECTIONS

Based on the different typologies presented throughout the chapter, it would be interesting to analyze the extent to which the expatriation process made expat-preneurs more entrepreneurial and how they perceive business opportunities in their expatriation processes. It will be important to analyze whether these opportunities are developed before or after expatriation and to what extent the expatriation experience has served to make the expat-preneur business more global. It would also be important to explore whether there are some differences between male and female expat-preneurs and, if there were, how they understand the evolution of the business and the expat-preneurs over time.

In order to complement the knowledge about AEs, it would be interesting to understand to what extent the career of these expatriates is influenced by the cultural diversity of the countries where they have been expatriated to over time. On the other hand, it would be interesting to analyze to what extent the expatriate cultural intelligence evolves over time regarding international assignments in homogenous or heterogeneous countries. Moreover, it would be of added value to understand if female expatriates are given the same opportunities to pursue an international career *vis-à-vis* male expatriates, and how those assignments influence their families.

REFERENCES

Agha-Alikhani, B. (2018). Adjustment in international work contexts: Insights from self-initiated expatriates in academia. *Thunderbird International Business Review, 60*(6), 837–849. doi:10.1002/tie.21928

Black, J. S., & Mendenhall, M. (1991). The U-Curve adjustment hypothesis revisited: A review and theoretical framework. *Journal of International Business Studies, 22*(2), 225–247. doi:10.1057/palgrave.jibs.8490301

15

Bonache, J., Brewster, C., Suutari, V., & Cerdin, J.-L. (2018). The changing nature of expatriation. *Thunderbird International Business Review*, *60*(6), 815–821. doi:10.1002/tie.21957

Chiang, F. F., Van Esch, E., Birtch, T. A., & Shaffer, M. A. (2018). Repatriation: What do we know and where do we go from here. *International Journal of Human Resource Management*, *29*(1), 188–226. doi:10.1080/09585192.2017.1380065

Eisenberg, J., Pieczonka, A., Eisenring, M., & Mironski, J. (2015). Poland, a workforce in transition: Exploring leadership styles and effectiveness of Polish vs. Western expatriate managers. *Journal for East European Management Studies*, *20*(4), 435–451. doi:10.5771/0949-6181-2015-4-435

González, J. M., & Oliveira, J. A. (2011). Os efeitos da expatriação sobre a identidade: Estudo de caso. *Cadernos EBAPE.BR*, *9*(4), 1122–1135. doi:10.1590/S1679-39512011000400011

Guttormsen, D. S. (2018). Does the 'non-traditional expatriate' exist? A critical exploration of new expatriation categories. *Scandinavian Journal of Management*, *34*(3), 233–244. doi:10.1016/j.scaman.2018.05.004

Jokinen, T., Brewster, C., & Suutari, V. (2008). Career capital during international work experiences: Contrasting self-initiated expatriate experiences and assigned expatriation. *International Journal of Human Resource Management*, *19*(6), 979–998. doi:10.1080/09585190802051279

Nunes, I. M., Felix, B., & Prates, L. A. (2017). Cultural intelligence, cross-cultural adaptation and expatriate performance: A study with expatriates living in Brazil. *Revista ADM*, *52*(3), 219–232. doi:10.1016/j.rausp.2017.05.010

Ribau, C. P., Moreira, A. C., & Raposo, M. (2018). SME internationalization research: Mapping the state of the art. *Canadian Journal of Administrative Sciences*, *35*(2), 280–303. doi:10.1002/cjas.1419

Richardson, J., & Mckenna, S. (2002). Career development international leaving and experiencing: Why academics expatriate and how they experience expatriation. *Career Development International*, *7*(2), 67–78. doi:10.1108/13620430210421614

Selmer, J., & Lauring, J. (2012). Reasons to expatriate and work outcomes of self-initiated expatriates. *Personnel Review*, *41*(5), 665–684. doi:10.1108/00483481211249166

Selmer, J., McNulty, Y., Lauring, J., & Vance, C. (2018). Who is an expat-preneur? Toward a better understanding of a key talent sector supporting international entrepreneurship. *Journal of International Entrepreneurship*, *16*(2), 134–149. doi:10.100710843-017-0216-1

Shaffer, M., Kraimer, M., Chen, Y.-P., & Bolino, M. (2012). Choices, challenges, and career consequences of global work experiences: A review and future agenda. *Journal of Management*, *38*(4), 1282–1327. doi:10.1177/0149206312441834

Shaffer, M. A., Harrison, D. A., & Gilley, K. M. (1999). Dimensions, determinants, and differences in the expatriate adjustment process. *Journal of International Business Studies*, *30*(3), 557–581. doi:10.1057/palgrave.jibs.8490083

Stone, I., & Stubbs, C. (2007). Enterprising expatriates: Lifestyle migration and entrepreneurship in rural Southern Europe. *Entrepreneurship and Regional Development*, *19*(5), 433–450. doi:10.1080/08985620701552389

Tahir, R. (2018). Expanding horizons and expatriate adjustment: Perceptions of Western expatriate managers in multinational companies in the United Arab Emirates. *Cross Cultural & Strategic Management*, *25*(3), 401–424. doi:10.1108/CCSM-02-2017-0024

Tharenou, P. (2010). Women's self-initiated expatriation as a career option and its ethical issues. *Journal of Business Ethics*, *95*(1), 73–88. doi:10.100710551-009-0348-x

Vance, C. M., McNulty, Y., Paik, Y., & D'Mello, J. (2016). The expat-preneur: Conceptualizing a growing international career phenomenon. *Journal of Global Mobility: The Home of Expatriate Management Research*, *4*(2), 202–224. doi:10.1108/JGM-11-2015-0055

Wang, X. (2002). Expatriate adjustment from a social network perspective: Theoretical examination and a conceptual model. *International Journal of Cross Cultural Management*, *2*(3), 321–337. doi:10.1177/147059580223003

KEY TERMS AND DEFINITIONS

Company-Assigned Expatriates: Individuals expatriated through the organizations they represent and for which they will perform a particular function outside their country of origin. Normally, their assignments are clearly defined in terms of managerial tasks to be performed abroad and time horizon of the assignment.

Expat-Preneurs: An individual temporarily living abroad who initiates an international new venture, based on a self-employment opportunity in a host country.

Expatriate: A person who lives outside her/his native country.

Immigrant: A person who comes to a country to take up permanent residence.

Lifestyle Migration: This concept involves melting migration (as individuals who move from one country to another, seeking better living conditions) with Lifestyle (a 'free choice' to pursue a particular way of living through migration). It normally involves identity-making projects of individuals who approach migration as a form of consumption in contrast to the typically production-orientated migration flows.

Repatriation: It is normally the inverse process of expatriation. It corresponds to the fist job of an individual/manager after returning from as international assignment, that normally dos not last more than two years.

Self-initiated Expatriate: Is an individual who initiates and usually finances her/his own expatriation and are not transferred by organizations. Ii is an individual who relocates to a country of his/her choice to pursue cultural, personal, and career development experiences, often with no definite time frame in mind.

Digital Transformation Journeys:
The Future Is Now

15

Jurgen Janssens

asUgo Consulting, Belgium

INTRODUCTION

Big Data and Digital Transformation are hot topics since many years. Big Data are large volumes of data from one or more sources, analyzed through innovative information processing to develop insights, resulting in better business decisions and process adaptation[1]. In 2018, human and machine data were expected to grow from 33ZB in 2018 to 175ZB by 2025 - of which a third in real-time (Reinsel, Gantz & Rydning, 2018).

Digital Transformation implies often Big Data powered changes (Mayhem, Saleh, & Williams, 2016). Whereas concrete outcomes of the latter are booming, Digital Transformation is still seen as a faraway, conceptual future. Nowadays, however, organizations should not ask themselves anymore how to prepare for the upcoming Digitization, but how to adapt to and in today's Digitized/Digitizing World.

To get there, they need to understand how to evolve by embracing new technological potential and by looking through the blurring frontiers between offline and online reality. They have to take changing habits and continuously transforming customer segments into account. They have to look beyond the mere 'product' and 'selling to customers' angle (Richter, & Wee, 2016). To keep their value, companies, organizations and even governments need to understand that mental mobility of people and their data-stimulated ecosystem have turned people's need for products in a need for shaped services.

This has a significant impact on the strategic vision, in for-profit and non-profit sectors alike. Typically, this requires a new way of working adapted to the redefined borders between reactivity and proactivity, and to the attention for real-time service and contextual adaptation. An organic compromise has to be found that answers the need for creative freedom and the need for an environment where management and development of human capabilities are possible in a structured way.

This article will shed light on core components for Digital Transformation. Concrete methodologies will also be analyzed that can guide the process of reviewing company fundamentals in the Digital Reality.

It will be explained that human means and data power need to be developed to develop a company's digitally quantified intuition[2] and to provide most value for the customer journey.

Altogether, this article will illustrate that the success of Digital Transformation goes through integrating technological possibilities and dynamic customer journeys in the corporate DNA. It will require a new internal perspective on projects, and create a new dynamic that, in the end, will allow people, companies and public and private organizations to be in the driving seat of this Fourth Industrial Revolution.

BACKGROUND

Reflections about Digitization and Digital Transformation exist since several years, also on intergovernmental level[3]. With technology developments in various fields amplifying one another, this will

DOI: 10.4018/978-1-7998-3473-1.ch176

continue. It is laying the foundation for a revolution more all-encompassing than anything seen so far (Schwab, & Samans, 2016), putting additional pressure to leaders and organisations that are de facto already operating in a turbulent context with frequent and unpredictable change (De Stobbeleir, Peeters, Pfisterer, & Muylle, 2019).

There are several risks if the dynamic is not engineered and managed correctly. First of all, companies need to be aware that Digital is not an add-on, but the very essence of the transformation journey to remain in the game (Henke, Libarikian, & Wiseman, 2016). It involves a change in leadership, new business models, and an increased use of technology to improve the customer experience. It is only by integrating this Digital backbone that Digital strategies can have a lasting effect. Digital is one of the main reasons half of the companies on the Fortune 500 have disappeared since 2000 (Nanterme, 2016). The growing impact of the GAFAs and the NATUs[4] only confirms this. Failing to understand its functioning can thus lead to companies losing their relevancy.

Traditionally, Digital Transformation is covered from separate angles. Certain sources analyze the impact of technology on job markets and human employability (Van Driessche, 2014). Others focus more on specific pieces of the corporate landscape – ranging from the need to extend the CxO suite with a Digital Officer, to the development of a new way of thinking, or the analysis of managerial choices to be made for techn(olog)ical transition.

Solely focusing on subsections risks to lead to an incomplete integration of the Digital dynamic. At best, the initiative will be an intermediary step. At worst, it will create a negative spiral that funnels means, time and potential - a risk further reinforced by the speed at which Digital is unfolding.

On the methodological level, a similar tendency can be observed. Agile frameworks like scrum[5] or Kanban[6] ensure guidance of essential aspects for agile product delivery (Galen, 2013). It is however less common to have agile covered for more profound transformations like those observed in the Digital Age.

The author wants to bring the components of the Digital journey together. Shaping their complementarity should open the possibilities of a new way of thinking about customers, organizations and projects, about shaping service and product delivery, about interacting with the ecosystem - and about creating value.

SOLUTIONS AND RECOMMENDATIONS

Changing Ecosystems, Dynamic Needs

Companies are continuously challenged to raise the bar, or to reinvent themselves. Digital Transformation is seen as one of the means to get there. This transformation is already well underway. Early 2016, the World Economic Forum in Davos called it the Fourth Industrial Revolution (Schwab & Samans, 2016).

Every industrial revolution is driven by new technologies. From a corporate perspective, new technologies get combined in the Fourth Industrial Revolution with technologies that finally become mature and affordable, like computing power, connected devices, genetic sequencing, artificial intelligence and the like.

From a human perspective, the way people live, work and interact is transforming at high speed: more than 2 billion people were on Facebook in 2017; some predict that more people will have mobile phones by 2020 than will have electricity or running water in their homes or villages; and children born in 2017 may never drive a car (Arbib & Seba, 2017; Schwab, 2016 ; Van Driessche, 2014).

The transformation of physical and digital worlds entails great potential. At the same time, this leads to (pressure for) increased human productivity. Customers expect businesses to anticipate their needs and provide personalised service through any communication channel. Business-to-Business (B2B) and Business-to-Consumer (B2C) businesses alike need to shift therefore from a model focused solely on selling products, to a service model driven by deeper connections with customers (Janssens, 2017).

This deeper connection is embodied through the concept of 'customer journeys'. Customer journeys are the sum of experiences and touchpoints that customers go through when interacting with a company, before, during and after the main interaction (Kalbach, 2016; Schadler, 2018; Truog, 2018; Van den Brink, 2018). By improving customer journeys, companies can continue to remain relevant in the Fourth Industrial Revolution.

ANTICIPATION AND ADAPTABILITY

Before analyzing strategy development or actionable translations, it is important to agree on what Digital really is. For some, it is about adding high tech niches to the portfolio. Others see it as collecting zealous amounts of data, being in constant communication with customers, or completely reshaping the company.

In practice, it is a dynamic sequencing of each of the above. It is a new way of thinking about service and product delivery, about organizing a company, about understanding and interacting with the larger ecosystem - and about creating value.

Data is the New Currency

In the Digital Age, people are using connected devices, privately and professionally, and are sharing large amounts of data every day.

By 2025, more than 6 billion consumers will interact with data every day, or 75% of the world's population. In 2025, each connected person will have at least one data interaction every 18 seconds. Many of these interactions are because of the billions of IoT devices connected across the globe, which are expected to create over 90ZB of data in 2025 (created by 150 billion devices). This is even before the advent of the nearly automated car, which is supposed to produce between 11 and 150 TB of data per day per car. At 30TB per car per day, this would equally roughly the data produced by hundreds of millions of Twitter users, all together on one year (Reinsel, Gantz & Rydning, 2018 ; Rossi 2018).

Through the data fuel, Artificial Intelligence (AI) is driving innovation across growing numbers of products and services. In 2017, organisations with AI expected to see a 39% increase on average in their revenues by 2020, alongside a 37% reduction in costs (Economic Times, 2017).

The higher the quantity and quality of the data, the higher the quality of the artificial learning. Machine learning algorithms and the like are therefore able to help businesses anticipate trends in consumer demands, personalize promotions for individual customers, and optimize pricing. Consumer sentiments towards a specific brand(s) can be unveiled (Stephen, 2017), supply chain operations can be further optimised (Gaus, Olsen & Deloso, 2018) and different types of cancer cells can be spotted through AI improved imagery (Tucker, 2018).

360° View of the Customer

To make data tangible, 360° views are key. A 360° view is the ability to see everything around you with no blind spots. It allows companies to capture every single part of the end-to-end relationship(s) it has with its customers. It includes sales and service information, marketing data, and information about who they are. From a B2B perspective, it also includes information about their business, what businesses they relate to, who has the buying power and the like (Loesel, 2014).

Figure 1. 360° view of the customer
Source: Own elaboration

In addition to creating an organisation's institutional memory, 360° information helps a company to understand who are in practice the largest accounts, identify whitespace to discover cross-selling opportunities, and connect in a more meaningful way with the biggest customers (Digital Marketing Institute, 2018).

In the past, this information got captured through different systems. Luckily, an increasing number of platforms, like Salesforce or Microsoft Dynamics, allows to capture this in a smooth way. To get there, clean and complete data are key (Sebastian-Coleman, 2013). It is therefore crucial to make it, on the one hand, easy for people to capture qualitative data, and, on the other hand, required to do so. By combining both aspects, contributing to the data power will become an organisational norm.

New Customer Journey(s)

One of the biggest changes is the transition from a product and competition-based economy to a service and customer journey focused reality (Janssens, 2017). That is a profound shift. The opportunity, on a service perspective, is to rethink the way to satisfy a customer's need through a service (Schadler, 2018; Van den Brink, 2018), especially as many of the services that can be created were not there before.

Through data and 360° views, companies need to understand how to evolve to continue to matter. They need to embrace new technological possibilities and look through the blurring frontiers between offline and online realities (Hinssen, 2014, Kablach, 2016; Truog, 2018). Understanding this requires courage and commitment, especially as pressure on delivery and results remain constant.

Shaping Digital Transformations is thus about shaping a dynamical way of working. With a clear strategy, skilled people and powerful data, digitally activated companies should get a fine-grained sense of the interactive relations between customers and their ecosystem, take proactive decisions based and, ultimately, adapt their business models to shape people's journey-focused experience.

STRATEGIC VISION: MODELS AND METHODOLOGIES

Organizations are facing a major challenge to reinvent themselves. To help them, professionals have developed tools that make this Digital process more tangible and the outcome more actionable.

In the Digital Transformation process, a clear baseline reference can be built based on the Digital Quotient. This metric for the Digital Maturity of a company has been developed by consultancy company McKinsey, based on an evaluation of 18 practices related to digital strategy, culture and capabilities, in 150 companies around the world (Catlin, Scanlan, & Wilmott, 2015).

The Digital Quotient is driven by four main components.

- **Strategic Commitment**: Companies must not go for digital as an add-on of their core business, but by wholeheartedly committing to a clear strategy.
- **Development of Digital Capabilities**: Digital success depends on the ability to invest in the relevant capabilities. They need to be sized for and aligned with the strategy.
- **Adaptive Culture**: In complement of technical capabilities such as Big Data analytics and the like, a strong and adaptive culture helps to compensate for a lack of them.
- **Internal Coherence**: Organizations need to align their internal structure, talent management and key performance indicators with the chosen Digital strategy.

Companies that desire to launch the transition to becoming Digital-ready can shape their roadmap by making choices with regards to the components of the Digital Quotient. This vision is the foundation for future actions and the management with a clear sense of direction.

Various frameworks are available to make the strategy actionable. A holistic approach to structure it from conception to realization has been developed by Jo Caudron and Dado Van Peteghem (2014). The 'Digital Transformation Modeling' methodology aims at clarifying the potential impact of Digital on an organization's activities and builds an action plan based on these insights.

In essence, the process consists of five steps:

Step 1: Creating insights:

- Understanding that a company can be impacted by and needs to prepare for Digital Transformation. This is traditionally initiated by one of the company's stakeholders.

Step 2: Assessing potential impacts:

- Assessing impacts is done by evaluating the readiness of the company with regards to seven Drivers for Impact, and their respective constituents.
- Each of the Drivers for Impact is represented by an analogy: The Glasshouse, The Package, The Frog, The Gatekeeper, The Traveler, The Participant, The Cyborg[7].
- The 'Cyborg', for instance, represents the impact driven by a series of technological evolutions, like the growing automation, the possibilities coming with real time data power, or additional potential offered by the Internet of Things.
- The 'Frog' materializes the fact that evolution does not have to be gradual anymore, but can be driven by shortcuts. The speed of insights, for example, can allow much faster reactions. Virtualization fits in this logic as it allows companies to jump over competitors more easily.
- Figures 2 and 3 illustrate the evaluation of the Drivers of Impact for an existing Glass Manufacturing company, and an existing Consultancy company. The evaluation has been done companywide. The former has more medium risks (amber). The latter has more risk factors under control (more black/green, less amber), but more risks with high impact (red).

Figure 2. Evaluation of the drivers of impact for an existing glass manufacturing company
own elaboration

The GlassHouse	The Package	The Frog	The GateKeeper	The Traveller	The Participant	The Cyborg
Transparency	Monolithic vs Atomic	Bypassing	New gatekeepers	Place	Community	Internet of Things
Accountability	APPification	Virtualization	Recommendations	Utility	Gamification	Wearables
Proximity	Long Tail	Fragmentation of Touchpoints	"Good is good enough"	Empowered Self	Collaboration	Quantified Self
Responsiveness	Personalised		Ambassadorship	Instant Gratification	The power of the crowd	Robotics
Bi-directional	Experience			New way of working		Data
Humanization	Speed			Contextual Awareness		Monitoring
Authenticity	Value for Money					
	(Self-) Service					
	Scalability					

Team(s)/Departement(s)/Division(s) concerned by the assesment: All Glass Divisions

White: has 0 impact in a digital context.	Green: has an impact (in a digital context), plan is defined and actions in motion.	Amber: has an impact (in a digital context), plan is existing but nothing in motion yet.	Red: has an impact (in a digital context), but no plan or action put on paper.

Figure 3. Evaluation of the drivers of impact for an existing consultancy company
own elaboration

15

The GlassHouse	The Package	The Frog	The GateKeeper	The Traveler	The Participant	The Cyborg
Transparency	Monolithic vs Atomic	Bypassing	New gatekeepers	Place	Community	Internet of Things
Accountability	APPification	Virtualization	Recommendations	Utility	Gamification	Wearables
Proximity	Long Tail	Fragmentation of Touchpoints	"Good is good enough"	Empowered Self	Collaboration	Quantified Self
Responsiveness	Personalised		Ambassadorship	Instant Gratification	The power of the crowd	Robotics
Bi-directional	Experience			New way of working		Data
Humanization	Speed			Contextual Awareness		Monitoring
Authenticity	Value for Money					
	(Self-) Service					
	Scalability					

Team(s)/Departement(s)/Division(s) concerned by the assesment: All Consultancy Practices			
White: has 0 impact in a digital context.	Green: has an impact (in a digital context), plan is defined and actions in motion.	Amber: has an impact (in a digital context), plan is existing but nothing in motion yet.	Red: has an impact (in a digital context), but no plan or action put on paper.

Step 3: Developing scenarios:

- By developing scenarios, the reality resulting from the combination of two risk factors is evaluated. A risk factor is one of the main Drivers of Impact, or one of its major constituents.
- This leads to four possible scenarios: risk factor 1 and risk factor 2 have a high impact, 1 high and 2 low, 1 low and 2 high, 1 low and 2 low. In practice, this results only in three useable scenarios, as the last one offers little added value compared to the existing situation.
- Each combination represents a high risk environment that could become reality when both conditions are combined (or an existing risk reality for which a solution needs to be found).
- For each scenario a headline should be provided (Figures 4 and 5), as well as a detailed report of how to tackle the risks.

Step 4: Building Business Case(s):

- Based on the scenarios, actions need to be defined to avoid such a scenario to happen (or to turn the risks in opportunities). This will result in the building of one or more Business Cases.
- Once the Business Case is approved, the 'traditional' transformation lifecycle starts, at the organizational level, process level, IT level, or combined at multiple levels.

Step 5: Staying alert through trend watching:

- To ensure a lasting effect of the awakening created by the start of the Digital journey, it is important to stay alert through structural trend watching and periodic workshops.

Figure 4. Example of a scenario evaluation for a Glass Manufacturing company, based on the risks coming from a New Way of Working, and major Cyborg elements
Own Elaboration

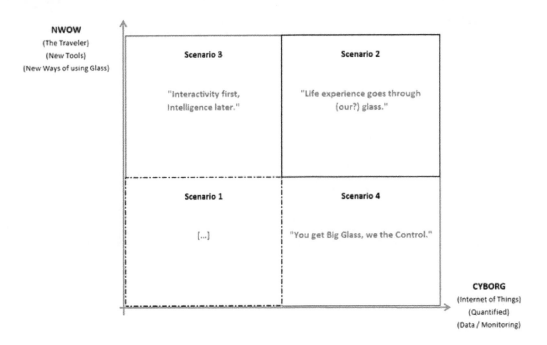

Figure 5. Example of a scenario evaluation for a Consultancy company, based on the risks coming from the Frog, and major Cyborg elements
Own Elaboration

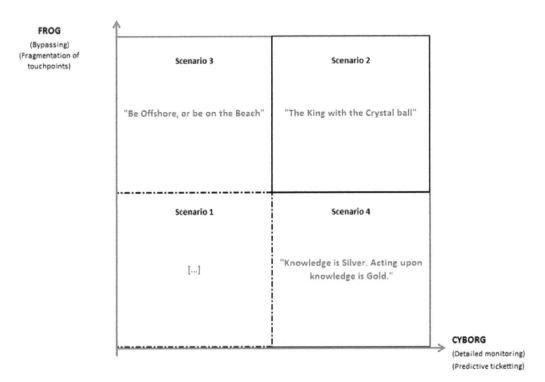

EMPOWERING DIGITAL PEOPLE

15

The Business Case might reveal gaps in terms of technical power or human capabilities. Whereas the data side can be managed through technological gear-up and anticipative sizing, human gaps have to be tackled by developing transversal capabilities.

The Business Case might reveal gaps in terms of technical power or human capabilities. Whereas the data side can be managed through technological gear-up and anticipative sizing, human gaps have to be tackled by developing transversal skills and capabilities. This implies shaping teams that are ready and able to take the leap, as well as a healthy dose of human understanding and people skills on project management side.

Management of skills disruption is an urgent concern in the Digital Age, and the rate of skills change accelerates across old and new jobs (Schwab & Samans, 2016). Consequently, project managers need to look for people that fit and that show, at the same time, a high level of adaptability.

Firstly, project managers need to nurture their people for and with the mental insights and technological catalysts of the Fourth Industrial Revolution, and create a stimulating environment (Bushnell & Stone, 2013; Knapp, Zeratsky & Kowitz, 2016). To do so, it has been increasingly important to do proactive workforce management, in collaboration with the out-of-project corporate organisation. With predictive HR management, for instance, companies can anticipate employee expectations and identify needs for mentoring. In turn, this will stimulate employee engagement and bottom-line project productivity.

Secondly, to make sure that the people adhere to the company and take ownership in project ecosystems, project managers need to consider the generational traits of teams (Bradt, 2014). This recurring concern has become increasingly relevant with the growing inflow of Millennials (also known as Generation Y) and Generation Z employees (Table 1).

Millennials value workplace satisfaction more than monetary compensation. Work-life balance and togetherness is considered essential. They are less likely than previous generations to put up with an unpleasant work environment. When satisfied, however, they are often passionate advocates for the organizations they work for (Tulgan, 2016). For projects, they are potent change agents.

Table 1. Generational composition of the US labour force

	Silent and Greatest generations	Baby Boom generation	Generation X	Millennial generation (Generation Y)	Post-Millenial generation (Generation Z)
Born	1945 or earlier	1946-1964	1965-1980	1981-1996	1997 and later
Age of working age adults in 2017	72 and older	53-71	37-52	21-36	16-20
% of US labour force in 2017	2%	25%	33%	35%	5%

Source: Fry, 2018

To Generation Z project members, company culture (and by extension project culture) is also more important than salary. They are looking for a sense of purpose (Stillman & Stillman, 2017). This does not mean that they are not ambitious. Generation Z 'work hard and play hard' and see their ambition as one of their most valuable assets, albeit in a different way. Rather than aiming at growing into the upper levels of the organisation, they want to strengthen their CVs through micro-careers. They want to grow through lifelong learning and providing a lot of value to the organisation through short projects (Stillman & Stillman, 2017).

Note that some research categorizes people between 1995 and 2005 as Generation K (Hertz, 2013). More than 75% of Generation K is concerned about climate change and social equality – and is vastly worried about getting a job. They can want to co-create and be committed. Similar to the analysis of Generation Z, they want to be part of a community that supports them whenever and wherever they need it.

To have Generation Y and Z/K project members motivated and really own their work, they expect to be led, rather than being managed in the traditional way. For managers this implies emphasizing feedback, focusing on the team (instead of focusing only on the project), and offering them independence and inspiration (Bradt, 2014).

From a project point of view, it might be challenging to apply each of the above, while respecting time, budget and other constraints. Applying one or more, or taking time for human value exchange, however, may already help to increase involvement, motivation and therefore ownership.

Thirdly, managers need to learn to talk digital, data and customer journey themselves. They do not need to know everything. They should be able to ask questions to their teams and understand the answer (Groysberg & Slind, 2012). It will reinforce faith in the project culture and will cascade down to other employees.

Specifically on AI, realism has to be injected in project boards. Organisations tend to expect magic coming out of the blue, delivering quickly unparalleled performance without having to skill-up competencies (Brooks, 2017). In practice, many innovations take far longer to be deployed than people in the field imagine, and with extrapolated targets that are downscaled to a more stringent reality. Moreover, AI is not only driven by technology. Exactly as in financial investment where ambiguity tolerance still beats artificial intelligence, AI and data science projects require a significant share of professional expertise (Schuller, 2017).

When working with people in the digital reality, it is therefore important to find a good balance between aiming for the sky and stating the reality. While it might temper the motivation of some people, it will strengthen the project focus towards targets that might remain aggressive, but that are perceived as more realistic. Doing so will create a climate of ambitious trust, which, in turn, will motivate the blended project teams to fully take up their work.

Having the appropriate human capital on board and managing them accordingly is thus one of the cornerstones for the Fourth Industrial Revolution. This implies creating an appropriate environment and project culture, nurturing people, and managing them with a solid understanding of what Industry 4.0 means for them and for the service to the customer.

RECONCILING STRATEGIC TRANSFORMATION WITH NEW HUMAN DYNAMICS

While aiming to reconcile digital strategy with human empowerment, organisations have worked on new organisational models at their own level. Some models are having a growing impact throughout the corporate world. One of them is the transformational approach of changing a company in a 'teal organisation'.

Formalised by Frederic Laloux (Laloux, 2014), Teal starts from the assumption that people are longing for better ways to work together. The approach wants to go far beyond a better life/work balance. Teal wants to develop a culture of self-management, wholeness, and a deeper sense of purpose.

Although this approach might seem hard to reconcile with corporate targets, experience in small to large companies supports the potential of this approach (Laloux, 2014). Organisations desiring to avoid radical change can introduce some elements separately. Over time, however, obtaining the full benefit depends on the extent to which the organisation embraces this approach on a structural level, including the organisation of the daily work as well as matters like the human resource management approach, strategy definition and financial management.

Digital web agency Yools, for example, decided to go through a profound transformation in 2015. After several years of existence and thousands of web development projects, they wanted to put the company focus back on the people. They wanted to create more happiness inside the company and trigger a positive impact on the business development dynamic, on the customers and on society. They transformed the organisation based on principles of meaningful mission, self steering and trust (Aerts, 2017).

Firstly, they proposed a new mission for the company, less based on money, but more driven by values. In complement, all employees got empowered to revise periodically the mission and the vision of the company, to keep their sentiment in line with the company's direction (Aerts, 2017).

Secondly, all 'Yoolsies' were mandated to take their own decisions. If people wanted to improve the company, they had to draft a proposal, ask others for feedback, and decide themselves if their project was worth it, before making things happen themselves. A foundational aspect was the increase in transparency. Yools decided to focus on transparency for decision taking, project cycles, and company results. Complete transparency on finance and salaries was deemed to radical of a change for a beginning (Aerts, 2017).

To guide this transformation process, Yools set up a series of daily and weekly ceremonies. This stimulated communication, canalised alignment and reinforced human bounding. Playbooks were created to support every process. One-on-one evaluations got replaced by group-driven peer feedback. Similarly, all employees got trained in new ways of self-expression and non-violent communication (Aerts, 2017).

Thirdly, trust was stimulated. The goal was to deliver qualitative project results without mandatory targets or timesheet controls. The idea was that the increased motivation would lead to increased ownership, which would ensure a regular delivery. To reinforce this aspect, coaches were appointed to help people in their new journey, in combination with moments of open sharing (Aerts, 2017).

Table 2. Evolutions in human collaboration

	Description	Guiding Metaphor	Foundations
ORANGE	Focus on beating competition; achieving profit and growth. Management by objectives.	Machine	Innovation Accountability Meritocracy
GREEN	Focus on culture and empowerment to boost employee motivation. Stakeholder replace shareholders as primary purpose.	Family	Empowerment Egalitarian Management Stakeholder Model
TEAL	Self-management replaces hierarchical pyramid. Organisations are regarded as living entities, oriented towards realising their potential.	Living organism	Self Management Wholeness Evolutionary Purpose

Source: Laloux, 2014

Subsequently, people left the company because they did not adhere to the new philosophy. To reinforce the company, the hiring process got adapted as the human fit had become the main catalyst for acceptance. The entire process could last from a couple of weeks to a couple of months (Aerts, 2017).

From a project perspective, all web projects were affected by this model based on trust, motivation and self steering. The initial phase of teal operation appeared to be extremely cumbersome for internal collaboration and external delivery. For senior employees, the long selection process of new resources appeared to be most challenging in periods of high demand. Strictly respecting the lack of managerial authority was not straightforward either, especially during periods of high pressure (Aerts, 2017).

After two years of human reshuffling, evolutive governance and growing understanding of and adherence to the model, project delivery attained a level of steady output and increased customer satisfaction. The company is growing and continues to hire new resources (Aerts, 2017).

For the employees that went through the transformation and that are still at Yools, the only 'major back draw' is that most Yoolsies would not want to work again in a traditional setting. Similarly, benchmarking with other teal companies indicated that the potential value in an era of digital transformation is tremendous, but highly dependent on a rigorous adherence to the teal philosophy, even in periods of project risk (Aerts, 2017).

DYNAMIC FEEDBACK AND AGILE PROJECTS

The biggest challenge for the execution of the Digital Strategy is the structural integration of the fundamental paradigm shift. Pre-Digital organizations focused on market share and people got managed accordingly. In the Digital Economy, companies need to be designed for reactivity, flexibility and agility. An integrated operational backbone is needed that embraces a continuously evolving service backbone, and a clearly articulated, but dynamic business strategy (Ross, 2016).

A fair share of this nimble way of working is initially coming from agile software development, focusing on rapid prototyping and getting releases out smoothly. This philosophy is now also influencing the development of business deliverables, especially as agile has grown into a maturing practice.

An increasing number of organisations has moved from using agile in pilot projects to accepting it as one of the main project management practices. Agile (and its subsequent versions) will therefore remain at the core of the projects of the coming years (Versione, 2018). For details on approaches, the author refers to dedicated literature[8]. Some attention points can nevertheless be highlighted.

Firstly, the fluidity associated with agile requires discipline of the main actors. Scope control, value driven priorities, failing fast, and regular iterations are part of the core principles. The success of agile comes from the unconditional availability of decision takers towards rapid feedback, during and after the iterations (Janssens, 2017).

Secondly, agile perimeters might have to integrate with more traditional ecosystems. To make such hybrid contexts work, managerial compromises must be made. When agile subsets are inserted in a waterfall environment[9], they must work with less autonomy and with a different time perspective. Similarly, waterfall entities will have to adapt to a flexible way of working – or agile Scrum might have to blend with agile Kanban (Reddy, 2015).

Thirdly, the overarching focus on agile should not become a goal on itself. Managers can start by developing personal agility, for instance by breaking large tasks into small steps and test working models, by streamlining activities to focus on the most valuable customer benefits, or by celebrating learning (Rigby, 2018). In the end, however, managers should not forget to focus on developing their quantified

Figure 6. Combining waterfall approaches and agile might be needed
Source: Janssens, 2016

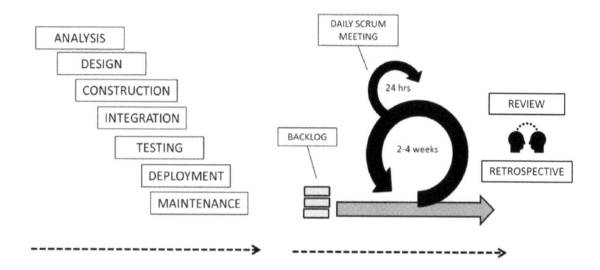

Figure 6. Combining waterfall approaches and agile might be needed
Source: Janssens, 2016

intuition and taking decisions that make a difference. The aim of agile is to be in support of the overall goal: providing appropriate solutions and value to customer needs and preferences (Highsmith, 2001).

Lastly, it should be noted that agile is not the same as agility. Agile is an iterative approach to software development and project management with specific principles. Agility, on the other hand, is an organisational trait characterized by durability, speed, flexibility and readiness (Prosci, 2017). It is a core competency and source of competitive advantage.

Agile and agility are related. As an organization grows agile project management practices, it can increase agility. Some reinforce their agility through adaptive leadership skills, for instance by reinforcing their vision and putting targeted efforts in strategy, people, structure and processes (De Stobbeleir, Peeters, Pfisterer, & Muylle, 2019). Similarly, many organizations working on improving their agility use agile development approaches given the desired outcome of agile and its inherent value for blended transformation leadership styles and strong teams (Viaene, 2018).

Overall, both agile and agility aim thus to equip organizations to more effectively respond to and seize opportunities. By combining the strengths of both, managers can reinforce the project management dynamic and contribute to shaping a company for reactivity and flexibility.

FUTURE RESEARCH DIRECTIONS

Algorithms power businesses like Amazon and Netflix. Health related apps are changing the medical world (Kirby, 2019). 5G is expected to redefine the data possibilities in all industries. And research about industries like hotels and retail indicate that benefits of skilled sales force may be diminishing in an increasingly data-driven world (Philips & van Ryzin, 2016).

Digital Transformation is thus providing society with substantial opportunities, as well as with challenges in the dynamic relation between agile organizations, rapid decision taking and the role of data powered artificial intelligence.

This raises the question whether machines or people should take decisions to provide the necessary value in the Digital Age. At the same time, it indicates that specialists and managers need to be able to sharpen their Digital Capabilities and elevate their quantified intuition to a higher level, in order to remain in control of their organization. To do so, several elements could be further explored.

From the methodological point of view, the project management toolbox has to be further enriched with actionable best practices. They will have to dedicate specific attention to the permeable delimitation between product delivery and service delivery. Likewise, cookbooks and exhaustive case reviews for hybrid contexts would be valuable. This will not dilute the role of project management frameworks and dynamic organizational management, but will improve compatibility with the Digital Reality.

Likewise, it will be valuable to analyze if best practices could be identified for specific sub-sectors. Also, attention to the public sphere would be valuable. By bringing public and private practices on par, it is imaginable to activate the potential of the public-private force field in domains like education, health, mobility or city management. In turn, this could benefit corporate and individual ecosystems.

Obviously, best practices will require continuous improvement. But the author believes that recurring efforts will be largely compensated by advantages in quality and outcome.

CONCLUSION

Managing the Digital Transformation is not a high-tech option for a faraway future. It is about how public and private organizations integrate technology to transform their activities - now. It involves a change in leadership, a different thinking, new business models, and increased use of technology to improve the customer experience. It is by integrating this backbone that Digital strategies can have a durable impact.

To get there, a series of key points have been addressed.

Firstly, it has been explained that a thorough understanding of the new reality is essential. The Fourth Industrial Revolution redefines borders between reactivity and proactivity, and creates the need for real-time service and contextual adaptation for the customer journey, based on a 360° understanding. It requires a dynamic silver lining, compatible with interactive work clusters and a hybrid organization.

It has been explained that this understanding needs to be translated through a strategy to profoundly revisit the company, encompassing the internal way of working, as well as the customer value proposition, the articulation of the product/service portfolio and the related follow-up dynamics.

Secondly, practical approaches have been analyzed that can guide this process. With the Digital Quotient, organizations have a baseline to put findings into perspective. Similarly, by embracing the Digital Transformation Modeling framework, a solid methodology is available to clarify the potential impact of Digital, create future scenarios for the Digital Age, and build an insight-based action plan.

Thirdly, it has been highlighted that putting a strategy into motion for Digital success implies an appropriate way of working and managing – encompassing the generational layers of the human work force and the collaborative maturity of the organization.

Lastly, it has been explained that the Digital way of working needs to be inspired by an agile philosophy. When doing so, organizations and managers are namely better prepared to develop their quantified intuition, and take relevant decisions for the company and the value provided to its customers.

Overall, Digital Transformation projects are thus part of a major change journey. A journey that shapes the present to be ready for an already ongoing future - and that will continue to transform at high speed. It is a new way of thinking about the interaction with customers, about shaping service and product delivery, about organizing an organization - and about creating value.

REFERENCES

Aerts, A. (2017, Dec). Reinventing Organisations: Een zinvolle missie en zelfsturing. Presented at the *Digital Experience sharing meeting*, Antwerp, Belgium.

Arbib, J., & Seba, T. (2017). *Rethinking Transportation 2020-2030: The Disruption of Transportation and the Collapse of the Internal-Combustion Vehicle and Oil Industries.* Retrieved June 23, 2018 from: www.RethinkX.com

Bradt, G. (2014). *Trying To Manage Millenials Give Up And Lead Them Instead.* Forbes.

Brillantes, K. (2015). *Hiring lessons from GV's design event series.* Retrieved March 7, 2016, from https://library.gv.com/

Brooks, R. (2017). *The Seven Deadly Sins Of AI Predictions.* MIT Technology Review.

Bushnell, N., & Stone, G. (2013). *Finding the Next Steve Jobs: How to Find, Hire, Keep and Nurture Creative Talent.* Headline Publishing Group.

Catlin, T., Scanlan, J., & Willmott, P. (2015). Raising your Digital Quotient. *The McKinsey Quarterly*, (June), 2015.

Caudron, J., & Van Peteghem, D. (2014). *Digital Transformation.* LannooCampus.

De Stobbeleir, K., Peeters, C., Pfisterer, M., & Muylle, S. (2019). *Adaptative Leadership: Shape your path through turbulence.* Vlerick.

Digital Marketing Institute. (2018). *The What, Why & How of the 360-Degree Customer View.* Retrieved Oct 12, 2018, from: https://digitalmarketinginstitute.com

Economic Times. (2017). *Artificial intelligence adoption driving revenue growth for businesses.* Retrieved May 16, 2018, from: https://economictimes.indiatimes.com

Galen, R. (2013). *Scrum Product Ownership: Balancing Value from the Inside Out.* RGCG.

Gaus, T., Olsen, K., & Deloso, M. (2018, May). Synchronizing the digital supply network. *Deloitte Insights*.

Groysberg, B., & Slind, M. (2012). *Talk, Inc.: How Trusted Leaders Use Conversation to Power their Organizations.* Harvard Business Review Press.

Henke, N., Libarikian, A., & Wiseman, B. (2016). Straight talk about Big Data. *The McKinsey Quarterly*, (October), 2016.

Hertz, N. (2013). *Eyes Wide Open: How to Make Smart Decisions in a Confusing World.* William Collins.

Highsmith, J. (2001). *The Agile Manifesto.* Retrieved Feb 28, 2018, from: http://agilemanifesto.org

Hinssen, P. (2014). *The Network Always Wins. How to Win in the Age of Uncertainty.* Mach Media.

Janssens, J. (2016). Blending Technology, Human Potential, and Organizational Reality: Managing Big Data Projects in Public Contexts. In *Managing Big Data Integration in the Public Sector*. IGI Global. doi:10.4018/978-1-4666-9649-5.ch007

Janssens, J. (2017). Digital Transformation journeys in a Digitized Reality. In *Encyclopedia of Information Science and Technology*. IGI Global.

Janssens, J. (2018). Project and Portfolio Maturity for Waterfall and Agile: Convergence of Layered Needs in Different Ecosystems. In *Developing Organizational Maturity for Effective Project Management*. IGI Global. doi:10.4018/978-1-5225-3197-5.ch013

Kalbach, J. (2016). *Mapping Experience: A Guide to Creating Value Through Journeys, Blueprints and Diagrams*. O'Reilly.

Kirby, A. (2019). *Digital RX*. Retrieved June 16, 2019, from: https://www.jwtintelligence.com/

Knapp, J., Zeratsky, J., & Kowitz, B. (2016). *Sprint: How to Solve Big Problems and Test New Ideas in Just Five Days*. Simon & Schuster.

Laloux, F. (2014). *Reinventing Organizations A Guide to Creating Organizations Inspired by the Next Stage in Human Consciousness*. LannooCampus.

Loesel, C. (2014). *Helpful Insights on Building the 360-Degree View of Your Customers*. Retrieved March 4, 2018, from: https://www.salesforce.com

Mayhem, H., Saleh, T., & Williams, S. (2016, Oct.). Making data analytics work for you—Instead of the other way around. *The McKinsey Quarterly*.

Nanterme, P. (2016). *Digital disruptions has only just begun*. Retrieved February 3, 2016, from https://www.weforum.org/agenda/2016/01/digital-disruption-has-only-just-begun

Philips, R., & van Ryzin, G. (2016). *Dealing in Data*. Retrieved February 12, 2016, from https://www8.gsb.columbia.edu/ideas-at-work/publication/1673

Prosci. (2017). *Stop confusing agile with agile*. Retrieved Oct 25, 2017, from: https://www.prosci.com

Reddy, A. (2015). The Scrumban [R]Evolution. Boston, MA: Addison-Wesley Professional.

Reinsel, D., Gantz, J., & Rydning, J. (2018). *Data Age 2025: The Digitization of the World from Edge to Core*. IDC White Paper. Retrieved May 11, 2018, from: http://www.seagate.com

Richter, G., & Wee, D. (2016, Oct.). Steering IT into the digital manufacturing era. *The McKinsey Quarterly*.

Rigby, D. K. (2018). *Develop personal, habitual agility*. Harvard Business Review Press.

Ross, J. (2016). *Digital Disruption: Transforming your Company for the Digital Economy*. Retrieved February 4, 2016, from http://cdn.executive.mit.edu

Rossi, T. (2018). *Autonomous and ADAS test cars produce over 11 TB of data per day*. Retrieved May 11 2019, from: https://www.tuxera.com/blog/autonomous-and-adas-test-cars-produce-over-11-tb-of-data-per-day/

Schadler, T. (2018). *Your Digital Experience Strategy Starts With A Customer Journey Map.* Retrieved Oct 10, 2018, from: www.forrester.com

Schuller, M. (2017). *Ambiguity Tolerance Beats Artificial Intelligence.* Retrieved Feb 18, 2018, from: http://www.panthera.mc

Schwab, K., & Samans, R. (2016). *The Future of Jobs: Employment, Skills and Workforce Strategy for the Fourth Industrial Revolution.* Global Challenge Insight Report. Geneva, Switzerland: World Economic Forum, p. V.

Sebastian-Coleman, L. (2013). *Measuring Data Quality for Ongoing Improvement.* Elsevier. doi:10.1016/B978-0-12-397033-6.00020-1

Stephen, A. (2017). *AI Is Changing Marketing As We Know It, And That's A Good Thing.* Forbes.

Terrar, D. (2015). *What is Digital Transformation?* Retrieved March 8, 2016, from http://www.theagileelephant.com/what-is-digital-transformation/

Truog, D. (2018). *Demystifying The Language Of CX and UX.* Retrieved Oct 12, 2018, from: www.forrester.com

Tucker, I. (2018). *AI cancer detectors.* London, UK: The Guardian.

Van den Brink, J. (2018). *Supercharge Your Journey Mapping.* Retrieved Oct 10, 2018, from: www.forrester.com

Van Driessche, W. (2014). *Modern Minds - Kan uw hoofd de 21ste eeuw aan?* Mediafin.

Versione. (2018). *The 12th annual State of Agile report.* Retrieved Oct 7, 2018, from: https://stateofagile.versionone.com/

Viaene, S. (2018). *Orchestrating Organizational Agility.* Ivey Business Journal.

World Economic Forum. (2016). *The Future of Jobs: Employment, Skills and Workforce Strategy for the Fourth Industrial Revolution.* Global Challenge Insight Report. Geneva, Switzerland: World Economic Forum.

KEY TERMS AND DEFINITIONS

360° View: Ability to capture every single part of the end-to-end relationship a company has with its customers. Includes sales and service information, marketing data, transactional information and information about who they are.

Agile: Project management methodology in which the development is characterized by the breakdown of tasks into short periods, with frequent reassessment of work and plans. Used in software related projects and digital transformation activities.

Customer Journey: Sum of experiences and touchpoints that customers go through when interacting with a company. Includes experiences and touchpoints before, during and after the main interaction.

Digital Quotient: Metric of the digital maturity of a company, based on the evaluation of a series of practices related to digital strategy, capabilities, and culture.

Digital Transformation: Process in which human and corporate society is shifted to new ways of working and thinking with digital and social technologies. Involves a change in leadership, a different mindset, the encouragement of innovation and new business models, and an increased use of technology to improve the experience of internal and external customers.

Fail Fast: Solution development approach used in volatile, uncertain and complex business contexts that focuses on trying something, getting fast feedback, and then rapidly inspecting and adapting. Sometimes referred to as Fail(ing) Forward.

Fourth Industrial Revolution: Industrial revolution driven by systems involving entirely new capabilities for people and machines. Represents new ways to embed technology in society, and induces new ways of working and thinking for human and corporate matters. Used as synonym for Digital Transformation, and, in specific cases, for Industry 4.0.

Kanban: Agile method to manage work by limiting work in progress. Team members pull work as capacity permits, rather than work being pushed into the process when requested. Stimulates continuous, incremental changes. Aims at facilitating change by minimizing resistance to it.

Quantified Intuition: Non-technical capability that helps in making impactful decisions at a fast rate, despite a high level of uncertainty and an important inflow of interconnected data.

Scrum: Iterative and incremental product development framework used in agile projects.

Teal: Stage in the evolution of human and organisational consciousness. Focuses on the development of a culture of self-management, wholeness, and a deeper sense of purpose.

Waterfall: Sequential project management methodology, in which project progress is regarded as a downwards process. Originally described as consisting of phases for Requirement Specifications, Design, Construction, Integration, Testing, Installation and Maintenance, variations exist on the naming and number of phases.

ENDNOTES

[1]   For more information on Big Data, the author refers to the 'Key Terms and Definitions' section.

[2]   For more information on quantified intuition, the author refers to: https://www8.gsb.columbia.edu/

[3]   For more information on international attention for Digital Transformation, the author refers to: http://www.digitaltransformation2016.eu/ and https://www.weforum.org/events/world-economic-forum-annual-meeting-2016

[4]   The growing impact of technology is symbolically embodied by to two groups of technology giants: Google, Apple, Facebook and Amazon (GAFA); and, increasingly, Netflix, Airbnb, Tesla, Uber (NATU).

[5]   For more information on scrum, the author refers to: https://www.scrum.org/ and https://www.scrumalliance.org/

[6]   For more information on Kanban, the author refers to: https://www.atlassian.com/agile/kanban

[7]   For a detailed explanation of each driver and the related analogy, the author refers to Caudron & Van Peteghem (2014).

[8]   For information on agile, the author refers to https://www.scrum.org/ and https://www.scrumalliance.org/ for scrum, and to https://www.atlassian.com/agile/kanban for Kanban.

[9]   For information on waterfall methodologies, the author refers to: https://www.pmi.org/PMBOK-Guide-and-Standards.aspx (PMBOK), http://www.prince-officialsite.com/ (Prince2).

Strategic HRM and Organizational Agility Enable Firms to Respond Rapidly and Flexibly to the Changing Environment

15

Nibedita Saha

https://orcid.org/0000-0003-0526-5289

University Institute, Tomas Bata University in Zlin, Czech Republic

INTRODUCTION

In the era of globalization and industrialization, the most pioneering and modern organizations are under excessive strain to work in a dynamic environment that always force them for prompt and quantifiable advantage in order to survive in this international competitive market. Under these circumstances, competitiveness and innovation as well as organizational resilience, i.e. organizational agility have become a hot issue of academic, business and managerial debates with regard to be agile and be able to sense and respond to market changes quickly and smoothly to sustain their efficiency, i.e. organizational competitiveness. Where, organizational agility is accountable for high ability to adapt, the ability to recognize change in the marketplace and allocate resources to take advantage of that change. Similarly, strategic HRM play the role of a facilitator that enables an organization to utilize its existing human resources in order to achieve its strategic goals and objectives. Additionally, strategic HRM also empowers organizations to enhance its business performance; develop an appropriate organizational culture, i.e. work culture which, will boost the organizational flexibility and innovation (Alsaadat,2019); (Jackson et al, 2014); (Oppong & Nasir, 2017). Research shows that nowadays, strategic HRM along with organizational agility specially with the presence of human capital plays a crucial role in gaining competitive advantage and improving organizational performance.

This sub-chapter highlighted the significant features of strategic human resource management that endeavored for enhancing organizational learning through organizational agility and organizational capability. According to Wahyono (2018) Agility is nowadays a key aspects of organizational excellence due to its distinctive characteristics that incorporates the aptitude of an organization or firms' to successfully respond to the ever changing environment especially when the transforming businesses is going on so firms are needed to fit for the fulfilment of the purpose in this digitally enabled world (Abraham and Perkin, 2017). Current research has explored the significant aspects or perspectives of organizational agility. However, this chapter has been organized to provide a unique integrative framework that encompasses all dimensions of organizational agility development. Hence, the purpose of this sub-chapter is to discourse this gap in order to enhance firms' competitiveness and sustainability by presenting a conceptual and thematic model that captures various critical extents to the development of agility within firms' or organizations. Moreover, this chapter also emphasized the linkage between SHRM practices and organizational agility that enable firms to respond rapidly and flexibly to keep pace with the changing environment. In this sub-chapter the focus has been given on how firms can develop an ability as well as capacity to respond rapidly and flexibly to the changing environment and why firms' realize that they are capable to accept these unwanted challenges for the benefit of their organizational

DOI: 10.4018/978-1-7998-3473-1.ch177

performance development. Finally, this subchapter highlights the important role that strategic human resource management plays in both developing organizational agility and strategic flexibility.

Accordingly, this study demonstrates that organization's capability for flexibility is developed through strategically managing human resources that enable to create competencies among the core employees at the organizational level. In addition, this flexible condition within the organization facilitate them to achieve the ability to respond and resist the unwanted shocks (Lengnick-Hall, Beck and Lengnick-Hall, 2011). Furthermore, to get the vivid description about the said topic this sub-chapter took effort to review two important elements about the possibilities of organizational capability to be flexible, i.e. organizations specific cognitive abilities (organizational agility), organizational behavioral characteristics, and contextual conditions (Strategic HRM capabilities) that enable them to respond rapidly in the dynamic environment (Saha et al, 2019). Similarly, in order to address a firms' competitiveness, it is necessary to highlight the strategic flexibility of a firm (i.e., their ability to accept the change for the benefit of overall performance) that empower them to face the prompt changes through organizational transformation. Hence it can be said that the outcome of this study envisaged the way SHRM practices affect the flexibility dimensions of an organization that enhance the robustness of firms, especially it significantly influences organizational agility and integrity (Bouaziz and Hachicha, 2018).

To comprehend the influence of strategic HRM on firms' competitiveness, it is necessary to indicate the key activities of human resources that facilitate businesses or organizations to create, undertake and maintain a sustainable organizational advantage. The theoretical framework of this study induces various approaches and models concerning organizational agility (OA), organizational learning, organizational knowledge. In this circumstances, it is necessary to mention that the notion of organizational learning is presently a subject of continuing debates between behaviorists and economists. Actually the concept of organizational learning was first introduced by Cyart and March, (1963) in the book *"a behavioral theory of the firm"*. According to them organizational learning is a field of academic research and professional practice with a relatively recent development. Thus, companies should learn from their experiences with the intention of adapting themselves to the conditions of the environment. Correspondingly, Basten and Haamann (2018) acknowledged that Organizational learning (OL) enables organizations to transform individual knowledge into organizational knowledge and enhance organizational effectiveness and guides the organizations to design the appropriate learning processes in order to improve long-term performance. This chapter reveals the perception of organizational agility and human resource management strategy as an emerging perspective for knowledge and performance-driven organizational capability. Precisely, this study put efforts to identify and classify, the way businesses or an organization can rapidly improve its sustainable organizational knowledge, skills and abilities (KSAs) development strategy through progressing their organizational performance.

Consequently, to foresee the modern business world, it is essential to remark that the essence of organizational knowledge, organizational agility and importance of human resource strategy is viewed as an eminent approach to meet the global challenges. Where, in the new phase of globalization, HR is responsible for empowering the effect of change in organizations and shielding employees against the unwanted effects. Therefore, the purpose of this sub-chapter is to tighten and elucidate a conceptualization of organizational agility and organizational learning process that discusses about the spirit of organizational agility, i.e. flexibility, nimbleness, and speed of an organization as well as key activities of HR. It also accentuates the way HR specialists are involved in operational matters and are progressively observed as a source of competitive advantage in order to meet the global challenges. Though, it is very difficult to enhance firms' sustainable growth quickly due to the urge of gradual expansion of the competitive marketplace and today's rapidly-changing business world. In another way, it can have said that nowadays organizational research, (i.e. administrative and managerial) deals with both the phases that are combined as well as inter- linked and focuses mainly on the following key elements, i.e. (human-centered and technology-oriented).

Henceforth, it is crucial to ensure that the success of any organization is based on the belief that an organization gains competitive advantage by using its people effectively and efficiently. Concerning this strategic role of HRM and organizational agility, this sub-chapter attempts to classify how firms can respond rapidly and flexibly to the changing environment without facing disturbance? How the HR competencies can really make a difference and influence on business performance? How firms' can enhance their organizational capability, organizational learning and organizational knowledge through the manifestation of strategic human resource management approach to meet the global competitiveness? Finally, this study suggested that strategic HRM and organizational agility both the approaches could be a very inspiring and demanding for the organizations of twenty first century. Specifically, it can be said that the key empowering factors of strategic HRM and organizational agility has a great influence on organizational competitiveness that enhances organizational learning capability as well as organizational knowledge development strategy, managerial competency, i.e. administration and technological upgradation, i.e. the advancement of information technology to achieve sustainable competitive Advantage.

This chapter has six additional sectors where, each sectors has distinctive remarkable part. Sector one provides a contextual overview of the whole the chapter by briefly describing the significant issues and conceptual approaches of strategic human resource management and its activities, organizational agility, organizational learning in relation to the present dynamic environment that empowering firms to act promptly during the phase of transformation as well as to resonate their (firms' / organizations) competitiveness. Sector two summaries the influence of organizational agility on strategic HRM that enhances firms' flexibility and competitiveness, along with the sub-sector, i.e. linkage between strategic HRM and organizational agility. Sub sector three presenting the challenging perspectives, key issues, deliberations and difficulties of organizational agility that fascinating organizational (managerial) of competitiveness. In this part it is obvious to discuss about the synergic consequence of human resource management strategy. Accordingly, subsection four extends the discussion by organizational agility and value of HRM strategy that can create a difference and influence on firms' performance. Later on, sector five proposed solutions and recommendations with the issues, influences and difficulties. At last sector six make conclusion, and accentuates the persuasion for additional coherent thinking on the proposed theme and topic that carried forward by the chapter as the implication of strategic HRM and its perspectives and positive approaches that strengthen organizational knowledge administrative competency as well as operational competency, (i.e. individual employees skills, and organizational capacity development skills) of an organization or firm can respond rapidly and flexibly to the changing environment without facing market turmoil through enhancing firms strategic capability.

Basically, the overall concern of this chapter is to point out the most possible way in which the significance of strategic human resource management (SHRM) as well as organizational agility concept can create and facilitate an organization to achieve a sustainable competitive advantage. It enables, whether the organization or firms are capable to achieves their two vital goals, such as: *the best possible way to enhance and maintain organizational flexibility* (both human resources and coordination flexibility) and *the best possible way to keep pace with the ever-changing dynamic environment* (both external and internal). With the aim to do so, this sub-chapter demonstrate a conceptual framework that delivers a theoretical groundwork for accepting the strategic role of human resources in an organization that empower them by supportive behavior, i.e. the appropriate and important aspects of the HR system to meet the strategic needs of the firm and enabling them by fabricating these components to facilitate flexible reaction to a variety of strategic requirements.

BACKGROUND: THE CONTEXTUAL PERSPECTIVES OF STRATEGIC HUMAN RESOURCE MANAGEMENT AND ORGANIZATIONAL AGILITY

In order to address the contextual perceptions of strategic human resource management (SHRM) and organizational agility (OA) it is required to reveal the present scenario of strategic HRM concept which, has progressively been acknowledged as a dominant managerial competence development strategy in an organization. The conceptual perspective of strategic HRM is seen as an excellent management style due to its value in implementing a normal basis for managing people. Research shows, that SHRM provides a very suitable alternative solution in order to tackle the critical success factors of the firms'. While considering the global perspectives of strategic HRM, numerous researchers realizes the significance of strategic HRM, among them Adler and Ghadar (1993) stated that during the new era of industrialization and globalization strategic HRM has been considered as one of the new approaches of managing research and development (R & D), production, marketing, and finance that are presently incorporating today's global realities and occurring rapidly. Subsequently, researcher and Marier (2012) mentioned about another new interesting concept and practice of SHRM in developed countries like Germany, a dominant economic power among the developed nations and Europe. He emphasized the way strategic human resource management concept has been occurred in order to recount the turbulent situation within the organization during the phase of influential emerging economy.

In this chapter the author's determination is to accentuate the contextual perspectives of organizational agility that confers organizational essence, competence, suppleness, nimbleness and speediness. Where, the perceptive approaches of this study is to illuminate the impression organizational agility (OA) and strategic HRM, as well as the linkage between them. Moreover, research shows that organizational agility (OA) and the strategic HRM perspectives considerately boost firms' in order to visualize their goals transparently and easily to improve their degree of functioning (Alaraqi, 2017; Harraf et al. 2015). On the other hand, to indicate the importance of strategic HRM Armstrong, (2006) quoted that human resource management (HRM) is a strategic and coherent approach to the management of an organization's that deals with the most valued assets, i.e. the people. According to him HRM, i.e. the people's collective contribution enables firms' to accomplishment their goals and objectives. Simultaneously, Eneh, and Awara, (2016) described that during the age of rapid technological development, the importance of human resources has been observed as the key factor to the development and growth of an organization. Thus, the concept of strategic HRM can be considered as a new approach, that directly and indirectly supports firms in aligning the skills and expertise of the employees within the organization and empowers them to enhance organizational competency.

The theoretical framework of this chapter refers to the base of the whole research is grounded upon. It mainly, explained and elaborated the relationships among the strategic HRM, organizational learning, organizational agility, organizational knowledge and performance that has been explained in light of theories and relevant studies in literature. This sub-chapter represents the significance of human resources a strategic approach that endows firms to apprehend the value of internal and external customers, knowledge of competitors, products, technology and sources of competitive advantage. It is all about people and significantly it ensures that the capability of a firm to enhance its competitive ability is initiated along with the belief that an organization gains a competitive advantage by using its people effectively and efficiently. Moreover, it emphasizes and explicate the contextual framework of organizational agility that deliberates about organizational spirit, capability, flexibility, nimbleness, and speediness. However, the key activities of strategic HRM intricate in operational matters that are increasingly observed as a source of competitive advantage in today's dynamic global market place.

Concerning to the perception of organizational agility various researchers from various fields stated different opinions for example researcher Albrecht, et al. (2015); Glenn, (2009) and Saha et al. (2017) considers that this issue can be considered as a multidisciplinary approach. Whereas, Nejatian et al. (2018) highlighted that the concept of agility is an organization's unique way of enhancing its competitive advantages in order to keep pace with the continuous changes of explosive markets. In addition, it is necessary to mention that in recent years much attention has been given to organizational capacity development in in order to face the global challenges that helps firms'/ organizations in the process of learning. Organizational agility concept is progressively developing its significance as one of the main tools for gaining and maintaining a competitive advantage in the disruptive technological innovation period (Žitkienė and Deksnys, 2018). Furthermore, it can be said that the capacity for enhancing organizational learning facilitates organizational learning process in which knowledge transfer takes place to achieve its advantages and helps to solve organizational problems and improve organizational performance, i.e. firms' competitiveness.

On the other hand, concerning the significance and distinctive features of organizational agility several researchers like (Nafei, 2016; Hugos, 2009; Mehrabi et al 2013; Tallon, and Pinsonneault, 2011; Yeganegi and Azar, 2012) have stated various opinions. Similarly, Alhadid (2016) and Najrani (2016) also addressed that actually the awareness of OA agility shows the impact of nimbleness in manufacturing firms', quickness in dealing with the market setting, and flexibility in dealing with manpower and fitness in technology for stimulating organizational or firms' performance. In addition, Ebrahimpour et al, (2012) emphasized that agility capabilities of an organization are considered for those today's forward-looking firms' that retain such characteristics in order to attain competitive advantage and gain an edge over competitors. Conversely, some researcher's such as Breu et al, (2001) ; Sull, (2009) ; Qin and Nembhard (2015) also highlighted that while considering the strategic activities of human resources as the most important assets in an organization that enables them to reconsider and transform the workforce to meet the business needs and to create organizational agility. More interestingly, according to Bill Gates, the success of an organization today requires the agility and drive to constantly rethink, reinvigorate, react, and reinvent." In another way, it can be said that to compete with the volatile market condition, organizational agility enhances the enterprises capability to consistently identify and capture business opportunities more quickly than its competitors do (Ganguly et al., 2009). Since, organizational agility is the capacity to sense and respond rapidly to changing customer needs, to make decisions rapidly, and to reallocate resource quickly as circumstances change Under this circumstance, organizational agility has become an important feature that has a noteworthy impact on employees' behaviour and organizational effectiveness (Kristensen and Shafiee, 2019; Chamanifard et al., 2015; Sull, 2009).

While discussing the contextual approaches of strategic HRM and organizational agility their effect on firms' competitiveness, it is obligatory to describe briefly the importance organizational leaning and its impact on firms' development. The activities of Strategic HRM and its effect on managerial skills and organizational performance offered some perceptions on how learning might occur at the organizational level to develop institutional capability as well as individual capability. To address the influence of strategic HRM there were plenty of research studies. However, there were some rare examples of linkages between SHRM and sustainable organizational learning practices that can improve firms' effectiveness and improve its performance through sufficient qualification, suitable working condition, and potential motivation. Nowadays, the strategic part of HRM practices which were integrated within the organization stated that the success of the organizational effectiveness fabricated in developing positive attitudes of individuals, groups, and organizations that mainly enhanced individual competence as well organizational competence through organizational learning. Therefore, the context of this study identified the key concept of Strategic HRM that influenced and boosted knowledge, skills, and abilities (KSA's) of employees.

THE INFLUENCE OF ORGANIZATIONAL AGILITY ON STRATEGIC HRM ENHANCE FIRMS FLEXIBILITY AND COMPETITIVENESS

Linkage Between Strategic HRM and Organizational Agility

To address and describe the influence of organizational agility on strategic HRM, it is necessary to demonstrate the alignment of human resource management; and its significant strategy discourse that has an insightful effect on significant agile organizations development concepts. Nowadays a robust discussion is going on among academicians, researchers, management experts and government on how firms can respond rapidly and flexibly for enhancing their business competitiveness. To highlight the relationship between strategic HRM and organizational agility on firms' performance development, the below mentioned Fig. 1 demonstrates the linkage between strategic HRM and organizational agilities influence on firm's flexibility and Competitiveness.

The below mentioned Fig.1 basically reveals the key concepts of strategic HRM practices such as: strategic planning, strategic capability and strategic responsiveness that strengthen strategic HRM practices in order to attain and enhance firms' strategic capability. Moreover, it can be said that the influence on human resources strategies, ensure the strategic role of HR, generate strategic ability of an organization that increase individual employees' skills (competence), managerial competence and group competence through strategic responsiveness and organizational flexibility. On the other hand, Fig. 1 also highlights the influence and importance of strategic HRM, which is inclusive with the key features of organizational agility, such as: organizational capability, adaptability, flexibility and organizational effectiveness that facilitate firms or organizations to realize their effectiveness. Additionally, recent study on organizational performance development says that through strategic HRM practices firms' need to find a research niche in the international research market to cope up with the strains of the present business environment. Conferring to this ideology of strategic HRM and organizational agilities linkage, numerous researchers like Teimouri et al, (2017); Holbeche, (2015); Battistella et al, (2017) and Dubey et al. (2018) and Keshavarz et al. (2015) identifies that human resource actions, i.e. (individual performance) are one of the major tools to accelerate firm's performance in order to fulfil organizational objectives quickly, flexibly and capably, i.e., through organizational agility.

In another way, it can be said that organizational agility (OA) and its initiatives enable firms' to augment organizations performance progress style, include HR approach and organizational progress attitude in order to efficiently respond to the ever changing world. Regarding this burning topic OA, researchers and practitioners and academicians from varied disciplines envisioned that this topic can be viewed as multidisciplinary perspective. Hence, it is rational to entitle that organizational agility and strategic HRM has a strong inter-personal relationship or linkage that facilitate firms' as well as business growth that enhance organizational efficiency, i.e. firms' competency. Relating to this issue, it is necessary to refer that organizational agility has been used in this research based on the influence

Figure 1. The linkage between strategic HRM and organizational agilities influence on firm's flexibility and competitiveness

of strategic activities of HR on organizational nimbleness, the way human resources drive their agile qualities in order to strengthen strategic HRM practices, as well as enhancing the positive influence on organizational learning. Illustrating the linkage between strategic HRM and organizational agilities influence on firm's flexibility and competitiveness this chapter performs to develop a relationship model (Fig.1), about the effect of strategic HRM on organizational agility that enables firms' to achieve their sustainable organizational efficiency, i.e. competitive advantage.

Challenges of Strategic HRM Enhancing Organizational Learning

To represent the challenging perspectives of strategic HRM, key issues and deliberations, it is obvious to discuss about the synergic consequence of human resource management strategy that fascinating organizational learning to enhance organizational knowledge (i.e. managerial and operational competency) and competitiveness. To better understand the significance of organizational learning and its impact on human resources strategic practices Kou, (2011) expresses that strategies of HRM consist better in *organizational learning*, *organizational innovation*, that enhances knowledge management capability which ultimately contributes to achieving organizational performance, (i.e. firms' effectiveness). In short it can be said that organizational learning improves organizational innovation and accumulates knowledge management capability, organizational innovation results in knowledge management capability. Thus firms need to create an environment to disseminate the use organizational knowledge in order to enhance organizational performance. Consequently, Cheng, Niu, and Niu, 2014; Chiva et al., 2014 remarked about the way organizational learning nowadays becoming a challenging perspective to strategic HRM due to its internationalization of knowledge and strategic organizational knowledge development capability. According to them, organizational learning is vital for the organizations or firms' when they are functioning in changeable environment in order to respond promptly to unpredicted circumstances than their competitors do (Garvin et al., 2008); (Basten and Haamann, 2018); (Saha et al., 2016).

Figure 2. Strategic HRM enhancing organizational knowledge through organizational learning

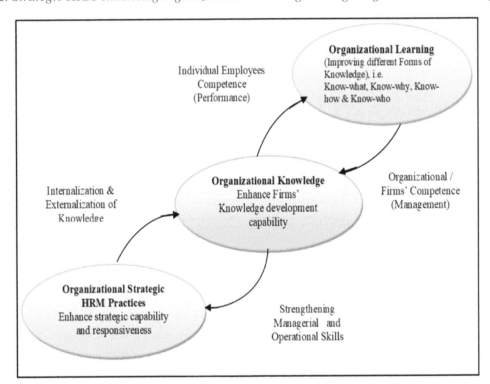

According to the findings of evolutionary economics, organizational behaviour and strategic HRM literature the author attempts to reveal the challenging perspective of Strategic HRM that enabling organizations or firms to enhance their knowledge development capability through organizational learning which has a great impact on firms' success and gain competitive advantage.

In this chapter the depicted Fig. 2 exemplify the challenging perception of strategic HRM that has been conducted in this study in order to explore the potential contribution of HRM strategy and its distinguishing features to gain some competitive advantages and enhance organizations' or firms' flexibility as well as capability and performance in relation to the implementation of organizational learning strategies (i.e. Know-what, know-why, know-how and know-who).

Organizational Agility and HRM Strategy on Firms Competitiveness

To visualize the significance of organizational agility and value of HRM strategy that can create a difference and influence on business performance, i.e. firms' competitiveness. On the other hand, the firm's competitiveness can respond rapidly and flexibly to the changing environment without facing market turbulence through organizational learning and strategic planning and strategic HRM practices. Through this concept, it intends to identify the key dimensions of organizational agility which focused on the right kind of people at the right time and at the right place to access to proper knowledge, skills and abilities (KSAs), innovative capability of the individual employee, and technological expansion. The strategic HRM approach within the organization or firms is considered to be a key player to enhance effectiveness, awareness, innovativeness, and competitiveness. The importance about organizational agility and HRM strategy on firms to competitiveness is expressed in Figure.3. The below mentioned represented Fig 3, discussed about the crucial elements and dimensions of organizational agility along with the key driving forces of human resource management. It demonstrates that basically organizational agility (OA) is consists of several key elements. Among them the most significant elements involve in organizational promptness and flexibility. For example: speed (which is responding to changes in the surrounding environment); adaptability (which enable institutions to cope up with the competitive world; and execution (Which is from the marketing perspective point facilitate institutions to enter in to the global market) Similarly, HRM is the strategic management that leads institutions to accomplish its goals through motivating and rewarding the right kind employees. Hence, it can be said that HRM consists of various driving forces and strategies that respond to face global challenges, namely knowledge skills and abilities(KSAs), i.e. organizational learning and strategic initiatives of human capital that encourage and stimulate enterprises to achieve sustainable competitive advantage.

Figure 3. Thematic model of organizational agility and strategic HRM's positive influence enhance firm's competiveness

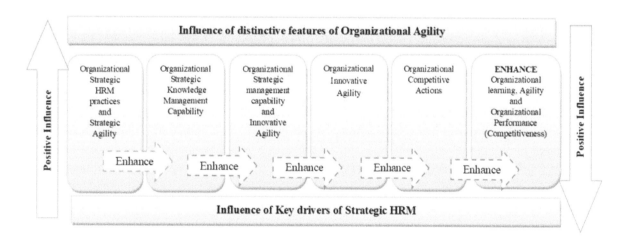

In order to justify the harmonization of organizational agility and strategic HRM that enable firms to enhance its effectiveness the described Fig. 3 demonstrates the way of organizational knowledge management proficiency and the innovative capability of an organization. The portrayed Fig.3 elucidates how rapidly and cost-efficiently firms can adapt and enter in to the global market with the influence of strategic HRM and its key drivers along with the key distinctive features of organizational agility. Therefore, this study emphasizes the influence of strategic HRM and organizational agility on the enhancement of organizational knowledge as well as organizational learning capability that influences on organizational excellence, i.e. firms' competiveness. Furthermore, this study explores and investigates the impression of OA and KM strategy as an identical perception of knowledge & innovation-driven growth of an organization. It describes that sustainability of an organization can be contingent on its agility, as the agile process of an organization promotes sustainable development. Simultaneously, from the organizational knowledge development point of view it enhances organizational strategic progress through its existing human capital's (human resources) innovative capability (Abbaspour et al., 2015); (Salamzadeh et al., 2014); (Doz and Kosonen, 2008). This perception has been already acknowledged by various scholars and researchers for example (Felipe, Roldán, and Leal-Rodríguez, 2016; Hatani and Mahrani, 2013; Mitchell, Obeidat and Bray, 2013; Bhatnagar and Sharma, 2005). Furthermore, from the organizational flexibility point of view, it is necessary to mention that in today's turbulence condition organizations need to share their risk along with their collaborative team members in order to compete successfully as well as to meet the global challenges (Page et al, 2016).Simultaneously, Trinh et al, (2012) also specified that the significance of organizational agility has been recognized by the organizations or firms who faced with challenges from a highly turbulent business environment. During that transition period they have realized and considered the agility concept as a novel approach of enhancing organizational capability in order to respond those changes and attain organizational competitiveness.

SOLUTIONS AND RECOMMENDATIONS

Finally, in order to identify the clarifications and recommendations concerning the debated issue of organizational agilities importance on firms' competitiveness, it has been viewed that the perception of strategic HRM enhances firm's competitive capability. It is mandatory to emphasize that in today's rapidly-changing business world, the impact of strategic human resource management (SHRM), and essence of organizational agility (OA) represents one of the most common strategic approaches to address the stresses of globalization and industrialization. Since, beginning of the 21st century, management development gradually becomes a part of the exclusive competence pillar. Hence, in recent years, many organizations or firms have attempted to manage their business performance using different strategies in order to achieve their mission, vision, and target as well as to meet the global challenges. Since all of us aware about the situation that to accelerate firms' knowledge and competitiveness organization need to have a proper organizational learning capability, i.e. employees' professional development facility, that enable them to regain their strength. The later experiences arguably enhance organizational learning. Different scholars have argued that harnessing the powers of human resources in institutional quality development strategy is one way to evoke the significance of institutional capacity development, i.e. organizational agility. Relating to this vibrant topic organizational agility and SHRM's key aspects and their role on enhancing firms' competitiveness this sub-chapter leads to the formation of significant research propositions and or hypothesis which states that SHRM is the key factor in HR development systems. Where, individual employee's proficiency (KSAs) creates value through them within their performance and individual creativity. In addition, this sub-chapter also expresses that organizational learning is used to strengthen the professional skills, and finally it can be said that organizational success enhances performance development of a firm or an organization.

15

Consequently, strategic HRM's activities and organizational agilities key features plays a motivating role to achieve sustainable organizational development, i.e. competitive advantage. In this chapter, the observed research expectations conclude that the currently organizations are under turbulence and due to that reason the importance of organizational agility is necessary for the firms in order to cope up with the changing world. Through organizational agility firms can enable to revive their effectiveness, i.e. (responsiveness, awareness and flexibilities) that promoting their competitiveness and aligning new business ideas.). Therefore, grounded on the said topic of research investigation, this study has drawn some significant managerial as well as operational approaches as recommendation for fostering firms' competitiveness. Initial clarifications of these recommendations have been exemplified below:

Recommendation 1: HR system in an organization is created by individual employee's talent, group talent, and organizational talent that outweighs the value through organizational learning. Thus, motivation, integration, and collaboration within the organization provides sustainable gains over the time, and balances the efforts for managing competence, namely management skills (managerial and operational) which, enables to maintain and extend the organizational success and long-term performance.

Recommendation 2: Organizations should change their mental as well as administrative setup in order to build systems, connection, collaboration for the new market growth, especially for those firms willing to cope up with global market opportunities. In this condition, organizational learning helps firms to strengthen the firms' competitive skill through improving four different types of knowledge, i.e. (Know-what), why it is necessary to achieve (Know-why), how it will be potential to make it (Know-how), who will be the right person to accomplish this task(Know-who) that can enhance organization's sustainability through internalization and externalization of knowledge (enhance firms' level of performance)

Recommendation 3: The third recommendation highlighted indicate that organizational performance in terms of flexibility and adaptability is achievable through organization's activities, especially, from the resource based perspective to process-based perspective. On the other hand, while discussing about the performance characteristics of an agile organization, it is required to state that organizations agile capacity is mainly existing on two important features, i.e. organizational adaptability and organizational flexibility; where, organizational adaptability mainly focuses on the way of an organization's procedure and structure, and status of reinforcement influence its capacity to quickly adapt to its business environment. Where, the opportunity (organizational or firms' excellence) with internal, i.e. HR's innovative capability to adapt the very fast response to sudden market changes and emerging threats by intensive customer interaction.

Recommendation 4: To overcome the excessive stress organizations need to enhance their competitive capability by collaborating as well as initiating a vibrant relationship between the academy and industry with the concept of performance –driven organizations innovative capability. So, for knowledge production organizations must put emphasis on academic fabric that can leverage and create strong driver for competitiveness. It is assumed that this conditions may help to take prompt decision and respond to the market need. It may also empower to build a business development strategy that substantiate a positive impact to achieve and sustain indigenous growth, i.e. organizational professional, commercial, managerial and operational benefit.

Recommendation 5: Finally, this chapter brings some hope for future which shows that human resource assets are the fundamental elements of success that they play a key role in the development of creating organizational agility. Thus author's feel that it is necessary to highlight that while considering human resources, strategic role, and its influence on organizational agility; decision makers of the organization are recommended to think about the capability to reconfigure and transform the employees to their business needs. Therefore, the firms' or organization need to be conscious about the fact that they can stimulate the expansion of attitudes, behaviors, and competencies. Thus, in short it can be said that this study highlights the importance of organizational agility and human resource's effectiveness, which have a great effect on enhancing organizational performance, i.e. firms' strategic capability to compete due to their competitive abilities.

FUTURE RESEARCH DIRECTIONS

In the current policy discourse, the philosophy and the urge of strategic HRM and organizational agilities potential influence for organizational development as well as for enhancing organizational competitiveness is overwhelming. Consequently, it is necessary to address the value of organizational learning in organization, it is obligatory to emphasize that currently organizations' have to face always competitive challenges and turn them into organizations knowledge development opportunities. Henceforth, from the organizational knowledge development perspective point of view, organizational learning can be considered as an opportunity to make changes and keep pace with the dynamically changing environment. This impression highlights that organizational learning is a fundamental factor in stimulating innovation and creativity within the organization. Therefore, the question of sustainable organizational learning and performance development become crucial elements in assessing and strengthening the overall development of organizational effectiveness. In this changeover condition, the notion of 'organizational learning' has become a key aspect of enhancing research organizations competitiveness through aligning organizational culture, which should be an integral factor when considering organizational competitiveness. Research shows that the significance of the association of organizational along with the organizational culture both act as a source of competitive advantage that enables organizations to enhance and influence on an organization's development strategy.

On the other hand, from the scientific as well as practical perspective point, it is expected that this research will extend to its outlook to another area of research where, organizational culture is perceived and considered as a principle that maintaining the connections with the mission, vision and a strategy, of an organization's structure and size, the management's activities, or functions within an organization. Though several researchers have also mentioned that organizational culture has a great influence in creating and maintaining a high performance oriented organizational effectiveness within the same culture and cross cultures. Thus to foresee the future prospect of this study, it is critical to emphasize the fact that at the present time, the manifestation of organizational learning concept as well as the significance of organizational agility along with organizational culture has been aligned with the perception of organizational performance development strategy. It aims to increase the efficiency and effectiveness of organizational behavior that constitutes a standardize operational environment, which acts as a vital stimulant for achieving the organizational competitive advantage. Finally, it can be said that organizational competency development enhances internal communication strategy in relationship with the organizational culture, knowledge, administration and technological upgradation that facilitate sustainable organizational learning.

CONCLUSION

To conclude, the prior discussion regarding the significance of organizational agility that foster firm's competitiveness through human resources strategic activities. To meet the global challenges, today it is

15

compulsory not only to improve the managerial and institutional competitiveness but also to find out the hidden know-how, i.e. the way organizations can enhance their existing resources competitiveness quickly, flexibly, and promptly in this continuously changing world. In addition, this thesis suggested that organizational agility and human resources strategic approach could be a very thought-provoking interesting idea to the organizations of the twenty-first century that have a good impact on human resource management and knowledge management strategy. To accomplish institution's competitiveness and enhance sustainable institutional excellence (performance) this thesis highlighted the integration of organizational competency awareness and its interpretation as well as knowledge dissemination to ensure not only the institution's success but also its sustainability. Consequently, there is a critical need for business leaders to assess their employee's talent (innovative skills and abilities) constantly, in order to determine whether the appropriate expertise is capable to accomplish the business goal or not. If not, then how to identify the skills of current employees for developing within the organization to perform better, according to the level required for the organization to be competitive. To resolve this tricky conditions of an organization, this thesis provides some evidence (presented in the list of publications) of how organizational proficiency and superiority that encompasses organizational aptitude on knowledge development and performance development.

Precisely, this chapter finally deliberates the significant issues of Organizational Agility (OA) and its effect on Strategic human resource management (SHRM) that enables businesses to sustain their organizational learning as well as to enhance organizational competitiveness. Furthermore, it is necessary to mention that chapter also highlighted the key enabling perspectives of strategic human resource management that endeavored for enhancing organizational learning through organizational agility and organizational capability. Since, nowadays the most pioneering and contemporary organizations are under excessive stress to work in a dynamic environment which, always enforces them for prompt and quantifiable advantage in order to survive in this internationally competitive market. Under these circumstances, competitiveness and innovation have become a hot issue of academic, business and managerial debates with regard to be agile and be able to sense and respond to market changes quickly and smoothly to sustaining their efficiency, i.e. organizational competitiveness. On the other hand, the conceptual framework of this study induces various approaches and models concerning organizational agility (OA), an organizations competency development approach that comprises human resources strategic approach and organizational progress attitude to efficiently respond to the dynamic world.

While addressing the key positive facets of strategic HRM, finally this chapter demonstrates some valuable features for instance (i) It is a flexible process of developing a sense of direction, making the best use of resources and ensuring it with strategic fit; (ii) It encourages to foresee the organizational capability of a firm which, depends on its resource (human capital) capability; (iii) It generate the best organizational managerial capability; (iv) It ensures that the organization has the skilled, engaged, committed and well-motivated employees in order to achieve sustained competitive advantage (v) It delivers added value and advantages to achieve sustainable competitive advantage through the strategic development of the organization's rare, hard to imitate and hard to substitute human resources. Thus, it is foreseeable that HR organizations of the future will have to reinvent the wheel to reinforce their talent management practices as well as driving agility in their organization and those who distress to do so may put their organizations in difficulty. Nevertheless, the subject matter that whether HRM Strategy is an enabler or act as an impeder of organizational agility still remains unanswered.

Finally, it is essential to designate that this chapter provides an understanding of the significance of organizational agility and its influence through organizational learning, i.e. the strategic initiatives of HRM and its effect on the occurrence of turmoil business environment as a novel approach. Moreover, while undertaking this study authors were mostly focusing on strategic HRM 's key driving forces that creates an enthusiasm among the researchers in order *to study the importance of learning at the organizational level,* how it influences an organization *to be flexible*; how it enables organizations *to develop an innovative way of indulgent rapidly during the period of technological turbulence*, (i.e. agility) that facilitates organizations either to create new knowledge or to modify the existing ones, (i.e. the impact of disrupting technological surveillance). Fundamentally, it is to be noted that strategic HRM influences RMHRM organizational learning (i.e. human resources learning capabilities, strategies within the organization) organizational agility (i.e. firm's fast-adopting capability, refinement and accepting the capability with the changing environment) and empower firms to take actions promptly and react flexibly to face the vibrant ever-changing business environment.

ACKNOWLEDGMENT

This work is supported by the institutional project entitled: "Process of implementing a Human Resources Strategy for Researchers (HRS4R)". Development of TBU research and development capacities in Zlín, Reg. No. CZ.02.2.69 / 0.0 / 0.0 / 16_028 / 0006243. The author of this chapter is thankful to the Director of the University Institute for providing management support system (MSS) and infrastructure facility in order to carry out this significant research. Also, the author dedicates this study to her only beloved son "Kanishka Binayak Saha" and beloved father "Chittaranjan Saha".

REFERENCES

Abbaspour, A., Golabdoust, A., Golabdoost, N., & Golabdous, T. T. (2015). A study on the relationship between organizational intelligence and organization agility in Tehran university of medical sciences. *International Journal of Asian Social Science*, 5(11), 626–640. doi:10.18488/journal.1/2015.5.11/1.11.626.640

Abraham, P., & Perkin, N. (2017). *Building the Agile Business through Digital Transformation*. Kogan Page Publishers.

Adler, N. J., & Ghadar, F. (1993). Strategic Human Resource Management: A Global Perspective. *Sun Yat-sen. Management Review*, (1), 1–40.

Alaraqi, A. K. (2017). Relationship between SHRM and Organizational Performance among Iraqi Oil Companies. *Journal of Global Economics*, 5(1), 1–12. doi:10.4172/2375-4389.1000241

Albrecht, S. L., Bakker, A. B., Gruman, J. A., Macey, W. H., & Saks, A. M. (2015). Employee engagement, human resource management practices and competitive advantage: An integrated approach. *Journal of Organizational Effectiveness: People and Performance*, 2(1), 7–35. doi:10.1108/JOEPP-08-2014-0042

Alhadid, A. (2016). The effect of organization agility on organization performance. *International Review of Management & Business Research*, 5(1), 273–278.

Alsaadat, K. (2019). Strategic human resource management technology effect and implication for distance training and learning. *Iranian Journal of Electrical and Computer Engineering*, 9(1), 314–322. doi:10.11591/ijece.v9i1.pp314-322

Armstrong, M. (2006). *Strategic human resource management: A guide to action* (3rd ed.). Thomson-Shore, Inc.

Basten, D. and Haamann, T. (2018). Approaches for Organizational Learning: A Literature Review. *SAGE Open - Literature Review,* 1–20.

Battistella, C., De Toni, A. F., De Zan, G., & Pessot, E. (2017). Cultivating business model agility through focused capabilities: A multiple case study. *Journal of Business Research, 73,* 65–82. doi:10.1016/j.jbusres.2016.12.007

Bhatnagar, J., & Sharma, A. (2005). The Indian perspective of strategic HR roles and organisational learning capability. *International Journal of Human Resource Management, 16*(9), 1711–1739. doi:10.1080/09585190500239424

Bouaziz, F., & Hachicha, Z. S. (2018). Strategic human resource management practices and organizational resilience. *Journal of Management Development, 37*(7), 537–551. doi:10.1108/JMD-11-2017-0358

Breu, K., Hemingway, C. J., Strathern, M., & Bridger, D. (2002). Workforce agility: The new employee strategy for the knowledge economy. *Journal of Information Technology, 17*(1), 21–31. doi:10.1080/02683960110132070

Chamanifard, R., Nikpour, A., Chamanifard, S., & Nobarieidishe, S. (2015). Impact of organizational agility dimensions on employee's organizational commitment in Foreign Exchange Offices of Tejarat Bank, Iran. *European Online Journal of Natural and Social Sciences, 4*(1), 199–207.

Cheng, H., Niu, M.-S., & Niu, K.-H. (2014). Industrial cluster involvement, organizational learning, and organizational adaptation: An exploratory study in high technology industrial districts. *Journal of Knowledge Management, 18*(5), 971–990. doi:10.1108/JKM-06-2014-0244

Chiva, R., Ghauri, P., & Alegre, J. (2014). Organizational learning, innovation and internationalization: A complex system model. *British Journal of Management, 25*(4), 687–705. doi:10.1111/1467-8551.12026

Cyert, R. M., & March, J. G. A. (1963). *A behavioral theory of the firm.* Prentice Hall.

Doz, Y., & Kosonen, M. (2008). The Dynamics of Strategic Agility: Nokia's Rollercoaster Experience. *California Management Review, 50*(3), 95–118. doi:10.2307/41166447

Dubey, R., Altay, N., Gunasekaran, A., Blome, C., Papadopoulos, T., & Childe, S. J. (2018). Supply chain agility, adaptability and alignment Empirical evidence from the Indian auto components industry. *International Journal of Operations & Production Management, 38*(1), 129–148. doi:10.1108/IJOPM-04-2016-0173

Ebrahimpour, H., Salarifar, M., & Asiaei, A. (2012). The Relationship between Agility Capabilities and Organizational Performance: A Case Study among Home Appliance Factories in Iran. *European Journal of Business and Management, 4*(17), 186–195.

Eneh, S. I., & Awara, N. F. (2016). Strategic Human Resource Management Practices and Organizational Growth: A Theoretical Perspective. *Global Journal of Social Sciences, 15*(1), 27–37. doi:10.4314/gjss.v15i1.3

Felipe, C. M., Roldán, J. L., & Leal-Rodríguez, A. L. (2016). An explanatory and predictive model for organizational agility. *Journal of Business Research, 69*(10), 4624–4631. doi:10.1016/j.jbusres.2016.04.014

Ganguly, A., Nilchiani, R., & Farr, J. V. (2009). Evaluating Agility in Corporate Enterprises. *International Journal of Production Economics*, *118*(2), 410–423. doi:10.1016/j.ijpe.2008.12.009

Garvin, D. A., Edmondson, A. C., & Gino, F. (2008). Is yours a learning organization? *Harvard Business Review*, *86*, 109–116. PMID:18411968

Glenn, M. (2009). *Organizational agility: How business can survive and thrive in turbulent times*. London, UK: The Economist.

Harraf, A., Wanasika, I., Tate, K., & Talbott, K. (2015). Organizational Agility. *Journal of Applied Business Research*, *31*(2), 675–686. doi:10.19030/jabr.v31i2.9160

Hatani, L., & Mahrani, S.W. (2013). Strategic human resource management practices: mediator of total quality management and competitiveness (a study on small and medium enterprises in kendari southeast sulawesi). *International Journal of Business and Management Invention*, *2*(1), 8-20.

Holbeche, L. (2015). *The Agile Organization: How to Build an Innovative, Sustainable and Resilient Business*. Kogan Page. Publishers.

Hugos, M. H. (2009). *Business agility: Sustainable prosperity in a relentlessly competitive world*. John Wiley & Sons.

Jackson, S. E., Schuler, R. S., & Jiang, K. (2014). An Aspirational Framework for Strategic Human Resource Management. *The Academy of Management Annals*, *8*(1), 1–56. doi:10.5465/19416520.2014.872335

Keshavarz, S., Heydari, M., & Farsijani, H. (2015). The strategic factors of knowledge management success in achieving organizational agility on the model (APQC) (Case study: automotive-related companies). *European Online Journal of Natural and Social Sciences*, *4*(1).

Kou, T. H. (2011). How to improve organizational performance through learning and knowledge? *International Journal of Manpower*, *32*(5/6), 581–603. doi:10.1108/01437721111158215

Kristensen, S. S., & Shafiee, S. (2019). Rethinking organization design to enforce organizational agility. *11th Symposium on Competence-Based Strategic Management (SKM 2019)*, Stuttgart, Germany.

Lengnick-Hall, C. A., Tammy, E., Beck, T. E., & Lengnick-Hall, M. L. (2011). Developing a capacity for organizational resilience through strategic human resource management. *Human Resource Management Review*, *21*(3), 243–255. doi:10.1016/j.hrmr.2010.07.001

Marier, J. H. (2012). Strategic Human Resource Management in Context: A Historical and Global Perspective. *The Academy of Management Perspectives*, 1–11. doi:10.5465/amp.2012.0063

Mehrabi, S., Siyadat, S., & Allameh, S. (2013). Examining the Degree of Organizational Agility from Employees' Perspective (Agriculture-Jahad Organization of Shahrekord City). *International Journal of Academic Research in Business and Social Sciences*, *3*(5), 315–323.

Mitchell, R., Obeidat, S., & Bray, M. (2013). The Effect of Strategic Human Resource Management on Organizational Performance: The Mediating Role of High-Performance Human Resource Practices. *Human Resource Management*, *52*(6), 899–921. doi:10.1002/hrm.21587

Nafei, W. A. (2016). Organizational Agility: The Key to Organizational Success. *International Journal of Business and Management, 11*(5), 296–309. doi:10.5539/ijbm.v11n5p296

Najrani, M. (2016). The endless opportunity of organizational agility. *Strategic Direction, 32*(3), 37–38. doi:10.1108/SD-02-2015-0026

Nejatian, M., Zarei, M. H., Nejati, M., & Zanjirchi, S. M. (2018). A hybrid approach to achieve organizational agility: An empirical study of a food company. *Benchmarking, 25*(1), 201–234. doi:10.1108/BIJ-09-2016-0147

Oppong, N. Y. (2017). Exploring the importance of human resource activities-strategies alignments: Interactive brainstorming groups approach. *Cogent Business & Management, 4*(1), 1–12. doi:10.1080/23311975.2016.1273081

Page, T., Rahnema, A., Murphy, T., & McDowell, T. (2016). *Unlocking the flexible organization: Organizational design for an uncertain future*. Deloitte.

Qin, R., & Nembhard, D. A. (2015). Workforce agility in operations management. *Surveys in Operations Research and Management Science, 20*(2), 55–69. doi:10.1016/j.sorms.2015.11.001

Saha, N., Chatterjee, B., Gregar, A., & Sáha, P. (2016). The impact of SHRM on sustainable organizational learning and performance. *International Journal of Organizational Leadership, 5*(1), 63–75. doi:10.33844/ijol.2016.60291

Saha, N., Gregar, A., & Sáha, P. (2017). Organizational agility and HRM strategy: Do they really enhance firms 'competitiveness? *International Journal of Organizational Leadership, 6*(3), 323–334. doi:10.33844/ijol.2017.60454

Saha, N., & Van Der Heijden, B. I. J. M. (2019). The Influence of SHRM and Organizational Agility-Do They Really Boosts Organizational Performance? In Handbook of Research on Contemporary Approaches in Management and Organizational Strategy. Hershey, PA: IGI Global. doi:10.4018/978-1-5225-6301-3

Salamzadeh, Y., Nejati, M., & Aidin Salamzadeh, A. (2014). Agility Path Through Work Values in Knowledge-Based Organizations: A Study of Virtual Universities. *Innovar (Universidad Nacional de Colombia), 24*(53), 177–186. doi:10.15446/innovar.v24n53.43942

Sull, D. (2009). How to Thrive in Turbulent Markets. *Harvard Business Review, 87*(2), 78–88.

Tallon, P. P., & Pinsonneault, A. (2011). Competing perspectives on the link between strategic information technology alignment and organizational agility: Insights from a mediation model. *Management Information Systems Quarterly, 35*(2), 463–486. doi:10.2307/23044052

Teimouri, H., Jenab, K., Moazen, I. R. H., & Bakhtiari, B. (2017). Studying effectiveness of human resource management actions and organizational agility: Resource management actions and organizational agility. *Information Resources Management Journal, 30*(2), 61–77. doi:10.4018/IRMJ.2017040104

Trinh, P., Molla, A., & Peszynski, K. (2012). Enterprise systems and organizational agility: A review of the literature and conceptual framework. *Communications of the Association for Information Systems, 31*, 167–193. doi:10.17705/1CAIS.03108

Wahyono. (2018). A conceptual framework of strategy, action and performance dimensions of organizational agility development. *Industrial and Commercial Training, 50*(6), 326-341. doi:10.1108/ICT-12-2017-0103

Yeganegi, K., & Azar, M. (2012). The Effect of IT on Organizational Agility. *Proceedings of the 2012 International Conference on Industrial Engineering and Operations Management.*

Žitkienė, R., & Deksnys, M. (2018). Organizational Agility Conceptual Model. *Montenegrin Journal of Economics, 14*(2), 115–129. doi:10.14254/1800-5845/2018.14-2.7

ADDITIONAL READING

Arbussa, A., Bikfalvi, A., & Marquès, P. (2017). Strategic agility-driven business model renewal: The case of an SME. *Management Decision, 55*(2), 271–293. doi:10.1108/MD-05-2016-0355

Cegarra-Navarro, J. G., Acosta, P. S., & Wensley, A. K. P. (2016). Structured knowledge processes and firm performance: The role of organizational agility. *Journal of Business Research, 69*(5), 1544–1549. doi:10.1016/j.jbusres.2015.10.014

Elgamal, M. A. (2018). Dynamic Organizational Capabilities: The Joint Effect of Agility, Resilience and Empowerment. *Journal of Human Resource Management., 6*(2), 44–49. doi:10.11648/j.jhrm.20180602.11

Fayezi, S., Zutshi, A., & O'Loughlin, A. (2017). Understanding and development of supply chain agility and flexibility: A structured literature review. *International Journal of Management Reviews, 19*(4), 379–407. doi:10.1111/ijmr.12096

Ordóñez de Pablos, P., & Tennyson, R. D. (2014). *Strategic Approaches for Human Capital Management and Development in a Turbulent Economy.* IGI Global. doi:10.4018/978-1-4666-4530-1

Panda, S., & Rath, S. K. (2018). Modelling the Relationship Between Information Technology Infrastructure and Organizational Agility: A Study in the Context of India. *Global Business Review, 19*(2), 424–438. doi:10.1177/0972150917713545

Polychroniou, P., & Trivellas, P. (2018). The impact of strong and balanced organizational cultures on firm performance: Assessing moderated effects. *International Journal of Quality and Service Sciences, 10*(1), 16–35. doi:10.1108/IJQSS-09-2016-0065

Raj, R., & Srivastava, K. B. L. (2013). The Mediating Role of Organizational Learning on the Relationship among Organizational Culture, HRM Practices and Innovativeness. *Management and Labour Studies, 38*(3), 201–223. doi:10.1177/0258042X13509738

Sekhar, C., Patwardhan, M., & Vyas, V. (2018). Linking Work Engagement to Job Performance Through Flexible Human Resource Management. *Advances in Developing Human Resources, 20*(1), 72–87. doi:10.1177/1523422317743250

Teena, B., & Sanjay, S. (2014). SHRM: Alignment of HR function with business strategy. *Strategic HR Review, 13*(4/5). Advance online publication. doi:10.1108/SHR-03-2014-0023

KEY TERMS AND DEFINITIONS

Competitiveness: In this chapter, the term competitiveness has been considered as the capability of a firm or organization that are willing to meet the organizational requirement and sustain in long-run as well to compete globally. From the organizational development point competitiveness can be reflected as managerial and operational competency.

Organizational Agility (OA): In this chapter the notion of organizational agility (OA) is a novel reasonable and practical approach. It is very essential for the organizations looking forward to visualize themselves in the new millennium. It can be considered as strategic approach that facilitates organizations to take challenges in a very flexible way which empowers them to reinforce their existing resources that act as an elixir to enhance organizational effectiveness.

Organizational Development: In this chapter, the term organizational development can consider as an arena for research, where it is dedicated to intensifying the organizational knowledge and organizational effectiveness through enhancing individual employees' performance management.

Organizational Learning (OL): In this chapter, the term organizational learning has been regarded as the inquisitiveness (desire for knowledge development) of employees learning capability. It may also have regarded as a tool for organizational knowledge development process or media that encapsulate organizational performance.

Strategic Human Resource Management (SHRM): In this chapter, the term strategic HRM has been viewed as the process of organizational tactical planning that influence human resources in order to enhance individual employees' skill and group capability as well as strengthen managerial skill.

Learning Organisation:
An Effect on Organisational Performance

Chandra Sekhar Patro

(iD) https://orcid.org/0000-0002-8950-9289

Gayatri Vidya Parishad College of Engineering (Autonomous), India

INTRODUCTION

A learning organization is an institution, which has the skills to change behaviour in order to form new information and understanding through the creation, gathering and transfer of information based on a continuous learning cycle. Organizations that could shed light on the future are those with learning capacity and enthusiasm and are able to form and use valid and reliable information. It is essential for the staff of an organization to be open to innovation and learning, in order to increase service quality, and convey the impact of being a learning organization to the forefront. Similar to the growing importance of being learning organizations in all fields and institutions, it is also gaining importance in educational institutions in terms of reforming information and adapting to change (Volante, 2010). Especially, gaining awareness of the characteristics of learning organizations can result in dynamism and innovation, as well as increased motivation and enthusiasm in the institutions (Tasargöl, 2013).

Organizations include multiple and intricate networks of relationships, which are sustained through communication and other forms of feedback with varying degrees of inter-dependence. With the rapid pace of growth, organizations face some challenges in training and retaining the intellectual capital of their workforce. First, due to the rapidly changing technologies, there is a need for continuous adaptation and retraining of the employees. Second, the training has to address a wide range of people with different backgrounds and abilities, ranging spectrum of needs and availability of time to study, etc. Further, as these learners are adults with considerable experience and awareness of what they would like to learn, training methods need to evolve to meet the needs of a modern knowledge society (Minch & Tabor, 2003). In addition, organizations are facing a number of key changes that focus attention on efficiency in relation to delivery methods. New opportunities are being offered by information technology (IT) which could facilitate major changes in the delivery of training and provide greater flexibility for learning (Littejohn & Watson, 2004).

In the digital age where information is regarded as the most important power, learning can be considered as an effective process of collecting, developing and transferring information (Alipour & Karimi, 2011). The concept of the learning organization has been linked to innovation and performance in organizations (Power & Waddell, 2004). The capacity for change and continuous improvement to meet the challenges in the environment in which organizations operate has been associated with the capability of these organizations to learn (Armstrong & Foley, 2003). Thus, organizations that learn will be able to keep abreast with developments and improvements in the business environment to operate successfully.

Organizations of the future will not survive without becoming communities of learning. It is absolutely essential for organizations to learn from their environments, to continually adjust to new and changing market dynamics, and just as is the case with the individual, to learn how to learn from an uncertain and

DOI: 10.4018/978-1-7998-3473-1.ch178

unpredictable future. Continuous improvement requires a commitment to learning. Solving a problem, introducing a product, and reengineering a process all require seeing the world in a new light and acting accordingly. In the absence of learning, organizations and individuals simply repeat old practices. Change remains cosmetic, and improvements are either fortuitous or short-lived.

BACKGROUND

The learning organization perspective is perhaps the most popular within the management and business at the moment. Senge (2006) suggests that the most successful organizations are learning organizations and that the ability to learn faster than competitors is the only sustainable advantage. It might, therefore, be reasonable to assume that being a learning organization would manifest itself in an excellent performance, given that this must be a key area of competitive advantage. Senge (1990, 1996) developed five interrelated dimensions that are considered vital to building organizations that can truly learn known as 'Five Disciplines'. These disciplines include mental models, personal mastery, shared vision, team learning, and systems thinking. The five disciplines have remained as the core elements of the learning organization.

Pedler, et al. (1997) argued that there has been a shift within the field away from looking at the learning organization as the 'panacea' for any organizational improvement, towards a more pragmatic emphasis on the process of the learning organization. The learning organization is referred to as a journey with a number of maturity stages based on eleven characteristics that need to be developed on the way. These eleven characteristics include learning approach to strategy, participative policymaking, informative, formative accounting and control, internal exchange, reward flexibility, enabling structures, boundary workers as environmental scanners, inter-company learning, a learning climate, and self-development opportunities for all.

Watkins & Marsick (1993) viewed the learning organization as an integrative model, where learning is a continuous process, used strategically, and is integrated with overall work processes. This model integrated both structure and people as they are focusing on leveraging learning on three levels like the individual, team and organizational or system learning (Watkins & Marsick, 1996). At the individual level, continuous learning opportunities need to be created, allowing members in the organization to acquire knowledge and skills. At the team level, individuals learn as teams, focusing on collaboration and teamwork. This is followed by learning at the organization level incorporating individual and group learning and capture all in standard operating procedures, work processes, operations manuals, information systems, and the organizational culture. Learning at the organizational level is described as the most difficult, and least practised by companies as it requires the establishment of effective systems to capture and share learning, and gaining organizational consensus and commitment from all employees through empowering them toward a collective vision, resulting in increase in organizational performance (Watkins & Marsick, 2003).

Örtenblad (2002) developed a typology of the idea of a learning organization. He suggested that there are four understandings of the learning organization concept. The first is the old learning organization perspective, which focuses on the storage of knowledge in the organizational mind. Learning is viewed as applications of knowledge at different levels. The second type is the learning at work perspective, which sees a learning organization as an organization where individuals learn at the workplace. The third is the learning climate perspective, which sees the learning organization as one that facilitates the learning of its employees. The fourth is the learning structure perspective, which regards the learning organization as a flexible entity (Örtenblad & Koris, 2014). Naser, et al. (2017) found that there is a high degree of importance of organizational dimension, knowledge management, the focus of continuing education, strategic partnerships and alliances, and keep up with the labour market in the organization. There is a fair level agreement about the axis of interest teams/committees, and scientific research. There is a moderate agreement about the importance of the human dimension, institutional culture, cognitive dimension, and consulting and training.

Dekoulou & Trivellas (2015) brought to light that learning-oriented operation is a crucial predictor of both employee job satisfaction and individual performance, while job satisfaction proved to be a mediator of the relationship between learning organization and job performance. Huili, et al. (2014) demonstrated the linkage mechanism of building a learning organization and business performance. The study found that learning dimension has the most significant impact on firm performance. Learning and innovation have a significant impact on performance, whereas, culture and leadership have a relative influence on non-financial indexes. Macpherson & Antonacopoulou (2013) identified that uneven outcomes were attributed to three critical contributing factors such as the leadership and governance structures, the meaningful ways in which members can participate and interact with others, and their identity and sense of belonging.

García-Morales, et al. (2012) argued that transformational leadership influences organizational performance positively through learning organization and innovation, learning organization influences organizational performance positively, both directly and indirectly through organizational innovation, and organizational innovation influences organizational performance positively. Singh (2016) argued that the learning organization have a great impact on organizational effectiveness. An organization can maintain a cordial learning environment within the organization through the senior managers by regulating data creation and data sharing among the employees within the organization. This will help in bringing the innovation capabilities and increasing the competitive advantage. The employees should continuously adapt to and learn for organization effectiveness. Abu-Shanab, et al. (2014) explored the relationship between different variables like information technology infrastructure, supportive organizational policies, knowledge sharing motivation, knowledge sharing practices and ongoing learning organization. The study indicated that there is a significant positive relationship between knowledge sharing practices and ongoing learning organization. Firms need to emphasise the role of learning organization in sustaining competitive advantage and furnish needed tools to encourage knowledge management practices. It is vital for organizations to set up an environment for social interaction as a means for knowledge sharing.

Moh'd Al-adaileh, et al. (2012) explored the influence of the knowledge conversion processes (KCP) on the success of a learning organization (LO) strategy implementation. The study revealed that socialisation, internalisation and their combination have a significant impact on the success of a learning organization strategy. Socialisation is the major influential factor, having the strongest impact on learning organization whereas, externalisation was found to have no statistical influence on learning organization. Aydin & Ceylan (2009) ascertained the impact of learning organization capacity (LOC) on organizational effectiveness. The study found that a company that features a high level of learning organization could have a higher level of worker satisfaction which can successively improve the money and growth performance of a company resulting in positive effects within the organization. Garvin et al. (2008) stated that learning organization is the place where the staff excel in the creation, acquisition, knowledge transfer, and consists of three basic building blocks like the internal supportive environment to learn, processes and practices to learn, and the behaviour of leadership that supports and enhances learning. A learning organization is different from other traditional organizations in terms of educational leadership, restructuring, allowing employees to participate and move effectively, and adopting

Figure 1. Disciplines of learning organization

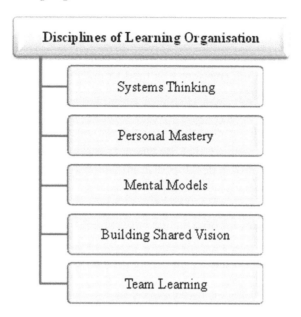

participation strategy. A learning organization also provides opportunities for exchange of knowledge, information, strategy and culture.

LEARNING ORGANIZATION DISCIPLINES

Learning organization theory first gained major recognition in 1990 with the publication of The Fifth Discipline: The Art and Practice of the Learning Organization by Peter Senge. According to Senge (1990), an organization should be a place where "people continually expand their capacity to create the results they truly desire, where new and expansive patterns of thinking are nurtured, where collective aspiration is set free, and where people are continually learning to see the whole together." Senge (2001) outlined five basic disciplines or components of a learning organization viz., personal mastery, mental models, building shared visions, team learning, and systems thinking. The five components of the learning organization were conceptualised to help people become active participants in understanding their reality at present and shaping it for the future. In his view, simply following best practices can do more harm than good, often leading to incomplete implementation and disappointing outcomes. He is not denying the value of learning from other organizations, or from well-conducted research. Rather, suggesting the importance of understanding and accommodating the nuances of each organization, and recognizing and responding to unavoidable changes in organizations' environment as they occur. The five disciplines of the learning organization are shown in figure 1.

1. Systems Thinking

Systems thinking is looking at the interrelated parts of a process and recognizing and examining patterns and possibilities. In the context of learning organization theory, Senge (1990) refers to systems thinking as the fifth discipline. It is the discipline that integrates the other four disciplines, viz., personal mastery, mental models, building shared visions, and team learning into a coherent body of theory and practice. Organizations are systems, comprised of interrelated parts and actions which often take years to fully play out their effects on each other. When an individual is inside an organizational system, it is hard to see or perceive full patterns of interactions and change, but can only see snapshots. When the decisions are made based on such limited information, it is hard to make good choices that solve fundamental problems (Kofman & Senge, 1995).

Systems thinking states that all the characteristics must be apparent at once in an organization for it to be a learning organization. If some of these characteristics are missing, then the organization falls short of its goal. However, some believe that the characteristics of a learning organization are factors that are gradually acquired, rather than developed simultaneously. It is the discipline that integrates all the employees of the organization, fusing them into a coherent body of theory and practice (Senge, et al., 1999). Systems thinking ability to comprehend and address the whole and to examine the inter-relationship between the parts provides for both the incentive and the means to integrate various disciplines in the organization.

2. Personal Mastery

Personal mastery is taking the time, and intellectual and emotional effort, to clarify, and then deepen one's personal vision. In essence, it is an individual figuring out what he or she considers truly important (Senge, et al., 1999). The central principle of personal mastery is creative tension. This involves using the gap between one's personal vision and one's current reality to generate energy for change. In order to do this effectively, individuals must have a clear view of both their vision and their reality (Senge, 2001).

Individuals striving for personal mastery are committed to life-long learning, and ever-increasing proficiency in their work, which they approach almost like a work of art. They are particularly interested in understanding how their actions affect others around them. Their goal is to attain expertise which can be shared with others, not to dominate others. They focus their energies on desired results and are much less concerned with the particular means or processes used to attain those results, which leaves their mind open to innovate and create solutions to problems (Senge, 1990). It is a process and lifelong learning discipline. People with a high level of personal mastery are acutely aware of their ignorance, their incompetence, and their growth areas. Therefore, it is important to develop a culture in the organization where personal mastery is practised in daily life.

3. Mental Models

Mental models are deeply ingrained assumptions/generalisations that influence how one understands the world behaves in the world and believes the world works. Mental models are the lenses through which individuals view their world (Senge, 1990). In order to examine mental models, one must first turn the mirror inward to unearth one's internal pictures of the world, and then bring those pictures to the surface and scrutinise them. Once an individual has accomplished this process, he or she must share his or her own thinking with others and expose it to their influence, so limitations in his or her worldview can be recognised.

In creating a learning environment it is important to replace confrontational attitudes with an open culture that promotes inquiry and trust. To achieve this, the learning organization needs mechanisms for locating and assessing organizational theories of action. Unwanted values need to be discarded by the process called 'unlearning' (Senge, 2001). If the organization is to develop a capacity to work with

15

mental models, then it is necessary for the employees to learn new skills and develop new orientations. For this, there need to be institutional changes in order to foster such a change. It involves seeking to distribute organizational responsibly far more widely while retaining coordination and control.

4. Building Shared Visions

Building shared visions is the process of translating individual visions into a shared picture of the future that an organization or a workgroup within an organization, wants to create. A shared vision is much more than the vision statements, which are often the vision of a single person or small group imposed on the rest of an organization. A truly shared vision is a common caring about a goal shared by all members of a working group and provides the focus and energy for subsequent team learning (Senge, et al., 1999). The development of a shared vision is important in motivating the employees to learn, as it creates a common identity that provides focus and energy for learning. The creation of a shared vision can be hindered by traditional structures where the organizational vision is imposed from above. Therefore, a learning organization tends to have a flat decentralised organizational structure.

The shared vision is often to succeed against a competitor for which there can be transitory goals. There should be long term goals that are intrinsic within the organization. The only way to arrive at a genuinely shared vision is to give each person with a stake in the organization's future a legitimate voice in the process. One can not dictate a vision, but it can emerge when all parties are brought into the process and have a long-term commitment towards it (Senge, 1990). When there is genuine vision, employees' excel and learn, not because they are told to, but because they want to. But many leaders have personal visions that never get translated into shared visions that galvanize the organization.

5. Team Learning

Team learning is a process in which co-workers in an organization "think together" until there is a consensus about how to reach a particular goal. Team learning is vital because teams, not individuals, are the fundamental learning unit in modern organizations. Unless teams in an organization can learn, the organization cannot learn (Reason & Bradbury, 2001). Team learning starts with dialogue. Three basic conditions must be present for dialogue to occur. First, team members must suspend their assumptions. This means they must be cognizant of their assumptions and willing to hold them for personal and group examination. Second, they must regard one another as colleagues, and give up any privileges of rank they normally are granted. Third, they must be guided, at least in the early stages of the process, by a facilitator. The facilitator's responsibilities include helping team members maintain ownership of the process and outcomes, keeping the dialogue moving, and reminding others of the conditions of dialogue (Senge, 1990).

Effective team learning balances dialogue and discussion. In dialogue, complex issues are explored, and no agreement is sought. In the discussion, different views are presented and defended, and decisions are made. Both dialogue and discussion can lead to new behaviours and actions. However, these behaviours and actions are simply a by-product of dialogue, while they are often the focus of discussion (Senge, et al., 1999). Team members who enter into dialogue regularly tend to develop a deep trust and an understanding and respect for one another's perspectives that carry over into discussions. Good teams are often in conflict, the free flow of conflicting ideas is essential for creative thinking. Negative patterns of interaction, such as defensiveness, can undermine dialogue, but if such patterns are recognized

Table 1. Summary of five disciplines of learning organization

Discipline	Description
Systems Thinking	This is a conceptual framework that allows people to study businesses as bounded objects. Learning organization uses this method of thinking when assessing the organization and has information systems that measure the performance of the organization as a whole and of its various components.
Personal Mastery	The commitment by an individual to the process of learning is known as personal mastery. Personal mastery is the discipline of continually clarifying and deepening employee's personal vision, of focusing their energies, of developing patience, and of seeing reality objectively. It goes beyond competence and skills, although it involves them.
Mental Models	The discipline of mental models starts with turning the mirror inward; learning to unearth our internal pictures of the world, to bring them to the surface and hold them rigorously to scrutiny. It also includes the ability to carry on 'learning' conversations that balance inquiry and advocacy, where people expose their own thinking effectively and make that thinking open to the influence of others.
Building Shared Vision	The development of a shared vision is important in motivating the employees to learn, as it creates a common identity that provides focus and energy for learning. The most successful visions normally build on the individual visions of the employees at all levels of the organization. Therefore, a learning organization tends to have a flat, decentralized organizational structure. The shared vision is often to succeed against a competitor for which there can be transitory goals.
Team Learning	A team or shared learning is that the employees grow more quickly and the problem-solving capacity of the organization is improved through better access to knowledge and expertise. A learning organization has structures that facilitate team learning with features such as boundary crossing and openness. The discipline of team learning starts with 'dialogue', the capacity of members of a team to suspend assumptions and enter into a genuine 'thinking together'.

Source: Peter Senge (1990)

and addressed, they can actually accelerate learning (Bennett & Brown, 1995). When teams are truly learning, they can produce extraordinary results.

In Senge's view, if all of the five disciplines are developed independently, much of the potential value of each discipline will be lost. On the other hand, if all five disciplines develop as an ensemble, and if an organization's employees consistently look at how each of the disciplines is connected to the others, the whole (the outcomes) can far exceed the sum of its parts (the inputs). The summary of the five basic disciplines of learning organizations is presented in table 1.

DIMENSIONS OF LEARNING ORGANIZATION

The organizations have experienced a trend of rapid transformation as global markets, and external political and economic changes make it impossible for any business or service-whether private, public, or non-profit to cling-to past ways of doing work. A learning organization arises from the total change strategies that institutions of all types are using to help navigate these challenges. Learning organizations proactively use learning in an integrated way to support and catalyse growth for individual workers, teams and other groups, entire organizations, and the institutions and communities with which they are linked (Marsick, 2000). Organizations have attempted to become learning organizations to establish or maintain their competitive advantage. This strategy has led to the formation and development of validated instruments to assess learning organization culture. Such diagnostic tools can be important, as organizational change necessitates the diagnosis of the current state of organizational culture at the first stage of the efforts (McLean, 2006).

Watkins & Marsick (1996) proposed an integrated model for a learning organization and defined a learning organization as "one that learns continuously and transforms itself. Learning is a continuous, strategically used process integrated with and running parallel to work." To measure an organization's learning culture, they developed the 'Dimensions of a Learning Organization Questionnaire (DLOQ)', an instrument that was also validated by relating it to organizational performance. Watkins & Marsick (1993) suggested that the design of learning organization requires six action imperatives including empowering people toward a collective vision, promoting inquiry and dialogue, encouraging collaboration and team learning, creating continuous learning opportunities, connecting the organization to the environment, and establishing systems to capture and share learning. These action imperatives are expected to occur at four different levels for an organization to have the capacity of continuous learning and change i.e., individual (continuous learning and dialogue and inquiry), the team (collaboration and team learning), organization (empowerment and systems), and societal levels (connection to the environment) (Watkins & Marsick, 2013).

In addition, Watkins & Marsick (1993) provided seven characteristics (7Cs) of continuous, collaborative, connected, collective, creative, captured and codified, and capacity building of an organization that has an enhanced ability to change as a result of the achievement of the six action imperatives. These 7Cs are the framework used to audit an organization's present capacity while identifying the gap between the current and the desired state for a learning organization. Watkins & Marsick (1997) published the DLOQ which was designed to measure the presumed seven dimensions of learning organization including continuous learning, dialogue & inquiry, collaboration, embedded system, empowerment, system connection, and strategic leadership. While some have suggested the underlying framing of the DLOQ is a theory (Swanson & Chermack, 2013). Watkins and Marsick have consistently indicated that the basis for the DLOQ is actually a model as shown in figure 2.

Figure 2. Dimensions of the Learning Organization

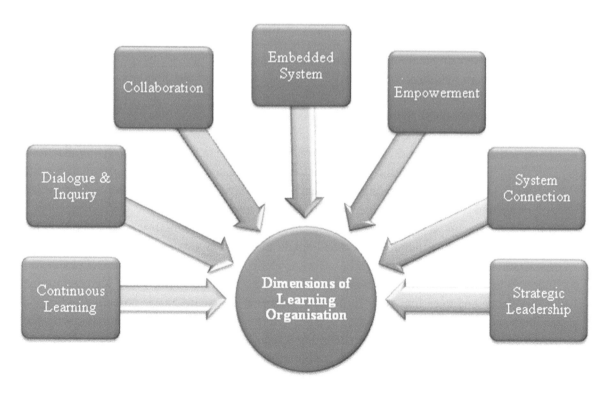

1. **Continuous Learning:** Continuous learning helps individuals to obtain new competencies to be applied to the work. When the individuals are rewarded for learning, it creates greater motivation for the individuals to become more receptive towards learning and develop high self-efficacy, which in return improves the individual's performance leading to improved organizational performance (Laatikainen, 2014). Vijjuprabha (2015) referred to continuous learning as providing opportunities to learn from the problems that people encounter, using incentives to support both formal and incidental learning and better planning.

2. **Dialogue& Inquiry:** The dimension dialogue& inquiry is concerned with learning from the experience of others (Pokharel & Choi, 2015). Dialogue provides a platform for questioning, being open to new ideas and understanding the opinion of other people (Watkins & Marsick, 2003). It ultimately serves in building a common understanding and cognition among individuals and a shared understanding of the organization. Inquiry involves questioning the views of others yet does not attack the individuals.

3. **Collaboration:** Organizations have continued to depend on teams to achieve effectiveness through task performance (Klein et al., 2011). Through team learning the members can adapt to changing circumstances, discover new ways of achieving team objectives, and continually refine practices and processes leading to the discovery of better ways of achieving team objectives, which finally results in better team performance (Bunderon & Sutcliffe, 2003). Kayes & Burnett (2006) developed a three-stage learning behaviour model of team learning and performance. The three identified behaviour models are tacit coordination, adapting and problem-solving.

   ○ Tacit coordination is the continuous and inferred organization of diverse roles, coordination of knowledge and responsibility in a team. Coordination here focuses on the synchronisation of knowledge and skills within a team. Tacit coordination between and among team members facilitates team processes such as decision making, exchange of information and interpersonal awareness thus enhances team performance.

   ○ The second behaviour is adapting which means responding to internal and external demands through adjusting actions and beliefs. The ability to continuously adapt to the environment allows team members to constantly change strategies and redefine goals in the middle of projects whenever the need arises. This behaviour keeps the team and organizational performance up to par due to the pro-activeness of teams.

   ○ Problem-solving as the last behaviour involves focusing and addressing problematic activities through collaboration. Collaboration involves channels that foster synchronization of skills and knowledge within the team. It facilitates decision-making, interpersonal awareness and knowledge sharing among team members. The level of performance depends on collaboration and shared interdependence between team members.

4. **Embedded System:** At the organizational level, relationships become structured while individual learning and some of the common understandings developed by groups become institutionalised; thus organizations are able to change to reflect new knowledge and learning (Yang, 2012). Organizations find ways to store knowledge and use it to sustain themselves during periods of high environmental turbulence and even high staff turnover (Watkins & Marsick, 2003). To be able to capture, maintain and integrate new information that is useful for improving organizational performance, a system to effectively capture and share learning is required (Tippins & Sohi, 2003). A good system to capture and share learning can improve organizational performance through people's access to critical knowledge and appropriate information (Lipshitz, et al., 2007). According to Weldy (2009), learning organizations have a memory to acquire, store, retrieve and manage information

and disseminate knowledge through the organization to new staff members to ensure improved organizational performance.

5. **Empowerment:** Another dimension of organizational learning is the empowerment of people towards a collective vision. Employee empowerment means involving employees in decision making by giving them the power in form of autonomy, the information in form of feedback, knowledge in form of training and reward in form of job enrichment (Demirci & Erbas, 2010). Empowerment enhances the employee's psychological attachment and commitment to the organization. An organizational learning system is supported by a common vision through ways such as keeping people committed to the vision and encouraging them to identify them with the vision that promotes organization goals (Garvin, et al., 2008). According to Yang & Choi (2009), employee empowerment is a powerful management tool and if managed well can cause an increase in performance, productivity and job satisfaction. Through empowerment, employees feel energized and become willing to do whatever it takes to get the work done thus enhancing the better performance of the organization (Ibua, 2014).

6. **System Connection:** The other dimension is connecting the organization to its environment or developing system connections. Organizational members are helped to note the effect of their work on the entire organization. The organization is linked to the community and members often scan the environment and use the information gathered to adjust their work practices (Watkins & Marsick, 2003). Organizations that take long to heed to environmental changes might end up being left with fewer options if they regain their desired position at all.

7. **Strategic Leadership:** The primary function of strategic leadership is to distribute organizational resources in such a way that gives the organization a competitive edge thus rip benefits from the dynamic environment (Weldy, 2009). Pazireh, et al. (2014) acknowledge that the vision and mission are one of the most important characteristics of a high performing organization. Developing an organization's vision and the organization's ability to manage change brought about by that vision brings competitive advantage. Strategic leadership is also involved in developing an organization's core competencies. A core competency is an organizational capability to perform in a manner consistently superior to its competitors thus achieving above-average organizational performance (Wendy, 2012). To enhance organizational performance, strategic leadership can influence organizational culture, rituals, symbols, reward systems and boundaries. Here, leadership uses learning strategies to enhance business performance and results.

According to Mrisha, et al. (2017), increased emphasis on an examination of the individual, team, and organizational level learning practices have stimulated tremendous interest in the concept of the learning organization (Ellinger, et al., 2000). The summary of the findings related to the dimension of the learning organization questionnaire (DLOQ) framework based on organizational levels is shown in table 2.

FRAMEWORK AND HYPOTHESES

The dimensions of the learning organization help the employees to increase their performance in the organization. The question is do the seven dimensions of learning organization have an impact on employees' efficiency and organizational performance? Therefore, an enquiry into the employees' response to learning organization has become essential. The framework of a learning organization is developed

Table 2. Dimensions of learning organization questionnaire (DLOQ) framework

Dimension	Description
Individual Level Learning	
Continuous Learning	The extent of developing learning in the organization by learning how to learn new knowledge, values and skills and creating continuous learning opportunities through experiments for personal and career development on the job.
Dialogue & Inquiry	Dialogue is the extent to which the culture of organization allows members to have open communication with open minds to talk, discuss, and explain their experiences and skills. Inquiry involves questioning the views of others yet does not attack the individuals.
Team Level Learning	
Collaboration	The degree to which an organization tries to design work for organizational members to achieve a unified action on common purposes has shared the vision and personal mastery to exchange their views and ideas and learn how to work collaboratively.
Embedded System	The extent of creating organizational capacity through both high and low technology systems and finding ways to maintain what is learned.
Organizational Level Learning	
Empowerment	The process of enabling organization members to participate in policy making, to know how to get something done, to assess their needs, to influence others and to create a shared and collective vision. This process continues to get feedback from organization members to recognize the gap between the current status and the new vision.
System Connection	The extent to which an organization has open systems to connect the organization to its external and internal environment to help organization members to see the impact of their work on the entire organization and think worldwide.
Strategic Leadership	Strategic leadership refers to organizational leaders' competence to think strategically, being a model, champion, support learning and energize the organization to create change. This also develops a collective vision to help organization members to move in the new direction.

Source: Watkins & Marsick (1997)

Figure 3. Learning organization framework

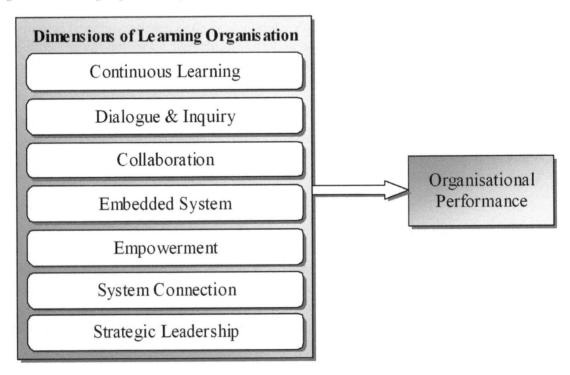

based on the Dimensions of Learning Organization Questionnaire (DLOQ) Framework proposed by Watkins & Marsick (1997) as shown in figure-3.

To know the effect of the dimensions of a learning organization on organizational performance, the following hypotheses (H) are developed:

H_1: Continuous learning does not show a significant impact on organizational performance.

H_2: Dialogue & Inquiry does not show a significant impact on organizational performance.

H_3: Collaboration does not show a significant impact on organizational performance.

H_4: Embedded system does not show a significant impact on organizational performance.

H_5: Empowerment does not show a significant impact on organizational performance.

H_6: System connection does not show a significant impact on organizational performance.

H_7: Strategic leadership does not show a significant impact on organizational performance.

METHODOLOGY

The current chapter measures the effect of the dimensions of the learning organization on organizational performance. The required data were collected from both primary and secondary sources. The secondary data was collected from books, journals, magazines, unpublished theses and institution websites to know the various concepts of the learning organization. The primary data resources are collected using a survey method from the employees working in different private business units of Visakhapatnam, India. To get the required data, a structured questionnaire was designed and distributed to the employees through emails and some respondents were interviewed personally. The purpose of the survey was explained to the respondents and they were assured of the confidentiality of their responses. A total of 216 valid responses were considered for statistical data analysis.

To measure the impact of the seven dimensions on organizational performance, a 5-point Likert rating scale technique was used ranging from highly satisfied (5) to highly dissatisfied (1). For evaluating the responses, inferential statistics are used to make a conclusion based on the results and significance. Descriptive analytical tools such as mean, standard deviation, values, factor loadings, composite reliability, Cronbach's alpha, and average variance extracted were used to summarize the respondents' opinion on learning organization. The seven dimensions were tested for their relationship with organizational performance using correlation, and the hypotheses were tested using multi-regression and ANOVA analysis.

STATISTICAL DATA ANALYSIS

To analyse the employees' opinion on learning organization, seven imperative dimensions like continuous learning, dialogue & inquiry, collaboration, embedded system, empowerment, system connection, and strategic leadership are identified. The descriptive statistic results regarding the employees'opinion on learning organization are shown in table 3. The mean scores, standard deviation, t-values, factor loadings, average variance extracted, composite reliability and Cronbach's alpha are computed as shown in table 3. The Cronbach's alpha value reveals that all variables have internal consistency as they are above 0.80. The composite reliability values also show the validity of the variables is above 0.80.

The descriptive statistics show that the overall mean values are in the range of 3.27- 3.85 indicating that the employees are satisfied with the concept of learning organization and agreed that it helps in increasing organizational performance. The standard deviation values range from 0.640- 1.011. Among the seven dimensions, the highly rated dimension is 'empowerment' with a mean value of 3.62 followed by the dimension's'system connection (3.58)', 'dialogue & inquiry (3.57)', 'strategic leadership (3.56)', 'collaboration (3.50)', 'embedded system (3.49)', and 'continuous learning (3.27)'. The organizational performance is rated at 3.85 indicating the usefulness of learning organization in an organization.

The dimension continuous learning assessed based on four parameters reveal that, 'I have the materials and equipment to do my work right (3.37)' got the highest rating from the respondents followed by 'there is someone at work who encourages my development (3.34)', 'supervisor provides feedback on my areas for improvement (3.25)', and 'I have opportunities at work to learn and grow (3.11)'. In the case of dialogue & inquiry, 'I know what is expected of me at work (3.62)' secured the highest rating followed by 'I am strongly encouraged to report unsafe conditions (3.60)', 'issues are resolved by constructive discussions with supervisor (3.54)', and 'safety information is always brought to my attention (3.51)' by the respondents. With regard to collaboration the variable, 'there are always enough people available to get the job done safely (3.52)' is highly rated followed by the variables 'co-workers often give tips to each other on how to work safely (3.44)', 'I am clear about what my responsibilities are for health and safety (3.66)' and 'my supervisor encourages me on innovative ideas (3.37)' by the respondents.

The respondents' opinion on the dimension embedded system reveals that 'management clearly considers the safety of employees of great importance' got the highest rating with a mean value of 3.43 followed by the variables 'a no-blame approach is used to persuade people acting unsafely when their behaviour is inappropriate (3.69)', 'customers are encouraged to provide feedback (3.49)', and 'I feel a culture of an organization can be correlated with vision and mission statement (3.35)'. With regard to empowerment, the variable 'I have received recognition or praise for doing good work (3.87)' secured higher rating by the respondents followed by the variables 'at work my opinions seem to count (3.94)', 'I have enough opportunity to build capability through technical/behavioural training (3.48)' and 'I am comfortable in discussing personal/professional matters with my reporting officer (3.17)'.

The respondents' opinion on strategic leadership reveals that the variable 'management acts decisively when a safety concern is raised (3.74)' secured highest rating following by the variables 'corrective action is taken when management is informed about unsafe practices (3.42)', 'at my location, prompt resolution of customer issues is recognised (3.14)' and 'I have sufficient time for transformational thinking rather than transactional issues (3.92)'. With regard to organizational performance, the variable 'qualitative improvements are achieved in the work' secured highest rating from the respondents with a mean value of 3.90 followed by the variables 'able to find solutions to the challenges being faced (3.98)', 'managers have been successful in driving productivity and performance (3.71)' and 'managers have been inspirational and instrumental in bringing a change in the attitude of employees (3.82)'.

From table 3, it can be observed that all the t-values are significant at $p < 0.05$ significance level (2-tailed). The test shows that the embedded system (t=34.65) is a highly significant dimension among the seven dimensions of the learning organization. The other dimensions of learning organization collaboration (t=27.75), system connection (t=26.75), empowerment (t=26.26), continuous learning (t=25.16), strategic leadership (t=24.20), and dialogue & inquiry (t=23.26) also show a significant positive impact on organizational performance.

The factor loadings ranged from 0.598-0.985 reveal that all the dimensions of learning organization have a positive impact on the employees' efficiency and organizational performance. In the case of continuous learning, the highest loaded factor is 'the supervisor provides feedback on my areas for improvement (0.985)'. The variable 'safety information is always brought to my attention (0.848)' is the highest influential factor in case of dialogue & inquiry. In the case of collaboration, the variable 'my supervisor encourages me on innovative ideas (0.832)' got higher factor loading. With regard to the

Table 3. Respondents opinion on dimensions of the learning organization(n=216)

Dimensions	Mean	SD	t	FL	AVE	CR	CA
Continuous Learning	**3.27**	**0.640**	**25.16**		**0.770**	**0.930**	**0.91**
There is someone at work who encourages my development	3.34	0.604	27.18	.782			
I have the materials and equipment to do my work right	3.37	0.497	30.15	.761			
The supervisor provides feedback on my areas for improvement	3.25	0.627	24.10	.985			
I have opportunities at work to learn and grow	3.11	0.831	19.21	.959			
Dialogue & Inquiry	**3.57**	**0.651**	**23.26**		**0.643**	**0.878**	**0.88**
I know what is expected of me at work	3.62	0.616	25.06	.795			
Safety information is always brought to my attention	3.51	0.714	20.18	.848			
I am strongly encouraged to report unsafe conditions	3.60	0.610	22.78	.818			
Issues are resolved by constructive discussions with the supervisor	3.54	0.663	25.01	.743			
Collaboration	**3.50**	**0.783**	**27.79**		**0.582**	**0.847**	**0.90**
There are always enough people available to get the job done safely	3.52	0.756	27.78	.719			
Co-workers often give tips to each other on how to work safely	3.44	0.819	25.85	.743			
I am clear about what my responsibilities are for health and safety	3.66	0.721	36.38	.752			
My supervisor encourages me on innovative ideas	3.37	0.836	21.15	.832			
Embedded System	**3.49**	**0.705**	**34.65**		**0.531**	**0.818**	**0.86**
Management considers the safety of employees of great importance	3.43	0.713	31.50	.825			
A no-blame approach is used to persuade people acting unsafely when their behaviour is inappropriate	3.69	0.661	26.55	.690			
Customers are encouraged to provide feedback	3.49	0.680	32.69	.734			
I feel a culture of an organization can be correlated with Vision and Mission statement	3.35	0.764	47.87	.653			
Empowerment	**3.62**	**0.729**	**26.26**		**0.502**	**0.799**	**0.89**
I have received recognition or praise for doing good work	3.87	0.708	30.14	.598			
At work, my opinions seem to count	3.94	0.673	32.23	.759			
I have enough opportunity to build capability through technical/ behavioural training	3.48	0.715	21.76	.633			
I am comfortable in discussing personal/professional matters with my reporting officer	3.17	0.819	20.92	.821			
System Connection	**3.58**	**0.717**	**26.75**		**0.729**	**0.914**	**0.93**
The mission/purpose of my company makes me feel my job is important	3.84	0.610	17.40	.918			
I do not receive praise for working conditions	3.39	0.818	45.65	.826			
Management operates an open door policy on working conditions	3.63	0.648	21.74	.766			
I have work profile matching to my passion	3.44	0.791	22.19	.896			
Strategic Leadership	**3.56**	**0.996**	**24.20**		**0.593**	**0.851**	**0.85**
Management acts decisively when a safety concern is raised	3.74	0.965	25.84	.791			
Corrective action is taken when management is informed about unsafe practices	3.42	1.005	23.19	.841			
At my location, prompt resolution of customer issues is recognised	3.14	1.059	21.32	.584			
I have sufficient time for transformational thinking rather than transactional issues.	3.92	0.954	26.46	.836			
Organizational Performance	**3.85**	**1.011**	**22.23**		**0.777**	**0.931**	**0.86**
Qualitative improvements are achieved in the work	3.90	0.913	22.66	.985			
Able to find solutions to the challenges being faced	3.98	0.883	24.84	.959			
Managers have been successful in driving productivity and performance	3.71	1.109	19.28	.918			
Managers have been inspirational and instrumental in bringing a change in the attitude of employees	3.82	1.137	22.12	.614			
Note: All the t-values are significant at the 0.05 level (2-tailed)							

SD-Standard Deviation, FL-Factor Loadings, AVE-Average Variance Extracted, CR-Composite Reliability, CA-Cronbach's Alpha embedded system, the highly loaded factor is 'management clearly considers the safety of employees of great importance (0.825)'. 'I am comfortable discussing personal/professional matters with my reporting officer (0.821)' is the highest factor in the case of empowerment. In the case of system connection, the highest factor loading is 'the mission/purpose of my company makes me feel my job is important (0.918)'. In the case of strategic leadership, the factor 'corrective action is taken when management is informed about unsafe practices (0.841)' is a highly rated factor. With regard to organizational performance, the variable 'qualitative improvements are achieved in the work (0.985)' got the highest factor loading. Thus, it can be observed that the loadings of seven dimensions are in the acceptable range.

The average variance extracted (AVE) values show that continuous learning (0.770) got the highest

Table 4. Correlation Matrix

Dimensions	1	2	3	4	5	6	7	8
1. Continuous Learning	1							
2. Dialogue & Inquiry	.647**	1						
3. Collaboration	.631**	.909**	1					
4. Embedded System	.715**	.716**	.754**	1				
5. Empowerment	.509**	.592**	.698**	.370**	1			
6. System Connection	.662**	.235*	.279**	.224*	.189*	1		
7. Strategic Leadership	.628**	.328**	.375**	.021	.490**	.832**	1	
8. Organizational Performance	.825**	.656**	.698**	.735**	.216*	.726**	.541**	1
**. Correlation is significant at the 0.01 level (2-tailed).								
*. Correlation is significant at the 0.05 level (2-tailed).								

variance, whereas empowerment recorded (0.502) the lowest variance. The inter-item correlation between the dimensions of learning organization was also examined and it was found that all the paired correlation measures are significant at $p < 0.01$ and $p < 0.05$ level (2-tailed), as shown in table 4. Therefore, the validity of the research has been achieved to a satisfactory level.

Table 5. Model summary

Model	R	R Square	Adjusted R Square	Std. Error of the Estimate
1	.841[a]	.819	.801	.16863
a. Predictors: (Constant), continuous learning, dialogue & inquiry, collaboration, embedded system, empowerment, system connection, strategic leadership				

RESULTS AND DISCUSSION

The statistical significance of all the dimensions of the learning organization was examined to determine the validity of the hypothesised paths. The results of the model summary, ANOVA, and regression coefficient values for the relationship between dimensions of a learning organization and organizational performance were analysed and interpreted.

Table 6. ANOVAa

Model	Sum of Squares	df	Mean Square	F	Sig.
Regression	7.234	6	8.470	143.13	.001[b]
Residual	2.438	200	.035		
Total	78.672	216			
a. Dependent Variable: organizational performance					
b. Predictors: (Constant), continuous learning, dialogue & inquiry, collaboration, embedded system, empowerment, system connection, strategic leadership					

The model summary table5 reveals that the linear regression coefficient (R=0.841) indicating a maximum correlation between the dependent and independent variables. In terms of variability R-Square (0.819) shows that the independent variables continuous learning, dialogue & inquiry, collaboration, embedded system, empowerment, system connection, and strategic leadership can predict 82 per cent

Table 7. Coefficients[a]

Dimensions	Unstandardized Coefficients		Standardized Coefficients	t	Sig.
	B	Std. Error	Beta		
(Constant)	.652	.155		3.32	.000
Continuous Learning	.390	.163	.314	1.29	.023
Dialogue & Inquiry	.469	.141	.446	3.27	.008
Collaboration	.371	.134	.331	1.60	.015
Embedded System	.257	.119	.229	1.11	.012
Empowerment	.047	.128	.045	1.26	.038
System Connection	.547	.132	.327	3.23	.005
Strategic Leadership	.231	.121	.321	2.44	.014
a. Dependent Variable: organizational performance					

Note: All the t-values are significant at 0.05 levels.

of the variance in the dependent variable organizational performance.

The results of the ANOVA test shown in table 6 indicates that the dependent variable organizational performance (F=143.13, p=0.001< 0.01) shows a significant relation with the independent variables continuous learning, dialogue & inquiry, collaboration, embedded system, empowerment, system connection, and strategic leadership.

The coefficient results shown in Table 7 reveals the relationship between the dimensions of the learning organization and organizational performance. The dimension continuous learning (t=1.29; p=0.023 < 0.05) shows a significant positive relationship with organizational performance not supporting the hypothesis H_1. Dialogue & inquiry (t=3.27; p=0.008 < 0.05) shows a significantly positive relation with organizational performance not supporting the hypothesis H_2. The dimension collaboration has a positive significant relationship with organizational performance (t= 1.60; p=0.015< 0.05) rejecting the hypothesis H_3. Embedded system dimension shows a strong positive significant relation with organization performance (t=1.11; p=0.012 < 0.05) and thus, the hypothesis H_4 is also not supported. Empowerment dimension shows a significant positive relationship with organizational performance (t=1.26; p=0.038 < 0.05), hence,the hypothesis H_5 is not supported. The dimension system connection has a strong positive significant relationship with organizational performance (t=3.23; p=0.005< 0.05), rejecting the hypothesis H_6. The strategic leadership dimension also reveals a significant positive relationship with organizational performance (t=2.44; p=0.014< 0.05) not supporting the hypothesis H_7. Thus, the regression analysis results provide strong support for the rejection of the null hypotheses relating to the relationship between independent variables continuous learning, dialogue & inquiry, collaboration, embedded system, empowerment, system connection, and strategic leadership with the dependent variable organizational performance.

CONCLUSION AND MANAGERIAL IMPLICATIONS

The strategic importance of adopting learning orientation has become essential for organizations as it could contribute towards organizational success. The capability to learn does not naturally and readily occur within organizations. However, it is imperative for the organizations to ensure that the resources are allocated and efforts made to instil learning within the organizations. The research concludes that the seven dimensions of learning organizations viz., continuous learning, dialogue & inquiry, collaboration, embedded system, empowerment, system connection, and strategic leadership have a significant positive effect on the employees' efficiency and organizational performance.

The organizations need to establish systemic interventions to create a continuous learning culture within the company across the strategic business units in order to leverage the skills. The managers need to pay attention to the factors that facilitate organizational learning since they have a direct influence on innovation and organizational performance. It is essential to have the tolerance to ambiguity, uncertainty and errors. Promoting dialogue and inquiry among the team members' fosters team learning, and helps organizations to agile in the highly dynamic and competitive landscape. In essence, teams provide vehicles for learning from others by creating peer group virtual team network in the company through various IT interventions and tools. This helps in facilitating the organizations to have a broad understanding of the employee needs and expectations, which help to evaluate their performance in terms of learning and competencies. Good communication between the managers and employees can improve the distribution of knowledge within the organization. Managers can use formal mechanisms to ensure sharing of best practices among employees and departments, making employees talk to each other using multi-functional work teams.

LIMITATIONS AND FUTURE RESEARCH DIRECTIONS

The scope of the study is limited only to the employee's opinion on the effect of the learning organization dimensions on organizational performance in Visakhapatnam district, Andhra Pradesh, India. It is essential to know the employee's perception of learning organization in various other regions and at different levels of the organization. Future research is required to measure the variables over a long period and establish how long it takes before changes in learning can lead to changes in performance. The findings can be further used for conducting future studies focusing on ascertaining the relation of the emotional quotient with the performance management system. The practitioners can develop a performance matrix to measure the business outcomes and cascade it to different levels of the organization. The research can be undertaken on individual and group learning related to organizational change and transformation.

REFERENCES

Abu-Shanab, E., Haddad, M., & Knight, M. B. (2014). Knowledge sharing practices and the learning organization: A study. *IUP Journal of Knowledge Management, 12*(2), 38.

Alipour, F., Idris, K., & Karimi, R. (2011). Knowledge creation and transfer: The role of learning organization. *International Journal of Business Administration, 2*(3), 61–67. doi:10.5430/ijba.v2n3p61

Armstrong, A., & Foley, P. (2003). Foundations of a learning organization: Organization learning mechanism. *The Learning Organization, 10*(2), 74–82. doi:10.1108/09696470910462085

Aydin, B., & Ceylan, A. (2009). Does organizational learning capacity impact on organizational effectiveness? Research analysis of the metal industry. *Development and Learning in Organizations: An International Journal, 23*(3), 21–23.

Bennett, S., & Brown, J. (1995). Mindshift: Strategic dialogue for breakthrough thinking. In S. Chawla & J. Renesh (Eds.), *Learning organizations: Developing cultures for tomorrow's workplace* (pp. 167–184). Productivity Press.

Bunderon, J. S., & Sutcliffe, K. M. (2003). Management Team Learning Orientation and Business Unit Performance. *The Journal of Applied Psychology, 88*(3), 552–560. doi:10.1037/0021-9010.88.3.552 PMID:12814303

Dekoulou, P., & Trivellas, P. (2015). Measuring the impact of a learning organization on job satisfaction and individual performance in Greek advertising sector. *Procedia: Social and Behavioral Sciences, 175,* 367–375. doi:10.1016/j.sbspro.2015.01.1212

Demirci, M. K., & Erbas, A. (2010). Employee Empowerment and Its Effect on Organizational Performance. In *2nd International Symposium on Sustainable Development*, (pp. 142-146). Sarajevo: Academic Press.

Ellinger, A. D., Yang, B., & Ellinger, A. E. (2000). Is the Learning Organization for Real? Examining the Impacts of the Dimensions of the Learning Organization on Organizational Performance. In *Adult Education Research Conference* (pp. 1-8). New Prairie Press.

García-Morales, V. J., Jiménez-Barrionuevo, M. M., & Gutiérrez-Gutiérrez, L. (2012). Transformational leadership influence on organizational performance through learning organization and innovation. *Journal of Business Research, 65*(7), 1040–1050. doi:10.1016/j.jbusres.2011.03.005

Garvin, D. A., Edmondson, A. C., & Gino, F. (2008). Is yours a learning organization? *Harvard Business Review, 83*(3), 109–116. PMID:18411968

Huili, Y., Shanshan, W., & Yanping, M. A. (2014). The Impact of Building a Learning Organization on Firm Performance: An Empirical Analysis Based on Software Company in Shanghai Pudong Software Park in China. *International Business and Management, 8*(1), 10–14.

Ibua, M. P. (2014). *The Influence of Institutional Factors and Job Related Attitudes on the Relationship between Employee Empowerment and Performance of Public Universities in Kenya* (Unpublished PhD Thesis). University of Nairobi.

Kayes, C., & Burnett, G. (2006). Team Learning in Organizations: A Review and Integration. In *Organization Learning, Knowledge and Capabilities 2006 Conference* (pp. 1-29). Coventry, UK: University of Warwick.

Kim, J., Egan, T., & Tolson, H. (2015). Examining the Dimensions of the Learning Organization Questionnaire: A Review and Critique of Research Utilizing the DLOQ. *Human Resource Development Review, 14*(1), 91–112. doi:10.1177/1534484314555402

Klein, K., Knight, A., Ziegert, J., Lim, B., & Saltz, J. (2011). When team members' values differ: The moderating role of team leadership. *Organizational Behavior and Human Decision Processes, 114*(1), 25–36. doi:10.1016/j.obhdp.2010.08.004

Kofman, F., & Senge, P. (1995). Communities of commitment: The heart of learning organizations. In S. Chawla & J. Renesh (Eds.), *Learning organizations: Developing cultures for tomorrow's workplace* (pp. 15–43). Productivity Press.

Laatikainen, E. (2014). *Employees Continuous Learning and Job Satisfaction - Effects on Productivity* (Unpublished Master's Thesis). Lappeenranta University of Technology, Lappeenranta, Finland.

Lipshitz, R., Friedman, V. J., & Popper, M. (2007). *Demystifying Organizational Learning*. Sage.

Littlejohn, D., & Watson, S. (2004). Developing graduate managers for hospitality and tourism. *International Journal of Contemporary Hospitality Management, 16*(7), 408–414. doi:10.1108/09596110410559096

Macpherson, A., & Antonacopoulou, E. (2013). Translating strategy into practice: The role of communities of practice. *Journal of Strategy and Management, 6*(3), 265–285. doi:10.1108/JSMA-11-2012-0061

Marsick, V. J. (2000). Learning Organizations. In *From the Learning Organization to Learning Communities: Toward a Learning Society* (pp. 5–20). Center on Education and Training for Employment Center Publications.

McLean, G. N. (2006). *Organization development: Principles, processes, performance*. Berrett-Koehler.

Minch, R. P., & Tabor, S. W. (2003). Networking education for the new economy. *Journal of Information Technology Education Research, 2*, 51–59. doi:10.28945/312

Moh'd Al-adaileh, R., Dahou, K., & Hacini, I. (2012). The impact of knowledge conversion processes on implementing a learning organization strategy. *The Learning Organization, 19*(6), 482–496. doi:10.1108/09696471211266947

Mrisha, G., Ibua, M., & Kingi, W. (2017). Effect of Learning Organization Culture on Organizational Performance among Logistics Firms in Mombasa County. *Journal of Human Resource Management, 5*(2), 32–38. doi:10.11648/j.jhrm.20170502.11

Naser, S. S. A., Al Shobaki, M. J., Amuna, Y. M. A., & Al Hila, A. A. (2017). Trends of Palestinian Higher Educational Institutions in Gaza Strip as Learning Organizations. *International Journal of Digital Publication Technology*, *1*(1), 1–42.

Örtenblad, A. (2002). A typology of the idea of learning organization. *Management Learning*, *33*(2), 213–230. doi:10.1177/1350507602332004

Örtenblad, A., & Koris, R. (2014). Is the learning organization idea relevant to higher educational institutions? A literature review and a "multi-stakeholder contingency approach". *International Journal of Educational Management*, *28*(2), 173–214. doi:10.1108/IJEM-01-2013-0010

Pazireh, M., Akhlagh, E. M., & Akbari, M. (2014). Evaluation of the Role of Strategic Leadership in Organizational Performance. *Universal Journal of Management and Social Sciences*, *4*(9), 23–28.

Pedler, M., Burgoyne, J., & Boydell, T. (1997). *The Learning Company* (2nd ed.). McGraw-Hill Publishing Company.

Pokharel, M. P., & Choi, S. O. (2015). Exploring the relationships between the learning organization and organizational performance. *Management Research Review*, *38*(2), 126–148. doi:10.1108/MRR-02-2013-0033

Power, J., & Waddell, D. (2004). The link between self-managed work teams and learning organizations using performance indicators. *The Learning Organization*, *11*(3), 244–259. doi:10.1108/09696470410533003

Reason, P., & Bradbury, H. (2001). *Handbook of action research*. Sage.

Senge, P., Kleiner, A., Roberts, C., Ross, R., Roth, G., & Smith, B. (1999). *The dance of change: The challenges to sustaining momentum in learning organizations*. Currency/Doubleday.

Senge, P. M. (1990). *The fifth discipline: The art and practice of the learning organization*. Doubleday.

Senge, P. M. (1996). Leading Learning Organizations: The Bold, the Powerful, and the Invisible. In F. Hesselbein, R. Marshall, & R. Bechkard (Eds.), *The Leader of the Future* (pp. 41–57). Jossey-Bass.

Senge, P. M. (2001). The learning organization. In W. E. Natemeyer & J. T. McMahon (Eds.), *Classics of organizational behaviour* (3rd ed., pp. 468–472). Waveland Press.

Senge, P. M. (2006). *The Fifth Discipline: The Art and Practice of the Learning Organization* (Revised Edition). Doubleday Dell.

Singh, E. (2016). Learning Organization and Its Impact on Organizational Effectiveness: A Literature Review. *CLEAR International Journal of Research in Commerce & Management*, *7*(4), 37–39.

Swanson, R. A., & Chermack, T. (2013). *Theory building in applied disciplines*. Berrett-Koehler.

Tasargöl, A. (2013). *Ilkögretim Kurumlarinda Görev Yapan Yöneticilerin Görüsleri: Okullarin Ögrenen Örgüt Olarak Deggerlendirilmesi. Yayinlanmamis Yüksek Lisans Tezi. Egitim Bilimleri Enstitüsü*. Yakin Dogu Üniversitesi.

Tippins, M. J., & Sohi, R. S. (2003). IT competency and firm performance: Is organizational learning a missing link? *Strategic Management Journal*, *24*(8), 745–761. doi:10.1002mj.337

Vijjuprabha, D. (2015). The Guidelines for the Development of Logistics Learning Organization. *International Journal of the Computer, the Internet and Management, 23*(2), 65-69.

Volante, L. (2010). Assessment of, for, and as learning within schools: Implications for transforming classroom practice. *Action in Teacher Education, 31*(4), 66–75. doi:10.1080/01626620.2010.10463536

Watkins, K. E., & Dirani, K. M. (2013). A meta-analysis of the dimensions of a Learning Organization Questionnaire looking across cultures, ranks, and industries. *Advances in Developing Human Resources, 15*(2), 148–162. doi:10.1177/1523422313475991

Watkins, K. E., & Marsick, V. J. (1993). *Sculpting the learning organization: Lessons in the art and science of systemic change*. Jossey-Bass.

Watkins, K. E., & Marsick, V. J. (1996). *In action. Creating the Learning Organization*. American Society for Training and Development.

Watkins, K. E., & Marsick, V. J. (1997). *Dimensions of the Learning Organization Questionnaire*. Partners for the Learning Organization.

Watkins, K. E., & Marsick, V. J. (2003). *Making Learning Count! Diagnosing the Learning Culture in Organizations*. Sage Publications.

Weldy, T. (2009). Learning organization and transfer: Strategies for improving performance. *The Learning Organization, 16*(1), 58–68. doi:10.1108/09696470910927678

Wendy, L. (2012). *The relationship between strategic leadership and strategic alignment in high perfomancing companies in South Africa* (Unpublished PhD Thesis). University of South Africa.

Yang, S. B., & Choi, S. O. (2009). Employee empowerment and team performance: Autonomy, responsibility, information, and creativity. *Team Performance Management: An International Journal, 15*(5/6), 289–301. doi:10.1108/13527590910983549

Yang, Y. (2012). Bilateral inter-organizational learning in corporate venture capital activity governance characteristics, knowledge transfer, and performance. *Management Research Review, 35*(5), 352–378. doi:10.1108/01409171211222278

KEY TERMS AND DEFINITIONS

Educational Leadership: Educational leadership is a collaborative process that unites the talents and forces of teachers, students and parents to improve the quality of education and the education system itself.

Innovation: Innovation is the process of translating an idea or invention into a product/service that creates value or for which customers pay.

Knowledge Management: Knowledge management is the systematic process of managing the organization's knowledge assets for the purpose of creating value and meeting tactical & strategic requirements.

Knowledge Sharing: Knowledge sharing is an act of exchanging information or understanding between individuals, teams, communities, or organizations.

Leadership: Leadership refers to the ability of an individual or a group of individuals to influence and guide followers or other members of an organization.

Learning Cycle: Learning cycle is referred to as how individuals learn from past experiences.

Learning Organization: An organization that facilitates the learning of its employees so that the organization can continuously transform itself is referred to as a learning organization.

Organizational Learning: Organizational learning can be seen as the collaborative learning process of individuals and analysing learning processes without concerning the outcomes.

Social Interaction: A social interaction is an exchange of communication between two or more individuals and is a building block of society.

Strategic Learning: Strategic learning is referred to as a means of evaluation to assisting the organizations or groups to learn quickly from their work and adapt their strategies.

Unified Communication Technologies at a Global Automotive Organization

Anthony D. Bolton

 https://orcid.org/0000-0002-1259-7479
University of South Africa, South Africa

Leila Goosen

 https://orcid.org/0000-0003-4948-2699
University of South Africa, South Africa

Elmarie Kritzinger

 https://orcid.org/0000-0002-5141-4348
University of South Africa, South Africa

INTRODUCTION

Information and Communications Technologies (ICTs) influence and shape the world and society (See-burger, Foth, & Tjondronegoro, 2015). This influence spans organizations and society, stemming from the foundational influence of electronic and computing technologies, spanning over six decades of the third industrial revolution (Skilton & Hovsepian, 2018).

The purpose of this study was to address the challenges of integrating and managing both the complex technology-oriented advancements in a multitude of organizations and fields, in terms of the developing Internet of Things (IoT), and human-centered, in the daily lives of people. Demands for communication between devices, sensors and systems are reciprocally driving an increased demand for people to communicate using, and manage, the undeniable rapid acceleration of the digital ecosystem of the IoT, and an unprecedented volume of data. This study will offer insights into key topics, such as organizational structure, strategic leadership, information technology management, business analytics, and digital transformation in the context of a global automotive organization, among others. It will be comprised of content allowing for greater breadth and range that highlights major breakthroughs, discoveries, and authoritative research results as they pertain to reference work, which should greatly benefit the expansion of coverage into aspects of organizational research, growth and development.

The main research question raised in the study was: *To what extent does digital transformation, implemented through Unified Communication and Collaboration (UC&C) technologies, impact improved productivity and enhanced facilitation of innovation within a global automotive organization?* A framework for the implementation of UC&C technologies was developed and implemented in one of the world's largest automotive organizations, General Motors (GM).

Following the development and implementation of the framework and digital transformation, qualitative and quantitative research were conducted, establishing observational and metric driven data to support analysis. A critical realist interpretation of the authoritative research results suggested that digitally transformed UC&C technologies can change the work practices of employees. The study concluded that

DOI: 10.4018/978-1-7998-3473-1.ch179

15

digital transformation, delivered via a UC&C technologies framework, can impact productivity and create opportunities for driving innovation within a global automotive organization.

In terms of practical managerial significance and appropriateness for this book, this chapter is properly directed to the proposed target audience of the book, in that it presents findings for researchers, educators, students, professionals, and knowledge seekers all around the world.

Now that the general perspective of the article has been described, the objectives of this chapter will therefore specifically be to determine what the factors are impacting:

1. The digital transformation of UC&C technologies within global automotive organizations, and how can these be best applied?
2. Productivity and innovation within a global automotive organization during digital transformation via UC&C technologies, and to what extent?

BACKGROUND

This section will provide broad definitions and discussions of the topic and incorporate the views of others (literature review) into the discussion to support, refute or demonstrate the authors' position on the topic.

The Combinatorial Effect of Mobile, Transmission Control Protocol/ Internet Protocol (IP) and Sensor Technology

According to Sathi (2016), the potential impact of the Internet of Things from an organizational perspective will be between $4 and $11 trillion per year by the year 2025. Central to this forecast is the introduction of data and information services, powered by IoT enabled sensor technology. It has been predicted that driverless autonomous vehicles, enabled via connected mobile infrastructure, internet connectivity and an array of intelligent sensor-based technologies, will take dominance in taxi and ride sharing fleets by the year 2030.

Evolving through the Internet of Things and associated concepts, such as Industry 4.0, connected mobile sensor technologies provide opportunities for the creation of a context aware internet. Combined with machine learning and intelligent data strategies, this evolution of capability holds the potential to transition from data and information transmission to automated and assisted cognitive decision making (Perara, Zaslavsky, Christen, & Goergakopoulos, 2014).

The ability to sense, process and make decisions on information in real time is already opening up opportunities in new areas of the cognitive internet related innovation, such as the 'cognitive Internet of Energy' (Vermesan & Friess, 2015).

Challenges in Digital Transformation

A workplace is no longer only the physical office space, but rather a combination of physical, virtual, social, and mental spaces, which are interlinked with each other to form a collaborative working environment. The challenge for digital organizations within the age of the IoT extends beyond the digitization of organizational processes, connectivity, system integration and automated analysis of data; it is how to make these four spaces support the knowledge workers' tasks in a distributed work setting. There is no one rule to follow. Organizations should start the process by analyzing the work of knowledge workers.

While this challenge garners much attention in research and industry, the impact of resulting complex interconnected systems and technologies on people is often left unaddressed (Liska, 2018). From the perspective of digitization within a large organization, only considering human interaction, integration and adoption as afterthoughts represents a barrier, if not carefully considered during planning.

The landscape of challenges associated with digital transformation can be as broad and far-reaching as the technology landscape of the internet of everything, from which they arise. In parallel to the changing digital landscape, challenges associated with digital transformation can be expected to morph and grow over time. Karacay (2018) points out that the roles and skills needed by employees will require ongoing and significant transformation.

People Challenges: Culture, Skills, Communication

Employees within a digital organizational model need to adapt to an environment of increased real-time collaboration with other people, and with automated and intelligent data-driven systems. An increase in real-time communication drives a requirement for employees to handle continuous change, as systems adjust for performance and enhancement, based on digital intelligence gained from data analytics and digital systems. The types of demands for change on employees with digitization have occurred in the past, but transition planning is required to mitigate significant adverse impacts on the organization and its employees (Liska, 2018).

Many organizations fail at change, because often, leaders have not given change management the proper attention. Effective management of change increases the effectiveness of the implementation and acceptance of changes. Ineffective management of change oftentimes affects employees negatively and makes the next change objective more difficult to implement. Additionally, the fear of managing the change is a leading cause of anxiety in managers.

To meet such challenges, digital-first organizations are viewing these challenges in the context of their digital organizational strategy. This approach blends talent, disciplines, digital systems and technologies (Cognizant, 2016).

The Fourth Industrial Revolution

Prior to Industry 4.0, there were three previously recognized industrial revolutions. The first three industrial revolutions brought about innovation and leverage of the steam engine, electrification, and finally, computers and communication within organizations. Each revolution brought about dramatic changes in organizational production, output and processes. The fourth industrial revolution anticipates the elimination of the barriers between man and machine, extending the cyber-physical characteristics of the Internet of Things to the industrial world (Salkin, Oner, Unstundag, & Cevikcan, 2018).

Industry 4.0 represents an extensive portfolio of integrated modular capabilities (Thramboulidis, Vachtsevanou, & Solanos, 2018), customized to each organization's unique needs, as opposed to a large, rigid, monolithic end-to-end solution.

THEORETICAL MODEL AND DESIGN

The study of documentation associated with the literature review of this research served as the primary source for concepts leveraged by the researcher in the study. These concepts were further applied in the establishment and construction of appropriate categories for evaluation of the hypotheses associated with the study and its theoretical model. While sharing general scope and character, there are many varied definitions on the meaning and interpretation of theory and theoretical models in literature (Strayhorn, 2013).

Theoretical Model

The definition of theory supplied by Schneider (2006) suggests that theories make general, yet explicit statements, about observed phenomena in the world, and how they work. The establishment of theories is essential in the process of the development of science and technology.

The theoretical model for the research study facilitates the development of theory associated with the research study through the identification of core concepts, and exploration of relationships between these concepts in terms of propositions. Theories in themselves are not taken for granted and propositions can result from established theories; however, the researcher creates, develops and tests theories through the observation of lesser understood phenomena (Ridder, 2016). As a core component of the research design and associated theoretical model, theoretical propositions assist in guiding the process for data collection and analysis.

Theoretical Background

According to Mioara (2012, p. 263), "knowledge and communication constitute a vital necessity to the social, organizational, human being", which is so important that it can "cause its stagnation and even its disappearance". People and organizations often take the exchange of information between people for granted; after all, communication is a foundational element of societal and organizational life and behavior of every individual and group.

Research (see e.g. Ebadi & Utterback, 1984) suggests that communication on several levels, including centrality, network cohesiveness and diversity, positively impact and contribute to technological innovation within groups and organizations. Studies relating to education and training (see e.g. Mioara, 2012) suggest that approaches to new technology **adoption**, organizational application and fostering of a technology-enabled information culture is required to fully capitalize on the potential of communication to drive innovation.

This study seeks to evaluate the *extent of the impact* of digital *transformation,* in the form of *UC&C* technologies deployment within the context of *improved* productivity and *enhanced facilitation of* innovation in a global automotive manufacturing, engineering, design, sales and marketing *organization*.

The research associated with the primary question has been operationalized via three sub-questions around which the study was structured:

1. What is the sequence and drivers that are causing a shift and bias towards the digital transformation of global automotive organizations and where is such digital transformation of UC&C technologies implied?
2. What form should a model for digital transformation UC&C technologies take to deliver successful integration of people within an organization?
3. Which factors impact digitally transformed UC&C technologies in terms of improved productivity and the enhanced facilitation of innovation within a global automotive organization?

The first part of the first sub-question relates to the economic, technological and organization **factors** that are *sequencing and driving* the rapid shift towards digital transformation and **adoption** within automotive design, engineering and sales. This sub-question also explores the potential impact of *UC&C* technologies within the organization.

The second sub-question explores the landscape of emerging and existing *UC&C* technologies that are leveraged within organizations and influenced by the shift towards greater *digital transformation*.

The final sub-question focuses on, explores and seeks to evaluate the impact that digital transformation, enabled and implemented via a UC&C technologies eco-system and framework, can have on productivity and capacity towards innovation within a global automotive organization.

Research Variables

Independent variables associated with the study include the *sequence and drivers* of *transformed* change towards digitization in automotive organizations, and the characteristics of associated *UC&C* technologies. These variables are established against the broader area of automotive organizations that encompass traditional large-scale manufacturing operations, sales and marketing functions, and automotive specific design and engineering processes.

Non-independence may arise due to several factors, for example, the sampling of individuals from too narrow a selection of groups, influenced, for example, by related social interactions. Non-independence due to sequence may occur where observations are taken repeatedly from a single unit over time and space, where units observed lack special independence. Stevens (2009) highlights the importance of the assumption of independence of observations and the serious implications in research associated with violation of such assumptions.

The sub-assessment of these variables aligned within the sphere of an automotive organization, versus organizations in general, may infer the existence of an active-independent variable within the study (automotive). Per Gliner, Morgan and Leech (2009), an active independent variable is attributed to a given group of participants within the scope and period of a study on at least one level. The outcome and analysis of the dependent variables are thus constrained to the influence of the field of the automotive organization, versus environments across all organizations as a whole.

Parke (2013) emphasizes the importance of avoiding issues associated with multi-collinearity in research, due to moderate or high relationships among the independent variables. To avoid outcomes within the study associated with multi-collinearity of research variables, the variables associated with the **second sub-question**, relating to the characteristics of emerging and existing *UC&C* technologies in digitally transformed organizations, is positioned independent of any specific organization. This avoids narrow alignment of the relationship between the variables associated with the **first sub-question**, which is focused within the sphere of the automotive organization and resulting technologies and associated strategies identified in the **second sub-question**.

In order to evaluate the primary research question and develop related hypothesis, the relationships between the independent and dependent variables of the study were assessed. Suggested outcomes of the variable analysis align to positive, negative/inverse and curvilinear relationships and seek to provide a link between the research questions, purpose of the study and its observed phenomenon, and possible hypotheses that were subsequently developed (Rubin & Babbie, 2009).

Within the scope of this study, the dependent variables of *productivity* and *innovation* were proposed. The design of the study avoided the leverage of specific control variables associated with specific functions of the automotive practice. A common model and set of technologies were applied within the case study across all organization functions. This approach aligns with that advocated by Collins, Joseph and Bielaczyc (2004) in their study of Design Research issues. While not directly related to the educational context of Design Research, the case study associated with the latter research was set in a large organization environment. Many variables associated with such a large global organization cannot be specifically controlled. To characterize the research situation and optimize current and future associated research, a process of incremental design refinement via quantitative and qualitative observation was required.

Diversity of Participation

Since GM is a global organization and has offices in different countries, employees from each of GM's business regions, North America (38.81%), Europe & Middle East (21.46%), South America (22.68%) and Asia (17.05%), were sampled during the survey. North America hosts the largest population of GM employees, accounting for the slightly higher cohort from that region engaged in the survey. No specific provision was, however, made for possible cultural differences.

Although the survey did not specially account for the age distribution of participants (e.g. so-called Millennials, X-generation, etc.), the demographics collected for interview participants did include measures relating to their self-assessed technical proficiency, as well as indications relating to the number of years that a participant had experience in the industry and in the particular role at that time.

THEORY DEVELOPMENT

The theoretical model presented within this study has been developed in order to investigate whether digitally transformed UC&C technologies positively impacts productivity and innovation. The study specifically focused on a broad set of workgroups and functions within a global automotive organization, including manufacturing, design, sales, marketing, corporate functions (Information Technology, Human Resources) and engineering.

It is proposed within the theoretical model of the study that multi-mode digital transformation through a UC&C technologies eco-system facilitates increased interactions between individuals and functions. The study seeks to explore the **hypothesis** that digital transformation increases communication and fosters relationships among teams, leading to a perceived impact on productivity and the enhanced facilitation of innovation within the organization. The proposed model conveys the *sequence and drivers* associated with the path to increased perceived productivity and innovation through digital transformation via an UC&C technologies model and deployment.

This consolidated model facilitated the compression of the research questions and the establishment of related research hypotheses, supporting perceived impact on productivity and enhanced facilitation of innovation.

Digital Transformation via UC&C Technologies Impacts Inclusion of Individuals Within Groups Across a Global Automotive Organization

The concept of enhanced connectedness supporting more effective **relationships** is supported in many areas of literature and research relating to digital communities and engagement. Raine and Wellman (2012) highlight the emergence of networked individualism facilitated through lose and fragmented digital communities and networks that provide succor. While many of these communities pre-dated their digital manifestations, Raine and Wellman (2012) also underline how the advancement and growth of these groups has been facilitated through digital communications technologies and infrastructure.

Digitally Transformed UC&C Technologies Impact Productivity

The social and information richness theory suggest that user performance will be enhanced if the social presence of a medium is matched to the communication requirements of a task (Karahanna & Straub, 1999). The latter authors therefore posit that forms of media that are perceived as high in social presence are more appropriate in situations, such as conflict resolution, asserting influence and personal communication.

De Kort, IJsselstijn and Poels (2007) highlight that developments in digital communication technology and internet connectivity has opened up wider channels that facilitate improved social interaction. Many elements, including visual facial cues, language, tone of voice and body posture, contribute to the establishment of social presence, as the process of computer mediated communication escalates through the various levels of available digital mediums (chat, voice, video).

Establishment of virtual physical presence is a fundamental element of the establishment of a digital persona and social presence within the digital world. Short, Williams and Christie (1976) developed one of the earliest descriptions of a digital social presence, defining it as the existence of a personal or human element in a medium. Establishing and maintaining a digital persona is not limited to organizations. Research indicates that the maintenance of a *digital self* is becoming a common practice in daily life. For example, over 81% of adults between the ages of 18 and 29 are wireless internet users and 73% of American teens with access to wired internet connectivity use social networking technologies to communicate and engage with their peers (Lenhart, Purcell, & Smith, 2010). Research has also shown that 54% of online adults maintain an identity on at least one social network, and the maintenance of multiple identities on separate networks is on the rise.

Within the scope of UC&C technologies, rich presence functionality helps to establish a virtual social presence for the user through the provision of status **indicators** at multiple levels, such as online/office, availability status (working/busy/free), group status (membership and group availability), device status (phone, PC, tablet) and physical location (country, city, building).

Digital Transformation Through UC&C Technologies Impact Innovation

Social context is important when people engage in multi-party interactions. Computer mediated communication is central to the formation of collective emotion across the virtual human community on the internet (Skowron, Rank, Garcia, & Holyst, 2017). Virtual environments are a digital representation of the real world. These digital environments seek to replicate the natural processes of human social interaction and communication. The processes associated with communication have developed and refined over the history of mankind's development as a species.

The term 'rich media' has been used in literature to describe media, which has broad capacity for communication, supporting digital interaction in multiple forms (Martinik, 2015). UC&C technologies and the associated presentation of integrated, digital rich-media pathways for communication have the potential to address the shortcomings of computer mediated communication highlighted in both media richness theory (Daft & Lengel, 1986) and media naturalness theory (Kock, 2005). Media richness theory suggests that outcomes will be negatively affected if knowledge intensive tasks are carried out via media that is low in multi-modal (richness) capability. Media naturalness theory suggests that communication carried out via computer and digital mediation can be perceived as lacking elements of communication found via face-to-face communication (audible and visual ques) and potentially pose obstacles for effective communication (Kock, 2013).

Digitally transformed UC&C technologies facilitate mediated interaction, communication and the sharing of both information and emotion. Combined, these features facilitate and influence visible and audible social queues, emotional display and expression (Gonzalez, Diaz-Herrera, & Tucker, 2014).

The cognitive model of media choice proposed by Robert and Dennis (2005) highlights the apparent paradox that exists in communication between the transmission and subsequent processing of information (Dennis, Fuller, & Valacich, 2009). Robert and Dennis (2005) also suggested that the leverage of asynchronous communication methods and media, such as those found in UC&C solutions, can enhance the processing of information. Through a media naturalness hypothesis, Kock (2005) underscores the potential for synchronous communication to increase psychological arousal.

If the technologies and their targeted enabling features are appropriately positioned for ease of integration, this can positively impact trust relationships within the work system, reduce inhibiting **factors** impacting interaction and engagement, and increase organizational efficiency, safety and productivity (Demerouti, Derks, Lieke, & Bakker, 2014). With its intuitive and converged presentation of blended digital multi-media, as well as synchronous and asynchronous communication channels, UC&C is well positioned to support balanced interpersonal and cognitive participation.

Factors, including the trend towards the digital transformation of organization processes, and changing work practices through collaborative innovation, have led to organizations having started changing their approaches to work practices through the digital transformation of UC&C technologies. This approach places a requirement on employees to organize and carry out their work practices in a more creative manner by leveraging 'new ways of working' (Demerouti, et al., 2014). The latter authors, however, warned that the introduction of new technologies to work practices can lead to a negative impact on organizational trust, if the technologies are not **easy to use**.

DEPLOYED MODEL

Hill (2018) argues that recognizing the value of iterative development as key to organizational and functional strategies. The production model that was deployed within the scope of the research study in General Motors was modified and improved via an iterative phased development and release approach. Hill (2018) also suggests that strategy development is frequently characterized through infrequent engagement and aggregation of executive opinion.

The model proposed within the scope of this research provides an architecture that can be leveraged to guide the development of a strategy and the downstream deployment of specific technical and operational components aligned to pre-defined outcomes.

Core Governance Domain

The Core Governance Domain is focused on the design and specification of key stakeholders and governance processes that are essential to framing and guiding digital transformation. Horizontally, the specified sub-modules represent elements of the strategy that are foundational in the overall specification of requirements and outcomes. These sub-modules also play a key role in horizontally influencing the development and validation of established outcomes, in terms of the resulting strategy, technologies and functional operation.

The preliminary model design specified four modules within the Core Governance Domain, inclusive of Organizational Architecture, Organization Stakeholders, "IT Transformation Governance, and Program Governance" (Bolton, Goosen, & Kritzinger, 2016, p. 7). The iterative development of the model identified redundancy between the IT Transformation Governance and Program Governance modules. Sperate specification of processes and artefacts proved to introduce redundancy and increase complexity in practical operation. Objectives and outcomes identified with these modules were found to significantly overlap, specifically in defined goals and objects, Program Governance and key performance indicators, resulting in a decision to collapse and consolidate the specification of these two modules into one.

The Organization Architecture module leveraged the existing architectural governance processes managed by GM's Information Technology organization. This approach ensured reusability of developed artefacts within other common, existing processes within the model (for example, technology standards within change control), and ensuring compatibility for integration with existing and future strategic adjacent technical service models within GM.

Operational Management Domain

Please note that further details regarding the Operational Management Domain are contained in Bolton et al. (2016).

Integrated Feature Domain

Features selected for inclusion as solutions within the Integrated Feature Domain were subject to evaluation modelled on the innovation decision process suggested by Rogers (2010). The latter author proposed a process with five main steps, described as knowledge, persuasion, decision, implementation and confirmation, which facilitates decision making relating to the **adoption** or rejection of the implementation of an innovation. The process moves from forming of a general attitude towards innovation, through to the specific decision to adopt or reject.

This model was adapted from the knowledge and persuasion steps as specified in the model by Rogers (2010). Adaptions included the removal of a specific module attributed to the 'trialability' of new features, with the integration of the trialability concepts into a more generalized end user observation module.

Unified Services Domain

The Unified Services Domain (USD) is focused on establishing the integrated technical services and components that support upper layer end user features and applications exposed via the Integrated Feature Domain modules. The Unified Services Domain includes horizontal service components identified in the UC&C functional architecture. These components are focused on service integration versus feature delivery.

The core modules of USD are associated with the provision of underlying network services, such as IP services, voice and video codecs, session management, media resource allocation, physical and logical (software) end point devices and services, carrier transport services, quality and performance management systems. While many management, software engineering, computer and communications models exist, such as eTOM, ONAP, DevOps and OSI, no single existing model is structured to ubiquitously cover the computer, telecommunication, middleware and application environment represented by an organizationally transformed UC&C technologies solution.

The Unified Service Domain element of the GM model is critical in facilitating the specification and inter-relationship of core services, features and components within the targeted state collaboration eco-system. The GM ICT team utilized the Enhanced UC&C (E-UC&C) model as guide for designing and building the underlying solution architecture. The depicted reference architecture relates to the real-time voice, instant messaging and audio services sub-system developed within the scope of the research study, and operationally deployed in GM. The underlying system components and applications are overlaid against the E-UC&C primary domain structures. This system reference architecture was employed to map out the primary signaling protocol paths, sub-system relationships, border, internal and external endpoint elements and core communication integration and session management systems.

The reference architecture associated with the integrated video broadcast sub-system developed and deployed within the GM case study is highlighted. This parallel communication system was developed to integrate real-time multi-cast and unicast transmission of media across the GM organization to all users and locations. The broadcast sub-system was similarly designed aligned to the E-UC&C model, ensuring layered compatibility with the real-time audio, video and instant messaging sub-system.

SOLUTIONS AND RECOMMENDATIONS

This section will discuss solutions and recommendations in dealing with the issues, controversies, or problems presented in the preceding section.

Discussion and review of findings associated with the established research hypotheses are essential in relation to the evaluation of the overall outcome of the research. Did the observations, findings and identified results validate the hypotheses developed in association with the research problem and questions? The following discussion outlines the summary conclusions of the study and the context of the established hypotheses.

Digital Transformation via UC&C Technologies Impacts Inclusion of Individuals Within Groups Across a Global Automotive Organization

Evaluation of the end user survey and interviews supports the view that digitally transformed UC&C technologies enhanced the ability of people and groups to engage and **collaborate**. Findings from the research data show that users reported a positive experience aligned with leverage of the multi-channel features associated with UC&C technologies. Through the use of these features, users reported that it was easier to engage with and **collaborate** effectively with virtual teams. Users described the ability to engage in ad-hoc meetings with peers and virtual teams and obtaining answers to questions quickly.

These observations contrast with legacy communication and collaboration technologies that required face-to-face communication to facilitate information exchange at any level beyond audio conference, or basic slide sharing using external technologies. Users also described positive attitudes relating to the ability to engage personally with peers and partners when working in remote locations. The new digitally transformed capabilities made it easier to include other parties in media rich virtual meetings and facilitated their direct participation. Tracking of feature-use across regions and room-to-room tele-presence engagements supports the view of increased cross-region and function engagement, inferring a high level of inclusion of people in virtual meetings outside of their workplace locations.

UC&C technologies, which are intuitively easy to use and adopt, combined with positive results from quick engagement when desired versus restricted schedule were experienced, lead users to positively associate the UC&C technologies with supporting their innovation processes, specifically **creativity**. Findings within the study showed that the consolidated features within the UC&C technologies, combined with the intuitively easy-to-use and adopt interface, resulted in many users establishing **changing work practices** and increasing organizational efficiency.

A small number of users reported having some difficulty in easily using, adopting, realigning and/or **changing** their **work practices** to the UC&C technologies; however, they still identified the technologies as having the potential to improve their productivity. After being introduced to digital transformation through UC&C technologies, most users preferred to keep 'their' new technologies, leading to legacy technologies' reduction and eventual elimination. Especially data from transformation and adoption metrics showed indicators of cultural change in terms of method of communication employed by users' post-adoption of the digitally transformed UC&C technologies. Finally, the results from the post-application and deployment of the digitally transformed E-UC&C framework and eco-system could be tracked and validated as generating direct savings to General Motors.

Digitally Transformed UC&C Technologies Impact Productivity

Findings indicate that the virtual persona and presence established by the end users have a positive impact on personal productivity, as it increases the opportunity to engage in real-time **collaboration** when needed. Feedback from end users indicates that digital presence **indicators** are useful in identifying other users or groups, who may be available for immediate ad-hoc communication and engagement.

Also, it is likely that the custom presence **indicators** help set a baseline expectation for the requesting party in establishing the probable timeframe for response. For example, when a user is in an ad-hoc or scheduled meeting, that user's presence and status will be set to 'busy', indicating that the user is already engaged in **collaboration** or work of some form. When a user is presenting using their laptop or PC, the presence indicator is set to 'presenting', and blocks instant messaging pop-ups for the requested user, setting the expectation that an immediate response is unlikely to occur. It is likely that users reporting their experience of the UC&C technologies as having the effect of removing the sense of distance from their peers and partners is tied to the presence **indicators**, as they get real-time status views of their colleagues' location and engagement status. This status develops an arguable perception of virtual presence. Users can additionally place commentary on what their current or planned daily activities are in the 'What's happening today' field of the UC&C technologies, further establishing their digital presence and persona.

Both survey respondents and interviewees described the digitally transformed UC&C technologies as leading to increased organizational efficiency, with the latter also indicating the increased speed of their communication processes and finding access to all of the features in one technology convenient. Convenience in having one technology to access multiple channels for communication, both within the office and remotely when travelling, or at home, is likely to be associated with end users' perception of productivity. The more convenient it is to do something and/or execute a task, the more productive users are when executing the task. Findings within the research also indicated that digitally transformed UC&C technologies and systems facilitate the opportunity for users to establish and maintain working relationships with colleagues and organization partners. Relationship building is enhanced and enabled through the facility of a virtual team and peer engagement. The research data shows that users perceived the ability to flexibly escalate communication through different levels and modes of communication to assist them in building relationships through rich information sharing in a virtual workspace. Finally, data from the interviews suggested that participants gained a sense of <u>satisfaction</u> from seeing their peers and business partners <u>changing</u> their <u>work</u> <u>practices</u> in line with changes associated with the **adoption** of the new toolset and features.

Digital Transformation Through UC&C Technologies Impact Innovation

Four factors relating to innovation was identified from the interviews, which are related <u>to changing</u> <u>work</u> <u>practices</u>, <u>collaboration</u>, <u>creativity</u> and <u>generating</u> <u>savings</u>. Users reported that the capabilities of the digitally transformed UC&C technologies and methods led to them <u>changing</u> their <u>work</u> <u>practices</u> and enhanced their ability to engage in <u>collaboration</u>. Users also found that multi-channel features facilitated richer virtual engagements supporting <u>creative</u> engagement, even when users were remote from each other. Within the <u>creative</u> process, the ability to engage in an ad-hoc <u>collaboration</u>, as needed, helps users capitalize when they have ideas, or need problems and questions quickly addressed. Engaging quickly through the digitally transformed UC&C technologies increases speed-to-action <u>creative</u> thoughts or tasks. It is reasonable to assume that the speed-to-engage offered by the new technologies helps maintain velocity and immediacy in <u>creative</u> <u>collaboration</u>, tied to innovation generation, such as sharing and working through new ideas or rapidly developing plans and proof of concepts. Many users identified <u>generating</u> <u>savings</u> associated with leveraging the digitally transformed technologies within their <u>work</u> <u>practices</u>, and this is likely due to users seeing the generation of innovation as an asset of the organization. Innovation leads to new products, or product enhancement, and ultimately higher margins and revenue. If the users can engage and drive more innovation through digitally transformed technologies, or speed up innovation generation, the organization will benefit financially.

The factor related to **convenience and speed** (mentioned regarding productivity) within the UC&C toolset is likely to align with the <u>changing work practice</u>s that users reported.

RECOMMENDATIONS

The inception of digital technology and associated innovations have been used by organizations to improve and innovate their products and services. Organizations are increasingly recognizing the value of patterns of social interaction within their organizational models and associated value chains. Patterns of social interaction apply both to the organizational workforce and customers, uncovering value within service-based organizations and connected consumer product lines. Intelligent digital organizations leverage these patterns of social interactions and associated data, in combination with 'big data' strategies and real-time analytics, to enable contextualized and automated decisions (Gilchrist, 2016). These strategies enable the establishment of predictive recommendations and rapid decisions focused on increasing productivity.

"The population associated with the target deployment outcome" represented "100% of GM's full-time salaried employees. The target population for" pre- and post-validation "deployment was focused on a representative subset of management and non-management employees. A" Z-score "of 2.576 with corresponding confidence level of 99% was used with a standard deviation of" 0.5 "and confidence interval of +/-5% to calculate the **recommended** survey sample and interview sample sizes. Based upon these variables a minimum target sample population of 664" was adopted (Bolton, et al., 2016, p. 7).

FUTURE RESEARCH DIRECTIONS

This section will discuss future and emerging trends and provide insight about the future of the encyclopedia's theme from the perspective of the article focus. The viability of a paradigm, model, implementation issues of proposed programs, etc., may be included in this section. Future research opportunities within the domain of the topic are suggested.

Further research is required to fully validate the impact of digitally transformed UC&C technologies on the organizational processes and end user communities of large organizations. While this research study provides valuable insight into the experiences of one such a global organization, further research should be carried out to contrast and validate the developed theories of increased productivity and the ability to drive innovation within a broader set of organizations. Opportunities exist to build on the theories and findings developed in association with this study; for example, the execution of a longitudinal study of digital transformations within a cross-section of organizations. This approach would allow for contrast and validation of the theories presented within this article against a broader set of organizations of similar size and complexity.

This research also highlights phenomenon relating to end user **adoption** of new technologies, specifically communication and collaboration technologies and the potential of new technologies to rapidly change end user work practices. In the case of this study, evidence exists of users rapidly changing well-established work practices relating to communication and collaboration and aligning those changes to the **ease of use** and perceived benefits of using the new technologies. Following this, an opportunity to focus research on the identification of specific drivers influencing positive **adoption** and change could be established. The experience of user **adoption** rates and magnitude of changing work practice can be contrasted against similar transformations of communication and non-communication related digital processes, to identify common drivers, with a view to establishing a framework for more predictive positive transformation outcomes.

CONCLUSION

This conclusion section will provide discussion of the overall coverage of the article and concluding remarks. The **purpose** of the empirical study was to observe and compare theories using real-life data. The process of empirical study enabled the researcher to develop and evaluate new concepts, processes, technologies, methods and techniques. Output from empirical studies can facilitate improving existing processes by using evidence and evaluating hypothesis formed during the study. Shdaimah, Stahl and Schram (2011) argued that one of the benefits derived from an empirical study is the establishment of facts about problems that can subsequently be analyzed and addressed. The research study was carried out over a five-year period leveraging General Motors, one of the world's largest automotive manufacturing and sales organizations, as a case study focus. Demands and changes in the organizational landscape of General Motors, including a significant shift to globalized operations and increased infusion of technology into their organization processes, drove a reciprocal demand for digital transformation and optimization of communication and collaboration among employees. Under the scope of the study, a unique E-UC&C model was developed and tailored to guide the establishment of a technical and service architecture, facilitating broad digital transformation across multiple facets of employee-to-employee, employee-to-partner, employee-to-customer and organization-to-employee communication and collaboration. Digitally transformed UC&C technologies were deployed across organizational systems. An impact assessment and summary of results attributed to the implemented framework, deployed under the E-UC&C model, was presented.

15

REFERENCES

Bolton, A., Goosen, L., & Kritzinger, E. (2016). Enterprise Digitization Enablement Through Unified Communication and Collaboration. In *Proceedings of the Annual Conference of the South African Institute of Computer Scientists and Information Technologists*. Johannesburg: ACM. 10.1145/2987491.2987516

Cognizant. (2016). *People - Not Just Machines - Will Power Digital Innovation.* Retrieved October 24, 2016, from https://www.cognizant.com/whitepapers/People-Not-Just-Machines-Will-Power-Digital-Innovation-codex1850.pdf

Collins, A., Joseph, D., & Bielaczyc, K. (2004). Design Research: Theoretical and Methodological Issues. *Journal of the Learning Sciences, 13*(1), 15–42. doi:10.120715327809jls1301_2

Daft, R., & Lengel, R. (1986). Organizational information requirements, media richness and structural design. *Management Science, 32*(5), 554–571. doi:10.1287/mnsc.32.5.554

De Kort, Y., IJsselstijn, W., & Poels, K. (2007). Digital Games as Social Presence Technology: Development of the Social Presence in Gaming Questionnaire (SPGQ). *Proceedings of PRESENCE*, 195-203.

Demerouti, E., Derks, D., Lieke, L., & Bakker, A. (2014). New ways of working: Impact on working conditions, work-family balance, and well-being. In C. Korunka & P. Hoonakker (Eds.), *The impact of ICT on quality of working life* (pp. 123–141). Springer. doi:10.1007/978-94-017-8854-0_8

Dennis, A., Fuller, R., & Valacich, J. (2009). Media Synchronicity and Media Choice: Choosing Media for Performance. In T. Hartmann (Ed.), *Media Choice: A Theoretical and Empirical Overview*. Routledge.

Ebadi, Y., & Utterback, J. (1984). The effects of communication on technological innovation. *Management Science, 30*(5), 572–585. doi:10.1287/mnsc.30.5.572

Gilchrist, A. (2016). *Industry 4.0 benefits: The Industrial Internet of Things.* Apress.

Gliner, J., Morgan, G., & Leech, N. (2009). Methods. In *Applied Settings: An integrated approach to design analysis*. Routledge.

Gonzalez, T., Diaz-Herrera, J., & Tucker, A. (2014). *Computing Handbook: Computer Science and Software Engineering*. CRC Press.

Hill, T. (2018). *Operations Strategy: Design, Implementation and Delivery*. MacMillan Education Palgrave.

Karacay, G. (2018). Talent Development for Industry 4.0. In A. Ustundag & E. Cevikcan (Eds.), *Industry 4.0: Managing the Digital Transformation* (pp. 123–135). Springer. doi:10.1007/978-3-319-57870-5_7

Karahanna, E., & Straub, D. (1999). The psychological origins of perceived usefulness and ease-of-use. *Information & Management, 35*(4), 237–250. doi:10.1016/S0378-7206(98)00096-2

Kock, N. (2005). Media richness or media naturalness? The evolution of our biological communication apparatus and its influence on our behavior toward e-communication tools. *IEEE Transactions on Professional Communication, 48*(2), 117–130. doi:10.1109/TPC.2005.849649

Kock, N. (2013). *Interdisciplinary Applications of Electronic Collaboration Approaches and Technologies*. IGI Global. doi:10.4018/978-1-4666-2020-9

Lenhart, A., Purcell, K., & Smith, A. (2010). *Social Media & Mobile Internet Use Among Teens and Young Adults*. Washington, DC: Pew Research Center. Retrieved August 10, 2017, from http://www.pewinternet.org/files/old-media/Files/Reports/2010/PIP_Social_Media_and_Young_Adults_Report_Final_with_toplines.pdf

Liska, R. (2018). Management Challenges in the Digital Era. In R. Brunet-Thornton & F. Martinez (Eds.), *Analyzing the Impacts of Industry 4.0 in Modern Business Environments* (pp. 82–99). IGI Global. doi:10.4018/978-1-5225-3468-6.ch005

Martinik, I. (2015). Rich-Media Technologies and Their Using in Crisis Management Communication. In J. Park, I. Stojmenovic, H. Y. Jeong, & G. Yi (Eds.), *Computer Science and Its Applications: Ubiquitous Information Technologies* (pp. 437–442). Springer. doi:10.1007/978-3-662-45402-2_66

Mioara, M. (2012). The impact of technological and communication innovation in the knowledge-based society. *Procedia: Social and Behavioral Sciences*, *51*, 263–267. doi:10.1016/j.sbspro.2012.08.156

Parke, C. (2013). *Essential First Steps to Data Analysis: Scenario based examples using SPSS*. Sage. doi:10.4135/9781506335148

Perara, C., Zaslavsky, A., Christen, P., & Goergakopoulos, D. (2014). Context aware computing for the internet of things: A survey. *IEEE Communications Surveys and Tutorials*, *16*(1), 414–454. doi:10.1109/SURV.2013.042313.00197

Raine, L., & Wellman, B. (2012). *Networked: The new social operating system*. MIT Press. doi:10.7551/mitpress/8358.001.0001

Ridder, H.-G. (2016). *Case Study Research: Approaches, Methods, Contribution to Theory*. Rainer Hampp Verlag.

Robert, L., & Dennis, A. (2005). Paradox of Richness: A Cognitive Model of Media Choice. *IEEE Transactions on Professional Communication*, *48*(1), 10–21. doi:10.1109/TPC.2004.843292

Rogers, E. (2010). *Diffusion of Innovations*. The Free Press.

Rubin, A., & Babbie, E. (2009). *Research Methods for Social Work*. Cengage. doi:10.1093/OBO_dataset_home

Salkin, C., Oner, M., Unstundag, A., & Cevikcan, E. (2018). A Conceptual Framework for Industry 4.0. In A. Ustundag & E. Cevikcan (Eds.), *Industry 4.0: Managing the Digital Transformation* (pp. 3–22). Springer. doi:10.1007/978-3-319-57870-5_1

Sathi, A. (2016). *Cognitive (Internet of) Things: Collaboration to Optimize Action*. Palgrave Macmillan. doi:10.1057/978-1-137-59466-2

Schnieder, M. (2006). *Theory Primer: A Sociological Guide*. Rowman & Littlefield Publishers Inc.

Seeburger, J., Foth, M., & Tjondronegoro, D. (2015). Digital Design Interventions for Creating New Presentations of Self in Public Urban Places. In M. Foth, M. Brynskov, & T. Ojala (Eds.), *Citizen's Right to the Digital City: Urban Interfaces, Activism, and Placemaking* (pp. 3–21). Springer. doi:10.1007/978-981-287-919-6_1

Shdaimah, C., Stahl, R., & Schram, S. (2011). *Research: A Case Study on Collaborative Methods for Social Workers and Advocates.* Columbia University Press.

Short, J., Williams, E., & Christie, B. (1976). *The Social Psychology of Telecommunications.* Wiley.

Skilton, M., & Hovsepian, F. (2018). *The 4th Industrial Revolution: Responding to the Impact of Artificial Intelligence on Business.* Palgrave MacMillan. doi:10.1007/978-3-319-62479-2

Skowron, M., Rank, S., Garcia, D., & Holyst, J. (2017). Zooming in: Studying Collective Emotions. In J. Holyst (Ed.), *Cyberemotions: Collective Emotions in Cyberspace* (pp. 279–304). Springer. doi:10.1007/978-3-319-43639-5_14

Stevens, J. (2009). *Applied Multivariate Statistics for the Social Sciences.* Routledge.

Strayhorn, L. (2013). *Theoretical Frameworks in College Student Research.* University Press of America.

Thramboulidis, K., Vachtsevanou, D. C., & Solanos, A. (2018). *Cyber-Physical Microservices: An IoT-based Framework for Manufacturing Systems.* arXiv preprint arXiv:1801.10340

Vermesan, O., & Friess, P. (2015). *Building the Hyperconnected Society: Internet of Things Research and Innovation Value Chains, Ecosystems and Markets.* River Publishers. doi:10.13052/rp-9788793237988

ADDITIONAL READING

Brenny, S., & Hu, J. (2013). Social connectedness and inclusion by digital augmentation in public spaces. *8th International Conference on Design and Semantics of Form and Movement (DeSForm)*, (pp. 108-118). Wuxi.

Chmiel, A., Sienkiewicz, J., Thelwall, M., Paltoglou, G., Buckley, K., Kappas, A., & Hołyst, J. (2011). Collective emotions online and their influence on community life. *PLoS One*, 6(7), e22207. doi:10.1371/journal.pone.0022207

Dale-Bloomberg, L., & Volpe, M. (2019). *Completing Your Qualitative Dissertation: A Road Map From Beginning to End.* London: Sage.

Dattalo, P. (2013). *Analysis of Multiple Dependent Variables.* Oxford University Press. doi:10.1093/acprof:oso/9780199773596.001.0001

Fain, J. (2017). *Reading, Understanding and Applying Nursing Research.* F.A. Davis Company.

Fehér, P. (2012). Integrating and Measuring Business and Technology Services in the Context of Enterprise. In V. Shankararaman, L. Shao, & J. K. Lee (Eds.), Business Enterprise, Process, and Technology Management: Models and Applications (pp. 148-163). Hersey: IGI Global. doi:10.4018/978-1-4666-0249-6.ch008

Fiorentino, G., & Corsi, A. (2014). Cyber Physical Systems give Life to the Internet of Energy. *ECRIM News*, *98*, 39–40.

Fortino, G., & Trunfio, P. (2014). *Internet of Things based on Smart Objects: Technology, Middleware and Applications*. Springer Science & Business Media. doi:10.1007/978-3-319-00491-4

KEY TERMS AND DEFINITIONS

Digital Transformation: Although digital transformation has existed in the lexicon of human thought for over fifty years and propelled humanity towards new horizons in terms of possibilities, the potential for digital transformation to enhance communication in our society and across our industries is beginning to be realized.

Global Automotive Organization: A global automotive original equipment manufacturer facing challenges as it digitally transforms its systems, service and work practices are likely to be familiar to many large global organizations.

Impact: The central issue addressed in this chapter is the relationship between the transformation of communication through digital methods and tools and the resulting impact within a global automotive organization on people and their social interactions.

Innovation: Organizations drive combinatorial innovation through technology convergence and standardization.

Internet of Things (IoT): Towards building the hyperconnected society, the Internet of Things is based on smart objects in terms of technology, middleware, and applications, with research in this regard including innovation value chains, ecosystems, and markets.

Productivity: Productivity improvement can be introduced rapidly through combinatorial digital innovation.

Unified Communication and Collaboration (UC&C) Technologies: UC&C technologies provide an integrated suite of presence-aware communication and collaboration capabilities.

Social Media and Organizational Communication

Victor-Alexandru Briciu

(iD) https://orcid.org/0000-0002-7506-8099

Transilvania University of Brasov, Romania

Arabela Briciu

Transilvania University of Brasov, Romania

INTRODUCTION

The online environment is a whole new channel of social interaction. For an organization, however, the online environment is a form of bidirectional communication, with the ultimate goal of gaining profit or various benefits from the image of such an entity. These aspects help us acknowledge the importance of using the Internet, as an organization, to maintain the relationship with both the public and the staff. Nowadays, when we think about the online environment, we automatically think about Social Media: social networks, Social Bookmarking sites, business blogs, and many other web pages where users can interact and can generate or access content, as well as static sites, generating unidirectional information.

Social Media is not only used to announce or promote a new product. This channel can also be used for direct sales, online advertising, maintaining the relationship with the public and especially for brand awareness. In addition to this component, that is specific to marketing, public relations or advertising, the online environment also plays an important part in human resources. With the development of Web 2.0, the selection and integration processes, as well as staff management, have become much easier, with the help of various online platforms offering professional services, as "organizations increasingly rely on online communication (social networks, blogs, official site, newsletter, digital marketing)" (Briciu, Briciu and Găitan, 2019, p. 44).

Therefore, public content management on the Internet becomes a specific activity for specialists in organizational communication. Thus, the organization involved in a Social Media campaign or simply existing in the virtual environment creates a presence that is meant to provide greater visibility and awareness. Through the channels it uses (website, blog, social networks, etc.), the organization maintains a permanent dialogue with its audience and uses its own resources to attract as many stakeholders of its virtual messge as possible.

This chapter's objective is to take into consideration the online environment as the new channel for social interaction, putting into focus the organizational communication and its development from Web 1.0 to Web 2.0. The chapter will also discuss the implication of Social Media characteristics and defining the terms, such as social bookmarks, wikis, social networks, photo and video sharing, etc. The chapter will also include a case study discussing the communication strategy using Social Media channels of a renowned Romanian brand from the petroleum and gas industry.

DOI: 10.4018/978-1-7998-3473-1.ch180

Figure 1. Web 1.0 vs. Web 2.0 features

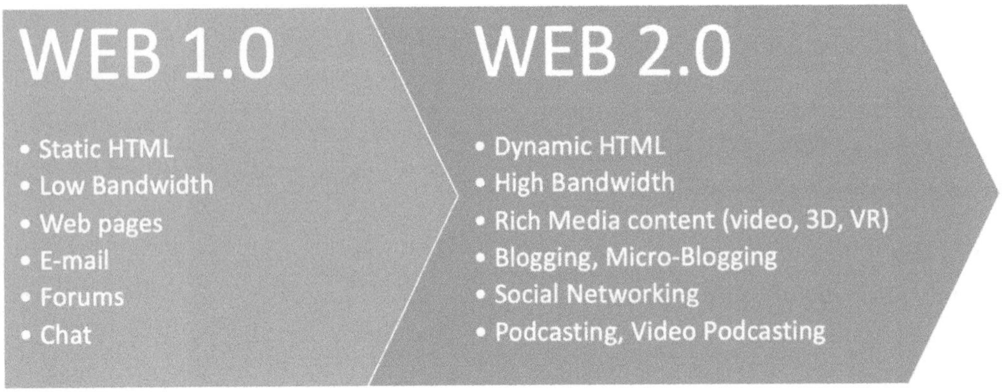

WEB 1.0	WEB 2.0
• Static HTML	• Dynamic HTML
• Low Bandwidth	• High Bandwidth
• Web pages	• Rich Media content (video, 3D, VR)
• E-mail	• Blogging, Micro-Blogging
• Forums	• Social Networking
• Chat	• Podcasting, Video Podcasting

BACKGROUND

In the past decades, information technology developed significantly, both in terms of hardware and software. This has had a major impact in simplifying organizational communication processes, especially in the business sphere. Originating from the United States, the Internet is based on "a network of linked computers, each one connected to a set of others, supporting the electronic communication between computers around the world" (Henslowe, 1999, p. 87). In order to better understand the evolution of the Internet and the emergence of Social Media, we need to take into consideration the relevant distinction between Web 1.0 and Web 2.0, and especially between the concepts of static and dynamic (See Figure 1).

In the beginning of the '90s, with free access to the Internet globally, users accessed pages via Web 1.0. Subsequently, the transition to Web 2.0 was a subtle one, with users being able to interact through content generation. In Web 1.0 there is limited interaction between websites and users. "Web 1.0 is simply an information portal where the public passively receives information without being able to post comments and feedback." (Mitruț and Stoica, 2016, p.3). The content is static and the users cannot change it. Digital content is generated only by writing code in text editors. Users cannot generate content; they can only view the information that is displayed on the website by its administrator. "We can say that the transition to Web 2.0 was made when Content Management Systems emerged, allowing users to create their own web pages. They were open-source, and hosting was free." (Mitruț and Stoica, 2016. p.6). Web 1.0 is a static environment, a place where you could find information instead of a forum for sharing ideas or creating new products together. Moreover, Lincoln (2009) states that Web 1.0 is a world of simple transactions, opposing the emergence of Web 2.0, the new medium where "people can interact and participate rather than just read" (p. 8).". These can be categorized as dynamic sites. "This appears to be quite innocuous stuff, very open and honest, customer-orientated and very much in line with the way corporate should be behaving in a Web 2.0 world" (Brown, 2009, p. 36). Today, Web 2.0 is associated with a large range of tools and software used for viewing and developing the websites, but what is also important is allowing the user to interact directly with any web content in order to obtain custom products. As a short conclusion to what was presented above, Lincoln (2009, p. 8) strongly states that "because of the ambiguity of the term Web 2.0, many people prefer to use the term social media".

15

New technologies are used to change the dynamics of the environment in which people create and discover value through publication. A first definition refers to Social Media as being "any highly scalable and accessible communications technology or technique that enables any individual to influence groups of other individuals easily" (Blossom, 2009, p. 29) or, from a different point of view, "Social media is synonymous with community. People want to connect. They want to talk. They want to share. They belong to whatever community they want – no matter how big or small." (Lincoln, 2009, p.14), but also "the next step of Web 2.0 technology development" (Briciu, Briciu and Găitan, 2019, p. 43).

According to Kaplan and Haenlein (2010, p. 61), Social Media is a group of Internet-based applications that have the purposes, ideological and technological foundation of Web 2.0 and that allow the creation and exchange of user-generated content. In other words, Social Media is more about "the ideas that you share, collaborate on, create and participate in rather than observe" (Lincoln, 2009, p. 10), because in these platforms users should be able to create and access digital content (Kane et al., 2014). There is a lot of controversy surrounding the definitions of Social Media as it is a trend to update old definitions or to create a new one, as it is the case with the development of technology, use and adoption of social media (Kapoor et al., 2017; Briciu, Mircea and Briciu, 2020).

Brown (2009) considers that Web 2.0 is not a different version of the web, but can be viewed as a gradual update of the former. Content is no longer offered to visitors or generated only by administrators and employees of various organizations, but can be created by users that are connected via existing informal networks on the Internet. They contribute and actively participate in spreading information through the web. Typical examples for this new aspect are blogs, as well as portals or platforms for sharing images, music, video, text and software such as Facebook, Flickr, YouTube, or Dropbox.

SOCIAL MEDIA SPECIFIC APPLICATIONS IN AN ONLINE ORGANIZATIONAL CONTEXT

According to Phillips and Young, "communication today is an adventure playground for people with an interest in the subject. There are so many ways people can communicate" (2009, p. 10). Social Media is booming nowadays with the emergence of more and more modern technologies, becoming essential in people's lives, with the use of specific applications increasing as well. Garcia-Morales, Martín-Rojas & Lardón-López (2018, p. 359) suggests that "organizations that exploit social media connections in their innovation processes can expect successful innovation activities that improve the organization's overall long-term performance".

This subchapter provides an overview of social media channels that were available in recent years. There are many other forms of organizational communication, such as blogs, microblogs, social bookmarking, wikis, social networking sites and more. The list is not exhaustive (and how it could be, when new Social Media services become available in the online environment and gain user popularity so quickly), but the most significant ones will be briefly outlined.

Blogs. A blog is a website owned by an entity (a person, a group of people, a company, etc.) where articles are posted on specific topics, and people who visit the blog can add comments. The author can edit the articles using different colors or fonts for the text, pictures, videos, audio and everything that he considers relevant, or thinks will make the article more appealing to the public. Once the Blogger platform was launched in 1999, the concept exploded on the Internet and led to the emergence of a large number of bloggers (Brown, 2009, p. 26). Unlike other sites, blogs usually allow people who access them to add comments and express their opinion. The word "blog" is a truncation of "weblog", and the content generators are called "bloggers". They write various types of texts and publish them on web pages that are dedicated to a certain topic or organize them in posts that are displayed in reverse chronological order, and made available to the general public. Blogs can be edited online using web browsers or content editing programs. Bloggers can attach pictures, charts, or audio-video recordings to their posts. According to Quesenberry (2019, p. 55) businesses that have prioritized blogging are thirteen times more likely to receive positive return on investment.

Microblogging is a different form of blogging that limits the author to 140-200 characters (extremely short blogs). The most popular microblogging platform is Twitter, while Facebook was also considered a microblogging platform because of the Status option. Users can then choose to publish their posts for anyone to read or restrict them to a certain group. The character limit allows these messages to be uploaded through a variety of means, especially SMS, which means they can be published anywhere, anytime.

Social Bookmarks Phillips and Young (2009, p. 13) show that "Social bookmarks allow you record web pages of interest through online lists that can be sorted, indexed, shared with small groups of colleagues or made available to the wider public. The most popular of these sites is Delicious. These are very useful services for practitioners." One of the ways a site can be developed is that its main pages are indexed on Delicious. News pages, as well as product and service pages on sites could benefit from allowing readers to quickly insert the page into their collections on the Delicious site.

Wikis are series of websites created and used to access information on a specific topic quickly and easily. Unlike for other websites, no technical knowledge is required for creating or adding content to them. The largest wiki platform is Wikpedia, which is an encyclopedia of wikis (Brown, 2009, p. 39). Wikipedia offers information related to a wide range of topics, but the validity of the information can not be ensured, because anyone can edit the articles. Whether we are a specialist in organizational communication or not, whether we promote a product, image or brand, the way we approach a particular topic cannot be objective. According to these ideas, there are cases where a company employee is entitled to modify the content of an article, for example, to delete spam messages or to correct the mistakes of the original author. It is important to note that "wikis are mostly used inside organizations to allow a group of people to create, reference and edit web pages to form an evolving body of knowledge for the group" (Phillips and Young, 2009, p. 31).

Social networks sites are websites that allow the exchange of information through interactive content between multiple people. "They are micro-websites that allow people to exchange interactive, user-submitted content among a network of friends through personal profiles, blogs and comment discussion lists" (Philips and Young, 2009, p. 26). These social networking services can be easily configured, and content-wise you can upload photos, videos, and audio recordings. Facebook, Instagram, Snapchat are social networks used globally by both individuals and companies. Social networking sites have emerged in the '90s, starting with *classmates.com* which aimed to help people find former school mates. They increased in number, expanded, and became online communities (Brown, 2009, p. 50). The created communities are based on different interests, connections or people you know. These networks are "all built around groups of friends or contacts coalescing around each other. They can send messages, they can share music and video and sometimes play games with each other. There are common interest groups, a variety of utility platforms and applications" (Brown, 2009, p. 165). LinkedIn is also a social network, but it is business and employment-oriented: "the network allows signed-up users to maintain a contact list, with career histories of people they know and trust through business" (Brown, 2009, p. 167). LinkedIn is a much safer network than Facebook in terms of data security, because it only allows the connection between users who have previously interacted. Thus, direct connections are created between people, which are grouped into networks of mutual connections. This may facilitate the recruiting process for some companies, as potential candidates can be recommended by other network users, and they have all their professional background published on LinkedIn.

The chat is a technology that allows messaging between two or more people in real time. One of the first programs that allowed chatting was "ICQ (Internet Relay Chat) and a number of other technologies were commonly used as stand-alone services in the early days of the internet and were among the forerunners of today's social media" (Philips and Young, 2009, p.13). Chatting exists in many forms, such as online chats, instant messaging, online forums and virtual worlds. Large companies use chats both inside the organization (intranet) and embedded in their website, wikis, blogs to optimize communication with the public. Even though this online communication channel is one of the most affordable ones out there, there is a risk of messages not being transmitted correctly when we use it, because of duplication, use of abbreviated words, etc.

Photo sharing is the act of transferring digital photos online and sharing them with others, whether limited to a selection of people or making them accessible to the wider public (Brown, 2009, p. 169). There are dedicated platforms for photo sharing, such as Flickr and Photobucket. Another platform that gained popularity in recent years is Pinterest, which managed to gradually eclipse the other two. Carr (2012) argues that Pinterest is a social network that is supported by the visual content it carries. The platform provides a virtual space where users can save or send images, quotes, or DYI projects. Pinterest practically allows users to make a collection of things they are interested in, to which they can give access to acquaintances. Instagram, a mobile photo (and now also short video) capturing and sharing service, has been in spotlight in the recent years gaining more than one billion users (Clement, 2019). According to Quesenberry (2019, p. 54) "Instagram has played an integral role in helping to lift sales for brands such as Gatorade which saw a 3 percent increased household penetration and 4 percent increased sales". He also considers that Snapchat can be the ideal place to reach younger target markets like millennials (Quesenberry, 2019).

Video sharing. There are countless video sharing sites and platforms, and one of them is familiar to everyone: YouTube. Brown states that YouTube is "the gold standard for sharing video on the internet" (2009, p. 164). It is easy to use: you upload videos and watch videos uploaded by others. The large number of users and the large amount of content provide a much richer experience than suggested by the simplicity of the concept. Broadcasters and TV producers upload content and use YouTube as a music tone (there is even the possibility of creating a playlist). Video sharing sites can pose a threat to companies if consumers share their unfavorable customer experience or malfunctions that they encountered.

Search engines are the most used websites because they help their users find information. In order to stand out, a company website should appear among the top search results. Google, the most popular search engine, uses the number of sites that are linked to that website as an algorithm (Phillips and Young, 2009, p. 24). Most search engines work based on a very simple principle: they search for pages or specific content on certain web pages by looking for and tracking hyperlinks (web page navigation items). In organizational communication, it is very important to gain the "trust" of a search engine. People often find out about organizations, events, or other things that interest them by accessing search engines. If an organization does not promote itself well enough and does not get enough attention from people, it will not get it from the search engine, either. Thus, the organization must be popular and record a high number of searches to be "favored" by the search engine.

Mashups. Brown (2009, p. 177) indicates that "mashups are web applications that combine things from multiple sources and bring them together to form something that is greater than the sum of its parts." A mashup is any combination of elements in the online environment. For example, websites may include mashups, as they may have embedded video content from YouTube to be viewed on the site, or a map in the contact section, provided via Google Maps. Facebook is also a great source of mashups due to the content diversity on the network and the multitude of embedded applications such as games, chat, video calls, etc.

Podcasting. A podcast is an audio file (usually an MP3 file) embedded in a web page (usually a blog) that works on almost the same principle as the syndication of RSS (i.e., Really Simple Syndication) content and allows users to add comments or respond to the content it offers. They can also provide information about events, conferences or festivals, facilitating participation in different events for people who can not be physically present. First of all, to be uploaded to a podcast channel, a podcast must contain ID3 tags, like files that tell us the title of the song, the artist, the album, and so on. Then the podcast has to be enabled for RSS, so subscribers get updates every time new episodes are uploaded. Podcasts must also exist on a third server (different from the one on which it is uploaded and the one on which it is loaded), allowing any user to download it at any time. "There are many other ways of publishing podcasts. For example, a number of blogging programs will allow you to embed audio in your blog and also have the facility to syndicate. Once you have set up the feed the blog host will detect whenever you load audio into your blog and will syndicate it as a podcast. Where the podcast is embedded in the blog it is sometimes referred to as a blogcast." (Brown, 2009, p. 47). Influenced by the development on technology (mostly on smartphones and Bluetooth devices), podcasts had grown in the last years "reaching new audiences on apps such as ITunes, SoundCloud, Stitcher, Tune In, and can be a great engagement tool and distribution channel for content marketing efforts" (Quesenberry, 2019, p. 198). Kampoor et al. (2017) consider that these platforms have reestablished the dynamics between organizations, employees, and consumers. Social media give users, managers, and developers new capabilities to act and interact in ways that were difficult or impossible in earlier online or offline settings (Kane et al., 2014). Kwayu, Lal & Abubakre (2017) emphasize how social media platforms enhance the competitiveness and creates business affecting with a faster rate some processes and practices within an organisation.

ORGANIZATIONAL COMMUNICATION IN THE ONLINE CONTEXT

Online organizational communication has become a phenomenon, along with technological development and the need for economic actors to communicate effectively and at a low cost. Also, this changed the communication boundaries allowing "communications among people outside the company through web-based social media platforms that cannot be controlled by the firm" (Kane et al. 2009 cited in Kane et al. 2014, p. 298).

Web 2.0 technologies and the widespread use of online applications place online communication in the present day, when the content display process is no longer in the hands of programming specialists and the use of tools by communicators with no technical studies is facilitated. Technologies become accessible, from a knowledge point of view, many of them being open access and adaptable to the needs of the organization.

The Internet is generating a new type of interaction. "Internet use threatens to erode time that was previously allocated to human interaction (...) Large media corporations have taken a keen interest in monitoring the Internet because it provides access to a market for their goods, products, and services" (Wicks, 2001, p. 163). In other words, measuring audience in the online environment and the presence of organizations in this virtual space is becoming a modern way to meet institutional interests, in the context where the user network is more accessible than in real life. Institutions that are active in this type of media produce messages that are meant to attract this virtual audience. "In order to offer products or services in the current economic context, organizations must offer the consumer a more dynamic role in both offline and online environments" (Hosu, Culic, and Deac, 2014, p. 21). Organizations conduct market research in the online environment. Audience and user preference measurements are made for specific channels or topics so they can be present in those places. Once they understand the online presence of their target audience, companies act. "The Internet provides users with a sense of companionship by enabling them to join virtual communities (...) Because the Internet provides such varied offerings, it quickly became a major competitor for the time and attention of the consumer" (Wicks, 2001, p. 165).

Organizations are present in the online environment in a variety of ways, starting with exposure through an official website and social media profiles (LinkedIn, Facebook, Instagram, etc.), to pop-ups and cookies. In addition, they often use databases to distribute certain messages through e-mail platforms or even social network feeds. These online activities are managed by either company employees or consulting and advertising firms. Online presence can be provided either free of charge, simply by generating accounts, or by using paid and sponsored accounts that are paid monthly or annually based on visibility. Most companies show their contact information and activity in the online environment so that the audience can easily keep in touch with the organization. Companies can even allocate large budgets for end-to-end image campaigns to create an online presence. Various activities can be hosted to attract the desired segment, such as contests, CSR campaigns, games, raffles, and more (Briciu, Briciu and Găitan, 2019, p. 48).

Social media technologies have a major impact on organizational performance directly and indirectly through the innovation capability of changing the way different stakeholders and organizations communicate and transfer information and knowledge (Aral et al., 2013, Garcia-Morales, Martín-Rojas & Lardón-López, 2018). The online environment is useful not only in terms of communication with the external public. Organizations also use this channel to facilitate communication with the internal public. This type of interaction "takes the form of electronic mail, distribution lists (i.e., listserves), multi-user dungeons (MUDs; also called multi-user object domains [MOOs]), chatrooms, and Usenet (...) to enable employees within companies to communicate and work collaboratively on company documents. Employees conducted electronic brainstorming sessions with individuals or groups of employees to solve problems or develop plans" (Wicks, 2001, p. 168). Thus, time and costs are reduced, and interaction is much easier to accomplish.

Castelló, Etter & Årup Nielsen (2016) emphasize with their study the importance of legitimacy building in a globalized networked society for corporations in order to maintain commmunication with stakeholders who have multiple, often conflicting sustainable development agendas. After a study that investigates social media assimilation in firms Bharati, Zhang & Chaudhury (2013, p. 268) consider that "assimilation of wikis, web services, and LinkedIn in an organization is influenced by the organization's ability to integrate existing technologies with new technologies, which is a measure of its absorptive capacity". So, the management should encourage employees spending time on Social Media for learning and for enabling multiple ways of communication with customers.

It's relevant the way Quesenberry (2019, p. 54) reflects on how companies are using the social media platforms just few of them moving beyond the main social platforms to "strategically add social channels well suited to their business goals and target audience". Even that the data is few years outdated, he remarks that "the high percentage of Fortune 500 companies on LinkedIn, Facebook, and Twitter, only two-thirds (66 percent) are using YouTube and just over one-third (36 percent) have corporate blogs. Under half of Fortune 500 brands are using other social channels like Instagram (45 percent) and Pinterest (33 percent) and only 40 percent of Fortune 500 CEOs are active on social media".

Also, for the employer branding the presence on social media is very important and also it gives the companies the opportunity to create a link between their brand and employees (e.g., Linkedin) so they gain more brand ambassadors. Nowadays, recruiters use social media to post job advertisements and to recruite. Singh and Sharma (2014, p. 236) consider that the social media is becoming an important tool in the recruitment process, companies gaining major benefits as: wider access and geographical spread "with real-time interaction and 24x7 job search activity", increased job visibility, a better candidate quality, finding hard-to-reach candidates, better ROI and competitive advantage on the market.

CASE STUDY – OMV PETROM AND ORGANIZATIONAL COMMUNICATION THROUGH SOCIAL MEDIA IN ROMANIA

To illustrate the importance of a company's presence in the online environment and the use of the specific Social Media applications presented above, an example of Petrom business activity in the living space is presented below.

About the Company

According to the data on the official website in 2018, OMV Petrom is a solid and modern company and the largest energy company from South-East Europe, operating more than 200 commercial oil and gas fields, onshore and offshore. This company was developed at the end of 2004 when the national petroleum company Petrom was privatized, with Austrian OMV AG being the new majority shareholder. The company underwent a vast reorganization and restructuring process but remains the most powerful brand from this industry in Romania. In the online environment, OMV Petrom's carries out an intense activity, both as a commercial brand and as an employer brand. It is present in the form of sponsored advertising messages in Social Media, websites, forums, articles and many other mentions on various pages.

Presence on Social Media (September 2019)

As far as the Social Media component is concerned, OMV Petrom has a presence on some of main platforms used on Romania: Facebook, Instagram, Linkedin and YouTube. Romania has 15.04 million internet users (77% penetration) with 11 million active social media users (56% penetration), 9.8 million being mobile social media users (50% penetration) (Hootsuite & We are Social, 2019). The same report shows that there are 10 million monthly active users of Facebook, 3.8 millions monthly active users of Instagram, 2.6 million monthly active users of LinkedIn, 1.4 million monthly active users of Snapchat and just 348 thousands of Twitter monthly active users in Romania. So, the OMV Petrom 's social media presence just on those platforms it's understandable as Snapchat is targeted mostly for teenagers and younger people, reaching with adverts just 8.2% percentage of Romanians aged 13+ and Twitter, not so popular among Romanians reaches with adverts just 2% percentage of people aged 13+ (Hootsuite & We are Social, 2019). According to Ioana Bucalău, Digital & Online Expert at OMV (SMARK, 2019), they considered the expansion on different social media platforms, but because of the content applicability on customers they didn't sow the sense, even with the growth on other platforms, they keep the social media communication mainly on Facebook. So, on Facebook (2019), OMV Petrom has two official pages (See Figure 2), the official page of the brand (@Petromro) that has 54,879 people who rated the page and 55,047 followers. They post on average three times on a week with an average

Figure 2. OMV Petrom Facebook Official pages: @PetromRo and @StatiilePetrom (Facebook, September 2019)

of just 6 comments/ post. For the share component, the numbers are higher with an average of 50 times. The page contains an About section, sections for photos, posts and videos, events and community. The other Facebook page is for the gas stations (@StatiilePetrom) and has 92,495 people who rated the page and 92,999 followers. This one is more interactive with posts once/ day with an average of 13 comments and 50 share by each post. For this page the producer responds to the comments within the hour, which means that the profile is managed by someone permanently. The page contains an About section, a Shop section with price offerts for products within the gas stations,sections for photos, posts and videos, also a section with the terms and condition for their promotional campaigns and contests.

The cover video is specifically addressing the Romanian public on both pages, presenting on @ Petromro page the last social responability campaign an in the @StatiilePetrom page the last advertising campaign for the gas stations. Both pages have also affiliate a Messenger account where users can communicate with the organization. Also, Ioana Bucalău, Digital & Online Expert at OMV (SMARK, 2019) specified that with the collaboration between their Petrom Brand Manager and the digital agency Atelieru + Cohn & Janssen, they growth the engagement, gaining sometimes one million viral reach on Facebook.

OMV Petrom's Instagram Page has 197 posts (40 posted on 2019), 1,272 followers, and links to the official website. The interactions are small with rarely one comment/post and with an average of 110 hundred appreciation/ post (See Figure 3).

On LinkedIn (2019), OMV Petrom is only present as an organization profile and has 54,304 followers within 5,076 employees. Posts are taken from the Facebook official account. The content on LinkedIn is a formal one, based on sources, specific to a respectable employer. There is an About field, a section with important employees, a corporate overview, and a section presenting the last CSR campaigns. On the OMV Petrom's Youtube account there are 242 videos uploaded since September 2009 with 34,075,929 views and 7,390 K followers (See Figure 4).

Employer Brand

OMV Petrom shapes its employer brand from its own website that is linked with each profile on social media. Here on the section Jobs and careers we can fiind their recruitment policy, employees success stories, training and internship programmes and jobs available within the OMV Group. Another important presence for the employer brand is on Glassdoor - a platform that allows employees to comment about their jobs and salaries and for the employer to advertise the job offer and to recruit. On this platform, OMV Group has 104 reviews, 11 jobs, 32 salaries, 22 interviews, a list of 75 benefits and 11 photos (Glassdoor, 2019).

Figure 3. OMV's Instagram posts on September 2019

SOLUTIONS AND RECOMMENDATIONS

Doorley and Garcia (2007, pp. 122 - 125) build a connection between organizational communication practices and online presence through Social Media for successful promotion. These recommendations are still viable and take place in several steps, as follows:

1. **Start with the Customer, Not the Medium:** The message must be built on the characteristics of the consumers or potential business partners. The press should only be the binder of communication, not its purpose. It is the only way the impact of the brand can be certain.
2. **Develop Solid Positioning:** Even the "best media-reaching techniques cannot compensate for undifferentiated positioning" (Doorley and Garcia, 2007, p. 123). Positioning is the way you want

Figure 4. OMV's Petrom LinkedIn and YouTube profiles (September 2019)

your brand to be seen by consumers. For example, Volvo is the car brand that is known for safety, while BMW is well-known for technical quality.

3. **Target, Tailor and Personalize Your Messages:** Digital technology has leveled the playing field in marketing and organizational communication. Connecting to the Internet is easily accessible nowadays so any user can search for and find a multitude of responses to their requests, so it is important that the message used to promote a particular product is original, innovative and attracts public attention. If the message meets these requirements, technology can further help with transmitting it to the target audience.

4. **Integrate (or Strategically Align) all Communication Elements and Campaigns:** Integrated marketing refers to the use of all means of promotion during a campaign to provide the correct message. Joining old media techniques with new media and Social Media is the most effective way to promote, so TV and radio commercials, written press articles, and online media are indispensable tools in this process.

5. **Personalize and Measure:** In the new context that is Social Media, measuring audience, hits, or consumption is mandatory. If a company is aware it is losing consumers, it can change or adjust the campaign, depending on the public's discontent.

6. Recognize and Accept the Fact that Every Published Communication Is Potentially

Accessible Anywhere - In this case, reference is not made only to official press releases, but also to a simple anonymous comment posted on a social network. Social Media brings such easy ways to advertise, but it's equally simple for these tools to become the main enemy in a time of crisis.

Use Technology as a Means, Not an End - Technology does not have to replace human creativity and intelligence. It is only a means of making communication faster, easier and more dynamic.

FUTURE RESEARCH DIRECTIONS

In the next decade, the process of replacing humans with machines will increase. Smarter, more reliable and faster technologies will emerge, capturing all existing industries under the new Web 3.0 concept (Funk, 2009; Briciu, Rezeanu and Briciu, 2020), which is the natural transition from the current Web 2.0 form or a semantic Web, that "opens new technological opportunities for web developers in combining data and services from different sources" (Mika, 2007, p. 24). Of course, with this process, unemployment will further increase, which can only be solved by re-qualification for other newer specializations in the online environment. This will be the beginning of a "new kind of partnership with machines that will build on our mutual strengths, resulting in a new level of human-machine collaboration and codependence." (Davies et al., 2011, p. 3) as, nowadays, our technical systems reside "in large data-driven organizational and administrative systems and even social media platforms that provide the frames within which much work and human interactions of all kinds take place" (Redström & Wiltse 2018, p.108).

The five trends and technologies in Web 3.0, according to Funk (2009, p. 128) are: (1) The Semantic Web and Artificial Intelligence; (2) Cloud computing; (3) Universal, portable, and online identities; (4) 3-D internet and (5) True convergence of web, mobile devices, and other equipment (See Figure 5).

Any aspect of the surrounding world will be transformed into data systems, "the diffusion of sensors, communications, and processing power into everyday objects and environments will unleash an unprecedented torrent of data and the opportunity to see patterns and design systems on a scale never before possible" (Davies et al., 2011, p.4). This change will also have an impact on a social level, leading

Figure 5. Adapting Web 3.0 features (according to Funk 2009, p.128)

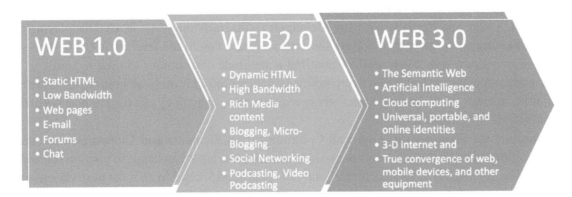

to the discovery of new models and relationships that have not yet been discovered. Technologies will become more sophisticated, being compressed into much smaller objects than the ones we now have. Caring for the environment will make future technologies environmentally friendly. Also, as Kapoor et al. (2017) remark most of the research on this field focus on the organizational structure and setting and so is a lack of studies in analyzing stakeholders' potential in adopting social media technologies to accomplish their work goals and to share their life within.

CONCLUSION

Finally, we can consider that the online environment is a second reality in terms of professional activity. Specialists become users and vice versa, networking and communicating permanently. That is why organizations need to feel their presence in this environment, which has become, almost as important as real life. The online environment is therefore in favor of any organization that wants to be connected to this technologically and professionalized world.

The need for digital competences is indisputable as an essential feature in everyday professional services. Nowadays, specialists are acquiring information, comparing and discussing in the virtual environment, which means that any company must be able to expose its message in an efficient way. The online environment has become an incredible network of interconnected users at the level of humanity, which allows the creation of professional trends and a global framework of expectations. This phenomenon is unprecedented in history, when messages were spread on paper.

The online environment and the other digital media have revolutionized human interaction. This is the network effect that organizations must use to reach their goals. This online presence of billions of people can be used both in organizational communication activities and in other areas, for research or facilitating professional activities. The fast transmission of information with great visibility no longer depends on a single issuing agent but is spread by tens, hundreds or thousands of users. With one share, the content becomes visible to all contacts who use the same channel in real time. Software resources also support daily managerial and production activities. The online environment is, therefore, in favor of any organization that wants to be connected to this world of technology and professionalism, considering the following key points:

- Social Media brings more power and attitude to people, helping them promote and express their point of view about a particular product.
- Companies can use various social media channels to connect with their customers and attract new ones. Those who have decided to take this step only saw benefits.
- Traditional media suffers because of Social Media, where content is rediscovered, having new value every time.
- Influence is what helps reach objectives in Web 2.0, not control.
- To increase your chances of success, the online environment must be seen as an offline one, with an appropriate behavior.

REFERENCES

Aral, S., Dellarocas, C., & Godes, D. (2013). Introduction to the special issue 'social media and business transformation': A framework for research. *Information Systems Research, 54*(1), 3–13. doi:10.1287/isre.1120.0470

Bharati, P., Zhang, C., & Chaudhury, A. (2013). Social media assimilation in firms: Investigating the roles of absorptive capacity and institutional pressures. *Information Systems Frontiers, 16*(2), 257–272. doi:10.100710796-013-9433-x

Blossom, J. (2009). *Content Nation. Surviving and Thriving as Social Media Changes Our Work, Our Lives, and Our Future.* Wiley Publishing, Inc.

Briciu, V., Mircea, I., & Briciu, A. (2020). Communication and Entrepreneurship in Romania: Dissimulation of First Impression in 30 Seconds. In Masouras, A., Maris, G., & Kavoura, A. (Ed.), *Entrepreneurial Development and Innovation in Family Businesses and SMEs* (pp. 22-38). doi:10.4018/978-1-7998-3648-3.ch002

Briciu V-A, Rezeanu C-I, Briciu A. (2020). Online Place Branding: Is Geography 'Destiny' in a 'Space of Flows' World? *Sustainability, 12*(10),4073. doi.org/10.3390/su12104073

Briciu, V.-A., Briciu, A., & Găitan, Ş.-M. (2019). *New Media and Organizational Communication. A Multiple Analysis of Romanian Bank Online Environment.* In *6th International Multidisciplinary Scientific Conference on Social Sciences and Arts SGEM 2019, Conference Proceedings* (pp. 41-52). Sofia: STEF92 Technology Ltd. 10.5593gemsocial2019V/6.1/S07.006

Brown, R. (2009). *Public relations and the social web: using social media and Web 2.0 in communications.* Kogan Page Limited.

Carr, K. (2012). *Pinterest for Dummies.* John Wiley & Sons, Inc.

Castelló, I., Etter, M., & Årup Nielsen, F. (2016). Strategies of legitimacy through social media: The networked strategy. *Journal of Management Studies, 53*(3), 402–432. doi:10.1111/joms.12145

Clement, J. (2019). *Number of monthly active Instagram users 2013-2018.* https://www.statista.com/statistics/253577/number-of-monthly-active-instagram-users/

Davies, A., Fidler, D., & Gorbis, M. (2011). *Future Work Skills 2020*. Institute for the Future for the University of Phoenix Research Institute.

Doorley, J., & Garcia, H. F. (2007). *Reputation Management. The Key to Successful Public Relations and Corporate Communication*. Routledge Taylor & Francis Group.

Funk, T. (2011). *Social Media Playbook for Business. Reaching Your Online Community with Twitter, Facebook, LinkedIn, and More*. Praeger.

Garcia-Morales, V., Martín-Rojas, R., & Lardón-López, M. (2018). Influence of social media technologies on organizational performance through knowledge and innovation. *Baltic Journal of Management, 13*(3), 345–367. doi:10.1108/BJM-04-2017-0123

Gibson, R., & Ward, S. (2000). A Proposed Methodology for Studying the Function and Effectiveness of Party and Candidate Web Sites. *Science Computer Review Journal, 18*(3), 301–319. doi:10.1177/089443930001800306

Henslowe, Ph. (1999). *Public Relations. A Practical Guide*. Kogan Page Limited.

Hootsuite & We are Social. (2019). *Digital 2019. Romania.* https://datareportal.com/reports/digital-2019-romania

Hosu, I., Culic, L., & Deac, M. (2014). Comunicarea Online, Provocări Manageriale. *Revista Transilvană de Științe Administrative, 2*(35), 19–28.

Kane, G. C., Alavi, M., Labianca, G., & Borgatti, S. P. (2014). What's different about social media networks? A framework and research agenda. *Management Information Systems Quarterly, 38*(1), 275–304. doi:10.25300/MISQ/2014/38.1.13

Kapoor, K. K., Tamilmani, K., Rana, N. P., Patil, P., Dwivedi, Y. K., & Nerur, S. (2017). Advances in social media research: Past, present and future. *Information Systems Frontiers, 20*(3), 531–558. doi:10.100710796-017-9810-y

Kwayu, S., Lal, B., & Abubakre, M. (2017). Enhancing Organisational Competitiveness Via Social Media - a Strategy as Practice Perspective. *Information Systems Frontiers, 20*(3), 439–456. doi:10.100710796-017-9816-5

Lincoln, S. R. (2009). *Mastering Web 2.0: transform your business using key website and social media tools*. Kogan Page Limited.

Mika, P. (2007). Social Networks and the Semantic Web. New York, NY: Springer Science+Business Media.

Mitruț, D., & Stoica, L. G. (2016). *Modelarea proceselor sociale. Web 2.0*. Academia de Studii Economice.

Phillips, D., & Young, Ph. (2009). *Online Public Relations. A practical guide to developing an online strategy in the world of social media* (2nd ed.). Kogan Page Limited.

Quesenberry, K. A. (2019). *Social Media Strategy. Marketing, Advertising, and Public Relations in the Consumer Revolution* (2nd ed.). Rowmnan & Littlefield.

Redström, J., & Wiltse, H. (2018). *Changing Things. The Future of Objects in a Digital World*. Bloomsbury Visual Arts.

Singh, K., & Sharma, S. (2014). Effective use of social media for talent acquisition and recruitment. *International Journal of Intercultural Information Management*, *4*(4), 228–237. doi:10.1504/IJIIM.2014.067932

SMARK. (2019). *Ioana Bucalau (OMV Petrom): Ne vom diversifica abordarea cand vom fi pregatiti sa ducem comunicarea cu clientul nostru in 2.0.* https://www.smark.ro/articol/45119/some-2019-ioana-bucalau-omv-petrom-ne-vom-diversifica-abordarea-cand-vom-fi?fbclid=IwAR2atRHT2mHWVJe7-pgReD0YPOiJhlsD14XgZ1Fg8AxAYaamjG-za-5a_o4

Wicks, R. H. (2001). *Understanding audiences: learning to use the media constructively.* Lawrence Erlbaum Associates.

ADDITIONAL READING

Blankespoor, E. (2018). Firm communication and investor response: A framework and discussion integrating social media. *Accounting, Organizations and Society*, *68-69*, 80–87. doi:10.1016/j.aos.2018.03.009

Crompton, D., & Sautter, E. (2011). *Find a job through social networking: use LinkedIn, Twitter, Facebook, blogs, and more to advance your career* (2nd ed.). JIST Works.

Eisenberg, E. M., Goodall, H. L. Jr, & Trethewey, A. (2010). *Organizational Communication. Balancing Creativity and Constraint* (6th ed.). Bedford/ St. Martin's.

Evans, D. (2008). *Social Media Marketing. An Hour a Day.* Wiley Publishing, Inc.

Harris, T. E. (2002). *Applied organizational communication: principles and pragmatics for future practice* (2nd ed.). Lawrence Erlbaum Associates, Inc., Publishers.

Kirkatrick, D. (2010). *The Facebook effect: the inside story of the company that is connecting the world.* Simon & Schuster.

Scott, D. M. (2010). *The New Rules of Marketing and PR. How to Use Social Media, Blogs, News Releases, Online Video, & Viral Marketing to Reach Buyers Directly* (2nd ed.). John Wiley & Sons, Inc.

She, C., & Michelon, G. (2018). Managing stakeholder perceptions: Organized hypocrisy in CSR disclosures on Facebook. *Critical Perspectives on Accounting.* Advance online publication. doi:10.1016/j.cpa.2018.09.004

Treem, J. W., & Leonardi, P. M. (2013). Social Media Use in Organizations: Exploring the Affordances of Visibility, Editability, Persistence, and Association. *Annals of the International Communication Association*, *36*(1), 143–189. doi:10.1080/23808985.2013.11679130

Turner, J., & Shah, R. (2011). *How to make money with social media: an insider's guide on using new and emerging media to grow your business.* Pearson Education, Inc., FT Press.

Tuten, T. L. (2008). *Advertising 2.0. Social media marketing in a web 2.0 world.* Praeger Publishers.

White, K., & Chapman, E. (1996). *Organizational Communication. An Introduction to Communication and Human Relations Strategies* (1st ed.). Simon & Schuster Custom Publishing.

KEY TERMS AND DEFINITIONS

Internet: A global system of interconnected computer networks that facilitates data communication services.

Online Environment: The virtual space in which a computed defined system can function being connected to other(s) connected systems through a communication electronic channel and sharing content.

Online Organizational Communication: A web-based online communication targeted to specific publics used in the organizational context.

Organizational Communication: Various communication channels, strategies, and techniques through which the corporation interacts with customers and other audiences.

Social Media: A range of different Web 2.0 internet-based tools that increase and enhance the exchange of information.

Web 1.0: Online activities centered on client-server architecture, where processing is done by the server, and the client is only used to display the content.

Web 2.0: A term that designates a whole range of interactive and collaborative aspects of the internet.

Organizational Behavior

Rilla J. Hynes
Northwood University, USA

INTRODUCTION

As organizations adapt to the challenges of technology an understanding of organizational behavior (OB) theories supports the development of new management and leadership behaviors, but OB is a dynamic multifaceted field with ambiguous definitions and conflicting articulated structures (Borkowski, 2015; Cummings, 1976; Vasu, Stewart, & Garson, 2017). According to Kaifi and Noori (2011), OB is an applied discipline, but its study requires a basic understanding of sociology, psychology, philosophy, anthropology, social psychology, economics, and axiology. Studies in organizational leadership, organizational culture, organizational development, organizational theory, organizational management, and change management are also constructs of OB (Otaghsara & Hamzehzadeh, 2017; Schaerer et al., 2018; Stouten, Rousseau, & De Cremer, 2018). OB applied in organizations uses scientific methods and practical experience to recognize, explain, and influence the attitudes and behaviors of individuals and teams in the organization (Kafi & Noori, 2011; Otaghsara & Hamzehzadeh, 2017; Schaerer et al., 2018; Stouten, Rousseau, & De Cremer, 2018).

With the expansion of global business and rapid changes in technology there has been a paradigm shift in management, calling for the use of positivity rather than negativity, expansion of collaboration across departments, and a growing emphasis on diversity and inclusion to support innovation. This shift promotes positive organizational policies and procedures while maximizing resources (Otaghsara & Hamzehzadeh, 2017). According to Bakker (2008), negative approach-based terms influenced organizational culture undesirably, and Luthans and Avolio (2007) claim developing a positive organizational behavior framework is a source of an organization's competitive advantage. This article will discuss the evolving theories of organizational behavior addressing the challenges of technology and change, as well as placing the discussion within the context of seminal theories.

BACKGROUND

The practice of OB is multifaceted, based on multiple organizational theories, management theories, organizational disciplines, and the intersection of research and practice (Cummings, 1976; Frederick, 2014; Vasu, Stewart, & Garson, 2017). Moorhead and Griffin (1995,pg. 4) defined OB as "the study of human behavior in organizational settings, the interface between human behavior and the organization, and the organization itself." Frederick (2014, pg. 564) discusses it as "…an applied behavioral science that involves integration of studies undertaken in behavioral disciplines such as psychology, sociology, anthropology, social psychology, and political science." Kafi and Noori (2011, pg. 89) describe OB as "a field of study devoted to recognizing, explaining, and eventually developing the attitudes and behaviors of people (individual and group) with organizations." Kafi and Noori further state OB is based on "scientific knowledge and applied practice."

DOI: 10.4018/978-1-7998-3473-1.ch181

The goal of OB is to provide tools through theories and concepts, to aid in understanding, measuring, analyzing, describing, and managing attitudes of individuals, groups, and the organization itself. OB allows managers to make effective use of resources to meet organizational goals. Various definitions of OB reflect the multiple perspectives, disciplines, and uses of the evolving discipline. The following review of disciplines and theories applied in OB focuses on creating an understanding of the foundational constructs of the various facets supporting OB, contributing to an understanding of the evolution of OB to the current positive focus.

Organizational Behavior (OB) literature references multiple constructs, including Organizational Theories, Organizational Development, and Leadership Theories. OB tools appear in strategic decision-making, communication strategies, organizational learning, managing change, driving innovation, and accomplishing the goals of the organization through understanding and influencing individual and group behaviors within the organization. A review of a sampling of the classic theories OB evolved from follows.

The development of classical organizational theories at the beginning of the 20th Century leaned heavily on Frederick Taylor's *scientific management theory* (Hatch, 1997; Taylor, 1911). "Taylorism" included 4 basic principles: 1) find the 'best way' to perform each task, 2) match each work to the 'best fit' task, 3) use transactional leadership, closely monitoring works and motivate through reward and punishment, 4) management's duty is planning and control. While Taylor improved production in the simple industrialized organizations, it proved too limited to respond to the major challenges and changes of the 21st century (Wagner-Tsukamoto, 2007).

Max Weber, expanding on the scientific management theory to install even more authority and control, reducing diversity and ambiguity in organizations, developed the *bureaucratic theory*. Weber (1947) focused on the hierarchy structure of power, division of labor and specialization, and creating stability and uniformity. He also discussed the idea that organizational behavior is a network of human interactions, where all behavior might be understood by looking at cause and effect. Mooney and Reiley (1931) continued in this vein, emphasizing the establishment of a universal set of management principles that applied to all organizations (Walonick, 1993). During this same time, Henri Fayol (1949) created a management theory called *Fayolism* emphasizing staffing, recruitment, strategic planning, and policies and procedures to support efficiency. Sometimes referred to as the father of operational theory, Fayol focused on management, as opposed to Taylor's focus on the task (Ott, 1989).

Classical management theory was limited, rigid, transactional, and framed all motivation within the context of economic reward. During the early manufacturing era, as society moved toward the urban industrial base it served as a transition tool. However, individuals did not respond well to the transactional, mechanistic approach that ignored their basic humanity and throttled individual creativity and innovation (Carroll & Gillen, 1987; Ott, 1989). According to Scott (1961)"…classical organization theory has relevant insights into the nature of organization, but the value of this theory is limited by its narrow concentration on the formal anatomy of organization." (pg. 10).

As research continued in the field of maximizing workers' efforts, the Hawthorne Experiment, 1929-1932, applied the clinical methods of Jean Piaget, a noted psychologist, to the field of business research (Hsueh, 2002). These studies influenced organizations as management began to understand the importance of interactions of groups and individuals, social relationships in the workplace, and people-management skills (Carroll & Gillen, 1987; Hatch, 1997; Hsueh, 2002). Maslow's Hierarchy of Human Needs was introduced in the 1940s, and integrated into the business lexicon as a motivational tool, explaining how individuals' inborn needs motivate them and influence their actions (Hatch, 1997; Maslow, 1954). The acceptance of the behavioral sciences in business developed into the Neoclassical Organization Theory.

According to Scott (1961) Neoclassical Organization Theory evolved as a reaction to the authoritarian structure of Classical management theories. Focused on informal organizational structure, human needs, and creating an atmosphere of cohesive values and purpose, organizational success became linked to leadership styles that emphasized managerial power based on acceptance. Barnard (1939), identified as a transitional theorist, built a body of work combining elements of both classical and neoclassical theories. Simon (1945) contributed a model of "limited rationality" to explain unpredictable worker reactions to management attention, legitimizing reductionism, quantification, and deductive logic as methods of studying organizations (Walonick, 1993). Despite the introduction of elements of the evolving human relations movement, these theorists shared the attitude management's duty is to maintain equilibrium through controlling and manipulating workers and their environment.

Within the context of the neoclassical theories, the importance of the social system as part of management motivational tools was established. While classified as neoclassical, the concept of the social system as an interactional part of the organization points the way to modern theories (Scott, 1961).

Various theories emerged throughout the 1950s and 1960s, particularly in America. Douglas McGregor contrasted the philosophical differences between the human relations approach and the scientific management school of thought (Augier, 2013; Carson, 2005) while Drucker (1954) popularized Management by Objectives, emphasizing participative goal setting, choice of actions, and decision making. These works contributed to the understanding of implementing organizational missions throughout organizations, as well as introducing collaborative perspectives. The concept of collaboration of team members of all ranks and positions in determining best practices and strategies is the foundation of modern organizational and leadership theories focused on managing change and supporting innovation. As the focus on planned change grew, Organizational Development (OD) emerged as a body of theory and practice (McGill, 1947).

Organizational Development describes multiple social-science approaches to planned organizational change (Anderson, 2016; Namada, 2018). It is a sustained, long-range process of reflective, self-analytical planned change. It builds on past and present research to create a collaborative system inclusive of data collection and diagnosis, as well as OB disciplines (Anderson, 2016; Namada, 2018). Contemporary models of OD change include Design Thinking, Spiral Dynamics, and Continuous Change (Beck & Cowan, 1996; Brown, 2008; Martin & Martin, 2009; Weick & Quinn, 1999).

While there is a practical value in the classical and neoclassical theories, if adapted to changing conditions, contemporary approaches often use the System Theory. The Systems Theory looks at the organization as a whole with mutually connected parts (Martz, 2013). Other approaches analysis pieces of the organization, viewed from the perspectives of the various disciplines, while the System Theory views the organization in its totality. In the 1960s, the Open Systems Perspective emerged, as human relations concerns expanded to include a focus on organizational growth and survival (Augier, 2013; Martz, 2013). Daniel Katz and Robert Kahn wrote a seminal work on the open systems perspective, stating organizations will continue to expand and survives only as long as they import more energy from the environment than they expend (Ashmos & Huber, 1987; Katz & Kahn, 1978). Emery and Trist called for different responses to varied environmental conditions to manage change, even as the environmental contexts in which organizations existed were increasing in complexity (Emery, 2000). In the 1980s, the productivity improvements made by Japanese companies led to Theory Z, a blending of American and Japanese practices (Lunenburg, 2011). Within the Open Systems Theory, complexity and expanding global markets drove the need for adaptation to change, and Change Management Theories evolved.

According to Cummings, Bridgman, and Brown (2016) Kurt Lewin's work on the change process is regarded as the classic approach to managing change. Lewin's approach lists the three steps to change as unfreezing, changing, and freezing. Lewin is often called the "founding father of change management" and the "intellectual father of contemporary theories "(Schein, 1988, pg. 239). Kotter (1978; 1996) is another seminal author of change management, with his 8- step Change Model. The 8- steps include: 1) create urgency, 2) form a powerful coalition, 3) create a vision for change, 4) communicate the vision, 5) remove obstacles, 6) create short-term wins, 7) build on the change, and 8) anchor the change in organizational culture. As organizations continued to seek ways to adapt to the rapid change of globalization and technology challenges, new change management models emerged, exploring leadership concepts, collaborative teams, and organizational learning to support organizational innovation and efficiency.

Organizational learning demonstrates an integration of disciplines. David Kolb (1984) created a learning model of experiential learning, building an understanding of the different stages of acquiring knowledge. His model is a learning cycle demonstrating the learner making sense of the experience. King (2009) expanded on organizational learning, including knowledge management as a key piece of learning within global organizations. Managing teams and diversity is not a new topic, as seen in Eckrel and Grossman's (2004) discussion on the growth of teams in the workplace and the need for diversity. Behavioral management, or leadership, is built into organizational learning and collaboration of teams. Senge (1990) was a pioneer of learning organizations, claiming without continual learning, supporting people growing and expanding their capacity to create as well as work in teams, organizations would not be flexible enough to adapt to rapid change. While known for his work with learning organizations, Senge's theories are often included in leadership models as well.

One of the recognized founders of the field of OD, Richard Beckhard, applied behavioral sciences to real life situations, describing an approach that was an innovative bottoms-up change effort (Fry, 2017). His work with collaborators McGregor, Bennis, and Schein initiated the Network of Organizational Development. Beckhard and Harris (1987) claimed the basic units of change are groups, not individuals; decision-making should be located where the information sources are without regard to role of hierarchy; open communication, mutual trust and confidence across divisions and level is needed; and people support what they create. Beckhard was instrumental in creating change models that influenced change management leadership styles. (Fry, 2017)

Leadership studies include seminal works such as the work of historian James Burns (1998) on Transformational Leadership and discussions by Bass and Avolio (1994; 1997) analyzing Transactional and Transformational Leadership. Situational/Contingency Models of leadership with their emphasis on being flexible and adaptable are part of the classic models of managing change. Some of the major models include: Kurt Lewin's Three Styles model, Tannenbaum and Schmidt's Leadership Continuum model, The Fiedler Contingency model, Path-Goal theory, the Situational Leadership model championed by Hersey and Blanchard (1969), and Bolman's and Deal's Four-Frame model (Scouller, 2011). Greenleaf (1977) espoused the Contingency Leadership Model and continued his leadership studies, creating the model for Servant Leadership. Kouzes & Posner's Leadership Model emphasized transformational features to build a model based on five leadership practices. More process-oriented theories include learning organizations. In these models, the work of leaders supports the followers, and includes an element of social responsibility (Bass & Avolio, 1997; Nawaz & Khan, 2016). Leadership models have moved from acquired traits to adaptive, situational styles, to models focused on the interactions of groups and group members to improve the organization as well as the individual (Asrar-ul-Haq& Anwar, 2018; Nawaz & Khan, 2016) .Recent leadership models developed in response to the call for innovation and creativity. .Models include Peter Senge's (1997, 2006) work developing learning organizations through leadership, Authentic Leadership built on followers' trust of the leader r(Avolio & Gardner, 2005), the Creative Leadership Model (McCauley & Van Velsor, 2004) used to support innovation with an emphasis on diverse work teams, and global/ sustainable leadership models, with an emphasis on Organizational Citizenship Behavior (Lane & Maznevski, 2019).

Focus

Organizations have always faced challenges, but today change is faster than at any time in history. According to Sayles (2017), a myriad of experts and workers will need to collaborate, emphasizing the communication challenges between teams with multiple visions. Some organizational visions have looked to the past, relying on increasing amounts of data driven analysis for strategic decisions. As technology improves, the data appears limitless, at times overwhelming the human decision makers (Yang, Choi, & Lee, 2018). Gladden (2016) posits the 'posthuman' organization has arrived. The discussion of creating a management style inclusive of AI, social robotics, and human augmentation emphasizes the interaction between processes and humans, as well as the need to grow people in their new roles. Humans and non-humans interact in increasingly digital and virtual worlds, in our social culture, personal life, and work life. The use of new technologies to enhance information gathering and physical strength is changing the workplace including the leadership styles needed to manage the change.

Transactional leadership emerges in the effort to mesh human workers with technology, including robotic tools (Gladden, 2016; Siciliano & Khatib, 2016). At the same time, calls for more innovation and creativity indicate the need to support transformational models of leadership. Assessing the organizational theories, classical theories might be employed to ensure the smooth functioning of manufacturing processes, supply chain management, and repetitive duties. Many rote actions should fall to technological devices, including robots and analysis programs. Assistant robots and exoskeletons augment human strength while protecting human bodies from the wear and tear of physical labor. Artificial intelligence allows mass data gathering and analysis in faster timeframes. The enhancement of humans in the organization is part of the future management process as changes in the organization drive changes in occupations and duties. Resilient organizations are able to respond effectively, reinventing themselves through innovation and creativity.

However, history shows organizations and workers traditionally resist change (Namada, 2018; Yang, Choi, & Lee, 2018). As radical organizational change occurs, OB knowledge provides models of change and paths of individual growth. Retaining valuable employees, retraining workers, developing collaborative teams, and embracing new technologies are suggested models for the future (Gladden, 2016; Namada, 2018; Yang, Choi, & Lee, 2018). Inherent in the need to manage change is the need for creation of knowledge, organizational learning, and the building of trust of followers.

SOLUTIONS AND RECOMMENDATIONS

Organizational Behavior is a complex merging of multiple disciplines. The need to integrate qualitative viewpoints with quantitative approaches continues to challenge the field (Rastrollo-Horrillo & Martín-Armario, 2019). Much as a mixed-approach to research has become the accepted norm, a mixed approach to managing approach may benefit organizations struggling to modify organizational behavior and culture. According to Hornstein (2015) it is essential project management and organizational change are integrated within the organizational behavior model. Despite recommendations to use projects as a way to institute and manage change (Crawford & Nahmias, 2010; Parker et al., 2013; Söderlund, 2010). While project management and change management use different terminologies and methodologies, having developed out of different parts of organizational behavior disciplines, they are complementary with mutually supportive disciplines. The success of the project is based on a wide array of factors and skills, and change management and project management should be viewed as multi-dimensional, combining traditional measures of project management and the broader field of organizational change management (Hornstein, 2015). The quantitative project management merged with the qualitative aspects of change management including culture building and communication, will allow a more inclusive approach to change, building a measurable yet innovative pathway to change.

According to Yang, Choi, and Lee (2018) organizations adapting to rapid changes in technology and the environment need to depart from the past macro-system focused view and recognize the individual-level factors influencing organizational change. Further discussion focuses on the need to consider" the multidimensionality of change behaviors in dynamic organizational environments" (Yang, Choi, & Lee, 2018, Pg.1659). Cross-functional collaboration enhances product innovation and development, while merging system-oriented change with people- oriented growth is vital to future growth of global organizations (Lin, Wang, & Kung, 2015). To spur innovation, diversity and horizontal organizational structures are preferred pieces of the organizational culture (Namada, 2018).

Lee and Edmondson (2017) discuss self-managing organizations as a means to flatten hierarchical structures and increase communication and knowledge sharing, while Luthans and Avolio (2007) advocate Positive Organizational Behavior, with criteria of hope, confidence, and resiliancy. Otaghsaram and Hamzehzadeh (2017) argue applying a positive psychological approach to research, practice, and work supports a competitive edge for organizations. They call for a paradigm shift from negativity to positivity, as increasingly turbulent situations spur the need for the use of authentic leadership styles to create an organizational climate that emphasizes the individual and developing positive characteristics of people, much as Senge advocated in building resilient organizations.

A key tenet of horizontal or flat organizations is openness within the organization. Openness, a norm within contemporary societies and flat organizations, has introduced greater transparency of information, expanded accountability throughout the organization, and increased inclusion (Hautz, 2017). Openness stands in contrast to traditional organizational views of confidentiality, authority, and competitive advantage, changing the fundamental ways organizations function. According to Dobusch, Dobusch, and Müller-Seitz (2019) the previous bureaucracy and organizational culture sometimes limit the benefits of openness. Their study indicates a two-pronged approach to implementing openness, procedural and contextual, allows a more accurate assessment of the efficiency of organizational openness.

FUTURE RESEARCH DIRECTIONS

Rapid change within organizations will continue, driven by globalization, uncertain markets, and new technologies. Tied to technology is a need for a deeper understanding of the effect of virtual teams and workplaces on the organizational culture. The restructuring process influenced by new information technologies opens doors for new models of management to cope with new working conditions and styles. The need to provide cohesive tools that support interaction between virtual and traditional teams includes processes, evaluations, and an inclusive culture (Alsharo, Gregg, & Ramirez, 2017).

Furthermore, Peters (2015) calls for a better understanding of digital technology, the media, and organizational use of new technology. As digital technologies shape our personal and social lives, so too do they shape organizational culture and structures. The use of new technologies and their implications on society and organizational transformation including innovation, learning, and communications is an area worthy of more exploration.

Granqvist and Gustafsson,(2016) point out the need for more understanding of perspectives on temporal institution work during times of change. In particular, they call for insights into how temporal maintenance work occurs, how synchronization and desynchronization affects institutional change, and how temporality acts as a source of institutional complexity. The expansion of current theories through temporal views might better inform innovation while integrating approaches to research across various disciplines. According to the European Group for Organizational Studied (2019), the concept of combining perspectives across levels from day-to-day activities to higher levels of the organization in research might help build understanding of time beyond 'clock time' to the social concept of time as used in organizing.

Future research is needed on the effect of diversity on knowledge creation and management focusing on communities within different socio-cultural contexts, including communities of practice (Manuti, Impedovo, & De Palma, 2017).). Diversity is still an intangible asset, mainly linked to a strategic use of human and social capital. Diversity is not yet fully defined, nor are the various aspects understood, especially in the context of innovation in AI, Deep Learning, and robotics. Olsen and Martins (2012) present a discussion of Diversity Management, indicating organizations do not understand how the context of their policies influences workforce diversity and outcomes, as well as calling for exploration into whether and how DM might adapt to environmental demands. Finally, organizations do not yet fully understand the consequences of new technologies. The need to explore the effects of an overload of diverse information on creativity, or the stress generated by constant connection to work and the lowering of personal interaction that supports innovation might help managers develop a culture that supports the highest level of creativity, diversity, interaction, and innovation (Oldham & Da Silva, 2015).

CONCLUSION

Global organizations face change on a large scale, using technology to create virtual teams, developing complex supply chains, promoting networks allowing asynchronous collaboration between developers, and the need for technology that can process vast amounts of data. With the advent of AI, robotics, and deep learning, organizations must manage the inclusion of technology in their teams, using the new knowledge to augment, rather than diminish, their people. Learning based organizations with positive and transparent organizational cultures will be situated to respond to the coming changes in all areas of the organization. OB must lead the way; ensuring leaders support innovation and change through the development of both technology and people, allowing new work models to emerge.

REFERENCES

Alsharo, M., Gregg, D., & Ramirez, R. (2017). Virtual team effectiveness: The role of knowledge sharing and trust. *Information & Management*, *54*(4), 479–490. doi:10.1016/j.im.2016.10.005

Anderson, D. L. (2016). *Organization development: The process of leading organizational change*. Sage Publications.

Ashmos, D. P., & Huber, G. P. (1987). The systems paradigm in organization theory: Correcting the record and suggesting the future. *Academy of Management Review*, *12*(4), 607–621. doi:10.5465/amr.1987.4306710

Asrar-ul-Haq, M., & Anwar, S. (2018). The many faces of leadership: Proposing research agenda through a review of literature. *Future Business Journal, 4*(2), 179–188. doi:10.1016/j.fbj.2018.06.002

Augier, M. (2013). The early evolution of the foundations for behavioral organization theory and strategy. *European Management Journal, 31*(1), 72-81. doi:10.1016/j.emj.2012.11.005

Avolio, B. J., & Gardner, W. L. (2005). Authentic leadership development: Getting to the root of positive forms of leadership. *The Leadership Quarterly*, *16*(3), 315–338. doi:10.1016/j.leaqua.2005.03.001

Basadur, M. (2004). Leading others to think innovatively together: Creative leadership. *The Leadership Quarterly*, *15*(1), 103–121. doi:10.1016/j.leaqua.2003.12.007

Bass, B. M., & Avolio, B. J. (1994). *Improving organizational effectiveness through Transformational leadership*. Sage.

Bass, B. M., & Avolio, B. J. (1997). *Full range leadership development: manual for the Multifactor Leadership Questionnaire*. Mindgarden.

Beck, D. E., & Cowan, C. C. (1996). *Spiral dynamics: Mastering values, leadership and change*. Blackwell Publishers, Inc.

Beckhard, R., & Harris, R. T. (1987). *Organizational Transitions: Managing Complex Change*. Addision-Wesley.

Brown, T. (2008). Design thinking. *Harvard Business Review*, *86*(6), 84. PMID:18605031

Burns, J. M. (1998). Transactional and transforming leadership. *Leading Organizations, 5*(3), 133-134.

Carroll, S. J., & Gillen, D. I. (1987). Are the classical management functions useful in describing managerial work? *Academy of Management Review*, *12*(1), 38–51. doi:10.5465/amr.1987.4306460

Carson, C. M. (2005). A historical view of Douglas McGregor's Theory Y. *Management Decision*, *43*(3), 450–460. doi:10.1108/00251740510589814

Crawford, L., & Nahmias, A. H. (2010). Competencies for managing change. *International Journal of Project Management*, *28*(4), 405–412. doi:10.1016/j.ijproman.2010.01.015

Cummings, S., Bridgman, T., & Brown, K. G. (2016). Unfreezing change as three steps: Rethinking Kurt Lewin's legacy for change management. *Human Relations*, *69*(1), 33–60. doi:10.1177/0018726715577707

Dobusch, L., Dobusch, L., & Müller-Seitz, G. (2019). Closing for the benefit of openness? The case of Wikimedia's open strategy process. *Organization Studies*, *40*(3), 343–370. doi:10.1177/0170840617736930

Eckel, C. C., & Grossman, P. J. (2005). Managing diversity by creating team identity. *Journal of Economic Behavior & Organization*, *58*(3), 371–392. doi:10.1016/j.jebo.2004.01.003

Emery, M. (2000). The current version of Emery's open systems theory. *Systemic Practice and Action Research*, *13*(5), 623–643. doi:10.1023/A:1009577509972

European Group for Organizational Studies. (2019). *SWGs*. Retrieved from: https://www.egosnet.org/

Fayol, H. (1949). *General and industrial management* (C. Storrs, Trans.). Pitman.

Fry, R. (2017). *Richard Beckhard: The formulator of organizational change. In The Palgrave Handbook of Organizational Change Thinkers.* Palgrave.

Gladden, M. E. (2016). *Posthuman Management: Creating Effective Organizations in an Age of Social Robotics, Ubiquitous AI, Human Augmentation, and Virtual Worlds.* Synthypnion Press.

Granqvist, N., & Gustafsson, R. (2016). Temporal institutional work. *Academy of Management Journal, 59*(3), 1009–1035. doi:10.5465/amj.2013.0416

Greenleaf, R. K. (2002). *Servant Leadership: A Journey into the Nature of Legitimate Power and Greatness.* Paulist Press.

Hatch, M. (1997). *Organization Theory: Modern, Symbolic, and Postmodern Perspectives.* Oxford University Press.

Hautz, J. (2017). Opening up the strategy process–a network perspective. *Management Decision, 55*(9), 1956–1983. doi:10.1108/MD-07-2016-0510

Hersey, P., Blanchard, K. H., & Johnson, D. E. (2007). *Management of organizational behavior* (Vol. 9). Prentice hall.

Hornstein, H. A. (2015). The integration of project management and organizational change management is now a necessity. *International Journal of Project Management, 33*(2), 291–298. doi:10.1016/j.ijproman.2014.08.005

Hsueh, Y. (2002). The Hawthorne experiments and the introduction of Jean Piaget in American industrial psychology, 1929-1932. *History of Psychology, 5*(2), 163–189. doi:10.1037/1093-4510.5.2.163 PMID:12096759

Katz, D., & Kahn, R. L. (1978). *The social psychology of organizations* (Vol. 2). Wiley.

King, W. R. (2009). *Knowledge management and organizational learning.* Springer. doi:10.1007/978-1-4419-0011-1

Kotter, J. P. (1978). *Organizational Dynamics: Diagnosis & Intervention.* AddisonWesley.

Kotter, J. P. (1996). *Leading Change.* Harvard Business School Press.

Kouzes, J. M., & Posner, B. Z. (2006). *The leadership challenge* (Vol. 3). John Wiley & Sons.

Lane, H. W., & Maznevski, M. L. (2019). *International management behavior: Global and sustainable leadership.* Cambridge University Press. doi:10.1017/9781108637152

Lee, M. Y., & Edmondson, A. C. (2017). Self-managing organizations: Exploring the limits of less-hierarchical organizing. *Research in Organizational Behavior, 37,* 35–58. doi:10.1016/j.riob.2017.10.002

Lewin, K. (1948). *Resolving Social Conflicts: Selected Papers on Group Dynamics* (G. Lewin, Ed.). Harper & Row.

Lin, Y., Wang, Y., & Kung, L. (2015). Influences of cross-functional collaboration and knowledge creation on technology commercialization: Evidence from high-tech industries. *Industrial Marketing Management, 49,* 128–138. doi:10.1016/j.indmarman.2015.04.002

Lindebaum, D., & Jordan, P. J. (2014). A critique on neuroscientific methodologies in organizational behavior and management studies. *Journal of Organizational Behavior*, *35*(7), 898–908. doi:10.1002/job.1940

Lunenburg, F. C. (2011). Organizational culture-performance relationships: Views of excellence and theory Z. *National Forum of Educational Administration and Supervision Journal*, *29*(4), 1-10.

Luthans, F., Avolio, B. J., Avey, J. B., & Norman, S. M. (2007). Positive psychological capital: Measurement and relationship with performance and satisfaction. *Personnel Psychology*, *60*(3), 60. doi:10.1111/j.1744-6570.2007.00083.x

Manuti, A., Impedovo, M., & De Palma, P. (2017). Managing social and human capital in organizations : Communities of practices as strategic tools for individual and organizational development. *Journal of Workplace Learning*, *217*(3), 217–234. doi:10.1108/JWL-07-2016-0062

Martin, R., & Martin, R. L. (2009). *The Design of Business: Why Design Thinking is the Next Competitive Advantage*. Harvard Business Press.

Martz, W. (2013). Evaluating Organizational Performance: Rational, Natural, and Open System Models. *American Journal of Evaluation*, *34*, 385–401. Retrieved from http://search.ebscohost.com/login.aspx?direct=true&AuthType=shib&db=eric&AN=EJ1015377&site=eds-live&scope=site

Maslow, A. H. (1954). *Motivation and personality*. Harper & Row.

McCauley, C. D., & Van Velsor, E. (Eds.). (2004). *The center for creative leadership handbook of leadership development* (Vol. 29). John Wiley & Sons.

McGill, M. E. (1974). The evolution of organization development: 1947-1960. *Public Administration Review*, *34*(2), 98–105. doi:10.2307/974932

Namada, J. M. (2018). Organizational learning and competitive advantage. In *Handbook of Research on Knowledge Management for Contemporary Business Environments* (pp. 86–104). IGI Global. doi:10.4018/978-1-5225-3725-0.ch006

Nawaz, Z., & Khan, I. (2016). Leadership theories and styles: A literature review. *Leadership*, *16*, 1–7.

Nawaz, Z., & Khan, I. (2016). Leadership theories and styles: A literature review. *Leadership*, *16*, 1–7.

Nicklin, J. M., & Spector, P. E. (2016). Point/Counterpoint introduction: The future of theory in organizational behavior research. *Journal of Organizational Behavior*, *37*(8), 1113–1115. doi:10.1002/job.2116

Oldham, G. R., & Da Silva, N. (2015). The impact of digital technology on the generation and implementation of creative ideas in the workplace. *Computers in Human Behavior*, *42*, 5–11. doi:10.1016/j.chb.2013.10.041

Olsen, J., & Martins, L. (2012). Understanding organizational diversity management programs: A theoretical framework and directions for future research. *Journal of Organizational Behavior*, *33*(8), 1168–1187. doi:10.1002/job.1792

Önday, Ö. (2016). Neoclassical organization theory: from incentives of Bernard to organizational objectives of Cyert and March. *Global Journal of Human Resource Management*, *4*(1).

15

Otaghsara, S. M. T., & Hamzehzadeh, H. (2017). The Effect of Authentic Leadership and Organizational Atmosphere on Positive Organizational Behavior. *International Journal of Management, Accounting & Economics, 4*(11), 1122–1135. Retrieved Http://search.ebscohost.com/login.aspx?direct=true&AuthType=shib&db=bth&AN=127683538&site=eds-live&scope=site83-94

Ott, J. S. (1989). *The organizational culture perspective*. Dorsey Press.

Pardo del Val, M., & Martínez Fuentes, C. (2003). Resistance to change: A literature review and empirical study. *Management Decision, 41*(2), 148–155. doi:10.1108/00251740310457597

Parker, D., Verlinden, A., Nussey, R., Ford, M., & Pathak, R. D. (2013). Critical evaluation of project-based performance management: Change intervention integration. *International Journal of Productivity and Performance Management, 62*(4), 407–419. doi:10.1108/17410401311329634

Peters, J. D. (2015). *The marvelous clouds: Toward a philosophy of elemental media*. University of Chicago Press. doi:10.7208/chicago/9780226253978.001.0001

Rastrollo-Horrillo, M. Á., & Martín-Armario, J. (2019). Organisational barriers to nascent born-global growth: Learning from the inside. *Journal of International Entrepreneurship, 17*(3), 1–20. doi:10.100710843-019-00256-1

Sayles, L. R. (2017). *Managing large systems: organizations for the future*. Routledge. doi:10.4324/9780203786437

Scott, W. G. (1961). Organization Theory: An Overview and an Appraisal. *Journal of the Academy of Management, 4*(1), 7. doi:10.2307/254584

Scouller, J. (2011). The Three Levels of Leadership: How to Develop Your Leadership Presence, Know-how, And Skill. Oxford, UK: Management Books 2000.

Senge, P. (1990). The leader's new work: Building learning organizations. *Sloan Management Review, 32*(1), 7–23.

Senge, P. (2006). *The Fifth Discipline: The Art and Practice of the Learning Organization*. Penguin Random House.

Siciliano, B., & Khatib, O. (Eds.). (2016). *Springer handbook of robotics*. Springer. doi:10.1007/978-3-319-32552-1

Söderlund, J. (2010). Knowledge entrainment and project management: The case of large-scale transformation projects. *International Journal of Project Management, 28*(2), 130–141. doi:10.1016/j.ijproman.2009.11.010

Wagner-Tsukamoto, S. (2007). An institutional economic reconstruction of scientific management: On the lost theoretical logic of Taylorism. *Academy of Management Review, 32*(1), 105–117. doi:10.5465/amr.2007.23463879

Weick, K. E., & Quinn, R. E. (1999). Organizational change and development. In J. T. Spence, J. M. Darley, & D. J. Foss (Eds.), *Annual Review of Psychology* (Vol. 50, pp. 361–386). Annual Reviews.

Yang, Y., Choi, J. N., & Lee, K. (2018). Theory of planned behavior and different forms of organizational change behavior. *Social Behavior and Personality, 46*(10), 1657–1671. doi:10.2224bp.6832

Yukl, G. (1989). Managerial leadership: A review of theory and research. *Journal of Management*, *15*(2), 251–289. doi:10.1177/014920638901500207

ADDITIONAL READING

Andrews, K., & Mickahail, B. (2015). Business and Social Media: Collaboration for the Sixth Discipline. In *Social Media and the Transformation of Interaction in Society* (pp. 158–172). IGI Global. doi:10.4018/978-1-4666-8556-7.ch008

Bakari, H., Hunjra, A. I., & Niazi, G. S. K. (2017). How does authentic leadership influence planned organizational change? The role of employees' perceptions: Integration of theory of planned behavior and Lewin's three step model. *Journal of Change Management*, *17*(2), 155–187. doi:10.1080/1469701 7.2017.1299370

Boiral, O., Talbot, D., & Paillé, P. (2015). Leading by example: A model of organizational citizenship behavior for the environment. *Business Strategy and the Environment*, *24*(6), 532–550. doi:10.1002/bse.1835

Chou, D. C. (2018). Applying design thinking method to social entrepreneurship project. *Computer Standards & Interfaces*, *55*, 73–79. doi:10.1016/j.csi.2017.05.001

Evans, M., Dalkir, K., & Bidian, C. (2015). A holistic view of the knowledge life cycle: The knowledge management cycle (KMC) model. *Electronic Journal of Knowledge Management*, *12*(1), 47.

Fillion, G., Koffi, V., & Ekionea, J. P. B. (2015). Peter Senge's learning organization: A critical view and the addition of some new concepts to actualize theory and practice. *Journal of Organizational Culture. Communications and Conflict*, *19*(3), 73.

Lozano, R. (2015). A holistic perspective on corporate sustainability drivers. *Corporate Social Responsibility and Environmental Management*, *22*(1), 32–44. doi:10.1002/csr.1325

Mickahail, B. K., & de Aquino, C. T. E. (Eds.). (2019). *Effective and Creative Leadership in Diverse Workforces: Improving Organizational Performance and Culture in the Workplace*. Springer. doi:10.1007/978-3-030-02348-5

Senge, P., Hamilton, H., & Kania, J. (2015). The dawn of system leadership. *Stanford Social Innovation Review*, *13*(1), 27–33.

KEY TERMS AND DEFINITIONS

Adhocracy: A highly informal organizational design that is organic rather than mechanistic. The configuration allows specialists to work in teams.

Authentic Leadership: A leadership model based on follower trust earned by the leader. The leader emphasizes honesty and positivity.

Benchmarking: Comparing products, processes, and people with competitors in a systematic comparison to imitate and improve on them.

15

Change Agent: Someone who supports, promotes, and enables change within a group or organization. Sometimes called a Change Champion.

Collectivism: Cultural influencing the degree of collaboration preferences to act in groups.

Decentralization: Decision-making is distributed throughout the organization, a flat or horizontal hierarchy.

Entrepreneurial Leadership: A leadership perspective where a leader strongly exhibits characteristics and behaviors of an entrepreneur.

Organizational Climate: The current work environment and atmosphere of an organization, as perceived by employees.

Organizational Socialization: The process that introduces new employees to the organizational culture.

Positivist Organization Theories: Based on research methods from the natural sciences, positivist researchers advocate knowledge produced from an accumulation of facts.

Practical Intelligence: An individual's ability to unravel everyday problems and find solutions. It includes the ability to get things done effectively and collaborating with others.

Visible Culture: A culture expressed visible with symbols and narratives.

Examination of Quality of Life in Workplace Environments

Lesley Clack

University of Georgia, USA

INTRODUCTION

Understanding how to enhance satisfaction of employees in the workplace is of significance to managers, and quality of life is an important construct that relates to job satisfaction and overall wellbeing of employees. Quality of life is an estimate of an individual's health status, defined as satisfaction or happiness within eight dimensions: vitality, physical functioning, bodily pain, general health perceptions, physical role functioning, emotional role functioning, social role functioning, and mental health (Ware, Kosinski, & Gandek, 2000). Quality of life is a common measurement in healthcare, in determining the effectiveness of treatment on patients. But, quality of life in healthcare workers is often overlooked. Healthcare organizations are commonly known to be high-stress environments due to the life-or-death nature of the work. Thus, examining the quality of life in healthcare professionals is of significance, and is related to one of the Healthy People 2020 Occupational Safety & Health Objectives, which is to "increase the proportion of employees who have access to workplace programs that prevent or reduce employee stress" (Office of Disease Prevention and Health Promotion, 2017).

The objectives of this article are to identify and examine the factors that impact quality of life in healthcare professionals and to identify solutions and recommendations for how healthcare managers can assist in reducing the impact of these factors in the workplace. This topic is timely because the well-being of healthcare professionals is important to the effective functioning of the health system (Selanu, Thornicroft, Fekadu, & Hanlan, 2017). While there are many factors that impact quality of life, this article will focus on four factors that are most prevalent in healthcare settings: occupational stress, burnout, workplace violence, and employee well-being. Research has shown that occupational stress, burnout, and workplace violence all can have a significant impact on employee well-being and overall quality of life (Brandstatter, Job, & Schulze, 2016).

BACKGROUND

The Institute for Healthcare Improvement (IHI) introduced the Triple Aim- enhancing patient experience, improving population health, and reducing costs- as the model for optimizing performance in the health system (Berwick, Nolan, & Whittington, 2008). Recently, there has been increased interest in changing the Triple Aim to a Quadruple Aim, thereby addressing the goal of improving the life of healthcare professionals (Bodenheimer & Sinsky, 2014). This push for a change even further highlights the significance and timeliness of exploring the negative consequences that affect quality of life in healthcare professionals.

Often healthcare professionals find it difficult to seek help for their health problems for a variety of reasons, such as workload and the fear of stigma and adverse effects on their career (Brooks, Gerada,

DOI: 10.4018/978-1-7998-3473-1.ch182

& Chalder, 2016). Particular types of healthcare professionals are even more susceptible to negative consequences that impact quality of life. For example, healthcare professionals working in an Intensive Care Unit (ICU) are at higher risk of stress, burnout, and anxiety (Vandevala, Pavey, Chelidoni, Change, Creagh-Brown, & Cox, 2017). Workplace violence is also an area of concern.

Healthcare managers have a pivotal role in healthcare organizations as they set the professional standard, oversee quality and training, and serve as role models (Maza, Shecter, Eizenberg, Segev, & Flugelman, 2016). According to the World Health Organization (WHO), "a healthy workplace is one in which workers and managers collaborate to use a continual improvement process to protect and promote the health, safety, and well-being of all workers and the sustainability of the workplace" (Burton, 2010). Thus, implications for how managers can assist in reducing stress, burnout, and workplace violence, and enhance employee well-being, will be explored.

FOCUS OF THE ARTICLE

Occupational Stress

Stress has been reported to be increasing in all full-time employees in the U.S. by as much as a 31% increase from 1983 to 2009 (Cohen & Janicki-Deverts, 2012). Stress can have a negative impact on individuals, such as mental health issues or burnout, and an impact on organizations, such as reduced performance and increased absences (Oginska-Bulik, 2006). Prior studies have surveyed healthcare workers and found that 28% reported stress to be a work-related health problem (Oginska-Bulik, 2006). In 2012, 63% of physicians surveyed reported they were more stressed than three years prior, and 34.3% reported being much more stressed than three years prior (Privitera, Rosenstein, Plessow, & LoCastro, 2014). A 2006 study by Oginska-Bulik concluded that there is a need for programs aimed to prevent work-related stress in healthcare organizations.

Occupational stress is the negative psychological response to job demands in the workplace and has been defined as a feeling of unease and discomfort that workers may experience when presented with extraordinary work demands and pressures (De Sio, Cedrone, Saruta, Ricci, Corbosero, Di Traglia, Greco, & Stansfeld, 2017). Occupational Stress has been reported at a prevalence of 52.7% in healthcare professionals (Kazmi, Amjad, & Khan, 2008). Other studies have also noted the significance of occupational stress and its relation to negative consequences in healthcare professionals (Gaither & Nadkarni, 2012). In a survey conducted in 2011, 87% of physicians reported that the leading cause of their occupational stress was due to paperwork and administration, and 63% reported that their stress is increasing (Bodenheimer & Sinsky, 2014). Healthcare managers should devise strategies to reduce the level of occupational stress and should provide support to healthcare professionals in order to help them deal with job-related stress (Sharma, Davey, Davey, Shukla, Shrivastava, & Bansal, 2014). If healthcare managers implement programs to reduce occupational stress in the workplace, the impact on quality of life in healthcare professionals could be significant. Intervention programs should be aimed at reducing an employee's experience of stressors (Awa & Plaumann, 2010).

Burnout

Burnout in healthcare professionals threatens the Triple Aim, as dissatisfied healthcare professionals are associated with lower patient satisfaction (McHugh, Kutney-Lee, Cimiotti, Sloane, & Aiken, 2011; Haas,

Cook, Puopolo, Burstin, Cleary, & Brennan, 2000). Burnout has been defined as "physical or emotional exhaustion, usually caused by stress at work" (Felton, 1998, p. 238). Burnout is typically assessed in terms of three dimensions that develop in response to chronic work-related stress: emotional exhaustion, depersonalization, and reduced personal accomplishment (Maslach, Schaufteli, & Leiter, 2001). Emotional exhaustion refers to the draining of emotional resources (Rasumussen, Turnell, Butar, Juraskar, Kirsten, Wiener, Patenaude, Hoekstra-Weebers, & Grassi, 2016). Depersonalization is characterized by negative and cynical attitudes towards patients (Demerouti, Bakker, Nachreiner, & Schaufeli, 2000). Burnout is associated with a reduction in motivation, job satisfaction, and job performance (Parker & Kulik, 1995). Burnout can occur when individuals fail to effectively control work-related stress (Langade, Modi, Sidhwa, Hishikar, Gharpure, Wankhade, Langade, & Joshi, 2016). Prior studies have identified a relationship between quality of life and job performance (Rastegari, Khani, Ghalriz, & Eslamian, 2010). Another study attempted to explore the relationship between burnout, occupational stress, and anxiety symptoms. The results of the study found a positive correlation, thus authors recommend burnout management in order to reduce the impact of occupational stress (Ding, Qu, & Wang, 2014).

Prior research has found that as many as half of all U.S. physicians meet the criteria for burnout syndrome (Shanafelt, Hasan, Dyrbye, Sinsky, Satele, Sloan, & West, 2015). In a study conducted by Shanefelt et al in the U.S. in 2012, 7,288 physicians completed a survey in which 45.8% of the physicians reported at least one symptom of burnout. The results of the study showed an approximately 10% higher level of burnout in physicians as compared to the general study population (Shanafelt, Boon, Tan, Dyrbye, Sotile, Satele, West, Sloan, & Oreskovich, 2012). In addition, a 2011 study by the American Academy of Orthopedic Surgeons reported that, out of 2,000 North American physicians, 87% described themselves as being in a state of burnout on a daily basis (Rosenstein, 2012). Other studies have reported that the prevalence of burnout among all categories of healthcare professionals ranges anywhere from 12.6% to 29.9% (Abdulla, Al-Qahtani, & Al-Kuwari, 2011; Abdulghafour, Bo-hamra, Al-Randi, Kamel, & El-Shazly, 2011). Emotional exhaustion, which is a component of burnout, has been reported to affect 20.1% of healthcare professionals (Johnson, Osborn, Araya, Wearn, Paul, & Stafford, 2012).

Burnout syndrome is a public health issue, considering its impact on quality of life (Gil-Monte, 2009). Since burnout is linked to patient safety and quality of patient care, examination of the impact on quality of life is warranted (Carta, Preti, Portoghese, Pisanu, Moro, Pintus, Pintus, Perra, D'Oca, Atzeni, Campagna, Fabrici Pascolo, Sancassiani, Finco, D'Aloja, & Grassi, 2017). Particular specialties, such as pediatrics (Al-Youbi & Jan, 2013), oncology (Rasmussen, Turrell, Butar, Juraskara, & Kirsten, 2016), and ICU workers (van Mol, Kompanje, Benoit, Bakker, & Nijkamp, 2015), are at increased risk for burnout. Other studies have found burnout to be particularly prevalent in emergency department physicians, general internists, neurologists, and family physicians (Shanafelt, Boone, Tan, Dyrbye, Sotile, Satele, West, Sloan, & Oreskovich, 2012). In a survey conducted in 2014, 68% of family physicians and 73% of general internists reported that they would not choose the same specialty if they could start their careers over (Kane & Peckham, 2014). In a study conducted in 2011, 34% of hospital nurses and 37% of nursing home nurses reported burnout, compared with 22% of nurses working in other settings (McHugh, Kutney-Lee, Cimiotti, Sloane, & Aiken, 2011).

Burnout syndrome may be associated with negative consequences, such as anxiety (Ding, Qu, Yu, & Wang, 2014). Prior studies have found that healthcare workers have a greater risk of developing anxiety due to occupational stress (Fiabane, Giorgi, Sguazzin, & Argentero, 2013; Patel, Weiss, Chowdhary, Naik, Pednekar, Chatterjee, Bhat, Araya, King, Simon, Verdeli, & Kirkwoods, 2011) Anxiety is a psychological and physiological state that has been described as "a feeling of fear related to some uncertain or future event or mental distress that is caused by a threat to a person or his/her values" (Ding et al, 2014, p. 1).

Other research has investigated whether burnout and depression are essentially the same thing and cover the same symptoms. Findings suggest that while similar symptoms may accompany both burnout and depression, that burnout is indeed a distinct problem (Bianchi, Schonfeld, & Laurent, 2014). Managers may be able to more easily recognize symptoms of anxiety and depression, which could indicate potential burnout in employees. The challenge for healthcare managers is to understand factors that would increase or decrease an employee's response to burnout (Rafii, Oskouie, & Nikraesh, 2004). If managers can identify employees who are showing signs of symptoms of burnout, anxiety, and depression, they can potentially implement interventions that could have a positive impact on the employee's quality of life.

Workplace Violence

Workplace Violence, such as bullying and harassment, is an occupational hazard in healthcare organizations that can lead to negative consequences, such as burnout and mental health issues (Lin, Wu, Yuan, Zhang, Jing, Zhang, Luo, Lei, & Wang, 2015). Workplace violence is defined as incidents where staff have been abused, threatened, or assaulted in job-related circumstances which impacted their safety, well-being, or health (ILO, ICN, WHO, & PSI, 2003). The World Health Organization (WHO) categorizes workplace violence into 2 types, physical violence and psychological violence (ICN, PSI, WHO, & ILO, 2002). Physical violence is defined as beating, kicking, slapping, stabbing, shooting, pushing, biting, and pinching; and psychological violence is defined as the threat of physical force against another person or group that can result in harm to physical, mental, spiritual, moral, or social development (Zhao, Liu, Ma, Jiao, Li, Hao, Sun, Gao, Hong, Kang, Wu, & Qiao, 2015). Prior studies have identified a relationship between workplace violence and quality of life (Wu, Lin, Li, Chei, Zhang, Wu, & Zhu, 2014; Chen, Huang, Hwang, & Chen, 2010), and have reported the incidence of workplace violence in the U.S. to be 78% (Benham, Tillotson, Davis, & Hobbs, 2011).

In 2010, the healthcare sector employed approximately 18.9 million workers (13.6% of the total workplace) making it the largest industry in the U.S. (Bureau of Labor Statistics, 2011). Additionally in 2010, the healthcare sector accounted for 11,370 nonfatal workplace violence injuries, with approximately 67% of nonfatal violent injuries occurring in all industries (Bureau of Labor Statistics, 2012). Over the last eight years, healthcare professionals on average accounted for 62% of the nonfatal workplace violence injuries that required time off from work (Bureau of Labor Statistics, 2012). The risk of healthcare professionals experiencing an assault that requires time off from work is 4.5 times greater than that of the general workforce (Bureau of Labor Statistics, 2012). The literature also suggests that the number of assaults is greatly underreported by healthcare professionals (Hartley, Ridenour, Craine, & Morrill, 2015).

Workplace violence has been reported to be a major problem for healthcare professionals globally (AbuAlRub & Al-Asmar, 2014). Prior studies have reported the prevalence of workplace violence to be as high as 89% (Boafo, Hancock, & Gringart, 2016; Franz, Zeh, Schablon, Kuhnert, & Niehaus, 2010). A study by Boafo in 2018 surveyed 592 nurses and found that 52.7% of participants reported having been abused verbally, and 12% reported having been sexually harassed in the workplace in the previous 12 months (Boafo, 2018). Workplace violence should not be tolerated, and managers should both recognize the issues and implement strategies in order to reduce occurrence and discipline the culprits.

Employee Well-Being

Occupational stress, burnout, and workplace violence can all impact employee well-being. Negative experiences and stress from workplaces often spill over into employees' personal lives, which impacts employee well-being (Yoo & Lee, 2018). Employee well-being (emotional and psychological) can be defined as employees' attitudes and lived experiences within the organization (Diener, 2000). Employee well-being can be conceptualized as subjective well-being, which refers to an individual's own cognitive and affective evaluation of their lives in terms of satisfaction with certain aspects, such as job satisfaction (Pasamar & Alegre, 2015). The fast-paced, demanding work environment in healthcare, and increasing demand for learning and using the latest technology, can lead to significant occupational stress and burnout in employees that impacts employee well-being (Raya & Panneerselvam, 2013). Burnout, in terms of exhaustion, has been most commonly used as a measure for employee well-being (Petrie, Gayed, Bryan, Deady, Madan, Savic, Wooldridge, Counson, Calvo, Glozier, & Harvey, 2018). Higher levels of burnout and exhaustion are more typical of lower levels of employee well-being. Prior research investigating the link between workplace violence and employee well-being found that employees who had greater exposure to workplace violence reported lower levels of quality of life (Yoo & Lee, 2018).

Managers play an important role in employee well-being. Research has consistently shown that a good social environment in the workplace is associated with employee well-being (Daniels, Watson, & Gedikli, 2017). Prior studies have found that creating an organizational culture that supports employees in their work and family roles is important for employee well-being (Odle-Dusseau, Herleman, Britt, Moore, Castro, & McGurk, 2013). Other research examining the importance of different aspects of manager support in healthcare settings highlighted the significance of the role of management in using organizational and team-level interventions to promote employee well-being (Petrie, Gayed, Bryan, Deady, Madan, Savic, Wooldridge, Counson, Calvo, Glozier, & Harvey, 2018).

SOLUTIONS AND RECOMMENDATIONS

Research studies have noted that the well-being of healthcare workers is dependent on the quality of their work environment (Portoghese, Galletta, Coppola, Fince, & Campagna, 2014), which is within a managers span of control. Studies have found that social support from managers can modify a healthcare professional's response to negative consequences, such as burnout (Rafii, Oskouie, & Nikravesh, 2014). Managers should focus on how to reduce stress, burnout, and workplace violence. In order to control risk of burnout, healthcare managers should use strategies aimed at increasing an employee's sense of control and reducing employee workloads (Portoghese, Galletta, Coppola, Finco, & Campagna, 2014). Healthcare managers can improve workers' sense of control by promoting their autonomy in the workplace, as job autonomy is considered an important coping strategy for decreasing occupational stress (Karasek & Theorell, 1990; Hausser, Mojzisch, Niesel, & Schulz-Hardt, 2012). Other recommendations for managers include providing support to employees to assist them in better dealing with the demands experienced in the workplace, and providing employees with training to help them deal with challenges faced at work (Gauche, de Beer, & Brink, 2017). Managers can also implement training programs in areas such as stress management and conflict management. There is some evidence that individual-focused web-based interventions relaxation and mindfulness techniques are effective for supporting employee well-being and reducing occupational stress (Ryan, Bergin, Chalder, & Wells, 2017).

FURTHER RESEARCH DIRECTIONS

15

Additional research in the area could explore further ways in which managers can improve each of these areas in order to reduce the impact on quality of life in healthcare professionals. Future research should also examine the impact of stress and burnout in healthcare managers, and how the stress level of managers impacts the quality of life in healthcare professionals. A lot of emphasis in research is placed on the support that employees need from managers, but one area that has not received a lot of attention in the support that managers need in order to know how to support employee well-being. Further research investigating how best to train and support managers in creating a supportive culture for employees is needed.

CONCLUSION

Quality of life in healthcare professionals can be significantly impacted by negative consequences in the workplace, such as occupational stress, burnout, and workplace violence, which can in turn impact employee well-being. Improving quality of life in healthcare professionals can have a substantial impact on their job satisfaction, thus improving patient care delivery.

While there are many factors that contribute to quality of life, research has consistently studied the impact of occupational stress, burnout, and workplace violence on employee well-being and quality of life. Many researchers have noted the significance of the impact that issues such as stress and burnout can have on well-being and quality of life. The involvement of healthcare managers in identifying these issues and reducing their impact in the workplace may be the key to improving quality of life in healthcare professionals.

REFERENCES

Abdulghafour, Y., Bo-hamra, A., Al-Randi, M., Kamel, M., & El-Shazly, M. (2011). Burnout syndrome among physicians working in primary health care centers in Kuwait. *Alexandria Journal of Medicine*, *47*(4), 351–357. doi:10.1016/j.ajme.2011.08.004

Abdulla, L., Al-Qahtani, D., & Al-Kuwari, M. (2011). Prevalence and determinants of burnout syndrome among primary health care physicians in Quatar. *South African Family Practice*, *53*(4), 380–383. doi:10.1080/20786204.2011.10874118

AbuAlRub, R. F., & Al-Asmar, A. H. (2014). Psychological violence in the workplace among Jordanian hospital nurses. *Journal of Transcultural Nursing*, *25*(1), 6–14. doi:10.1177/1043659613493330 PMID:23835894

Al-Youbi, R. A., & Jan, M. M. (2013). Burnout syndrome in pediatric practice. *Oman Medical Journal*, *28*(4), 252–254. doi:10.5001/omj.2013.71 PMID:23904917

Awa, W., Plaumann, M., & Walter, U. (2010). Burnout prevention: A review of intervention programs. *Patient Education and Counseling*, *78*(2), 184–190. doi:10.1016/j.pec.2009.04.008 PMID:19467822

Begat, I., Ellefsen, B., & Severinsson, E. (2005). Nurses' satisfaction with their work environment and the outcomes of clinical nursing supervision on nurses' experience of well-being: A Norwegian study. *Journal of Nursing Management, 13*(3), 221–230. doi:10.1111/j.1365-2834.2004.00527.x PMID:15819834

Benham, M., Tillotson, R. D., Davis, S. M., & Hobbs, G. R. (2011). Violence in the emergency department: A national survey of emergency medicine residents and attending physicians. *The Journal of Emergency Medicine, 40*(5), 565–579. doi:10.1016/j.jemermed.2009.11.007 PMID:20133103

Berwick, D. M., Nolan, T. W., & Whittington, J. (2008). The triple aim: Care, health, & cost. *Health Affairs, 27*(3), 759–769. doi:10.1377/hlthaff.27.3.759 PMID:18474969

Bianchi, R., Schonfeld, I. S., & Laurent, E. (2014). Is burnout a depressive disorder? A reexamination with special focus on atypical depression. *International Journal of Stress Management, 21*(4), 307–324. doi:10.1037/a0037906

Boafo, I. M. (2018). The effects of workplace respect and violence on nurses' job satisfaction in Ghana: A cross-sectional survey. *Human Resources for Health, 16*(6), 1–10. doi:10.118612960-018-0269-9 PMID:29334969

Boafo, I. M., Hancock, P., & Gringart, E. (2016). Sources, incidence, and effects of non-physical workplace violence against nurses in Ghana. *Nursing Open, 3*(2), 99–109. doi:10.1002/nop2.43 PMID:27708820

Bodenheimer, T., & Sinsky, C. (2014). From triple to quadruple aim: Care of the patient requires care of the provider. *Annals of Family Medicine, 12*(6), 573–576. doi:10.1370/afm.1713 PMID:25384822

Brandstatter, V., Job, V., & Schulze, B. (2016). Motivational incongruence and well-being at the workplace: Person-job fit, job burnout, and physical symptoms. *Frontiers in Psychology, 7*(1153), 1–11. doi:10.3389/fpsyg.2016.01153 PMID:27570513

Brooks, S. K., Gerada, C., & Chalder, T. (2016). The specific needs of doctors with mental health problems: Qualitative analysis of doctor-patients' experiences with the practitioner health programme. *Journal of Mental Health (Abingdon, England), 26*(2), 161–166. doi:10.1080/09638237.2016.1244712 PMID:27841030

Bureau of Labor Statistics (BLS). (2011). *Employed persons by detailed industry, sex, race, & Hispanic or Latino ethnicity.* Retrieved from https://www.bls.gov/cps/cpsaat18.pdf

Bureau of Labor Statistics (BLS). (2012). *Occupational injuries/illnesses and fatal injuries profiles.* Retrieved from https://data.bls.gov/gqt/InitialPage

Burton, J. (2010). *World Health Organization health workplace framework & model: background and supporting literature and practices.* World Health Organization.

Carta, M. G., Preti, A., Portoghese, I., Pisanu, E., Moro, D., Pintus, M., Pintus, E., Perra, A., D'Oca, S., Atzeni, M., Campagna, M., Fabria Pascolo, E., Sancassiani, F., Finco, G., D'Aloja, E., & Grassi, L. (2017). Risk for depression, burnout and low quality of life among personnel of a university hospital in Italy is a consequence of the Impact One Economic Crisis in the welfare system? *Clinical Practice and Epidemiology in Mental Health, 13*(1), 156–167. doi:10.2174/1745017901713010156 PMID:29238392

Chen, W. C., Huang, C. J., Hwang, J. S., & Chen, C. C. (2010). The relationship of Health-Related Quality of Life to workplace physical violence against nurses by psychiatric patients. *Quality of Life Research: An International Journal of Quality of Life Aspects of Treatment, Care and Rehabilitation, 19*(8), 1155–1161. doi:10.100711136-010-9679-4 PMID:20521131

Cohen, S., & Janicki-Deverts, D. (2012). Who's stressed? Distributions of psychological stress in the United States in probability samples from 1983, 2006, and 2009. *Journal of Applied Social Psychology, 42*(6), 1320–1334. doi:10.1111/j.1559-1816.2012.00900.x

Daniels, K., Watson, D., & Cigdem, G. (2017). Well-being and the social environment of work: A systematic review of intervention studies. *International Journal of Environmental Research and Public Health, 14*(8), 918–934. doi:10.3390/ijerph14080918 PMID:28813009

De Sio, S., Cedrone, F., Saruta, D., Ricci, P., Corbosero, P., DiTraglia, M., Greco, E., & Stansfeld, S. (2017). Quality of life in workers and stress: Gender differences in exposure to psychosocial risks and perceived well-being. *BioMed Research International, 2017*, 1–6. doi:10.1155/2017/7340781 PMID:29349081

Demerouti, E., Bakker, A. B., Nachreiner, F., & Schaufeli, W. B. (2000). A model of burnout and life satisfaction among nurses. *Journal of Advanced Nursing, 32*(2), 454–464. doi:10.1046/j.1365-2648.2000.01496.x PMID:10964195

Diener, E. (2000). The science of happiness and a proposal for a national index. *The American Psychologist, 55*(1), 34–43. doi:10.1037/0003-066X.55.1.34 PMID:11392863

Ding, Y., Qu, J., & Wang, S. (2014). The mediating effects of burnout on the relationship between anxiety symptoms and occupational stress among community healthcare workers in China: A cross-sectional study. *PLoS One, 9*(9), 1–7. doi:10.1371/journal.pone.0107130 PMID:25211025

Felton, J. S. (1998). Burnout as a clinical entity- Its importance in health care workers. *Occupational Medicine, 48*(4), 237–250. doi:10.1093/occmed/48.4.237 PMID:9800422

Fiabane, E., Giorgi, I., Sguazzin, C., & Argentero, P. (2013). Work engagement and occupational stress in nurses and other healthcare workers: The role of organizational and personal factors. *Journal of Clinical Nursing, 22*(17-18), 2614–2624. doi:10.1111/jocn.12084 PMID:23551268

Franz, S., Zeh, A., Schablon, A., Kuhnert, S., & Niehaus, A. (2010). Aggression and violence against healthcare workers in Germany- A cross sectional retrospective survey. *BMC Health Services Research, 10*(51), 1–8. PMID:20184718

Gaither, C. A., & Nadkarni, A. (2012). Interpersonal interactions, job demands and work-related outcomes in pharmacy. *International Journal of Pharmacy Practice, 20*(2), 80–89. doi:10.1111/j.2042-7174.2011.00165.x PMID:22416932

Gauche, C., de Beer, L. T., & Brink, L. (2017). Exploring demands from the perspective of employees identified as being at risk of burnout. *International Journal of Qualitative Studies on Health and Well-being, 12*(1), 1–13. doi:10.1080/17482631.2017.1361783 PMID:28784048

Gil-Monte, P. (2009). Some reasons to consider psychosocial risks in the work and its consequences on public health. *Revista Espanola de Salud Publica, 83*(2), 169–173. doi:10.1590/S1135-57272009000200003 PMID:19626246

Haas, J. S., Cook, E. F., Puopolo, A. L., Burstin, H. R., Cleary, P. D., & Brennan, T. A. (2000). Is the professional satisfaction of general internists associated with patient satisfaction? *Journal of General Internal Medicine*, *15*(2), 122–128. doi:10.1046/j.1525-1497.2000.02219.x PMID:10672116

Hartley, D., Ridenour, M., Craine, J., & Morrill, A. (2015). Workplace violence prevention for nurses on-line course: Program development. *Work (Reading, Mass.)*, *51*(1), 79–89. doi:10.3233/WOR-141891 PMID:24939112

Hausser, J. A., Mojzisch, A., Niesel, M., & Schulz-Hardt, S. (2012). Ten years on: A review of recent research on the job demand-control (-support) model and psychological well-being. *Work and Stress*, *24*(1), 1–35. doi:10.1080/02678371003683747

International Council of Nurses (ICN), Public Services International (PSI), World Health Organization (WHO), & International Labor Office (ILO). (2002). Framework guidelines for addressing workplace violence in the health sector. Geneva, Switzerland: International Labor Office.

International Labor Office (ILO), International Council of Nurses (ICN), World Health Organization (WHO), & Public Services International (PSI). (2003). Workplace violence in the health sector: country case studies. Geneva, Switzerland: World Health Organization.

Johnson, S., Osborn, P., Araya, R., Wearn, E., Paul, M., Stafford, M., Wellman, N., Nolan, F., Killaspy, H., Lloyd-Evans, B., Anderson, E., & Wood, S. J. (2012). Morale in the English mental health workforce: Questionnaire survey. *The British Journal of Psychiatry*, *201*(3), 239–246. doi:10.1192/bjp.bp.111.098970 PMID:22790677

Kane, L., & Peckham, C. (2014). *Medscape physician compensation report 2014*. Retrieved from https://www.medscape.com/features/slideshow/compensation/2014/public/overview#24

Karasek, R., & Theorell, T. (1990). *Stress, productivity, and the reconstruction of working life*. Basic Books.

Kazmi, R., Amjad, S., & Khan, D. (2008). Occupational stress and its effect on job performance: A case study of medical house officers of District Abbottabad. *Journal of Ayub Medical College, Abbottabad*, *20*(3), 135–139. PMID:19610539

Langade, D., Modi, P. D., Sidhwha, Y. F., Hishikar, N. A., Gharpure, A. S., Wankhade, K., Langade, J., & Joshi, K. (2016). Burnout syndrome among medical practitioners across India: A questionnaire-based survey. *Cureus*, *8*(9), 771–783. doi:10.7759/cureus.771 PMID:27833826

Lin, W. Q., Wu, J., Yuan, L. X., Zhang, S. C., Jing, M. J., Zhang, H. S., Luo, J. L., Lei, Y. X., & Wang, P. X. (2015). Workplace violence and job performance among community healthcare workers in China: The mediator role of Quality of Life. *International Journal of Environmental Research and Public Health*, *12*(11), 14872–14886. doi:10.3390/ijerph121114872 PMID:26610538

Liu, H., Zhao, S., Jiao, M., Wang, J., Peters, D. H., Qiao, H., Zhao, Y., Li, X., Song, L., Xing, K., Lu, Y., & Wu, Q. (2015). Extent, nature, & risk factors of workplace violence in public tertiary hospitals in China: A cross-sectional survey. *International Journal of Environmental Research and Public Health*, *12*(6), 6801–6817. doi:10.3390/ijerph120606801 PMID:26086703

Maslach, C., Schaufeli, W. B., & Leiter, M. P. (2001). Job burnout. *Annual Review of Psychology*, *52*(1), 397–422. doi:10.1146/annurev.psych.52.1.397 PMID:11148311

Maza, Y., Shecter, E., Eizenberg, N. P., Segev, E. G., & Flugelman, M. Y. (2016). Physician empowerment programme: A unique workshop for physician managers of community clinics. *BMC Medical Education, 16*(269), 1–6. doi:10.118612909-016-0786-y PMID:27741943

McHugh, M. D., Kutney-Lee, A., Cimiotti, J. P., Sloane, D. M., & Aiken, L. H. (2011). Nurses' widespread job dissatisfaction, burnout, and frustration with health benefits signal problems for patient care. *Health Affairs, 30*(2), 202–210. doi:10.1377/hlthaff.2010.0100 PMID:21289340

Odle-Dusseau, H. N., Herleman, H. A., Britt, T. W., Moore, D. D., Castro, C. A., & McGurk, D. (2013). Family-supportive work environments and psychological strain: A longitudinal test of two theories. *Journal of Occupational Health Psychology, 18*(1), 27–36. doi:10.1037/a0030803 PMID:23276196

Office of Disease Prevention and Health Promotion. (2017). *Healthy People 2020 topics & objectives: Occupational Safety & Health*. Retrieved from https://www.healthypeople.gov/2020/topics-objectives/topic/occupational-safety-and-health/objectives

Oginska-Bulik, N. (2006). Occupational stress and its consequences in health professionals: The role of Type D personality. *International Journal of Occupational Medicine and Environmental Health, 19*(2), 113–122. doi:10.2478/v10001-006-0016-7 PMID:17128809

Parker, P. A., & Kulik, J. A. (1995). Burnout, self- and supervisor-related job performance, and absenteeism among nurses. *Journal of Behavioral Medicine, 18*(6), 581–599. doi:10.1007/BF01857897 PMID:8749987

Pasamar, S., & Alegre, J. (2015). Adoption and use of work-life initiatives: Looking at the influence of institutional pressures and gender. *European Management Journal, 33*(3), 214–224. doi:10.1016/j.emj.2014.09.002

Patel, V., Weiss, H. A., Chowdhary, N., Naik, S., Pednekar, S., Chatterjee, S., Bhat, B., Araya, R., King, M., Simon, G., Verdeli, H., & Kirkwoods, B. R. (2011). Lay health worker led information for Depressive and Anxiety Disorders in India: Impact on clinical and disability outcomes over 12 months. *The British Journal of Psychiatry, 199*(6), 459–466. doi:10.1192/bjp.bp.111.092155 PMID:22130747

Peek-Asa, C., Howard, J., Vargas, L., & Kraus, J. F. (1997). Incidence of non-fatal workplace assault injuries determined from employer's reports in California. *Journal of Occupational and Environmental Medicine, 39*(1), 44–50. doi:10.1097/00043764-199701000-00009 PMID:9029430

Petrie, K., Gayed, A., Bryan, B. T., Deady, M., Madan, I., Savic, A., Wooldridge, Z., Counson, I., Calvo, R. A., Glozier, N., & Harvey, S. B. (2018). The importance of manager support for the mental health and well-being of ambulance personnel. *PLoS One, 13*(5), 1–13. doi:10.1371/journal.pone.0197802 PMID:29791510

Portoghese, I., Galletta, M., Coppola, R., Finco, G., & Campagna, M. (2014). Burnout and workload among healthcare workers: The moderating role of job control. *Safety and Health at Work, 5*(3), 152–157. doi:10.1016/j.shaw.2014.05.004 PMID:25379330

Rafii, F., Oskouie, F., & Nikravesh, M. (2004). Factors involved in nurses' responses to burnout: A grounded theory study. *BMC Nursing, 3*(6), 1–10. doi:10.1186/1472-6955-3-6 PMID:15541180

Rasmussen, V., Turnell, A., Butar, P., Juraskara, I., & Kirsten, L. (2016). Burnout among psychosocial Oncologists: An application & extension of the Effort-Reward Imbalance Model. *Psycho-Oncology*, *25*(2), 194–202. doi:10.1002/pon.3902 PMID:26239424

Rastegari, M., Khani, A., Ghalriz, P., & Eslamian, J. (2010). Evaluation of quality of working life and its association with job performance of the nurses. *Iranian Journal of Nursing and Midwifery Research*, *15*(4), 224–228. PMID:22049285

Raya, R. P., & Panneerselvam, S. (2013). The healthy organization construct: A review and research agenda. *Indian Journal of Occupational and Environmental Medicine*, *17*(3), 89–93. doi:10.4103/0019-5278.130835 PMID:24872666

Rosenstein, A. H. (2012). *Physician stress and burnout: prevalence, cause, & effect*. Retrieved from http://www.physiciandisruptivebehavior.com/admin/articles/31.pdf

Ryan, C., Bergin, M., Chalder, T., & Wells, J. S. G. (2017). Web-based interventions for the management of stress in the workplace: Focus, form, and efficacy. *Journal of Occupational Health*, *59*(3), 215–236. doi:10.1539/joh.16-0227-RA PMID:28320977

Selamu, M., Thornicroft, G., Fekadu, A., & Hanlan, C. (2017). Conceptualisation of job-rFelated well-being, stress, and burnout among healthcare workers in rural Ethiopia: A qualitative study. *BMC Health Services Research*, *17*(412), 1–11. PMID:28629360

Shanafelt, T. D., Boone, S., Tan, L., Dyrbye, L. N., Sotile, W., Satele, D., West, C. P., Sloan, J., & Oreskovich, M. R. (2012). Burnout and satisfaction with work-life balance among U.S. physicians relative to the general U.S. population. *Archives of Internal Medicine*, *172*(18), 1377–1389. doi:10.1001/archinternmed.2012.3199 PMID:22911330

Shanafelt, T. D., Hasan, O., Dyrbye, L. N., Sinsky, C., Satele, D., Sloan, J., & West, C. P. (2015). Changes in burnout and satisfaction with work-life balance in physicians and the general U.S working population between 2011 and 2014. *Mayo Clinic Proceedings*, *90*(12), 1600–1613. doi:10.1016/j.mayocp.2015.08.023 PMID:26653297

Sharma, P., Davey, A., Davey, S., Shukla, A., Shrivastava, K., & Bansal, R. (2014). Occupational stress among staff nurses: Controlling the risk to health. *Indian Journal of Occupational and Environmental Medicine*, *18*(2), 52–56. doi:10.4103/0019-5278.146890 PMID:25568598

Sun, W., Fu, J. L., Chang, Y., & Wang, L. (2012). Epidemiological study on risk factors for Anxiety Disorders among Chinese doctors. *Journal of Occupational Health*, *54*(1), 1–8. doi:10.1539/joh.11-0169-OA PMID:22156318

van Mol, M. M. C., Kompanje, E. J. O., Benoit, D. D., Bakker, J., & Nijkamp, M. D. (2015). The prevalence of compassion fatigue and burnout among healthcare professionals in Intensive Care Units; a systematic review. *PLoS One*, *10*(8), 1–22. doi:10.1371/journal.pone.0136955 PMID:26322644

Vandevala, T., Pavey, L., Chelidoni, O., Chang, N. F., Creagh-Brown, B., & Cox, A. (2017). Psychological rumination and recovery from work in Intensive Care professionals: Association with stress, burnout, depression, & health. *Journal of Intensive Care*, *5*(16), 1–8. doi:10.118640560-017-0209-0 PMID:28174662

15

Ware, J. E., Kosinski, M., & Gandek, B. (2000). *SF-36 Health Survey: Manual and Interpretation Guide.* Quality Metric Inc.

Wu, S., Lin, S., Li, H., Chei, W., Zhang, Q., Wu, Y., & Zhu, W. (2014). A study on workplace violence and its effect on Quality of Life among medical professionals in China. *Archives of Environmental & Occupational Health, 69*(2), 81–88. doi:10.1080/19338244.2012.732124 PMID:24205959

Yoo, G., & Lee, S. (2018). It doesn't end there: Workplace bullying, work-to-family conflict, and employee well-being in Korea. *International Journal of Environmental Research and Public Health, 15*(7), 1548–1561. doi:10.3390/ijerph15071548 PMID:30037131

Zhao, S., Liu, H., Ma, H., Jiao, M., Li, Y., Hao, Y., Sun, Y., Gao, L., Hong, S., Kang, Z., Wu, Q., & Qiao, H. (2015). Coping with workplace violence in healthcare settings: Social support & strategies. *International Journal of Environmental Research and Public Health, 12*(11), 14429–14444. doi:10.3390/ijerph121114429 PMID:26580633

ADDITIONAL READING

Ang, S. A., Bartram, T., McNeil, N., Leggat, S. G., & Stanton, P. (2013). The effects of High-Performance Work Systems on hospital employees' work attitudes and intention to leave: A multi-level and occupational group analysis. *International Journal of Human Resource Management, 24*(16), 3086–3114. doi:10.1080/09585192.2013.775029

Bartram, T., Casimir, G., Djurkovic, N., Leggat, S., & Stanton, P. (2012). Do perceived High Performance Work Systems influence the relationship between emotional labor, burnout, and intention to leave? A study of Australian nurses. *Journal of Advanced Nursing, 68*(7), 1567–1578. doi:10.1111/j.1365-2648.2012.05968.x PMID:22384981

Bartram, T., Karimi, L., Leggat, S. G., & Stanton, P. (2014). Social identification: Linking High Performance Work Systems, psychological empowerment and patient care. *International Journal of Human Resource Management, 25*(17), 2401–2419. doi:10.1080/09585192.2014.880152

Harley, B., Allen, B. C., & Sargent, L. D. (2007). High Performance Work Systems and employee experience of work in the service sector: The case of aged-care. *British Journal of Industrial Relations, 45*(3), 607–633. doi:10.1111/j.1467-8543.2007.00630.x

Harley, B., Sargent, L., & Allen, B. (2010). Employee responses to 'High Performance Work System' practices: An empirical test of the disciplined worker thesis. *Work, Employment and Society, 24*(4), 740-760.

Leggat, S., Bartram, T., Casimir, G., & Stanton, P. (2010). Nurse perceptions of the quality of patient care: Confirming the importance of empowerment and job satisfaction. *Health Care Management Review, 35*(4), 355–364. doi:10.1097/HMR.0b013e3181e4ec55 PMID:20844360

Leggat, S. G., Bartram, T., & Stanton, P. (2011). High Performance Work Systems: The gap between policy and practice in Health Care reform. *Journal of Health Organization and Management, 25*(3), 281–297. doi:10.1108/14777261111143536 PMID:21845983

Scotti, D. J., Harmon, J., & Behson, S. J. (2007). Links among High-Performance Work Environment, service quality, and customer satisfaction: An extension to the healthcare sector. *Journal of Healthcare Management, 52*(2), 109–125. doi:10.1097/00115514-200703000-00008 PMID:17447538

KEY TERMS AND DEFINITIONS

Anxiety: A feeling of worry or fear that is associated with nervousness and restlessness.

Burnout: A state of physical or emotional exhaustion that is typically the result of stress.

Occupational Stress: Stress that is particularly related to a person's job.

Quality of Life: The overall well-being of an individual in terms of things such as physical health, life satisfaction, and job satisfaction.

Stress: Physical, mental, or emotional tension caused by a situation.

Well-Being: The overall physical, mental, and social wellness of a person.

Workplace Violence: Verbal or physical threats against a person in a workplace.

Coworking Spaces, New Workplaces

Diane-Gabrielle Tremblay
Université TÉLUQ, Canada

Arnaud Scaillerez
Université de Moncton, Canada

INTRODUCTION

While technologies now allow the emergence of new collaborative working environments, these new organizational methods, new spaces and new objectives also refer to a set of issues and challenges that are not yet well studied. However, they bring significant results without necessarily being costly or complex to put in place. However, research on coworking spaces is emerging and increasing every year.

This is precisely the basis of the originality and purpose of this chapter. After defining coworking, the chapter presents the implementation of coworking spaces, as well as the advantagesoffered by these places for the benefit of entrepreneurs, businesses and employees, but also the limits.

The challenges related to the emergence of these new collaborative environments as new ways of organizing work are also adressed. We also bring a critical look at the reality of the coworking phenomenon.

BACKGROUND

Coworking spaces are part of the category of third places. The study of third places emerged from the work of the sociologist Ray Oldenburg in the late 1980s. The author describes new places of life, neither the house, "first place," nor the company, "second place". Oldenburg is one of the first researchers to have conceptualized third places and especially coworking spaces. In his seminal work "Celebreting the Third Place" (2000), he suggests the existence of these places which would be at the heart of the vitality of societies and indispensable to the smooth functioning of modern democracies.

Third places (Good place), correspond to spaces that are neither in the private or the public sphere, but having characteristics that are common to the private sphere and the professional sphere. These places were originally created to revive social interactions in North American cities that were in economic decline. Since then, different authors have added some criteria to the definition, making it broader and thus including other circumstances (Smits, 2015) and other countries. Therefore, to be considered as a third-place, this place must be:

- Neutral (therefore neither at home nor at the employer's place), hence the third place (Oldenburg, 1989);
- Free access, therefore open to all without any restriction, especially as regards the type of activity done in this space (Oldenburg, 1999);
- Facilitating meetings and exchanges (the configuration of the place must be conducive to conversation, with the presence of meeting rooms in particular - or simply places of conviviality like that reserved for the coffee break or lunch (Guenoud, Moeckli, 2010);

DOI: 10.4018/978-1-7998-3473-1.ch183

With these first elements, one could for example imagine that cafes providing free wifi (such as Starbucks) could be considered as a third places. However, this is not the case, because to be considered as a third place, two other elements must also be present:

- Frequency of use by the same users (also in fact, with this fourth element, Starbucks could represent a third-place for customers accustomed to come and work and exchange, Gershenfeld, 2005);
- And above all for a third place to be recognized as such, it is necessary that the knowledge (product, service or other result) that is produced and that emanates from the exchanges between the persons regularly present in the place subsists even after the end of the collaboration, even after the closing of the venue and the end of the meetings between the actors. And it is undoubtedly this element that differentiates places open to the public (such as Starbucks for example), from a third place conducive to work and knowledge sharing (Liefooghe, 2016).

FOCUS OF THE ARTICLE

Setting Up Coworking Spaces

Over the last 20 years or so, depending on the cities or countries, a new form of open space has emerged, the coworking space. The coworking movement, which is part of this evolution, originated in the mid-2000s in San Francisco, in the Californian world of Web 2.0. Coworking thus fits into the wider context of the development of "third places" (Oldenburg, 1999, 2000), places that lie between the place of residence and the place of work. This phenomenon continues to grow and in particular the coworking spaces have multiplied in many cities and villages across the world. Indeed, they can be found not only in the large capitals of the world (Paris, London, New York, Mexico, etc.), but also in many smaller cities and rural areas across the globe (Tremblay &Vaineau, 2020), and not only in industrialized countries, but also in what we refer to as developing countries (Mexico, Brazil, Senegal, Kenya, Maroc and others). Indeed, over time, these coworking spaces have emerged, first within metropolitan areas and then outside urban centers, including in remote rural areas, where they can contribute to develop economic activity.

There are several categories of creators. The creators of coworking spaces are for the most part self-employed workers who are workingin these places. They have come together to unite their efforts and their means to find premises that can accommodate them.

Some coworking spaces have been created by government authorities in order to boost a territory with a loss of economic attractiveness (as in the Cantal region in France in particular). Others were created within the premises of a company to make the site profitable by renting some parts of it. At the same time, in Europe and North America, numerous Internet platforms and hotels (the Accor hotel group for example) offer their customers (business travelers) coworking spaces established within the hotel. In addition, some start-ups also make a part of their space available to a large public in order to facilitate coworking. We find this trend in Berlin where German start-ups provide digital services and platforms running for the benefit of coworkers. A process of communication around the existence of the place was therefore initiated, but often it was mostly word of mouth that was enough to attract other workers in the premises. The initiative for the creation of these third-places is individual and supported by private or mostly private funds

In the world, the number of spaces has indeed been multiplied by 32 in 10 years, by 12 in 6 years and by 5 in the last 4 years alone. Thus, in 2013, there were 2,423 spaces, and it is estimated there were 13,800 worldwide as of December 31, 2017 (Deskmag, 2017).

These workspaces are not, initially, spaces dedicated to work, they are places that have been partially diverted from their original function, such as cafes or libraries. In many cases they are also associated with the revitalization of certain deindustrialized zones and buildings in cities (Ananian, 2019). Often created by individuals, often self-employed workers who wanted to offer themselves access to meeting rooms, printers or other technological devices, they are hybrid spaces that offer better working conditions than those that one can have at home, in a workshop or at the office (Scaillerez, Tremblay, 2019, 2016a). However, over time, and especially around large metropolises in Europe, salaried workers also came to work in some of these spaces, when they found some closer to their homes. Finally, some countries or cities also support these spaces in order to facilitate access to work for individuals who have difficult access to the labour market, or cannot finance access to a private office, with all the necessary equipment. Thus, in some countries, such as France, local politicians have been interested in these spaces for various socioeconomic objectives, such as labour market integration and training for work (see various chapters in Krauss and Tremblay, 2019).

Hosting salaried or independent teleworkers for both economic and social reasons, collaborative workspaces are gaining popularity, and the numbers have exploded as we indicated above. But why this interest? The shared cost is less than what a self-employed worker would pay for renting his own office, and this gives access to better spaces, that are more centrally located, for many coworkers. They also allow to break the isolation of working at home and contribute to expanding professional networks, sometimes increasing contracts for workers and economic activity for cities. These coworking spaces are places where people gather to work, but also to interact in a friendly atmosphere. They are alternatives to the daily routine that many employees can experience in large firms in particular and can also offer many benefits to employers through the access to new networks, new ideas, even the development of innovative products or services (Tremblay & Vaineau, 2019, Scaillerez & Tremblay, 2016b).

In addition, some places are open primarily or exclusively to women. They indicate they want to promote women's entrepreneurship and also enable women to have a continuous professional career, without the need to interrupt or reduce it, by facilitating work-family balance via the coworking space. It is both to meet these needs and to contribute to its development that some coworking spaces have favored the sharing of values and help between women entrepreneurs. For example, *Soleilles cowork* in Paris is a space founded in 2011 by five women with the aim of creating a place of collaboration and sharing for the benefit of all entrepreneurial activities, but especially for women. This is a women-friendly space. To this day, out of 30 workstations offered, the space is attended by 40% men and 60% women. Some coworking spaces also offer coworkers the opportunity to come with their children who can be kept on site. This option is offered in many countries, we can mention the significant initiatives of My outspace in London, Coworking Village in Chicago or Mamaworking in Brazil. In these spaces, as many men as women come to work bringing their children. This allows men to play their role of father and women to continue their professional career. Of course these initiatives cannot replace regular daycare, so they can only be temporary options if there is no regular daycare service, but these initiatives do favor the reconciliation of social times for the benefit of both sexes.

However, they can also be oriented towards social economy or third sector initiatives, as is the case in a few coworking spaces in Montreal or in Paris for example. Coworking spaces seem to be conducive to the development of social entrepreneurship since the sharing of values and the collaborative exchanges between coworkers stimulate the professional activities of each and facilitate this type of business opportunities. For example, the co-working space Esplanade, in Montreal, is one of the most significant examples since their users share values related to the desire to counter economic decline, to find alternative modes in the face of neoliberalism, which increases their value, solidarity and professional support.

Some of these places are grouped by category of work or professional interests which lead to develop networks or relations with other coworkers (Scaillerez, Tremblay, 2016b). Whether the creators of these places want to establish a professional logic or not, there is an overrepresentation of categories of work and professional activities related to new technologies and the digital world (programmers, Web developers), writing and communication (editors, translators, freelance journalists, or similar professions in publicity or marketing) or creation (designers, architects, graphic designers).

Over the years, large real estate firms have become interested in this formula in order to revitalize some partially empty buildings in city centers. Indeed, companies such as WeWork, but also many real estate companies in various cities have looked towards this formula to rent spaces on a few floors in large centrally located downtown buildings. They often contract out to designers to develop very modern and attractive open spaces, and offer them on the office market. Collaborative workspaces are also beginning to be established in the peripheries located around large cities, and this highlights a possible positive effect of coworking spaces, that is that they can contribute to reducing traffic congestion and travel times for a good number of workers, which can also reduce pollution and greenhouse gas emissions (Scaillerez, Tremblay, 2016a and b).

Membership formulas are diverse and characterized by their flexibility. There are flat rates for office rentals by the hour, half-day, day, week, month, semester or "à la carte", with a sliding scale. The time of attendance is also very variable, some packages offering rentals from Monday to Friday or only on weekends, with traditional working hours (8 am to 18 pm) or unlimited access (24 hours a day). Prices vary depending on the formula chosen, the length of the rental and the office you wish to occupy: cubicle, closed office, open space, mobile office or permanent office . In Quebec (Canada), the monthly costs to use a full-time floating office (five days a week) range from $ 250 to $ 400CAN (or about 300 $US) before taxes. The difference in price from one place to another also depends on the nature of the packages offered, as well as on local real estate prices. The traditional packages offer at least an office equipped with all the necessary equipment (photocopier, printer, telephone, Internet access at high or very high speed, meeting rooms and videoconferencing). Most of the time, the coworker brings his or her own computer. These work places also offer spaces of conviviality like a place to rest, with comfortable sofas and chairs, as well as a kitchenette with a coffee machine, and even kitchen equipment (fridge, oven, etc.), all this favoring meetings and exchanges between the coworkers. Some offer additional packages, permanent or occasional services, such as a facilitator, animator or secretarial services, subject to some supplementary charges.

Coworking, a New Form of Work Organization

Coworking also brings important changes in the organization of work. It is a type of work organization that refers both to the sharing of a workspace, but also to a form of networking of workers within the same space, encouraging cooperation and exchanges in a specific space of work. These spaces avoid the potential isolation that can be experienced by someone who teleworks from home. They can also contribute to a better concentration than at the office and to facilitate meetings with other users of the place. Coworking spaces are thus considered as places of socialization for various individuals who benefit from the effects of networks produced in these workspaces. True communities can be formed through the creation of relationships of trust, mutual aid and shared values among project leaders (Fabbri, 2015,

2016, Garrett et al., 2017). It needs to be mentioned however that even if the objective of cooperation, network creation and creativity or innovation are often put forward by the initiators of coworking spaces, research has shown that it is not all individuals who want to cooperate, nor all spaces that lead to this cooperation. Indeed a few cases apparently show that some coworkers appreciate working in these spaces but do not particularly seek exchanges and networking with other coworkers (see chapters by Ferchaud and Krauss, in Krauss and Tremblay, 2019).

On the contrary, some collaborative workspaces have also been established in reference to a common identity, with the desire to create a community of belonging or collective identity, as is the case for examples in coworking spaces that refer to the social economy, third sector or associative activity. Users of these locations want to work in a place where they have affinities and common objectives or interests with others, which can lead to a common or shared identity, and thus lead to more interaction and collaboration with other coworkers. In some of these places, they come together because they share common values such as those of the social economy, which can be very strong in creating collective interest and identity (Tremblay and Vaineau, 2020; Scaillerez, Tremblay, 2019, 2016a and b). Collaborative workspaces naturally create a network where everyone has their activity and where, if necessary, it will be possible to use the skills, experience and even the network of these workers. This type of activity leads to a feeling of belonging to the same place, a desire to share, a climate of trust and a form of emulation between the coworkers.

Finally, coworking spaces are also places of life and animation. Most collaborative workspaces regularly organize, in various forms, meetings and activities for the benefit of ite users or events around a specific theme. This brings animation to the place and promotes it to make other workers want to come there for their work or their activity. The objective is also to facilitate meetings between the workers who use these places while reinforcing the feeling that one belongs to the same place and to the same professional family (Scaillerez, Tremblay, 2019, 2016b,), again with the objective of giving workers supplementary value for their payment to access the space.

To further facilitate the meetings and open the coworking spaces to more people, some organizations have set up:

- *networks* (such as the International Co-working Movement ; the League of Extraordinary Coworking Space (LEXC), a North American network of coworking spaces that promotes coherence and the quality of the place ; or in Quebec, the QC co-working movement.
- *tools*, such as maps designating all coworking spaces in a territory. We can cite in particular the map produced by coworking Quebec or another one developed in Europe1.

Coworking and Entrepreneurship

Today, businesses, especially small businesses and self-employed, need to access new markets and increase their efficiency and productivity to adapt to the circumstances of increasingly fierce competition. This search for performance and markets leads them to rethink the organization of work and to seek greater flexibility (Scaillerez, Tremblay, 2016c). The type of philosophy found in a collaborative workspace, which is based on mutual support and sharing, and not only on financial (a company rents space for several workers) but also professional objectives (promoting networking, innovation, etc.) apparently presents many advantages from this point of view. Indeed, coworking spaces are intermediary places that aim to promote sharing and exchanges, thus creating communities where information and knowledge flow, generating as many opportunities for innovation and creativity (Tremblay and Scaillerez, 2019;

Scaillerez, Tremblay, 2017). This sociability can be at the heart of their performance and new markets or contracts through the possibilities of new formal and informal meetings and the creation of extended social networks. Undertaking in these places seems to correspond to our time when the mechanisms of solidarity compensate the uncertainties related to the future.

Coworking spaces can directly or indirectly support the development of the projects of the entrepreneurs they host and promote collaborative dynamics (Fabbri and Charue-Duboc, 2013, 2016) based on relationships of trust and / or cooperation. As mentioned above, this is not always the case, but indeed in many cases, the exchange of ideas and collaborative work do give rise to innovations of all kinds. This is often found in the context of socialized organization, even if some cases the question of private property is all the more acute when it comes to, for example, to file a patent, to evaluate the participation of different stakeholders. For the entrepreneurs and self-employed who chose a coworking space, the objective is often to develop one's project in an autonomous way, in the absence of any hierarchical relationship.

THE LIMITS OF COWORKING

Over the years, depending on the cities or countries, coworking has become a new way of organizing work based on a shared work space, set up with the aim of fostering exchanges and synergies between coworkers, and fostering creativity and innovation. It is thus generally presented as a real revolution in the organization of work. However, coworking covers very diverse realities, as has been observed in recent research (Krauss and Tremblay, 2019). Coworking indeed translates into a wide variety of situations, and the link with third places is not necessarily self-evident, since coworking spaces are more general workspaces (Fabbri, 2017). While these are workspaces that want to offer new types of spaces and working environments, as well as better working conditions in terms of work organization, and technologies, they can also offer an interesting balance between more autonomy and collaboration with others. Coworkers are not subject to any rigid work schedules and are masters of their own time and can take advantage of the other users present in the premises to develop their knowledge and their activities (Scaillerez and Tremblay, 2019).

The level of autonomy that is possible in these spaces is however quite contrasted depending on the type of work content, or work status (salaried or self-employed). Coworking spaces do not only attract people with a high propensity to create and innovate, but also people looking for work, which in this way create their own job as self-employed, or even nomadic workers who exercise a professional activity fora large company, or an association. All workers do not necessarily have a strong capacity or desire to innovate, but it is more common to find ideas in an open space, a place where it is possible to meet others, including for individuals who were excluded from salaried employment but have found in coworking a way to create their own job or economic activity. Indeed, the synergistic relationships mentioned above between coworkers belonging to the same workspace are not always present, and this is one of the limits of some coworking spaces. If you can talk with other coworkers about your project in the cafeteria, a coworking center usually consists of independent individuals, small businesses, associations, entrepreneurs or auto-entrepreneurs, and not all are interested in cooperation and synergistic types of relationships. The objective is not always to develop ideas or projects with others.

In addition, the methods of access to coworking spaces are different. Some have a selection process for access to the space, based either on the type of professional activity or on collective identity (territorial belonging, social economy, etc.), others do not. In this sense coworking spaces are very different depending on the country, region or city where they are located, but also depending on the creators' objectives.

Coworking spaces can be created by entrepreneurs who have identified a market opportunity, public initiatives that see this as an opportunity to create employment in their territory, or by large companies favoring a form of nomadic salaried work (i.e. working in different places at different times). Depending on the different scenarios considered, governance arrangements will also be different, more or less user-friendly, more or less market oriented. For example, for large companies, this can also be a way to reduce the fixed costs of creating office space. In the context of Covid-19, firms needing to adapt their work environments to social distancing might see in coworking spaces the opportunity to offer different working spaces to their employees, without needing to build or rent more space on a permanent basis. Coworking spaces can offer space for salaried workers, as is more often the case in Europe and Asia, and less in North America, at least to this day. For the owners of a building, this can be an opportunity to maximize the profitability of their real estate by offering for rent a new variety of office space, again which may be occupied by firms needing to adapt to social distancing.

FUTURE RESEARCH DIRECTIONS

In terms of scientific research, the main question for the coming years will be how these spaces adapt to a pandemic and post-pandemic context. As most have open spaces, there will surely be some adaptation, and at the same time, they can receive guests from companies wanting to externalize some workers in order to facilitate social distancing or to reduce transportation time for some workers. (Tremblay, 2020a,b) Comparative studies of modes of adaptation to Covid between cities and countries will surely be of interest.

Also, a lot of research on coworking only refers to one disciplinary field. Few multidisciplinary studies exist for the moment.

In addition, studies on the relationships between coworking spaces with innovation and entrepreneurship are developing, but research on the subject is scarce, which for the moment makes it impossible to deduce significant results regarding the impact in these two areas. One can even add that most research is rather uncritical to coworking spaces; a more analytical perspective would be welcome.

The possible limits, risks,and other dysfunctions that one could meet in this type of place should be investigated. Yet, even though coworking spaces are multiplying, others close their doors or go bankrupt each year, but there are too few studies to explain the reasons for these failures at the moment. Data explaining the reasons for these failures would be useful, but few creators or managers of coworking spaces report on these failures. However, entrepreneurial failure is also a reality and understanding the reasons for these failures would be interesting in order to improve the activities of coworking spaces and increase their viability. Still, the Covid and post-Covid adaptation remains the main research question for the future.

CONCLUSION

Working spaces continue to change, and the COVID-19 virus has strongly increased the percentage of telework from home in all countries. It has demonstrated that it is no longer necessary to work in the office building of the employer, or even during traditional working hours. The relationship between time, space and work has been radically modified with the COVID pandemic. Coworking spaces are part of this modification of work and arouse great interest for workers as well as firms by introducing a new dynamic in working space, allowing people to work closer to home, not take public transit and remain master of their work organization and time.

In many industrial and emerging countries, coworking has become, over the last twenty years, a new way of organizing work based on a shared work space, set up with the aim of fostering exchanges and emulation between coworkers, to fuel creativity and innovation (Brown, 2017). The reality is however much more complex, and will continue to evolve in the post-pandemic context. Indeed, coworking designates a diversity of situations according to the territory in which it develops, but also the intention of the creators of the space and the coworkers themselves. Each coworking space has a history, a given trajectory, although it can be said that this new phenomenon of coworking is clearly part of a major transformation of the organization of work.

REFERENCES

Brown, J. (2017). Curating the "third Place"? Coworking and the mediation of creativity. *Geoforum, 82,* 112–126. doi:10.1016/j.geoforum.2017.04.006

Deskmag. (2017). *Final results of the global coworking survey in charts.* Author.

Fabbri, J. (2015). *Les espaces de coworking pour entrepreneurs. Nouveaux espaces de travail et dynamiques interorganisationnelles collaboratives.* Thèse en Ecole polytechnique, Palaiseau.

Fabbri, J. (2016). Les espaces de coworking: Ni tiers-lieux, in incubateurs, ni fab-Lab. *Entreprendre et Innover, 31*(4), 8–16. doi:10.3917/entin.031.0008

Fabbri J. (2017). Les espaces de coworking: ni tiers-lieux, ni incubateurs, ni fab.labs. *Entreprendre & Innover, 31,* 8-16.

Fabbri, J., & Charue-Duboc, F. (2013). Un modèle d'accompagnement entrepreneurial fondé sur des apprentissages au sein d'un collectif d'entrepreneurs: Le cas de La Ruche. *Management International, 17*(3), 86–99. doi:10.7202/1018269ar

Fabbri, J., & Charue-Duboc, F. (2016). Les espaces de coworking: nouveaux intermédiaires d'innovation ouverte? *Revue française de gestion, 254,* 163-180.

Garrett, L., Spreitzer, G., & Bacevice, P. (2017). Co-constructing a sense of community at work: The emergence of community in coworking spaces. *Organization Studies, 6*(38), 821–842. doi:10.1177/0170840616685354

Geldron, A. (2013). L'obsolescence programmée est-elle une stratégie répandue? *Pour la Science, 425.*

Gershenfeld, N. (2005). *FAB: The Coming Revolution on Your Desktop – From Personal Computers to Personal Fabrication.* Basic Books.

Krauss & Tremblay. (Eds.) (2019). *Tiers-lieux – travailler et entreprendre sur les territoires: Espaces de co-working, fab labs, hack labs.* Academic Press.

Liefooghe, C. (2016). Tiers-lieux, coworking spaces et fab labs: nouveaux lieux, nouveaux liens et construction de communautés de connaissance créatives. In Lille, métropole créative? Nouveaux liens, nouveaux lieux, nouveaux territoires. Lille: Presses universitaires du Septentrion.

Oldenburg, R. (1989). *The great good place: Cafes, coffee shops, community centers, beauty parlors, general stores, bars, hangouts and how they get you through the day*. Paragon House.

Oldenburg, R. (1999). *The great good place: Cafes, coffee shops, bookstores, bars, hair salons, and other hangouts at the heart of a community*. Marlowe.

Oldenburg, R. (2000). *Celebrating the Third Place: Inspiring Stories about the Great Good Places at the Heart of Our Communities*. Marlowe.

Scaillerez, A., & Tremblay, D-G. (2016a). Co-working: une nouvelle tendance qui favorise la flexibilité du travail, Volet économie. *Revue État du Québec*, 215-218.

Scaillerez, A., & Tremblay, D-G. (2016b). Les espaces de co-working, les avantages du partage. *Revue Gestion de HEC Montréal, 41*(2), 90-92.

Scaillerez, A., & Tremblay, D-G. (2016c, May). Le télétravail, comme nouveau mode de régulation de la flexibilisation et de l'organisation du travail: analyse et impact du cadre légal européen et nord-américain, *Revue des Organisations Responsables*, 21-31.

Scaillerez, A., & Tremblay, D.-G. (2017). Coworking, fab labs et living labs, État des connaissances sur les tiers-lieux. *Territoire en mouvement Revue de géographie et aménagement, 34*. http://tem.revues. org/4200

Smits M. (2015). *Les tiers-lieux sont-ils reproductibles à grande échelle? Étude de la viabilité de l'intégration de ces espaces dans un processus d'aménagement formalisé*. Projet de fin d'étude, ENPC, 61.

ADDITIONAL READING

Bilandzic, M., & Foth, M. (2016) Designing hubs for connected learning: Social, spatial and technological insights from coworking, hackerpaces and meetup Groups. *Place-Based Spaces for Networked Learning*. Consulté à l'adresse http://eprints.qut.edu.au/83742/

Bilandzic, M. V. (2013) The embodied hybrid space: designing social and digital interventions to facilitate connected learning in coworking spaces. Consulté à l'adresse http://eprints.qut.edu.au/62872

Capdevila, I. (2013). Knowledge dynamics in localized communities: Coworking spaces as microclusters. *Available at SSRN 2414121*. Consulté à l'adresse https://papers.ssrn.com/sol3/papers.cfm?abstract_id=2414121

Capdevila, I. (2014). Coworking spaces and the localized dynamics of innovation in Barcelona. *Proceedings of ISPIM Conferences*, n°26, 1-25. 10.2139srn.2502813

Capdevila, I. (2014). *Coworking spaces and the localized dynamics of innovation. The case of Barcelona*. Working Paper. Consulté à l'adresse https://www.researchgate.net/profile/Ignasi_Capdevila/publication/269401092_Coworking_spaces_and_the_localized_dynamics_of_innovation._The_case_of_Barcelona/links/5489bc910cf214269f1aba30.pdf

Foth, M., Forlano, L., & Bilandzic, M. (2017). The City is My Office: Mapping New Work Practices in the Smart City. *Handbuch Soziale Praktiken und Digitale Alltagswelten*. Consulté à l'adresse http://eprints.qut.edu.au/96279/

Fuzi, A., Clifton, N., & Loudon, G. (2015) New spaces for supporting entrepreneurship? Co-working spaces in the Welsh entrepreneurial landscape. International Conference for Entrepreneurship, Innovation and Regional Development. Consulté à l'adresse https://repository.cardiffmet.ac.uk/dspace/handle/10369/7478

Gandini, A. (2016). Coworking: The Freelance Mode of Organisation? In The Reputation Economy (p. 97-105). Palgrave Macmillan UK. doi:10.1057/978-1-137-56107-7_7

Hartmann, P. D. M. (2016). Coworking oder auch die (De-) Mediatisierung von Arbei. In J. Wimmer & M. Hartmann (Eds.), *Medien-Arbeit im Wandel* (pp. 177–204). Springer Fachmedien Wiesbaden., doi:10.1007/978-3-658-10912-7_9

Pierre, X. (2015). L'apport des espaces de travail collaboratif dans le domaine de l'accompagnement des entrepreneurs : L'animation de réseaux de pairs. *Revue de l'Entrepreneuriat, 1*(13), 51–73.

Pierre, X., Burret, A. (2014) Animateur d'espaces de coworking, un nouveau métier ? *Entreprendre & Innover*, n°23, 20-30.

KEY TERMS AND DEFINITIONS

Business Opportunity: Opportunities that can be offered to users in the same coworking space, provided that coworkers are open to this opportunity to collaborate together on a business project.

Collaboration: This is one of the major goals of a coworking space. It is an attempt to organize meetings between coworkers in order to encourage professional cooperation.

Community Manager: Person in charge of the management and animation of a coworking space. This feature greatly contributes to the success of a coworking space and its profitability. The job is however little recognized and low paid. It also happens that coworking spaces do not have the financial means to remunerate the function. The tasks are then entrusted to the founders of the place or to trainees or volunteers.

Coworkers: Users of coworking spaces. They are generally entrepreneurs or nomadic workers, and sometimes employees of companies, or even employees of public administrations. They use these places for several reasons such as improving their business opportunities, reducing their business expenses by sharing premises, fighting isolation, or better reconciling their private and professional lives.

Coworking Spaces: Sharing place to connect coworkers in order to facilitate their meeting and possibly to create business opportunities.

Networking: Opportunity created by the presence in the same place of several people with various professional activities and skills. Networking allows coworkers to pool their knowledge and clients to create new profitable business opportunities for each participant.

Sharing: We can consider that two forms of sharing can be found in coworking spaces. These places allow first of all an acquired sharing which is the sharing of premises and also professional equipment (photocopiers, printers, meeting rooms ...) and equipment of conviviality (collective kitchen, free coffee, rest room ...). They can also spark a second form of sharing, but that depends on the coworkers' will. Here, we refer to the sharing of the professional network, good practices between coworkers with related activities or exchange of ideas and development of common business opportunities.

Third Places: New workplaces that allow users to get closer to their home work by reducing the time and commuting distance between home and workplace, thus offering them a better work-family balance.

These third places can also allow remote work without staying at home. These places are inclusive (open to all) and seek to promote the sharing and improvement of working conditions, as well as user activity.

15

ENDNOTE

[1]   MAP OF EUROPEAN. SPACES OF COWORKING. By Irene León, Big Data Technician and Digital Analyst for FACE Entrepreneurship (pdf): link www.face-entrepreneurship.eu/images/Face/knowledge/88/Europe_Coworking.pdf

Jeans, Flip Flips, and Suit Jackets:
The Mixing Bowl of Today's Business Attire

Sara Joy Krivacek

Clemson University, USA

INTRODUCTION

In a competitive nature to recruit and keep the most talented workers, companies are constantly evolving to meet different generations' needs and preferences. One factor, in particular, that has evolved overtime is the accepted norm for work attire. While there lies a wide spectrum of variables that determine a company's dress code, companies, as well as current or potential employees, have an increased awareness about work attire. Steve Jobs, Mark Zuckerberg, and Mark Cuban are successful people who believe in or wear casual attire in the workplace. Steve Jobs wore a black turtleneck religiously with jeans and sneakers. According to a Forbes article, Jobs not only felt comfortable in this clothing, but it also allowed him to focus less on his choice of attire, and more on work (Smith, 2012). Zuckerberg wears jeans and a t-shirt for similar reasons. Finally, Cuban passionately expresses his opinion against suits as he once stated in his blog, "I just could never think of any good reason for any sane person to wear a suit in the first place. Exactly what purpose does a suit serve?...Does wearing a tie make us work harder or smarter?" (Blog Maverick, 2007). Whether it is for marketing purposes, making a statement, or other various reasons (Clifford, 2011), employees, specifically millennials, have had an immense impact on the attire policy in the workplace.

This chapter utilizes the intrinsic business case study analysis to better understand work attire and its evolution, and offer recommendations for companies. The chapter first defines work attire and provides a literature review and useful theories on its impact in the workforce. Then, the author categorizes and details the three different types of work attire: business professional, business casual, and casual. Finally, the author analyzes three different companies that contain a variety of dress policies and represent each of the three categories mentioned prior. It is important to note that the topic, discussion, and purpose of the chapter is work attire, and the business cases incorporated in the chapter play a supportive role in understanding the topic. Arguments for and against different work attire and final recommendations are made based on the research.

BACKGROUND

Work attire can be defined in several ways, whether it is "the clothing (e.g. jacket, skirt, pants) and artifacts (e.g. name tag, smock, jewelry) that employees of an organization wear while at work" (Rafaeli & Pratt, 1993, p. 34), or "an assemblage of body modifications and/or supplements displayed by a person in communicating with other human beings" (Eicher & Roach-Higgins, 1992, pg. 15). Overall, it can be seen as nonverbal communication and expression in the workplace. Rafaeli and Pratt (1993) developed a framework for the study of organizational dress. This framework addressed how extra-organizational factors (societal and institutional standards) as well as intra-organizational factors (values and structure)

DOI: 10.4018/978-1-7998-3473-1.ch184

15

significantly influenced organizational dress. In addition, dress can impact multiple factors, including first impressions (Davis, 1984), the way a person behaves (Adam & Galinsky, 2012; Davis & Lennon, 1988; Johnson, Yoo, Kim, & Lennon, 2008), as well as the way a person feels about him/herself (Peluchette, Karl, & Rust, 2006). It is important to note that there are various factors, outside of the company's policies and guidelines, that impact employee dress.

Several theories have been useful in explaining various influences and impacts that work attire can have on an employee, as well as other coworkers. First, in alignment with role theory, an employee may dress according to his/her part in the company in order to exemplify how he/she wants others to perceive him/herself. According to role theory, which was developed in the 1920s and 1930s through theoretical works of Mead, Moreno, Parsons, and Linton, people may behave in a predictable, context-specific situation based on social situations, hierarchical chains, and other factors (Biddle, 1986; Hindin, 2007). For example, a new manager in a company may dress more professionally in hopes to receive respect and set the level of expectation of appropriate attire for other employees. The manager may feel the need to dress business professional due to his/her role in the company. In addition, impression formation theory can help explain the impacts attire has on the workforce. Impression formation (Fiske & Neuberg, 1990) describes an impression made on a person's character based on available information, such as attire. In other words, employees may perceive one another based on the attire that he/she is wearing. This theory is especially important in relation to work attire policy when considering if a company is client-focused.

Defining and categorizing work attire can be difficult as there are countless options and interpretations. Eicher and Roach-Higgins (1992) declare "that systems for defining and classifying types of dress are frequently incomplete, and that the terminology used is ambiguous and inconsistent" (p. 13). For instance, many definitions of dress do not consider "body modifications, from skin coloring to perfumes and hairdress" (Eicher and Roach-Higgins, 1992, p.13). Colbert (2014) defined dress categories according to three attributes: color, material, and style of clothing. There are endless qualitative observations when analyzing a person's dress. Therefore, for the purposes of this paper, work attire will be strictly defined as the clothing, shoes, and accessories (i.e. jewelry, scarves, hats, etc.) both men and women wear in the workforce. Similar to the definition, the categories of work attire can be endless. To remain consistent within the scope of this paper, three categories of work attire are addressed for both genders: business professional, business casual, and casual. Each category will be discussed in further detail in the following section.

DRESS CATEGORIES

Business Professional

The business professional attire can be viewed as the traditional clothing policy that many corporations have adopted since the 19th century. More specifically, this is the attire that millennials are rejecting. Business professional can vary according to gender, but for simplicities sake, it can be viewed as the suit-and-tie, dress pants, suit jackets, dresses, and so forth. Many corporations require this type of attire, especially when interacting with customers. It is almost expected, unless otherwise stated, that interviewees wear traditional business professional clothing in the job application process. In fact, Mosca and Buzza (2013) establish three main effects in "dressing for success: maintain respect, establish credibility, and establish yourself as an authority figure" (p. 63). Many employees utilize this dress category also to establish strong first impressions. In fact, college students are taught that first impressions are made within the first minute of interaction, and this can be critical for potential hiring success rates (Burgess-Wilkerson & Thomas, 2009). There are many studies that argue for the benefits of business professional attire in the workplace, which will be discussed in the following section.

Arguments for Business Professional

"Dress for success" has been popular advice for employees in the workforce. Employees should essentially dress the part, whether it is to be taken more seriously, impress for an interview, or dress for a desired position. "Dress for success" can even stem outside of the workforce. McMillian (2014) believes in encouraging undergraduate students to dress professionally for "better practice for the world and increase student opportunities" (p. 1). Professional dress can be very specific and send strong messages. Eicher and Roach-Higgins (1992) even note that "specific differences in color, structure, surface design, volume, or texture distinguish dress of males and females, differences in social rank and power can be made obvious" (p. 20).

Professional attire can be seen as an indication of conformity (Burgess-Wilkerson & Thomas, 2009). Thus, there can be less distractions in the workforce when everyone is dressed to the same code. A business professional dress code can limit any confusion on what to wear to work. McMillan (2014) states his students perform better when they dress professionally. There have also been concerns that work ethic will weaken when business professional clothing is not mandated. Business consultant Andrew Jensen notes that if an office has more of a traditional environment (i.e. not as relaxed), then casual dress would negatively impact the work ethic (Goodman, 2016); therefore, business professional would be the appropriate option. Moreover, attire can have a significant impact on the way employees work and think. Research shows that formal dress workers feel more powerful and are more adept to higher level of abstract thinking (Slepian, Ferber, Gold, & Rutchick, 2015; Goodman, 2016).

Finally, if a company interacts with clients or customers frequently, it is important to establish trust and create a good impression. Business consultant Andrew Jensen argues that "customers will judge a business's productivity based solely on its level of professionalism" (Jensen, 2018). Therefore, attire communicates and sends strong messages about the employee as a person, as well as the company he/she represents.

Arguments Against Business Professional

Conversely, conformity is not necessarily always a positive aspect for employee dress attire. There should be a limit to which employees conform with the attire and workplace norms (Burgess-Wilkerson & Thomas, 2009). The word "conform" in itself may carry a negative connotation and limit the freedom of expression or individuality for an employee. Company morale may not be as high when restricting employees to a specific attire code, especially if competitors are allowing looser dress codes. Most businesses were relaxing their dress code by the mid-1990s (Kiddie, 2009).

Furthermore, this strict dress code is costlier to employees (Gutierrez & Freese, 1999). Besides the high-quality clothing that employees are expected to wear every day, proper maintenance such as dry cleaning is also another cost the employee has to bear. If an employee is not conducting an outside meeting or scheduled with a customer, it can be questioned why business professional attire is mandated. As stated earlier, Mark Cuban questions why a person has to wear a suit and tie in order to be successful. In alignment with this, it can be argued that an employee is more productive, happy, and creative when he/she wears clothes that are laxer than formal business attire (Goodman, 2016; Gutierrez & Freese, 1999).

Business Casual

15

In between the two extremes, a majority of employees play it "safe" by finding an option somewhere in the middle, or business casual. Shri and Nair (2009) define business casual as "dressing professionally, looking relaxed, neat and pulled together. A more pragmatic way of putting this would be that business casual dress is the mid ground between formal business clothes and street clothes" (p. 102). While a suit and tie may be too formal, open-toed shoes and tank tops may be too casual. Therefore, this category leans more toward the "conservative casual" type, and "looser business professional" type. Gragg (2004) does a nice job defining the business casual attire, which can consist of the following items:

- Nice jeans and a clean tee-shirt with no slogan
- Khakis and a company logo polo shirt
- Khakis and a nice polo shirt
- Khakis, oxford shirt, and blazer
- Dress pants and oxford shirt
- Dress pants and dressy shirt with a blazer, or a mid-calf skirt or dress for women with a blazer—unbuttoned on Friday's

Many companies have adopted a business casual attire. However, it is not uncommon for employees to bring a suit jacket into work in case he/she needs to interact with a customer or attend an important meeting.

Arguments for Business Casual

As stated previously, this attire may be more appropriate and relevant if an employee does not have an outside meeting or is not scheduled with a customer. According to one study, people felt more productive in business casual clothes (Shri & Nair, 2009). Franz and Norton (2001) found in their study that performance outcomes were not negatively affected with business casual attire, and thus recommend to continue this dress code as long as employees desire it. A study based on a survey response showed that candidates enjoy wearing casual clothing at work as it makes them feel more comfortable, and can be viewed as an incentive to attract new employees (Gutierrez & Freese, 1999). Thomas Kiddie (2009) even noted that his decision to accept Bell Labs offer over IBM was the casual dress code. This middle ground attire is a "safe" call for employees, which still offers them some freedom. Business consultant Andrew Jensen notes that if the culture and office environment is already relaxed, then a more casual dress would not negatively impact the work ethic (Goodman, 2016).

Arguments Against Business Casual

Business casual can cause some confusion on the guidelines of what is acceptable to wear. Some employees may lean on the more conservative side of business casual, while others may take more advantage of the "casual" aspect, which engenders less conformity and more confusion. More specifically, Shri and Nair (2009) note that "business casual dress code has no generally-accepted definition; its interpretation differs widely among organizations and is often a cause of sartorial confusion among workers."

Research also shows that there are gender differences in perception of business casual (Shri & Nair, 2009). Depending on what gender is in charge of regulating appropriate dress attire, this can be conflicting. Rafaeli, Dutton, Harquail, & Mackie-Lewis (1997) conducted an in-depth interview with women to learn more about perceptions and efforts in choosing attire. The results demonstrate that many women dress to "be emotionally comfortable and confident in their current position" (Rafaeli et al., 1997; Sullivan, 1997, p. 91). Some women prefer to dress for the job they want, and business casual may be too casual for women who choose attire to help them achieve their organizational roles (Rafaeli et al., 1997).

Casual

The final dress category can be seen as the most relaxed and has the least amount of restrictions. Companies that allow a casual attire offer many options for the employee. Clothing can range from jeans, t-shirts, flip flops, and even tank tops to distressed jeans. The employee has much independence and authority in choosing what he/she wears to work. However, it can be difficult to clearly differentiate between the lines of business casual and casual. For instance, a conservative employee that dresses on the nicer side of the "casual" category and a person who dresses on the looser side of the "business casual" category can create a blur between the two attires. Therefore, it should be noted that there is a "gray space" between dress codes. Casual attire also tends to have more options in terms of the types of clothes to wear; therefore, it can be difficult to clearly establish what is and what is not acceptable in the workplace.

Arguments for Casual

Casual attire allows for many different options, offering employees more freedom to choose what to wear. Therefore, employees that have more options in choosing what to wear will help them be emotionally comfortable and confident in their job (Rafaeli et al., 1997; Sullivan, 1997). Employees should not feel uncomfortable or restricted in the clothes they choose to wear all day. Rather, their choice of clothing should allow them to feel comfortable and offer them more time to focus on work, and less on blistering heels or tight collared shirts. Companies have noted that casual dress even increases morale and productivity (Gardin, 1998; Gutierrez & Freese, 1999), and is considered an added employee benefit (Gutierrez & Freese, 1999). One of the most important benefits to casual attire is making the employees feel comfortable and happy. These two positive results can lead to an increase in productivity (Goodman, 2016). As seen in the prior examples of Mark Zuckerberg and Mark Cuban, it can be argued that what an employee wears does not define how successful he or she is going to be.

While specific roles may require the business professional attire, the Wall Street Journal makes an argument for the casual attire for many different business settings. The article points out that this new trend is not only for and about young people, but rather to showcase a unique and modern statement for the employees and potential customers (Binkley, 2008). Companies are gradually changing their dress codes, thus sending out an important message to employees and customers.

Arguments Against Casual

A concern for companies may be that "relaxed" clothing may mean "relaxed" employees, in that the urgency of getting the job done becomes nonexistent. A professor of Psychology at the University of Hertfordshire, Dr. Karen Pine, told Forbes that "when we put on an item of clothing it is common for the wearer to adopt the characteristics associated with that garment. A lot of clothing has symbolic meaning for us, whether it's 'professional work attire' or 'relaxing weekend wear,' so when we put it on we prime the brain to behave in a way consistent with that meaning" (Tulshyan, 2013). Similar with this notion is the blurred lines of professionalism in the workplace. In affecting employees' performance and attitude, some argue that casual attire can lead to laziness and decrease in professionalism (Goodman, 2016). Companies are concerned that dressing casually will harm their professional image (Gutierrez & Freese, 1999). If a company frequently interacts with customers or clients, trust is also another important issue. Customers may be less trusting or cautious in a meeting with an employee who dresses casually. Therefore, the casual attire may negatively affect company performance in the client-oriented world.

Gardin (1998) notes four "taboos" that can occur when wearing too casual: short shorts, after-five attire, sheer blouses, and distressed jeans. She notes that it is not appropriate to wear the same clothes to work to "go out" in after work. She also argues that sheer blouses and distressed jeans can be distracting and make it difficult for coworkers to concentrate. The menu of various options can be overwhelming for women. More specifically, the emotional costs for women with relaxed dress codes "may lead to even greater stress for employees because they must learn new definitions of appropriate work attire" (Sullivan, 1997, p. 91).

Finally, besides the impression the attire will present to other coworkers, clients, or customers, employees may also face difficulty in understanding what is acceptable. As Gragg (2004) phrases it, everyone knew the "code" with business professional. It could even be argued that there is less room for confusion with business causal also. However, there is much more room for interpretation, and difficulty in understanding the "code" for casual attire. With the various and unlimited options, employees may feel overwhelmed and uncertain, thus increasing the stress level about work attire.

METHODOLOGY

This current chapter explores different dress policies via the business case study method. The intrinsic research method in this chapter does not aim on building theory or understanding a phenomenon, but rather provides insight into this topic. The selected business cases offer support for the three categories of work attire, and create a sound argument when ultimately making a recommendation to companies. Three companies were analyzed for this paper: American Eagle Outfitters, General Motors, and UBS. The author selected the following companies because they were significantly different from one another in regards to dress code policy, and each followed along with the three different spectrums discussed above. Each company has a unique or specific dress code, some vastly different from others. The goal is to provide information on companies with dress codes on a wide spectrum in order to offer a valid argument and recommendations. Information about each company will entail an overview of the business, how successful the company has been in the past, and its required (if so) dress code for the employees and its associated work attire category. Unless stated otherwise, information about each company has been retrieved from the company's website. There are no hypotheses in this case study, but rather the author analyzes the different categories and makes a recommendation based on the research and presented companies.

BUSINESS CASES

Case 1: American Eagle

American Eagle Outfitters (AEO) is a retailer company that offers apparel to a variety of customers. Originally founded in 1977, AEO offers products to both men and women, ranging from teens to young adults. In addition, the company offers intimate products under the Aerie Brand. The company operates over 1,000 stores and ships to eighty-one countries through its online channel. AEO has its main headquarters located in Pittsburgh, Pennsylvania and its design and production office located in New York City, New York. For the purposes of this paper, it can be assumed that referring to AEO means both AE and Aerie sectors in the Corporate environment.

According to the work attire categories mentioned above, AEO falls under "casual" attire. Employees have significant freedom in their choice of attire. For instance, jeans, flip flops, tank tops, distressed jeans are all acceptable options. A casual attire can give employees more confidence and make them feel comfortable to be productive in the workforce. AEO's website reiterates the importance of high morale and expression of individuality: "We believe that our associates are our most valuable assets and we want them to feel motivated and have the freedom to be themselves at work. We strive to be an employer of choice – a place where people are excited to come to work because they believe in what we do, enjoy working with each other, and have fun doing it" (American Eagle; Aerie: Who We Are). In addition, reviews for working at the company were positive from both Indeed and Glassdoor (American Eagle Outfitters: Pittsburgh, PA). Multiple reviews included the relaxed and casual atmosphere as a "pro" for working for the company (American Eagle Outfitters). AEO is just one example of a company that offers a casual attire for employees every day of the week.

Case 2: General Motors

General Motors, or GM is American multinational corporation. While the company has a vast array of services, it is most known for creating automobiles. The company's goal has been aimed at advancing technology and transportation in order to bring the number of crashes, emissions, and congestion to a halt. GM is headquartered in Detroit, Michigan, where it employs almost 200,000 people. Innovation is at the heart of GM, and dress code is no exception. The company has evolved drastically with its attire policy for employees (Murphy, 2018). In prior years, GM held a strict and complex dress code policy that ran about ten pages long (Murphy, 2018). However, after bankruptcy hit the company in 2009, vice-president of global human resources at the time Mary Barra made drastic changes to the work attire expectations. From ten pages, Barra cut down the expectations to a two-word policy: "dress appropriately" (Murphy, 2018). Barra's determination to improve morale and change the company culture resulted in her promotion to CEO in 2014. She gives much credit to the dress code as the "smallest biggest change" made at GM, which helped lead the company to a record sales year in 2014 (Feloni, 2015). Despite giving employees much freedom in expression, there were many different interpretations and much pushback from higher-level employees (Murphy, 2018).

According to the work attire categories, GM can be classified as a mix between business casual and casual. The company was once a business professional attire setting, but Barra's changes allowed the employees to dress between the business casual and casual. It is not uncommon for employees to wear jeans to work, however, after some complaints by managers, it was decided that employees bring nicer clothes to work in case of a meeting (Murphy, 2018). Therefore, employees may decide to lean towards a more casual style, and change when necessary.

Case 3: United Bank of Switzerland (UBS)

Union Bank of Switzerland, or UBS, is an investment banking company founded and based in Switzerland. This global firm provides financial services in over fifty countries, including the United States. In addition to private banking, UBS provides an array of services including wealth management, asset management, and investment banking for private, corporate, and institutional clients. Founded over one hundred fifty years ago, their strongest presence now lies in the United States. UBS's strategy is "focus[ed] on businesses that have strong competitive position in their targeted markets, are capital efficient and have an attractive long-term structural growth or profitability outlook." The company further credits its success to the talented and hard-working employees that comprise the company. Therefore, it is always important to keep morale high and create incentives for high-skilled prospective workers.

Similar to General Motors, UBS has seen some changes within the dress code. Originally forty-four pages long, the company's business attire is strictly business professional (Wachtel, 2011). As the company interacts with current and new clients every day, it is very important for the company to present a professional image. However, the forty-four-page document goes into much depth to outline detailed requirements, such as skin-colored underwear and how to smell nice (Wachtel, 2011). After much backlash and ridicule, the company decided to revise its dress code. The company revised to a more modest guide, compared to the detailed guide that told women how to apply make-up, men how to tie a tie, and reminded all to trim their toenails (Berton, 2010). Currently, the company does not have a formalized dress code for the staff, but rather leaves the decision to bankers' discretion as to what is appropriate ("Dress Code Draws Cool Reception", 2017).

DISCUSSION

After analyzing the companies above, it can be seen that there are various dress codes and policies enforced (or not) in the workforce. American Eagle Outfitters, General Motors, and UBS all offer unique dress codes, and some have altered it over time in order to stay relevant. While these companies lie on different ends of the spectrum, it is important to provide opposing views in order to make a sound argument. The recommendation in the following section is based on the above companies discussed and the prior research on employee attire in the workforce.

Recommendations

It is very difficult to recommend a "one-size-fits-all" approach. In fact, according to a study done on physician dress on patient perceptions, it was concluded that this "one-size-fits-all" approach is "improbable" (Petrilli, Mack, Petrilli, Hickner, Saint, & Chopra, 2015, p. 14). The study shows that there are many outlying factors, such as age, geography, and interaction, rather than just clothing, that impact patient trust, confidence, and perceptions (Petrilli et al., 2015). Likewise, with attire in the business setting, there are many additional factors that can impact morale, productivity, and performance. However, it is important to argue for guidelines that businesses can refer to when implementing, or considering to change, new dress code policies. Overall, a more flexible dress code that offers the employee more freedom is recommended to all companies, but this chapter also keeps in mind certain situations.

First, it is important to establish if the company is customer-oriented, and if so, what message (i.e. appearance) the company wants to send to the customer. Attire can serve as a form of non-verbal communication, thus, it is vital to form good impressions. In alignment with impression formation theory, it is essential for client-focused companies to maintain a respectable and trustworthy reputation. While research has supported benefits to both the person and surrounding people of the person wearing professional attire, a too structured atmosphere can create an "impersonal" and "mechanic" experience (Barrick, Dustin, Giluk, Steward, Shaffer, & Swider, 2012). Therefore, it may not always be necessary to have business professional attire in the presence of customers, but it is important to keep in mind the drawbacks discussed earlier that can arise with a laxer appearance. If the company interacts frequently with customers or clients, it is advised that employees first match the customer's attire or err on the more formal side when in doubt. Therefore, business casual to business professional would be advised in these situations of doubt. In alignment with role theory, an employee in a client-focused company can dress in a way that ties to the duties, expectations, and responsibilities of his/her current role. This more formal wear also is important in the face-to-face interview setting. If an interviewee has uncertainty on what is appropriate, it is recommended to err on the more formal side.

If the company is not customer-oriented, it is recommended to allow employees to express more freedom of individuality in their attire. As Millennials are gradually taking over the workforce, freedom in choice of attire will continue to have a strong presence. Therefore, employees can have the freedom to choose attire ranging from business casual to casual. According to prior research, there are numerous benefits to a more relaxed attire. In order to keep up with the competition in recruiting the best employees, companies need to adjust prior traditional habits and allow more freedom of expression to the employee. As seen in the provided examples above, companies have already started to focus on improving morale.

Second, unless the dress code is business professional, companies need to form clear guidelines that would eliminate any points of confusion for employees. For instance, a company with a casual attire policy could enforce no tank tops, skirts shorter than finger-length, or open-toed shoes. Whatever image the company wants to present, it is important to lay out a clear policy that addresses what is *not* permitted in the workforce. Instead of suggesting what is appropriate to wear to work, it is advised to allow the employee creativity and freedom, and only state what is not appropriate. By allowing an employee to dress creatively, it may cognitively help him/her to think more creatively as well (Slepian et. al, 2015). Although Barra's goal was to allow employees the autonomy and responsibility to "dress appropriately," that loose guideline may cause too much confusion and conflict as there are numerous interpretations of what would be considered acceptable. However, it is important to be mindful when creating guidelines, as an extensive and thorough review (i.e. 10 pages) can become a drawback.

Finally, it is advised that companies stick with the dress code for all days the employee works. For instance, it is not recommended to have business casual Monday through Thursday, and casual "jean day" on Friday, or "casual" summers. This can cause change in employee attitude, performance, and motivation in the workforce (Goodman, 2016; Sullivan, 1997). Businesses should be consistent and stick with one attire, and outlined in a policy if necessary. It is recommended that businesses create a change in the dress code policy that aligns with the culture, or vision of the culture, of each company. Drastic changes can cause significant shifts in employees and the environment.

FUTURE DIRECTION FOR RESEARCH

As evident in the chapter, attire can be difficult to define. There are several variables that comprise an employee's attire. Opportunities for future research include analyzing work attire beyond the strict clothing and accessories of an employee. For instance, hair styling, makeup, tattoos, and so forth should all be considered for the overall "look" for the employee. Therefore, research on productivity, performance, motivation, and morale can all be better judged according to the whole "look" of the employee.

Next, there is opportunity to study how work attire impacts other variables. Future research, for instance, can expand into how casual dress can impact the hierarchy and managerial style in a business. Longitudinal studies or even comparison studies of different firms can be analyzed to determine differences that might originate from work attire. There must be constant awareness from a business perspective in what the current trend for employees is, and also what direction it will take in order for businesses to be successful and recruit the best candidates.

Managerial Implications

Each company identified in the chapter represents one-way employees adhere to proper work attire. It should be noted that not all dress codes in the workforce have been addressed. The research conducted by the author only provides a small framework for future research. Therefore, the small number of firms could be a limitation. However, the author believes that the companies represent varying options of attire, and that the recommendations could be transferrable to other industries, subject to further study.

Other implications include the blurred line between the work attire categorizations. It can be a challenge, and a matter of interpretation, to distinguish between "business casual" and "casual." This confusion between the categories can make it difficult to clearly define a company's attire, and more importantly, recommend what should be the appropriate attire. Furthermore, it is difficult to make a sound argument for a company without prior knowledge of the current business culture. For instance, if a company has a current traditional and stricter environment, changing the dress code to more casual may have a larger impact on performance compared to making that change to a company that has a current relaxed culture and environment. The author made recommendations based on the research and from an external look at each company.

Overall, the research provides insight into the transformation of attire in the workforce, and also offers direction of how companies can change in the future. It is possible that attire will continuously change in the workforce in the immediate and long-term future.

CONCLUSION

It is vital for companies to continuously evolve to meet employees' preferences and needs. In a fast-changing work environment, companies need to stay in tune with competition, the current trend, and preferences in order to recruit and retain the best employees. Work attire is one variable that different generations have seen evolve over the years. Companies need to first establish the "look" they want to convey to other employees, potential customers, and the public before deciding on an appropriate work attire. Second, companies should allow more freedom to their employees if possible. Flexibility in options for the employee and freedom in choice of attire can pose as a desirable quality for a company, especially to Millennials. Although there can be conflicting issues with any work attire policy, it is important to establish important guidelines from beginning. An increased awareness into the work attire evolution and willingness to adapt is crucial for employee morale and success of a company.

ACKNOWLEDGMENT

The author wishes to thank the reviewers for their valuable contributions and input into the final paper.

REFERENCES

Adam, H., & Galinsky, A. D. (2012). Enclothed Cognition. *Journal of Experimental Social Psychology*, *48*(4), 918–925. doi:10.1016/j.jesp.2012.02.008

American Eagle. (n.d.a). *Aerie: Who We Are*. Retrieved March 13, 2019 from https://aeo.jobs/info/page1

American Eagle. (n.d.b). *Aerie: Corporate Opportunities*. Retrieved March 8, 2019 from https://aeo.jobs/page/corporate-opportunities-at-aeo-23

American Eagle Outfitters. (n.d.). *Indeed*. Retrieved March 15, 2019 from https://www.indeed.com/cmp/American-Eagle-Outfitters/reviews?fcountry=US&floc=Pittsburgh%2C+PA

American Eagle Outfitters. Pittsburgh, PA. (n.d.). *Glassdoor*. Retrieved March 13, 2019 from https://www.glassdoor.com/Location/American-Eagle-Outfitters-Pittsburgh-Location-EI_IE2642.0,25_IL.26,36_IC1152990.htm

American Eagle Outfitters, Inc (AEO). (n.d.). *Reuters*. Retrieved March 8, 2019 from https://www.reuters.com/finance/stocks/financial-highlights/AEO

Barrick, M. R., Dustin, S. L., Giluk, T. L., Steward, G. L., Shaffer, J. A., & Swider, B. W. (2012). Candidate characteristics driving initial impressions during rapport building: Implications for employment interview validity. *Journal of Occupational and Organizational Psychology*, *85*(2), 330–352. doi:10.1111/j.2044-8325.2011.02036.x

Berton, E. (2010). UBS Dress Code is a Smart Idea. *The Wall Street Journal*. Retrieved March 19, 2019 from https://blogs.wsj.com/source/2010/12/15/ubs-dress-code-is-smart-idea/

Biddle, B. J. (1986). Recent developments in role theory. *Annual Review of Sociology*, *12*(1), 67–92. doi:10.1146/annurev.so.12.080186.000435

Binkley, C. (2008). How to Pull Off 'CEO Casual': The Goal: Shed the Stodgy Suit but Keep The Authority; One Executive's Views On Custom Shirts and Chest Hair. *Wall Street Journal*. Retrieved February 25, 2019 from https://www.wsj.com/articles/SB121806871823918831

Burgess-Wilkerson, B., & Thomas, J. (2009). Lessons From *Ugly Betty*: Business Attire As A Conformity Strategy. *Business Communication Quarterly*, *72*(3), 365–368. doi:10.1177/1080569909340684

Clifford, S. (2011). Power of Apparel: A Look That Conveys a Message. *The New York Times*. Retrieved February 25, 2019 from https://www.nytimes.com/2011/03/05/business/05uniform.html

Colbert, C. (2014). *The Impact of Work Attire on Employee Behavior*. Retrieved March 4, 2019 from https://www.researchgate.net/publication/270890459_THE_IMPACT_OF_WORK_ATTIRE_ON_EM-PLOYEE_BEHAVIOR

Davis, L. L. (1984). Clothing and Human Behavior: A Review. *Home Economics Research Journal*, *12*(3), 325–339. doi:10.1177/1077727X8401200308

Davis, L. L., & Lennon, S. J. (1988). Social Cognition and the Study of Clothing and Human Behavior. *Social Behavior and Personality*, *16*(2), 175–186. doi:10.2224bp.1988.16.2.175

Dress Code Draws Cool Reception. (2017). *Finnews*. Retrieved March 20, 2019 from https://www.finews.com/news/english-news/27909-finance-dress-code-basler-kantonalbank-bkb-style-guide-ubs

Eicher, J., & Roach-Higgins, M. (1992). Definition and Classification of Dress: Implications for Analysis of Gender Roles. Berg Publishers, Inc.

Feloni, R. (2015). GM CEO Mary Barra explains how shrinking the dress code to 2 words reflects her mission for the company. *Business Insider*. Retrieved March 17, 2019 from https://www.businessinsider.com/gm-ceo-mary-barra-on-changing-gms-dress-code-2015-3

Fiske, S. T., & Neuberg, S. (1990). A Continuum of Impression Formation, from Category Based to Individuating Processes: Influences of Information and Motivation on Attention and Interpretation. *Advances in Experimental Social Psychology*, *23*(C), 1–74.

Franz, T., & Norton, D., S. (2001). Investigating business casual dress policies: Questionnaire development and exploratory research. *Applied H.R.M. Research*, *6*(2), 79–94.

Gardin, D. (1998). Summer Days Usher in Casual Work Attire. *Network Journal*, *5*(9), 7.

Goodman, C. (2016). Workers are dressing more casually. Does that affect productivity? *Miami Herald*. Retrieved March 18, 2019 from https://www.miamiherald.com/news/business/biz-columns-blogs/cindy-krischer-goodman/article90019197.html

Gragg, E. (2004). What do you mean "Business Casual?" *Office Solutions*, *21*(2), 42–44.

Gutierrez, T., & Freese, J. (1999). Benefit or Burden? Dress-Down Days. *The CPA Journal*. Retrieved March 18, 2019 from http://archives.cpajournal.com/1999/0499/Features/F320499.HTM

Hindin, M. J. (2007). Role theory. The Blackwell Encyclopedia of Sociology, 3959-3962.

Jensen, A. (2018). *How Does Workplace Attire Affect Productivity?* Retrieved March 18, 2019 from https://www.andrewjensen.net/how-does-workplace-attire-affect-productivity/

Johnson, K. K. P., Yoo, J.-J., Kim, M., & Lennon, S. J. (2008). Dress and human behavior: A review and critique of published research. *Clothing & Textiles Research Journal*, *26*(3), 3–22. doi:10.1177/0887302X07303626

Kiddie, T. (2009). Recent Trends in Business Casual Attire and Their Effects on Student Job Seekers. *Business Communication Quarterly*. Retrieved March 20, 2019 from http://homepages.se.edu/cvonbergen/files/2013/01/Recent-Trends-in-Business-Casual-Attire-and-Their-Effects-on-Student-Job-Seekers.pdf

McMillan, S. (2014). Dressing Up Our Students: Reasons Why Faculty Should Encourage Professional Attire in Undergraduates. *The Political Science Educator*. Retrieved March 18, 2019 from https://www.academia.edu/9288795/Dressing_Up_Our_Students_Reasons_Why_Faculty_Should_Encourage_Professional_Attire_in_Undergraduates

Mosca, J. B., & Buzza, J. B. (2013). Clothing and The Affects On a Teacher's Image: How Students View Them. *Contemporary Issues in Education Research*, 6(1), 59–65. doi:10.19030/cier.v6i1.7603

Murphy, B. (2018). GM Has a 2-Word Dress-Code, and It's Actually Brilliant. *Inc*. Retrieved March 17, 2019 from https://www.inc.com/bill-murphy-jr/this-giant-company-has-a-2-word-dress-code-its-actually-kind-of-brilliant.html

Peluchette, J. V., Karl, K., & Rust, K. (2006). Dressing to Impress: Beliefs and Attitudes Regarding Workplace Attire. *Journal of Business and Psychology*, 21(1), 45–63. doi:10.100710869-005-9022-1

Petrilli, C. M., Mack, M., Petrilli, J. J., Hickner, A., Saint, S., & Chopra, V. (2015). Understanding the role of physician attire on patient perceptions: A systematic review of the literature—targeting attire to improve likelihood of rapport (TAILOR) investigators. *BMJ Open*, 5(1), 1–18. doi:10.1136/bmjopen-2014-006578 PMID:25600254

Rafaeli, A., Dutton, J., Harquail, C., & Mackie-Lewis, S. (1997). Navigating by attire: The use of dress by female administrative employees. *Academy of Management Journal*, 40, 9–45.

Rafaeli, A., & Pratt, M. (1993). Tailored Meanings: On the Meaning and Impact of Organizational Dress. *Academy of Management Review*, 18(1), 32–55. doi:10.5465/amr.1993.3997506

Shri, C., & Nair, R. (2009). Gender Differences and Business Casual Attire. *SIES Journal of Management*, 6(2), 102–109.

Slepian, M. L., Ferber, S. N., Gold, J. M., & Rutchick, A. M. (2015). The Cognitive Consequences of Formal Clothing. *Social Psychological & Personality Science*, 6(6), 661–668. doi:10.1177/1948550615579462

Smith, J. (2012). Steve Jobs Always Dressed Exactly the Same. Here's Who Else Does. *Forbes*. Retrieved February 22, 2019 from https://www.forbes.com/sites/jacquelynsmith/2012/10/05/steve-jobs-always-dressed-exactly-the-same-heres-who-else-does/#5bc5196a5f53

Sullivan, S. (1997). Do clothes really make the woman? The use of attire to enhance work performance. *The Academy of Management Executive*, 11(4), 90–91. doi:10.5465/ame.1997.9712024841

Tulshyan, R. (2013). Is Casual Dress Killing Your Productivity At Work? *Forbes*. Retrieved February 25, 2019 from https://www.forbes.com/sites/ruchikatulshyan/2013/10/17/is-casual-dress-killing-your-productivity-at-work/

Wachtel, K. (2011). That Crazy 44-Page Long UBS Dresscode Got Ridiculed So Much That Now It's Getting 'Revised'. *Business Insider*. Retrieved March 19, 2019 from https://www.businessinsider.com/swiss-bank-ubs-changes-much-mocked-dress-code-garlic-underwear-smell-shower-january-2011-1

Why I Don't Wear a Suit and Can't Figure Out Why Anyone Does! (n.d.). *Blog Maverick: The Mark Cuban Weblog*. Retrieved February 22, 2019 from http://blogmaverick.com/2007/01/16/why-i-dont-wear-a-suit-and-cant-figure-out-why-anyone-does/

ADDITIONAL READING

Cardon, P. W., & Okoro, E. A. (2009). Professional Characteristics Communicated by Formal Versus Casual Workplace Attire. *Business Communication Quarterly, 72*(3), 355–360. doi:10.1177/1080569909340682

Easterling, C. R., Leslie, J. E., & Jones, M. A. (1992). Perceived importance and usage of dress codes among organizations that market professional services. *Public Personnel Management, 21*(2), 211–219. doi:10.1177/009102609202100208

Executive Views on Employee Dress. (1970). *Management Review, 59*(8), 49–53.

Howlett, N., Pine, K., Cahill, N., Orakcioglu, I., & Fletcher, B. (2015). Unbottoned: The Interaction Between Provocativeness of Female Work Attire and Occupational Status. *Sex Roles, 72*(3-4), 105–116. doi:10.100711199-015-0450-8

Karl, K., Van Eck Peluchette, J., & Collins, A. (2017). Employee Self-Perceptions Regarding Workplace Attire in Turkey. *Journal of Organizational Psychology, 17*(6), 112–125.

Rag, P., Khattar, K., & Nagpal, R. (2017). "Dress to Impress": The Impact of Power Dressing. *The IUP Journal of Soft Skills, 11*(3), 45–54.

Shao, C. Y., Baker, J. A., & Wagner, J. (2004). The effects of appropriateness of service contact personnel dress on customer expectations of service quality and purchase intention: The moderating influences of involvement and gender. *Journal of Business Research, 57*(10), 1164–1176. doi:10.1016/S0148-2963(02)00326-0

Yan, R.-N., Yurchisin, J., & Watchravesringkan, K. (2011). Does formality matter? Effects of employee clothing formality on consumers' service quality expectations and store image perceptions. *International Journal of Retail & Distribution Management, 39*(5), 346–362. doi:10.1108/09590551111130775

KEY TERMS AND DEFINITIONS

Attire: An outfit, look, or style that creates the visual appearance of a person.

Business Casual Attire: Attire that lies somewhere in the middle between business professional attire and casual attire. Many interpretations of this category exist. Outfits generally consist of a more comfortable and relaxed feel compared to business professional attire.

Business Professional Attire: Formal, conservative, and clean-cut attire that typically consists of suit jackets, ties, blazers. The material usually is, or appears as, good quality.

Casual Attire: Relaxed attire that can have multiple interpretations. The clothing usually consists of jeans, flip flops, and other relaxed items.

Customer-Oriented Company: A company that interacts with customers on a frequent basis.

Dress Code Policy: The guidelines, which can range in depth, a company provides for the employees on the appropriate, and sometimes not appropriate, attire in the workplace.

Work Attire: The clothing, jewelry, shoes, and any other accessories that create the style, dress, and overall look of an employee.

Is Psychological Contract Relevant in the Healthcare Sector?

Nitu Ghosh

 https://orcid.org/0000-0002-5744-1670

REVA University, India

Fazeelath Tabassum

REVA University, India

INTRODUCTION

Businesses in the present digitized millennium considers the skilled and competent knowledge workers along with their complex bundle of values as the assets of an organization and the main key to innovation and growth. Commitment, engagement, involvement and integrity of the employees are the values that lead an organization towards sustainability and progress by creating long-lasting relationships with external and internal stakeholders (Robert, G. E. et al., 2012). It is beyond doubt that, high customer experience and business value is achieved through well-trained, committed and competent employees, who are the ones coordinating between customers and organizational goals. It is crucial for any organization to maintain positive interpersonal relationships with the employees in order to achieve its ultimate goals (Patrick & Priscilla, 2019). Psychological contract explains the root of existence of contemporary employment relationships in modern workplaces (Maria Tomprou, 2011) leading to values of commitment, engagement and empowerment among the employees irrespective of the nature of job and industry. The dynamism in the business environment, depreciating labor market and organizational transitions has made it challenging to retain talented and productive employees in the fast-booming Healthcare sector.

Globally, healthcare sector is projected to grow at an annual rate of 4.1% in the period between 2017-2021, up from simply 1.3% in 2012-2016 (Economic Survey report, 2017-18). Robust growth mandates committed employees and effective talent management programs. This is where Psychological contract becomes an inevitable key to enabling organisations balance the increased expectations of healthcare professionals (doctors, nurses etc.) and maintain commitment and contributions as per organisational goals. The concept of psychological contract has captured the attention of researchers as a framework for understanding the employment relationship (Coyle-Shapiro, Jacqueline A-M. & Parzefall, M., 2008), managing mutual expectations, needs, commitment and reciprocal contributions as per organisational standards contributing to talent management and growth (Taylor & Tekleab, 2004).

India is expected to rank amongst the top three healthcare markets worldwide in terms of incremental growth by 2020 as per the SEPC report. According to a study by National Healthcare Retention and Registered Nurse Staffing Report, the average hospital turnover rate in 2017 was 18.2%, which is the highest recorded turnover in the industry for almost a decade (Wells, M., 2015). The rising turnover rate of employees in healthcare industry is possibly due to lack of work engagement, lower job security and personal safety of healthcare professionals, lack of training and professional development, less adoption of newer technologies, challenging work-life balance and high stress levels in the hospitals (Warrier, 2017).

DOI: 10.4018/978-1-7998-3473-1.ch185

The high stress levels, challenges and accountability involved in the job roles mandates psychological contract to exist as a talent retention strategy. The healthcare professionals need to deal with patients who may be upset or scared, the doctors are often required to disclose tragic news to patients and their family members that leads to critical attacks on them. Safety, security and stress of the healthcare professionals is a major concern in an emerging country like India, raising constraints for doctors and nurses to perform their job better. Healthcare professionals do not often have a choice in their day-to-day lives and find it difficult to find social support from the hospital management. This impacts their psychological contract adversely leading to burnout, low commitment, poor behavioural outcomes and degrading healthcare services offered to the patients. Psychological contract describes the understandings, beliefs and commitments that exist between an employee and employer (Patrick, H., 2008). It is important to identify the determinants that affect the psychological contract of professionals in healthcare sector and to identify the reasons beyond it as well as consequences. The ultimate outcome is retention and undeterred employee performance.

Psychological contract involves informal assumptions and perceptions of the workplace relationships that exists between leader and worker (Chang, 2007). Although these contracts are rarely written down formally and explicitly, they have a powerful impact on employee motivation and performance leading to enduring commitment and reducing turnover intentions (Conway et al., 2011; Zhao et al., 2007). Relational contracts, a form of psychological contract have been found to deal with the maintenance of quality of emotional and social relationships between employer, employee and peers (Chang et al., 2013). Extant researches have revealed that psychological contract improves the relationship between employer and employee; leading to engagement, productivity and in some cases better workplace (Naidoo et al., 2019). As stated in Equity theory, the variable 'Fairness' is an important dimension of psychological contract, which leads to sustenance of healthy relational and transactional contracts, as employees need to perceive that they are being treated fairly in order to develop the feeling of commitment (Strong, E.V., 2003). Researches have revealed that there is often breach in psychological contract. It can be observed in weekly working life due to factors like excessive workload in combination with a lack of job resources to cope with these job demands (Bal, 2016).

This chapter deals with the concept of psychological contract, its antecedents, consequences and the relevance of psychological contract in healthcare sector. The main aim of this chapter is to highlight the importance of psychological contract in motivating and retaining healthcare professionals (doctors and nurses) and developing a secured work environment for them. The study throws limelight on the trends and status of the healthcare professionals in India. The intention is to communicate to healthcare management in India that a key strategy to prevent the growing rate of brain drain and encourage healthcare professionals to take up long-lasting career in this country is to retain them through the development of psychological contract.

BACKGROUND

Evolution of the Concept of Psychological Contract

Levinson et al. (1962) first introduced the psychological contract theory, which has continued to evolve, and has more significant practical implications in management and organisations presently. Psychological contract is the perception of a mutual agreement between two parties (Argyies, 1962; Levinson, 1962; Rousseau, 1998). According to Rousseau (1995), "the psychological contract consists of individual beliefs regarding terms of an exchange agreement between individuals and their organization". Psychological contracts are individual beliefs in a reciprocal exchange of obligations between the individual and the organization. Restoration of the relationship can involve the re-establishment of stable patterns of interaction over time, often accompanied by active efforts at open communication (Rousseau, 1989). Psychological contract has drawn the attention of researchers to understand the relation between employer and employee (Coyle-Shapiro, Jacqueline A-M. & Parzefall, M., 2008). It is related to greater job satisfaction, productivity, and reduced turnover than other contracts (Kotter, 1973). Employees are more likely to stay in an organisation for a longer duration, if they are promised certain benefits by the employer in terms of both monetary and non-monetary forms (Ellershaw, 2014).

Employees with transactional contract recognize only financial benefits as their motivators and are less loyal and maintain short-term commitment. Individuals who perceive higher psychological contract breach will intend to show decrease in job satisfaction, organisation support, commitment and intention to stay with the organisation (Nichole, 2013). Researchers identified nine factors such as inclusive welfare, trust and commitment, transactional relationship, initiative, employee involvement, reciprocity, sense of belongingness, growth prospects, and work-pay continuum that determine the commitment of an employee through psychological contract (Bhattacharya, 2018). The inclusive welfare factor has been considered the most important which includes components like job security, skill development, rewards, performance appraisal, and growth opportunities. The healthcare professionals undergo high stress at workplace, which ultimately is not shared among the colleagues, possibly due to nature of their job roles involving individual accountability. Bal et al. (2013) asserted that stability in work engagement, turnover intention and employer obligations tends to be much stronger for high tenure employees than for their low tenure counterparts, and mainly determined through the degree of psychological contract built between the employee and management.

Psychological contract depends on various socio-demographic factors like marital status, designation, years of experience in total as well as in the current organization (Bhattacharya, et al., 2018). According to (Najjum et al., 2016) the transactional factors, relational factors and organizational support has an effect on healthcare professionals' level of commitment. In addition, poor pay and rewards, lack of support from the employer and poor work environment were noted as key factors that were likely to affect their commitment and hence adversely impacting the quality of healthcare service delivery. According to Vantilborgh (2016), employees perceiving high demands and low resources were the ones who were more likely to report that their organization is not fulfilling its obligations. Undeterred commitment of an employee, high engagement, behavioral outcomes like trust, integrity, bonding, and overall performance are the outcomes of psychological contract (Ballou, Nichole Simone, 2013).

Figure 1 illustrates a model of psychological contract. This model explains the psychological drivers and external drivers resulting in the process of building psychological contract. The anticipatory expectations of employees like pre-entry expectations, cognitive bias and previous work experiences influence the post-entry expectations, individual expectations and work ideologies, mediated by the influence of facilitators like contract makers, power and authority and promises leading to emotional reactions. This further leads to psychological contract creation, updated expectations, reciprocated exchange of promises and emotional fluctuations (Maria, 2011). This psychological process of relational and transactional contract building is complex and mediated by various external and internal variables.

The social exchange theory (Homans,1958; Blau,1964 and Gouldner,1960) offers valuable insight into the foundational theoretical roots of psychological contract. Homans (1958) described in one of the primary theories of social behavior stated social behavior as 'exchange'. Social behavior often involves social exchanges, where people are motivated to attain some valued reward for which they must forfeit

Figure 1. A model of psychological contract
(Source: Maria, 2011)

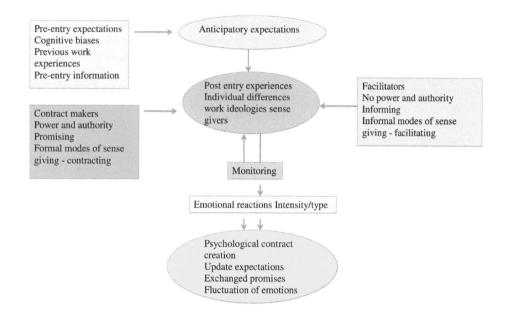

something of value (cost). Individuals choose those alternatives from which they expect the maximum profit and value. Employees choose those alternative outcomes that promise better long-term outcomes, job security, and choose alternatives that promise the greatest financial gains for the least financial expenditures.

Visualization of Social Exchange Theory -

Exchange = Trade something of value (cost) for something needed/valued (reward)

Rewards – Costs = Positive Outcomes (profits) or Negative Outcomes (net loss)

Inequity = Cost > Reward or My Costs > Your Costs or My Rewards < Your Rewards

The Social exchange theory includes the factor- 'the Quality of work life', which when fulfilled can invariably increase morale and motivation among employees and lead to positive attitude towards jobs and the organization (Seyda, 2018).

Figure 2. Social exchange theory
Source: (Şeyda, 2018)

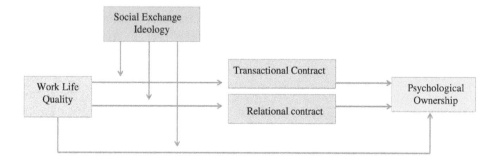

Figure 3. A Proposed model of social exchange theory and an extension
Source: (Haemoon Oh, 2017)

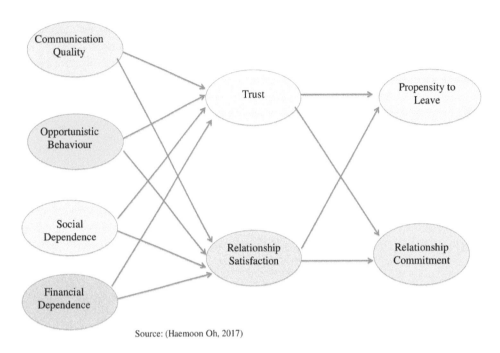

Source: (Haemoon Oh, 2017)

The study conducted by Haemoon (2017) claimed that satisfaction may be a more powerful explanatory variable than trust for non-economic, psycho-social dimensions of organisation relationships. This is related to the development of psychological contract. Thus, various researches have provided clear views on the concept of psychological contract (PC), its antecedents and causal factors as well as its outcomes.

Trends in Indian Healthcare Sector

In the current scenario, Healthcare sector is gaining rapid momentum due to growing demand for high quality healthcare services. Global health care expenditures are expected to continue rising and increase at an annual rate of 5.4 percent between 2017-2022, from USD $7.724 trillion to USD $10.059 trillion. Quality healthcare services require well-trained professionals comprising of nurses, doctors and administrative staff, who are committed and competent in their job roles beyond expectation. An aging workforce, rising demand for healthcare services, moral and well-being concerns are driving shortage of appropriately skilled healthcare staff in both developed and developing economies (Deloitte Global Health Care Outlook, 2019).

As per the recent Economic Times report, the long-term outlook of the healthcare sector is stable with annual revenues projected to grow at 12-14 per cent over the next five years. Despite having 5 million professionals employed in the healthcare sector in India, it continues to have scarcity of skilled workforce with figures being below those of Sri Lanka, China, Thailand, UK and Brazil, according to a World Health Organisation database. This data has placed the country into the status of 'critical shortage of health-care providers'. Bihar, Jharkhand, Uttar Pradesh and Rajasthan are the worst hit while Delhi, Kerala, Punjab and Gujarat compare favourably (Bindu, The Hindu, 2019). India plans to establish 200 new medical colleges in the next 10 years to meet the projected huge shortage of 6 lakh doctors (Madhav, 2013).

The Indian Healthcare sector has become largest sector in terms of revenue and employment. Indian Hospital Industry stood at US$ 61.79 billion during the FY2017 and is expected to reach US$ 132.84 billion by 2022. But India spends 1.02% of gross domestic product (GDP) on public health care, lower than most low-income countries, which spend 1.4% of their GDP on health care. Indian healthcare sector has established number of multispecialty hospitals and healthcare groups and the Indian government have focused on providing better facilities. Indian Government has shown a great interest in the development of telemedicine and started investing in this segment to provide better healthcare facilities in rural India. Medical tourism from the Sub-Saharan countries is expected to grow by nearly 20% in the future (Economic Times, 2019). Indian public health care is under-financed, short-staffed, particularly rural areas are poorly affected. According to a study conducted by a private body, India will need to invest a minimum of Rs 8 lakh crore over the next 20 years to establish two million new patient beds in the healthcare organisations. These Health care organizations are supposed to plan for the future by undertaking comprehensive workforce planning, establishing a robust talent pipeline and focusing on retaining their current employees. India is expected to face an acute skill gap of 12.7 million in the field of health care by 2022 if sufficient measures are not taken up to tackle the challenge of talent management and retention.

There is a skill gap among healthcare professionals such as the inadequate ability to adhere to standard hospital procedures, inadequate ability to think differently and the tendency to have a limited thought process, inadequate communications skills, less knowledge of basic languages needed to communicate with multiple set of patients. There is shortage of medical technologists, surgical and intervention technology connected health professionals, medicine connected employees, medical laboratory professionals and radiography (Manju Chhugani, Economic Times, 2015). India's ratio of 0.7 doctors and 1.5 nurses per 1,000 people is dramatically lower than the World Health Organisation's (WHO) global average of 2.5 doctors and nurses per 1,000 people. Estimates suggest that our country needs an additional 1.54 million doctors and over 2.4 million nurses today to match the global average. There are 70% of complaints due to medical negligence and wrong treatment against private hospitals and government hospitals (Durgesh, Times of India, 2017). The key problem is lack of clear communication about this skill gap and lack of staffs in the hospitals.

Estimates state that a premier public institution like AIIMS spends over one crore rupees to train a single doctor. Firstly, in India there is need to improve salary structures for public health staff, which further enhances staff retention and make the public healthcare system more attractive to professionals. Secondly, the government must work towards expanding the number of seats available for healthcare professionals across the board. Thirdly, a mismatch between skill availability needs has to be adequately addressed. Developing healthcare human resources for India would need an active and seamless coordination for resource planning, course development, skilling, training, employment, emoluments and compensations (Karan Thakur, 2017). Thus, in such a scenario focus on psychological contract development emerges as significant HR strategy facilitating building up of a committed, satisfied and skilled workforce.

How Does a Psychological Contract Impact Behavioural Outcome?

The organisation's care and value for employees positively influences their job-related outcomes and behaviours. There is a growing need to identify to what extent employers are concerned about the employees, in order to meet expectations and ensure procedural justice in the administration of rewards in an era of labour shortage, growing demographic dividend and the role of employee share ownership in retaining key employees (Flood, 2001). This would allow investigation of the impact of different socialization processes and employer strategies on the psychological contract to be studied in-depth. Employers can earn the trust of their employees and employees will be less likely to perceive a contract breach in the first place and more likely to retain their trust despite possible changes or breaches in the employment agreement (Robinson,1996). Psychological contract violations are likely to have a pervasive negative impact on employee attitudes and behaviours, including increased neglect of in-role job duties, reduced willingness to engage in voluntary behaviours supportive of the organization, and increased attempts to leave the organization altogether (William, 2000).

The psychological contract also influences the employees with positive outcomes, which will result in desirable behaviour at the workplace. Employees with high initial trust in their employers may have overlooked or forgotten actual breaches by their employer, whereas employees with low initial trust may have actively searched for or remembered incidents of breach, even when no actual breach occurred (Robinson, 1996). Psychological contract fulfillment results in increased employee performance both in terms of in-role and citizenship behaviour (Turnley, 2003). An effective measure to improve quality of service and productivity of human capital mandates a strong psychological contract fulfilment policy as such efforts can motivate employees to arrive at work early, be productive to meet expected production levels, use time effectively, encourage voluntary contributions at work, as well as work to meet deadlines (Jones, L. A. & Mildred F. K., 2017). Training effectiveness designed to improve skill deficiencies in psychological contract fulfilment, behaviour modelling, and the development of skills and abilities, competence in collecting information related to employers' interests, skills, and personalities is critical for the effective application of Psychological contract fulfilment (Noe et al., 2014).

Research Objectives

To be a successful in healthcare sector it's important to be the best in providing healthcare facilities to the patients in the hospital by sourcing and retaining competent healthcare professionals. In order to source and manage best healthcare talent, it is necessary to meet the expectations and needs of the professionals, besides gaining their trust, loyalty and dedication. The current study believes that there is a major gap and this issue could be addressed by understanding the psychological contract among the healthcare professionals. The aim of the paper is to identify the antecedent variables that determine psychological contract amongst Healthcare professionals, leading to their undeterred commitment and performance. This study would also help to determine the significant influence of socio-demographic factors, psychological factors and organizational factors on the psychological contract of doctors and nurses and highlights the significant influence of psychological contract on their behavioral outcomes and healthcare service quality. This chapter intends to answer the question whether psychological factor is useful in healthcare sector and can be practically applied to tackle the challenge of skill gap, attrition and brain drain.

METHODOLOGY AND DISCUSSION

Human Resource (HR) experts, doctors and senior nurses from four Private Hospitals located in Bangalore were interviewed for the study. A qualitative analysis was adopted using Case based approach and content analysis design approach to analyze and provide better insights into psychological contract in the health care sector. Primary data was recorded from focus group interviews of senior Human Resource (HR) professionals of healthcare organizations and senior doctors. Purposive sampling technique was considered for the study. Experts were identified based on experience and position in the Healthcare organization for the study as they offer an effective way to gather perspectives on psychological contract. The interviews were semi-structured in nature using the telephone as well as face-to-face. These methods help to disclose the experiences of psychological contract between employer and employees.

Table 1 presents the information of four cases of private healthcare organizations in Bangalore along with their profiles and participants details. These hospitals were identified based on the following criteria – registered hospital; having a prominent brand, logo and established in the market; active in social media with the registered website. These companies are well recognized in terms of implementing various strategies of psychological contract fulfillment, employee motivation and received appreciations at the national and international level. The data was collected from three HR managers using a semi-structured interview method (two face-to-face and one telephonic interview). The respondent details and company details are anonymized.

The participants were interviewed for 30 minutes in various aspects. Interview procedure initiated with the collection of the archival documents of the hospital activities and relevance of psychological contract. Based on the information gathered from both internal and external sources, sets of open-ended questions were framed to interview the participants. They were interviewed on various aspects of psychological contract – personal opinion about the idea of psychological contract (expectations of both employer and employees) at the workplace and the perceptions about factors determining psychological contract. The interview and discussion were carried out in English.

Figure 4 depicts the overall data gathering and a collection procedure for the study from four Healthcare sectors. The study adopted content analysis technique for qualitative analysis of the data collected through interviews (Berg, 2001). It started with reading and understanding the entire interview descriptions and narrations. Secondly, the study examined the data to identify the patterns and similarities within the data. Later, researchers refined and combined the common themes and were thematically mapped and grouped for conceptual consistency. From the previous literature works, comparisons were made between academic and practitioner approaches on psychological contract to develop a holistic framework.

The archival documents and other information sources clearly stated that the four hospitals have fully accepted the idea of psychological contract. All of them have adopted different approaches to psychological contract fulfillment and meet the expectations of employees. The Human Resources (HR) staff of private hospitals believe that understanding the expectations of doctors and nurses will definitely benefit and yield better outcomes. One HR manager stated that providing career growth opportunities enhances desirable behavior at the workplace. Another hospital stated that providing better equipment and skilled doctors and nurses would help them to be more effective at the treatment of patients. Most believe that behavioral outcomes are positive with quality customer/patient service, when they focus on achieving higher psychological contract among healthcare professionals through better work environment, skill enhancement through training and other HR benefits. The study identifies which factors are common and consistent in making the psychological contract relevant and successful in healthcare sector, various factors involved is vital and exhibits different levels of success in the process. The analysis of interview responses reveals the factors that build psychological contract and yield employee behavioral outcomes.

The four key variables of psychological contract that emerged through the analysis of collected data are as follows – a) Reciprocates, b) Career growth, c) Employee welfare and security, d) Trust and commitment.

Table 1. Profile of the company, participants and interview type

Code	Profile	Participant proof	Interview type
Hospital A	Ownership: Private Limited Established: 2016 Corporate office /Headquarter: Bangalore Total employees: 26000 Area served: National	Designation: HR Experience: 6 Years Location: Bangalore	Face to face
Hospital B	Ownership: International private healthcare company Established: 1996 Headquarter: Kuala Lumpur, Malaysia Revenue: $2 million Total employees: 120098 Area served: Global	Designation: HR Experience: 8 Years Location: Bangalore	Face to face
Hospital C	Ownership: Corporate Established: 1983 Headquarter: Chennai Revenue: 2,332 million Total employees: 81798 No of hospitals: 70 Area served: Global	Designation: HR Experience: 11 Years Location: Bangalore	Face to face
Hospital D	Ownership: Trust, Healthcare Headquarter: Bangalore Total employees: 23000 Area served: National	Designation: HR Experience: 11 Years Location: Bangalore	Face to face

Source: Compiled by authors from website of respective hospitals and personal interview with each respondent.

Figure 4. Data collection and analysis process
Note – Revised from " Biswan & Suar, (2018)" for the study

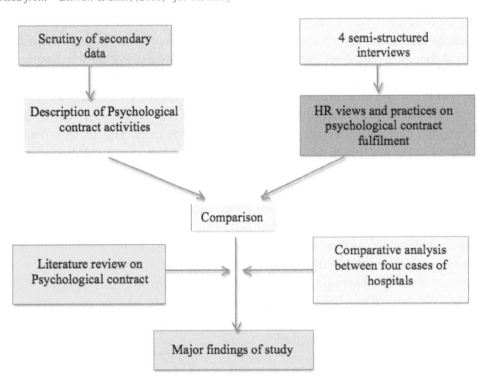

ANTECEDENTS OF PSYCHOLOGICAL CONTRACT

15

Reciprocates: Psychological contract is an unwritten agreement encompassing beliefs and expectations between the employer and employee. The employers reciprocate the needs of its employees. It makes healthcare professionals to be loyal at the workplace, as the doctors and nurses work hard and make sacrifices in daily life.

Employer has to understand the expectations of the employees and reciprocate to it. Same would be reciprocated through loyalty, commitment, trust and undeterred performance.

We provide induction program to new comers. Try to understand the expectations of employees and provide regular training and support (Manager of hospital A).

We know the importance of monetary benefits based on performance, performance-based promotions, intimation of benefits as per the eligibility, enroll for benefits as per the eligibility which ultimately satisfy the employees and implement the same (Manager of hospital B & D).

Healthcare professional's engagement is about managing relationships between doctors, nurses, administrative staff and more importantly patients in an efficient and effective manner. The better the relationship between each one of them, more satisfying is the experience for each healthcare staff and hence higher the engagement levels (Manager of hospital C).

The psychological contract variables of autonomy (delegation of power, accountability and authority), involvement (engagement), and clarity of organizational goals influence job satisfaction indirectly through psychological contract breach; performance feedback directly and indirectly, through psychological contract breach and affects job satisfaction (Hartmann, 2015).

Employee Welfare and Security: Psychological contract fulfilment for higher productivity should pay focussed attention to the provision of job security, safety at workplace, good benefits and incentive packages, and provision of identity and worth for employees in the healthcare sector. Such measures will ultimately develop and sustain the efforts and contributions of employees (Lewis, 2017).

We provide fair compensation, equal opportunity, a safe and healthy workplace specially to deal with patient's aggressive behaviour and other monetary and non-monetary commitments to adhere to human rights policies. This invariably reflects our belief that the success of this hospital is directly linked with employee satisfaction and well-being (Manager of hospital A, B).

Employees are provided with welfare facilities which included healthcare insurance, pension plans, performance bonus, maternity and paternity leaves, vacations and Paid time off, sick leave, salary and benefits. Various initiatives are been taken by the hospital management to ensure work life balance is maintained by the Doctors and nurses. We have a good doctor: nurse: patient ratio and ample human resources to tackle emergency situations and avoid work overload and employee stress (Manager of hospital D).

As part of the employee welfare program, 98% of our employees are administered through an Annual Health Check. This is believed to develop higher commitment and ownership among the employees as a reciprocate behavior to the welfare policies" (Manager of hospital C).

Career Growth: Psychological contract is believed to be the result of well-crafted HR policies of career growth and development. Better opportunities to grow and develop in one's career provided in the organization, provides motivation to the employee to keep contributing with higher commitment and loyalty.

It is imperative for every employee to go through relevant growth and development interventions to broaden their skills and competencies and to help them progress further in their career (Manager of hospital A).

Management conducts monthly and yearly tracker of all internal and external training programs. On the job training is conducted to ensure that employees perform their job safely and efficiently in their respective work environments. Competency mapping is done and anybody (Doctor, nurse, lab managers or administrative staffs) are not allowed to take up specific job roles till they achieve the required competencies (Manager of hospital B).

Skill development and learning, career growth and opportunity, challenging and interesting work and organising new activities that expose professionals to diverse competency enhancement platforms is focused to lead to employee motivation, trust, ownership and commitment (Manager of hospital C).

Our nurse's focus on patient safety and the prevention of any harm to patients, platform to learn new skills in nursing field such as about new equipment, new technologies in medical health are provided (Manager of hospital D).

Providing better career growth and welfare facilities definitely adds competitive edge to healthcare professionals and boosts their confidence in order to provide quality services to patients and to be dedicated. This eventually leads to psychological contract fulfilment on either sides.

Consequences of Psychological Contract

Employer contract fulfilment features an important result on employees' perceived support, commitment and organisation citizenship behaviour. Employees tend to balance the relationship between the variables through reducing their commitment and their willingness to engage in organizational citizenship behaviour when they perceive their employer as not having fulfilled its part in the exchange process (Coyle, 2000).

Trust and Commitment: According to researches, majority of healthcare professionals look forward to improve the quality of work assigned, but few indicated that they can easily leave the hospital, if they get another opportunity elsewhere (Najjuma, 2016).

The aim of the hospital is to grow in a transparent and accountable manner, which develops trust and commitment among employees. (Manager of hospital A).

Engaging with our key professionals and materiality process helps us in deciding on issues to focus, in order to mainstream sustainability into our decision-making (Manager of hospital B).

As we are continuously conducting satisfaction surveys, grievance redressal, open forums, various committees, which understand the employee's expectations and meet them, we expect the values of trust and ownership to be integrated within our organizational culture and behavior of our skilled healthcare professionals (Manager of hospital C).

Healthcare professionals are committed towards hospital management and constitute very efficient team players with growth orientation by fixing self driven targets (Manager of hospital D).

We provide job security, safe work environment for the doctors and nurses in our hospital, thereby facilitating in the development of long-lasting loyalty and commitment (Manager of hospital A, B, C, and D).

Providing safe and secured working environment fulfills the safety needs of employees as per Maslow's Need Hierarchy theory (Maslow, A., 1943) and would allow the doctors and nurses to work in focused manner.

FUTURE RESEARCH DIRECTIONS

The study has strong practical implications in strengthening the relationships by identifying the factors of psychological contract. The study creates an awareness among the management in healthcare sector to provide more time and scope in order to help professionals to handle the stress at workplace by providing supportive network and clear understanding of employer and employee expectations enabling psychological contract fulfilment. This study states that care and value for the healthcare professionals will positively influence job related outcomes and behaviours. Healthcare sector are using different ways to develop the psychological contract of its skilled professionals through practices and techniques for differentiating themselves from the competitors in terms of satisfying the needs of professionals, providing safe working environment, better rewards, resources at workplace and effective HR policies (Fasolo, 1995; Wayne et al., 1994, 1997). It has strong practical implications in terms of developing commitment, loyalty, trust, dedication towards high quality service to patients, positive behavioral outcomes, job satisfaction, motivation and better performance. Doctors and nurses who develop the values of ownership and commitment are most valuable assets of any hospital.

But the question here is to understand to what extent does the employer safeguard the needs and expectations of its doctors and nurses, provide best in the industry compensation, suitable equipment and resources and manage scarcity of human resources through training and caring for skilled workforce. This is among the few studies exploring potential employee behavioural outcomes due to various psychological contract variables (reciprocates, career growth, employee welfare, trust and commitment) of healthcare professionals. According to (Vantilborgh, 2016) employer should react quickly to prevent negative affect from causing psychological contract breach perceptions, by investing in job resources to stimulate positive affect. This is done by a successful long-term strategy to build enduring personal resources that prevent psychological contract breach perceptions.

Future research should try to capture employees Psychological contract levels and their behavioral reactions following a Psychological contract breach as a causal source, and employees' contributions and expected reactions when a Psychological contract breach is perceived (Griep, 2018). A detailed investigation supported by empirical evidence about the level/degree of psychological contract and breach caused due to various factors may provide better information and this can also be considered under future research.

CONCLUSION

From the qualitative interviews, it has been observed that HR departments association is responsible within the hospital. In-depth understanding can be done by conducting empirical research and involving doctors and nurses in the surveys, which may give strong support to the argument. This study has made an attempt to understand the view of HR managers about the term psychological contract and its relevance in the healthcare sector. The observed characteristics of psychological contract have been described. HR managers believe that psychological contract is a process of understanding the expectation of both the parties in the healthcare industry for better understanding and smooth working.

During the process, employees try to build a psychological contract with the employer based on reciprocates, career growth opportunity, employee welfare, trust, commitment, safety and security features of the psychological contract (Katou, A.A., 2013). The psychological contract fulfillment will help the healthcare professionals to be motivated and maintain accentuated work engagement. There is a need to understand implied expectations of the professionals in healthcare, which leads to job outcomes such as job performance, work behaviour and job security. Psychological contact discharge is likely to originate from successful practices like fulfilling the expectations of employees, providing training and learning activities, trust employees, flexi-working hours, career advancement, safety at work which is requested by the healthcare professional in order to work peacefully. It will reduce turnover, increase the level of satisfaction and commitment. According to (Mensah, 2018) employer should attempt to understand and discharge the expectations of talented employees so that employees can reciprocate with positive outcomes. Finally, the study would like to set a path for more research in association with psychological contract fulfilment and strategies for better understanding the variables of psychological contract among healthcare professionals.

REFERENCES

Argyris, C. (1960). *Understanding Organisational Behaviour*. Dorsey Press.

Arnold, J. (1996). The psychological contract: A concept in need of closer scrutiny? *European Journal of Work and Organizational Psychology*, *5*(4), 511–520. doi:10.1080/13594329608414876

Bal, M., De Cooman, R., & Mol, S. T. (2013). Dynamics of psychological contracts with work engagement and turnover intention: The influence of organizational tenure. *European Journal of Work and Organizational Psychology*, *22*(1), 107–122. doi:10.1080/1359432X.2011.626198

Bal, P. M., Hofmans, J., & Polat, T. (2016). Breaking Psychological Contracts with the Burden of Workload: A Weekly Study of Job Resources as Moderators. *Applied Psychology*, *66*(1), 143–167. doi:10.1111/apps.12079

Ballou, N. S. (2013). *The Effects of Psychological Contract Breach on Job Outcomes*. Master's Theses. Paper 4327.

Bhattacharya, S., Trehan, G., & Kaur, K. (2018). Factors Determining Psychological Contract of IT Employees in India. *International Journal of Human Capital and Information Technology Professionals*, *9*(1), 37–52. doi:10.4018/IJHCITP.2018010103

Biswas, M. K., & Suar, D. (2018). Employer Branding in B2B and B2C Companies in India: A Qualitative Perspective. *SA Journal of Human Resource Management, 5*(1), 76–95. doi:10.1177/2322093718768328

15

Blau, P. (1964). *Exchange and power in social life*. Wiley.

Challenges in Indian Healthcare Industry. (n.d.). https://www.civilserviceindia.com/current-affairs/articles/challenges-in-indian-healthcare-industry.html

Chang, H.-T., Hsu, H.-M., Liou, J.-W., & Tsai, C.-T. (2013). Psychological contracts and innovative behavior: A moderated path analysis of work engagement and job resources. *Journal of Applied Social Psychology, 43*(10), 2120–2135. Advance online publication. doi:10.1111/jasp.12165

Chang, K. T., Rousseau, D. M., & Lai, L. (2007). *Going the Extra Mile: Psychological Contracts and Team Learning from a Social Network Approach*. Working paper.

Conway, N., Guest, D., & Trenberth, L. (2011). Testing the differential effects of changes in psychological contract breach and fulfilment. *Journal of Vocational Behavior, 79*(1), 267–276. doi:10.1016/j.jvb.2011.01.003

Coyle-Shapiro, J. A-M., & Parzefall, M. (2008). Psychological contracts. In The SAGE handbook of organizational behaviour. SAGE Publications.

Coyle-Shapiro, J., & Kessler, I. (2000). Consequences of The Psychological Contract for the Employment Relationship: A Large scale Survey. *Journal of Management Studies, 37*(7), 903–930. doi:10.1111/1467-6486.00210

Durgesh Nandan Jha. (2017). *Medical negligence: Wrong treatment biggest grouse*. https://timesofindia.indiatimes.com/city/delhi/wrong-treatment-biggest-grouse/articleshow/61954358.cms

Ellershaw, J., Steane, P., McWilliams, J., & Dufour, Y. (2014). Promises in psychological contract drive commitment for clinicians. *Clinical Governance: An International Journal, 19*(2), 153–165. doi:10.1108/CGIJ-01-2014-0003

Fasolo, P. M. (1995). Procedural justice and perceived organizational support: hypothesized effects on job performance. In R. S. Cropanzano & K. M. Kacmar (Eds.), *Organizational Politics Justice and Support: Managing the Social Climate of the Workplace*. Quorum Books.

Flood, P. C., Turner, T., Ramamoorthy, N., & Pearson, J. (2001). Causes and consequences of psychological contracts among knowledge workers in the high technology and financial services industries. *International Journal of Human Resource Management, 12*(7), 1152–1165. doi:10.1080/09585190110068368

Gouldner, A. W. (1960). The norm of reciprocity. *American Sociological Review, 25*(2), 161–178. doi:10.2307/2092623

Griep, Y., & Vantilborgh, T. (2018). Reciprocal effects of psychological contract breach on counterproductive and organizational citizenship behaviors: The role of time. *Journal of Vocational Behavior, 104*, 141–153. doi:10.1016/j.jvb.2017.10.013

Hartmann, N. N., & Rutherford, B. N. (2015). Psychological contract breach's antecedents and outcomes in salespeople: The roles of psychological climate, job attitudes, and turnover intention. *Industrial Marketing Management, 51*, 158–170. doi:10.1016/j.indmarman.2015.07.017

Homans, G. C. (1958). Social behavior as exchange. *American Journal of Sociology, 63*(6), 597–606. doi:10.1086/222355

Homans. (1958). Social Behaviour as Exchange. *American Journal of Sociology, 63*(6), 597-606. http://www.jstor.org/stable/2772990

Jeong, M., & Oh, H. (2017). Business-to-business social exchange relationship beyond trust and commitment. *International Journal of Hospitality Management, 65,* 115–124. doi:10.1016/j.ijhm.2017.06.004

Jones & Kolson. (2017). Psychological contract fulfillment and its implication on performance of employees: The case of Asanko Gold Mine, Ghana. *Journal of Public Administration and Policy Research, 9*(2), 17-25. DOI: doi:10.5897/JPAPR2017.0402

Katou, A. A. (2013). The link between HR practices, psychological contract fulfilment, and organisational performance in Greece: An economic crisis perspective. *Journal of Industrial Engineering and Management, 6*(2), 568–594. doi:10.3926/jiem.501

Kotter, J. P. (1973). The Psychological Contract: Managing the Joining-up Process. *California Management Review, 15*(3), 91–99. doi:10.2307/41164442

Levinson, H., Price, C. R., Munden, K. J., Mandl, H. J., & Solley, C. M. (1962). *Men, management, and mental health.* Harvard University Press.

Levinson, H., Price, C. R., Munden, K. J., & Solley, C. M. (1962). *Men, Management and Mental Health.* Harvard University Press. doi:10.4159/harvard.9780674424746

Maria, T. I. N. (2011). A model of psychological contract creation upon organizational entry. *Career Development International, 16*(4), 342–363. doi:10.1108/13620431111158779

Maslow, A. H. (1943). A theory of human motivation. *Psychological Review, 50*(4), 370–396. doi:10.1037/h0054346

Mensah, J. K. (2018). Talent Management and Employee Outcomes: A Psychological Contract Fulfilment Perspective. *Public Organization Review.* Advance online publication. doi:10.100711115-018-0407-9

Mishra, A. (n.d.). *Indian Healthcare Industry in 2018 and Forecast for 2019.* https://health.economictimes.indiatimes.com/news/industry/indian-healthcare-industry-in-2018-and-forecast-for-2019/67286959

Naidoo, V., Abarantyne, I., & Rugimbana, R. (2019). The impact of psychological contracts on employee engagement at a university of technology. *SA Journal of Human Resource Management, 17.* Advance online publication. doi:10.4102ajhrm.v17i0.1039

Najjuma, S. S., Okiria, J. C., & Nanyonga, R. C. (2016). Care Workers' Commitment in Public Health Sector in Uganda: A Case Study of Medical Doctors in Mulago National Referral Hospital (MNRH). *International Journal of Science and Research, 5*(4), 2.

Nichole. (2013). *The Effects of Psychological Contract Breach on Job Outcomes.* San Jose State University, Master's theses. 4327.

Noe, R. A. (2014). Employee Development: Issues in Construct Definition and Investigation of Antecedents. In Improving Training Effectiveness in Work Organizations. Mahwah, NJ: Lawrence Erlbaum.

Patrick, H. (2008). Psychological Contract and Employment Relationship, *The ICFAI University. Journal of Organizational Behavior*, 7.

Patrick, N. N., & Priscilla, O. O. (2019). Interpersonal Relationship at Work; Enhancing Organizational Productivity of Deposit Money Banks in Port Harcourt. *Journal of Research in Business and Management*, *7*(1), 22–33.

Robert, G. E., Kathleen, M. P., & George, S. (2012). How to become a sustainable company. *MIT Sloan Management Review*, *53*(4), 43–50.

Robinson. (1996). Trust and Breach of the Psychological Contract. *Administrative Science Quarterly*, *41*(4), 574-599.

Rousseau, D. M. (1989). Psychological and Implied Contracts in Organizations. *Employee Responsibilities and Rights Journal*, *2*(2), 121–139. doi:10.1007/BF01384942

Rousseau, D. M. (1995). *Psychological Contracts in Organizations: Understanding Written and Unwritten Agreements*. Sage.

Şeyda. (2018). *A research on work life quality, psychological contract and psychological ownership relationship in the context of social exchange theory*. Yorum-Yönetim-Yöntem Uluslararası Yönetim-Ekonomi ve Felsefe.

Strong, E. V. (2003). *The role of the psychological contract amongst knowledge workers in the reinsurance industry* (Unpublished master's thesis). Gordon Institute of Business Science. Pretoria: University of Pretoria.

Taylor, M. S., & Tekleab, A. G. (2004). Taking stock of psychological contract research: assessing progress, addressing troublesome issues, and setting research priorities. In J. A.-M. Coyle-Shapiro, L. M. Shore, M. S. Taylor, & L. E. Tetrick (Eds.), *The Employment Relationship: Examining Contextual and Psychological Perspectives* (pp. 253–283). Oxford University Press.

Thakur, K. (2017). *Mind the gap: Health workforce shortage, the pioneer*. https://www.dailypioneer.com/2017/columnists/mind-the-gap-health-workforce-shortage.html

Turnley. (2003). The Impact of Psychological Contract fulfilment on the Performance of In-Role and Organizational Citizenship Behaviours. *Journal of Management*, *29*(2), 187–206. DOI:10.1.1.864.7207

Turnley, W. H., & Feldman, D. C. (2000). Re-examining the effects of psychological contract violations: Unmet expectations and job dissatisfaction as mediators. *Journal of Organizational Behavior*, *21*(1), 25–42. doi:10.1002/(SICI)1099-1379(200002)21:1<25::AID-JOB2>3.0.CO;2-Z

Vantilborgh, T., Bidee, J., Pepermans, R., Griep, Y., & Hofmans, J. (2016). Antecedents of Psychological Contract Breach: The Role of Job Demands, Job Resources, and Affect. *PLoS One*, *11*(5), e0154696. Advance online publication. doi:10.1371/journal.pone.0154696 PMID:27171275

Wayne, S. J., Shore, L. M., & Liden, R. C. (1994). *An examination of the effects of human resource practices on leader–member exchange and perceived organizational support*. Presented at the *Academy of Management Meeting*, Dallas, TX.

Wayne, S. J., Shore, L. M., & Liden, R. C. (1997). Perceived organizational support and leader–member exchange: A social exchange perspective. *Academy of Management Journal*, *40*, 82–111.

William, L. J., & Anderson, S. E. (1991). Job satisfaction and organizational commitment as predictors of organizational citizenship and in-role behaviors. *Journal of Management, 17*(3), 601–617. doi:10.1177/014920639101700305

Zhao, H., Wayne, S. J., Glibkowski, B. C., & Bravo, J. (2007). The impact of psychological contract breach on work-related outcomes: A meta-analysis. *Personnel Psychology, 60*(3), 647–680. doi:10.1111/j.1744-6570.2007.00087.x

KEY TERMS AND DEFINITIONS

Psychological Contract: The psychological contract is the unwritten set of expectations of both employee and employer at the time of employment contract.

Psychological Contract Breach: Psychological contract breach arises when employer fails to meet the expectations of employees.

Psychological Contract Fulfilment: Psychological contract fulfilment is created when the employer keeps the promises of employees.

Organisational Citizenship Behaviour: Organizational citizenship behaviour deals with positive and desirable behaviour of employees that benefit the team and encourage greater organizational functioning and efficiency.

Reciprocates: Reciprocates means both the parties' employer and employee enter into agreements mutually, making the obligation of one party corresponding to the obligation of the other.

Relational Contract: Relational contract the contract that gets affected based on relationship of trust between both the parties (i.e., employer and employee).

Transactional Contract: Transactional contracts focus more on explicit elements in which employees are less career oriented, lack of trust in employer and greater resistance to change.

Imbibing Organizational Health Practices With Ambidextrous Approach as a Solution to Higher Education Institution Staff Turnover Predicaments

Farooq Miiro

Islamic University in Uganda, Uganda

Azam Othman

International Islamic University, Malaysia

INTRODUCTION

In the era of globalization and internationalization, high education institutions (HEIs) have been challenged to cope up with high competition whose labor market and determinants require severe strategic and transformational plans. And this can be done by opening up boarders to both national and internationals levels with an intention of attracting skilled human resources who can ably help these institutions provide solutions to humanity in general. To stay competitive and sound, fundamental strategic business plan must be laid to enhance excellent academic achievement coupled with performance by both staff and students (Zakuan, Yusof, Saman, & Shaharoun, 2010). To achieve these strategies, managers of these institutions are required to imbibe organizational health practices using both ambidextrous and sine qua non approach since these are the only ways through which attraction of highly qualified staff can be achieved while reducing staff turnover. The issue of organizational health practices is taken as a cornerstone for acquisition of quality services and products in an organization. World over, institutions that have so far realized what the forces of demand dictate in the academic arena have opted to imbibe these forces and gain competitive advantage through highly qualified staff to help them attain high and extra ordinary levels of performance at the same time providing needed human resources to the world market. This is done to ensure that HEIs from faculty level change their operational mechanisms so as to remain compatible with the changing market scope. For HEIs, to survive in the era of volatility, there is need to ensure that elements related to task contingence, intellectual stature development and favorable working conditions of both talented and highly skilled staff and take care of since they are bedrock and cornerstone for institutional survival and failure to use both the left and right hand approaches for an institution's survival may be in jeopardy (Douglas & Selin, 2012). By adopting strategies that address the global concerns, leaders of HEIs must be aware that the forces that lead to turbulence within these institutions are mostly shaped by political, social, religious and economic hegemony of super powers whose sole aim is to control the spectrum of human development and behavior (Douglas & Selin, 2012; Frontiera, 2010; Meyer, Bushney, & Ukpere, 2011; Miiro, 2016b; Miiro & Otham, 2016). Even though universities are re-structuring their ways of operation and infusing the global changes into their culture and policies, a lot is still desired in terms of imbibing organisational health practices so as to recruit and retain highly qualified who must in turn, attract a big number of students with high levels of performance both at national and international levels. It is therefore imperative to note, that imbibing organisational

DOI: 10.4018/978-1-7998-3473-1.ch186

health practices in HEIs operations is not only a necessity but it is a way through which rebranding of institutional approaches towards staff welfare can be realized. Conversely, leaders must take care of organisational health practices by using both the right and left hand approaches without its due diligence employees cannot survive longer in an institution.

Moreover, this challenge of not being swift with new demands of time towards staff employment can be attributed to the traditional manner through which many of the university employees in influential positions have remained rigid while forgetting the dictates of the time (Meyer et al., 2011). Thus the purpose of this paper is to expose the readers to ways through which organizational health (OH) and how its nine (9) dimensions can be imbibed in HEIs to curtail the staff turnover predicament.

BACKGROUND

Staff Turnover

Staff turnover has of recent turned into cancerous especially in HEIs. Moreover, it is unhealthy due to unpleasant effects that normally affect the usual operation of an organisation. This is experienced through loss of talented staff who are normally envisaged as would be future leaders. It curtails the smooth growth and customer trust whenever it happens in a work place. For staff to leave an institution, is a natural behavior and it may sound nice while in the actual sense it affects the corporate image of an institution.

Turnover can be termed as staff mobility around the labour knowledge market. Today, many professionals from the academic arena are moving from one university to another at both national and international levels due to several reasons. This kind of gesture, poses a lot of challenge to HEIs' sector due to the fact that there is an increased number of people with diverse background that want to join this sector with several purposes that relate to growth, exposure, creativity and live not only usefully but also reflectively and responsibly.

In the face of HEIs, challenges of staff moonlighting, loss of highly qualified staff to private sector have been experienced because of qualified personnel looking for higher pay and better conditions of working. Moreover, there are also different factors that push and pull individuals to different working places. In a study conducted by Owence, Pinagase, & Mercy (2014), it was found that poor systems, presence or absence of good team, innovative culture, poor leadership, excessive workload, poor career opportunities, burnout, frustration and disillusion and better pay lead to staff turnover in South African HEIS. Also in a quantitative study done on 4651 employees by Erasmus, Grobler, & Plessis (2015), it was established that employees with low performance levels had resigned. However, the same study recommended that organisational citizenship, leadership style, supervision, organisational climate and compensation should be given due attention so as to influence staff stability. In a study conducted by Figueroa, (2018), it was realized that Biological characteristics (ex. age, education), prior experiences, human resource roles, structural features and staff expectations plus self-development were the factors for staff turnover. Meanwhile, Musah & Nkuah, (2013) found out that the lack of motivation in Ghana HEIs which is also a key element of OH was the influential factor for staff turnover. Conversely, in a study done in Tanzania by Demetria & Mkulu, (2018), it was opined that staff mobility was due to low remuneration, leadership style, lack of proper job description, security and poor mechanism of staff development. Moreover, a study conducted in Uganda by Ddungu, (2014) found out that low professionalism and empowerment levels were the causative factors for staff attrition in HEIs.

Basing on the issue raised above pertaining to staff turn over, it can be observed worldwide HEIs face serious challenges of staff turnover. Moreover, the causative factors seem to be the same though their magnitude differ from location and level of different of development. But all the situations can be taken us being unhealthy for the employees, the customers and the institutions themselves. For this matter, this paper unpacks the model of OH as an ingenuity that requires both ambidextrous and sine qua none approaches to curtail staff turnover predicament.

OVER VIEW OF ORGANIZATIONAL HEALTH

Organizational health is a management aspect that has of recent attracted several studies and research. Through these efforts, many researchers have provided different meaning to the concept. For instance it is derived from occupational health. Organizational health can be termed as the ability of an organization to align its strategy, culture and a clear vision with an aim of providing quality services and excellent products to outcompete other organizations on the world market (De Smet, Schaninger, & Smith, 2014; Franciska & Welly, 2013). The amalgamation of these key aspects of key elements of organisational health should rhyme with the financial input and employ performance. It implies that when institutional leadership commit themselves to attracting staff input beyond performance, they are likely to attain staff commitment, willingness to perform beyond supervision, citizenship and the gaps of losing staff will be closed (Yüceler, Doğanalp, & Kaya, 2013).

Also for HEIs to attain a competitive advantage, they must be ready to keep their staff with necessary skills to accept the changing demands while putting into consideration issues of acceptance to change which leads to innovative ideas and strategies (Hussein, Mohamad, Noordin, & Amir, 2014). The essence of organisational health is to ensure that priorities are stated and geared towards achievement of institutional goals. Scholars argue that to achieve higher levels of performance, key performance indicators must be set in line with employ satisfaction to avoid absenteeism while targeting high levels of productivity coupled with cultural practices, collegiality and emotional factors.

Moreover, in Uganda HEIs staff seem to hold institutions at ransom to the extent of showing that they have the carte blanch to determine policies and if not supported, they can turn against any leaders of the institution. Meanwhile the paper unpacks the nine elements of organisational health elements as enshrined in the findings of Keller and Price, (2010) as mechanisms for addressing staff turnover if imbibed in HEIs sector using ambidextrous and sine qua non approaches.

Leadership

Leadership is the pivot and steering of institutional activities in that when an institution suffers from challenge a leader can see opportunities where others reach deadlocks for him he finds solutions. It is one of the key aspects of institutional management that should not be given to any one without through scrutiny and revision of one's history. World over many institutions have suffered from myopic and egocentric tendencies due to leadership. It is therefore imperative that supervisors of intuitional affairs take key note and self-sacrifice on who should be at the helm of all decision. Especially in Africa many higher institutions are still lagging behind due to leadership vacuums. Whoever reaches at PhD level or professorship thinks that he or she is a leader without examining himself or herself of what he or she is capable of. Since leadership plays an important role towards organisational health, it should be given due diligence and respect for future prosperity of institutional agendas, mission and vision.

A leader should be able to listen, prepare himself or herself before meeting others, be ready to listen and avoid saying ''No'' all the time without listening to others. A leader should be ready for advice and at the same time set committees for think tanks. Unnecessary talks and jokes should be avoided since some of the followers learn a lot from their leaders. A leader should be a servant who moves extra mile to understand how business move within an organization and at the same time take note of the reports generated with firm actions and strategies that can lead to change institutional cooperate image. Leaders should stop sitting in offices every now and then without reaching the ground and inspect how things are done and what challenges are faced by change agents and hustlers.

It is therefore important to note that knowing leadership is not enough. It also requires imbibing strategic leadership styles with positivity so as to harness talents and sustainable leadership practices. When this practice is done well, staff will be willing to learn and exchange ideas that lead to innovative strategies and change with all their efforts. However, when leaders differ or divert from the common goals, their followers and members of the institution normally reduce their efforts towards supporting them. Accordingly, respecting them and ensuring that the integrity of the institution is protected should always remain at heart. It is a shame for the workers of an institution to embark on their leadership and while forgetting that whatever they say or write puts the corporate image of an institution at risk. Therefore, to curb this kind of practice and attitude, leadership should put in place avenues that help staff to develop their skills and knowledge in order to come up with innovative ideas. The gesture of increased staff development and skills enhancement among employees should be supported with all intuitional structures and systems knowing that without it, staff support towards administration will remain a myth and hence killing the spirit of innovation and learning

Innovation and Learning

Innovation and learning is done by accepting diverse ideas and strategies that emanate from different units and levels of staff with an aim of moving an organization to higher horizon. To achieve this aspect of OH, there should be proper ways of facilitating staff to engage them in research and publication that leads to new knowledge and ideas that can help the future generation attain fabulous living (Yüceler, Doğanalp, & Kaya, 2013). Through innovation and learning there will be willingness to accept diversity and at the same time unlearn old habits that do not suit the current and new generations to come. Being able to adjust and act accordingly to new trends with an open mind ready to learn from newness and then be ready to move and think in novel ways, is a sine qua non gesture that helps an institution and its staff reposition themselves on the world market (Miiro, 2016b). To achieve these practices, it needs an ambidextrous approach that enables staff to come up with ways that lead to institutional economic development and resumption of which in the end may lead to provision of solutions to challenges of the community hence leading to consultancy services. Without moving in this direction, HEIs will continue to displace themselves and fail to cope up with customer needs and at the same time remain passing over irrelevant information that does not lead to skills development and provision of solutions to human challenges. Innovation should be categorized into technology, services, products and these activities should be coupled with entrepreneurship skills that help learners to come up with ideas and insights that lead to both self and community development. Findings from a study conducted by (Jafarzadeh, 2015) revealed that acquisition of knowledge, information distribution and interpretation coupled with strong memories are the key segments that drive both the conscious and unconscious trends of organisational change. It means that for such elements to be achieved, organizations will require a conducive culture and climate as modes of the work place. Thus, culture and climate should be good and sound enough to attract and retain staff of higher qualifications.

Culture and Climate

Culture can be defined as the way organizations do their business, for example the formula, the goals and mission. Whatever business that is done must suit within the set customs and goals of an institution (Vilcea, 2014). Since HEIs are a specific organizations with specific cultures, their staff at all levels must embrace the true needs of the new generation and it is future breeds so as to remain relevant to both the internal and external stakeholders. The internal stakeholders are the staff, students and alumni whereas, the external are the government, quality assurance control agencies, employers and parents (Douglas & Selin, 2012; Franciska & Welly, 2013; Vilcea, 2014). However a conducive culture cannot be attained without favorable climate. Climate is defined as the characteristics and identity of an organization from others. It involves the way members interact, perceive and conceptualize, their dimensions, source of influence and shaping of behaviours, the way of interpreting situations, attitude and norms that shape their culture (Carlfjord, Andersson, & Nilsen, 2010; Chandra, 2014; Mcmurray, 2012).

Meanwhile, in the age of increasing environmental change coupled with increasing dynamic and controversies that affect life of both individuals and organizations, HEIs should invest in staff while capitalizing on the more experienced and old staff since many of them have vast experience on how management of business should be done. But to aspire and inspire future generations, leadership should always encourage the old and experienced staff to imbibe into themselves the heart of unlearning, relearning, learning, contextualizing, actualizing and then form a foundation of synthesizing new dimensions and trends that are a sine qua non to the existence of their institutions on the world market.

Moreover, this approach should be encapsulated with ambidextrous rigorous training to help both the shakers and hustlers in facilitating organisational business be on one page in terms of input and output. While doing training and refresher courses to the staff, members are exposed to change as an integral nature that requires constant generation of new knowledge that addresses new organisational challenges, its customers and the surrounding. Through knowledge generation, more involvement of students and staff in several business of educational institutions shall be realized other than putting emphasis on discipline management.

Furthermore through imbibing OH, organizations with staff who sit on several committees for years without training shall be shunned. For instance, members will be updating themselves on the new trends of management of both students and staff. Understanding culture and environment is done through learning and accepting differences. Staff should be encouraged to unlearn, learn, re-learn before actualizing and contextualizing issues that lead to new policy formulation and implementation in HEIs.

Nevertheless, orientation should be given priority for both staff and customers before accusing them of violating rules and regulations. Punishing in most cases does not change behavior but tolerance, counselling and guidance may be the best options towards reform of human beings. Man is bound to mistakes but before inflicting punishments through research, discussion and analysis of the magnitude of what he is or she has done is important if HEIs are to empower change agents to society. To ensure sanity and conducive environment, there is need to have smooth collaboration and networking within organisational structures and systems so as to ease customer gains and quality assurance.

Control and coordination are the ability to assess institutional performance and risks putting into consideration the challenges and opportunities. Through this process institutional leadership and their staff should rhyme their activities with job description, and psychological empowerment as dedicated towards achievement of staff commitment (De Klerk & Stander, 2014; Mendes & Stander, 2011). However control and coordination cannot be achieved without imbibing systems, with clear job roles and at the same time employ staff with competences that lead to quality working environment. Health organization do not stall activities or act in adhoc manner, staff are orientated and trained often to suit the demands of the time. Procrastination of activities should be avoided to ensure that time is not wasted and systems are not abused. Through this ambidextrous process, structure can function effectively and systems may be automated to answer customer concerns without delays.

Without taking control and coordination of activities as a sine qua none element, many organizations in all spheres of business have lost touch with customers and their funders to uncoordinated ways of running business. This can be experienced when members of the same group give different and varying information on a certain aspect of organisational element when approached by an outsider. When such scenarios happen they are clearly indicating that there is absence of clear communication channels with the outside world which in the end may lead to conflict of interest, unintended expenses and uncoordinated activities (Glenn, 2008; Hamid et al., 2011; Husain, 2013; Miiro, 2016a; Miiro, Othman, Sahari, & Burhan, 2017; Miiro, Othman, Sahari Nordin, & Burhan Ibrahim, 2017)

External Orientation

External orientation is the qualitative engagement of customers and other stakeholders and others in the process of transforming the institution. Given the nature of market dictates and recipe spectrum, the external forces that pressurize change in mode of operation do not leave HEIs as isolated organizations due to the fact that they have a lot of attachment and influence on the way business should be conducted in the outside community (Mitchell & Nielsen, 2012). It is therefore important that these educational institutions avoid closed systems that do not give the true picture of what these institutions are offering.

A strong relationship with external forces should not only focus on what customers want but they should put in place ties that lead them to their competitors, business partners, policy makers and community to help them understand the nature of human resources needed in the market. This is because these stakeholders shape the market dictates without clear relationship and interaction with HEIs which can lead to irrelevance of either party when it comes to products and services.

Furthermore interacting with the outside community helps HEIs to understand what is not offered by sister organizations and then capitalize on how to rebrand and blend her services against their competitors. It can also act as a catalyst to examine the nature of graduates given to society, their level of performance and ability to change lives and innovate in line with the market demands. Without tracer studies and benchmarking countries like Uganda where many institutions remain enclosed without understanding where their alumni are employed shall remain isolated while at the same time providing the same ingredients for years.

Conversely the best way is for these organizations to have a shared vision, with forums of meeting and make themselves understand to develop products that are in line with the markets demands whereas at the same time providing consultancy to the challenges of the community. With this kind of strategy, these organizations shall be able to take on the market, shape it and dictate the kind of services, products and human resources that should be trained.

Meanwhile, HEIs should also take a lead of advising the regulatory agencies and councils for quality standards before new policies come up. For instance; in Uganda NCHE comes up with regulations tailored with high costs(De Smet et al., 2014). This tendency of commoditizing every activity kills the nature of voluntarism, nature of humanity and the end of it all value for money and deadlines may not be adhered to.

The actual work of these enemies is to stress continuous improvement of quality and services among HEIs and in line with the vision of the country, customer demands and market dictates and at the same time avoid wastage and efficiency in their systems and structures. In a research done by Franciska & Welly, (2013) revealed that organisations that adhere to this kind of practice surpass others in terms of quality services, high levels of performance even though, they may be not be excellent in nature however, when they stick on health practices with leadership archetype mode attaining excellent levels becomes easy.

Organisational health is a pinnacle and precursor of all institutional activities without which business may be crippled down. Therefore, leadership must ensure that staff efficacy, timely performance evaluation and accountability are functional, efficient and effective are imbibed in both ambidextrous and sine qua none ways. This is due to the fact staff have a lot of influence on total quality, management and quality assurance. When staff are lackadaisical in nature they tend to do things at their pace without focusing on a bigger picture of an institution. Therefore leadership must pay greater attention to this aspect bearing in mind that no one wants to associate with failure. Weak staff yield kakistocracy in systems and structures. For HEIs such scenarios should not be called for since they impact a lot on societal development and vice versa. To attain institutional goals there should clear communication channels, commitment with distribution of power, favorable utilization of resources, knowledge sharing, collaboration and networking to secure favorable working environment and proper planning for transformation purposes that can lead to attraction of highly skilled staff and their retention.

To supplement the above element, there is need for infused proper communication channels into our working behavior. Communication should be used as a process of delivering information and data to the right offices. Through this process effective and efficient means of executing institutional business will be attained without struggling with the systems and structure. Without proper channels of communications; rumors, distortion and misinformation can mislead institutional business and drag the system into a state of quagmire. It is therefore important for leadership and institutional staff to ensure that their tongues and hands are used to pass over rightful information with good intention. Communication channels sometimes are manipulated and misused by self-seekers to inform customers of what is not worth while forgetting that they are shooting themselves in the feet. Public relations officers and the corporate image's officer should always have their ears open to address all the unclear situation before the media can take on the lead. Customers in this case, students must be listened to and have their concerns addressed without delay. Through proper communication channels institutions shall be able to keep in touch with both the internal and external community. Communication of the real life business must reach the community while well packaged to attract their attention and trust. Lecturers and administrators must understand that tongues and hands create and destroy societies therefore their use in downplaying institution's business must be discouraged to avoid self-seekers. In the same vein leaders must be able to learn from their enemies because it is not true that whatever they say is wrong. Platforms must be availed to help people speak with respect and sense while airing out their nerves and anger.

Meanwhile, through communication, networking and collaboration within and outside the world may be achieved. This can be done through direct links at both personal and group interaction. Members can set up strategies of implementing decisions at all levels when information is understood, communicated and implemented well. For HEIs institutions that do not give due diligence to this aspect of organisational management will still lag behind and have their activities either sabotaged or jolted down. In a study done by Guidetti, Converso, & Viotti, (2015), it was found that managing educational institutions is not an easy task due to the many activities that surround its efficiency for instance management of parents concerns, customer, discipline, low salaries whereas the energy exerted is too much. It is therefore important that management and staff keep themselves informed of what is taking place in and outside the institutions and thus communicate effectively and efficiently putting into consideration that what they say and do must be accounted for.

ACCOUNTABILITY

Under the term accountability, the stated job description and key performance indicators upon which staff understand their designated responsibility, have the authority and are responsible for the results. Accountability can still be taken as a management terminology used as a framework for measuring employ performance with a focus on the stakeholder's interest (Harrison, Rouse, & De Villiers, 2012). It is a ground under which a staff of an organization takes responsibility of his decisions, actions towards execution of institutional duties. In this case staff are given autonomy and powers to execute duties within their dockets on behalf of the chief accounting officer however at the end of the year or contract, each person must show tangible results that must act as a basis for salary increment and renewal of his or her contract. Before reaching this period, staff's performance can be on scene basing on the way work is done daily.

Abscentism in this situation is uncalled for and staff are supposed to write officially whenever they feel that some time should be given for off duty. In areas where staff do not perform well, organisational systems should give that kind of staff a leave and subject him or her to training and renew his skills and knowledge to cope up with the technological demands.

However, some institutions tend to ignore some people especially in big posts even when there is a lot of misconduct in the management of organisational business. This kind of attitude does not only dwindle the progress of an organization but it also yields bad behavior and attitude among other staff and hence ruin the corporate image of the entire orgnaisation. To arrest this kind of embarrassment within organisational performance, staff who are seated in influential positions of an institution should be required to give mini reports on the progress of their departments and units for close monitoring.

Auditing of services and products should also be done critically with verification of the organizations daily expenditure on units to examine whether performance and expenditure on departments is commensurate with staff performance levels. In this era, HEIs should lay down policies that help to streamline the mode of operation and offer of services. The new generation calls for systematic evaluation of institutional systems, structures, values and at the same time recruit skilled human resources with rigor and vigor attached to high pay that attracts their commitment and diligence towards change. Through taking this direction, institutions shall be able to change from management theories to performance management and meet the necessities of the time (Annan-prah & Coast-ghana, n.d.; Carrera, 2010; Sokol, Gozdek, Figurska, & Blaskova, 2015). Without imbibing accountability into institutional operations, the mission and vision of an institution may be lost or ignored. For smooth running of organisational business, there is need for regular staff training, workshops, attending conferences, regular meetings and annual staff evaluation. Failure to implement accountability through use of modern systems for instance, key performance indicators, balance score card model, international organization for standardization (Iso) framework institutions are likely to fail in achieving their agendas. Moreover, when there is employment of ambidextrous and sine qua non approach, institutions will have clear direction defined with achievable mission, vision and shared values.

Direction

Direction is a clear sense of focus where an institution is strategizing to get. For an institution to achieve its targets there should be a clear vision, mission and stated values. In that whenever any plan for pushing the institution ahead in terms of networking and collaboration must fit within the stated vision and mission. However, as time changes with new dynamics that shape up life, the vision, mission structures, systems and shared values must be revisited to bridge the gap and at the same time address the necessities of the time.

Organisations that take long to review their ways of doing things tend to lose customers and also fail to cope with strategies that lead to quality management achievement. It is therefore important to note HEIs are capitalized on teaching and learning therefore their combined efforts towards integrating customer concerns and with skilled human resources that meet the market demands are a must do without which they may seize to exist (Leary, Walker, Shelton, & Fitt, 2013). Likewise just and reliable methodologies of teaching and testing learner's ability while relating to professionalism must be employed in order to remain relevant to the new trends of the time (Adamu, 2014; Hargreaves, Halász, & Pont, 2007; Moreno-Murcia, Silveira Torregrosa, & Belando Pedreño, 2015; Moreno-Murcia et al., 2015; Wößmann & Hanushek, 2007).

Furthermore staff development and training should be also revisited to ensure that the skills and knowledge tend to address institutional objectives. This is because staff play a central role in the management of organisational affairs when ill skilled and poor attitude personnel are positioned at the center stage of all activities a lot of damage both intended and untended plus sabotage may be encountered.

Moreover those who do work according to the expectations of the organizations should be rewarded and praised for purposes of raising their morale and encouraging others to copy from them(Harrison, Rouse, & De Villiers, 2012; Leary et al., 2013; Leithwood, Day, Sammons, Harris, & Hopkins, 2006). Defining the direction without infusing the willingness to lead the walk, talk and at the same time show the way. It is very unlikely that an institution will move especially when it is full of employees with diverse backgrounds and experiences. It is therefore imperious that organisational leadership becomes firm and support whoevers moves into the desired goal of an institution since it's the only option for survival in the competitive world.

Motivation

Motivation is the availability of enthusiastic drives that attract employees to invest extraordinary efforts to deliver results. This should be done through provision of meaningful values that require to be revisited all the time to suit the demands of the time. In addition, inspirational leadership career development opportunities should be strategized to motivate staff that move on with academic development and career growth.

Meanwhile, financial incentives, rewards and recognition should be tailed to work done and results showed by any member of an organization. In systems where staff work and they are not appreciated in anyway, morale for moving extra miles get killed. In moments where junior officers are placed in high offices orientation and management of human resources skills should be done to avoid frustration and embarrassment of elders, departments that deal with finances should always address staff concerns quickly.

Over questioning and writing on staff requisition even when what is requisitioned for is clear dwindles staff efforts towards positive perception of institutional programs implementation. Without clear and well stated systems of staff motivation, strategies of staff development and capabilities of acquiring reasonable human resources will be frustrated and killed mysteriously. Since motivation is a complex aspect in the management of universities, for managers to achieve the targets and set goals, motivation should be the top priority and its strategy must be laid down in white and black to achieve improved organisational performance (Zlate & Cucui, 2015).

In addition, Kuchava, Allay, Georgia, & Allay, (2016) state that motivation of staff in HEIs both public and private is a key to drive staff to more productivity and high performance levels leading to job satisfaction. It implies that institutions with clear motivation strategies achieve plausible results from their staff due to their levels of satisfaction, care and zeal to provide quality services. When an institution puts in place clear mechanisms of motivation for both intrinsic and extrinsic demands, staff will be subjected to key performance indictors at the same time evaluated through the use of proper appraisal standards of job performance. By employing of these modern management practices, HEIs will have the audacity and the nerve to attract skilled and experienced staff who will ably compete the world of academia

Moreover, to achieve capabilities and proper tools of securing highly qualified staff leadership style, the level of trust, awareness, and openness to discussion and communication play an important role(Blašková & Blaško, 2013).

Capabilities

Capability is the availability of skilled human resource who can be able to execute the designated duties to achieve strategy in the competitive market. At the time when some countries still lag behind in education and transformation of their countries, educational institutions through their leadership and staff should come to an understanding that time of attaining and developing high skilled labour is not an option but a must do (Miiro, 2016b). For instance; in most of African countries the methods of teaching used to not suggest any future development. This is because students study under threatening environment, lecturers are moonlighting, many imparters of knowledge are used to dictation of notes to students, independent to individual reading and reasoning is not yet given due respect. And it is because of this reason and others that many of their graduates do not have true skills of survival and job creation (Miiro & Otham, 2016). Adopting the modern ways of teaching and learning with an aim of helping students to attain skills of critical thinking, logic and reasoning. HEIs' human resources needed to address the challenges of Y generation and generations to come must be opted for rebranding their teaching skills, employ wisdom and other technological ways of imparting knowledge. Talents with quick mindset and reasoning should be nurtured and created in abundance to bridge the gap that many educational organisations are going through especially in Africa. Staff with master's degree and have not been in research and writing should stop teaching students at postgraduate diploma. Students at postgraduate must be exposed to all style of research and publication writing with an agenda of developing them into experts (Miiro, 2017). Many countries suffer brain drain and lack of experts due to lack of proper ways of retaining them and at the same time facilitate their efforts of attracting others and better levels of academic development. Furthermore, for organizations that endure to survive in the era of change, they should also put in place strategies of attaining staff commitment towards high level of performance (Miiro, Othman, Sahari, & Burhan, 2016; Miiro, 2018, 2018). Attracting staff with high qualification is important but also gaining their moral, commitment and quality products and services is the main agenda that must be paid greater attention to (Yüceler, Doğanalp, Kaya, Prof, & Yüceler, 2013). Since employee welfare and organisational effectiveness are always intertwined and their separation causes disastrous effect to organisational survival, HEIs leadership should always be more vigilant and put in place all avenues that lead to staff stability. Institutions that do not lay a firm strategy of securing commitment from their staff and at the same time attract others from sister institutions as a necessity for survival, they are bound to poor quality products. This kind of practice and strategy of ensuring OH implementation, should be accompanied with firm decisions and their implementation strategy should be penned down and followed in order to improve staff development, identification, retention, replacement and nurturing to avoid any vacuums that can be brought with either natural or artificial factors (Kaweesi & Miiro, 2016).

FUTURE RESEARCH DIRECTIONS

The ultimate goal of implementing OH elements as espoused in the model of Keller and Price (2010) is to achieve quality services, products and customer satisfaction. This can be achieved through staff stability, innovation and development. With future researchers therefore, emphasis may be centered on issues like organisational health and customer satisfaction, organisational health and total quality management, safety, security, business continuity, performance measurement and accountability, HEIs staff stability and community change. It is therefore emphatic that managers of these institutions play an important role towards stabilizing their staff by attending to key issues that relate to OH so as to compete favorably in the knowledge economy. Also the new world order of HEIs will focus more on staff influence towards customer service and community change due the needs of the time that are focusing on sustainable development goals. All the above will still not be achieved without proper strategies that focus on organisational health elements efficiency and effectiveness to curtail staff turnover.

CONCLUSION

It is therefore important to note that while imbibing OH model into HEIs operations through the sine qua non and ambidextrous approach to avoid situations that can lead to staff turnover, all avenues employed for its effectiveness should ensure that all organisational health elements relate with one another to ensure smooth delivery of organisational business. More so this approach should be coupled with new trends of digital transformation, virtual connection, agility approach, quantum leadership, cloud leadership and being on top of trends. By adopting these trends, HEIs are likely to consolidate their developed staff and at the same time attract potential skilled human resources

REFERENCES

Adamu, A. Y. (2014). *Ethnic and Religious Diversity in Higher Education in Ethiopia: The Case of Bahir Dar University*. The University of Tampere.

Annan-prah, E., & Coast-ghana, C. (n.d.). *Improving Productivity through Performance Management in Public Sector Organizations in Ghana: Is Change Management the Answer?* Department of Management Studies School of Business College of Humanities and Legal Studies University.

Blašková, M., & Blaško, R. (2013). Motivation of University Teachers and its Connections. *Human Resources Management & Ergonomics, 7*(2), 6–21.

Carlfjord, S., Andersson, A., Nilsen, P., Bendtsen, P., & Lindberg, M. (2010). Linköping University Post Print The importance of organizational climate and implementation strategy at the introduction of a new working tool in primary health care. *Journal of Evaluation in Clinical Practice*, 6(16), 1326–1332. doi:10.1111/j.1365-2753.2009.01336.x PMID:20738475

Carrera, E. G. (2010). *The Area of Freedom, Security And Justice Ten Years On Successes and Future Challenges Under The Stockholm Programme*. Academic Press.

Chandra, S. (2014, Feb.). Organisational Culture: A Case Study Organisational Culture. *International Journal of Knowledge Management and Practice*.

Ddungu, L. (2014). *University Lecturers' Professional Empowerment and Turnover in Uganda*. Academic Press.

De Klerk, S., & Stander, M. W. (2014). Leadership Empowerment Behaviour, Work Engagement and Turnover Intention: The Role of Psychological Empowerment. *Journal of Positive Management*, 5(3), 28. doi:10.12775/JPM.2014.018

De Smet, A., Schaninger, B., & Smith, M. (2014). The hidden value of organizational health— And how to capture it. *The McKinsey Quarterly*, 69–79. https://www.mckinsey.com/insights/mckinsey_quarterly/digital_newsstand/2014_number_2

Demetria, S., & Mkulu, G. (2018). *Academic Staff Retention in Private Universities in Southern Highland Zone Tanzania as a Strategy of Attaining Sustainable Development*. doi:10.30845/ijhss.v8n5p17

Douglas, E., & Selin, Y. M. (2012). Internationalization and Globalization in Higher Education. *Globalization - Education and Management Agendas*, 3–22. doi:10.5772/48702

Erasmus, B., Grobler, A., & Plessis, M. (2015). *An Employee Retention In A Higher Education Institution : An Organisational Development*. doi:10.25159/0256-8853/600

Figueroa, O. (2018). *The Influences Impacting Staff Turnover in Higher Education*. doi:10.5539/jms.v5n4p86

Franciska, V., & Welly, J. (2013). Formulating Company Health Aspiration To Achieve Organizational Excellence By Using Organizational Health Index (Ohi) : Case Study At Pt Bio Farma (Persero). *The Indonesian Journal of Business Administration*, 2(13), 1570–1579.

Frontiera, J. (2010). Leadership and Organizational Culture Transformation in Professional Sport. *Journal of Leadership & Organizational Studies*, 17(1), 71–86. doi:10.1177/1548051809345253

Glenn. (2008). *The future of higher education: How technology will shape learning*. Retrieved from http://www.nmc.org/pdf/Future-of-Higher-Ed-(NMC).pdf

Guidetti, G., Converso, D., & Viotti, S. (2015). The School Organisational Health Questionnaire: Contribution to the Italian Validation. *Procedia: Social and Behavioral Sciences*, 174, 3434–3440. doi:10.1016/j.sbspro.2015.01.1015

Hamid, M. R. A., Mustafa, Z., Idris, F., Abdullah, M., Suradi, N. R. M., Sains, F., ... Matematik, S. (2011). Measuring Value – Based Productivity : A Confirmatory Factor Analytic (CFA) Approach. *International Journal of Business and Social Science*, 2(6), 85–93.

Hargreaves, A., Halász, G., & Pont, B. (2007). *School leadership for systemic improvement in Finland A case study report for the OECD activity Improving school leadership.* Academic Press.

Harrison, J. A., Rouse, P., & De Villiers, C. J. (2012). Accountability and Performance Measurement: A Stakeholder Perspective. *Journal of Centrum Cathedra, 5*(2), 243–258. doi:10.7835/jcc-berj-2012-0077

Husain, Z. (2013). Effective Communication brings successful organizational change. *The Business Andd Management Review, 3*(2), 43–50. Retrieved from http://www.abrmr.com/myfile/conference_proceedings/Con_Pro_12315/7-dubai13.pdf

Hussein, N., Mohamad, A., Noordin, F., & Amir, N. (2014). Learning Organization and its Effect on Organizational Performance and Organizational Innovativeness : A Proposed Framework for Malaysian Public Institutions of Higher Education. *Procedia: Social and Behavioral Sciences, 130,* 299–304. doi:10.1016/j.sbspro.2014.04.035

Jafarzadeh, M. (2015). A survey on the Relation between Organizational Health and Prganizational Learning across Iran. *Research Journal of Recent Sciences, 4*(2), 20–24.

Kaweesi, M., & Miiro, F. (2016). Decision Making and Problem Solving in Higher Education Institutions. In *Applied Chaos and Complexity Theory in Education* (pp. 226–239). IGI Global Disseminator of Knowledge. doi:10.4018/978-1-5225-0460-3.ch015

Keller, S., & Price, C. (2010). Performance and Health: An evidence-based approach to transforming your organisation. *The McKinsey Quaterly.*

Kuchava, M. A. M., Allay, D. A., Georgia, T., & Allay, D. A. (2016). Staff Motivation in Private and Public Higher Educational Institutions (Case of International Black Sea University, Sokhumi State University and Akaki Tsereteli State University). *Journal of Education & Social Policy, 3*(4), 92–100.

Leary, H., Walker, A., Shelton, B. E., & Fitt, M. H. (2013). Interdisciplinary Journal of Problem-Based Learning Exploring the Relationships Between Tutor Background, Tutor Training, and Student Learning: A Problem-based Learning Meta-Analysis. *Interdisciplinary Journal of Problem-Based Learning, 7*(1), 3–15. doi:10.7771/1541-5015.1331

Leithwood, K., Day, C., Sammons, P., Harris, A., & Hopkins, D. (2006). Successful School Leadership What It Is and How It Influences Pupil Learning. *Leadership,* 132.

Mcmurray, A. J. (2012). The role of organisational climate factors in facilitating workplace innovation Kathryn von Treuer. *Int. J. Entrepreneurship and Innovation Management.* doi:10.1504/IJEIM.2012.048078

Mendes, F., & Stander, M. W. (2011). Positive organisation: The role of leader behaviour in work engagement and retention. *SA Journal of Industrial Psychology, 37*(1), 1–13. doi:10.4102ajip.v37i1.900

Meyer, M., Bushney, M., & Ukpere, W. I. (2011). The impact of globalisation on higher education: Achieving a balance between local and global needs and realities. *African Journal of Business Management, 5*(15), 6569–6578. doi:10.5897/AJBM11.205

Miiro, F. (2016a). Conflict Managememt in higher Educational Institutions: Acomplexity perspective. In Applied chaos and Complexity Theory in Education (p. 299). Information Science Reference.

Miiro, F. (2016b). Sustainable Leadership Practices in Higher Education Institutions : An Analytical Review of Literature. In Ş. Ş. Erçetin (Ed.), Chaos, Complexity and Leadership 2016, Springer Proceedings in Complexity, (pp. 235–245). Springer International Publishing AG.

Miiro, F. (2017). Holistic Personality Development of Youth Through Higher Education Using The Prophetic Practices. *Australian Journal of Humanities and Islamic Studies Research*, *3*(1), 1–5.

Miiro, F. (2018). An Exploratory Factor Analysis for Validation of a Measurement of Organizational Excellence Construct among Universities in the Central Region of Uganda. *Interdisciplinary Journal of Education*, *1*(1), 40–61. Available at: <https://journals.iuiu.ac.ug/index.php/ije/article/view/37

Miiro, F., & Otham, A. (2016). Talent Management Practices A Trajectory and Ingenuity in Higher Education Institutions : A Meta-analysis Review of Literature. In Chaos, Complexity and Leadership 2016, Springer Proceedings in Complexity, (pp. 111–123). doi:10.1007/978-3-319-64554-4

Miiro, F., Othman, A., Sahari, M., & Burhan, M. (2016). A Measurement Model of Talent Management Practices Among University Staff in Central. *Journal of Positive Management*, *7*(3), 3–19.

Miiro, F., Othman, A., Sahari, M., & Burhan, M. (2017). Examining Organizational Health Practices among Universities. *Journal of Positive Management, 8*(2), 69–86.

Miiro, F., Othman, A., Sahari Nordin, M., & Burhan Ibrahim, M. (2017). Analysing the Relationship Between Sustainable Leadership. *Talent Management and Organization Health As Predictors of University Transformation*, *32*(1), 32–50. doi:10.12775/JPM.2017.003

Mitchell, D. E., & Nielsen, S. Y. (2012). *Globalization – Education and Management Agendas: Internationalization and Globalization in Higher Education*. INTECH.

Moreno-Murcia, J. A., Silveira Torregrosa, Y., & Belando Pedreño, N. (2015). Questionnaire evaluating teaching competencies in the university environment. Evaluation of teaching competencies in the university. *Journal of New Approaches in Educational Research*, *4*(1), 54–61. doi:10.7821/naer.2015.1.106

Musah, A. A., & Nkuah, J. K. (2013). Reducing Employee Turnover in Tertiary Institutions in Ghana. *The Role of Motivation*, *4*(18), 115–135.

Owence, C., Pinagase, T. G., & Mercy, M. M. (2014). *Causes and Effects of Staff Turnover in the Academic Development Centre : A Case of a Historically Black University in South Africa*. doi:10.5901/mjss.2014.v5n11p69

Sokol, A., Gozdek, A., Figurska, I., & Blaskova, M. (2015). Organizational climate of higher education institutions and its implications for the development of creativity. *Procedia: Social and Behavioral Sciences*, *182*, 279–288. doi:10.1016/j.sbspro.2015.04.767

Vilcea, M. A. (2014). Quality Culture in Universities and Influences on Formal and Non-formal Education. *Procedia: Social and Behavioral Sciences*, *163*, 148–152. doi:10.1016/j.sbspro.2014.12.300

Wößmann, L., & Hanushek, E. (2007). The Role of Education Quality in Economic Growth The Role of School Improvement in Economic Development. *World Bank Policy Research Working Paper*, *4122*, 1–94. doi:10.2139srn.960379

Yüceler, A., Doğanalp, B., & Kaya, Ş. D. (2013). The Relation Between Organizational Health and Organizational Commitment. *Mediterranean Journal of Social Sciences*, 4(10), 781–788. doi:10.5901/mjss.2013.v4n10p781

Yüceler, A., Doğanalp, B., Kaya, Ş. D., Prof, A., & Yüceler, A. (2013). The Relation Between Organizational Health and Organizational Commitment. *Mediterranean Journal of Social Sciences*, 4(10), 781–788. doi:10.5901/mjss.2013.v4n10p781

Zakuan, N., Yusof, S. M., Saman, M. Z. M., & Shaharoun, A. M. (2010). Confirmatory Factor Analysis of TQM Practices in Malaysia and Thailand Automotive Industries. *International Journal of Business and Management*, 5(1), 160–175. doi:10.5539/ijbm.v5n1p160

Zlate, S., & Cucui, G. (2015). Motivation and performance in higher education. *Procedia - Social and Behavioral Sciences, 180*(November), 468–476. doi:10.1016/j.sbspro.2015.02.146

KEY TERMS AND DEFINITIONS

Ambidextrous: Application of management process using both right and left hand with an aim of causing positive change.

Imbibing: To absorb the new trends of organisational health into HEIs management practices.

Organisational Health: Organizational health is the ability of an organization to align its strategy, culture and a clear vision with an aim of providing quality services and excellent products to outcompete other organizations on the world market (De Smet, Schaninger, & Smith, 2014; Franciska & Welly, 2013).

Sine Qua Non: Is the application of essential management practices in day to day of running institutional business without an organization is bound to fail.

Leader Ambidexterity in Research Teams

Montserrat Boronat-Navarro

(iD) https://orcid.org/0000-0002-9062-4161

Jaume I University, Spain

María P. Mora-Crespo

Jaume I University, Spain

INTRODUCTION

Universities are increasingly developing an awareness about their so-called third mission, in which a scientific-economic paradigm is present (Chang et al., 2009). The institutions realize the importance of transferring knowledge to industry and society, with the possibility of exploiting the knowledge generated inside universities. The ability to combine conflicting demands that require different activities at universities, such as research publication and research commercialization, is an important challenge that must be addressed to effectively transfer knowledge and technology from universities to society.

Universities as organizations promote the transfer of knowledge and technologies to different industries, providing an adequate institutional framework and structure to researchers. We recognize the importance of this structure and the difficulty at the organizational level to cope with tension that requires research and entrepreneurial orientations, but we focus this study on the factors that have an influence at the micro-level of a leader of a research team. Because the main units at universities that develop knowledge are the research teams (Bayona-Sáez et al., 2002), in this study we analyse the ambidexterity of a leader of a research team. Research teams and specifically their main researchers must deal with dualities that arise if they want their research to become commercialized.

The ambidexterity concept shows the importance of coping with this tension, as studied from organization learning literature (e.g., March, 1991), management and strategic literature (Ghemawat and Ricarti Costa, 1993), and innovation studies (e.g., Jansen et al., 2006; Smith and Tushman, 2005). Ambos et al. (2008) interpret the concept in the context of universities as the ability to simultaneously produce knowledge-focused research or scientific contributions and property-focused research or commercial contributions. Chang et al. (2016) define individual research ambidexterity as "the ability by which academic scientists can simultaneously achieve research publication and research commercialization at the individual level". We analyse this concept in the case of the main researcher of a research team, who acts as the leader of the team.

The aim of the present research is to determine the antecedents that make it possible for the main researchers to successfully achieve both research and commercialization activities. First, the concept of ambidexterity is presented and then translated to the university context. Next, we review the ambidexterity literature to propose the antecedents that must be studied at the level of an individual leader of a research team. Then, we present the methodology and illustrate our framework with an analysis of two research teams at different Spanish universities that have achieved academic as well as commercial results. Finally, we present our results and derive our conclusions.

DOI: 10.4018/978-1-7998-3473-1.ch187

BACKGROUND

Ambidexterity

The literature on management, innovation, and organization has discussed the contradictions that managers must reconcile to be efficient and effective, to develop incremental and radical innovations, to focus on the short- and long-term, or to cope with variation and stability. March (1991) outlines these contradictory firm demands in the concepts of exploration and exploitation in organizational learning. Exploration refers to risk taking activities, variation in learning, experimentation, flexibility and discovering, while exploitation means refinement, efficiency, and learning by doing. His seminal paper on the necessity of balancing both activities has been highly studied, and the later concept of organizational ambidexterity reflects the organizational capability to achieve exploration as well as exploitation. The difficulty in achieving ambidexterity is the conflicting demands of exploration and exploitation. Exploration requires variance-increasing activities and distant search, whereas exploitation is rooted in variance-decreasing activities and local search (Smith and Tushman, 2005). The importance of the concepts ambidexterity, and exploration and exploitation has grown in the literature and has been applied in different areas, while a variety of definitions have proliferated as Gupta et al. (2006) recognized. For example, in distinguishing between exploration and exploitation, Baum et al. (2000) focus on the distance of knowledge and variation, thus providing closed definitions to March's original concepts (March, 1991) and to Smith and Tushman's (2005) explanations. Other authors centre their definitions on the differences in the innovative output achieved, such as Benner and Tushman (2002) or He and Wong (2004). After reviewing a variety of definitions, Li et al. (2008) propose a framework that integrates different perspectives to better understand these differences. The authors distinguish between the 'function domain' and 'knowledge distance domain'. Whereas in each step in the value chain the organization can create familiar knowledge (exploitation) or more unfamiliar knowledge (exploration) ('knowledge distance domain'), "the 'function domain' regards each function on the value chain as unique in its type of learning" (Li et al., 2008: 118). Considering science, technology and product market knowledge as a sequence in the value chain, the early stages correspond to exploration during which organizations search for new knowledge, while the last steps have more exploitative characteristics for applying that knowledge (Li et al., 2008). In this sense, the next section explains the consideration of exploration and exploitation in this study, which agrees with this conceptualization of differences in the 'function domain'.

Furthermore, the three major approaches identified within the literature at the organizational level to achieve ambidexterity are the temporal, structural, and contextual (Gibson and Birkinshaw, 2004; Tushman and O'Reilly, 1996). In the temporal view of ambidexterity, organizational resources are concentrated in exploration or exploitation at different times, since periods of exploitation are followed by periods of exploration. Structural ambidexterity is achieved by organizational mechanisms, formal structures and coordination mechanisms, by concentrating some units on exploration and others on exploitation and then coordinating the units (Tushman and O'Reilly, 1996). We follow the third approach, contextual ambidexterity because it applies to the individual level, on which this study is focused. Contextual ambidexterity means to simultaneously achieve exploration and exploitation by building systems in which individuals could develop ambidexterity and make their own judgements about dividing their time between the conflicting demands for alignment and adaptability (Gibson and Birkinshaw, 2004). In this sense, we concentrate on the individual level of ambidexterity.

Ambidexterity at Universities

Research publication and commercialization require the development of very different abilities and tasks (Ambos et al., 2008; Chang et al., 2016). Academia rewards knowledge dissemination while industry demands ownership and control of intellectual property rights in different ways, which also means a delay in the possibility of publication of the findings that underly the commercial output (Ambos et al., 2008). Academics develop their routines and abilities while performing scientific research, which are highly linked with their professional evolution and opportunities for career development. The transfer of knowledge to companies in the form of patents, licenses, spin-offs, spin-out companies, and other ways of technology transfer require that academics, and more specifically, the leaders of the research teams, develop other types of abilities that are contradictory with their usual behaviour (Ambos et al., 2008), and divide their time and efforts between research and commercialization. In this sense, ambidexterity refers to the ability to simultaneously produce knowledge-focused research or scientific contributions and property-focused research or commercial contributions (Chang et al., 2016).

We focus on the main antecedents of achieving this ambidexterity at the individual level, specifically at the level of the leader of a research team. Although recognizing the importance of the context and the structural support from universities in other levels of analysis, such as the full organization, departments and other formal structures, the attention of this research is on the individual level. Ambidextrous managers are considered to be one of the most relevant elements to promote ambidexterity (Mom et al., 2009; O'Reilly and Tushman, 2011). Managers acting as a leader of a group represent a key element since they are going to be in charge of directing both the exploitative and explorative efforts.

Specifically, our research is based on the concept of individual research ambidexterity proposed by Chang et al. (2016: 9), which is defined as "the ability to which academic scientists can simultaneously achieve research publication and research commercialization at the individual level".

Antecedents of Individual Ambidexterity

Ambidexterity at the level of a leader and/or manager has been studied in the management literature. To achieve organizational ambidexterity, individuals play an important role (Gibson and Birkinshaw, 2004), and specifically managers or leaders must address the contradicting dualities. Mom et al. (2009) define ambidextrous managers as those that organize contradictions, can multitask, and can refine as well as renew their knowledge and abilities. Chang et al. (2016) analyse, at the individual level, the ability to recognize opportunities to exploit their research opportunity, whereas Chang et al. (2009) propose networking and personal entrepreneurial capabilities as the main antecedents. Ambos et al. (2008) are more centred on individual scientific excellence, the embeddedness in academia and the motivation to pursue commercial outputs. Together, these antecedents compose the framework proposed in this study to analyse the ambidexterity of the leader of a research team; we will now analyse this framework.

Networking

Personal networking, both inside and outside the organization and the team, has been recognized in the literature as one of the main characteristics of ambidextrous leaders (Cao et al., 2010), especially in a university context (Ambos et al., 2008; Chang et al., 2009). Networking means creating interactions between academic scientists, and between academics and firms and other organizations (Ambos et al., 2008; Chang et al., 2009). A network provides information and knowledge that could have a potential value (Cao et al., 2010). This gives the leader a deeper understanding of the internal and external situations, which provides more opportunities for a comprehensive picture of how to explore and exploit (Cao et al., 2010). Links with industry actors provides opportunities to understand their needs as well opportunities for financing projects or other commercial outputs (Chang et al., 2009; Jensen et al., 2003). Connectedness with other academic researchers provides opportunities to enhance their research as well as meet members that may possibly be needed for future projects. Additionally, it is important to know potential candidates to include additional human resources in their laboratories and teams. This network provides possibilities of incorporating new knowledge and experiences outside the team's usual trajectory (Chang et al., 2009).

Entrepreneurial Capabilities

Considering that the entrepreneurial process comprises discovering, evaluating and exploiting opportunities (Chang et al., 2009; Shane and Venkatraman, 2000), which includes proactiveness and risk taking, ambidextrous leaders must have entrepreneurial abilities. The importance of entrepreneurial capabilities has been shown in a variety of areas. The Council of the European Union has even included entrepreneurship as a key competence for lifelong learning, considering it as "the capacity to act upon opportunities and ideas, and to transform them into values for others" (Council of the European Union, 2019: 23).

To overcome the difficulties in the process and to be able to cope with the ambiguous environment, this ability must also include a strong motivation to obtain commercial applications for their research (Chang et al., 2009; Chang et al., 2016; Gibson and Birkinshaw, 2004). These time-consuming processes could be detrimental for the scientific production (Chang et al., 2016; Smith and Parr, 2003); therefore, leaders must be conscious of the risk it implies.

Paradoxical Thinking

The literature has stressed the importance of ambidextrous managers addressing conflict and having paradoxical thinking (Gibson and Birkinshaw, 2004; Mom et al., 2009; Smith and Tushman, 2005). It implies motivation and the ability to be sensitive to, to understand, and to pursue a range of seemingly conflicting opportunities, needs, and goals (Mom et al., 2009). In fact, the 'paradoxical' view of ambidexterity considers the simultaneous achievement of exploration and exploitation and their mutual reinforcement (both/and), as opposite to the trade-off view (either/or) (Gibson and Birkinshaw, 2004). According to Mom et al. (2009) and O'Reilly and Tushman (2004), managers continuously must cope with contradictions which implies that "they have the motivation and ability to be sensitive to, to understand and to pursue a range of seemingly conflicting opportunities, needs, and goals" (Mom et al., 2009: 813). In the context of the leader of a research team, this means that he or she must integrate contradictions regarding the different tasks, processes, norms and routines that research publication and research commercialization require (Chang et al., 2016). Paradoxical thinking is a fundamental trait to manage those contradictions (Smith and Tushman, 2005). Moreover, managers must also reconcile conflicts regarding the team's long- and short-term goals. For example, sometimes a long-term goal could be focused on developing totally new knowledge and processes that could result in a patented solution, but it is common that younger members of the team need short-term results in terms of publications necessary to continue with their careers. Therefore, managers must resolve these conflicting demands between the long- and short-term and between differences among the team's members. Paradoxical thinking implies embracing contradictions instead of choosing between contradictory goals (Smith and Tushman, 2005).

Multitasking

The development of exploration and exploitation also means performing diverse tasks and activities. In this sense, ambidextrous managers must accomplish multiple tasks within the same period (Mom et al. 2009), representing different roles (Floyd and Lane, 2000; Sanchez et al., 1996). They must recognize the strategic direction and ratify and monitor its development but also command the deployment of resources (Floyd and Lane, 2000). Moreover, they usually develop nonroutine activities in the more creative side of their tasks but must also implement routine activities (Adler et al. 1999). In the context of the leader of a research team, the tasks and even the roles to perform exploration and exploitation show clear differences, since the process of developing a patent or another commercial goal must support other relationships, such as with firms, as well as different processes, norms, and regulations to have success with a commercial output.

Refining and renewing knowledge and abilities

The literature also emphasizes the need for ambidextrous leaders to refine their knowledge and skills through reliability-enhancing learning activities, while simultaneously renewing their knowledge with variety-increasing activities (Holmqvist, 2004; McGrath, 2001; Mom et al., 2009). These processes require managers to acquire diverse knowledge and information from different sources, engaging in local and distant searches (Mom et al., 2009).

Scientific Excellence

Although we propose that leaders must be ambidextrous to produce commercial and also academic outputs, concentrating too much on the academic aspect could be detrimental to obtaining industrial applications. Strong academic excellence means also having academic influence, and it can only be achieved by being embedded in academia, which also means having a higher commitment to certain norms and behaviour (Ambos et al., 2008). Academia defines what is valuable and rigorous research, and it could be detrimental to deviate from these norms to obtain commercial applications. Academia usually rewards the academic aspect; therefore, a reduction of the commercial results could be expected (Ambos et al., 2008). Researchers with higher commercial results are usually different from researchers that traditionally focus on producing academic results (Ambos et al., 2008).

After the review of these antecedents, the next sections illustrate the framework with two real examples.

ANALYSIS

Methods

After proposing the framework for leader ambidexterity in research teams, we analyse the framework in two research teams that have made scientific as well as commercial contributions. This research constitutes an initial approach to further develop the empirical part in future with more data and over a longer period in a full case study. Case studies are an inductive-based methodology (Eisenhardt, 1989; Yin, 2009) suitable for answering how and why questions (Yin, 2009) and has been used in similar contexts

15

(e.g., Mckelvey et al. 2015). The examples in the present research are designed to illustrate the proposed theoretical framework of leader ambidexterity in research teams.

The decision about the number of examples to include in the research was based on the recommendation of having more than one case to have literal replication, that is, for predicting similar results (Yin, 1994). The aim is to illustrate the theory.

The selection of the specific examples was made according to their suitability for the theoretical framework (Eisenhardt, 1989; McKelvey et al., 2015). Accordingly, we select two research teams from different Spanish universities and different areas of research. The areas are purposefully selected to include fields where the demands of commercial research are relevant. Specifically, we search for scientists with results in terms of published scientific papers as well as transference to industry. We search for academic leaders that have a specific sensitivity to the commercial aspect, since it is more difficult to find. The two selected cases reflect as a mission of their team and/or as a personal goal on their webpages the necessity of transferring knowledge to society.

We focus on the individual as the unit of analysis since our aim is to illustrate the antecedents of leaders' ambidexterity in research teams. Therefore, we contact the two main academics who coordinate research teams with knowledge- and property-focused research.

Data are collected during March and April 2018 through semi-structured interviews with the leaders that are recorded, transcribed and analysed, and completed through the collection of secondary data obtained from public sources including the universities' webpages, the research teams' and institutes' webpages (of which they are members), news, the Web of Science, Scopus database, and published patents. Having primary and secondary data allows us to have different sources of evidence (Yin, 2009). In the interviews, both authors are present, and both analyse the results to increase objectivity in the interpretation. The protocol for the interviews includes semi-structured questions to get information about the antecedents in a fluent manner. Following other studies that use interviews for data collection in case studies (e.g. Bonesso et al., 2014), we reformulated questions from previous empirical studies that analyse and/or measure ambidextrous leadership and different antecedents (Ambos et al., 2008; Chang et al., 2009, 2016; Mom et al., 2009). An example of a question is: How often do you collaborate with other research teams? The interviews last on average one hour.

The leaders are also contacted after the interviews by mail or phone to confirm some data. Furthermore, after interpreting the examples, analysing results, and redacting the final manuscript of this research, the two leaders read the final document. Two members of the research team of the second leader interviewed have also read the final manuscript and confirmed that it reflects the leader's orientation towards research and commercialization.

Presentation of the two Illustrative Examples

After choosing and contacting the research teams, we obtain the collaboration of two scientists that act as coordinators of research teams from two different Spanish public universities. Both universities have research excellence and promotion of knowledge transfer as strategic objectives. The first (in which the first leader presented undertakes his work) is more active in promoting transference with specific structures (institutes and research centres) and a detailed budget for transference. Nevertheless, its global budget is also higher than in the second institution, which has more limited resources.

The selection of these teams is based on their special sensitivity to the transfer of knowledge, that they have both types of outputs (commercial and academic), that they belong to different institutions and research areas, and that they agree to participate in the present research. The selected leaders are in the areas of Information and Communication Technologies (referred to as Leader 1) and Chemical and Advanced Materials (presented as Leader 2).

Leader 1

The team that Leader 1 manages, conducts theoretical and experimental research to develop basic metrology and specific and accurate measurement devices for radiofrequency and microwave. The institute where Leader 1 performs research has the mission of improving society through the transfer and application of knowledge from research in the field of Information and Communications Technology. The institute has a specific organizational structure inside the university to promote research and commercialization. It gives support to researchers with an adequate infrastructure to promote both aspects of research and transference. The research team led by Leader 1 is composed of more than 14 researchers.

The leader is a full professor and has published 86 papers in journals belonging to the Scopus database, has developed 4 patents, and has promoted more than 50 contracts with industry.

Leader 2

Leader 2 coordinates a team that analyses polymers for energy applications, coatings, composite materials, biomaterials and technologies of corrosion, electrochemical characterization and material spectroscopy. The team was founded in 2010 with the mission of generating and transferring applied knowledge in the area of advanced materials to improve the innovation capacity of the industry. It is composed of six researchers and two technicians, and several Ph.D. students and master and undergraduate students from the same university. They collaborate in an established way with other research groups at other universities that specialize in different areas, such as clinical, chemistry, proteomic and biotechnology.

Leader 2 is a full professor with 65 scientific papers (according to the Scopus database), as well as many other publications. He participates in the subject Master's Thesis, where master's students must develop a professional oriented project in industrial engineering. The leader also appears as the inventor in 6 patents (4 of them licensed or in exploitation), and a promotor of 2 spin-off companies, and the principal researcher of 50 contracts with industry. The team was able to promote one of the first International Organization for Standardization (ISO) standards proposed by Spain (ISO 17463:2014).

Results

The results are presented following the structure of the theoretical framework, analysing results from the characteristics/antecedents of the leaders' ambidexterity.

Interactions

Both leaders stress the importance of creating a network outside their research groups. Table 1 shows the main statements from the interviews that outline the relevance of these networks. While *Leader 1* stresses both aspects of these networks (i.e., industry and academia), Leader 2 gives more relevance to the industry aspect of a network. Regarding contacts with academia, Leader 1 seems to be equally concerned about the interaction with academia and industry, specifically organizing an academic international conference with the goal of reinforcing their network and creating new contacts. By contrast, Leader 2 only remarks that once they have created a research structure with another research team that belongs to a different

Table 1. Examples of quotes from the interviews regarding the importance of networks

Networking (Ambos et al., 2008; Chang et al., 2009)	
Leader 1	**Leader 2**
"We organize an international conference to maintain our relationships and to create new ones." "We have a network of contacts with research groups from other countries, contacts with research groups in other areas at the university and also a network of contacts with companies." "A network is very important, and it takes much time to build a network. Once the companies know what you are doing, when they have a problem or a new challenge, they contact us." "Previous contacts allow us to develop new ideas, new developments."	"Collaboration with other groups that specialize in different areas in an established way is critical for the success of the research lines." "The team who develops patents consists of two research groups from different universities." "We carry out virtual and face-to-face meetings with the full group, which includes teams from other universities." "We collaborate with researchers in other areas." "The team members themselves belong to different knowledge areas and we must try to find a common language." "I am in contact with firms that know the necessity of patents." "It is impossible to transfer a patent… if you don't know which need the market has, the firms are who know the needs." "The firm gives us the need and we develop solutions to solve this need." "The firm gives us more contacts." "We create a network of industrial contacts through this first contact."

university, the important thing is having industry contacts. However, Leader 2 recognizes the necessity of collaborating with other researchers, but with an exploitation-oriented goal—they collaborate with studies in other areas as needed to develop a patent. Moreover, data analysed from other documents (i.e., publications or the Web) show that Leader 2 also maintains a collaboration with researchers that belong to other institutions where he has been previously employed.

Regarding the interaction with industry, both stress its importance and share the idea that firms are the starting point to develop a patent when they communicate a need or a problem, because it is from this moment that teams start to perform research to solve the challenge, a process that could, in turn, end with the development of a patent. Furthermore, in both cases, it is the leaders of the teams who create and are the visible interlocutor with firms. Leader 2 stresses this point by claiming that he is the person who is in contact with companies.

Entrepreneurial Abilities

Both leaders share a strong motivation to serve society through the development of knowledge with practical applications. In fact, we select both leaders because this motivation clearly appears in their main webpage or as a mission of the institute they manage. In the interviews, Leader 1 demonstrates how they are required to know all the phases to successfully achieve a commercial application (Table 2). In addition to the mission that appears for the group, Leader 2 also includes in his professional webpage his goal of transferring the group's developments to the productive sector. In the interview, Leader 2 recognizes the difficulties of being centred on transferring knowledge to the productive sector and the risks they assume, because it requires more time and money and could be detrimental for their own scientific production.

Paradoxical Thinking

The results show the importance of addressing contradictions for both leaders (Table 3). Paradoxical thinking is necessary to develop a solution according to Leader 1. In the interview with Leader 2, his

Table 2. Examples of quotes from the interviews regarding the importance of entrepreneurial abilities

Entrepreneurial abilities (Chang et al., 2009; Chang et al., 2016)	
Leader 1	**Leader 2**
"As leaders, we propose the areas or topics of research." "Our projects with firms are development projects in which we must discover a new solution for a problem." "Some contracts with companies require patenting the development." "Previous contacts allow us to develop new ideas, new developments." "We are strongly oriented to carry out both basic research and contracts with companies (that allow commercialization)." "Contracts provide us more resources to continue our research." "We must act as a seller in some sense."	"I am the person in the team who is in contact with firms to discover opportunities." "It's a risky decision to develop a patent, in terms of money, time and my own career."

role of managing contradictions and conflicts among the team clearly surfaced. Both stress the necessity of coping with different demands for the long- and short-term. They must also possess this paradoxical thinking to be able to find a solution to problems not yet resolved in their development projects.

Multitasking

Regarding multitasking, both leaders fulfil multiple roles of teaching at the University, performing management tasks as leaders of their teams, being a chair director (Leader 2), and being researchers and developers of their projects from the initial phases to the end. Some statements in the interviews also outline their multiple tasks (Table 4). As leaders of the research teams, they must align the team members to achieve the objectives in an efficient way. As directors, they must also be involved in management tasks, in obtaining and managing resources for the institute, and must also work with companies to establish long-term relationships with them. In the entrepreneurial characteristic, we have also outlined how they perform diverse activities.

Table 3. Examples of quotes from the interviews regarding the importance of organizing contradictions

Organize contradictions and paradoxical thinking (Mom et al., 2009)	
Leader 1	**Leader 2**
"We have new ideas and develop new knowledge that we must 'sell' in terms of projects, papers or contracts with firms and have some procedures that we must follow. Additionally, firms contact our group to solve problems that do not have a current solution, and we develop new solutions. Our projects are development projects." "As a leader, I must think of the long-term; my decisions have consequences on the work of my team." "Some issues require prompt consideration, whereas others are less vital. I must prioritize tasks and make decisions within the group."	"We continuously need to manage contradictions among the team because we belong to different areas of knowledge where the language is different, and it is different from the firm's language." "We focus on the long-term. The process to develop a patent is very long in this area, but we also need to obtain more short-term goals regarding the project itself (different phases) and regarding the younger members of the team because they need publications to advance their careers."

Table 4. Examples of quotes from the interviews regarding the importance of performing multiple tasks

Multitasking (Mom et al., 2009)	
Leader 1	**Leader 2**
"We must teach in our classes, create new knowledge to carry out basic research, and apply this research; we also have other academic positions."	"I am the person who is in contact with firms." "I need to understand their language." "I think of the ideas for how to develop the project."

Refining and Renewing Knowledge and Abilities

We outline in Table 5 examples of the statements both leaders made regarding the necessity of acquiring distant knowledge. To develop new projects, they need interdisciplinarity, which Leader 1 remarks is addressed with their approach to other knowledge areas based on their contacts as well as inside the team. The leader said that it is important to understand the main principles as the leader, but that specialized people are also needed to execute the full projects. Leader 2 even remarks the solution comes sometimes by breaking the established rules of a given area.

Scientific excellence

Regarding scientific excellence, both leaders have a high number of published papers in the Scopus database (Table 6) which includes Scimago Journal Rank (SCR). Table 6 also shows the H index and the total number of citations received by both leaders. Table 6 also includes data from the Web of Science for one of the most cited researchers in each area, although the Web of Science only provides the ranking of the Highly Cited Researchers in more generic areas. It does not provide this list in each of the specific sub-areas of both leaders, which would be more realistic for comparison. Of course, the figures of the top scientists are higher, but the numbers of both leaders demonstrate high research-oriented results. Furthermore, both are full professors, which means that they have achieved at least the minimum level of excellence for this position. Leader 2 clearly realizes in the interview that academia has its own rules and that following them, until now, means to not give value to the transference to industry; therefore, concentrating on the commercial aspect is a risky decision for his own career. In this case, the leader has assumed these risks because he has been convinced of his main role as providing useful output to society.

In general, these results illustrate the importance of factors proposed to achieve ambidexterity for the leaders of the research teams. Both leaders are ambidextrous and need to manage the tension between both activities to have success from both aspects.

Table 5. Examples of quotes from the interviews regarding the importance of refining and renewing knowledge

Refining and renewing knowledge and abilities (Mom et al., 2009)	
Leader 1	**Leader 2**
"When we need new developments in other areas, we know who can help us within our network. For example, we have contacts with other areas that help in analysing materials." "In our team, some members are approaching different areas of knowledge, so they must learn new skills and knowledge."	"We must understand other areas of knowledge because our projects are interdisciplinary." "We enter other areas." "We need to break the rules of different areas to find a solution." "We need to enter new areas of knowledge to develop our projects and we enter like elephants in a china shop." "Breaking the rules often gives up new ideas."

Table 6. Information concerning the number of publications and citations

Scientific excellence (Ambos et al., 2008)	
Leader 1*	**Leader 2**
86 papers in SJR H index = 11 Total number of citations = 425	65 papers in SJR H index = 19 Total number of citations = 1091
Data for a researcher that appears in the list of Highly Cited Researchers in the area of computer science**	*Data for a researcher that appears in the list of Highly Cited Researchers in the area of chemistry*
H index = 55 Total number of citations (excluding auto-citation) = 25,976	H index = 46 Total number of citations (excluding auto-citation) = 7,280
*Data concerning the leaders were extracted from the Scopus database **Data concerning other researchers were extracted from the Web of Science database	

SOLUTIONS AND RECOMMENDATIONS

To transfer knowledge and technologies from universities to the productive sector, research teams and their leaders must address the tension generated by the different abilities and resources needed to achieve research- and commercialization-oriented results. The ambidexterity literature helps us to identify the clues for ambidexterity at the individual level of the leader.

The factors reviewed in this study are illustrated with two empirical examples in which the importance of these factors has been shown. The establishment of a network within academia and with industry, entrepreneurial abilities, paradoxical thinking, multitasking ability, and prioritizing the refinement and renewal of knowledge and abilities have been showed to be important characteristics for achieving ambidexterity. Specifically, the determination of the leaders to achieve exploration and exploitation, i.e., their entrepreneurial capabilities, is one of the main factors to successfully transfer knowledge and technology to industry. Contacts with firms are also crucial since they begin the process of producing commercial-oriented research when firms propose a need or a problem without a current solution. The importance of creating a network outside their research teams has emerged as a crucial factor. The initial process for an innovation often begins with these contacts. The data show that the leaders have a high number of publications, which demonstrates their scientific excellence. Ambos et al. (2008) propose that this factor has a negative influence at the individual level in regard to achieving commercial-oriented outputs because time restrictions cause scientists to develop some specific routines; scientists with higher commercial results are usually different from researchers who traditionally focus on producing academic results. Nevertheless, the authors also recognize other studies in which a positive relationship exists between academic excellence and commercial outcomes because the best scientists are also likely to have more abilities to commercialize their own knowledge (e.g., West 2008; Zucker et al. 2001). We need to study this factor more deeply by comparing our results with the best researchers in a specific area with a higher scientific excellence and with scientists that have more commercial-oriented research.

The results clearly show that the process of achieving individual ambidexterity in the context of leaders of research teams is difficult. One determining factor according to Leader 2 is the context in the sense that for career development exploration and exploitation have not had the same value until now. This conclusion also confirms the results from Ambos et al. (2008) in the sense that the tension at the individual level is high. To advance in this sense, universities should provide the same support for both activities.

FUTURE RESEARCH DIRECTIONS

This research topic could be broadly amplified. An interesting factor to take in account would be the other individuals conforming the Research Team and their contribution to the ambidextrous environment or their opinions about the leadership style. To complete the analysis, we must also focus on some developments made in the teams and examine them in detail over a longer period, in order to devise a complete case study. As well, it would be useful to increment the sample of subjects and analyse more cases to find differentiating factors in the leaders. Comparisons with researchers in other areas could also provide a more complete picture of these factors. Another point to take in account for future research would be to provide an analysis on the valuation by the universities with regard to exploitation and exploration tasks and how they are appraised in the University context.

Some of the theoretical concepts included in this study, such as entrepreneurship or paradoxical thinking, require further analysis. A study of the literature that first introduced and then focused on these constructs, along with an analysis of the similarities with the dimensions introduced by each one, could represent a theoretical advance to avoid terminology confusion.

CONCLUSION

We contribute to the ambidexterity literature by proposing and analysing factors affecting the achievement of ambidexterity at the individual level in a specific context. We also contribute to the technology transfer topic by applying ambidexterity to the transfer of knowledge between universities and industry by reviewing and illustrating the more important individual aspects.

The factors analysed in this study contribute to a better comprehension of the importance of specific traits and characteristics leaders must develop to address the dualities required to successfully transfer their knowledge into the productive sector and not only through academia. It could be an interesting starting point to encourage commercial results from research projects at universities by considering the factors analysed in this study and the difficulty to achieve both research- and commercial-oriented results at the individual level. For universities that want to improve their transference to society, it is important to realize the necessity of developing stronger supporting structures, formation and recognition of the two types of results so that scientists can overcome the drawbacks of achieving individual ambidexterity. The so-called third mission of universities is increasing in importance and providing support for individual ambidexterity is crucial in the sense that individuals and the leaders of research teams are those who are producing knowledge and could transform it into applications for society.

Regarding limitations of the present research, although we select examples to ensure we have two leaders with results in the two aspects of ambidexterity (exploration and exploitation), we do not compare our results with cases of superior researchers in the same area for a better understanding. It could also be useful to compare our results with other leaders that only concentrate their efforts on one of the aspects of ambidexterity to analyse the differences. Moreover, our data are based on interviews with the leaders and secondary sources. Performing interviews with the network of contacts and with other members of the research teams could add more value to the results. Another limitation is that we focus only at the individual level, but interactions with variables regarding the organizational level could provide a richer analysis. Future research should address these questions.

REFERENCES

Adler, P. S., Goldoftas, B., & Levine, D. (1999). Flexibility versus efficiency? A case study of model changeovers in the Toyota production system. *Organization Science, 10*(1), 43–68. doi:10.1287/orsc.10.1.43

Ambos, T. C., Mäkelä, K., Birkinshaw, J., & d'Este, P. (2008). When does university research get commercialized? Creating ambidexterity in research institutions. *Journal of Management Studies, 45*(8), 1424–1447. doi:10.1111/j.1467-6486.2008.00804.x

Baum, J. A., Li, S. X., & Usher, J. M. (2000). Making the next move: How experiential and vicarious learning shape the locations of chains' acquisitions. *Administrative Science Quarterly, 45*(4), 766–801. doi:10.2307/2667019

Bayona-Sáez, C., García-Marco, T., & Huerta-Arribas, E. (2002). Collaboration in R&D with universities and research centres: An empirical study of Spanish firms. *R & D Management, 32*(4), 321–341. doi:10.1111/1467-9310.00264

Benner, M. J., & Tushman, M. (2002). Process management and technological innovation: A longitudinal study of the photography and paint industries. *Administrative Science Quarterly, 47*(4), 676–707. doi:10.2307/3094913

Bonesso, S., Gerli, F., & Scapolan, A. (2014). The individual side of ambidexterity: Do individuals' perceptions match actual behaviors in reconciling the exploration and exploitation trade-off? *European Management Journal, 32*(3), 392–405. doi:10.1016/j.emj.2013.07.003

Cao, Q., Simsek, Z., & Zhang, H. (2010). Modelling the joint impact of the CEO and the TMT on organizational ambidexterity. *Journal of Management Studies, 47*(7), 1272–1296.

Chang, Y. C., Yang, P. Y., & Chen, M. H. (2009). The determinants of academic research commercial performance, towards an organizational ambidexterity perspective. *Research Policy, 38*(6), 936–946. doi:10.1016/j.respol.2009.03.005

Chang, Y. C., Yang, P. Y., Martin, B. R., Chi, H. R., & Tsai-Lin, T. F. (2016). Entrepreneurial universities and research ambidexterity: A multilevel analysis. *Technovation, 54*, 7–21. doi:10.1016/j.technovation.2016.02.006

Council of the European Union. (2018). *Council Recommendation on Key Competences for Lifelong Learning*. http://data.consilium.europa.eu/doc/document/ST-9009-2018-INIT/EN/pdf

Eisenhardt, K. M. (1989). Building theories from case study research. *Academy of Management Review, 14*(4), 532–550. doi:10.5465/amr.1989.4308385

Floyd, S. W., & Lane, P. J. (2000). Strategizing throughout the organization: Managing role conflict in strategic renewal. *Academy of Management Review, 25*(1), 154–177. doi:10.5465/amr.2000.2791608

Ghemawat, P., & Ricart Costa, J. E. I. (1993). The organizational tension between static and dynamic efficiency. *Strategic Management Journal, 14*(S2), 59–73. doi:10.1002mj.4250141007

Gibson, C. B., & Birkinshaw, J. (2004). The antecedents, consequences, and mediating role of organizational ambidexterity. *Academy of Management Journal, 47*(2), 209–226.

Gupta, A. K., Smith, K. G., & Shalley, C. E. (2006). The interplay between exploration and exploitation. *Academy of Management Journal, 49*(4), 693–706. doi:10.5465/amj.2006.22083026

He, Z., & Wong, P. (2004). Exploration vs. Exploitation: An Empirical Test of the Ambidexterity Hypothesis. *Organization Science, 15*(4), 375–497. doi:10.1287/orsc.1040.0078

Holmqvist, M. (2004). Experiential learning processes of exploitation and exploration within and between organizations: An empirical study of product development. *Organization Science, 15*(1), 70–81. doi:10.1287/orsc.1030.0056

Jansen, J. J., Van Den Bosch, F. A., & Volberda, H. W. (2006). Exploratory innovation, exploitative innovation, and performance: Effects of organizational antecedents and environmental moderators. *Management Science, 52*(11), 1661–1674. doi:10.1287/mnsc.1060.0576

Jensen, R. A., Thursby, J. G., & Thursby, M. C. (2003). Disclosure and licensing of university inventions: The best we can do with the s**t we get to work with. *International Journal of Industrial Organization, 21*(9), 1271–1300. doi:10.1016/S0167-7187(03)00083-3

Li, Y., Vanhaverbeke, W., & Schoenmakers, W. (2008). Exploration and exploitation in innovation: Reframing the interpretation. *Creativity and Innovation Management, 17*(2), 107–126. doi:10.1111/j.1467-8691.2008.00477.x

March, J. G. (1991). Exploration and exploitation in organizational learning. *Organization Science, 2*(1), 71–87. doi:10.1287/orsc.2.1.71

McGrath, R. G. (2001). Exploratory learning, innovative capacity, and managerial oversight. *Academy of Management Journal, 44*, 118–131.

McKelvey, M., Zaring, O., & Ljungberg, D. (2015). Creating innovative opportunities through research collaboration: An evolutionary framework and empirical illustration in engineering. *Technovation, 39*, 26–36. doi:10.1016/j.technovation.2014.05.008

Mom, T. J., Van Den Bosch, F. A., & Volberda, H. W. (2009). Understanding variation in managers' ambidexterity: Investigating direct and interaction effects of formal structural and personal coordination mechanisms. *Organization Science, 20*(4), 812–828. doi:10.1287/orsc.1090.0427

O'Reilly, C. A. III, & Tushman, M. L. (2011). Organizational ambidexterity in action: How managers explore and exploit. *California Management Review, 53*(4), 5–22. doi:10.1525/cmr.2011.53.4.5

Sanchez, R., Heene, A., & Thomas, H. (1996). *Dynamics of Competence Based Competition*. John Wiley and Sons.

Shane, S. A., & Venkataraman, S. (2000). The promise of entrepreneurship as a field of research. *Academy of Management Review, 25*(1), 217–226. doi:10.5465/amr.2000.2791611

Smith, G. V., & Parr, R. L. (2003). *Intellectual Property: Licensing and Joint Venture Profit Strategies* (2nd ed.). John Wiley & Sons.

Smith, W. K., & Tushman, M. L. (2005). Managing strategic contradictions: A top management model for managing innovation streams. *Organization Science*, *16*(5), 522–536. doi:10.1287/orsc.1050.0134

Tushman, M. L., & O'Reilly, C. A. III. (1996). Ambidextrous organizations: Managing evolutionary and revolutionary change. *California Management Review*, *38*(4), 8–30. doi:10.2307/41165852

West, J. (2008). Commercializing open science: Deep space communications as the lead market for Shannon Theory, 1960–73. *Journal of Management Studies*, *45*(8), 1506–1532. doi:10.1111/j.1467-6486.2008.00807.x

Yin, R. K. (2009). Applied Social Research Methods Series: Vol. 219. Case Study Research: Design and Methods, Essential guide to qualitative methods in organizational research. Academic Press.

Zucker, L. G., Darby, M. R., & Torero, M. (2001). Labour mobility from academe to commerce. *Journal of Labor Economics*, *20*(3), 629–660. doi:10.1086/339613

ADDITIONAL READING

Lubatkin, M. H., Simsek, Z., Ling, Y., & Veiga, J. F. (2006). Ambidexterity and performance in small- to medium-sized firms: The pivotal role of top management team behavioral integration. *Journal of Management*, *32*(5), 646–672. doi:10.1177/0149206306290712

O'Reilly, C. III, & Tushman, M. (2013). Organizational Ambidexterity: Past, Present and Future. *The Academy of Management Perspectives*, *27*(4), 324–338. doi:10.5465/amp.2013.0025

O'Reilly, C. A. III, & Tushman, M. L. (2011). Organizational ambidexterity in action: How managers explore and exploit. *California Management Review*, *53*(4), 5–22. doi:10.1525/cmr.2011.53.4.5

Perkmann, M., Tartari, V., McKelvey, M., Autio, E., Broström, A., D'Este, P., & Krabel, S. (2013). Academic engagement and commercialisation: A review of the literature on university–industry relations. *Research Policy*, *42*(2), 423–442. doi:10.1016/j.respol.2012.09.007

Raisch, S., Birkinshaw, J., Probst, G., & Tushman, M. (2009, July–August). Organizational Ambidexterity: Balancing Exploitation and Exploration for Sustained Performance. *Organization Science*, *20*(4), 685–695. doi:10.1287/orsc.1090.0428

KEY TERMS AND DEFINITIONS

Ambidexterity: Capability or ability to effectively combine exploration and exploitation activities.

Contextual Ambidexterity: Type of Ambidexterity obtained by the alignment of all the different elements of the organization towards specific tasks in order to foster exploration and exploitation at the same time.

Entrepreneurial Capability: The ability to identify opportunities and aligning the suitable resources and efforts to seize these opportunities.

Exploitation: Activities or actions oriented to develop the existing capabilities/objectives.

Exploration: Activities or actions oriented to develop new or innovative capabilities/objectives.

Paradoxical Thinking: Being able to cope with contradictions, to think on situations with a whole and integrative perspective.

Structural Ambidexterity: Type of ambidexterity managed through two different units in the organization each one focused on exploration or on exploitation only.

Innovation Management Capabilities for R&D in Pakistan

Zeeshan Asim

Electrical Engineering Department, Institute of Business Management, Pakistan

Shahryar Sorooshian

University of Gothenburg, Sweden

INTRODUCTION

Today major issues are: unpredicted global business climate in every business sector. The significant emergences of domestic and international business dynamism, challenging business competition, rising growth in knowledge driven economies with all comprehensive technological tools have browse innovation and innovative capabilities as major instrument that used to compete global business dynamism. Number of studies and publication in context of evaluating effectiveness of innovation management capabilities on R&D activities particularly during the developing on National innovation system (NIS) (Naqvi, 2011) for the developing economies like Pakistan,

A national innovation system- as theoretical framework- is generally translated as a specific cluster or range of linkages among the factors implied in innovation processes, and interrelationship among these factors determines the performance related to innovation process (i.e. innovation efficiency) (Freeman, 1987; Metcalfe, 1995; Nelson, 1993; Numminen, 1996). This interpretation attracts many researchers to draw their conclusion on new structure of knowledge based economies in case of both developing and developed economies (Correa, 1998; Foray, 1994; Lundvall, 1998)

Innovation capability influence imperative stake in developing R&D activities in recognized to confront the uncertain business environment and counter domestic and global business competencies, it encourages firms to reduce their production expenditure, starched the business potential and excel societal source of revenue (Pannirselvan et al., 2016; Sorooshian et al, 2013). The existing circumstances recognized as knowledge era, and the global business challenges experience to "Knowledge revolution" drive by the accelerating growth of scientific and technological progression (Gilani, 2015a)

Pakistan has made inspiring pace towards creating an advance infrastructure for R&D through aggressive policy with potential financial backing but the expected targets could not be accomplished. It finds quite reluctant to R&D and innovative activities developed through academia, while some limited momentum adds up from the private sector (Naqvi, 2011). Developing capabilities in various sectors consider as significant step to superimpose the innovation effectiveness (Lau, 2010), In this context, number of scholar's have understood such innovation capabilities considers as key factor to influence overall innovation effectiveness that impact on R&D spending specifically translating into innovational design with respect to market environment (Paolo Landoni, 2016; Yam, 2011).

In holistic view, there is certainly a problem with determining innovation inputs and outputs, particularly in context of a dynamic business environment. There are few other complex issues for instance: Emergences of domestic and international business dynamism, and challenging business competition, rising growth in knowledge driven economies. In general narrative all the estimations related to innova-

DOI: 10.4018/978-1-7998-3473-1.ch188

tion inputs explicitly and implicitly comprise of elements that depends on R&D spending (or developing the circumstance for increasing R&D spending) (Jankowska et al., 2017).

There are comparatively unexplored literature regarding criteria for general decision guideline about involvement of innovation capabilities as useful under limited expenditure and lack of empirical evidence regarding supportive indictors to cater policy making in order to propel research and development (Dimitrios Kafetzopoulos 2015; HaoJiaoa, 2016; Mei-Chih Hu, 2016; Samson, 2014; Yam, 2011; Zhu, 2014). However, there are more investigation and in depth emphasis required on relationship among the dimensions and criteria's of innovation capabilities and their influence to R&D to draw a general guideline that helps decision makers to develop policies by using these criteria's to strategies R&D configuration in order to expend and achieve business competitiveness (Alberto Di Minin 2012; Hosseinia, 2016; Martin, 2015)

In contrast developed economies, finite research is being done on R&D with science and technological advancement in Pakistan (BPTC, 1998; Naim, 2001; Qureshi, 1998) but specifically with angle of innovation and technological advancement system in Pakistan. Pakistan council of Science and Technology (PCST) highlights Science and Technology (S&T) Indictors (Gilani, 2015b) over a period of time. One of research purpose is to evaluate S&T significant drivers with a specific dimension of innovative mechanism in order to screen progressive national innovation initiative. But due to the instable government political drawback creates difficulties for sustaining R&D activities (Naqvi, 2011).

BACKGROUND

Developing innovation capabilities consider as an expensive and uncertain process. From business perspective, in general argument innovation can be describe as a complicated systemic process of developing new conceptual ideas- start with the procedure of their development, process of their modeling, and commercial application- using technical knowledge, technological capabilities, and comprehensive firms resources (W. Artz, M. Norman, E. Hatfield, and L. Cardinal., 2010; Karlsson, 2015a). Similarly, number of firms used innovation an instrument for consistent growth because it drives to influence number of complex functional strategies such as (marketing, production and product). Number of experts and scholars figure out innovation capabilities as crucial enabler of business competencies and recognized as essential indicator to the overall productivity and business growth (Karlsson, 2015a; Subrahmanya, 2012). In general, firms accomplished their innovation process by either developing in house innovation capabilities through concrete internal R&D process or by acquiring R&D capabilities through external collaboration. The initial aim to strength a extensive progress in technological drivers that retain the existing process capabilities and starched the product range with minimum production cost (Ganotakis, 2011).

Most of the innovation literature argues that innovation is the most essential resource for firm's accomplishment and survival (Abbing, 2010; Cho & Pucik, 2005) in dynamic business environment Innovation capabilities are consider as significant drivers for influencing innovation (Teece et al., 1997) and regard as the foundation of firms transformation to conceive competition, new market opportunities and external circumstances (Guan & Ma, 2003; M.Elmquist & Masson, 2009). Accordingly, there have been numerous and extensive discussion on innovation capabilities, which direct to various approaches to classify such capabilities.

There are various approaches to characterize innovation capabilities in prior studies are twofold. One has to observe the capabilities from the holistic angle for instance from outcome perspective, in which innovation outcome can be split into various components. For instance: Sulistiyani and Harwiki (2016) translate innovation capabilities as 'product with enhance quality', innovative product and advance production strategy. Plessis (2007) suggested three main dimensions related to innovation capabilities based on innovation management, product and process. Similarly, According to Adam and Comber (2013) interpretation they suggested innovation capabilities were based on three factors: improve product quality, product innovation and potential market growth

An innovation capability is a significant and indefinable input character that is crucially linked to R&D. The process of Innovation management requires adequate investment in order to drive retainable R&D activities (Czarnitzki, 2011) because R&D enhance firm's existing knowledge strength that can utilized to generate new product range or used as for the purpose of process modification (W. Artz, M. Norman, E. Hatfield, and L. Cardinal. 2010., 2010). Similarly, number of scholars and expert identified in house development of innovational capabilities as key enabler to internal R&D that retained the firm's performance without disclosing the firm's potential capabilities (Conte, 2013; Hall, 2002; Karlsson, 2015b; Pellegrino, 2014.). In general perception innovational capabilities consider as driving instrument to R&D that not only sustain the R&D activities during dynamic business environment but support R&D as influences firms to absorb potential knowledge spillovers form external collaboration. This advocate that R&D with concrete innovation management capabilities consider is crucial gauging factor for quantifying firms absorptive ability (Gallie, 2012)

But in case of acquiring capabilities externally as most of the firms may no longer to retain and rely on their in-house R&D capabilities or firm's internal capacity unable to aligned their operational activities with respect to the changing behavior to business environment, Because of the lack of availability skill set, lack of retaining the innovational capabilities due to higher cost, with low product range due to the short lifecycle, and incompatibility due to the complex technological constrain (Berchicci, 2013; Bergman, 2010).

This organizational shift from in- house R&D activities on toward open innovation external R&D encourage to create range of new product and modified processes with minimum cost factor. Furthermore, the core advantage of such acquisition is to distribute the risk and cost associate during the develop of innovation capabilities internally and exploiting economics of scale (Colombo, 2011; Hagedoorn, 1990; Nieto, 2010; Peltier, 2012; Pullen, 2012). Similarly, innovation capabilities also defined as abilities to measure innovation effectiveness for national innovation mechanism precisely based on outcomes for product innovation, market growth, new production system, and product quality. Akman and Yilmaz (2008) suggested innovation capabilities as proficiency for the in-depth understanding towards organizational internal culture and external situation that acknowledge to them. Lawson and Samson (2001) suggested innovation capabilities as competency to transform knowledge in to new product or process

CURRENT CHALLENGES IN CASE OF PAKISTAN

Approximately, 26% of overall GDP and 45% of total employment is obtained from agriculture sector till 2010, now the economic scope shifted towards the service and manufacturing based economies. It also adds significantly to Pakistan exports and to excel as potential supplier of raw materials to manufacturing sector. Also Major portion of countries population approximately 66% living in rural density and directly and indirectly connected to the agriculture sector. The agriculture contributes around 20.8% as compared to manufacturing sector which add around 24.3% while the service sector shares more than half of the GDP approximately add up around 54.9%. But from previous two decades Pakistan GDP growth pattern is 6.4% clearly represents that Pakistan has to join in with at least average economies

Table 1. World economic outlook (IMF, 2016)

	Real GDP			Consumer Prices			Unemployment		
	Projections			Projections			Projections		
	2015	2016	2017	2015	2016	2017	2015	2016	2017
Pakistan	2.5	3.1	3.5	5.7	5.2	4.8	-	-	-

cross the region (China 9.8% and India 7.4%) (Economist, 2007), But due to the economic instability because of the regional politics Pakistan GDP growth decrease up to 6.1% in year 2006 and it remain stagnant at rate of 3.1 year 2016 as show Table 1 (IMF, 2016).

According to Pakistan Science and Technology Council, STI policy 2015 (Anwar-ul-Hassan Gilani 2015) Pakistan has established comprehensive infrastructure 160 High Education Institute (HEIs) and these keep rising along with 100 R&D organizations. But unfortunately due to the distributed financial mechanism and different organization structures there has been no coordination and protocol exchange mechanism among these institutions. At current circumstance without proper coordination R&D activities deteriorate specifically when there has been no correlation among knowledge, Innovation and Technological capabilities. According to STI, 2015 indicator overall National innovation system productivity remain low and not reach to predicted projection as compare to the other regional economies, the situation getting even worst according to global innovation index (GII, 2015) (Soumitra Dutta, 2015-2016) Pakistan rank 131 position out of 141 countries and similarly according to the global competitive index (GCI, 2015) (Schwab, 2015–2016) Pakistan made up 129th mark among 141.

Eighteen-year publication data defines the rising and falling pattern in research publication from 1996 onward Pakistan, which can be the accredited to the significant rise in the R&D spending, as show in Table 2. Pakistan frequently emerges in the category as 'rising stars' for accomplishing maximum citation of scientific publication in number of fields (UNESCO, 2016).

The existing innovation capabilities development structure in Pakistan acquires major funding from the government agencies. As according to the current available statistics accumulate by Pakistan council of Science and Technology the Gross expenditure on R&D in Pakistan is float in between 0.29% to 0.59%

Table 2. Scientific publications in Pakistan

Years	Scientific publications in Pakistan
2007	4156
2008	5032
2009	6285
2010	7437
2011	9021
2012	9675
2013	8932
2014	9069
2015	9375
2016	10863
2017	13101

Table 3. Gross domestic R&D expenditure

GERD($ millions)	2005	2007	2009	2011	2013	2014	2015	2016	2017
Pakistan	2043	4097	3119	2471	2454	-	-	-	-
India	26532	32866	39402	48063	-	-	8532610		
Malaysia	-	-	5400	6457	-		15058344		
Turkey	4617	7049	8867	11246	13315				
Japan	128695	147602	136954	148389	160247				
Israel	6966	8749	8507	9523	10774				

of their GDP (Table: 3) shows the amount total spend with respect to the percentage of their GDP. The major contribution in gross domestic expenditure came from the government side which around 83%. While the contributor includes private funding non-profit agencies, business firms and the universities with 1%, 3%, 10% respectively, if further looking in detail the R&D major portion is used to spend in agriculture sector consider recipient of major source of funding followed by defense, Health sciences, industrial production and engineering and technology in a respective other (Muhammad Bashir, 2014). These statistical indictors illustrate that long way to go for developing more advance innovational capabilities that required more funding agencies particularly for the private sector need to jump in to promote domestic R&D. Furthermore, allocation of investment fund needs to distribute equally to create balance in innovation structure (Muhammad Anwar ulHaq 2014).

Pakistan remain bottom in the region with all the significant instruments used for measuring innovation capability according to GII, 2016 (global innovation index 2016), Pakistan face a serious challenges as compares to their regional counterparts regarding to acquires knowledge and technology output. Pakistan place at 89th position in out of 140 countries, the innovation and capacity output indicating unit basically comprises on country overall ability to have capacity for innovation, quality of scientific research institute, company spending on R&D, university and industry collaboration in R&D and availability of engineers and scientist with overall knowledge impact actually influence research and development

Particularly when developing the new knowledge based economy, Similarly India place at 42nd out of 140 countries with slightly higher GDP growth spending on R&D. While on the other hand Malaysia and Turkey is more progress middle income economies that place their mark 20th and 41st out of 140 countries, In case developed economies Israel and South Korea mark their position 03rd and 6th respectively.

FUTURE RESEARCH DIRECTIONS

Under the light of statistical data that shows the present status of Pakistan internationally: in order to boost or improve the international standing of Pakistan National innovation mechanism extensive efforts must be paid on "human capital", "institutions", "scientific output", and "creative output". While, government target 2025 vision and implement certain process for reconfiguration of current innovation mechanism as main dimension to accomplish the vision. As innovation consider as continuous process and according to present situation no country attempt to claim its saturation without adding any new approach to improve innovation at national level in long term perceptive. Similarly, to this Pakistan have a positive and supportive infrastructure but due to the lack of overall innovation policies may redeem the expected vision.

Table 4. Present status of Pakistan in global innovation index

Pillars of GII	2011	2012	2013	2014	2015	2016	2017
Global Innovation Index	26.8	23.1	23.3	24	23.1	22.6	23.8
Institutions	46.7	39	40.2	40.1	37.1	37.1	38
Human capital & research	14	10	7.7	9.8	12.8	13	12.8
Infrastructure	19.5	20.9	19.8	22.2	23.1	26.5	29
Market sophistication	28.1	23.4	29.6	35.8	35.8	35.7	38.3
Business sophistication	24.7	28.3	21.1	19.3	22.5	25.3	29
Scientific outputs	17.5	18.1	19.7	21.9	20.2	19.6	18.9
Creative outputs	36.3	25.6	26.3	23.2	19.6	15.9	17.4

The R&D activities in Pakistan mostly practiced among the public sector research organizations and in few universities. The initial structure of R&D mechanism in public sectors organization based under federal and provincial ministries depend upon under which authority the public sector organization serves. The public sector research organization basically involve in research of Advance agriculture science and development, science and technology, Advance medical sciences, life stock, civil and water resource, Advance engineering science, Energy Management and Advance bioengineering (Muhammad Anwar ul Haq 2014). In public sector research institute majority of R&D activities belongs to agriculture science and development more than 40 organizations currently active in this sector. While, approximately 19 public sector R&D institute involve in conducting research in science and engineering. There are less 6 institutes involved in conducting research in Advance Medical science and biotechnology (Technology, 2009). However, in spite the higher number of research institutes belong to agriculture Pakistan unable to reached with self-reliance in agriculture sector. There is huge rectification also required in Medical science and Engineering sector due to the lack of connectivity among the universities and enterprises that are not as much active to carry out internal R&D activities.

CONCLUSION

The initial perception on efficiency related to national innovation structure is directly linked with fundamental theory of productivity. An innovation mechanism (more related to policy development) is designated as proficient based on some precise parameter for instance: when the similar magnitude of effort exerts for innovation inputs firms were expected to have same amount of innovation outputs; similarly, when less effort has made for innovation input same amount of innovation has been drive at outcome.

Developing innovation capabilities with systematic approach in Pakistan has understand over period of time bust still need aggressive approach. In effort to established comprehensive systematic approach regarding to develop innovational capabilities require aggressive policy formulation which needs a comprehensive contribution of all stakeholders from government body to private sector. Still more options need to discover other domain of research field and develop supportive structure to encourage private R&D firms to carry out research activities and R&D investment to industrial scale as most as Pakistan need to adopt the same approach as other emerging economies do by implement R&D incubators as to provide interconnectivity in between the academia and industrial sectors

REFERENCES

Abbing. (2010). *Brand-driven Innovation SA*. AVA Publishing.

Adam, M., & Comber, S. (2013). Knowledge Transfer for Sustainable Innovation: A Model for Academic-industry Interaction to Improve Resource Efficiency Within SME Manufactures. *Journal of Innovation Management in Small & Medium Enterprises*, 1-21.

Akman, G., & Yilmaz, C. (2008). Innovative Capability, Innovation Strategy and Market Orientation: An Empirical Analysis in Turkish Software Industry. *International Journal of Innovation Management*, *12*(01), 69–111. doi:10.1142/S1363919608001923

Alberto Di Minin, J. Z. (2012). Chinese foreign direct investment in R&D in Europe: A new model of R&D internationalization? *European Management Journal*, *30*(3), 189–203. doi:10.1016/j.emj.2012.03.004

Anwar-ul-Hassan Gilani, F. L. A. (2015). STI, policy. *STI Voice Quarterly Newsletter, 1*(4).

Artz, W., Norman, M., Hatfield, E., & Cardinal, L. (2010). A Longitudinal Study of the Impact of R&D, Patents, and Product Innovation on Firm Performance. *Journal of Product Innovation Management*, *27*(5), 725–774. doi:10.1111/j.1540-5885.2010.00747.x

Artz, W., Norman, M., Hatfield, E., & Cardinal, L. (2010). A Longitudinal Study of the Impact of R&D, Patents, and Product Innovation on Firm Performance. *Journal of Product Innovation Management*, *27*(5), 725–774. doi:10.1111/j.1540-5885.2010.00747.x

Bashir. (2014). *PCST R&D Survey 2013-14* [Press release].

Berchicci. (2013). Towards an Open R&D System: Internal R&D Investment, External Knowledge Acquisition and Innovative Performance. *Research Policy, 42*(1), 117–129.

Bergman. (2010). *Internal and External R&D and Productivity—Evidence from Swedish Firm-Level Data*. Department of Economics Lund University.

BPTC. (1998). *Building Pakistan's technological competence*. Author.

Cho & Pucik. (2005). Relationship between innovativeness, quality, growth, profitability, and market value. *Strategic Management Journal, 26*, 555-575.

Colombo, Laursen, Magnusson, & Rossi-Lamastra. (2011). Organizing Inter- and Intra-Firm Networks: What Is the Impact on Innovation Performance? *Industry and Innovation*, *18*(6), 531–538.

Conte, A., & Vivarelli, M. (2013). Succeeding in Innovation: Key Insights on the Role of R&D and Technological Acquisition Drawn from the Company Data. *Empirical Economics*, *47*(4), 1317–1340. doi:10.100700181-013-0779-1

Correa, C. (1998). Argentina's national innovation system. *International Journal of Technology Management*, *15*(6-7), 721–760. doi:10.1504/IJTM.1998.002627

Czarnitzki, D., & Hottenrot, H. (2011). R&D Investment and Financing Constraints of Small and Medium-Sized Firms. *Small Business Economics*, *36*(1), 65–83. doi:10.100711187-009-9189-3

Dimitrios Kafetzopoulos, E. P. (2015). The impact of innovation capability on the performance of manufacturing companies: The Greek case. *Journal of Manufacturing Technology Management, 26*(1), 104–130. doi:10.1108/JMTM-12-2012-0117

Economist. (2007). *The World in Figures: Countries*. London: Economist Intelligence Unit.

Foray, D. (1994). Production and Distribution of Knowledge in the New Systems of Innovations: The Role of Intellectual Property Rights. *STI Review, 14*, 119–152.

Freeman, C. (1987). Technology and Economic Performance: Lessons from Japan. London: Academic Press.

Gallie, E., & Legros, D. (2012). Firms' Human Capital, R&D and Innovation: A Study on French Firms. *Empirical Economics, 43*(2), 581–596. doi:10.100700181-011-0506-8

Ganotakis, P., & Love, J. (2011). R&D, Product Innovation and Exporting. Evidence from UK New Technology Based Firms. *Oxford Economic Papers, 63*(2), 279–306. doi:10.1093/oep/gpq027

Ganotakis, P., & Love, J. (2011). R&D, Product Innovation and Exporting. Evidence from UK New Technology Based Firms. *Oxford Economic Papers, 63*(2), 279–306. doi:10.1093/oep/gpq027

Gilani, A.-u.-H. (2015a). STI Policy. *STI Voice Quarterly Newsletter, 4*(1).

Gilani, A.-u.-H. (2015b). Science, Technology, Innovation. *STI Voice, 1*(3).

Guan, J., & Ma, N. (2003). Innovative Capability and Performance of Chinese Firms. *Technovation, 23*(9), 737–747. doi:10.1016/S0166-4972(02)00013-5

Hagedoorn. (1990). Organizational Modes of Inter-Firm Cooperation and Technology Transfer. *Technovation, 10*(1), 17–30.

Hall, L., & Bagchi-Sen, S. (2002). A Study of R&D, Innovation, and Business Performance in Canadian Biotechnology Industry. *Technovation, 22*(4), 231–244. doi:10.1016/S0166-4972(01)00016-5

Hao Jiaoa, Gaoc, & Liud. (2016). the more interactions the better? The moderating effect of the interaction between local producers and users of knowledge on the relationship between R&D investment and regional innovation systems. *Technological Forecasting and Social Change, 101*.

Hosseinia, P. A. S. M. (2016). Social capital, knowledge sharing, and innovation capability: An empirical study of R&D teams in Iran. *Technology Analysis and Strategic Management, 28*(1), 96–113. doi: 10.1080/09537325.2015.1072622

Hu, Chen, & Tseng. (2016). Determinants of university–industry research collaborations in Taiwan: The case of the National Tsing Hua University. *Research Evaluation Advance*, 1-15.

IMF. (2016). *World Economic Outlook: Subdued Demand: Symptoms and Remedies*. IMF.

Karlsson & Tavassoli. (2015). *Innovation Strategies and Firm Performance*. Working Paper Series in Economics and Institutions of Innovation. Center for Excellence for Science and Innovation Studies.

Lau, A. K. W., Tang, E., & Yam, R. C. M. (2010). Effects of Supplier and Customer Integration on Product Innovation and Performance: Empirical Evidence in Hong Kong Manufacturers. *Journal of Product Innovation Management, 27*(5), 761–777. doi:10.1111/j.1540-5885.2010.00749.x

Lawson, B., & Samson, D. (2001). Developing Innovation Capability in Organisations: A Dynamic Capabilities Approach. *International Journal of Innovation Management, 5*(03), 377–400. doi:10.1142/S1363919601000427

Lundvall, B. A. (1998). Why study national systems of innovations and national styles of innovation. *Technology Analysis and Strategic Management, 10*(4), 407–421. doi:10.1080/09537329808524324

Martin, M. (2015). Effectiveness of Business Innovation and R&D in Emerging Economies: The Evidence from Panel Data Analysis. Journal of Economics. *Business and Management, 4*(3), 440–446. doi:10.7763/JOEBM.2015.V3.225

Metcalfe, S. (1995). *The Economic Foundations of Technology Policy: Equilibrium and Evolutionary Perspectives*. Blackwell Publishers.

Naim. (2001). Science and technology development in Pakistan. *Science, Technology and Society, 6*(1), 97–132.

Naqvi, I. B. (2011). National innovation system in a least developing country: The case of Pakistan. *Int. J. Technology. Policy and Management, 11*(2), 139–152.

Nelson, R. (1993). *National Innovation Systems. A Comparative Analysis*. Oxford University Press.

Nieto, M., & Santamaria, L. (2010). Technological Collaboration: Bridging the Innovation Gap between Small and Large Firms. *Journal of Small Business Management Decision, 48*(1), 44–69. doi:10.1111/j.1540-627X.2009.00286.x

Numminen, S. (1996). National Innovation Systems: Pilot Case Study of the Knowledge Distribution Power of Finland. Helsinki, Finland: Academic Press.

Pannirselvan, M. D., Bin Rahamaddulla, S. R., Muuhamad, P. F., Maarof, M. G., & Sorooshian, S. (2016). Innovative solution for barriers of green logistics in food manufacturing industries. *International Journal of Applied Engineering Research, 11*(18), 9478–9487.

Paolo Landoni, C. D. E. (2016). Design Contribution to the Competitive Performance of SMEs: The Role of Design Innovation Capabilities. *Creativity and Innovation Management, 25*(4), 484–499. doi:10.1111/caim.12165

Pellegrino, G., Piva, M., & Vivarelli, M. (2014). How Do New Entrepreneurs Innovate? *Economia e Politica Industriale, 42*(3), 323–341. doi:10.100740812-015-0015-4

Peltier, J., & Naidu, G. M. (2012). Social Networks across the SME Organization Lifecycle. *Journal of Small Business and Enterprise Development, 19*(1), 56–73. doi:10.1108/14626001211196406

Plessis, M. D. (2007). The Role of Knowledge Management. *Journal of Knowledge Management, 11*(11), 20–29. doi:10.1108/13673270710762684

Pullen, A., Weerd-Nederhof, P., Groen, A., & Fisscher, O. (2012). SME Network Characteristics vs. Product Innovativeness: How to Achieve High Innovation Performance. *Creativity and Innovation Management, 21*(2), 130–146. doi:10.1111/j.1467-8691.2012.00638.x

Qureshi, M. M. K. (1998). 50 Years of Research and Development in Pakistan. Pakistan Council for Science and Technology.

Samson, D., & Gloet, M. (2014). Innovation capability in Australian manufacturing organizations: An exploratory study. *International Journal of Production Research, 21*(52), 6448–6466. doi:10.1080/00 207543.2013.869368

Schwab, K. (2015). *The Global Competitiveness Report. Retrieved from Soumitra Dutta, B. L., and Sacha Wunsch-Vincent.* Effective Innovation Policies for Development.

Sorooshian, S., Jambulingam, M., & Mousavi, M. (2013). Business green shift based on innovation concepts. *Research Journal of Applied Sciences, Engineering and Technology, 6*(9), 1632–1634. doi:10.19026/rjaset.6.3881

Subrahmanya, M. H. B. (2012). Technological Innovation in Indian SMEs: Need, Status and Policy Imperatives. Current Opinion in Creativity. *Innovation and Entrepreneurship Theory and Practice, 1*(2), 1–6.

Sulistiyani, R., & Harwiki, W. (2016). How SMEs Build Innovation Capability Based on Knowledge Sharing Behavior? Phenomenological Approach'. *Procedia: Social and Behavioral Sciences, 219,* 741–747. doi:10.1016/j.sbspro.2016.05.070

Technology, P. C. S. a. (2009). Islamabad: Ministry of Science and Technology.

Teece, D. J., Pisano, G., & Shuen, A. (1997). Dynamic capabilities and strategic management. *Strategic Management Journal, 18*(7), 509–533. doi:10.1002/(SICI)1097-0266(199708)18:7<509::AID-SMJ882>3.0.CO;2-Z

ul Haq, Phulpoto, & Usman. (2014). Analysing National Innovation System of Pakistan. *Journal of Developing Countries Studies, 4,* 133-139.

UNESCO. (2017). *Expenditure on R&D.* Retrieved from uis.unesco.org/en/country/pk?theme=science-technology-and-innovation

Yam, R., Lo, W., Tang, E., & Lau, A. (2011). Analysis of sources of innovation, technological innovation capabilities, and performance: An empirical study of Hong Kong manufacturing industries. *Research Policy, 40*(6), 391–402. doi:10.1016/j.respol.2010.10.013

Zhu, X., & Xu, L. (2014). Evaluation of Independent Innovation Capability of Enterprises Based on Factor Analysis. Paper presented at the 2014 International Conference on Education Reform and Modern Management (ERMM-14). 10.2991/ermm-14.2014.107

ADDITIONAL READING

Ganotakis, P., & Love, J. (2011). R&D, Product Innovation and Exporting. Evidence from UK New Technology Based Firms. *Oxford Economic Papers, 63*(2), 279–306. doi:10.1093/oep/gpq027

Paolo Landoni, C. D. E. (2016). Design Contribution to the Competitive Performance of SMEs: The Role of Design Innovation Capabilities. *Creativity and Innovation Management, 25*(4), 484–499. doi:10.1111/caim.12165

Subrahmanya, M. H. B. (2012). Technological Innovation in Indian SMEs: Need, Status and Policy Imperatives. Current Opinion in Creativity. *Innovation and Entrepreneurship Theory and Practice, 1*(2), 1–6.

Sulistiyani, R., & Harwiki, W. (2016). How SMEs Build Innovation Capability Based on Knowledge Sharing Behavior? Phenomenological Approach'. *Procedia: Social and Behavioral Sciences*, *219*, 741–747. doi:10.1016/j.sbspro.2016.05.070

Yam, R., Lo, W., Tang, E., & Lau, A. (2011). Analysis of sources of innovation, technological innovation capabilities, and performance: An empirical study of Hong Kong manufacturing industries. *Research Policy*, *40*(6), 391–402. doi:10.1016/j.respol.2010.10.013

Zeeshan, A., Surriyya, A., Sorooshian, S., & Muhammad, S. A. (2017a). Disabilities in Pakistan's R&D Sector: Knowledge Management Capability. *Information*, *20*(10(A)), 7209–7216.

Zeeshan, A., Surriyya, A., Sorooshian, S., & Muhammad, S. A. (2017b). Overview on Pakistan R&D Sector in Context Adopting Technological Capabilities. *Information*, *20*(10(A)), 7217–7226.

KEY TERMS AND DEFINITIONS

Capability: The approach which enable broad spectrum of fields, most significantly in creative thinking, economical welfare, and social policies this reflects individual's wellbeing and social planning.

Innovation: It refers to the act of developing new idea, technique, or product.

Innovation Management: Innovation Management is ability to managing innovation practices, starting at the initial stages of conceptualization, to its final stage of successful implementation.

Knowledge Management: Knowledge management describe as process to encourage knowledge growth, extensive sharing of knowledge among the function of organization.

Pakistan: It is a country in Asia, along the Arabian Sea and Gulf of Oman and it is bordered by India, Iran, Afghanistan, and China.

Research and Development (R&D): It refers to the activities for betterment of existing technology, knowledge and/or products.

Technology Management: Technology management is set of management disciplines that allows organizations to manage their technological fundamentals

About the Contributors

For full author biographies, please visit the book's webpage at:

https://www.igi-global.com/book/encyclopedia-organizational-knowledge-administration-technology/242894

Index

F

P

Q

R

U

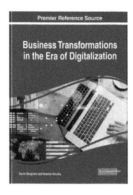
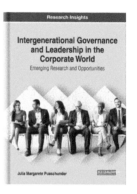

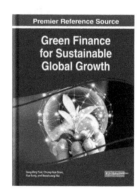

Ensure Quality Research is Introduced to the Academic Community

Become an IGI Global Reviewer for Authored Book Projects

The overall success of an authored book project is dependent on quality and timely reviews.

In this competitive age of scholarly publishing, constructive and timely feedback significantly expedites the turnaround time of manuscripts from submission to acceptance, allowing the publication and discovery of forward-thinking research at a much more expeditious rate. Several IGI Global authored book projects are currently seeking highly-qualified experts in the field to fill vacancies on their respective editorial review boards:

Applications and Inquiries may be sent to:
development@igi-global.com

Applicants must have a doctorate (or an equivalent degree) as well as publishing and reviewing experience. Reviewers are asked to complete the open-ended evaluation questions with as much detail as possible in a timely, collegial, and constructive manner. All reviewers' tenures run for one-year terms on the editorial review boards and are expected to complete at least three reviews per term. Upon successful completion of this term, reviewers can be considered for an additional term.

If you have a colleague that may be interested in this opportunity, we encourage you to share this information with them.

IGI Global Proudly Partners With eContent Pro International

Receive a 25% Discount on all Editorial Services

Editorial Services

IGI Global expects all final manuscripts submitted for publication to be in their final form. This means they must be reviewed, revised, and professionally copy edited prior to their final submission. Not only does this support with accelerating the publication process, but it also ensures that the highest quality scholarly work can be disseminated.

English Language Copy Editing

Let eContent Pro International's expert copy editors perform edits on your manuscript to resolve spelling, punctuaion, grammar, syntax, flow, formatting issues and more.

Scientific and Scholarly Editing

Allow colleagues in your research area to examine the content of your manuscript and provide you with valuable feedback and suggestions before submission.

Figure, Table, Chart & Equation Conversions

Do you have poor quality figures? Do you need visual elements in your manuscript created or converted? A design expert can help!

Translation

Need your documjent translated into English? eContent Pro International's expert translators are fluent in English and more than 40 different languages.

Email: **customerservice@econtentpro.com**   **www.igi-global.com/editorial-service-partners**